Instant Money Savers

Expert Secrets for Spending Smart, Getting the Best Discounts, and Living Well for Less

Reader's
Digest

The Reader's Digest Association, Inc.
New York, New York | Montreal

A READER'S DIGEST BOOK
Discounts, Deals & Steals
Copyright © 2011 The Reader's Digest Association, Inc.
Previously published in hardcover as *Early Bird Specials*

Amazing Insider Secrets
Copyright © 2007 The Reader's Digest Association, Inc
Previously published in hardcover as *Forbidden Advice*

ISBN: 978-1-60652-497-8

PROJECT STAFF

Discounts, Deals & Steals
Executive Editor: Elissa Altman
Writers: Sharon Bowers, Susan Randol, Karen Kelly
Designers: Michele Laseau, Erick Swindell
Copy Editor/Proofreader: Marcia Mangum Cronin
Illustrations: © Chuck Rekow

Amazing Insider Secrets
Project Editor: Don Earnest
Project Designer: Michele Laseau
Editor: Daryna Tobey
Copy Editor: Jeanette Gingold
Illustrator: Travis Foster
Editor/Lead Writer: Jeff Bredenberg
Writers: Mary Beausoleil, Jeff Edelstein, Kelly Garrett, Debra Gordon, Dougald McDonald, Eric Metcalf, Elizabeth Shimer, Logan Ward
Health and Fitness Advisors: Mary Hardy, M.D., Jeff Novick

READER'S DIGEST TRADE PUBLISHING

U.S. Project Editor: Kim Casey
Project Designer: Rich Kershner
Senior Art Director: George McKeon
Editor-in-Chief, Books & Home Entertainment: Neil Wertheimer
Associate Publisher, Trade Publishing: Rosanne McManus
President and Publisher, Trade Publishing: Harold Clarke

We are committed to both the quality of our products and the service we provide to our customers. We value your comments, so please feel free to contact us.

The Reader's Digest Association, Inc.
Adult Trade Publishing
44 South Broadway
White Plains, NY 10601

For more Reader's Digest products and information, visit our website: www.rd.com (in the United States)

Printed in China

1 3 5 7 9 10 8 6 4 2

NOTE TO READERS

The information in this book should not be substituted for, or used to alter, medical therapy without your doctor's advice. For a specific health problem, consult your physician for guidance. The mention of any products, retail businesses, or websites in this book does not imply or constitute an endorsement by the authors or by The Reader's Digest Association, Inc.

contents

Amazing Insider Secrets

Outsmart the Experts
with *the* Consumer Guide
for Getting the Best Deals—
from Skin Care to Home Repairs

Jeff Bredenberg

Reader's
Digest

The Reader's Digest Association, Inc.
New York, New York | Montreal

1,703 **Ways to Win!**

You've thought it a thousand times: If I'd
only known the full story ... the hidden
facts ... the way the system really works ...
the inside dope. I could have saved my hard-
earned cash. I could have made a lot better
use of my time. I could have used my energy for
something much more important or enjoyable.

The fact is, we've all been victims of either misinformation or withheld information that ultimately cost us precious resources of money, time, and energy. Call it the silence of the experts. It's not that they are outright lying, or even consciously being deceptive. But sometimes they know information that could help you—and they just don't tell it to you. They're bored, they're lazy, they assume you know, or worse, they don't want to jeopardize a sale. And yes, sometimes experts withhold information for the worst of reasons—to make a quick buck off you. Whatever the reason, withheld expert advice is rampant, touching every aspect of our lives.

Oh, to be a mind reader! Wouldn't you love to know what's *really* going through the mechanic's mind when he peruses your engine? The dark secret your banker is hiding from you when you sign up for a checking account? The few words you need to murmur to your pharmacist before you save a bundle on your prescription?

A Boatload of Insider Secrets

If the answers to those questions are "yes," then you are about to be quite delighted. For much of a year, we have searched out as many expert insider secrets as we could find. Tips that are not only guaranteed to preserve your valuable resources but will make you feel like a genius to boot. And here they are!

In the pages ahead you'll find hush-hush hints and tips from pros, experts, and other insiders that will give you the upper hand at home, at work, in stores, on the road and on vacation, anywhere, anytime, even in casinos. They range from food industry secrets that can magically slash your food costs and health risks from food to crucial appliance care instructions that should be in every owner's manual. Our inside secrets tell you what corporations and marketers don't want you to know, from the drug company that wants you to ignore perfectly effective home remedies to the established, well-reputed website that slides hidden software onto your home computer.

Amazing Insider Secrets gives you the facts that will make you the smartest, sharpest consumer on the block. Over and over again, we found shockingly effective ways to outsmart the sneaky pros and beat them at their own game. Each of the 1,703 pieces of "forbidden advice" in this book come straight from the mouth of knowledgeable insiders (reluctant though they were to give it up). Here are just some of the things that you'll discover:

- games that supermarkets play to get you to buy the priciest product
- inexpensive home treatments that your doctor and drugmakers don't want to you know about
- unspoken rules that HR and office bigwigs actually follow
- sneaky ways the slim-and-trim get their edge
- rarely revealed info that will make the steely car salesman blush
- tricks that insurance companies are hiding up their sleeves
- corner-cutting tricks of seasoned travelers
- $95-an-hour subterfuges that repair people use
- expiration dates that are just a ploy to steal your money

You'll be amazed at how surprisingly enlightening and simple many of these expert remedies and professional solutions are. You'll discover the secrets for navigating a health food store … the pitfalls of travel websites … the gadgets that clever home-makers use … a notorious tightwad's negotiating tips. You'll find out when you can safely ignore that oil-change sticker, why you should skip the expensive sports drink, how a simple squirt bottle can cut the need for expensive on-the-road dry cleaning, and why you should always get a player's card when you go to casino. You'll even discover that yogurt may be your best bet for avoiding a cold this winter.

Unrigging the Game

Of course, you're no bumpkin. You probably already knew—or at least strongly suspected—that the game is rigged. And by "the game" we mean absolutely everything around you—repair people, credit cards, supermarkets, clothing stores, car dealers, hotels, airlines, restaurants, medical care, insurance, your job, the educational system. It's a fact: Mixed in undetected among the many well-intentioned professionals is the occasional sneaky glad-hander who has laid a trap that's ready to snap closed on your money. It's a complex world, getting more and more confounding all the time, and no matter how hard the average person tries, it seems at times to be almost impossible to keep up with all of the distorted information and all the smooth talkers who are out to make a fast buck at your expense.

That's why we wrote *Amazing Insider Secrets*. It's the book that all the penny-pinching companies, scheming marketers, and sneaky bigwigs didn't want published. Anywhere your finances or well-being is at risk, we hounded expert insiders until they surrendered their secrets. Oh, scores of our informants provided the inside dope openly—because they believe in giving us regular folks an even break. But many more experts, fearing for their jobs and their professional reputations, insisted on anonymity. Picture these experts testifying in shadow behind a screen, while their less reputable colleagues squirm and squeal when their underhanded tricks come to light.

What's Inside

In this book, you will learn the times when you're most likely to get a rookie doctor at the hospital. About the heart-damaging sweetener you find in just about every processed food on the market. About the scary chemicals that sneak into your home in household products and building materials. Not only do we reveal these health threats, but we also tell you what to do about them. (While we're on the subject of health, we'd like to give special thanks to two professionals who helped ensure the accuracy of our health advice—Dr. Mary Hardy, an integrative medicine expert at the University of California, Los Angeles, and Jeff Novick, director of nutrition for the Pritikin Longevity Center & Spa in Aventura, Florida.)

You also will find out how manufacturers gouge extra money out of your wallet every day. Learn the inexpensive dandruff cure that you keep in a bottle by the sink—but it's not shampoo! Get the over-the-counter sleep aid you need—without that hefty price tag. Revive the musty air in your house without those pricey air fresheners. Buy cosmetics for pennies on the dollar. And learn about the secret clothing codes that will lead you to enormous discounts.

You'll discover easy, low-cost solutions to problems around the house—annoyances that you have been throwing big money at. Learn the most common, simple fixes that you could easily do yourself, but that instead keep repair people laughing all the way to the bank. Find out the common lawn care mistake that will kill your trees. Read about the common kitchen item that will keep your icemaker running smoothly and prevent huge repair bills.

Speaking of fixes, this book was written for both U.S. and Canadian readers, so we've included metric measurements as well as traditional "pound-foot" ones. But even in metricized Canada, traditional units are commonly used for some products and materials such as lumber. When in doubt about a size, consult a knowledgeable staffer at your local harware store, home center, or lumberyard.

As this book hits the streets, you can just about hear the collective howl from all the schemers and other sneaks who have been getting a free ride up to now off your goodwill and trusting nature. No more. We've turned a big, bright spotlight onto those closely guarded secrets, and now all of us everyday Janes and Joes can fight back!

—Jeff Bredenberg

Contents

part **One**

YOUR WELL-BEING

Psst! We've got a lot of secrets to share about matters that affect you personally. Want to know how a simple vitamin can replace an expensive cholesterol prescription? How a certain fruit juice will supercharge your workout? How to snoop out the lowest prices in a supermarket? How to instantly tell if a packaged food is healthy? How paying a few cents more at the grocery will help you shed the pounds? Want to know how to make fries that are actually healthful? Or why you should always buy herbs at health food stores? How about an easy trick that chefs use to make any steak taste like a million bucks? It's here: all this, and much, much more.

Saving Your Skin

8 Simple Tricks for Preventing and Treating Skin Maladies

Take vitamin B to prevent insect bites. These days, a mosquito bite is more than an itchy nuisance—it could also mean the transmission of the nasty West Nile virus. Sure, you can spray chemicals on yourself. Or you can try this hunter's trick from Lou Schlachter, Ph.D., R.N., a former dean at the University of North Carolina who now teaches herbal and folk medicine at the College of William & Mary in Williamsburg, Virginia. She recommends taking 100 milligrams of vitamin B_1 or brewer's yeast every day to prevent bites from mosquitoes, chiggers, deer flies, and ticks. The benefits kick in after a week, she says, and continue as long as you keep taking the vitamin.

SECRET WEAPON

Crisco

The red rash of eczema is not only unsightly, but can drive you nuts with the itchiness. Instead of steroid creams, coat the area with Crisco (or a similar product) and cover with plastic wrap. Now, *that's* something your doctor never learned in medical school!

Soothe a sting with vinegar or baking soda. There's no better way to ruin a day at the beach than with a jellyfish sting, or to destroy the Zen of a picnic with a bee sting. But since the venom in most stings is composed of either acid or alkaline substances, using the opposite immediately relieves the stinging sensation, says Dr. Schlachter. So carry a small spray bottle of white vinegar and a little container of baking soda with you when you head to the great outdoors. If you get stung, spray with the vinegar first. If the sting persists, slather on a paste of baking soda (just mix a tiny amount with some water or even your spit). If the stinger is still in your skin, gently rub it with a wet bar of soap—the stinger will come right out, she says.

Use yogurt to dry up cold sores.

Why is it that a cold sore seems to pop out just as you have an important event coming up, like your daughter's wedding? Probably because most cold sores are caused by the common herpes virus. It lives quietly in your body until some kind of stress (aforementioned wedding) wakes it up. To quickly get rid of the ugly cold sore, do what Dr. Schlachter does: Put a teaspoon of cultured yogurt on the area several times a day. The active microorganisms in the yogurt "attack" the virus, she says, reducing the itching and helping the sore heal faster.

Use an onion to remove a splinter.

So your grandkid was playing on your back deck barefoot and now he's got a 1/4-inch (6.35-mm) splinter stuck deep in his foot. When you pull out the needle and matches, he begins screaming like you've suggested cutting off the foot. No need for those tears. Just take a 1/4-inch-thick piece of onion, place it over the splinter site, and wrap a bandage around it to keep it close to the skin. Leave overnight. In the morning, the splinter will have worked its way out of the skin with no pain, thanks to chemicals in the onion that shrink the skin.

Put an onion on that bruise. If you

bruise so easily that your coworkers have begun leaving brochures about domestic abuse on your desk, try this folk remedy. Place a slice of yellow onion on the bruise for 15 minutes. The same compound in onions that makes your eyes water—allicin—stimulates the lymphatic flow in your body, helping flush away the excess blood in the tissue that creates the bruise. This only works, however, if you apply the onion *immediately* after the injury.

Treat a bruise with witch hazel. If

the onion remedy just isn't doing it for you, try rubbing the bruise with witch hazel (available in health food stores and drugstores) and covering with ice for five minutes. The two together constrict blood vessels, reducing bleeding into the tissue and speeding healing, says Dr. Schlachter.

Use baking soda to prevent athlete's foot. Snatch that box of baking

soda out of the fridge and sprinkle it on your feet and between your toes. By absorbing moisture, it can help prevent itchy, unsightly athlete's foot. Need the baking soda for biscuits? No problem. Just crush six garlic cloves in two tablespoons olive oil and let it sit for a few days, then strain and apply the oil to the area once a day. The active ingredient in garlic, ajoene, is a powerful antifungal substance, says Dr. Schlachter.

Prevent contact irritation with nail polish. Your husband just bought you a

set of gorgeous (and expensive) diamond stud earrings (and he didn't even do anything wrong!). Problem is, you're having an allergic reaction to the metal. Before getting your doctor to write a prescription for a steroid cream, try coating the backs with clear nail polish to provide a barrier between the metal and your skin. ◁

Hair and Nail Care
4 Secrets for Keeping Your Hair Healthy and Your Nails Strong

Wash your hair in Listerine. Why? Because your hair stinks. No, not really. Turns out that Listerine is an effective cure for dandruff, says Dr. Schlachter. Mix your own dandruff rinse by combining one part mouthwash with nine parts water. After shampooing with your regular shampoo, apply the mixture to your scalp and leave it on. Your dandruff will improve, your hair won't be sticky, and you can be assured people won't accuse your hair of having bad breath. You don't actually have to use Listerine. Most drug chains carry a much cheaper house-brand antiseptic mouthwash that has the same active ingredients as Listerine. Just compare labels.

Give your hair a mint rinse. Okay, the Listerine remedy works, but if you'd rather not have your hair smelling like mouthwash, try this other remedy from Dr. Schlachter: Mash a handful of fresh or dry peppermint leaves and cover them with vodka (sounds good already, doesn't it?) Let it steep for a full day (no tasting), then strain. Add 1/4 teaspoon water at a time to the mix until it becomes cloudy. After shampooing, apply the mix to your scalp and leave it on. You should see results by the second shampoo, and if not, you can always drink the stuff (the vodka mix, not the shampoo).

Take B vitamins for strong nails. Nails as strong as horses' hoofs, to be exact. It's a secret veterinarians have long known—that the B vitamin biotin strengthens horses' hoofs. The hoofs are made from keratin, the same substance that makes up fingernails (the natural ones, at least). Several studies find it works just as well in humans. One from Swiss researchers found that patients with brittle nails who supplement with 2,500 micrograms of biotin for six months increased their nail thickness 25 percent. Take 300 micrograms of the vitamin four to six times a day.

Skip the quick-drying nail polish. Most quick-drying polishes contain more formaldehyde and alcohol than regular polishes, and those fluids can dry and split your nails. The best way to fast-dry your nails is by freezing them. Dump a tray of ice cubes into your bathroom sink, add enough cold water to cover them, then dip your wet nails into the cold water for a minute or two after each coat. ◁

Stifling the Sniffles

6 Secrets for Dealing with Colds, Allergies, and Other Respiratory Difficulties

Eat raw honey to prevent hay fever. It's spring, and while everyone else is outside enjoying the warmth, you're a prisoner in your air-conditioned house, not even an open window to bring the season inside. That's because you're allergic to some form of pollen. Well, start eating raw honey. Since it contains grains of pollen, it helps to gradually accustom your overactive immune system to the pollen so it doesn't go nuts when it encounters the grains every spring. Aim for 3 or 4 tablespoons a day. You can lick it right off the spoon, mix it into your tea, or drizzle it onto your toast or corn muffin. Make sure you're using *raw* honey, and use local honey so it contains pollens from your local region. You can usually find this type of honey at roadside vegetable stands and farmers' markets.

Try algae for allergies. Here's another trick for controlling those seasonal sniffles: Try sucking down green drinks or supplements that contain spirulina, a blue-green algae. This strong anti-inflammatory can quell the overreactive immune response to allergy triggers that leads to your miserable symptoms. That's what University of California, Davis, researchers found when they gave 24 people with allergies either 2,000 milligrams a day of spirulina or a placebo. The algae group produced 32 percent fewer inflammatory chemicals that trigger those symptoms—the placebo group saw no change. Now, just

WHAT YOUR DOCTOR DOESN'T WANT YOU TO KNOW ABOUT Homeopathy

Homeopathy, a 19th-century form of medicine in which you take a highly diluted form of a component capable of causing the symptoms you're exhibiting to cure your condition, has some serious scientific backing behind it. In 1991 a review of 107 studies on homeopathy published in the *British Medical Journal* found 81 trials whose positive results couldn't be attributed to placebo. In 1997 the renowned British journal *Lancet* published another well-done analysis of 89 placebo-controlled clinical studies on homeopathy, concluding the treatment provided twice the therapeutic benefit of a placebo. Another study published in the *Annals of Internal Medicine* in 2003 concluded that while more and better research is needed, "it is important that physicians be open-minded about homeopathy's possible value and maintain communication with patients who use it." The therapy seems to work best for treating the flu (*Oscillococcinum*), hay fever (*Galphimia glauca*), and pain and bruising (*arnica*).

For other conditions, seek out someone trained in homeopathy to develop individually mixed preparations for you.

imagine your allergist's face when you cancel your next six appointments!

Prevent colds with yogurt. If the thought of downing live bacteria turns your stomach, stop reading now. But if, like the rest of us, you'd like to avoid the sneezing, sniffling annoyance of colds this winter, then this tip is for you—and we're pretty sure your doctor never heard of it. Two six-ounce servings of Stonyfield Farm yogurt, or any other yogurt that contains the healthy live bacteria *Lactobacillus reuteri,* can cut your sick days in half. That's what researchers in Sweden (capital of yogurt) found when they had factory workers drink a concoction with 100 million units of the little bugs or a placebo for 2 1/2 months. Just 11 percent of the bacteria guzzlers took a sick day during the study compared to 23 percent of those taking a placebo. Why? These little guys help your immune system work better.

Actually, the yogurt itself may also help fend off colds. In another study from researchers at the University of California, Davis, people who eat a cup of yogurt a day have 25 percent fewer colds than non-yogurt eaters. And it didn't matter whether the yogurt was live culture or pasteurized. Start your yogurt eating in the summer to build up your immunity before cold and flu season starts. The manager of your local drugstore will wonder why his cold remedies aren't moving as well as they used to.

Go salt-free when gargling. Remember your grandmother forcing you to gargle every winter morning with salt water, swearing it would keep away colds and flu? Well, she was right. But if, like us, the idea of gargling with warm salt water makes you gag, skip the salt. Studies find gargling plain water works just as well, says Susan Montauk, M.D., professor of clinical family medicine at the University of Cincinnati's College of Medicine, who recommends it for her patients. In fact, she says, statistically you'll do better with plain water than with salt water.

Get a CRP for sinusitis. Instead of just swallowing the antibiotics your doctor hands you—and the line that all sinus infections are bacterial in nature—ask for a CRP test, an inexpensive blood test that measures levels of an inflammatory marker and is given primarily to test for heart problems (see page 18). If levels are high, you have a bacterial infection and will need antibiotics, thank you very much. But if levels are low, your infection is viral and only time will clear it up. One Danish study found doctors using the CRP test for sinusitis wrote 20 percent fewer prescriptions for antibiotics than those who didn't—great news as we try to stem the growth of antibiotic-resistant bacteria.

Get a CT scan for that chronic cough. Doctors are pretty bad at diagnosing the reason behind a chronic cough. Instead, they'll probably just write you a prescription for a nasal medication to dry up secretions. But a study from Mayo Clinic doctors who performed CT scans on the sinuses of those with chronic cough found more than a third of them had chronic sinusitis, an infection, or inflammation that could cause coughing and sneezing. The treatment? Antibiotics, nasal steroids, or decongestants. ◁

Staying Heart-Healthy
10 Little-Known Ways to Help Prevent Heart-Related Disorders

Take your niacin. LDL, LDL, LDL. If that's all you're hearing when you ask for your cholesterol results, then you're only getting half the story. High levels of HDL—the so-called good cholesterol—are just as important, if not *more* important, in predicting heart attack risk as LDL levels and other blood fat markers. But if all your doctor does is prescribe a statin, you're missing the boat. Talk to your doctor about high-dose niacin—a B vitamin shown to increase HDL levels. Don't be thrown by negative talk about flushing as a side effect of niacin. Today, new formulations, including an over-the-counter form called SLO-niacin and a prescription form called Niaspan, provide all the benefits of niacin without the red face. Problem is, there aren't any drug companies pushing vitamins, so your doctor may not be up on the latest about this important treatment.

Get heart-healthy with chocolate. It seems to go against all of the nutritional advice Mom ever gave, but dark chocolate truly is a healthful food—proven in studies to lower your blood pressure. With its heart-healthy monounsaturated fat, antioxidants, and other beneficial plant chemicals, dark chocolate is actually more akin to nuts than it is to candy. It also provides fiber and magnesium. Scientists who fed people 100 grams of dark chocolate every day for two weeks found that their blood pressure dropped a significant amount—on average, 5 points on the systolic reading (the top number) and 2 points on the diastolic (the bottom number). The one hitch: The test subjects had to forgo other sweets or junk food in their diets to compensate for the added calories. So eat 100 grams of Hershey's Special Dark Chocolate every day, and pass up 531 calories' worth of pies, cakes, ice cream, and chips that you would have eaten otherwise.

Replace butter with avocados in your food. We have nothing personal against dairy farmers, but avocados are a tasty, heart-protecting substitute for butter and cream. When you mash them, they take on the same creamy texture as butter. Use them to thicken your soup or make your mashed potatoes creamier. Avocados are one of the only two fruits (along with olives) that are high in fat—but it's the heart-healthy variety called monounsaturated fat.

SECRET WEAPON

Milk

Mom always told you to drink your milk to build strong bones. We're telling you to drink it to reduce blood pressure. A study published in the journal *Hypertension* that evaluated nearly 5,000 men and women found those getting three or more servings of low-fat dairy a day were 36 percent less likely to have high blood pressure than those eating half a serving a day.

Ask about diuretics for high blood pressure. Pity the poor doctor. With dozens of medications available to treat high blood pressure, patients coming and going at all times, and that stack of medical journals piling up on her desk, who can blame her for prescribing what she knows best—rather than what the research shows works best. And that would be simple diuretics, one of the oldest—and cheapest—classes of drugs to treat high blood pressure. Yet the most-prescribed drugs for high blood pressure are beta blockers. Now an analysis of more than 13 studies involving 105,000 patients finds that people on beta blockers have a 16 percent higher risk of stroke than those on diuretics. The difference was so striking that the Swedish researchers conducting the study recommended beta blockers *not* be the first choice to treat hypertension. Talk to your doctor about switching.

Get tested beyond HDL/LDL. Bad news, your doctor says with a grim look. Your cholesterol is a bit high. Before he can whip out his prescription pad and start you on a statin, ask for more details. Specifically, a lipoprotein phenotyping, which, in addition to measuring HDL (good) and LDL (bad) cholesterol, measures amounts of two other types of blood fats: chylomicrons and very low-density lipoproteins (VLDL). High levels of either can be far more risky in terms of developing heart disease than a high LDL. Plus, statins may have no effect on VLDL or chylomicron levels. The results of the tests will let you know how serious your cholesterol levels are and whether you should start immediately on a statin or give lifestyle changes a try first.

Ask your doctor to check your CRP. Chances are your doctor hasn't. Yet this simple, $15 blood test can tell you more about your risk of a heart attack than ten cholesterol tests. The high-sensitivity C-reactive protein (hs-CRP) test measures a marker for inflammation—a risk factor for stroke or heart attack. In fact, a study published in the *New England Journal of Medicine* found the test is twice as effective as a standard cholesterol test in predicting heart attacks and strokes. The good news? Statins, the most commonly prescribed drug for high cholesterol, also reduce CRP levels.

Take horse chestnut extract to prevent clots when flying. Although you'd rather have your fingernails pulled out with pincers than fly in a cramped coach seat these days, sometimes there's no way to avoid it. If you simply must suffer through a long flight, take double the recommended dose of horse chestnut extract before heading for the airport, says Mary Hardy, M.D., director of Integrative Medicine at the Ted Mann Family Resource Center at the University of California, Los Angeles. The herb helps reduce leg swelling, minimizing your risk of blood clots.

Measure your waist to determine heart risk. That beer belly you're toting around does more than force your pants down around your knees; it's also a big, fat sign that you're at risk for a heart attack (and/or diabetes). Abdominal fat is more inflammatory than fat on your rear or hips, and those inflammatory chemicals it puts out are devastating to your coronary arteries. A simple tape measure can tell you if you're carrying around this risk factor, but the Shape of the Nations Report from the World Health Federation in Switzerland found 62 percent of doctors surveyed said they don't measure their patients' waistlines to check for overweight and obesity. The survey quizzed doctors and patients in the United States, Canada, and 25 other countries. Ninety-five percent of women at risk for heart disease said their doctors never measured their waist circumference, and 71 percent said that their doctors never told them that excess weight, including high-risk abdominal fat, boosted their risk for heart disease. So bring a tape measure with you to your next doctor visit and teach your physician how to do a waist measurement:

- Raise your shirt above your stomach.
- Place the measuring tape around your waist halfway between the top of your hip bone and the bottom of your rib cage.
- Relax and breathe out while measuring. If your waist is no more than 35 inches (89 cm) for women or 40 inches (101 cm) for men, you're okay. Any more and you better hit the gym.

Get a roommate to cut heart disease. And no, your cat doesn't count. Given the latest research out of Denmark, we think it's worth giving up a bit of privacy and learning to share the refrigerator shelves. The Danish study found that people living alone have twice the risk of serious heart disease compared to those who live with someone. We hear craigslist (the online bulletin board at www.craigslist.org, where you can find everything from roommates to a used dining room table) is a good place to advertise that spare room!

Keep working to reduce heart risk. Yeah, yeah, you're two years away from retirement and your boss makes the Meryl Streep character in the movie *The Devil Wears Prada* look good. You're dying to quit or even get yourself fired so you can take early retirement and get out of the rat race. Hold on. A study of more than 12,000 Americans finds that losing your job late in your career dou-bles your risk of heart attack or stroke. So suck it up, keep your head down, and document everything. In fact, continuing to work through your golden years, volunteering, and even just taking the stairs instead of the elevator are the kind of daily activities researchers at the National Institute on Aging found could help you live longer. Even better? The researchers found these non-exercise activities packed as much longevity punch as actually working out! ◁

If you've been relying on cholesterol readings or treadmill tests to judge your risk of a heart attack, you're missing the boat. William Davis, M.D., medical director of Milwaukee Heart Scan and author of the book *Track Your Plaque,* notes: "Using cholesterol testing to identify people with heart disease is like trying to predict who is going to die on a high-speed freeway." That's because half of all heart attacks occur in people with levels of the "bad" LDL cholesterol below 134 (anything over 129 is borderline high).

Instead, he recommends a ten-minute, $200 test called an electron beam computed tomograph, or EBCT. The scans take fast pictures of the heart for 20 seconds inside an open machine that uses about the same amount of radiation contained in dental x-rays. The scans show the amount of calcium in your coronary arteries (20 percent of artery-clogging plaque is calcium) and provides a far more accurate picture of your heart disease risk.

Why hasn't your doctor recommended this simple test? "Everyone focuses on LDL cholesterol because high cholesterol is a profitable disease," says Dr. Davis. Doctors are also waiting for the results of a long-term trial of the screening test due in 2008. We say, don't wait. Three studies published in major medical journals in 2006 found the test worked great at predicting heart attack risk. It's recommended for all American men over age 45 and most women over 55.

Secrets of Good Sleep

7 Easy but Rarely Disclosed Ways to Make the Most of Your Slumber Time

Get your ZZZ's for better memory. If you go to your doctor complaining that you no longer remember the cat's name and you forgot your dentist appointment twice, he might give you a short quiz, pat you on the back, and tell you that you're fine—we're all getting older. But will he ask you the critical question: How much sleep are you getting? Probably not. And that's a shame, because a major study from Harvard Medical School sleep researchers found that the amount and quality of sleep you get significantly affects your memory, particularly the type of memory that helps you remember facts and events in time.

Skip the sleeping pill. Ever wonder why docs are so quick to whip out the prescription pad when you complain about insomnia? Because it's easy, quick, and it works—temporarily. They also have only five minutes before they need to see their next patient, and it would take longer than that to explain the most effective therapy for insomnia—cognitive behavior therapy, or CBT. This therapy teaches you to realistically evaluate your insomnia and find ways to address it. For instance, you might learn that missing a night's sleep isn't so terrible. That, in turn, helps you feel less anxious about not falling asleep so you can, well, fall asleep! One study followed 63 adults with insomnia for eight weeks and found CBT worked better than the prescription medication Ambien (zolpidem).

Check your meds if you can't sleep. Doctors are always supposed to ask you what medications you're taking (or know by looking at your chart), but we've found they rarely do. So when you complain of insomnia, they may not think to connect your sleeplessness with some drug you're taking. Yet many medications can interfere with sleep, says Dr. Mary Hardy of UCLA. These include beta blockers, thyroid medication, certain antidepressants like the selective serotonin reuptake inhibitors (SSRIs), decongestants, corticosteroids, and medications with caffeine (like Excedrin). If you're seeing your doctor about insomnia, make a list of all drugs you're taking—including over-the-counter medications and herbal and nutritional supplements. List the dosages you're taking, too, and take them to the doctor with you.

Boil some lettuce for a good night's sleep. It sounds yucky (and might make a bit of a mess) but lettuce contains a compound called lectucarium, which works similarly to opium in your brain. Since opium is a bit difficult to get these days (not to mention illegal), try this: Simmer three to four large lettuce leaves in a cup of water for 15 minutes. Remove from heat, add two sprigs of mint, strain, and sip just before bed. Any kind of lettuce works, so go for the cheapest—plain ol' iceberg.

Calm those restless legs with a bar of soap. It's a common cause of insomnia: You go to bed, tired and ready to get a solid eight hours. Just as you're drifting off, however, your legs jerk. And they continue to do this throughout the night, either keeping you from falling

☐ The most frequently prescribed medications for chronic insomnia have never been tested or approved for that purpose. In fact, while the antidepressant Desyrel (trazodone) is the most prescribed drug for insomnia, just one quality study has been published on its use for insomnia. That study found that after a week, Desyrel worked no better at relieving insomnia than a placebo.

☐ All over-the-counter sleeping aids, from Tylenol PM to Sominex and everything in between, contain the same active ingredient—diphenhydramine or some other antihistamine. So for the occasional sleepless night, Dr. Mary Hardy says, skip the expensive store brands and pick up any generic antihistamine. Just make sure it doesn't say "non-drowsy" on the label!

asleep or waking you up. While there is now an approved prescription medication for restless legs syndrome (there seems to be a drug for everything these days) side effects include confusion, dizziness, nausea and hallucinations. We have a better solution: Slip a bar of Ivory soap under your legs and the restlessness should disappear in about 3 to 5 minutes, says Dr. Lou Schlachter. It must be plain soap, she says, not a deodorant bar like Dial or Zest. The high magnesium content of the soap helps, she says. And, indeed, research links low levels of magnesium to restless legs. In one study of ten patients with restless legs syndrome, those taking 150 to 300 milligrams of elemental magnesium and 300 to 600 milligrams of calcium a half hour before bed woke less often and experienced fewer jerks after supplementing for four to six weeks.

Take a vitamin for better sleep.
If your restless legs are keeping you awake, by all means try the bar of soap recommended above. But also pop a B vitamin. In one small study, researchers found that women with restless legs syndrome were deficient in folic acid, which is required for proper brain and nerve function. Supplementing with this vitamin, however, improved symptoms. Take 400 to 800 micrograms of folic acid a day, along with a 50-milligram B complex supplement to maintain a balance of B vitamins.

Exercise at the right time. It has been shown time and again that even mild exercise, like a half-hour of walking, can help you sleep better. But *when* you exercise is also important. Exercise is stimulating; it's not something to do just before bedtime. Instead, plan your exercise for early evening—about four to six hours before bedtime. This is the time it takes for your body's metabolism and temperature to drop after exercise, which primes your body for sleep. ◄|

Alleviating Depression

6 Secrets for Handling Distressing Down-in-the-Dumps Moods

Find a new friend to prevent depression. Research finds that fewer of us have close friends today than people did 30 years ago. Research also finds much higher rates of depression today than 30 years ago. While there's no evidence (yet!) that the two are linked, we think they might be. That's because there's so much evidence showing that supportive relationships—whether friend or family—can protect you against major depression, particularly if you're a woman. Since family members are all too often the *cause* of depression, we think finding new friends is important. How to make friends when you're no longer in school? Join a group, sign up for a committee, invite a coworker out to lunch or for an after-work drink.

Get a dog to lift your spirits. With more than 147 million prescriptions for antidepressants like Prozac written each year in the United States and Canada, it might seem like everyone and their mother is popping happy pills. Shoot, veterinarians are even prescribing Prozac and its cousins for puppies. But instead of medicating your dog, you should play with it, especially if you're sad or depressed. That's what researchers from the University of Missouri found when they studied levels of mood-related chemicals in people after they'd played with a dog for just a few minutes. Playing with Fido increased levels of feel-good hormones. Rufff!

Find happiness in eating fish. Why are so many of us depressed? Could it be that we're not getting enough fish? That's what a growing body of evidence shows. The link, researchers say, is related to omega-3 fatty acids, "good" fats that help nerve cells, like those in the brain, communicate with one another. Among the many studies looking at fish consumption and depression, one found that people eating a healthy diet with fatty fish like salmon two or three times a week for five years had significantly fewer feelings of depression and hostility than a similar group of people who weren't getting as much fish. If you can't stand fish, you have a couple of other options: 3 grams a day of fish oil or 2 tablespoons a day of ground flaxseed, another great source of omega-3s. ◁

WHAT THE DRUG COMPANIES DON'T WANT YOU TO KNOW ABOUT Therapy

Cognitive therapy, a form of therapy that helps patients view the world differently as a way of addressing their depression, is at least as effective as drugs when it comes to treating severe depression. And the therapy has no side effects and costs less. Those findings come from researchers at the University of Pennsylvania and Vanderbilt University who followed 240 patients for 16 months—an unusually large and long study for depression. They even found that the therapy's effects lasted longer after patients stopped the therapy than when they stopped the medication.

Plan an outdoor vacation for winter. Unless you live in Florida or California, you know that February is actually 35 days long—at least, that's how it feels. By this point in the winter, you're likely dragging from the lack of sunshine, the lousy weather, the lack of a significant break, and the general crappiness of the world. So cruising the islands or even skiing in Utah can give you a powerful dose of mood-lightening natural light, says UCLA's Dr. Mary Hardy. You don't have to be super-wealthy for such a trip. Even a cut-rate hotel in Florida will work—as long as it has a balcony for sunbathing. Once you return home, you'll not only be refreshed and revitalized but you'll only have a few weeks left until spring arrives.

Skip a night of sleep to end depression. If you struggle with depression, here's a surprising finding that might give your spirits a lift: Researchers find that skipping an entire night of sleep can quell depression for as long as a month. No one's sure why this works, but speculation is that depriving yourself of sleep "resets" your internal clock and enables people who are depressed to actually sleep better.

Indulge yourself to avoid regrets later. You only order a single scoop of vanilla, shop at Wal-Mart, and fly coach—and then only to visit your aunt Ruth in Topeka. Someday, you say, you'll upgrade to first class, buy cashmere, indulge in a banana split every week. Don't wait too long ... a study from researchers at Columbia University found that denying yourself life's little pleasures leads to more than a dull life. It leads to serious regret as you age. Over time, the regret gets worse, while the guilt over indulging fades.

Alleviating Anxiety
12 Little-Known Ways to Deal with Anxiety and Life's Stresses

Ask your doctor for this blood test for anxiety. We've always said how great it would be if there were a simple blood test to diagnose mental health conditions like depression and anxiety. Now there is, at least for anxiety. A blood test to measure levels of the protein acetylcholinesterase, a chemical you release when you're under stress, and the enzymes butyrylcholinesterase (BChE) and paraoxonase (PON), accurately predicted the presence of an anxiety disorder 90 percent of the time in Israeli trials. Although the researchers hope to have a commercial test for these chemicals on the market soon, your doctor can order the test through a hospital or specialty laboratory.

SECRET WEAPON

Basil Tea

If you're feeling rattled, rankled, and wound up, relief is as close as your herb garden or your supermarket. Basil tea is a calming concoction for many people. Just put three fresh basil leaves in a cup of hot water and steep for ten minutes before drinking. Fresh basil is easy to find in the produce section of your supermarket too.

Avoid the stress of telling lies. Pinocchio learned well: No good can come from lying. Not to mention it increases levels of stress hormones that, over time, can cause lasting harm. Don't believe us? How do you think polygraph tests work? By picking up on your body's response to stress, such as increased blood pressure, heart rate, and breathing rate. The stress response is so strong that researchers are developing a "sniffer test" to measure stress hormone levels on your breath.

Quit the caffeine to reduce jitters. We have one question for you: If you have a tendency to get anxious, and you know that coffee and other highly caffeinated beverages and foods make people jittery, then what are you doing with a Starbucks card? Seriously, quit the caffeine. It blocks the calming effects of the brain chemical adenosine, which usually helps promote calmness and sleepiness. And you don't have to chug it all at once to get these effects; one study found drinking the equivalent of two cups of coffee over five hours could make you as jittery and anxious as if you'd chugged two cups of coffee all at once.

Learn the calming effect of breath control. You know how when you're anxious, your heart beats like a locomotive coming full speed up the tracks, and try as you might, you can't seem to get enough oxygen in your lungs? Forget the old breathe-in-a-paper-bag trick. Instead, try this the next time you feel the beginnings of that anxious feeling, says Michael Crabtree, Ph.D., a professor of psychology at Washington & Jefferson College in Washington, Pennsylvania, and a licensed clinical psychologist.

- Lie on the floor, place your hand on your chest, and try to reduce the amount of movement, while continuing to breathe normally. You need to breathe for five minutes and allow your hand to feel the breathing. But you don't want your chest to move, you want the other parts of your body to take over the breathing—using your diaphragm, instead of the big chest inhalation and exhalation.

- Make yourself aware of your breathing in non-stress situations, such as reading or watching television.

- Try to employ the breathing you experience in non-stress situations in more stressful situations—such as traffic jams or conflicts with the kids. "Use the power of getting yourself more focused and relaxed," says Crabtree.

- Develop this non-stress type of breathing as your sustained way of life. "Make it your normal way of breathing," he says.

- Be aware that chest breathing still has a purpose, but only as a point of context. It should only be used in periods of extreme emotional arousal—like running away or fighting.

Try an antibiotic to cut fear of public speaking. Given the growing problem of antibiotic resistance, getting your doctor to prescribe one is getting as difficult as convincing an accountant to take a week off in April. But here's one reason to prescribe the drug: to help you get over socially related anxiety quicker. This type of anxiety hits when you have to do something in public, like give a speech. When researchers from Emory University gave 13 patients undergoing therapy for their anxiety the antibiotic D-cycloserine (DCS) and compared them to a similar group undergoing therapy but not getting the drug, they found those getting the antibiotic learned to overcome their social fears quicker. D-cycloserine is typically used to treat tuberculosis, but studies find it can also enhance learning, which may be why it helped, the researchers speculate.

How I Do It A Spirituality Expert Counters Anger

The secret is selective silence. "As soon as you realize that you are about to express anger over a situation, hush up," says Mick Quinn, the author of *Power and Grace: The Wisdom of Awakening*. "This was the position Gandhi took, and note the fantastic results."

As you interact in your relationships …

☐ Pay attention to the arising of thoughts (or feelings) of anger or anxiety.

☐ Ask yourself this question: "Do I care more about this other person than I do about myself?" A positive response reveals a truly selfless person and a friend anyone would want to have, keep, and cherish.

☐ Be prepared for the sometimes overwhelming need to express negative thoughts or emotions without regard for the consequences on your relationship(s).

☐ Choose to not express those thoughts and feelings by being *selectively silent*.

☐ "Discern, decide, and disregard." Discern that a thought is not beneficial to your current objective, decide not to express it in conversation or action, and through introspection and selective silence, disregard it.

Pop some sunflower seeds to lower anxiety. You've got a big speech to deliver tomorrow and already you can feel your palms sweating and heart racing. Here's what you do, says Dr. Mary Hardy: Munch on sunflower seeds for a few hours before the presentation. Why? Because low levels of magnesium contribute to anxiety. Anxiety, in turn, depletes your body of magnesium as a result of the fight-or-flight response. But magnesium-rich sunflower seeds can break this vicious cycle. One more thing: Before you go to bed tonight and first thing in the morning, take 200 milligrams of this valuable mineral.

Watch some funny movies to bust stress. Yes, line up an Adam Sandler marathon, the complete works of The Three Stooges, and the last three seasons of *Seinfeld*. Then every day you'll have something funny to look forward to. That in itself is enough to boost stress-busting hormones like endorphins and growth hormones, and drop stress-inducing hormones like cortisol and epinephrine, according to a University of California-Irvine College of Medicine study. Researchers there tested 16 men, half of whom knew they were going to watch a funny video three days before they did. The ones who knew the yucks were coming had huge decreases in stress-inducing hormones and increases in relaxation-enhancing hormones even before watching the film. Those who didn't get to see the movie had no changes.

Bang on a drum to relieve stress. It might sound a little New Age, but drumming—yeah, beating on a drum with a group of people—is a great way to relieve stress (especially if you picture your boss's head as the drum). Researchers at Meadville Medical Center in Pennsylvania compared 50 people who either participated in a drumming circle or just listened to drumming and found the drummers had much lower levels of the stress hormone cortisol and much higher levels of immune-enhancing chemicals called natural killer cells. You can find a drumming circle in your area by looking in the newspaper or checking with an alternative health center or practitioner.

Create a space where you can cool out.
Paint the room a calming light blue or green. Add a scented candle designed to help relax you, such as lavender, lights on a dimmer switch, and a comfortable chair with a soft throw. This is your relaxing room, a place you can go when you need to calm down—after work, for instance. The colors are important because they've been shown to help people feel calm and relax, says Larina Kase,

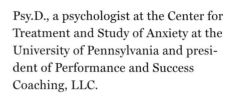

Psy.D., a psychologist at the Center for Treatment and Study of Anxiety at the University of Pennsylvania and president of Performance and Success Coaching, LLC.

Become an art lover to cut stress.
You could start attending art auctions, visit a museum, or simply frame and hang your kids' pictures on your walls. Regardless, studies find that viewing works of art, no matter how much they're worth monetarily, can reduce stress hormones! Another option: Make your own art. Any kind of creative activity like painting or drawing also reduces stress hormones. Oh, and talk to your doctor about those blank white walls in her office.

Ask for a prescription before a stressful situation.
We're not one to advocate medication for all woes, but this one from Susan Montauk, M.D., professor of clinical family medicine at the University of Cincinnati College of Medicine, really made sense. She prescribes a 24-hour beta blocker called atenolol (Tenormin) for patients who have test anxiety or become anxious in other situations. "It's wonderful for those who get a little bit of heart palpitation," she says. You know, that feeling you get just before giving a presentation like you've had six cups of coffee and run two miles? Dr. Montauk has her patients take the medication on a day when they're not going to have any anxiety, just to make sure it works and doesn't have any side effects. Of course, you need to talk to your health care provider about this. Beta blockers are only available with a prescription.

Just say no to stressful demands.
Repeat after me: "No, I cannot serve on the bake sale committee." "No, I do not want to spend every night and weekend driving vast distances to take my child to elite soccer games." "No, I cannot loan you the money for a new car ... allow you to move back home ... take on the fired employee's job." Yeah, it sounds simple, but most of us have no clue how to say the "n" word without feeling guilty; and if you're feeling guilty, what's the point? So Susan Newman, Ph.D., a social psychologist and author of *The Book of No: 250 Ways to Say It—and Mean It*, provides this handy five-step plan:

- Count the number of yeses you've given out during the past week. Make a list of them. The number will shock you.

- For one week, track how you spend your time every hour and who you're with. You may discover one friend is monopolizing you or one family member is very demanding. If you're managing your time well, however, you'll keep some in reserve for yourself.

- Decide who is first on your list: your spouse, child, boss. What about yourself?

- Know your limits. How long can you listen to a friend's sad story again without choking her? How many more PTA meetings can you sit through without screaming?

- Pick one thing a week to cede control of. Maybe it's paying the bills, cutting the grass (does it *have* to be perfect, or can your 12-year-old do it?), fixing dinner every night (there's some great, healthy takeout available these days). ◁

Dental Secrets
9 Simple Tricks You Can Use to Keep Tooth Problems at Bay

Use an extract on that sore tooth.
The pain from your sore tooth is so bad you're ready to tie one end of a string around it and the other around a doorknob and slam the door shut. Hang on. Before you destroy that beautiful grin, put a couple of drops of oil of clove on a cotton ball, put the cotton ball over your sore tooth, and bite down. Hold for several minutes. This elixir made from the dried, unopened flower buds of the tropical clove tree is a great multitasker when it comes to tooth pain—numbing the pain and killing bacteria and other germs that could make whatever's causing the pain worse. You can do the same thing with vanilla extract. After three or four minutes of biting down, spit out the cotton ball and swish 6 ounces water mixed with 1/4 teaspoon salt and several drops of the extract in your mouth for 30 seconds. This will kill more bacteria. Spit—don't swallow. This solution is only temporary, however; make an appointment with your dentist to see what's causing the pain.

Chew gum to prevent cavities.
Chewing gum used to *cause* cavities, but these days it can actually prevent them. Just make sure your gum contains xylitol, says Dr. Mary Hardy. Not only does the gum chewing help maintain saliva flow to flush away bacteria, but studies find that it makes bacteria less likely to adhere to your teeth. You may want to avoid gum altogether, however, if you have bridges, crowns, veneers, or other reconstructive dental work; the constant chewing may help loosen the materials.

You don't really need to have your teeth checked every six months unless you have gum disease, smoke, or have other high-risk factors for dental problems (such as diabetes). Studies comparing dental problems to the number of dentist visits find that visiting the dentist at least once a year (along with regular flossing and brushing) provides good dental health.

Another tooth-friendly chewing gum. Next time you're in the checkout line at the grocery store, toss a few packs of Big Red chewing gum onto the counter. The spicy cinnamon gum contains the ingredient cinnamic aldehyde, a plant oil that keeps nasty bacteria from growing, helping reduce cavities and gum infections. Don't like cinnamon? You can get similar results with Arm & Hammer Baking Soda Gum and gum made from the tree bark pycnogenol (available in health food stores).

Brew a pot of tea for oral health. It's the second most commonly drunk beverage on the planet (second only to water), yet tea gets a bad rap when it comes to your teeth because the tannins in tea can stain. We say, fuggedaboutit. With all the great tooth bleaching tools out there, today you can have your tea and drink it too. That's a good thing, since studies find that tea drinkers have fewer dental cavities, while rinsing with green tea after brushing can reduce overall plaque and the risk of gum disease.

Floss, floss, and then floss again. Sure, it's something you *tell* your dentist you do, but deep inside you know it's been at least three years since you bought that unopened container of dental floss gathering dust at the bottom of your bathroom drawer. Well, it's time to pull it out. Study after study confirms that having gum disease significantly increases your risk of not only tooth loss but also heart disease, and flossing can prevent gum disease. Diseased gums apparently release high levels of compounds that increase inflammation—everywhere in your body. So pull out the floss, toss it into your purse or pocket, and use it after every meal and before bed.

Try this new way to floss. Admit it—you'd rather clean under your fingernails with a scalpel than floss your teeth. What if we told you about a tool that's easier to use and works better than regular dental floss at reducing plaque and gum inflammation? It's true—researchers at the University of Pennsylvania School of Dental Medicine compared flossing with BrushPicks (which have a narrow, three-sided blade at one end, and a probe with six bristles at the other end) with regular dental floss and found the "cleaning aid" was significantly better than the old-fashioned floss.

Avoid hidden sugar sources. You choose apples over apple pie, carrots over caramels and water over soda, but what about those hidden sources of sugar? Like a spy, cavity-contributing sugar lurks everywhere, including antacid tablets, cough drops, liquid medications, and chewable tablets, including vitamins. The sugar content of these over-the-counter preparations is particularly high in children's versions, and research shows they contribute to dental cavities. What to do? Your dentist won't tell you, but we will: Brush your teeth after chewing a couple of antacids or sucking a throat lozenge, just as you'd do after that piece of apple pie.

Swallow, don't chew, your vitamin C. Yes, they're as big as horse pills, but swallowing vitamin C supplements could save your teeth. Chewing them significantly increases the acidity of your saliva, which, combined with the high sugar content in the tablets, can really do a number on your tooth enamel.

Use an electric toothbrush. Put a little spin in your morning routine with an electric toothbrush instead of a manual one. A review of 21 studies over the past 37 years found less dental plaque and gum disease in people who used the battery-powered tools. ◁

Eat fish for dry eyes. How much fish have you been eating lately? And no, the fried shrimp at Captain D's doesn't count. If you find yourself rubbing your eyes a lot and practically mainlining Visine, then the two—lack of fish and dry eyes—could be related. Fish contains valuable omega-3 fatty acids, which make your tears oilier so they coat the surface of your eyes better. They also reduce inflammation, another cause of reduced tear production. Either eat a fatty fish like salmon or mackerel two or three times a week, or take 3 grams of fish oil daily.

SECRET WEAPON

Sunglasses

You wear sunscreen for your skin, don't you? Well, you need the equivalent for your eyes too. In fact, sun exposure is one of the leading contributors to potentially blinding diseases such as age-related macular degeneration and cataracts. Not just any pair of sunglasses will do, however, so listen up. You want glasses that transmit no more than 1 percent UVB and 1 percent UVA rays, wraparound to prevent sunlight from leaking in the sides of the glasses, and gray lenses because they provide the best protection. If you wear contact lenses, get yours with ultraviolet light protection. "Class 1" contact lenses, a designation from the U.S. Food and Drug Administration, provide the best sun protection. But since contacts don't cover the entire eye, it's best to wear proper sunglasses.

Eat spinach for eye nutrients. You know why Popeye is always affiliated with spinach? Because when he was invented back in the early 1930s, a misprint in a medical study gave spinach ten times the amount of iron it actually had. We don't really care where the idea linking spinach to strength came from. What's most important is that Popeye never went blind. Today we know that spinach is rich in eye-protecting carotenoids like lutein and zeaxanthin. Numerous studies find that diets rich in these nutrients can prevent or slow the progress of age-related macular degeneration. But raw spinach won't cut it; you need to cook spinach a bit to release the full amount of carotenoids. So sauté a bag of prewashed spinach in 2 tablespoons extra-virgin olive oil and a garlic clove just until the spinach wilts. Toss a pinch of dried red peppers over the greens, place over pasta, and sprinkle the whole thing with grated Parmesan cheese.

Get your bilberries for night vision. Here's a fact we're pretty sure neither you nor your doctor knows: Pilots in the Royal Air Force in Britain used to eat tons of bilberry jam to improve their night vision before flying sorties. They knew then what science is only now learning: Bilberries, also called English blueberries, can preserve the health and integrity of your retina and improve night vision. Take a 160-milligram supplement twice a day.

Try acupuncture for dry eyes. No, not *in* your eyes, but in other parts of your body. Numerous studies find that this ancient Chinese treatment significantly increases eye moisture, although, as with many alternative approaches, we're not sure why. But you know what? We also don't know why or how a lot of drugs work! And don't worry: If you're afraid of needles, most acupuncturists today can use acupressure or other non-needle approaches. ◂

Caring for Your Ears
6 Little-Known Tricks for Staving Off Problems with Hearing

Get exercise to hear better. Now, this is something we know your doctor doesn't know—but the more physically active you are, the better your hearing is likely to be! Why? Because aerobic activity such as biking and walking brings more oxygen into your lungs, which increases blood flow throughout your body (including your ears). That, in turn, improves your hearing! At least, that's what we hear from researchers.

Eat avocado to help your hearing. Mmm, like eating solid butter—but oh, so much better for you! The green fruit is rich in magnesium, a mineral that helps protect your hearing from noise-related hearing loss. Just make sure the fruit is uniformly dark when you buy it and yields slightly—but not too much—when you press on it. You can store a ripe avocado in the fridge for two or three days.

SECRET WEAPON

Earplugs

You don't have to have spent your youth following the Grateful Dead around to damage your hearing with loud noises. The noises of everyday life—lawn mower, leaf blowers, cars backfiring, even the ubiquitous iPods attached to everyone's ears these days—are more than enough. So get a few pairs of earplugs, scatter them around the house, in your car and purse, and use them to turn down the volume of your world.

Drink wine to prevent hearing loss. Okay, when's the last time your doctor told you to drink? Probably never, even though everyone, particularly Morley Safer of *60 Minutes,* knows that wine is good for your heart. But even Morley probably doesn't know it's also good for your ears. That's what researchers evaluating 3,000 people in Beaver Dam, Wisconsin, found. Just one to three glasses of wine or beer a day could actually protect against age-related hearing loss. Stop right there, though. Once you hit four or more servings of booze, not only do you have a drinking problem, but you may be contributing to hearing loss.

Take care of your teeth to protect hearing. Trust us, you want to keep your original teeth. The more teeth you have, it seems, the better your hearing as you age. That's what researchers found when they compared dental health and hearing loss in more than 1,000 veterans (why they thought to link the two, no one knows). Every tooth you lose more than doubles your risk of hearing loss. Scientists aren't sure why, but suspect it has something to do with the position of the jaw or maybe lack of muscle activity that affects the auditory tube. Regardless, brush and floss twice a day!

Be aware of your partner's snoring. While your doctor may warn you about obvious loud noises like gunshots and lawn mowers, you may never hear about the dangerous effects of snoring on your hearing. Yes, snoring. Research shows that the sound of snoring can be louder decibel-wise than the sound of city traffic. And any loud noise damages your ears over time. After proving to your partner that yes, he or she *does* indeed snore—a tape recorder may help—suggest a visit to a sleep center. Snoring can be a sign of sleep apnea, a breathing disorder that could lead to heart disease.

Take ginkgo biloba to open up your ears. If you have a doctor who recommends herbal supplements as part of a healthy life, good for you. The rest of us buy books like this. Because it's a rare doctor who's going to recommend ginkgo biloba for your hearing. Yet several European studies find that the herb improves hearing, even restoring hearing suddenly lost. One study compared it to the drug pentoxifylline, used to increase blood flow in cases of sudden hearing loss, and found the herb worked better than the drug! Take between 12 and 120 milligrams twice a day, depending on the extent of your hearing loss. ◁

Clean Out Your Own Ears (Thanks Anyway, Doc)

EXPERT INSTANT ADVICE

Ever notice your general practitioner is a little too, ahem, *eager* to get at the wax in your ears? No, it's not some strange fetish. But when they clean out your ears, they get to bill your insurance company (or you) for a separate service, since cleaning out earwax is actually considered a surgical procedure. Maybe that's why U.S. physicians clear impacted wax, or cerumen, from an estimated 150,000 ears each week! Save the money and do it yourself. Mix 1 tablespoon hydrogen peroxide with 1/2 cup warm water. Fill an ear bulb syringe (the blue things you use to clear an infant's nose) with the mixture, tilt your head sideways, and release the solution at the opening to your ear (don't stick the dropper tip into the ear). You'll hear and feel bubbling, but don't worry. Those bubbles help loosen the earwax so it can make its way to the surface for removal. Then, after a few seconds or when the bubbling stops, turn your head the other way to drain the ear.

For extensive earwax, get the over-the-counter wax softener Cerumenex (it's prescription-only in Canada). Fill the canal of the ear with several drops and plug with a cotton ball before going to sleep. In the morning, remove the cotton, shower, and wash your hair. This usually rinses out all but the most severe plugs.

Coping with M.D.'s

11 Tricks for Getting the Most Out of Medical Exams and Visits to Doctors

Get the first appointment of the day. What is it with doctors that they think *their* time is more valuable than yours, leaving you to cool your heels in the waiting room for an hour or more past your scheduled appointment? One way to get around this is to make sure you get the first appointment of the day or the first appointment after lunch, says UCLA's Mary Hardy, M.D. No one will have tied up the doctor or staff before you, and everyone will be more refreshed and less rushed than if they're running between you, the "chronic cough," and the "foot fungus."

Do your homework on your condition. The days of trusting implicitly in your doctor are over. These days, you have to be an active participant in your health care. And that means learning about your condition and the best way to treat it. No, you don't need to go to medical school. Thanks to the Internet, national guidelines for treating many health conditions are just a few mouse clicks away. Start with guidelines based on the latest scientific evidence at the National Guidelines Clearinghouse at www.guideline.gov. Then make sure you ask your doctor if *your* treatment is based on the latest evidence.

Find out what your doctor isn't telling you. There are procedures, tests, and treatments that could help you, but since your health insurance doesn't cover them, your doctor isn't telling you about them. That's the finding from a survey of 1,124 U.S. physicians, which showed that one in three docs withhold information from their patients about useful medical services that aren't covered by the patient's insurance. The remedy: Be an informed patient, do your own research, and look your doctor in the eye as you ask: "Is there anything else I could do? Even if it's not covered by my health insurance?"

Ask to sample a drug first. When your doctor prescribes a brand-name medication, ask if you can have samples. Drug company representatives often give doctors free samples, and it will cost your doctor nothing to pass them along to you. You'll get a "free ride" for several days, and if you have a bad reaction to the medicine, you'll find out without having paid a cent. You may actually end up giving that pharmaceutical company *less* of your cash for a change. One caveat: Check the expiration date on the drugs first.

Ask for three months of meds. The next time your doctor writes you a prescription, ask for enough to last you three months rather than a shorter duration. That way, you only have to pay one co-pay for a three-month supply, instead of three monthly co-pays for the same amount of medication. Check the prescription before leaving the doctor's office, however, to make sure it's written correctly.

Tell your doctor what you can afford. Studies find that doctors won't ask you if you can afford your medication, but if you tell them you can't, they'll come up with strategies so you can get your drugs and still have money to pay the rent and eat. Some options:

Many so-called objective patient websites and consumer health organizations are heavily funded by drug companies. Even some national campaigns highlighting a particular disease—like one that popped up in mid-2006 explaining that a virus causes cervical cancer—come from drug companies. That cervical cancer campaign? Funded by Wyeth-Ayerst in the months before it received FDA approval for the first HPV vaccine. The message: Be an informed consumer. Check websites for information on board members and funders and be aware of messages designed to steer you toward a particular drug or diagnosis.

writing prescriptions for generics instead of brand names, reducing dosages, stopping some medications, teaching you how to split pills, and referring you to pharmaceutical assistance programs. So forget the "don't ask, don't tell" policy on income when it comes to your health.

Schedule your skin checkup for winter. If you call your dermatologist in June and ask for an appointment for your annual skin check in August, is the receptionist going to say, "Why don't you wait until December when you don't have a tan and it's easier to see any irregularities?" No, most likely she will go right ahead and make your appointment without passing along this vital information. But now *you* know, so hold off on that exam until winter.

Time your Pap test. Okay, guys, you can tune out here. This is just for the ladies. Before you schedule that annual Pap test, check your calendar. The best time for the test is the week before or after you ovulate, usually the first or third week of your menstrual cycle, says Dr. Mary Hardy. This is when the cervical opening is widest, so it's easier to get a sample, and the cervical mucus is thinnest, increasing the accuracy of the test.

Time your mammogram. Another one for the ladies, so guys, consider this the book's version of a commercial you can tune out. Ladies, whether anyone talks about it or not, having your breasts squeezed between two glass plates in a futile attempt to make them as flat as a pancake *hurts*. But it must be done (every year or two from age 40 onward). To reduce the pain, time your mammogram for the week after your period, suggests the American Cancer Society. Your breasts are less tender and, an added bonus, a major study found mammograms taken during this time are more accurate. They're less likely to result in false positives, while mammograms taken during the second half of your menstrual cycle are twice as likely to miss a cancer.

Eat only liquids before a colonoscopy. Just the thought of it gives us the shivers, but once you turn 50, a colonoscopy should be as much a part of that passage as a midlife crisis.

You can make the whole thing easier on yourself by following a liquid diet for two days before the procedure so during the pre-procedure "clean-out" you don't have the, ahem, "matter" to clean out.

Ask for a warm blanket for that PET scan. No one likes lying on the cold metal bed of a PET scanner waiting to learn if he has cancer. But if you're covered with a warm blanket, the test will not only be more comfortable, but more accurate. That's because special tissue called "brown fat," the kind that keeps you warm, also tends to absorb the radioactive tracer used in a PET scan to identify cancers, misleading doctors into thinking the fat cells are cancer cells or even hiding actual cancer cells. The warm blanket, however, can reduce the amount of tracer the fat takes in by 62 percent. Other ways to ensure an accurate PET scan include abstaining from strenuous activity and caffeinated beverages before the scan. ◁

Hospital Savvy

5 Surprising Tips for Making Hospital Stays as Brief and Safe as Possible

Avoid hospitals and emergency rooms in July and August. In the U.S., new medical students, interns, and residents start work July 1 and medical errors spike. There's even a name for it: The "July phenomenon." One study found that the odds of interns nearly missing important information in a blood test were more than twice that in their first month on rotation as during the following 11 months of their intern years. A primary reason for the near misses? "Inexperience and unfamiliarity with hospital systems," say researchers. Another study found the average length of stay in hospitals increased 2 percent in July, August, and September, while the average death rate increased 4 percent. You can wait until Christmas for that hernia repair, can't you?

Never check into a hospital on a weekend. Unless it's an emergency—if you're just having tests or elective surgery—don't check into the hospital on a weekend (or a holiday). Chances are good that you will do nothing but lie in bed for the weekend at a cost of more than $1,200 a day. Doctors try to discharge patients by Friday, so hospitals want to fill the empty beds on weekends. For both your monetary and physical health, insist on checking in as close to the test or surgery time as possible.

Check out a hospital, especially if you're a woman. Hospitals today are spending millions to lure women as patients, splurging on such features as fancy atriums with three-story fountains, maternity wards with wood floors, down comforters, and flat-screen televisions. But we know that you can't judge a book by its cover. And, in fact, many of those hospitals wouldn't appear quite so inviting if they revealed that you're 40 percent more likely to die of a heart attack or stroke there than if you chose the hospital down the road for your cardiac bypass operation or to treat your heart attack. That's what a three-year study of more than 2.1 million hospitalizations at more than 2,100 hospitals found when it analyzed six heart-related procedures and diagnoses for the hospital's female patients. Overall, there was a 40 percent difference in death rates between the nation's best-performing hospitals and the nation's worst, and a 23 percent difference in death rates between the best-performing hospitals and those that were only average. If all the hospitals performed as well as the best hospitals, 30,548 additional women might have survived their hospitalization for heart disease and stroke. To find out where your hospital ranks, visit www.healthgrades.com.

Ask: Have you washed your hands?
How gross is this: The nurse changes the sheets of your roommate who just had his appendix out, then comes right over to work on yours. Did she wash her hands? Nooooo. In fact, although the primary way to reduce the spread of hospital-borne infections is hand washing, studies find most hospital workers comply with basic hand-washing requirements less than half the time. One way to make sure the nurses or doctors do wash their hands before examining you? Ask. One study found when patients checked whether health-care workers washed their

hands, the workers washed their hands more often and used more soap.

Ask for a less unpleasant catheter.
It's one of the most humiliating and painful parts of hospitalization (if you're a man). Having a nurse stick a catheter up your private part. It's also probably the reason you got that nasty urinary tract infection during your hospital stay. Next time you have to go to the hospital, ask for an external, or "condom," catheter. This form of catheter, also called a "Texas catheter" (don't ask), is a rubber latex sheath with a tube at the end that fits tightly on the penis, rather than having to be inserted *in* the penis. The first-ever study comparing the two types of catheters found the condom catheter, which is much more pleasant and less painful, reduced the risk of urinary tract infections by 80 percent. That could mean a shorter hospital stay, not to mention a quicker overall recovery. Of course, this type of catheter doesn't work if the reason for using a catheter is a constricted urinary tract because of prostate problems or bladder surgery. ◁

HOW YOU CAN
Reduce
Medical Errors

A groundbreaking Institute of Medicine report issued in 1999 found that 44,000 to 98,000 Americans die in hospitals each year, not from the medical conditions they checked in with but from preventable medical errors. While the health-care system as a whole is working on ways to reduce those dreadful figures, there are also things you, as a patient, can do. Here are the top ten recommendations from the U.S. Agency for Healthcare Research and Quality.

☐ Be an active member of your health-care team. Don't just blindly nod when your doctor hands you a prescription or says you need surgery. Question everything, ask for studies, find out about your doctor's experience in a particular procedure. Research shows that patients who are more involved with their care tend to get better results.

☐ Make sure *all* your doctors know *everything* you're taking. That includes prescription and over-the-counter medicines, and dietary supplements such as vitamins and herbs. But it also includes illegal drugs. Don't worry—your doctor is bound by confidentiality rules not to disclose the information to anyone. So once a year, toss all your meds into a paper bag and take them to your annual checkup.

☐ When your doctor writes you a prescription, make sure you can read it. If you can read it, chances are good the pharmacist can too. And that will help reduce medication errors.

☐ Ask for information about your medicines in terms you can understand—both when your medicines are prescribed and when you receive them. Studies find that doctors are terrible at explaining to patients how to take medications, what their side effects are, and how long they should be taken. Ask the following questions:

> What is the medicine for?
>
> How am I supposed to take it, and for how long?
>
> What side effects are likely? What do I do if they occur?
>
> Is this medicine safe to take with other medicines or dietary supplements I am taking?
>
> What food, drink, or activities should I avoid while taking this medicine?

☐ Make sure you understand the medication label. For instance, does "four doses daily" mean a dose every six hours or just during regular waking hours?

☐ If you have a test, don't assume that no news is good news. Ask about the results.

☐ When you're discharged from the hospital, ask your doctor to explain the treatment plan you will use at home. This includes learning about your medicines and finding out when you can get back to your regular activities. Research shows that at discharge time, doctors think their patients understand more than they really do about what they should or shouldn't do when they return home.

☐ If you're having surgery, make sure you, your doctor, and your surgeon all agree and are clear on exactly what will be done. In fact, ask your doctor to sign his/her initials on the site of the surgery—for instance, the left knee—then double-check that it's the correct site. That's what the American Academy of Orthopaedic Surgeons urges its members to do.

☐ Make sure that someone, such as your personal doctor, is in charge of your care. This is especially important if you have many health problems or are in a hospital.

☐ Ask a family member or friend to be there with you and to be your advocate (someone who can help get things done and speak up for you if you can't). Even if you think you don't need help now, you might need it later.

Using Meds Effectively
7 Secrets You Should Know About Taking Prescription and OTC Drugs

Buy drugs late in the month. Filling your prescription on the first of the month significantly increases the likelihood you'll get the wrong dose or drug. A study from researchers at the San Diego Center for Patient Safety found that since government checks such as Social Security go out at the beginning of the month, that's when many people get their prescriptions filled. That, in turn, overwhelms many already-overwhelmed pharmacists. And those overwhelmed pharmacists may be part of the reason that University of San Diego researchers found deaths related to pharmacy medication errors spiked 25 percent at the beginning of the month. So get yourself on a mid- or late-month refill schedule.

Check your meds at the drugstore. Before you hand over the charge card, check the medicine in the bag and ask, "Is this what my doctor prescribed?" A study from the Massachusetts College of Pharmacy and Allied Health Sciences found that 88 percent of medicine errors involved the wrong drug or the wrong dose.

Check the ingredients of cold remedies. If your child has the sniffles, you may be tempted to provide him with all manner of over-the-counter treatments to provide comfort. But you could be putting your child's health at risk unless you read the fine print carefully. The corner drugstore will happily sell you cold treatments by the basketload, but make sure that you aren't inadvertently harming your child by giving him too much of particular ingredients. You might give him the proper dosage of acetaminophen tablets, for instance, but not notice that the cough medicine you're also providing contains the same drug. Too much acetaminophen can cause liver damage. So check the fine print on the packaging of all medications.

Swallow your penicillin with live-culture yogurt. Your doctor isn't going to tell you this as he writes the prescription, but antibiotics can have some annoying side effects, including diarrhea and yeast infections (in women). The easy way to prevent these problems is by eating at least two cups of live-culture yogurt (you can find it in the dairy case) a day while taking antibiotics. The "good" bacteria in the yogurt restores the "good" bacteria that the antibiotic wipes out.

SECRET WEAPON

Water

Sure, it's the elixir of life. But did you know that studies find that getting at least five 8-ounce glasses of water a day, particularly if you're over 65, can reduce your risk of falls, constipation, coronary heart disease, and even bladder cancer (in men)? In fact, one study found that nearly half of older adults admitted to the hospital from the emergency room were dehydrated—and didn't even know it. A good way to get enough water is to fill one-third of a gallon-size pitcher with water and keep it in your refrigerator. When the pitcher is empty, you've consumed your 40-ounce minimum for the day.

Measure medicine properly.
Studies find that many people don't understand how to measure liquid meds. Too often, they use a regular teaspoon, which doesn't deliver the right amount. Save the teaspoon for cereal and pick up a medicine spoon or syringe for the drugs.

Get off the Pill to quit smoking.
You've tried the patch, the gum, even the inhaler, but nothing seems to work and you're still smoking half a pack a day. Now try switching your birth control pill for a nonestrogen form of contraception, such as an IUD or a diaphragm. Women apparently not only metabolize nicotine faster than men, but the effects are even more pronounced in women who are taking oral contraceptives. Researchers from the University of California, San Francisco, who conducted the study that found this effect, say this sex difference may be one reason women have a harder time quitting smoking than men.

Take your meds—or else. Or else you could die. No kidding. A report analyzing 21 studies found that people who take their medicine regularly—*even if their medicine is a sugar pill*—have a lower risk of dying during a certain time period than those who don't follow the instructions. Don't count on your doctor to remind you how important it is to take your meds, however; numerous studies find docs are notoriously bad when it comes to counseling patients regarding the most important thing about a prescribed drug: If you don't take it, it won't work! ◁

Alleviating Pain
8 Little-Known Facts You Should Know About Coping with Aches and Pains

Don't take Tylenol for arthritis.
If your doctor is still recommending Tylenol for arthritis pain, then she's not reading the medical journals. A major study published in the respected *Archives of Internal Medicine* found that Tylenol, or acetaminophen, worked no better than a sugar pill at relieving arthritis pain. Plus, in large doses it could cause kidney damage and liver damage. Instead, work with your doctor to find alternative means of managing your pain, ranging from exercise to non-steroidal medications like ibuprofen, which studies find works much better than acetaminophen for this type of inflammatory pain.

Don't mix pain relievers for different pains. You're taking ibuprofen for your arthritis and acetaminophen for your headache and an over-the-counter flu remedy that, unbeknownst to you, also contains acetaminophen. Whoa! You've just overwhelmed your liver. So read the labels of your pain relievers and cold and flu remedies before popping another pill.

Go for the lowest dose of painkillers. First you pop an all-day naproxen for your sore back. But a few hours later, your back still sore, you unthinkingly shake out a couple of Motrin from the bottle in your purse. That night before you go to bed, you take a couple of Tylenol PM to help you sleep. Keep on this way and you're putting yourself at risk for high blood pressure. Seems that women who consume high doses of non-aspirin pain

Many surgeries have little or no clinical evidence proving their effectiveness, and some show no more benefit than a placebo, or sham, surgery. That's because no government agency has to "approve" new surgical techniques in the way that the FDA approves new drugs.

Back surgery is a prime area to be cautious. Many doctors recommend spinal fusion surgery for chronic back pain. But a study comparing the surgery to exercise found that each was just as effective in reducing pain.

Disk bulges and protrusions found on MRI are just as common in people without back pain

as in people with back pain, according to a study published in the New England Journal of Medicine. That means if your surgeon tells you that you need surgery to correct a bulging disk, get a second opinion. The disk may not have anything to do with your pain.

Another major study found that a common surgery performed on patients with arthritis of the knee was no better at relieving pain or improving knee function than a sham, or fake, operation in which incisions were made but no surgery was performed.

Bottom line: If your doctor recommends surgery for chronic

pain or other chronic conditions, get a second and even a third opinion, and don't go under the knife until you exhaust all your other options.

relievers like acetaminophen and ibuprofen are much more likely to develop high blood pressure than women who don't. Start keeping a medication diary in which you note the time, dose, and type of over-the-counter drugs you're taking; the total amount just might surprise you.

Pick pain medication on price, not symptom. Even though it's become a major marketing ploy for over-the-counter pain relievers to tout their "specialty" on the label (for instance, Excedrin Migraine), such products all contain the same basic ingredient regardless of the type of pain they're purported to address. So check the label of the product you're interested in, note the amount of active ingredient in each

dose, then pick up the cheapest generic brand containing the same thing and save yourself a few bucks (and another headache!)

Burn out arthritis pain with chile-pepper salve. There are no fancy, 30-second television spots or national campaigns, and since no one is marketing it to your doctor, you may never hear about it, but chile peppers (to be more precise, the active ingredient in chile peppers—capsaicin) are one of the most effective pain relievers around for arthritis pain. You don't swallow capsaicin, however; you apply a cream containing it to the painful area. Experts think it works by depleting something called substance P, a chemical that transmits pain messages to your brain. Give it time: You have to apply capsaicin four times a day for several days before it kicks in, but the relief will be worth it. If you can find the cream combined with glyceryl-trinitrate (GTN), a compound that stimulates the release of nitric oxide, grab it. Not only does GTN reduce the stinging that occurs when you first apply the capsaicin cream, but the two together seem to work better than either alone at reducing pain. Keep your hands away from your face and eyes when applying, and wash your hands immediately after each application.

Take fish oil for neck and back pain. More than 70 million people in the U.S. alone take prescription non-steroidal anti-inflammatory drugs (NSAIDs) to reduce inflammation and pain. Yet these drugs are now the leading cause of health problems and death related to prescription medications, says the U.S. Food and Drug Administration. Imagine if there was a completely natural compound that would not only relieve your pain, but provide additional health benefits as well? No ifs, ands, or buts about it: fish oil supplements can. When researchers from the neurosurgery department at the University of Pittsburgh asked 125 people with back and neck pain who were already taking NSAIDs to add 2,400 milligrams a day of omega-3 fatty acids for two weeks, followed by 1,200 milligrams per day thereafter, 59 percent said they completely stopped their NSAID medication after two weeks and were pain-free, while 60 percent of the rest of the participants who were still taking NSAIDs said their overall level of pain had improved when they added the fish oil. Look for pharmaceutical-grade fish oil, which is guaranteed toxin-free.

Wrap your pain with warmth. The drug companies aren't going to tout this study, but you can get more pain relief from a muscle-warming wrap like ThermaCare Heat Wrap than you can from ibuprofen or acetaminophen. At least, that's what a well-designed study of 371 people with low back pain found. Plus, if you wear the wrap overnight, you'll have less pain for least two days—even without the wrap! However, in the interest of full disclosure, we should tell you that the wrap's manufacturer—Procter & Gamble—sponsored the study. We say, go ahead and try it anyway. It certainly isn't going to increase your risk of liver, kidney, and heart damage the way over-the-counter pain relievers can!

Try this nondrug tactic to relieve a headache. Got a headache? Before you make the cash registers ring at the local pharmacy, try this drug-free remedy: From a standing position, bend forward from the hips and settle your forehead onto the padding of a chair. Relax in this position for 30 seconds, feeling the gentle pressure against your head. Then sit down in the chair, spread your fingers, slide them into your hair, and make a fist. Pull your hair gently away from your scalp, hold for three seconds, and release. This relieves tension in the connective tissues underlying your scalp. Continue this process of grabbing handfuls of hair and pulling gently. Work your way from the top of your head to the sides and finally to the back. With the tension relieved in your entire scalp, you should feel refreshed and ready to resume your day. ◁

How to Navigate a **Health Food Store**

Finding your way safely around a health food store is much like navigating a minefield. There are a lot of traps—hidden behind a lot of hype, misinformation, and outright ignorance—to be on the lookout for while trying to find useful products. The following advice comes from UCLA's Dr. Mary Hardy.

Ask about employee training

The clerk behind the counter should know the difference between various forms of calcium, why liquid echinacea is preferred over tablets, and why you shouldn't take kava kava if you have liver disease. But he usually doesn't. In one published report, a researcher from the University of Hawaii posed as the daughter of a breast cancer patient and visited 40 health food stores. She was frequently told to take shark cartilage, a remedy linked to liver toxicity, nausea, fever, and other ill effects in cancer patients. A Canadian study in which employees of 34 retail health food stores were asked what they'd recommend for a patient with breast cancer found 33 different products recommended, none of which had any significant research behind them. Only eight employees discussed the potential for drug interactions, and one actually suggested the patient stop taking tamoxifen (a proven cancer treatment). So ask about the clerk's training (large chains say they invest in training) and don't follow any recommendations if the clerk doesn't at least ask about your health and other medications you're taking.

Stay away from memberships

If you're being pitched a membership in a health food club, get out of there. Health food stores should be dedicated to helping you find the best remedy for your needs, not plying you with stuff you don't need.

Do your research before you hit the store

Don't walk in looking for "something to help the pain in my knee." At least know to ask for glucosamine.

Read the labels

Compare the amounts of active ingredients and the types of ingredients in the supplement, dosages, and number of doses in the bottle. Such comparisons will lead you to the best value for your money.

Ask to see third-party literature

If all you're handed regarding the benefits of a supplement is literature from the manufacturers, you're in the wrong store. First of all, manufacturers can't make disease claims about their products (for instance, "improves fertility"). Second, you need some unbiased information. If the supplements don't mention the brand name and come from experts not connected with the manufacturer, ask to see additional information.

Supplement Secrets
8 Tricks for Getting the Most Out of Vitamins and Other Supplements

Take vitamins with food. Popping your multivitamin any old time is about as effective as trying to put out a fire with a watering can. If your body can't absorb the vitamins and minerals in that horse-size pill, it's not doing you any good. To maximize absorption, take all vitamins and minerals with food.

Don't take supplements with coffee. If you're used to popping a handful of vitamins and minerals with your morning coffee, you could be missing out on important benefits, says Viviana Simon, Ph.D., director of scientific programs at the Society for Women's Health Research. Seems caffeine interferes with your body's ability to absorb calcium, manganese, zinc and copper, as well as vitamins C, A and B. Wait an hour before consuming anything with caffeine after taking your supplements.

Take children's vitamins if you have a swallowing problem. Gummi vitamins for children are a godsend for older adults and anyone else who has problems swallowing vitamins, or who gets stomach irritation from a single large dose of several supplements. Instead, take two children's vitamins in the morning and two at night. Try the gummi vitamins—they're delish!

Be sure to take vitamin D. Vitamin D is beginning to look like the miracle vitamin. Also called the sunshine vitamin, it can protect against colon cancer, help maintain strong bone, reduce the risk of developing type 2 diabetes and multiple sclerosis, and improve immunity and brain function, among other benefits, according to research. Yet studies also find many North Americans, particularly those in northern climates, don't get enough of this vital vitamin because the sun is our primary source. In fact, findings showing significant vitamin D deficiencies in certain populations led the Institute of Medicine in 2005 to recommend higher daily intakes of this supplement. Dark-skinned individuals, elderly people, and those who don't get enough sunlight (most of us in the winter months) should get an extra 1,000 IU per day from food or supplements. You can get that with three cups of vitamin-D fortified milk, one cup of vitamin D-fortified orange juice, and 600 IU of vitamin D supplements. The rest of us should aim for at least 600 IU a day.

Check your calcium source. Drug company marketers don't exactly ballyhoo this on the packaging of their supplements, but the human body is better at absorbing one common form of calcium than another. Favor sources of calcium citrate (such as Citracal) instead of the other variety, calcium carbonate, which is often found in antacids such as Tums. Calcium citrate is absorbed two and a half times more easily. If you choose this form, however, says Dr. Mary Hardy, double your dose. Calcium citrate contains less elemental calcium (the stuff that matters) than calcium carbonate.

Stifle the gas with enzymes. First, the facts on flatulence: Everyone does it, on average about a pint a day or about 14 discharges a day (it doesn't take much to make the odor). Now, how to stop doing it so much: Take a dose of digestive enzymes, either fruit-based papain and bromelain, which come from papaya and pineapple, or animal-based trypsin and pepsin, with each meal. That's the recommendation of Dr. Hardy. Many over-the-counter digestive enzymes contain both types. The enzymes will help you better digest your food, leaving less to ferment in your colon and produce the stinky gas that gets you those weird looks in the elevator.

Check out a supplement before taking it. Supplements often don't contain the amount of active ingredient—or even *any* active ingredient—listed on their labels. If you want to check out the quality of your supplement before you plunk down $25, go to www.consumerlab.com. This independent laboratory tests supplements and provides reports on their ingredients. You'll need a membership for the full report, but even the partial reports provide good information. If the supplement isn't listed, it either wasn't tested or was tested and found wanting. The site only posts products that passed testing. Another way to ensure quality is to buy store brands from leading retailers such as Wal-Mart, CVS, and Eckerd Drugs. They have a reputation to protect and are more likely to use reputable manufacturers and manufacturing processes.

Stay away from sex-enhancement supplements. If you head online to buy herbs and other supplements to make you more powerful in bed, hold on. The U.S. Food and Drug Administration warns that numerous online sexual enhancement products contain drugs, herbs, and other products that aren't listed on the labels. These could be dangerous, potentially interacting with other drugs you're taking or triggering a life-threatening allergy. Specific ones to watch out for are Zimaxx, Libidus, Neophase, Nasutra, Vigor-25, Actra-Rx, or 4EVERON. If you need to get your blood moving, good old magazines and videos are a better choice. ◁

WHAT **SUPPLEMENT MAKERS** DON'T WANT YOU TO KNOW ABOUT Contaminants

We're so accustomed to assuming that anything sold in a drug or health food store is safe, that it probably never occurred to you that your Ayurvedic health remedies could contain dangerous levels of lead and other heavy metals. But when Boston doctors bought dozens of the remedies at stores throughout the region and tested them, they found 20 percent had significant amounts of lead, mercury, or arsenic, sometimes at very high levels. What to do? Buy your herbs from a trusted herbalist and ask where the remedy originated. Those grown in India, China, and other third-world countries are more likely to contain the contaminants.

10 MUST-HAVE
healing herbs
and Supplements

There's a whole new arsenal of supplements that natural medicine experts "prescribe" for themselves and their patients—because they're backed by compelling research that proves they really work. Your doctor isn't likely to tell you about them. You'll have to discover them for yourself. Here are the top ten natural remedies that live up to their promise. All are widely available at health food stores.

1 Andrographis

Although it isn't as well known as echinacea, andrographis has been used for centuries to treat colds and fevers, and it seems to work better, reducing inflammation and stimulating the immune system. TriMune (which also includes vitamin C, zinc, and echinacea) and Kold Kare are two common brands.

2 Arnica

Ointments and creams made from this herb can be used to ease swelling and promote healing of injuries that cause inflammation. Use it to treat bruises and burns; strains, sprains, and sore muscles; bursitis and tendinitis; and even carpal tunnel syndrome. Just take care not to use it on broken or bleeding skin.

3 Bromelain

Derived from pineapple stems, bromelain is an enzyme that encourages good digestion. Bromelain supplements help break down food and complete digestion, making them helpful for conditions such as flatulence or inflammatory bowel disease. Bromelain also eases swelling and bruising by blocking body chemicals that cause inflammation, helpful for treating bruises, muscle soreness, and bee stings.

4 Capsaicin

Capsaicin is the chemical that gives hot peppers their heat. It helps relieve pain by short-circuiting pain signals from skin nerves to the brain. It's available as a cream in strengths ranging from 0.025 to 0.075 percent. Apply it to the skin for osteoarthritis, shingles, neck ache, or carpal tunnel syndrome, or as a patch for back pain. An initial burning feeling fades quickly. Start with the mildest form and wash your hands after applying. Never use capsaicin on broken skin or blisters. Leaving a patch on too long may cause skin irritation.

5 Devil's Claw

This bitter-tasting African herb contains compounds called harpagosides that reduce inflammation, making it helpful for conditions such as chronic back pain, neck aches, and osteoarthritis. It's commonly available in a liquid and as a powder.

6 Elderberry and Elderflower

During flu season, keep Sambucol, a concentrated extract of elderberries, on hand. When you feel flu symptoms coming on, take a tablespoon four times a day for three to five days to boost your immune system and shorten the duration of the attack. Also keep a jar of elderflowers; a tea made from them will help you sweat and help break a fever.

7 Evening Primrose Oil

Made by pressing tiny seeds of the evening primrose flower, this remedy is rich in an essential fatty acid that eases inflammation and can be used to treat asthma, rheumatoid arthritis, PMS bloating and menstrual cramps, and impotence. It also helps moisturize skin, hair, and nails and can be taken orally to help brittle nails and dry hair from the inside out. It comes as an oil or in gel-filled capsules.

8 Lemon Balm

Lemon balm is an old-time remedy and as a tea is used for treating insomnia, shingles, and—mixed with dandelion and crushed fennel seeds—inflammatory bowel disease. It has been found to contain compounds that are potent virus fighters and is also available as a concentrated ointment that is used to speed recovery from a cold sore outbreak.

9 Lysine

Lysine is an amino acid that has been shown to help fight viruses, especially herpes, by blocking the activity of arginine, another amino acid that viruses need to replicate. Taking the supplement can help control outbreaks of oral and genital herpes, when combined with restrictions on arginine-rich foods, such as nuts, chocolate, and raisins. It also helps to eat lysine-rich foods, such as cheese, eggs, chicken, milk, and lima beans.

10 Quercetin

Quercetin is an antioxidant derived from plants that acts much like an antihistamine. Take it to relieve or help prevent allergy symptoms, such as watery eyes, stuffy nose, and sneezing, or to help ease airway inflammation in asthma.

Healthy Food Choices

11 Secrets for Selecting Foods That Will Make Your Meals More Nutritious

Start meals with vegetables. If you find it hard to get excited about the veggies on your plate, try starting your meal with veggies *only*. Before you even bring out the chicken or lasagna, eat a double portion of salad, green beans, or broccoli—whatever vegetable you're serving that night. Or a hearty vegetable soup. Then sit and chat with your dinner companion for 15 minutes before getting the next course. You'll eat less of the rest of the meal!

Choose cleaned, bagged veggies. While it may cost a bit more, cleaned, bagged vegetables are the best thing to hit grocery stores since Starbucks counters. Numerous consumer studies find that we're more likely to buy bagged salads and other produce. These days, you get much more than just lettuce. How about green beans, peeled and diced butternut squash, washed and chopped kale—we're all for it. In fact, the introduction of bagged, prewashed spinach in the late 1990s is touted as the main reason spinach consumption increased 16.3 percent in North America between 1999 and 2001.

Stock up on frozen vegetables. Probably not something your supermarket manager is going to like (fresh usually costs more), but frozen veggies may actually be more nutritious (since they're often flash frozen just hours after picking) and they're a heck of a lot more appealing than the mushy rotting mess that often fills our refrigerator vegetable drawer. Try microwaving an entire bag's worth of frozen broccoli or green beans (in a microwaveable container), drizzling a couple of tablespoons of low-fat dressing over them, and sprinkling with low-fat Parmesan cheese for a quick lunch or dinner.

Pop some soybeans. Soy is a high-protein, low-fat vegetable that tastes so good you might expect the nutrition police to come after you. But forget tofu. We're talking edamame, or soybeans. Buy them frozen or fresh, steam for 5 minutes, and sprinkle with some coarse salt. Now pop the beans out of the pod. Make a lot—you can't eat just one!

Make fries from sweet potatoes. Instead of plain potatoes, make sweet potato "fries." Slice a scrubbed, large sweet potato into one-inch (2.5-cm) strips, coat with a tablespoon of canola oil, and bake in a preheated oven (450°F or 230°C) for about ten minutes. Shake the pan to turn the fries and continue baking until crispy, about another 15 minutes.

Buy whole-grain bread. Bread manufacturers aren't going to tell you this, but all too often the "wheat" bread they're marketing is nothing but regular white bread browned with molasses. To make sure you're getting the real thing, the first ingredient in any whole-grain product should have the word "whole" in it, as in "whole wheat," or "whole grain." If it says multi-grain, seven-grain, nutria-grain, cracked wheat, stone-ground wheat, unbromated wheat, or enriched wheat, it's not whole wheat, and thus is lacking some of the vitamins and minerals, not to mention fiber, of whole grains.

Serve whipped butter at the table. Julia Child always said to use real butter when you wanted butter, and we agree. But she never told you what *type* of butter! We recommend whipped. It's still the real thing, but at 60 calories a serving compared to stick butter's 100, and with 5 grams of saturated fat compared to regular butter's 7, you'll use less, saving calories. Let it soften before using; it spreads easier, ensuring you'll use even less!

Eat mushrooms for antioxidants. If you're as sick of hearing about the health benefits of "brightly colored vegetables" as we are, here's some good news: Researchers at Pennsylvania

5 Great Uses for Beans

Beans are packed with fiber (15 grams in just a cup of black beans) and, since they come canned, they're so easy to use. Just rinse them first to remove excess sodium (or look for the no-salt-added variety). Not sure what to do with them?

1. Puree a can of cannellini beans with 2 garlic cloves, 1 tablespoon lemon juice, and 1 tablespoon olive oil. Use as a dip for veggies and whole-grain crackers.

2. Spread nonfat refried beans on a whole-wheat burrito and sprinkle with chopped chicken and shredded cheese.

3. Use 1/4 cup black beans and salsa as a filling for your morning omelet.

4. Make a bean salad with canned black beans, fresh or frozen corn kernels, chopped cilantro, chopped onion, and chopped tomato. Drizzle with olive oil and a dash of vinegar, salt, and pepper.

5. Make your own chili pizza. Top a prepared (whole-wheat) pizza crust with kidney beans, shredded cheese, and ground turkey cooked with chili flavorings.

State University found you can get the same levels of disease-fighting antioxidants in portobello and cremini mushrooms as in the ubiquitous carrots and green peppers. We prefer ours grilled, please, with just dash of balsamic vinegar.

An apple a day to keep fractures away. You already know about the benefits of calcium and vitamin D for strong bones. But what about fruit and vegetables? Yup, chalk up another health advantage to these amazing foods—the more fruits and veggies you eat, the higher your bone mineral content, a fancy way of saying you have stronger bones and are less likely to develop osteoporosis or fractures.

Eat chocolate—the right kind. In case you missed it on page 17, dark chocolate is packed with healthy antioxidants. But what you may not know is that it's also packed with magnesium, says Kevin Gianni, a personal trainer in Danbury, Connecticut, and creator of "The 50-Second Fitness Quick Fix" health and fitness tip video-zine. That magnesium can help moderate your appetite!

Buy condiments that add flavor. If you select the right condiments, you'll have the underpinnings for wonderful sauces, low-fat marinades, and even low-salt flavorings that will greatly improve the taste of your meals. Some of these condiments have a high salt or sugar content, so the secret is to use them judiciously to add flavor or to look for low-sodium or sugar-free versions. One great benefit of these tasty meal flavor-adders is that they'll help you stay away from less healthy fatty condiments, such as mayonnaise, butter, stick margarine, and creamy salad dressings. These delightful flavorings include:

- Flavored ketchups and barbecue sauces, chili sauce, and salsas (look for sugar-free varieties)
- Horseradish and various types of mustards
- Jarred spaghetti, bruschetta, and pesto sauces (the latter is luscious spooned atop salmon and baked)
- Jarred olives, capers, sun-dried tomatoes, anchovies, and roasted red peppers
- Worcestershire, hot pepper, soy, and teriyaki sauces (look for low-sodium varieties)
- Extra-virgin olive, sesame, and walnut oils (the healthy oils)
- Flavored vinegars and various kinds of marmalades. ◂

WHAT YOUR GROCER DOESN'T WANT YOU TO KNOW ABOUT Store Aisles

If you shop only on the periphery of the store—where the "real" foods are based—you're more likely to wind up with a healthier cart of groceries. Only venture down the internal aisles for staples such as spices, sugar, flour, canola oil, vinegar, and such. You may save more money in the long run, too, especially if you stick to fruits and veggies that are in season and meats and poultry on sale.

Better Breakfasts

6 Simple Strategies for Starting the Day Without All the Usual Grease and Sugar

Drink tomato juice for breakfast. Instead of high-sugar orange juice in the morning, substitute a cup of low-sodium tomato juice. It's more filling, is less likely to spike your blood sugar, and provides more nutrients and fiber.

Drink a fruit smoothie. What about drinking your fruit instead of eating it? No, not in fruit juice—which is often high in sugar and stripped of the fruit's fiber—but in a smoothie. Just toss a cup of berries—strawberries, blueberries, raspberries—and a sliced (but not peeled) apple, peach, or pear into your blender. Add 1/2 cup skim milk and a frozen banana, maybe a cup of ice if you like it thicker, and blend. Mmmmm good!

Mix your cereals half and half. We agree that eating some of those high-fiber cereals is tantamount to munching on cardboard. So try this: Mix 1/3 cup of the hearty stuff with your favorite cereal. Choose a high-fiber cereal such as All-Bran, with 8.5 grams of fiber, and you're more than one-third of the way toward the recommended 25 grams of fiber a day.

Eat an Israeli-style breakfast. Instead of the sugary cereals, starchy breads, and greasy meat and eggs that make up the typical North American breakfast, do what Robyn Frankel of St. Louis, Missouri, did after visiting Israel. She switched to Israeli breakfasts: hummus, cottage cheese, tomatoes or fruit, plus sometimes a slice of raisin bread. For the first time in her life she's eating breakfast regularly, which studies find is critical if you're going to lose weight and keep it off. The 57-year-old public relations consultant carries just 128 pounds on her 5-foot, 2-inch frame.

Eat half a grapefruit twice a week. Grapefruits are loaded with folate, which has been found to significantly reduce the risk of stroke. But be cautious if you're taking regular medications. Grapefruit and its juice can interact with medications that have to be processed through the liver. Check with your doctor about any possible interactions between grapefruits and any medications you are taking.

Sprinkle half a cup of blueberries on your cereal. Studies find that these tiny purple berries are loaded with valuable antioxidants that can slow brain aging and protect your memory. Not into cereal? Try baking blueberries into oatmeal to create your own oatmeal-blueberry granola bar or mixing them into whole-wheat pancake or waffle batter. ◁

Cooking Techniques
6 Tricks the Home Chef Can Use to Make Dishes More Healthy

Don't pour oil, mist it. Those super-sized jugs of olive oil you buy at warehouse stores may be a good deal financially, but they can get you in trouble calorically. To avoid pouring too much, get a nonaerosol sprayer (like a Misto) and fill with your favorite oil. Use for flavoring foods, coating pans and grills, or spraying directly on bread or salad. You'll use less—much less!

Fake the cream in sauces. You want to make your mother's famous cream of tomato sauce and creamy beef stroganoff, but you don't want the extra fat and calories of heavy cream. No problem! Just open a can of nonfat condensed milk. You'll get the creaminess without the fat and calories—promise!

Sneak vegetables into your entrées. Here are two simple ways to increase your intake of vegetables by adding them to main dishes as you cook:

- Always start with *mire poix* (pronounced MEER-pwah). This blend of onions, celery, and carrots (ratio of 2:1:1 or 3:2:1) with parsley and bay leaves is worth learning a bit of French for. It's a great way to sneak veggies into nearly every entrée you prepare. Sauté a cup (or more) of the mixture (which you can buy already cut up and prepared in some groceries) in a tablespoon of canola oil, then use as a starter for sauces, stews, and soups.

- Whether you're making homemade or jarred spaghetti sauce, adding 1/2 cup or more of pureed veggies (red peppers, cauliflower, carrots, or broccoli) provides just the right touch of antioxidants, vitamins, and—don't forget!—flavor. Or add 1 cup grated or mashed carrots, zucchini, squash, sweet potatoes, or pumpkin to muffins and other quick breads.

Try a different take on potatoes. If you are like most of us, you always make potatoes the same way—peeled, boiled, and mashed with lots of butter. It's a lot of carbs and a lot of calories. Here are two alternatives to try:

- Add boiled and pureed cauliflower to your mashed potatoes. You won't be able to taste the difference, but you'll get less starch and more fiber. Also, to cut back on the amount of butter you add, blend in a little low-fat milk.

- Instead of mashed, serve potatoes boiled with the skin on and cut into cubes. Even better, select new potatoes, which have fewer simple carbs than other types of potatoes.

Stretch the meat. This is a closely related trick—one your parents or grandparents probably used during the Depression, when a pound (500 grams) of hamburger had to feed 12. They stretched it with mashed potatoes, grated carrots, beans, and other vegetables. Well, even though you can afford sirloin these days, we recommend the same approach. Add grated vegetables (try carrots or onions) to ground turkey or beef to stretch the meat, reduce the fat, and punch up the fiber content of meat loaf, hamburgers, chili, and soups. You can buy veggies already cut up and prepared in many supermarkets. Even better: Learn to use soy, beans, and lentils as delicious protein sources instead of meat in dishes like stews, spaghetti sauce, and lasagna.

Add some fat to that salad. Your nutritionist may not tell you this, but the key to getting the most out of all those fruits and vegetables is … wait for it … *fat!* That's because many of those vitamins and other nutrients are fat soluble, meaning they need some fat present if your body is going to absorb them. For instance, researchers from Ohio State in Columbus compared salads and salsas made with and without avocado (high in monounsaturated fat). When it came to the salsa, participants absorbed up to 4.4 times more lycopene and 2.6 times more beta

5 Ways to Have Your Cheese and Eat It Too

1. **Choose hard cheeses.** Parmesan and Romano (the real stuff, not the stuff in the green can) pack a wallop of flavor in a small amount. Two grated tablespoons contain less than 4 grams of fat, about 2 of them saturated. Even better: Look for low-fat versions.

2. **Shred your cheese.** Then just sprinkle over your burrito or salad instead of laying on slices or tossing in chunks. You'll use less, saving calories and fat.

3. **Go for soft cheeses.** Skim or nonfat ricotta or farmer's cheese, goat cheese, and feta are often lower in fat than other cheeses. And like hard cheeses, a little goes a long way.

4. **Go for the flavor.** Just a tiny bit of strongly flavored cheese such as blue cheese can transform a salad without transforming your waistline.

5. **Have a slice.** An ounce (28 grams) of processed cheese has just 4 grams of fat per slice and 60 calories, compared to cheddar, with 9 grams of fat and 114 calories.

carotene (valuable antioxidants) than when they ate plain salsa.

The researchers saw similar results with the salad—adding avocado upped the absorption of lutein up to 7 times and of beta carotene by nearly 18 times! Without the added fat from the avocado, the salad had a mere 2 percent of its calories from fat, and participants absorbed barely any of the carotenoids. That doesn't mean you have to douse all your healthy veggies and fruits in fat. If you're eating a steak, for instance, you've got plenty of fat to carry the nutrients in the salad throughout your body, so stick to nonfat dressing and skip the cheese (and avocado) in that instance. ◄

9

WAYS TO GET

nine
servings

without even trying

You know you're supposed to get nine servings of fruits and vegetables, but the thought of all that healthy stuff makes you, well, nauseated. What if we told you that when it comes to fruits and veggies, a serving is really a relatively tiny amount? Here are easy ways to get your nine in one day (without throwing up):

1 Make a super salad

One 7-ounce (198-gram) bag of washed lettuce equals a bit more than one serving. Add a sliced tomato, a cut-up apple, and 1/4 cup raisins and you've just eaten four servings. Top your super salad with cooked chicken or diced, hard-boiled egg whites for protein and you've got lunch.

2 Munch 'em as a snack

Freeze 1/4 cup blueberries and 1/4 cup grapes and munch on them during your favorite TV program. That gets you up to six servings.

3 Dip 'em

For a before-dinner snack, dip 1/2 cup carrots into low-fat ranch dressing. Now you're up to seven.

4 Add some nuts

Sprinkle chopped, toasted pecans or walnuts over green beans.

5 Drink 'em

Eight ounces (225 ml) of low-sodium V8 juice provides two vegetable servings. Voilà! You've hit the magic nine and it's not even dinnertime.

6 Add some sweetness

Drizzle honey, maple syrup, or fruit juice on steamed carrots or sweet potatoes.

7 Roast 'em

Nothing brings out the natural sweetness of veggies like roasting. You can roast nearly anything, but our favorites are carrots, onions, beets, turnips, rutabagas, and Brussels sprouts. Just cut into chunks, mix with enough canola oil to coat, sprinkle with kosher salt, and spread in a single layer on a greased pan. Roast in a preheated 450°F (230°C) oven until browned on the outside and fork tender on the inside.

8 Make popcorn

Cut the florets off a cauliflower and cut them up into bite-size pieces. Mix the cauliflower pieces with 2 tablespoons canola oil and sprinkle with kosher salt. Preheat the oven to 450°F. Spread the pieces on a cookie sheet and bake them until they are brown, turning them once. Now pop a movie in the DVD player; then settle back and pop this healthy version of popcorn in your mouth.

9 Sauce 'em

There's a reason spaghetti squash got its moniker—the strands of golden squash really do look like spaghetti, only they pack a much more powerful punch. Take the pretend pasta one step further by topping the strands with tomato sauce and a curl of fresh Parmesan cheese.

Tracking Diet Progress
3 Simple Tricks for Creating a Revealing Record of Your Food Intake

Write down everything you eat. This is where the restaurant industry could be in trouble. If you start writing down everything you eat during the day, especially meals eaten out, the shock of how much is actually going in should be enough to get you to toss those neighborhood restaurant takeout menus. While you're at it, check your weight every day. Studies find that careful monitoring of what you eat and what you weigh helps you lose more weight than those who aren't tracking their progress. One study of 40 obese people found that those who followed the tracking advice lost nearly twice as much as those who didn't. Another study found that those who weighed themselves every day lost more weight (or gained less weight) than those who didn't.

Use your cell phone to track your food. Here's a new take on the traditional food diary—which numerous studies find can help with weight loss. Instead of writing down everything you eat, snap a picture with your cell phone or digital camera, then upload onto your computer. *Seeing* what you've eaten in a day can be far more effective in showing you where you're making nutritional, high-calorie mistakes than just reading about it. If you want a formal way to do this, you can sign up online for www.nutrax.com, a service that allows you to build an online food picture log. For $8 a week, a dietitian offers meal-by-meal feedback.

Give yourself a shiny star. It might sound elementary, but do it anyway: Buy a package of those little shiny metallic star stickers. Every day you meet your fitness or nutritional goal (for instance, a 30-minute walk and fixing a healthy meal instead of ordering pizza), give yourself a sticker. "As silly as it sounds, sometimes seeing a whole month of shiny stickers can make you really proud," says Lindsay Wombold, Healthy Horizons program assistant at Butler University in Indianapolis, Indiana. "It's tangible proof of how well you're doing." ◁

WHAT **WEIGHT WATCHERS** AND **ATKINS** DON'T WANT YOU TO KNOW ABOUT Diets

What's most important when it comes to losing weight is *following* the diet, no matter which weight-loss program you choose. That's what a study published in the *Journal of the American Medical Association* found. Researchers compared the effectiveness of Weight Watchers, which limits calories and portions; Atkins, which limits carbohydrate intake; the Zone, which moderates foods based on glycemic value; and the very-low-fat Ornish diets.

The scientists found that sticking with the plan is more important than the plan itself.

However, researchers also found that regardless of the diet, none of the participants stuck with it long-term, with 21 percent quitting before two months, and 42 percent quitting before six months.

Trimming Sugar and Salt
5 Simple Tricks for Cutting Your and Your Family's Intake of These Ingredients

Cut out high-fructose corn syrup. What if we told you that there's one ingredient in food today that, more than anything else nutritionally related, is making us fat? No, it's not fat. And it's not even sugar—at least, not all forms of sugar. It's high-fructose corn syrup (HFCS), which didn't even exist 40 years ago. Today, however, this sweetener is found in nearly every processed food you buy—from fast-food hamburger buns to ketchup, juice, cereal, and even mayonnaise. It's much more dangerous than plain sugar, because your body doesn't metabolize it in the same way, leading to higher levels of blood fats such as triglycerides and VLDL (very low density lipoprotein) cholesterol, which is even worse for you than regular cholesterol.

Even more frightening: It doesn't affect the hormones that suppress hunger. So even if you're getting an extra 500 calories a day from HFCS, your body still thinks it needs more, explains Linda Bacon, Ph.D., associate professor of nutrition at the University of California, Davis. The easiest way to avoid HFCS is to eschew processed foods and, when it comes to condiments and cereals, buy organic (and read the ingredients list carefully). You can make a big dent in your HFCS consumption just by giving up regular soda and fruit juices and other sweetened beverages such as tea, which has become very popular.

Crack the sugar code. Manufacturers are deathly afraid that you'll quit using their products if they aren't dripping with sugary taste. After all, North Americans slurp down about 34 teaspoons of sugar a day—more than three times the limit recommended by the USDA. So sugar gets hidden in products everywhere you turn, including cough medicine, chewing gum, tomato sauce, baked beans, and lunch meats. You'll even find sugar in some prescription medications. Identifying sugary foods can be tricky, however, because manufacturers often substitute code words on their labels. So look for these terms: corn syrup, dextrin, dextrose, fructose, fruit juice concentrate, high-fructose corn syrup, galactose, glucose, honey, hydrogenated starch, invert

---

WHAT CANDY MANUFACTURERS DON'T WANT YOU TO KNOW ABOUT Fruit

If you have a sweet tooth, you can assuage that need for sweets with fruit just as well as with candy, cakes, and cookies. It's a scientific fact. Researchers from Ohio State found that sweet-snack lovers eat more fruits than salty-snack lovers, and fruit lovers eat more sweet snacks than vegetable lovers. The moral of the research? Reach for a juicy peach next time you're craving a Mars bar and see if it doesn't fill that craving just as well.

sugar maltose, lactose, mannitol, maple syrup, molasses, polyols, raw sugar, sorghum, sucrose, sorbitol, turbinado sugar, and xylitol.

Substitute kelp powder for salt.
Sea vegetables have some of the highest mineral content of any plant on earth, says personal trainer Kevin Gianni. Plus, since they're from the sea, they're salty! You can find kelp powder at health food stores. Sprinkle it over vegetables, mix a tablespoon into sauces—use anywhere you'd normally use salt.

Look out for non-salt sources of sodium. Although salt is the prime culprit that adds sodium to our diets, it is not the only one. Check food labels for sodium, Na, monosodium glutamate or MSG, sodium citrate, baking soda, baking powder, and sodium bicarbonate. They are all forms of sodium.

Break the salt habit gradually.
Don't expect to be able to dramatically cut the amount of sodium you consume overnight—or even over a week. It takes time for your taste buds to adjust and begin to recognize the subtle favors masked by salt. Until then, everything that doesn't have salt will be bland tasting. When cooking, slowly cut back on the amount of salt you add to dishes. Another way to get on the path of less sodium intake is to mix low-sodium foods with regular salted foods. Mix no-salt peanuts with regular salted peanuts, unsalted peanut butter with regular peanut butter, or lite salt with regular salt, suggests Lila Ojeda, R.D., a bionutritionist at Oregon Health Services University. Slowly increase the amount of the salt-free product as you decrease the amount of the salted version until you're only eating the salt-free food. ◂

Your Eating Mind-Set
5 Ways Your Mind Can Triumph over Matter in Fighting the Battle of the Bulge

Learn to eat intuitively. It's the last thing the weight-loss and exercise industries want you to do, but if you simply stop trying to remake your body and accept it for the way it is, you're more likely to eat better and may even lose weight unintentionally. That's what researchers at Ohio State in Marion found through a series of studies on "intuitive" eating, which teaches people to eat based on feelings of hunger or fullness, not for emotional or situational reasons. The studies evaluated 597 college women, finding that those who were intuitive eaters appreciated their bodies more, and were more likely to agree with statements like, "Despite its flaws, I accept my body for what it is." An earlier study by the same researchers found that women who ate intuitively were also more likely to have a lower body mass index than women who didn't.

Hypnotize yourself. We do it all the time when we daydream or become so engrossed in a book, movie, or task that we lose track of time, says Susan Neri-Friedwald, a certified hypnosis therapist from New York and author of the CDs *Take Control of Your Eating* and *Eat What You Like and Lose Weight.* Every night, just before falling asleep, repeat four to five times out loud (whispering is fine, and any added emotional intensity strengthens it), "I am in the process of becoming thinner and thinner." Repeat every night for 30 consecutive nights, and it will become your automatic subconscious thought. The last thing you tell yourself before falling asleep will be repeated all night long by your subconscious, she says, and you should begin to see results almost immediately. The evidence supports her: Several studies find that adding hypnosis to weight-loss programs not only improves the amount of weight lost, but participants tend to lose more weight over the long term compared to those who aren't hypnotized.

Go interactive on the Internet.
Weight-loss programs like eDiets proliferate online, but they're probably not going to share this with you: You'd do better getting weekly advice from a behavioral therapist online than simply reading about diet and exercise and filling out tracking forms. That's the result of a study from Brown University. Researchers found that dieters who received such advice lost three times as much weight over six months as those who took a more passive approach to online weight-loss info. One reason is that those getting online advice logged on twice as often those who didn't. Another is that the structured program with continued contact simply works

better than just providing information. A later study by the same researchers found that it doesn't matter if the feedback is real, via e-mail from a human, or automated.

Pray your way to weight loss.
Several studies find that women enrolled in church-based weight-loss programs lose more weight than those who try to lose on their own. One of the best designed and most recent studies involved 15 Baltimore churches and 529 overweight women. During the yearlong study, one-third of the participants attended weekly nutrition and physical activity sessions at the church, one-third added spiritual content and prayer to the regimen, and one-third received education materials on healthy living. Those getting the on-site help—with or without the spiritual content and prayer—lost significantly more weight than those just handed educational materials, with women who weighed the most at the beginning of the study losing an average of 20 pounds.

Get ready for bed right after dinner.
No, you don't have to put your PJs on, but go ahead and brush your teeth and wash and moisturize your hands, says Marina Kamen, a 47-year-old mother of three who lost 100 pounds in her late 30s and has kept it off for more than ten years. "Now that you are fresh and clean, you might think twice before dipping your hand into a greasy bag of chips or messing up your minty mouth with a sugary cookie," she says. ◄

Subversive Habits

4 Surprising Changes in Everyday Non-Eating Behaviors That Can Help You Lose Weight

Turn off the television. There's probably no simpler way to lose weight than to stop watching television. A study involving 486 low-income-housing residents in Boston, two-thirds of whom were overweight or obese, found every hour of television viewing was associated with 144 fewer steps walked—or an average of 520 fewer steps a day for those who spent 3.6 hours in front of the television. Additionally, for each hour of television that participants watched, they were 16 percent less likely to achieve the 10,000-steps-per-day goal. For those who watched the 3.6 hours a day of TV on average, their odds of walking 10,000 steps a day were 47 percent less than non-television-watchers. Researchers estimate that 10,000 steps a day measured with a pedometer roughly approximates the recommended level of daily activity.

If you can limit yourself to just two hours a day of TV or less, you're likely to consume fewer calories and fewer nutritionally bereft snacks than those who watch more. And when you *do* watch TV, leave the snacks in the kitchen. Another study found that if you snack while watching TV, you're much more likely to be obese.

Don't overdo your hours at work. This isn't something your boss is going to encourage, but who cares what she thinks? The fact is, if you work more than nine hours a day (and lunch is included in here as part of your nine hours, whether you work through it or not) you're more likely to be overweight.

And while you're at it, find a less stressful job—the more stressful your job, the more likely you are to be overweight.

Get a solid eight hours of sleep. No, we're not recommending the "sleep diet" described on page 69, but there is compelling evidence that hitting the sack before midnight and getting a solid seven or eight hours can prevent obesity. Researchers from the University of Warwick in Coventry, England, reviewed the cases of more than 15,000 adults and found that sleep deprivation is associated with almost twice the risk of being obese. They also found that the less you sleep, the more your body mass index and waist size increase over time.

What would cause this? Probably hormonal changes produced by sleep deprivation. Other studies find that lack of sleep stimulates production of ghrelin, a hormone that stimulates appetite, and reduces production of leptin, a hormone that suppresses appetite.

Take a walk before dinner. Going for a short walk does more than burn calories. Like most exercise, it also cuts your appetite. And if you do it just before dinnertime, you won't want to eat as much as usual. In a study of 10 excessively overweight women conducted at the University of Glasgow in Scotland, 20 minutes of walking reduced appetite and increased the sensations of fullness as effectively as a light meal. ◂

10
FRUITS & VEGGIES TO
enhance
your meals

When you see them in grocery stores, you may turn up your nose at them, and even wonder, Who the heck buys this stuff? Well, starting today, *you* do. Here are ten to try, along with recipe ideas.

Garlic

We don't recommend doing this alone. Find someone you love, and share. Remove the loose paper covering from a head of garlic, cut off the tops, drizzle olive oil over it, wrap in foil, and bake in a 350°F (175°C) oven until soft, about an hour. Then squeeze the soft heads of garlic onto toasted bread and spread. You'll be getting fabulous amounts of plant nutrients called thioallyls that dramatically lower blood cholesterol levels, as well as prevent blood from becoming sticky and clumping into heart-damaging clots. Scientists believe you can lower your total cholesterol about 9 percent with just 1.5 to 3 cloves of fresh garlic daily for 2 to 6 months.

Avocados

Yeah, yeah, yeah, they're high in fat. But it's "good" fat—the monounsaturated kind that helps lower cholesterol. Try mashing a ripe avocado with a bit of lemon juice, onion, and chopped tomato as a topping for baked potatoes.

Fennel

Also known as sweet anise, fennel has a sweet, mild licorice flavor. The feathery fronds can be used as an herb, like dillweed, to flavor soups and stews. The broad, bulbous base is treated like a vegetable and can be eaten raw or sliced and diced for stews, soups, and stuffing. Try it roasted for a sweet treat.

Bok Choy

An Oriental cabbage, bok choy is like the Chinese version of spinach, only better. It doesn't get mushy, it retains its crunch, and it is the perfect vehicle for soy sauce. Serve it chopped and stir-fried in a bit of peanut oil and soy sauce. Or toss a chopped bunch into a hearty vegetable soup just before serving.

Jicama

Known as the Mexican potato, jicama (pronounced HE-kuh-muh) is a root tuber (like potatoes). Buy it smooth and firm with unblemished roots. Serve it cold and raw, or in soups, stews, or salads. Great as a substitute for water chestnuts.

Chayote Squash

A summer squash native to Latin America, chayote (pronounced chy-O-tay) squash is also known as the vegetable pear because of its shape and color. It has a mild taste, like zucchini, with a slightly citrus tang. You don't have to peel it, and the seeds inside are edible. Just cut into cubes, add 1/4 cup water, cover, and microwave for about 8 minutes.

Kohlrabi

A member of the turnip family, it is often called a cabbage turnip, but it's sweeter, juicier, crisper, and more delicate in flavor than a turnip. The cooked leaves have a kale or collard flavor. Trim and pare the bulb to remove all traces of the fibrous layer just beneath the skin, then eat it raw, boil it, steam it, microwave or sauté it, or add it to potato casseroles.

Belgian Endive

This type of lettuce has a mild, slightly bitter flavor and is packed with fiber, iron, and potassium. Use it in salads and instead of crackers with vegetable dips.

Guava

Yes, we never thought of actually *buying* it either, let alone eating it. But this fruit is awesome—and not just plain. Add the flesh to smoothies, dice it into fruit salads and salsas, and puree it for a fabulous sauce for fish or chicken. An added benefit? Researchers had 50 people with high blood pressure and high cholesterol eat four to seven guavas a day for 12 weeks. They found that the guava eaters had much lower blood pressure and LDL cholesterol (the bad stuff), and they had higher HDL cholesterol (the good kind) than 50 people who didn't add the fruit to their diets.

Prunes

These days the politically correct term is "dried plums," but we'll never stop thinking of them as prunes. Blend prunes with water into a puree and use this to replace oils and fats in baking, add prunes to stews for a delicious sweetness, or chop them and sprinkle over salads, yogurt, cottage cheese, or cereal. Prunes have a special kind of soluble fiber called pectin, which forms a gel in your intestines that absorbs excess cholesterol, sweeping it from your body. When 41 men with mildly high cholesterol levels added 12 prunes a day to their diets for four weeks, their LDL levels dropped more than when they drank grape juice for four weeks.

Cutting Calories

8 Secrets for Reducing the Temptations That Compel You to Eat More Than You Need

Clear out all tempting foods. You know the saying: "You don't miss what you don't have." Add another iteration on this: "You can't eat what you don't have." Go through every cabinet, the refrigerator, freezer, and pantry, and toss (or donate) every food product you don't trust yourself with. It's better to waste it by putting it in the trash than putting it in your mouth, says Lindsay Wombold, Healthy Horizons program assistant at Butler University in Indianapolis, Indiana.

Pay a few extra cents for smaller packs. Your accountant won't like it, since the small packs actually cost *more* per ounce (gram) than the large packs, but your doctor will. It turns out that people tend to eat less when they get several small packages than when they get one large package containing the same amount, says Raphael Calzadilla, exercise guru from eDiets.com. Part of the reason is that the smaller packages provide obvious stopping points at which to consider whether you want to keep eating. We have another reason: The added cost might persuade you to be more frugal with your snacks—for instance, sticking to one bag at a time instead of several in a day.

Shop at the supermarket, not the warehouse club. This carries the same idea one step further. Costco, Sam's, and BJ's may take a contract out on you, but you'll probably wind up eating less. Yup, it turns out that having large stockpiles of food products at home like those huge boxes and bottles of food you get at wholesale club stores makes the products more visible and appetite-provoking than less plentiful ones. So those mega-containers contribute to overconsumption and, possibly, to overweight.

Find lower-calorie alternatives to the foods you crave. You will shave off pounds without feeling deprived if you find reasonable substitutes for the high-calorie foods you crave. We're talking baked veggie chips in place of fried Lay's; nonfat, sugar-free ice cream or fruit pops in place of Häagan-Dazs; baked "fried" chicken instead of the real thing. You get the idea!

Hide the candy dish. If your major munching occurs at work, here's some advice that will not only cut back on the calories but also save you bucks in the candy aisle at Costco: Hide the candy dish, use an opaque dish, or better yet, get it off your desk. A four-week study looking at how much chocolate candy 40 secretaries ate found that people ate an average of 2.2 more candies each day when they could see them (for instance, in a clear dish), and 1.8 more candies when they were on their desks, as opposed to just a couple of feet away. (Hey, it's rough, but someone has to do the tough studies!)

Crack your own nuts. Don't buy shelled nuts, says Susan Burke, R.D., vice president of nutrition at eDiets.com. Shelled nuts make it too easy to eat too much. Besides, their nutrient value drops with processing. A little elbow grease with the nutcracker not only helps to limit portions but burns calories, provides the freshest nut, and gives the most nutritional bang for your buck.

Every meal, eat a pear, apple, or some strawberries. The snack-food industry will gasp in horror, but what they don't know won't hurt 'em. And what they don't know is that each of these fruits contains 4 grams of fiber. Getting just that much extra fiber a day (although more is better) is enough to reduce your risk of being overweight fivefold, according to a study from Tufts University. Not only does fiber fill you up without filling you out (because its calories are not absorbed), but it boosts hormones that send the "I'm full" message to your brain.

Try frozen dinners for portion control. Sometimes frozen is best, particularly when it comes to weight loss. That's what researchers from the University of Illinois at Urbana-Champaign found when they compared weight loss between two groups of overweight and obese men. One group ate two frozen meals a day (they could choose among 24 varieties of Uncle Ben's Bowls) plus other foods. The other group fixed their own meals. Both followed government nutritional guidelines and contained about 1,700 calories. While all participants lost weight, those who got their grub from the freezer lost an average of five more pounds (2.5 kg) than those fixing their own meals, and their average body mass index dropped more. A similar study showed similar results for overweight women. The reason for the difference? The automatic portion control. ◂

The following comes from Susan Burke, R.D., vice president of nutrition for eDiets.com, and Jeff Novick, director of nutrition for the Pritikin Longevity Center & Spa in Aventura, Florida.

1. **Fish.** Choose any fish for high-quality, lean protein that is low in saturated fat and cholesterol. (One caveat: Avoid large deepwater varieties such as tilefish, kingfish, and swordfish, which are chock-full of mercury.) Vary your fish choices: Fatty fish (salmon, sardines, mackerel, and tuna) are full of healthy omega-3 fatty acids, but you shouldn't eat them every day. And don't ignore shellfish: Although it contains dietary cholesterol, this type of cholesterol is not linked to heart disease.

2. **Beans.** Beans are the richest source of vegetable protein to be found. They're dense in nutrients, low in calories, and are loaded with fiber—especially soluble fiber, the type that lowers blood cholesterol.

3. **Fruit.** All fruits are fantastic as long as you eat them whole, as opposed to drinking processed juices. But super fruits like blueberries, kiwis, and strawberries pack the most nutritional punch in terms of antioxidants and fiber.

4. **Sweet potatoes.** When you see orange, think nutrition. Orange means beta carotene, which produces the antioxidant vitamin A. Sweet potatoes are also rich in vitamin C and B_6, and they're full of fiber.

5. **Oatmeal.** Studies find that people who eat oatmeal on a regular basis maintain a stable weight and a healthy cholesterol level. That's because oatmeal provides a high-fiber, high-protein source of magnesium and selenium. Just mix 1/2 cup whole oats and 1 cup water and microwave for 1 minute. Add blueberries or raisins for an additional treat.

Snack Control

3 Strategies for Limiting the Damage Caused by the Urge to Nibble

Don't be duped by "energy" bars. In food-industry lingo, energy doesn't mean vim and vigor; it means calories. And that's what "energy bars" have plenty of. They use the imagery of hard-driving athletes who need a quick dose of calories to supply their muscles enough energy to finish the marathon. However, there aren't enough marathoners or long-distance cyclists or cross-country skiers to provide the demand to keep all the high-profit energy bars on the shelves. So most of them wind up being bought by armchair athletes who eat them instead of lunch or just for snacks. Researchers say that most of the bars do contain some ingredients that are good for you (nuts, fruit, and oats, for example), held together with goo that makes them taste good. As a lunch, energy bars are better than corn chips and soda, but not as good as an apple and a salad. If you think you need them during your workout, just be sure you're burning more calories during the workout than you're eating in the bar. And if by chance you are eating these bars because you really *do* need a shot of calories, then eat the bars slowly, advise experts. Like one bite every ten minutes.

Choose the plain chips. Snack chip manufacturers fall all over themselves to entice you with new flavorings, backed up with glitzy advertising campaigns and fancy packaging. Mesquite this, sour-cream-and-onion that. What they don't tell you is that such chip flavorings typically come with hefty additional doses of salt—often twice the normal amount. And excessive salt can lead to high blood pressure, heart and kidney problems, and bone disorders. So save your exotic cravings for fresh foods and keep your chip choices simple.

Don't want to eat it? Don't buy it. Are you or your kids engaged in a constant struggle to resist those tantalizing chips, dips, and frozen desserts beckoning from the refrigerator and pantry? Here's a simple secret that the junk food manufacturers hope you don't catch on to: Once these foods have crossed the threshold of your house, they have already won the battle. Most likely, if you've bought it, you'll eat it. So the place to start just saying no is at the store. Research shows that among the factors contributing to our unfortunate tendency to stuff ourselves and get fat is proximity. If food is easy to get, you're more likely to eat too much of it. If you're trying to avoid specific foods or certain kinds of food, keep them out of the house. And it's not just for you. The person who does the shopping and fixes most of the meals has the most influence over what others in the household eat, according to Dr. Brian Wansink, director of the Food and Brand Lab at Cornell University. He calls that person the "nutritional gatekeeper" (no longer always the mother). Dr. Wansink has found that Americans make about 248 food decisions every day, many of them without much thought, and that the "gatekeeper" controls 72 percent of those decisions. ◂

Burning Calories

4 Tricks for Losing Fat by Increasing Your Metabolism and Your Daily Activities

Drink plain ice water. The Gatorade people aren't going to feature you in any commercials this way, but here's the truth: Not only does water have zero calories, but when it's very cold, you actually *burn* calories warming and absorbing it. Once you finish burning those calories, your metabolic rate remains 30 percent higher than before you quaffed the liquid—for another 90 minutes!

Keep a glass of ice water next to you all day and continually sip from it, refilling it with fresh water when it gets warm or you finish the glass. That way you'll never get dehydrated. Why should you care? When you're dehydrated, your metabolism slows so it can wring every drop out of whatever liquid it is getting, says Mary Hardy, M.D., director of Integrative Medicine at the Ted Mann Family Resource Center at the University of California, Los Angeles. In fact, it can actually lead to 45 fewer calories burned a day. That might not sound like much, but it adds up to 4.5 pounds (2 kg) a year!

Eat hot peppers to rev your metabolism. Don't you pity the vendors of "miracle" weight-loss products? While they're begging you to shell out big bucks for secret (and dubious) formulas, scientists have identified a simple and inexpensive food that may turbocharge your weight loss. It's right there in the produce section. Hot peppers not only liven up a meal, but some studies show that very spicy foods can temporarily increase your metabolism, or the rate at which you burn calories. Some enticing uses for hot peppers: Spice up your morning omelet with minced jalapeño, or fire up some beef stew with half a diced banana pepper.

Walk the stairs. Just four minutes of stair climbing a day can lead to a four-pound (1.8 kg) weight loss in just a year, says Michelle Cederberg, a Canadian fitness and wellness consultant. Here's the math: An average 160-pound (73-kg) person will burn about 50 calories climbing up stairs for four minutes (and down for one minute). If that same person takes the stairs for the same length of time five days a week, by the end of the year he'll burn about 12,700 calories (or about four pounds of fat). You can track your efforts at Health Canada's Stairway to Health online calculator at http://stairway.hc-sc.gc.ca/calcalc.aro.

Keep moving after dieting. You've heard the statistics: Most people who diet regain the weight they lost—and then some—when they end their diets. Well, you're not a statistic and you can avoid becoming one if you spend 30 minutes, four days a week, cycling, walking, or water jogging during and after your diet. That's because the low-intensity exercise can prevent the decrease in metabolism and fat burning that often occurs during and after a diet. ◁

Eating Out

6 Tricks for Avoiding Overconsumption When You Go Out to Eat at a Restaurant

Skip the romantic restaurants. It's not something any restaurateur is going to admit, but the reason they keep the lights low and play soft music is that they know this atmosphere encourages you to eat slower for a longer amount of time. It also makes you more likely to order dessert and another drink. How do they know? Research proves it.

Double up on appetizers. Your waiter will roll his eyes, because he wants you to order one of those oversized entrées. However, you can often trim back on calories—and cost too—if you order two appetizers for dinner and skip the entrée altogether—particularly if the restaurant has a nice selection of seafood- and vegetable-based starters. Just say *nada* to anything fried.

Keep your salad simple. Restaurant managers can't help themselves. They take a pleasantly simple offering like veggie salad and have to pile on the calorie-laden (and more expensive) extras—such as cheese, salami, spicy ham, croutons, and mayo-based dressing. By all means order a salad, but insist on vegetables only.

Skip the cocktail. What's the first thing the waiter wants to bring you in a sit-down restaurant? A cocktail, wine or beer, of course. Waiters know instinctively what was confirmed in a study in England—people who have an alcoholic drink before dinner tend to eat more. The study found that men who drank a glass of beer 30 minutes before a meal ate more during the meal than men who consumed a nonalcoholic beverage.

Those who drank alcohol also ate more fatty and salty foods and felt hungrier after the meal than men who didn't have alcohol. So if you're trying to control your weight, have your alcohol after your meal rather than before.

Check fast-food calories on the Web. Many of the highly hyped meals at fast-food restaurants are little more than a heaping helping of fat and calories. You won't be able to tell this by reading that menu over the service counter, of course. If you like the convenience of fast food but also want to keep your arteries free and clear, here's the best way to find the most healthful foods: Go to the Internet site of each chain store you frequent and click your way to the nutritional breakdowns for each offering. You'll quickly discover that the French fries, other fried foods, hamburgers, and mayo-based sauces are a shocking nutritional minefield. You'll see the wisdom of ordering smaller portions and heart-healthy sandwiches.

Keep your coffee order simple. That pricey coffeehouse wants you to order your brew in as fancy a form as possible. Not only does this drive up the tab for each visit, but it also stacks on hundreds of calories—from the whole milk, whipped cream, sugar and syrups. A regular cuppa joe made from good beans and with a dash of skim milk is heaven in itself, so protect your wallet and your arteries by keeping things simple. ◁

At the Table

7 Secrets for Reducing Your Food Intake When You Sit Down to Eat

Limit your food choices. This is something the owner of that Mongolian buffet down the road really doesn't want you to know, but the more variety you are offered in a meal, the more you'll eat. University of Pennsylvania researchers found this out when they offered people either three or one flavor of yogurt. Those with the choice ate an average of 23 percent more. So keep down the number of different things to eat on your home table.

Eat alone or with one other person. Pull a Greta Garbo and tell your partner you "vant to be alone." It might just save you unwanted weight. Researchers find that meals eaten with one other person are one-third larger than those eaten alone, and the amount increases as the number of people you're eating with increases. By the time you sit down to dine with six people, you're eating 72 percent more than if you'd just eaten alone.

Don't read or watch TV while eating. It's not on the Weight Watchers list of weight-loss tips, but distractions such as television, reading, movies, and even sporting events take your attention away from your eating to the point that you eat more. So no more meals on automatic pilot. Declare a media blackout and focus on what you are putting into your mouth.

Keep the physical sizes of dishes smaller. Researchers at Cornell University threw an ice-cream social to test whether oversized bowls (34 ounces [960 grams] versus 17 ounces [480 grams]) and extra-large ice-cream scoops (3 ounces [85 grams] versus 2 ounces [55 grams]) led to overeating. They found that doubling the size of someone's bowl increased how much participants took by 31 percent. The larger scoop increased the amount of ice cream by 14.5 percent. Yet all but 3 of the 85 participants finished all of the ice cream in their bowls. The moral of the story: Serve it up in smaller dishes!

Keep serving bowls smaller too. Rather than pile all of the mashed potatoes into one oversized bowl and bring it to the table, split it into two bowls. You'll wind up eating less. That's what Cornell University researchers found when they invited college students to a

Medicine That Cuts Weight

EXPERT INSTANT ADVICE

If you have a serious weight problem, you may want to talk to your doctor about prescribing a drug that is most commonly used to treat depression and smoking habituation but that has been shown to be effective in helping people lose weight. Researchers studied women who were taking bupropion, marketed as Wellbutrin for depression and Zyban for smoking cessation, for 24 weeks. The women followed a 1,600-calorie-a-day diet and lost significantly more weight and fatty tissue than women who only cut calories. Even better: The women taking bupropion kept the weight off for at least two years. The drug acts on the neurotransmitters norepinephrine and dopamine, which play a role in reward and pleasure in the brain.

Super Bowl party (get it, Super *Bowl?*) and offered them snacks from one of two tables. One table had a large bowl of snacks, and the other had two smaller bowls of snacks that, together, equaled the same amount as the large bowl. Students taking from the large bowls ate 56 percent more (142 calories) than those who served themselves from the smaller bowls.

Use chopsticks for all your food.
Using chopsticks might be messier, but you'll also eat less. When researchers compared patrons dining in Chinese restaurants, they found that those who were overweight were more likely to be using silverware than chopsticks, while normal-weight patrons chose the more labor-intensive chopsticks.

Add the color blue to your table.
The designers of fast-food restaurants avoid the color blue like the plague. For good reason: That particular color suppresses the appetite. So give yourself one more weapon in the war against bulging waistlines. Use blue dinner plates, cover the dinner table with a blue tablecloth, and dress in blue as well. Avoid using red, yellow, and orange in your dining areas. These colors encourage eating. ◂

Exercise Motivation
7 Surprising Ways to Set Your Mind on Getting Active and Getting Fit

Make your fitness goals known.
Tell your family, friends, and coworkers about your fitness goals and encourage them to ask you how you're doing with meeting them. Knowing that everyone is watching you provides great motivation to stick to your goals, says Lindsay Wombold, Healthy Horizons program assistant at Butler University in Indianapolis, Indiana.

Make an appointment with your doctor. This isn't something docs are very good at, so it's up to you to start the conversation. Ask about your health and how becoming more physically fit can help you become healthier. Then ask for some advice. A government study found just three hours of advice and counseling by doctors and other health-care professionals over two years boosted couch potatoes' physical fitness.

Hire a personal trainer for one hour. In addition to the workout you'll get, ask the trainer to set your fitness goals for the year. A study from researchers at McMaster University in Hamilton, Ontario, found that if you're new to exercising, you'll do better if you have a fitness professional determine your goals rather than going it alone. That means setting the weights on machines for you, determining how long you should walk or run, giving you a time limit for the treadmill, StairMaster, or elliptical trainer. The reason for the improved results? The self-confidence you get when an expert believes in you and thinks you can reach a certain goal. You only need to hire the trainer for an hour to get your goals set. Of course, if you want to continue working with him or her, that's a good thing too!

Think *fit living*, not just *workouts*. The exercise industry makes more money when everyone thinks of fitness only in terms of formal workouts. But even if you spend three hours a week in the gym, what of the other 100-plus waking hours we have each week? Truth is, fit people go about their entire day living in a high-energy way. Not only is it fun and motivating; these ongoing spurts of everyday activity add up to a whole lot of fitness. So how do you live fit? Here are easy examples:

- Stand up and walk around whenever you get on the phone.
- Always take the steps, not the escalator or elevator.
- And when you take the steps, try for two at a time!
- Stand up and move around during every TV commercial break.
- Routinely stretch your arms, legs, and back.
- Carry stuff more often—garden supplies, groceries, laundry.

Do it for charity. Some of us get greater satisfaction helping others than helping ourselves. If you fall in that category, then find a way to use your charitable nature to motivate you to exercise. For example, donate $1 to a favorite charity for every mile you walk. Donate $10 for every pound you lose. Or commit to several fund-raising events per year that involve walking, biking, dancing, or a sports match.

Be creative with your measurements. There are so many ways to measure fitness that you can quickly become paralyzed by them all. Is it my weight? Body mass index? Pulse? Is it mileage covered, pounds lifted, calories burned, minutes of activity? For maximum motivation, focus on what matters most to you: Do you feel better than you used to? Do you look better than you used to? Are your clothes less tight? Can you see a difference in the mirror? Are your improvements getting noticed by others?

Fly to your next race. Sign up for a walkathon or race that requires an airline flight to get there. Book your flight at the same time that you sign up for the race, even if it's six months away. The motivation to train for the race (which will cost you in terms of a lost reservation if you chicken out) will keep you more motivated than any personal coach. ◁

SECRET WEAPON

A Personal Trainer's Tool Kit

If these work for personal trainers and nutritionists, they can work for you, says Raphael Calzadilla, fitness expert for eDiets.com:

- Body composition calipers, for checking body fat vs. lean tissue
- A digital, easy-to-read scale, to help monitor the above
- A tape measure, to gauge inches lost or gained
- A camera, to take a "before" photo
- A workout chart, for monitoring strength increases
- A heart rate monitor, for gauging target heart rate during aerobic exercise
- Plastic replicas of five pounds (2.25 kg) of human fat and five pounds of human muscle, to show the value of gaining muscle and losing fat.

Working Out

6 Tricks for Making the Most of the Time You Spend Exercising

Increase your intensity, not your time. Forget hour-long spinning classes and five-mile (8-km) runs. A study from the exercise gurus at McMaster University in Hamilton, Ontario, found that just six minutes of intense exercise a week could provide the same physical benefits as hours of moderate exercise. Now, by "intense exercise," we're not talking about a stroll in the park, and the six minutes were spread over three exercise sessions that also included some recovery time. The researchers had their subjects do between four and seven 30-second "bursts" of all-out cycling on stationary bikes, each followed by four minutes of regular cycling three times a week for two weeks. (Another alternative would be full-out running for 30 seconds in the midst of a leisurely jog or walk.) All told, the time the "sprinters" spent exercising each week was 20 percent of the time spent by the moderate exercisers (1 1/4 hours versus 5 1/4 hours).

Exercise first thing in the morning. Don't think about it. Just roll out of bed, put on your shoes (oh, and please brush your teeth), and go. You're more likely to get your workout in if you do it in the morning, research shows. An added benefit: You'll sleep better at night.

Weigh the benefits of free weights. The salespeople hawking enormous—and expensive—multi-exercise workout machines hope you don't catch on to this: Inexpensive free weights actually offer a number of advantages in terms of fitness and convenience. When you use free weights, you can exercise both sides of your body separately, eliminating muscle imbalances. Only some exercise machines allow that. If you have a slight body, the typical exercise machine—designed for men—may not fit you no matter how much you fiddle with the settings. If you like working out at home, you may have trouble working a gargantuan machine into the décor of your family room. Dumbbells, on the other hand, are compact, inexpensive, and easy to use.

Drink a glass of cherry juice before working out. Who woulda thunk a glass of red juice could make a difference in muscle strength? But that's just what researchers at the University of Vermont in Burlington found when they had 14 volunteers drink either fresh cherry juice blended with commercial apple juice twice a day for three days before exercise and for four days afterward, or a dummy mixture containing no cherry juice. The cherry juice drinkers lost far less muscle strength in the days after their workouts than those drinking the fake mixture (4 percent vs. 22 percent). The cherry juice drinkers also had much less pain after working out than the other juice drinkers. Plus, the cherry juice drinkers said their pain peaked at about 24 hours, while it lasted twice that long for those getting the placebo juice. The researchers suspect the high levels of antioxidant and anti-inflammatory compounds in cherry juice are behind its benefits.

Stick to drinking water when exercising. The television ads show elite athletes slurping down sports drinks to

How I Do It **This Skinny PR Pro Hated to Exercise**

When Dan Collins graduated from college in 1984, he was 21, just a hair under 5 feet, 11 inches (180 cm), weighed 239 pounds (108 kg), and had high blood pressure.

"You're coming to see me once a month, every month," his doctor told him. And the fear of the white coat kicked in. "I'd tried other ways of losing weight, such as the 'sleep diet' during summer vacation when I slept as long as I could—the logic being if you're asleep, you're not eating," explains Collins, a senior director of media relations at Mercy Medical Center in Baltimore.

He lost the weight—but promptly gained it back, plus 20 pounds.

But the "power of the white lab coat," as he calls it, worked. Hearing he was in trouble from a doctor finally gave him the motivation he needed to lose weight permanently. He stopped night eating—the bane of many with a food addiction. As the weight came off, however, it became important for him to find some way to keep it off. The problem: He had never found a way of exercising that agreed with him. Until the day he stopped at the local YMCA. He had intended to

sign up for a class on automotive maintenance, but he became intrigued instead by a class called Fencing for Beginners.

"I felt good enough about myself at that time to dare to don the very unforgiving whites and met a man named Ray Gordon, the instructor." Twenty years later, Collins weighs a healthy 190 pounds. Gordon remains his closest male friend, and they continue to fence. At last word, the two swashbucklers were in training to set the first Guinness World Record in fencing.

---

replenish their body chemistry and thus enhance their performance. Well, this has little relevance to us normal folk. Research does show that top-performing endurance athletes need higher levels of sodium and far more to drink than everyday people. Sports drinks like Gatorade fill that need—they're rich in salt, which not only provides the needed sodium but also keeps the athlete thirsty for more fluids. Here's the reality check, however: The extra salt provides no benefit at all to everyday people. Even if you exercise regularly, unless you are testing your body's physical limits for extended periods, water will quench your thirst nicely.

Use music to help increase your pace. Program your iPod or other portable music player to start out with slow music (think classical and easy listening) and gradually build to rapid-fire dance music (any club music should do nicely). That arrangement, studies find, will result in your working harder and longer than those who start with fast or slow music and stick with it, or move from fast music to slow music.

And here's another use for your favorite toy: Use it when you're walking. A study published in the journal *Chest* found that people who listened to music while walking covered four more miles (6.4 km) during the eight-week study than a similar group that didn't listen to music. The participants had serious respiratory disease, and researchers think that listening distracted them from the negative symptoms of exercise (such as boredom and fatigue) and reduced shortness of breath. ◄

10

SECRETS FOR
choosing
a health club

Here's how to choose a gym—advice from Lindsay Wombold, who works for a health and wellness program at Butler University in Indianapolis, Indiana, and Raphael Calzadilla, a fitness expert for eDiets.com.

1 Health clubs can *always* waive the "enrollment fee." That fee is just a way for them to get more money out of you. If you don't want to pay it, just tell the sales rep you're going to join somewhere else. You're pretty much guaranteed to have the fee waived.

2 Make sure you can cancel at any time. You may even need to write on your contract that "per [salesperson's name], I can cancel this membership anytime with no fees." Have the salesperson sign and date it. Even better, have the manager sign and date it in case there's turnover and your salesperson no longer works there.

3 Find out when the gym is busiest, and make sure that works with your preferences. For instance, if you prefer to work out during a quiet time but the only time you can get to the gym is after work when the machines are mobbed, this might not be the best gym for you.

4 Ask for a one-week trial and bring a friend. Your friend might be able to spot problems you didn't see.

5 Insist on a free personal training session if you join. If they already provide one, ask for two.

6 Ask how often the equipment is serviced and cleaned. Cleaning should be done daily; servicing at least once a month.

7 When you get a tour of the facility, check for torn benches and antiquated-looking cardio equipment, and inspect the cleanliness of the locker area.

8 If the sales rep is wooing you with visions of Pilates and yoga classes, ask about additional fees. Many make you pay more for such classes.

9 Fitness clubs oversell memberships in the hope that people won't go. If just 20 percent of the members showed up at one time, most clubs would not have enough space or equipment to support them. Ask when the busiest times are, and show up then to see if the place is too crowded for your taste.

10 Personal trainers at gyms are on commission plus a small hourly rate. So beware of trainers who hound you to sign up for sessions—they're most likely under pressure to make a sales goal. Instead, get a sense of the trainer's genuine passion for fitness. If he or she doesn't pressure you, that's a good sign.

Women's Exercise Concerns
5 Things Every Woman Should Know to Get More Out of Her Workouts

Time your exercise to your menstrual cycle. Don't tell your health club manager, but the next time he sees you climbing like mad on the StairMaster, it's because you're in the latter part of your menstrual cycle. A study from the University of Adelaide in Australia found that women who exercise during this time of the month, when levels of estrogen and progesterone are highest, burn more fat for energy, leading to less exercise-related fatigue.

Check your iron levels. No, not the kind of iron you pump, the kind that enables your blood cells to carry much-needed oxygen to your body tissues. A study from Cornell University found that women with low levels of iron—but not low enough to be classified as anemic—find it more difficult to maintain exercise and training than women with normal levels. An estimated 16 percent of North American women have this level of iron deficiency and don't know it. Women who are physically active, dieting, or vegetarians are particularly at risk.

Don't despair! Supplementing with 100 milligrams a day of iron can double your exercise endurance compared to iron-deficient women who don't supplement. Don't try this on your own, however—this is prescription-strength iron that should only be taken under your doctor's supervision. Good sources of dietary iron include red meat, seafood, and citrus fruit or juice taken with meals to improve absorption from iron-rich foods such as legumes, whole grains, and green vegetables.

Ignore the mirrors at gyms. The designers of fitness clubs can't resist throwing up a wall of mirrors anytime they install an exercise room. The assumption is that you want to watch yourself work out. But observing your own stepping, lunging, and arm swinging might actually work against you. One study found that women who exercised in front of a mirror felt less calm and more fatigued after 30 minutes of working out than those who exercised without mirrors. Some exercise gyms are now catching on and offering "reflection-free" zones. If yours doesn't, talk to the gym manager.

Pass on star-centered videos. You could pack the Hollywood Bowl with all of the svelte models and skinny celebrities who are hoping you'll buy their exercise videos. But experts say such videos may actually undermine your motivation to work out. A study at McMaster University in Hamilton, Ontario, Canada, found that people felt less confident about their fitness and less inclined to exercise in the future when they used videos featuring super-slim models with amazing muscles and revealing thongs. Oddly enough, the effect was even worse with videos featuring an ultra-slender host leading a group of plumper, normal-looking women. Apparently that scenario further emphasizes the divide between exercise divas and everyday folks.

If you want a motivating exercise video or class, researchers say you should look for a teacher you can trust. Find a teacher with a fitness background who, like the rest of us, needs to exercise in order to look great. Videos created by personal trainers and exercise physiologists, or classes taught by them, are a good bet.

You can be both healthy and heavy.

Many women think they are too heavy to benefit from exercising; others get discouraged when they don't see significant weight loss after weeks of exercise. But the most important benefit of exercise is keeping your heart healthy. And research shows that the amount of activity you get, not your weight, is the chief predictor of heart disease. One study in particular, published in 2004 in the *Journal of the American Medical Association,* evaluated more than 900 women, three-quarters of whom were overweight or obese. Researchers assessed them for weight, body mass index, and level of physical activity, then gave them angiograms to detect heart disease. The results were clear-cut: Weight didn't matter, but exercise did: It wasn't the heaviest women who showed the most evidence of heart problems, but the least active women. So get moving, whatever your size.◄

Walking
7 Secret Ways to Make the Most of the Ultimate Healthy No-Cost, Low-Impact Activity

Walk to control your body weight.
Don't think this mild activity can help? In one significant study, a group of sedentary people were given a daily goal of 10,000 steps of brisk activity, as measured by their pedometers. They improved their fitness levels, blood pressure, and body fat just as much as a group that followed a traditional gym-based aerobic program. Overall, studies find that getting 8,000 to 10,000 steps a day (about five miles or 8 km) helps you lose weight, while adding to that another 2,000 steps (an extra one mile or 1.6 km a day), helps you maintain your current weight and stop gaining weight.

Walk for entertainment one day a week.
Instead of walking around your neighborhood, walk through the zoo, an art museum, or an upscale shopping mall. First, circle the perimeter of your location at your usual brisk pace. Then wander through again more slowly to take in the sights.

Walk in the prettiest neighborhood.
Okay, we admit it. Just circling the same streets can get plenty boring. Heck, even our dog got bored after two years of walking the same neighborhood. So do what we did: Get in the car and drive to a new neighborhood. And make it a nice one. When researchers from the University of Wollongong in New South Wales, Australia, surveyed walkers about their walking habits, they found that men who perceived their neighborhoods to be "aesthetic" were more consistent about walking around them. Other research finds that neighbor-

hoods with well-maintained sidewalks and safe and well-lit walking areas encourage walking more than neighborhoods that don't have those features. Also, people who live in so-called walkable neighborhoods walk an average of 70 more minutes each week than people who live in neighborhoods lacking such characteristics.

Walk faster earlier in your walk. If you want to increase the amount of fat you burn during your walk, add some bursts of faster walking toward the *beginning* of your walk. Many walkers wait until the end of the walk to speed up, treating their faster walking as a finishing kick. Yet a study published in the *European Journal of Applied Physiology* found that exercisers burned more fat and felt less fatigued when they inserted their faster segments toward the beginning of a workout rather than closer to the end. It works because you speed up your heart rate early and keep it elevated for the rest of your walk.

Walk when you shop. Online shopping is great in terms of convenience and selection, but it stinks when it comes to burning calories. Walking around the mall, however, can burn about 200 calories an hour, much more than what you'll burn sitting on your butt as you surf the Net. You can increase the effectiveness of your walk and shop time by doing a lap around the mall between store visits.

Walk to fund-raise for a cause. You, you, you. That's all you think about! Instead, start thinking about the Susan G. Komen Breast Cancer Foundation, the National Multiple Sclerosis Society, The Terry Fox Run, or the Red Cross. All are charities that sponsor walk- and

runathons to raise funds. You don't even have to formally join the event. Just pledge to contribute. You'll take pride in the fact that you're walking for something beyond yourself, which will motivate you to go longer and faster. After every walk, mark the amount you owe on a chart, and when you reach $100, send a check. Whoever thought exercise could be tax deductible?

SECRET WEAPON

Pedometer

The manager at your local gym will hate you, because once you figure out the benefits of this palm-size gadget, your days on the treadmill are history. You wear pedometers on your waist. The device senses your body motion and counts your footsteps, then converts the count into distance based on the length of your stride.

Don't skimp on quality when you buy a pedometer. A study published in the online edition of the *British Journal of Sports Medicine* found that cheap pedometers are not only less likely to accurately measure steps taken, but most overestimated participants' steps, which could lead to a false sense of accomplishment.

Walk around the office or house. Are you stuck at your desk working all day, practically chained to your PC? Get up and walk around for five minutes at least every two hours. A brisk five-minute walk every two hours will parlay into an extra 20-minute walk by the end of the workday. And getting a break will make you less likely to reach for snacks out of antsiness. It's good idea to get up and walk around for a few minutes every hour or so if you are sitting for long periods of time at home reading, watching television, Web surfing, or pursuing a hobby. ◂

Secret Workouts

8 Easy Ways to Sneak Some Beneficial Exercises into Your Daily Routine

Squeeze for a tight rear. Your gluteus maximus, also affectionately known as your butt, is the largest muscle group in your body. Fire it up and you'll burn calories, says Michelle Cederberg, a fitness and wellness consultant from Calgary, Alberta. Whether you're standing or sitting, an invisible butt squeeze (tighten, hold for two seconds, release) repeated 10 to 15 times, one to three times a day, will tighten your tush and burn calories.

Practice proper posture. By making an effort to stand "tall and proud," you contract dozens of muscles from your legs up to your neck, says Cederberg. This burns calories and builds muscle. Whether you're ironing, doing dishes, or standing in a line at the bank, concentrate on keeping a solid foot stance, a slight bend in your knees, an open chest (that is, standing tall, not slouched), with shoulders depressed and head up. Another secret workout: Imagine you're squeezing a pencil between your shoulder blades and you have to hold the muscles tight so the pencil doesn't fall. It doesn't take long before the muscles in your back start to fatigue. Anytime you realign your posture, sit or stand a bit taller, and get away from a slumped posture, you're exercising your back and core muscles.

Do leg exercises while doing laundry. Whether you're folding clothes, ironing (yes, some of us still iron!), or waiting for the rinse cycle, "captive time" is ideal for adding in some lovely leg work, Cederberg says. Perform 10 to 15 plié squats (think ballerina). Position your heels just beyond shoulder width with your toes rotated out to 45 degrees. As you drop into your squat, keep your knees in line with your toes and make sure your head, shoulders, and hips align, or "stack up," as you drop down. Return to the starting position, and squeeze the muscles in your butt as you stand tall.

Play games with the kids. Instead of sitting around watching your kids play sports, dive in. That's the advice from Beth Brody of Stockton, New Jersey, who lost 20 pounds (9 kg) and kept them off for a year by inventing active games with her five- and seven-year-old sons. Together they invented the game Mommy Monster, "an exhausting game of chasing them until I catch one for tickling," she explains. They also play dodgeball and soccer. "If I don't move fast enough, I get hit with the ball or kicked in the shin." These days, she's down to a size 6 dress from a size 10, and she doesn't get winded during her three-mile (4.8-km) jogs. Best of all: "Dodging the shin kicks has certainly made me more agile."

Do isometric exercises. Remember the term? It dates back to the Charles Atlas days. Isometric exercises, put simply, are exercises in which muscles are tensed without movement. For example, pushing as hard as you can against a brick wall is an isometric exercise, because neither you nor the wall moves. Research has shown that isometric exercises provide lots of value, particularly for those people with a limited range of motion. And you can do them anytime, anyplace. The basic rule: Hold the tension for 5 to 10 seconds, then relax for a few seconds. Repeat the cycle five to eight times. Here are some simple isometric exercises to try:

- Tense your abdominal muscles and hold.
- Put your hands together in front of you, as if praying, and press your hands together as hard as you can.
- Stand with your legs apart about a foot from a wall. Push against the wall with your hands as if you were trying to move it.
- Stand inside a doorway and, with your arms straight down and by your sides, put the backs of your hands against each door frame. Push your hands against the doorway as hard as you can, as if you were trying to widen the door space.
- While still inside the doorway, push your palms against the frame above you, as if you were trying to lift the building.
- Sit down in a chair, feet flat on the ground. Push your legs into the ground as hard as you can.

Get outdoors at least three hours every weekend. Ever notice how so much of the equipment at a health club—treadmills, stationary bikes, climbing walls, rowing machines— merely replicates what you would be doing if you were outside? Truth is, one of the best indications of a fit lifestyle is how much time you are outdoors. Why? Even if you are just strolling, gardening, washing the car, or taking a child to a playground, you are being far more active than you would be sitting indoors. Plus, it's terrific for your attitude—and a whole lot cheaper than paying for a health club membership. Best of all, once you get in the habit of

being outside on your free days, you'll soon be hankering for more active pursuits: bike riding, nature hiking, even taking up a sport again—anyone can shoot baskets in the driveway for fun and exercise!

Lengthen and speed up your stride while walking. Not just occasionally— all the time! Become a high-energy walker—fast, confident, with good posture and healthy arm swinging. Just this little everyday adjustment will deliver lots of extra calories burned, stronger legs, and a shapelier behind over time.

Make cooking an easy, everyday workout. By adjusting your gear, your food supplies, and your storage, you can make every meal healthier to create! Here are a few ways:

- Switch your primary cooking knife to a cleaver. It's heavier, giving your hands, wrists, and forearms a better workout while chopping.
- Switch to cast-iron skillets and soup pots. Again, they are much heavier to lift (plus, they cook terrifically well).
- Buy milk and other drinks in larger containers. This turns pouring into an exercise.
- Defy wisdom and put the pantry and cooking items you use most either very high or very low. Stretch slowly and deliberately as you reach up or squat down for items.
- Learn the master-chef trick of tossing your food while it cooks, rather than stirring. This means picking up your sauté pan by the handle and literally tossing the ingredients up in the air to turn them. It takes a lot more strength than mixing the food around with a spoon, and it looks impressive to those watching you cook! ◁

Food Labels

10 Tricks for Deciphering the Real Truth from the Information on Packaged Foods

Look for short ingredient lists. When you find a packaged food in the supermarket with a long list of ingredients on the label, just set it back on the shelf and look for a simpler version of the food. (We're talking here about the "Ingredients" part of the label. "Nutrition Facts" is another part, and more about that later.) The alarming truth is, many of those ingredients are various kinds of sugars and chemical additives, and they're not put there for you—they're there to benefit the company that processes the food. They "enhance" the looks, taste, or shelf life— which is all about marketing and shipping and not at all about your health. Most additives aren't known to be harmful (although the health effects of some are still open to question), but they aren't about nutrition or taste as nature intended taste to be. In fact, one of their main purposes is to make up for a lack of those things. So check the list of ingredients every time. Marion Nestle, a professor of nutrition at New York University, says that almost always, the shorter the better.

Think twice about "no cholesterol" claims. Cholesterol is a fat that occurs only in animal products (meat, fish, eggs, milk, and butter, for instance). So why do some plant-derived products claim in large letters that they contain no cholesterol? Because the food companies know that people care about their cholesterol levels, and they know that most people probably have forgotten or never knew that plants don't contain any. Some of the offenders are cereal, bread, cookies, salad dressings, and, especially, oils and margarine. Oils are obviously fats, so the makers think you'll be reassured to see that there's no cholesterol in the corn oil, safflower oil, or olive oil. Next time you see the claim, just say to yourself, "Duh! It's a plant product! Of course it doesn't contain cholesterol."

Learn what "organic" really means.
There's considerable confusion about the use of the word "organic" on food labels, just as there is about almost everything having to do with labeling. For starters, the organic label is earned through a certification process, and it means the producer adhered to a strict set of rules and procedures.

- *For organic fruits and vegetables,* U.S. Department of Agriculture rules—and virtually identical regulations in Canada—say that they must be grown without any of these things: genetically modified seeds, fertilizers made from chemicals or sewage sludge, chemical pesticides or herbicides, and irradiation. Growers are also required to keep records and present them upon demand by accredited inspectors. Foods may also be labeled "100 percent organic," "organic" (95 to 99 percent organic), "made with organic ingredients" (74 to 94 percent organic), or, for organic content of lesser amount, the specific organic ingredients may be listed.

- *On meat,* the organic seal means the animals may be fed only certified organic feed and no by-products of other animals. The animals can't be given hormones or antibiotics. They must be allowed access to the outdoors and treated humanely.

All organic farms must keep records and be inspected by accredited inspectors. There isn't enough organic food being produced to meet the demand for it, but its availability is increasing all the time. Many supermarkets now carry some organic food, and there is at least one chain (Whole Foods Market) that

WHAT THE FOOD INDUSTRY DOESN'T WANT YOU TO KNOW ABOUT Food Politics

The food industry would have you believe that buying food is all about price and convenience. To some degree, it is. But more importantly, buying food is about the health of you and your family. It's also about agriculture, the environment, and your local economy, to name just some issues that are involved every time you buy food. Think of your purchases as votes. You can vote for or against the use of pesticides, herbicides, antibiotics, chemical fertilizers, and preservatives. You can vote for food that is locally produced or food that has been trucked hundreds or even thousands of miles. You can vote for or against humane treatment of animals.

sells mostly organic. In addition, farmers' markets, health food stores, and individual farms are good sources of organic food.

Be suspicious of "natural" labels. The food labels "natural" and "organic" are pretty much interchangeable, right? That's exactly what food companies want you to think. But here's the truth: Use of "natural" on labels is a much more loosey-goosey affair than use of the term "organic." There's no single set of requirements for products claiming to be natural, but such labels are supposed to be accurate. If, for example, meat is claimed to be natural because the animal was not fed antibiotics or hormones, the label should say that and it should be true. Farmers or food companies that use the "natural" label are not subject to inspections as a condition of using the label. You just have to take their word for it.

Be wary of the serving size. Many "Nutrition Facts" labels are designed to make you think you're getting fewer calories than you really are. For example, labels list the nutrients on a per-serving basis. But be sure to check the "serving size" and "servings per container" lines. The candy bar that most people would eat all by themselves in a single sitting may say that it contains two servings. If you saw "100 calories" on the label, you must make a mental adjustment—you're actually eating two servings, so you're getting 200 calories.

Use a pocket calculator to compare items. A calculator is the best tool for helping you figure out what the food industry doesn't want you to know: the actual value of the nutrients in the food you're buying. For example,

say you're trying to find out which breakfast cereal is more nutritious, General Mills' Multi Grain Cheerios or Kellogg's Frosted Mini-Wheats (the whole-grain version). The Cheerios serving size is listed as one cup, but the Mini-Wheats serving is "about 24 biscuits." You can't really open the box in the store to see how that stacks up against the one cup, so the only way to compare unit to unit is to use grams, which are listed on both packages. The 59-gram Mini-Wheats serving is almost twice the size of the 29-gram Cheerios, so you have to cut in half the nutrients listed on the Mini-Wheats label. Gram for gram, their nutrients are very similar: roughly the same calories, fiber, carbs, protein, and fat. Even the amount of sugars is about the same, despite the fact that the Cheerios box proclaims the contents to be "lightly sweetened" and the Mini-Wheats have frosting! This might come as a surprise to a lot of nutritional gatekeepers.

Get the "whole" story. Marketers know that nutrition-conscious shoppers are interested in whole grains these days. Don't be deceived into buying a product that's labeled "wheat bread," however. What you really want is "whole wheat" or "whole grain" bread (for more, see page 47).

Don't confuse cereal hype with facts. If you want a healthy breakfast cereal, not one that just claims to be, ignore the large-type claims on the package and go right to the labels. Look for a short list of ingredients. Look for a whole grain as the first ingredient. Look for one that has no sugar. (You can always add sugar yourself if necessary.) Then look at the per-serving nutrients on the nutrition label. Look for a cereal with a lot of

No wonder North Americans are getting fat. If all the food production in North America were measured as calories and distributed evenly among the entire population, it would average about 3,900 calories per day for every person. Yet adults need only about 2,000 to 3,000 calories per day, except for those who get a lot of exercise. (And those who are overweight, as well as young children, should usually be eating fewer than 2,000.) What happens to all the calories you eat but don't burn? They get stored as fat, of course. So you can easily see part of the problem: One reason food companies go to such lengths to get you to buy more and eat more, without regard to the consequences, is that there's too much food being produced.

fiber in each serving. Highly sweetened cereals, when fed regularly to young children, condition their taste for sugar at an early age, forming habits that are hard to break. Nutrition professor Marion Nestle says that most breakfast cereals are now processed and sugared to such a degree that "they might as well be cookies—low-fat cookies."

Don't get soaked for watery foods. Water is the magic ingredient in prepared foods, and if it's first on the list of ingredients, that's a clue that there's a long list of additives to follow to give that water some taste and texture. You might not be surprised to see water at the top of the list of ingredients in soups. After all, soup does take a lot of water. It's more surprising to find it so prominent in SpaghettiOs. Many, many salad dressings contain more water than anything else, and since oil and water don't mix, it takes a bunch of additives to hold everything together. Water is cheap, so the food industry likes it.

Scan the can for MSG. Check out the ingredient list on the labels of prepared foods—on soups, for example. Keep reading, because it's pretty far down on a long list (although if there is no MSG, that's usually prominently mentioned at the top). MSG (monosodium glutamate) is sometimes listed under its own name but often under other names, among them hydrolyzed soy protein, autolyzed yeast, and sodium caseinate. MSG is a synthetic version of the substance *umami*, as it is known in Japan, which occurs naturally in some foods, including Parmesan cheese, soy sauce, and mushrooms. MSG, widely used in Asian cooking, went out of favor when it became associated with headaches and other unpleasant symptoms. Now many Asian restaurants proudly advertise "No MSG" on their menus, but the food industry still sneaks it in as a flavor enhancer. So if you're concerned about MSG, look for it under all of its names. ◁

Buying Produce
8 Strategies for Getting the Best-Tasting and Most Nutritious Fruits and Vegetables

Study "fresh" produce with a skeptic's eye. Unless the produce you're buying in your supermarket was locally grown, it has probably spent at least a week and possibly as much as 10 days being picked, trucked, packed, hauled, transferred, unpacked, displayed, arranged, misted, and rearranged. Furthermore, some fruits and vegetables are picked before they are really ripe so they won't spoil during the time lag. Some produce has been treated with gases, washed, cut, and bagged. Even then, it may sit in your refrigerator for a day or more before you use it. All the while, the produce is losing taste and nutritional value, which are affected by light, heat, and oxygen. If produce had to be labeled with its country of origin, that would offer a clue as to how long the produce had been on the road. But the food industry has resisted any such requirement for years. Some stores (Whole Foods Market, for example) voluntarily say where their produce comes from so customers can draw their own conclusions about just how fresh it might be. Otherwise, you're on your own.

Let common sense be your guide. If you live in Minnesota and your supermarket has strawberries in February, you can be pretty sure they've come a long way. Also, go by looks. If the lettuce is limp, it's been around too long. But paradoxically, fruits and veggies that are too shiny and waxy also may be stale. The spit and polish may be cloaking flaccid cukes or peppers, for instance. Stores do often label produce as "local," when they have it, because for many customers something locally raised is a real treat. Early in the season the locally grown may be a little more expensive, but as the season goes on, it gets cheaper.

For freshness, buy frozen. If you have any doubts about the freshness of the produce in your supermarket, here's an insider tip: Sometimes the frozen fruits and vegetables are fresher than what you'll find in the "fresh" produce section. How could that be? Frozen fruits and vegetables are picked when they're fully ripe, and they're frozen on the same day. Freezing does change the texture somewhat, but very little nutritional value is lost in the processing. The vitamin content may be somewhat reduced, but the protein, fat, minerals, fiber, and calories are the same. However, that only goes for the single-item packages of fruit and vegetables, which don't take up most of the real estate in the frozen-food aisles of your supermarket. Most of the space is given over to highly processed, prepared dishes or meals, which are more profitable for the food companies.

When it comes to limes, any (real) lime will do. Do you really need Key limes for Key lime pie or Key lime bars? Key lime growers want you to think you do, but tasters in a blind taste test split over which was better, the bars made with Key limes or those made with regular lime juice. Key limes are a trifle sweeter than the others, but the difference isn't great—except in the amount of work it takes to get at that juice. It takes about six Keys to get the same amount of juice you can get from one regular lime. Easiest of all is bottled lime juice, but testers found it bitter and an unacceptable substitute for any kind of lime, Key or otherwise.

Pick your own fruits and veggies. If you can't grow your own produce, then do the next best thing: Pick your own. PYO farms are one alternative to agribusiness food. Strawberries, raspberries, blueberries, apples, and pumpkins all lend themselves to the PYO treatment, and you get to trade your labor for part of the price of the produce. You'll get the freshest food possible, for less money than you'd have to pay in the grocery store, and you and the family will get some good exercise to boot. Some places also provide entertainment such as hayrides and petting zoos. You won't read about them in glossy magazine ads, but you might find out about one from a small ad in your local newspaper, a poster nailed to a telephone pole, or a roadside sign. Many do their best advertising by word of mouth.

Subscribe to a farm. Here's another non-agribusiness option: community-supported agriculture, or CSA. You get good, fresh food, and you also contribute to the survival of a small farm—the kind that big farms are always driving out. In a CSA, subscribers pay a farmer (usually at least partly up front) for a certain amount of food every week for the season. You get whatever's available, and the farmer gets cash to help keep the farm going. Your bag or box of food may be cheaper than what you'd pay for the same items at the grocery store, but that isn't always the case and isn't the only reason, or even the main reason, to try this arrangement. There's no requirement that CSAs be organic, but many are. One of the hardest parts is finding one, because they don't usually have marketing budgets. You won't find a flyer in your mailbox advertising the weekly specials. Ask at your local health food store for suggestions or contact a local or regional organic farming organization.

Eat for free in fields of greens. Some of the most nutritious vegetables in existence await you just outside your door. Plants with dark green leaves, such as dandelion greens, have more nutrients per ounce than any other food. Even the dandelion blossoms are good— in pancakes, fritters, salad and, with a little time and practice, as the basis for an interesting wine. And dandelions are just the beginning. Another good green

---

Use Imagery to Picture a Healthy Meal

EXPERT INSTANT ADVICE

Food companies make more money from their highly processed foods than from the simple ones, and that's why we're barraged with their advertising and images of snack food, cookies, complicated frozen dishes, chips, dips, and other salty, sugary food. Despite the best efforts of the U.S. Department of Agriculture and Health Canada to get us to eat more fruits and vegetables, we aren't. And the veggies eaten most often aren't the most nutritious ones. Dr. Douglas Husbands, a certified clinical nutritionist in San Carlos, California, has devised a way to help his patients visualize what they should be eating. He tells them to picture a plate of food divided like this: Half is filled with brightly colored or dark green, leafy vegetables. (Notice that French fries and iceberg lettuce don't qualify.) A quarter of the plate holds a serving of food with lean protein, such as fish, free-range chicken, or grass-fed beef. Finally, the last quarter has a healthy starch such as brown rice, a sweet potato, or a slice of whole-grain bread.

is *Chenopodium album*, commonly called pigweed or lamb's-quarters. (The Latin name is important because plants sometimes have different common names in different locales.) It's a common garden weed and grows just about anywhere in disturbed soil. Ramps, or wild leeks, are so prized that some communities in the South build whole festivals around them.

Two important warnings: Beware of gathering wild plants in any area where herbicides or other poisons have been applied, and avoid anything that can be mistaken for a poisonous plant. Buy a good field guide, such as *A Field Guide to Edible Wild Plants* by Lee Allen Peterson. If you're interested in mushrooms—and there are many wonderful wild ones—they're in a category all by themselves, and your best bet is to take a class from an expert. Wild food is about as anti-agribusiness as you can get. If you start learning about it and using it, you'll not only eat better, you'll have found an interesting new hobby.

Ripen fruit in a paper bag. Unless you're buying locally grown fruit, you rarely get it fully ripe from the supermarket. If it was picked at its peak, it would spoil during the time it takes to move the fruit from the grower to you. You may have heard that putting fruit in a paper bag concentrates the ethylene gas and speeds ripening. To make it ripen even faster, put some fully ripe fruit (bananas, for example) into the bag with it. The ripe fruit is giving off more ethylene, which the unripe fruit can use. Don't use plastic bags; the fruit will just spoil. The paper bag trick only works with fruits that will continue to ripen after they've been picked. Among them

are apples, avocados, bananas, blueberries, cantaloupe, kiwis, mangoes, peaches, pears, plums, and tomatoes. It pays to know which fruits don't ripen after picking, so you can avoid buying unripe ones in the first place. They include citrus fruits, pineapples, cherries, grapes, raspberries, strawberries, and honeydew melons.

Eat the fruit, skip the juice. The fruit juice industry has done a great job of persuading people that juice is a wonderful food, and the earlier you get your kids started on it, the better. Well, there's *some* truth in that. Fresh orange juice, with plenty of pulp, has vitamins, fiber, some minerals, just about no fat, and it tastes good. But there's little need to chug down OJ like it's water—a mere four ounces (125 ml), or half a cup, would supply about 60 mg vitamin C, well above the recommendations of 40 mg per day for men and 30 mg for women. What you don't hear so much about is all the calories in juice. Eight ounces (250 ml) of orange juice has 112 calories, a bit more than the 106 in the same amount of Coke. (Of course the diet version has no calories, but it does have artificial sweeteners—another story altogether.) These days, some young children nurse bottles of juice more or less all day. So the first problem is that juice drinkers usually drink way too much of it. Go for whole fruit instead. It's not as easy to chow down on a couple of oranges as it is to drink two cups of juice. A second problem is that the food companies have created tons of juice-like products, such as "juice drink," that are mostly sugar and water, with varying amounts of juice thrown in. Because these cost less, many people choose them over 100 percent juice. ◂◃

START YOUR OWN
community
Agribusiness

Who says growing, marketing, and distributing food has to be done on a global scale? A community-supported agriculture organization does it all on the local level. The marketing is rudimentary, and the distribution system usually extends less than 100 miles (160 km) from the farm—not the thousands of miles that big agribusiness covers.

Most CSAs are started by the farmer, who must go out and sell the idea to subscribers. But Sprout CSA in Richmond, Virginia, provides another model: a CSA started by the subscribers, who went out and found a farmer. Noah Scalin, a graphic artist, was the seed behind Sprout. When he returned to his native Richmond in 2001 after ten years in New York City, he soon began to miss the farmers' markets and other sources of organic food he had enjoyed in New York. So he organized a group of like-minded people, and they found a farmer to provide the food. Scalin did most of the marketing and he and other subscribers also helped with harvesting and distribution.

In 2002, Sprout's first year, there were nine subscribers, and the number grew every year until it reached 130. That turned out to be too big a workload, so it scaled back to 75 subscribers. At this writing, the subscribers were paying $575 for the season, May through October. Each week they received a box of whatever the farm had in its gardens. In one week in mid-July, for example, subscribers got cucumbers, cabbage, kale, onions, and potatoes.

A CSA doesn't supply all of the vegetables one might want, and the output can be hurt by bad weather. But Scalin said he not only loves the food but also loves the idea that he's contributing to healthy farming practices (Sprout's farm is organic, although not all are) and helping a small farm to sustain itself.

If you want to know more about community-supported agriculture, organic farming, and other alternatives to supermarket produce, these organizations will put you on the fast track:

Alternative Farming Systems Information Center, National Agricultural Library, ARS, USDA, 10301 Baltimore Avenue, Room 132, Beltsville, MD 20705-2351; 301-504-6559; afsic.nal.usda.gov

National Sustainable Agriculture Information Service, P.O. Box 3657, Fayetteville AR 72702; 800-346-9140; attra.ncat.org

Canadian Organic Growers, 323 Chapel Street, Ottawa, Ontario K1N 7Z2; 888-375-7383; www.cog.ca

Robyn Van En Center for CSA Resources, Wilson College, Fulton Center for Sustainable Living, 1015 Philadelphia Avenue, Chambersburg PA 17201; 717-264-4141, ext. 3352; www.csacenter.org

Biodynamic Farming and Gardening Association, 25844 Butler Road, Junction City, OR 97448; 888-516-7797; www.biodynamics.com

Organic Consumers Association, 6771 South Silver Hill Drive, Finland MN 55603; 218-226-4164; organicconsumers.org

Ecological Agriculture Projects, McGill University (Macdonald Campus), Ste.-Anne-de-Bellevue, Quebec H9X 3V9; 514-398-7771; eap.mcgill.ca

Organic Trade Association, P.O. Box 547, Greenfield MA 01302; 413-774-7511; info@ota.com; www.ota.com

Tomato Tricks

5 Surprising Ways to Make the Most of This Popular Vegetable That's Technically a Fruit

Store tomatoes at room temperature. Ripe, juicy, just-picked tomatoes have a rich, vibrant taste. But it isn't improved by refrigeration. Keep good tomatoes in the pantry in a basket so air can circulate around them.

Capture the flavor of tomatoes at their peak. Even if you don't grow your own, it's worth it to get good tomatoes in season from a farmers' market or farm stand and preserve them for future use. Older cookbooks told you how to can tomatoes, but canning takes a long time and makes a mess. To freeze tomatoes, just cut out the tough part of the core, put the whole tomatoes on a baking sheet and into the freezer, says Jyl Steinback, author of *The Busy Mom's Slow Cooker Cookbook*. After they've frozen, transfer them to a plastic zipper bag and put them back into the freezer. When you want to use them, you can easily peel them if you allow them to thaw until they're just barely soft on the outside. Then just rub off the skins. Or you can run warm tap water over them and peel them immediately. Use them in recipes for any cooked dish.

Avoid crushed and ground canned tomatoes. They're convenient, yes, because you don't have to cut up the tomatoes. But they're often packed in poor-quality tomato paste that has a metallic aftertaste. Use whole canned tomatoes instead. If you're making sauce in a hurry and don't have time to cook down all that juice, just pour it off and save it. And instead of cutting up the tomatoes, just break them up with your hands as you add them to the sauce. Canned tomatoes are often very good and always better than poor-quality fresh ones. While you're at it, avoid most plum tomatoes too. They are often used in cooking because they have more pulp and less juice and seeds, so they cook down faster than some of their juicier relatives. But plum tomatoes in general are quite tasteless, and Roma (the most common in North America) is one of the least flavorful.

Make tomato sauce without simmering all day. *Mamma mia!* The tomato sauce that simmers for hours does taste great. But a fresh tomato sauce that takes just minutes to cook has a charm all of its own—especially when it's made with local tomatoes at the height of their flavor. There are many excellent versions of this sauce. This one comes from *The Sopranos Family Cookbook: As Compiled by Artie Bucco*. Cook 2 large, smashed garlic cloves in 1/4 cup olive oil over medium heat for about 4 minutes or until the garlic is golden. Add 2 pounds (1 kg) very ripe tomatoes, peeled, drained, and chopped. (If fresh ones are not in season, use one 28–ounce [540-ml] can Italian tomatoes, drained and chopped.) Add salt to taste and simmer for 15 to 20 minutes, until the sauce is thick. Stir in 8 to 10 fresh basil leaves, torn into pieces. Serve over hot, cooked pasta. This sauce doesn't have the complexity of its long-simmered cousin, but that isn't the only kind of sauce, as the ads for the canned supermarket sauces would have you believe.

Keep the tomato seeds and skin.

A sauce with peels and seeds in it—horrors! That's some people's opinion, and they're entitled to it. But it's all a matter of taste. The skin and seeds both contribute a great deal to the flavor of a tomato sauce, but if you want to remove the evidence, put the sauce through a food mill. Or make a somewhat coarser sauce with a blender or food processor. Or let it be, with skins and seeds intact. Another sauce tip: When you've seen one tomato, you haven't seen them all. Different varieties have different tastes, and even a single tomato has several aspects to its character. It can be sweet, sour, and salty, all at the same time. You can choose different flavorings to bring out the different facets. Basil, chives, sweet peppers, and even mint will bring out sweetness. Wine, citrus, capers, and vinegars will bring out the sour. The salty aspect will respond to anchovies, olives, capers, and cured meats. ◅

Make Your Own Salad Dressings

EXPERT INSTANT ADVICE

The food companies don't want you to know this, but making salad dressings is not a big deal. You can make any oil-and-vinegar-based dressing from a basic vinaigrette and the additions of your choice. The vinaigrette is simple as can be.

> Mix 3 parts good olive oil to one part good vinegar, then add salt and pepper to taste.

Keep that on hand in the refrigerator all the time. If you want blue cheese dressing, add some blue cheese to it. If you want tarragon dressing, by all means add that. For garlic, add a crushed garlic clove. And so on. The quantities of the additions need not be precise; just keep tasting and stop adding when you like it.

Although salad dressings are a small part of an overall diet, they take up an inordinate amount of space on supermarket shelves. Why? Because these condiments are very high-profit items for their makers, who would like you to think there's such a huge difference between blue cheese and vinaigrette that you couldn't possibly do it yourself.

"Salads are ruined with bought dressings," Elizabeth David writes in her book *Italian Food*. They're usually made from water, bland soybean oil, flavorings, emulsifiers, and preservatives. Even if you want a dressing not based on oil and vinegar, such as ranch or Thousand Island, a basic cookbook will give you directions. You'll eat better, it will cost you less, and you'll free up about an acre of space in your refrigerator.

Egg Secrets
4 Things You Should Know About Buying, Cooking, and Storing This Versatile Food

Buy organic eggs. Of course, organic eggs are slightly more expensive than regular eggs, but we wouldn't be telling you to buy them unless they were better for you. The reason is they are much higher in the all-important omega-3 fatty acids, which have been shown to benefit everything from your mental health (by reducing the risk of depression) to your heart health (by reducing the risk of atherosclerosis and atrial fibrillation), says Fred Pescatore, M.D., author of *The Hamptons Diet* and a physician at Partners in Integrative Medicine in New York City.

There's more than one way to boil an egg. Do you want the control freak's method or the laissez-faire system? They both work. A lot of cookbooks want you to think there's only one way to do something—their way, of course! In some cases, that's true. If you want to beat egg whites for an angel food cake, you can't allow even a speck of yolk to get into the whites or they won't beat up into a meringue. But more often, there are several ways to do something—like boil an egg.

- *The control freak's way* is to bring the water to a boil and *then* place the eggs carefully into it. Cover the pan, and when the water returns to a boil, set the timer for 3 minutes for soft-boiled eggs or 13 minutes for hard-boiled. When the timer goes off, remove the pan from the stove and drain off the water. You'll probably be eating the soft-boiled egg immediately, but if you intend to refrigerate the hard-boiled ones, first run cold water over the eggs until they're no longer hot. (That will also make them easier to peel.)

- *The easygoing laissez-faire method* doesn't require a timer. Start by putting the eggs in the pan and covering them with cold water. Put the pan on a burner over high heat, and cook just until the water comes to a boil. Turn off the heat immediately and leave the eggs in the hot water, covered. After 20 minutes (you *can* use a timer if you want to—this is the laissez-faire way, after all) the eggs will be hard-boiled to the same degree as they are following 13 minutes of constant cooking. But you'll have helped combat global warming by saving 13 minutes of energy usage. There's nothing sacred about the 20-minute requirement; that's merely the minimum. You can let them sit in the water much longer, although eventually the whites will become a little rubbery and a greenish ring will form around the yolk. (It's harmless, but some people find it unsightly.) Eggs will be soft-boiled under this method after sitting in the hot water for 5 minutes. There's no reason for any supposed non-cook to lament, "I can't even boil an egg."

Prick eggs to make them peel easily. It's well known in Europe but not so well known in North America: Pricking eggs before boiling them makes them easier to peel. In Europe they even sell little gizmos for piercing the eggshell, but you don't need one of those.

Just take a pin and insert it about half an inch into the fat end of the egg. That lets in enough air to break the seal between the membrane and the egg white it wants to cling to. Other egg tips: Older eggs peel easier than fresh eggs. If you're making egg salad and won't be serving the eggs intact, don't peel them at all. After you've boiled and cooled them, crack them open and scoop out the egg. You're going to mash it up anyway, so why bother with all that peeling? If, on the other hand, you're planning on making deviled eggs or slices for a garnish, you do want perfect eggs.

Freeze leftover egg whites individually. How many times have you used a few egg yolks, then stored the leftover whites all together in the fridge—only to forget about them? Later, you come upon the container and can't remember how many whites are in it or when you put them there. So you toss it out. Here's a better way. Put each white into one compartment of a clean ice cube tray and freeze them. Then remove the cubes from the tray and store them in a plastic zipper bag. It's then obvious how many there are, and you can thaw them overnight in the refrigerator before using them. To lighten an omelet, add several whites to the whole eggs you use. You can even use them for angel food cake, but they won't beat up to quite as much volume as fresh ones. ◂

Cast Your Net for Sustainable Seafood

Fish is the best source of the "good" fatty acids, but buying fish and seafood, whether at the grocery store, fish market, or in a restaurant, has never been so complicated—that is, if you know what's going on behind the scenes. The fishmongers certainly aren't going to tell you.

"Wild" fish has become scarcer, and of course more expensive, as technology has enabled ever more fish to be caught by an increasingly automated fishing fleet. Overfishing has driven some formerly plentiful fish, such as Atlantic cod, to the verge of extinction.

Then along came fish farming, and for a while it seemed as if that would be the answer to, for example, the problem of declining numbers of Atlantic salmon. But even when farming solved the scarcity problem, aquaculture created new problems by possibly introducing diseases into the wild population and polluting waters. And the environmental concerns don't even address the issue of mercury contamination in the tissues of fish.

How can a fish lover sort it all out? Well, the Monterey (California) Bay Aquarium Foundation has undertaken to do it for you. It has divided many popular food fish into three categories:

- Best Choices
- Good Alternatives
- Avoid

Fish on the "Avoid" list got there either because they're so scarce or because of the methods used to farm or catch them. The list changes when changes in fishing or farming methods change, but you can keep up with it at www.seafoodwatch.org. There you can find downloadable, compact lists of fish in the various categories.

Serving Meat

9 Secrets for Getting Healthy and Tasty Results When Buying and Preparing Animal Protein

Buy grass-fed beef. Here's something the beef industry doesn't want you to know: Conventionally raised beef has more bad fat and less of the good kind than grass-fed beef. But all cattle eat grass, don't they? Yes and no. In the mass-production beef industry, cattle graze on grass for part of their lives, then they're sent to giant feedlots to pig out on corn until fat enough for slaughter. Only a small number are fed on grass for their whole lives. Irish researchers reported in 2000 that cattle fed on grass had less of the artery-clogging saturated fat in their tissues after slaughter than those fed grain, and they also had a higher proportion of omega-3 to omega-6 fatty acids. (Both are essential for humans, but omega-6 is much more common in the North American diet.) In addition, grass-fed beef contains conjugated linoleic acid (CLA), which is believed to help prevent cancer and heart disease. As if that weren't enough, the feedlot cattle also create giant manure piles that can't be absorbed by the land nearby, thus polluting water and air. Since cattle stomachs were made to digest grass, when they're fed a lot of grain they usually also have to be treated with antibiotics to prevent or treat illness. However, they get fat faster on grain than on grass; grain is cheap in America because it's subsidized by the taxpayers through the U.S. Department of Agriculture. No wonder the beef industry loves grain!

"Other white meat" is hogwash. Whoever penned the advertising slogan touting pork as "the other white meat" is clearly a marketing genius. Light coloring aside, the truth is that lean chicken is much less fatty than lean pork. A 3-ounce (85-gram) serving of broiled, skinless chicken breast provides 140 calories, 27 from fat, and only one-third of that fat is saturated. The same serving of roasted lean pork loin provides 275 calories, 189 of them from fat, half of it saturated. To top it off, the chicken serving has 6 more grams of protein than the same amount of pork.

Get Montreal's signature meat online. "Smoked meat" is available in many places in Canada, but the people who really know it say the best comes from Montreal, where it originated. And the best of Montreal's smoked meat, many say, comes from Schwartz's Montreal Hebrew Delicatessen. There are people who travel to Montreal just to eat the smoked meat at Schwartz's and consider it time and money well spent. Smoked meat is similar to pastrami but with somewhat different spices. Frank Silva, the general manager of Schwartz's, says Schwartz's didn't invent smoked meat but it has kept the same process since the deli opened in 1928. The process begins with marinating the meat, a brisket, in a special blend of spices for 7 to 10 days. That is followed by 7 or 8 hours of smoking, and 3 hours of steaming. No chemical preservatives or shortcuts are used, and that's what separates Schwartz's from the competition, Silva says. The company has refused many offers to franchise the business, but it does sell its smoked meat sliced by the pound or by the whole brisket, at www.schwartzsdeli.com.

Don't expect London broil to be tender. The name has a vaguely upscale sound to it, but in reality "London broil" signifies a rather tough cut, usually from the chuck or round. London broil doesn't exist in the same sense that a porterhouse steak exists, with the term meaning a certain cut of meat from a specific part of the carcass. London broil is a term invented by a New York restaurant in the 1930s, and it remains in use because it's so useful—to the supermarkets. It's much cheaper than cuts such as T-bone, porterhouse, or filet mignon, which are instantly recognizable as steak. Flank steak used to be among those cuts called London broil, but then it became popular in its own right and the supermarkets realized they could charge more for it under its real name. Still, London broil can be flavorful, and its toughness can be mitigated as long as you know what you're up against. *Cook's Illustrated* writer David Pazmino found that he could tenderize the meat for grilling by sprinkling about 2 teaspoons salt evenly over both sides, wrapping it in plastic wrap, and letting it sit in the refrigerator for at least 3 hours, but not more than 24 hours. After the grilling, slice the meat very thinly, on the diagonal. A really sharp knife is essential.

Try rubbing coffee on your steak. Ever had coffee on your steak? Probably not, unless you've eaten at Rippe's steak and seafood restaurant in Seattle. In 2003 a chef and waiter came up with the idea of smearing Starbucks on

their sirloin. It soon became a big hit, and Rippe's dubbed its creation Seattle's Signature Steak. Restaurants tend to be secretive about the recipes for their special dishes (with the exception of those that publish cookbooks, such as Chez Panisse, Moosewood, and the Silver Palate). Some home cooks make a game out of defying the restaurants and devising their own versions of their favorite restaurant fare.

Laure Dixon, a fine cook and wine connoisseur who lives in Nashua, New Hampshire, developed this version of coffee-dusted steak. She says to start with a good cut of meat and good coffee beans. (Some like espresso best.) Grind the beans to a fine powder. Then use that as a dry rub on the meat, rubbing it in with your hands. Shake off any excess. Then grill, broil, or pan-fry the steak to your preferred level of doneness. After she takes it off the heat, Laure swipes the steak across a plate containing a fine olive oil, then sprinkles sea salt all over it. (If you want less oil, just drizzle a little over the steak.) Other cooks have also attempted to re-create Rippe's steak, and you can find another version at www.supermarketguru.com.

If you have a favorite restaurant dish you'd like to duplicate, try searching the Web under the name of the restaurant or the dish. If you don't find anything, be fearless—try making it up yourself.

Dilute that serving of beef. The cattle industry would like you to saw your way through a large slab of steak for dinner. But do your arteries a favor and save the whole-steak approach for special occasions. For day-in-and-day-out dining, find ways to cook your steak with other ingredients. Examples: Slice raw beef and sauté it with peppers and onions, fajita style. Cook cut-up steak in a wok with lots of vegetables. Top a salad with steak slices. Or make shish kebab with steak cubes and veggies. You almost always eat less meat when you prepare it as part of a broader dish.

Cook your hamburgers however you want. Here's more proof that there's more than one way to do lots of things, despite what the experts say. Brothers Bob and David Kinkead, who are partners in the restaurant Sibling Rivalry in Boston, divide their loyalties when it comes to cooking burgers. Bob prefers his cooked in a pan because he says grilling gives you the taste of char, not meat. David says cooking over charcoal or wood brings out the most flavor. One thing they do agree on: Don't press on the burgers while they're cooking. That just extracts juices and dries them out.

Try healthier ground chicken or turkey. Whenever you find yourself reaching for a package of ground meat, switch over to the poultry section instead and pick up some ground chicken, ground turkey, or even some soy crumbles. All of them work just as well as ground beef for meatballs, meat loaf, or chili. However, this simple substitution can cut more than 30 percent of the calories and at least half of the fat and saturated fat in a three-ounce serving. When it's smothered in a zesty tomato sauce or flavored with seasonings, you'll never be able to tell the difference. If you are feeling a little gun-shy about abandoning the beef, use half turkey and half lean beef, or half soy crumbles and half beef.

Roast a chicken breast down. Cooked in the traditional way with breast side up, the white meat of a chicken is dry and worn out by the time the dark meat is done, but most cookbooks don't tell you what to do about it. Try flipping the bird over, as amateur (and admired) cook Laure Dixon does. Chicken cooked with its backside up and breast down produces meat that is moist and tender throughout. One small piece of special but inexpensive equipment, a V-rack, is helpful for the inverted roasting. But without that rack, you can prop up the chicken on a long cylinder of rolled-up aluminum foil. Roast in a preheated 400°F (200°C) oven until a meat thermometer inserted into the thickest part of the thigh reads 175°F (80°C). Another way to roast a chicken, favored by some cooks in the Provence region of France, is to set it on two pounds (1 kg) of garlic cloves (yes!) and roast as above. A more modest version calls for 40 cloves to be inserted into the cavity before roasting. Either way, the cooking makes the garlic much milder, and those who enjoy it can eat the cloves like a vegetable. ◂

Cookout Secrets

4 Ways to Make Your Outdoor Grilling Better Tasting—and More Fun as Well

Master the nuances of grilling. Most people never use their grills to their full potential, and restaurants that rely heavily on grilling are usually pleased not to demystify the process. There's a lot more to it than throwing on a slab of meat and trying not to burn it. Ron Rupert, executive chef at Seasons 52 restaurant in Orlando, Florida, is willing to share some of his secrets. He uses different parts of the grill for their different heat levels, and selects different woods for the subtle yet distinctive flavor they impart. For example, he uses mesquite for a slightly sweet, smoky flavor; when he wants a smokier taste, he burns oak. Also, he says, different woods burn at different temperatures. Mesquite produces a very hot fire, suitable for cooking fish, while oak burns at a temperature favorable for vegetables and meats. For a juicy steak, first sear the meat on a hotter part of the grill, then move it to a medium-hot area to allow the flavors to develop more slowly. He wows diners at his restaurant with grilled fresh vegetables (in addition to meat and fish, of course) cooked with very little added fat. The restaurant doesn't even have a deep fryer, never panfries, and rarely sautés. And each item on the menu promises to have fewer than 475 calories.

Butter up your grilled steak. When you order steak in a good restaurant, don't be dazzled by exotic spices or cooking techniques listed on the menu. There's an astoundingly simple chef's secret that provides the knock-'em-dead flavor that you can't seem to achieve when you grill steaks at home: butter. When you're grilling at home, as soon as you remove your steak from the grill, shave 1/2 tablespoon butter onto it and let the butter melt. Don't tell your guests—they'll wonder how you found the time for cooking school.

Take the spilling out of grilling. Those cute little wooden skewers were supposed to work fine if you soaked them in water first. Well, you can't soak them enough to keep them from catching fire—and then there goes the shish kebab. Round metal skewers were just fine until it came time to turn them over. You'd no sooner get the whole thing flipped over than gravity would take over, and all the stuff on the skewer would swing around too. Then there were flat skewers, which kept the food from flopping over, but they had to be bigger in order to be effective. That was fine for the meat, but the peppers, onions, and especially fragile mushrooms would often split while you were attempting to thread them onto the skewer. Kebab baskets eliminate both problems. They're a kind of long wire box with a lid and a long handle. You put the stuff into the box, close the lid, and place it on the grill or over the fire. The handle allows easy flipping.

Rediscover the campfire. Go ahead, if you want to, and buy a grill that practically duplicates your whole kitchen (including the price, if you buy one of the fanciest). But before there were grills, there were campfires, and they're still magical. You can have plenty of fun with a little fireplace in the backyard. Naturally, the grill makers don't advertise that! (Check your local ordinances to make sure it is allowed.) Here are two methods:

How I Do It A Chef Grills Ears of Corn and Lettuce

Chef Ron Rupert uses the grill not just for cooking but also as a flavor enhancer for vegetables. Here is his secret for corn on the cob, a summertime favorite. First, don't husk the corn. Place it on a medium-hot part of the grill and turn the ears as they brown. The object of this step is to cook the kernels, and that should take 20 to 25 minutes. Then peel back the husks (but leave them on the cob), remove the silk, spritz the kernels with a little olive oil, and season them with salt and pepper. Return to the grill and cook until nicely browned, 4 to 5 minutes.

Rupert even grills lettuce for one of his restaurant's signature salads. Using romaine, he first washes it and pats it dry. Then he cuts it in half lengthwise, spritzes it with olive oil, and adds salt and pepper. He cooks the lettuce briefly, over a hot fire, removing it when browned. He brushes the grilled romaine with a Caesar dressing and tops it with buffalo steak, grilled red onion rings, and corn salad.

- Dig a hole about four inches (10 cm) deep and two feet (60 cm) in diameter, and place some round stones in a circle, very close together, along the edge. A mere 10 or 15 rocks about the size of a softball will do the job—there's your fire pit.

- If you happen to have flat stones, and more of them, you can build a little fireplace. Pile the rocks on three sides and leave it open on one side to allow you to get at the fire. The stones should be piled high enough to shield the fire from the wind without cutting off the air supply. This is a simple device, not made according to a precise formula.

After you have your fire pit or fireplace, make the fire. If you're in the backyard, crumple up some paper (look for bark or dry leaves if you're in the woods). Loosely arrange small twigs over the paper, bark, or leaves to create a tepee. Add a layer of slightly larger twigs on top of that. Then light the paper. As soon as the twigs have caught fire, start piling on more twigs, using ever-larger ones as the fire gets going. When the fire will burn sticks of a couple of inches (5 cm) in diameter, pile on enough so that when they burn down, they'll create a nice bed of coals. That could take a half hour or more, depending on how big a fire you have.

Once you have red-hot coals, it's time to cook. In keeping with the primitiveness of it, find and cut a couple of nice slim branches. Sharpen one end of one with a jackknife, and poke it through a couple of hot dogs to roast over the fire. Toast a couple of rolls at the same time on the other stick. Add a piece of firewood occasionally if you don't want the fire to go out. When you've had your fill, use the sticks to toast a few marshmallows. Be sure to douse the fire completely when you're done, even if it looks as if it has gone out. The fire pit or fireplace can be used over and over again. ◁

Storing Food
5 Secrets for Keeping Food from Spoiling and for Using On-the-Edge Foods

Make cheese and milk last longer.
Good cheese is expensive. It also gets moldy fast. Mold is fine on blue cheese, but less than delectable on cheddar. You can delay the onset by wrapping the cheese in a piece of cheesecloth soaked in whiskey, then put that in a plastic bag. Or wrap the cheese in parchment paper and then foil and keep it in the crisper drawer. To keep the side of a piece of cheese from drying out, rub a little butter on it. To keep milk or cream fresh longer, add a pinch of salt to the carton.

Soften those rock-hard raisins. You can prevent raisins from getting hard, or at least slow the process a lot, by storing them in a jar with a tight lid. But you forgot to do that, and only got to eat a handful before the 15-ounce (425-gram) box hardened into stone. It feels like a shame to toss away that food, inedible though it may be. Don't scribble "raisins" on the shopping list just yet— you can revive those hardened nuggets. Drop them into a cooking pot and add water until they're submerged. Bring the water to a boil on the stovetop and then turn the stove off. Let the raisins steep in the water for 10 minutes. Set your colander in the sink and pour your soft-and-tasty raisins into it to drain.

Save the not-yet-rotten bananas.
When bananas get too ripe to be eaten whole or even to be presentable as slices, they're still fine for shakes or banana bread. If you can't use them immediately, peel them and freeze them individually in plastic wrap; thaw before using.

Make a portable root cellar. Rather than let your ginger shrivel up in the fridge or watch the carrots turn to slime in the crisper, try storing roots in a pot filled with clean sand. An unglazed flowerpot works well. Cover the roots, and pick them out as you need them. Store the pot in a cool, dark place.

Freeze the leftover tomato paste.
When you just want a tablespoon or two of tomato paste, remove that from the can and drop the remainder by spoonfuls (pretend you're making cookies) onto wax paper. Put these dollops, wax paper and all, in the freezer. Once they're frozen, peel them off the paper, drop the paste pieces into a zip-seal plastic bag, and store them in the freezer. Next time you need a little tomato paste, just add a "cookie" or two to your sauce or soup. There's no need to thaw them. ◁

Beware of Buying in Bulk

Some people are so seduced by the idea of bargains at warehouse stores that they momentarily lose their common sense when shopping there. The warehouse stores won't tell you, but sometimes an item costs the same or even less in regular stores. You have to study the unit price to determine that. Why buy and store 50 cans of tuna if you can buy it a few at a time for the same price per can? Before you buy a gross of hot dogs or three kilos of grated Parmesan cheese, stop and think about how you'll store your purchases. Do you have enough room in your freezer, refrigerator, or pantry? Why buy 6 pounds (2.7 kg) of grated cheese at a bargain price if it's going to mold before you can use it all, and you wind up throwing half of it away? When you're buying just because it's a bargain, be sure it really is.

Cooking Skills
5 Easy Ways to Get You on the Road to Becoming a Fantastic Cook

Ignore the hype—you *can* cook.
Cooking isn't an exotic art practiced only by cultists, although there are plenty of take-out restaurants, eat-in restaurants, delis, supermarket deli sections, and mini-marts that profit when you think that way. According to government statistics, almost half of U.S. consumers' food budget, and just under a third of Canadians', goes for meals prepared outside the home. Julia Child, the noted cook and cookbook author who brought detailed instructions for French cooking to American readers, took issue with the idea of cooking as a pastime open only to a few. "If you can read, you can cook," she wrote.

Get a back-to-basics cookbook.
Julia Child's statement may not be terribly reassuring to people who have no idea where to start reading—there is an incredible array of cookbooks on the market, after all, and often they only further intimidate the novice. (We won't even get into the intimidation factor of all of those cooking shows on TV.) If you want to learn to cook, don't start with one of the just-published, hyped-up, fancy-schmancy cookbooks prominently displayed in bookstores. You need a basic,

nuts-and-bolts guide, one that will explain something as obvious to an experienced cook as "roast" or "sauté" or "braise." Here's a recommendation: *Joy of Cooking*. It has been around since 1931 and has gone through six editions in order to keep up with changing North American tastes. The older editions explain how to can vegetables and make pickles, jams, and jellies. The latest edition doesn't have those sections, but it explains the basics of many dishes from ethnic cuisines that were practically unknown in North America decades ago. There are other good basic cookbooks, but few as comprehensive as *Joy*. Once you have obtained a basic book, then just follow the advice of Alice B. Toklas, an author of another sort of cookbook—the kind that's fun to dip into to supplement the basics. "The only way to learn to cook is to cook," she wrote in 1954 in *The Alice B. Toklas Cookbook*. Toklas was a companion to the American writer Gertrude Stein, and they lived for many years in France. Toklas's cookbook has never been updated, but neither has it ever been out of print, probably because of her recipe for "Haschich Fudge," popularly known as "hash brownies." Her cookbook is an amusing mix of recipes and anecdotes from the 1930s and 1940s and is a good illustration of the notion that cookbooks don't follow just one recipe for usefulness and success.

Find out what foods your family likes. Nothing will boost your confidence in your cooking skills more than having satisfied customers—that is, family members who are happy with what they are eating. While it helps to ask everyone what their favorite dishes are, and even get them involved in menu planning, you can't always trust what people say off the top of their head when asked a broad question like "What kind of dishes do you like for dinner?" A more reliable way is to observe what dishes your family enjoys at restaurants or at someone else's house. Consult your cookbooks or surf food sites on the Web for similar recipes and surprise them by duplicating those dishes at home.

Stay current with a magazine. There are so many cooking and food magazines that you can choke trying to digest the options. So here's another recommendation: *Cook's Illustrated.* Its articles deal with basic techniques and ingredients as well as more exotic ones. They advise on the usefulness of new products, and they always explain the reasoning behind their choices. *Cook's* has no advertising or product endorsements. Finally, it's beautifully designed and well written.

Read the directions all the way through first. That sounds pretty obvious, but many cooking attempts fail if you omit this step. In the middle of a recipe, wannabe cooks suddenly realize they have to cream the butter—and it's rock-hard in the fridge. Or they don't preheat the oven to the right temperature. Or they find themselves with no chocolate when they're trying to make brownies. For Southern-style barbecue, you must start with the right cut of meat and plan on hours for it to cook, or it will be tough. If you're making an omelet, getting the pan hot makes the difference between an omelet that is easily flipped and leaves the pan cleanly, or ending up with scrambled eggs— minus the half that's stuck to the pan. ◁

Adding Flavor
4 Surprising Flourishes That Will Improve the Way Your Food Tastes

Buy herbs and spices at a health food store. Instead of buying dried herbs and spices in those tiny bottles and cans (with the big price tags) in the supermarket, try your local health food store. Most health food stores sell them in bulk, and ounce for ounce, gram for gram, they're a whole lot cheaper than the grocery store kind. They're usually fresher, too, and many are organically grown. The per-pound (500 grams) prices, even at the health food store, can seem daunting ($15 per pound for dried parsley?), but you can scoop out a generous amount that is pretty cheap when it gets weighed up because dried herbs and spices are so light. In the sampling of spices and prices shown in the chart below, only chili powder was roughly comparable in price, although still a little cheaper at the health food store.

per ounce	SUPERMARKET	HEALTH FOOD STORE
Chili powder	$1.33	$1.19
Cinnamon (ground)	1.50	0.56
Oregano	1.24	0.75
Parsley flakes	3.32	0.94
Peppercorns	1.15	0.87

Source: Survey taken 7/12/06 at Price Chopper and St. Johnsbury Food Co-op in St. Johnsbury, Vermont

There were some differences in quality too. One of the ingredients in the supermarket's chili powder was salt, which was not included in the health food kind. (You can always add your own salt if you really need it.) The health food store chili powder had a richer spice mixture, with eight spices to five for the supermarket variety (not counting the salt). And the health food kind mentioned prominently that it had not been irradiated. Irradiation is a very common treatment in all kinds of herbs and spices.

Use wine for flavor. And say goodbye to bottled and dried mixes, bouillon cubes, and artificial flavors that the food industry would like you to use in soups, stews, and gravies. Elizabeth David writes, "If every kitchen contained a bottle each of red wine, white wine, and inexpensive port for cooking, hundreds of store cupboards could be swept clean forever of the cluttering debris of commercial sauce bottles and all the synthetic aids to flavoring." (Don't use *cooking* wine. It's not of good quality, and it's typically loaded up with sodium you don't need.) To make excellent gravy for roast meat, strain the fat off the pan drippings, add 1/2 cup wine, and scrape off the meat residue in the pan. Cook on high heat for a couple of minutes—that gets rid of the alcohol in the wine—add a little water, and cook for about 2 minutes more.

Celebrate celery. Celery doesn't get much respect. It appears most often in soups, stews, and casseroles, where, in a supporting role, it adds some of its distinctive flavor. But it's rarely the star, except in Cajun and Creole cookery, where with peppers and onions it is part of the "holy trinity." Why not let it shine? Add chopped celery—not cooked to death, but crunchy—at the last minute to creamed dishes. It adds taste, texture, and surprise. Here's another surprise: an easy relish that livens up a traditional accompaniment to pork. To a pint of applesauce, add 1 cup chopped celery and 1 tablespoon horseradish. You may like yours with more or less horseradish and celery, so feel free to adjust the quantities.

Don't be scared away from butter. Just don't use too much of it. We all know that butter has saturated fat, and too much saturated fat isn't good. But good health is less about avoiding one particular food than about your overall eating patterns. If you eat Pop-Tarts for breakfast and satisfy your daily vegetable requirement with French fries and potato chips, don't think you're protecting your health by using margarine instead of butter. The margarine makers would like you to think that, but don't let them kid you. They've made a whole industry out of fear of butter. Many great cooks—and healthy ones—swore by butter. Julia Child was ridiculed as the "cholesterol queen" for her love of butter and cream, but she remained an advocate for good butter and good food until the end, which came two days shy of her 92nd birthday in 2004. She also believed in enjoying butter (and everything else) in moderation. ◂

Gadgets and Gizmos
5 Things to Know About Buying and Using Food-Preparation Utensils and Aids

Ignore kitchen tool hoopla. A lot of manufacturers of kitchen gadgets, as well as the stores that sell them, would have you think you simply can't cook without this or that gizmo. What you never hear is that one cook's cool tool is another cook's clutter. There are fine cooks who don't have a food processor, a microwave, a blender, a slow cooker, a mandoline, a mango splitter, a gas grill, a ricer, a food mill, a toaster oven, a bread maker, a juicer, or even a coffee maker. There are other cooks who swear by any one of those items, and a whole lot more. There are cooks—good ones—who still prefer an old-fashioned, hand-cranked eggbeater to a wire whisk. When it comes to equipment, you must find your own way. Just don't think you have to figure it out all at once. If you don't want to spend a lot of money on equipment until you know what you really like, look for yard sales that advertise kitchen equipment among their wares. You can buy things for very little money, see how you like them, and either keep them or put them into your own sale.

Don't worry about wood vs. plastic cutting boards. Which side are you on, wood or plastic? The war over which type of cutting board is safest has entered a new phase: It's a draw. The battle went back and forth for more than a decade. Everyone assumed plastic could be cleaned more thoroughly, and was therefore better than wood, until some research in 1994 showed that wood retained less bacteria than plastic. More research followed, and it further confused the issue. Finally, researchers at *Cook's Illustrated* threw up their hands and declared: There isn't much difference. Just wash them with hot, soapy water, because bacteria persist on both for a long time.

Discover the double boiler. Here's a tool that's so old it never gets any hype, so it might as well be new and unknown. Cookbook author Virginia Bentley swore by a good old-fashioned double boiler. Several of them, actually, in big and small sizes. She loved them

---
SECRET WEAPON

A Brick

You don't need a special panini press, according to Jason Denton. He owns 'ino on Bedford Street in New York City, a tiny restaurant that for eight years has specialized in panini. First, he says, set the grill for about 250°F (120°C) or, if using charcoal, wait until the coals have cooled down a bit and are not too hot. Use some kind of substantial bread, such as a baguette, and slice off the domed part on top. Slice the loaf in half lengthwise. (Depending on the size, you can probably get several sandwiches from one loaf.) Put some cheese (Denton likes baby Swiss and provolone) on both sides of the bread, and the filling goes between the layers of cheese. For a filling, he uses what's in season—maybe zucchini or tomatoes with some simple cured meat. It's important not to stuff it too much, he says. Put the sandwich on the grill and weight it with an ordinary brick wrapped in aluminum foil. The brick helps everything melt together and keeps the heat even. It should be done in 3 to 4 minutes. Check Denton's book *Simple Italian Sandwiches* for a host of other ideas.

---

because they're guaranteed not to scorch, and they're great for keeping food warm. She liked to serve directly from them when she was entertaining. You can improvise a simple double boiler by placing a heatproof bowl (Pyrex is perfect) over a saucepan of simmering water. The bowl should sit over the water, not in it.

In with the new, but hang on to the old. Product makers will label their new-and-improved gadgets as "breakthroughs," new and better replacements for the old version that's sitting in your kitchen drawer. If you succumb to temptation and buy, don't throw out your old tool just yet. Take graters, for instance. The old-fashioned four-sided box grater, with different sizes of grating teeth, is still the best for grating tomatoes and cheeses such as cheddar. It also has small teeth that do a decent job on hard cheeses such as Parmesan. But a newer kind of grater, the rasp grater, does an even better job on hard stuff, like Parmesan cheese, garlic, nutmeg, and chocolate. But it does a lousy job with the softer things, so hang on to that old one.

Use coffee filters for straining. Many recipes call for using cheesecloth to strain things, but David Felton, executive chef at the Pluckemin Inn in Bedminster, New Jersey, often uses paper coffee filters instead. Straining through the filters takes a little longer, but it produces a clearer liquid and they're easier to use than cheesecloth. He uses coffee filters for broth and also to strain the juice from watermelon and fresh tomatoes to use in aperitifs. The straining produces a liquid nearly as clear as water but with a little surprise to the taste buds. If you're using a cone-shaped filter, set it into a funnel and put that over a container large enough to hold your liquid. Pour the liquid into the filter. If it's taking its time about going through (it depends on what the liquid is), go do something else for a while, then pour in some more. If you're using a basket-type filter, follow the same procedure, but set it into a sieve over a jar or bowl. ◁

Picnic Tricks

7 Little-Known Ways to Eat Better and More Safely When You Pack Your Basket

Make your own soft drink, and let it cool your picnic. You'd never freeze a commercial soft drink, so all they do is give you one more thing to keep cold. But before there was Coke and Pepsi, there was lemonade. You can still make your own, using about three lemons for a quart (liter). Squeeze the lemons, which should give you about 1/2 cup juice. Mix that with 1/2 cup sugar (or to taste), and add three cups water. Voilà! The night before your picnic, freeze the lemonade in plastic milk cartons. Then use the cartons to help keep the food cool in the cooler. Drink the lemonade as it thaws.

Make potato salad with oil and vinegar. Just hold the mayo and eggs. There's no picnic food that gets more bad press than potato salad—and justifiably so, when it's made with eggs and mayonnaise, which can harbor bacteria that cause sickness. There are many delicious variations on potato salad that use oil and vinegar instead—but few cookbooks tell you that they're safe for picnics. Here's a very simple version: Boil potatoes until they're tender. Drain and dice them. Then dress them while still warm with olive oil, vinegar, salt, pepper, finely chopped onions, and/or garlic. You can eat it hot, cold, or warm.

Don't expect a cooler to keep ice cream frozen. Ads for coolers suggest they can keep just about anything cold. But don't count on one to keep frozen things from turning to goop within a few hours. "Coolers cool; they don't freeze," writes Tom Bartlett in an article in the online magazine *Slate* that ana-

lyzed the performance of six picnic coolers. However, Bartlett's top-rated cooler, the Coleman Ultimate Xtreme, priced at $49.99, kept a six-pack of beer surrounded by ice cool for four days. His favorite for the esthetics was another Coleman, the Steel Cooler. It costs twice as much, but it kept beer cool for three days and looks great. Hard coolers did a better job than soft-sided ones, but you may want a softie for other reasons. Bartlett liked the Polar Bear Soft Side Cooler, $49.95, for being easy to store and clean. He has a few cooler tips too. One: A full cooler stays cool longer than a half-full one. Pack it full in layers: ice on the bottom, then drinks, then more ice, and soft stuff such as sandwiches and potato salad on top.

SECRET WEAPON

A Checklist

Many a picnic has been less than perfect because some essential item was left behind. Make a checklist of foods and all the equipment that you need to transport and serve it. If you go on picnics often, put together a special picnic basket that contains all the basics. Leave it packed from picnic to picnic. Make sure to include such indispensables as a corkscrew, bottle opener, clips for closing bags of chips, bug repellent, adhesive strips, and antiseptic. Also pack several medium-size garbage bags for disposing of trash and recyclables when you get home.

Think finger foods ... Let's be honest: Managing forks, spoons, and knives on a picnic isn't much fun. You can make a terrific meal with foods that require only two fingers to eat! Start with the healthy nibbles: berries, cherry tomatoes, grapes, celery and carrot sticks, asparagus spears, olives, cheese cubes, crackers, and so on. Next, consult your favorite cookbook for appetizers like stuffed mushrooms, chicken fingers, or foccacia that can be eaten by hand. Need more substantial food? Sandwiches, ribs, fried chicken, and burgers all fall in the no-cutlery category. You'll be grateful come cleanup time!

... but bring lots of hand sanitizer.
Bathrooms with warm water and good-quality soap are in short supply on picnics. So use the next best thing: waterless hand sanitizers. These cleaning gels kill germs instantly and dry nearly as fast. They're the perfect hand-cleaning solution, particularly if you are serving finger foods. Be sure to have a large bottle on hand.

Use lots of squirt bottles.
You can buy squeezable, plastic squirt bottles for next to nothing at any restaurant supply store. Use them for mayonnaise, ketchup, mustard, barbecue sauce, salad dressings, oils, and any other condiment or cooking liquid. They are easy to pack and super clean to use. They're one of the best secret tools of professional chefs.

Keep desserts simple.
For a hot summer day, there's nothing better than a slice of watermelon, a fresh-picked peach, or a bowl of cold strawberries for the perfect ending to an outdoor meal. Skip the fruit salad—and all its preparation, serving, and cleanup hassles. Or serve up your best brownies and cookies. Again, these are all finger foods that require no plates or cutlery—and that everyone will love. ◁

Restaurant Food
4 Ways to Protect Your Pocketbook and Health When You Go Out to Eat

Keep your coffee order simple. That pricey coffeehouse wants you to order your brew in as fancy a form as possible. Not only does this drive up the tab for each visit, but also stacks on hundreds of calories—from the whole milk, whipped cream, sugar and syrups. A regular cuppa joe made from good beans and with a dash of skim milk is heaven in itself, so protect your wallet and your arteries by keeping things simple.

Give gelato a try. Move over, Ben & Jerry. Gelato is an Italian ice cream that tastes great even though it isn't loaded with fat. (Gelato is 4 to 8 percent butterfat versus 10 to 18 percent for regular ice cream.) Nor is it all fluffed up with air. Cafés that specialize in gelato are popping up all over North America. Jan Horsfall, founder, president, and chief executive of Gelazzi, a gelato café in Denver, Colorado, makes his gelato fresh every day and says the quality of his extracts, cream, and eggs, makes his gelato rich and creamy. He travels to Italy several times a year to obtain the extracts. He also pairs his gelato with various liqueurs to make interesting gelato cocktails. If there is no gelato café near you and you want to try making your own, do a Web search for gelato and you'll find plenty of help.

Go when a restaurant has a downtime. Most restaurants go out of their way to attract customers at times when business is slow. Take advantage of them and you can eat for up to 25 percent less than when a restaurant is busy and the prices are at their highest. You can expect service to be much better too. Here are some examples:

- Any day of the year, early evening will usually produce "early bird specials" in restaurants.
- Lunchtime menus often offer the same dishes as in the evening for a sizeable discount. Or you can get a "businessman's special" in many restaurants.
- If you live in an area that draws tourists, the off-season forces many nearly deserted restaurants to offer specials to attract locals.
- Restaurants that have just opened often offer lower prices to attract customers, so keep an eye out for promising new restaurants.

When traveling, you can control food costs. Travel planners, local booster organizations, and food outlets of all kinds would like you to take all of your meals in restaurants when you're visiting. But you can extend your travel budget by having a few picnics instead. A trip to the local markets can furnish you with healthier and cheaper food, as well as an adventure in its own right. Buy fresh food, pack it in a sack you take for that purpose, and eat it at some lovely spot, even in the park in a city.

Also when traveling: When you do want to dine in a fine restaurant, if you eat your big meal at noon, you can do so more cheaply. ◂

Indulge in a Canadian Secret (If You Dare)

U.S. fast food has nothing on *poutine*, a Quebec concoction nicknamed "heart attack in a dish." Surprisingly, it's not at all well known outside Canada. It consists of a bed of French fries topped by thick gravy and cheese curds. It is more often eaten in restaurants than made at home, and as with any beloved dish, there are lots of opinions about how to make it.

The French fries must be large, not the skinny ones, because they support so much stuff on top. Some places have tried using cheese, not the curds, but the purists don't like that at all. And there are many versions of the gravy, as you'd expect: chicken, beef, vegetarian, and a gourmet version that calls for wine to be added to the pan drippings from roast duck and then reduced.

In Canada, *poutine* is available at restaurants throughout the country, but many authorities say the best still comes from Quebec, where it originated either in 1957 in Warwick or in 1964 in Drummondville. In Quebec, many fast-food restaurants (including the well-known American chains) offer poutine, but the purists say their versions aren't the real "mushy mess," or "pudding," as the name means in the French Acadian dialect.

TOP SECRET

part Two

AROUND THE HOUSE

That young man at the garden center is so outgoing and helpful you can't believe he's not being entirely up-front with you about how to control that infestation of aphids. It's not that he's lying; he's just not telling you about the 25-cent solution you already have at home. Contractors, decorators, repairmen, and the people who sell you appliances, clothing, and electronics all practice a similar code of silence. Well, we've managed to get a few of them to open up and let you in on their secrets. Learn about unnecessary fees and warranties, repairs so simple anyone can do them, low-cost decorating tricks, even how to get free computer security.

Decorator Secrets

3 Strategies Pros Use to Turn a Sow's Ear Room into a Silk Purse One

Learn to trick the eye with color. There's nothing quite like seeing before-and-after photos of a room transformed from dull to dazzling. The interior designers who achieve such magic are often considered intuitive and naturally creative—in fact, many do have a special knack. But most designers nurture that knack by going to school to learn hard-and-fast design rules. From these rules come their tricks of the trade. In other words, there is method to their magic. Which is where you, the homeowner, come in. You may not have been to decorator school, but you can benefit from a page out of a top designer's playbook. Follow her advice, and you might just work some magic of your own—without paying hundreds of dollars per hour in design fees.

- *Make your ceilings look taller.* Low ceilings got you down? Here's an optical illusion practiced by designers for artificially (and inexpensively) raising the roof: Add contrasting strips of fabric along the inner and outer edges of curtains. Say you've got beige curtains. Add chocolate brown fabric strips, and the ceiling will look taller.

- *Add "architectural" interest to a room.* Transform a plain-Jane room into something handsome and eye-catching with color. Paint the molding and the trim around windows and doors a shade or two darker than the walls, and paint the window sashes—the sliding parts that carry the glass—an even deeper shade. Guests will ask for the name of the designer you hired.

- *Draw the eye outside.* If you've got French doors—or another kind of glass doors—leading to an attractive yard, patio, or deck, paint them a deep, dark color to lead the eye to what's beyond.

Avoid the predictable seating arrangement.

You know: sofa, a pair of matching chairs, coffee table in between. Snooze. The solution is elegantly simple. It's a trick designers call the "pull-up chair"—a nonmatching chair tossed into the mix to keep the arrangement looking fresh and unique.

Make the most of everyday items.

Some of the top designers working today know that big bucks aren't a requirement for decorating creativity. In fact, having to stick to a tight budget often forces people to take chances they might not otherwise take with an expensive piece of furniture or fabric. Having to make do with everyday items can inspire some of the most attention-grabbing details in a home. Here are examples:

- *Recycle old sofa cushions.* If you're tossing an old couch, keep a couple of the pillows. Cover them in an attractive but durable outdoor fabric and use them as floor pillows for extra seating. The kids will love it, especially during Friday movie night.
- *Make a stylish porch swing.* Find an old garden bench at a flea market and cut off the legs. Attach chains or sturdy ropes and hang from hooks.
- *Customize off-the-shelf items.* Take a store-bought lampshade, for example. It's white, generic-looking, and—here's the good part—cheap. Glue a handsome red ribbon around the top and bottom edges, and you've got a personalized accessory. ◁

Clever Cover-Ups
6 Smart Ways to Transform a Room with Some Fabric or Wallpaper

Think of your sofa as your favorite shirt. In other words, cover it in a color you love to wear instead of in a neutral—what most people choose—that disappears in the room. If you choose your favorite color, one that looks best on you, the sofa will take center stage. And you'll never get tired of sitting on it.

Use bold fabric patterns in small doses. A little on a footstool or accent pillows will go a long way. It won't overwhelm, but it will still stand out. This is a good way to use an expensive fabric you love without having to break the bank buying several yards to cover an entire couch.

For large chairs, choose a small print. If you're covering a large chair, like a wingback, choose a small-print fabric. The chairs are dramatic enough. A small print helps balance that drama and looks more sophisticated.

Got kids? Choose a forgiving sofa fabric. Patterns help hide spills and crumbs. You probably know that by now. But did you also know that a fabric with a texture—a cotton velvet or some other textile with a pile—will do wonders for masking the mess? Try it. You'll worry less and enjoy more.

Dress up boring window shades. Those vanilla-colored roller shades are about as blah as it gets. But they're inexpensive, and they do their job. For a few dollars more, you can transform the shades—and an entire room in the process—by gluing a bold wallpaper print to the insides of the shades. This works best with shades 27 inches (68 cm) wide or less—the width of a standard wallpaper roll. Measure the length of the fully extended shade, and cut the wallpaper to fit, leaving an extra two inches. Roll out the shade and cover it with wallpaper adhesive using a sponge roller. Lay the wallpaper on the glue, letting the extra two inches wrap under the bottom of the shade. Use a rolling pin to smooth out air bubbles. Trim away any excess wallpaper. Because the wallpaper makes the shade a little harder to roll up and down, this trick works best on windows where you don't mind leaving the shade partially down.

Make a decorative bulletin board. Large acoustic ceiling tiles—the kind of thing you see in office drop ceilings—make great, inexpensive bulletin boards. Go to your big-box home store. Look for the size tiles that appeal to you. Two-foot-square (61-cm-square) tiles cost about $20 for a box of four. Wrap them in the decorative fabric of your choice (leave a few inches of overlap and glue the edges to the back). You can tack these directly into your wall. Or paint a lightweight hollow-core door and attach the fabric-wrapped tiles to the door in a neat row. Lean the door against the wall, and voilà! You've got an inexpensive message board. ◂|

Organizing Papers

4 Tricks for Keeping Papers and Photographs from Becoming an Insurmountable Problem

Categorize those papers. Office papers tend to pile up quickly on desktops, says Karen Lawrence, CEO of Space Matters, a home-organizing business in Richmond, Virginia. Not only do the desks become eyesores, but they result in lost documents and missed appointments. Here's a trick: Use stackable filers to sort papers on your desk into categories. Label them "Need action," "To be filed," "Read later," and "Outgoing mail."

Cast off old cards and crafts. Many people feel obliged to keep every greeting card they've ever received or every craft their child ever made. You'll enjoy these items more if you select a few and honor them by making a scrapbook, album, or wall decoration.

Weed out your photos. Instead of letting photos pile up and take over, take back your shelf space with a few simple steps. First, sort photos by person, event, or time frame (for example, "Family Beach Vacation" or "Wedding Weekend"). For each group, select the best 10 to 20 pictures, and place these pictures in an album or frame. Get rid of the rest, either throwing them away or spreading the memories by giving them away. There's no point in keeping 20 bad pictures when you have 10 good ones.

Organize and toss daily. Spend a few minutes every day picking up and organizing household paper clutter, especially newspapers and junk mail. Have special stacks or folders for bills, statements, and receipts. That way, things don't pile up and become unmanageable. ◂|

Clutter Control

5 Secrets for Cutting Down on the All the Nonessentials Filling Up Your Home

Organize your home like a pro.
Decluttering is big business these days. Professional home organizers know that busy people will shell out for peace of mind, which is why they charge fees of $200 to $900 per day. And while many of these professionals do good work, it's not rocket science. Home organizer Karen Lawrence offers these general tips for do-it-yourself organizing.

- Bear in mind that everything you buy is an investment of your time. Clothes must be laundered, dry-cleaned, and mended. Knicknacks have to be dusted. Toys need storing, cleaning, and fixing. As you buy items, mentally add this extra "cost" to the purchase price of the new item. You'll buy less and save money.

- Set small goals, such as decluttering one room a week or tackling one shelf or one drawer per day. If you try to organize your entire house in a weekend, you'll get so discouraged, you may quit altogether.

- Before decluttering, set aside bags and boxes labeled "Trash," "Donate," and "Belongs Elsewhere." This way, you break down a big pile of clutter into smaller, more manageable tasks.

- Sort like items together. You may be surprised that you have six black sleeveless dresses, four coolers, fifteen blue ties, or eight flashlights. Keep the best and get rid of the rest.

- Define important, clutter-producing activities, such as processing mail, paying bills, wrapping gifts, sewing or other crafts, or indoor gardening, and then create "centers" for doing these activities. Fill them with the necessary organizational tools and stay on top of the clutter. And make sure you have a wastebasket near each center.

EXPERT INSTANT ADVICE

Lazy Susan

Barry J. Izsak, founder of Arranging It All and president of the National Association of Professional Organizers, is a big fan of turntables. No, not those obsolete old record players. We're talking about storing items on a lazy Susan for easy access. "This is my favorite item for organizing kitchen cupboards and pantries," he says. There are tons of uses for them and they are very inexpensive (less than $5). Use them to organize your spices, containers, glassware, and canned goods.

Balance your closet. Clean out and organize your closet, getting it to a point that satisfies you. From now on, whenever you buy anything new—a winter coat, for example, or a pair of sandals—give away a like item, your old winter coat or your old sandals, for instance. Though your closet may need straightening every once in a while, it will remain at equilibrium, never again bursting at the seams.

Make regular donations to charity. Include furniture, clothes, and household items. Not only will you stay on top of clutter, but you'll be able to take a tax deduction for the things you donate. Keep empty boxes labeled "Donate" available. Make a run every month—or as needed—to your charity's drop-off center. Research specific charities in your area. Some groups collect old eyeglasses for children in underdeveloped countries, or barely worn interview suits for moms on public assistance.

Purge the fix-it pile. Fixing stuff is admirable. But hanging on to broken household items until you find the time to repair them burdens you mentally and clutters your garage or shop. Once a month, evaluate the items in your "someday" pile and either fix them, throw them away, or pay to have them repaired.

Have a yard sale. Whether you call it a yard, garage, or tag sale, it's a terrific way to dispose of a lot of discardable items that are cluttering up your house. Planning one is a good incentive to go through closets, cupboards, and storage boxes to gather material for the sale. ◄|

Container Magic
5 Creative Ways to Use Baskets and Other Holders to Bring Order to Chaotic Items

Use the basket trick. Place a decorative basket or crate in or near the most cluttered room of your house. Place items that belong in other rooms in the basket. Anytime you exit the room, grab items out of the basket and return them to their rightful place.

Sort those loose items. Loose items, such as batteries, buttons, lightbulbs, and matches, often end up scattered in junk drawers and can't be found when you need them. Keep them at hand by labeling containers for these items.

Label laundry baskets. Save time by presorting laundry. Label bags or baskets: "Whites," "Colors," "Permanent Press," and "Dry Cleaning." You will always know when it is time to deal with a particular load, and you will never waste time separating laundry again, says home organizer Karen Lawrence.

Use paraphernalia baskets. Keep baskets or small bins on tables to store small frequently used items, such as remote controls, nail clippers, and notepads. Similarly, put a small dish on the bureau top to collect loose change and earrings, and an old mug on the desk to hold pens, pencils, and scissors. Surfaces will appear neater.

Make kid stuff reachable. Create kid storage units that are lightweight and low to the ground—rolling crates and small plastic dressers, for instance—so that children can help keep toys organized. Tape a photo or drawing of the items to the outside of each drawer or crate. ◄|

How I Do It A Home Organizer's Container Secrets

A lot of what you'll hear from household organizers has to do with storage. And, indeed, proper storage is necessary for a clutter-free home. But some storage techniques are better than others. Here are dos and don'ts for storing things safely and more efficiently from Karen Lawrence:

☐ *Use cardboard for the short term.*
The basic cardboard box is ideal for moving and short-term storage. But cardboard boxes collapse under pressure when stacked. And since cardboard absorbs moisture, and moisture deteriorates cardboard, boxes aren't great for long-term storage, especially in humid attics, basements, and garages. Moist cardboard attracts insects, such as silverfish, that feed on paper. Weakened boxes allow easier access for rodents.

☐ *For long-term storage, plastic is best.*
When you use plastic containers, make sure stored items are dry before putting the lid on, because plastic can trap moisture *inside*, promoting mold and mildew growth. Also, if you are going to use plastic, use several small containers. People will often get huge plastic boxes, fill them up, and then not be able to move them.

☐ *Don't store clothes in dry-cleaning bags.*
This may seem like a good inexpensive solution for keeping clothes fresh and dust-free. But dry cleaning uses toxic chemicals, and the bags the clothes come in trap those chemicals. Also, mold and mildew can form on clothing sealed in plastic. Remove the bags before you hang the clothes in your closet—and certainly before you store clothes for the season. If you want to store them in something, use garment bags made from a breathable material like cotton.

☐ *Don't store precious photos in frames.*
If you choose to no longer display a framed photo, remove the photo from the frame and store it in an archival safe box, wrapped in acid-free tissue paper. The photo will take up much less space than the frame, which is now available for other photos. If you leave the photo in the frame, humidity will make the photo stick to the glass, and gas emissions from the materials used for framing—masking tape, cardboard, and rubber cement—may leave behind harmful residue, spotting the photo.

Housecleaning
9 Simple Secrets That Can Save You Time, Effort, and Money When Doing Housework

Use a certified germ killer. Use a cleaning product that carries the word "disinfectant" on its label when you're cleaning food-preparation areas in the kitchen such as the counters and sink. You may be impressed at how all-purpose cleaners remove visible grime, but what you're not seeing is the bacteria that are left behind, laughing at you. "Disinfectant" is a government-regulated term that means the product kills bacteria and viruses. So read the fine print of those squirt bottles.

Watch out for microfiber cleaning cloths. This isn't something the manufacturers of these little gems are going to tell you, but the authors of *The Complete Idiot's Guide to Cleaning*, Mary Findley and Linda Formichelli, will: Microfiber cloths are made out of plastic, and therefore they can scratch. Don't use them on sealed surfaces such as wood floors, marble, granite, Corian, and painted surfaces.

Clean your windows for pennies. Why should a gallon (3.7 liters) of glass cleaner, which is mostly water, cost you more than a gallon (3.7 liters) of gasoline? Because the manufacturers want you to pay for their fancy advertising campaigns. Here's how to whip up high-powered glass cleaner for pennies. Pour 1 gallon (3.7 liters) warm water into a bucket. Add 1 cup white vinegar and 1 teaspoon grease-cutting dishwashing liquid, and then stir. If you're cleaning a lot of large windows, apply the glass cleaner with a squeegee straight out of the bucket. Otherwise, pour the mixture into plastic squirt bottles and label them.

Dirty disposer? Dive in. Well, not literally. The point is to do it yourself rather than call a plumber or handyman. And don't pay for expensive foaming disposer cleaners. Disposers are easy to clean, since they provide the muscle. First, keep food waste from building up inside the disposer by only grinding small amounts of food at a time. And when you're done, run a steady flow of cold water through the spinning disposer for up to 30 seconds. Cold solidifies fatty and greasy wastes so they will be cut up and flushed down the drain. Hot melts them and smears the grease around the disposer and drainpipe.

To remove grease buildup, periodically grind a handful of ice cubes mixed with 1/2 cup baking soda. Together the powder and cubes (once again cold) will safely scour the inside of the disposer. Flush any residue by plugging the sink and filling it with 2 to 3 inches (5 to 8 cm) of water. Then run the disposer while the water drains. Grind lemon peels to freshen the smell.

Give your sink a bath. One of the most frustrating things about porcelain sinks is that they scuff if you so much as look at them the wrong way. Forget the Ajax. Instead, Linda Mason Hunter, coauthor of the book *Green Clean*, recommends an herbal bath. Steep several bunches of rosemary or thyme in hot water for a few hours, then strain. Stop up the sink, pour in the mixture, and let it sit overnight. In the morning you'll find a glistening white sink that smells like an herb garden.

Fizz your toilet clean. It's a shame you have to find room in your bathroom cabinet for a product like toilet cleaner that can do only one job around the house. Most toilet cleaners are a frighteningly caustic product, to boot. Here's the simpler path: Once a week, drop two denture tablets into your toilet and let them dissolve for at least 20 minutes. Then give your toilet's interior a quick brushing and flush. The same cleaning action that brightens dentures will leave the toilet bowl gleaming as well.

Clean your grill grate in the oven. Put away that time-consuming wire grill brush and leave that caustic oven cleaner in the cabinet. Here's the zero-effort, nontoxic way to clean the mess off your barbecue grill's grate. Simply remove it from the grill, pull the racks out of your oven, slide the grate into your oven, and set the oven on "self-clean." This same superheated cycle that incinerates everything inside a self-cleaning oven will scorch away any greasy remnants from the grate.

Clean your own curtains. Dirty drapes send some homeowners straight to the yellow pages. Too technical, they think. Then they find out that most professional drapery cleaners charge *by the pleat* to steam- or dry-clean curtains. At $10 per pleat or more, cleaning costs can add up fast. Here are some tricks for cleaning curtains yourself:

- Dust them regularly. Don't bother taking them down. Simply run your vacuum cleaner over them (from top to bottom) using the dusting brush or upholstery attachment. Focus on the tops and hems, where dust tends to gather. Avoid sucking the fabric into the nozzle by either reducing the vacuum pressure or grasping the bottom and holding the curtains tight. If you don't have the proper attachments, use a feather duster. Dusting drapes prevents dirt buildup and lessens the chances that the drapes will need a major cleaning.

- Wash the ones that can be washed. If your drapes do need cleaning, start by looking for the manufacturer's cleaning recommendations, which should be on a tag sewn inside the hem. No tag? Identify the fabric, including all trim and linings, and use that information to choose the best cleaning method. You will either machine-wash, hand-wash, or dry-clean your drapes. The delicate cycle is usually best for curtains that can be machine-washed. You never know how much the sun has weakened the curtain fibers. The same goes for the dryer—use the delicate cycle. And instead of tumbling curtains until they are dry (which could leave them in a wrinkled ball), remove them from the dryer and hang them damp. If you're lucky, you'll avoid having to iron them.

- Find an experienced dry cleaner. Few dry cleaners know how to properly handle drapes, but you won't see them advertising that fact. It's up to you to ask around. The best will measure your curtains beforehand and guarantee they will come back the same length.

Buying drapes? Check the tag. You may love those fancy silk or velvet curtains. They might even be on sale. But before you buy them, keep in mind the cost to clean them. Check the manufacturer's tag, inside the hem, for curtains that are machine washable, and you'll save big bucks in the long run. ◂

16

SCARY CHEMICALS THAT *sneak* Into Your Home

Companies using toxic chemicals in their cleaning products, building materials, and pesticides tend to focus on the benefits of their products, but they don't say much about the negative side effects. Air fresheners give off naphthalene, a suspected carcinogen. Ammonia-based window cleaners cause respiratory irritation. And some cleaners contain the nerve-damaging butyl cellosolve (also known as ethylene glycol monobutyl ether), which is absorbed into the skin. These are just a few examples of the harmful chemicals that sneak into our homes. Things are so bad, says Katie Albright of the Sierra Club of Canada, that "air quality studies show that the inside of homes is often worse than the outside." The icing on the cake? The chemical companies charge you a premium for the poisons hiding behind popular brand names.

Bad Guys

So what can be done? First, familiarize yourself with the chemical culprits, scan ingredient labels on all household products, and avoid these substances whenever possible:

butyl cellosolve

cresol

formaldehyde

glycols

hydrochloric acid

hydrofluoric acid

lye

naphthalene

PDCBs (paradichlorobenzenes)

perchloroethylene

phenol

propellants

TCE (trichloroethylene)

petroleum distillates

phosphoric acid

sulfuric acid

Good Guys

Next, keep healthy alternatives around the house. Not only will you reduce indoor pollution, but you'll save money while doing your body a favor. Here's the all-star team of effective chemical alternatives:

Baking soda. Effective mineral with mildly abrasive cleaning, whitening, and deodorizing properties. Very inexpensive. Great for carpet pet odors (page 116).

Vinegar. Derived from the fermentation of fruits or grains, vinegar has a high acid content that makes it great at killing germs, cutting grease, and dissolving mineral deposits.

Borax. A naturally occurring mineral (containing water, oxygen, sodium, and boron) with tremendously useful antiseptic, antifungal, deodorizing, and disinfectant properties. It stops the growth of mold and mildew and kills roaches (page 114).

Vegetable oil–based liquid soap. This biodegradable alternative to petroleum-based detergents can be found in health food stores.

Washing soda. Sometimes called soda ash, this mineral (sodium carbonate) cleans grease, oil, dirt, and lots of petroleum products. It is also a water softener and soap booster. Look for it in the supermarket laundry section.

Essential oils. The boiled-down essences of different plants—peppermint, lavender, and lemons, for instance—these oils can be used as natural air fresheners and to add pleasant scents to homemade cleaners. You can find some in the baking section of the grocery store.

Cleaning Valuables

4 Ways to Save a King's Ransom When Cleaning Jewelry and Other Expensive Items

Clean gold with dishwashing liquid. Jewelers are like car dealers. They sell you necklaces, bracelets, and rings and hope you bring your pieces back for service, including cleaning. But while resetting a loose diamond is beyond the skill level of the average ring owner, periodic cleaning is not. Here's how to clean that most common of jewelry items—gold. It may not tarnish like silver, but over time gold develops a dull film from lotions, soaps, and the oils secreted by your skin. To revive the luster of gold jewelry, clean it regularly in a bowl of warm water mixed with a squirt of mild dishwashing liquid. After a brief soak, gently scrub the gold jewelry using a soft toothbrush. Rinse under warm running water (careful of the drain—to be safe, put it in a wire tea strainer). Pat dry with a clean white cloth. For stubborn stains, mix equal parts cold water and ammonia. Soak the gold jewelry in the solution for half an hour. Scrub with a soft toothbrush. Rinse under cold water. Pat dry. Whatever you do, don't clean with toothpaste, which contains silica, an abrasive found in quartz, which can dull a glossy gold finish.

Wipe pearls often to keep them clean. A pearl's value is largely determined by color, luster, and the thickness of its fine coating, or nacre. Because pearls are highly sensitive to chemicals and salts, it's important that you wipe down your pearls after you wear them, using a slightly moistened, very soft cloth such as chamois. This removes harmful substances such as perspiration, perfume, and makeup that can penetrate the pearls' porous surface.

(As a preventive measure, always apply perfume, makeup, and hair spray *before* you put on your pearls.) To occasionally clean more thoroughly, use a mild bar soap such as Ivory and lukewarm water to create light suds. Dip your cloth in the suds and gently wipe the pearls. Rinse with clean water and dry on a soft cloth. Never soak pearls. And never hang them to dry, since that might stretch the string. Remove stubborn solids from their surface using your fingernail. Since your fingernail has a hardness of 2.5 or less on the Mohs' scale, and pearls register from 2.5 to 4.5, you probably will not scratch them.

Precautions with Gold and Silver

- ☐ Avoid getting chlorine on your gold or silver jewelry at any cost. Both of these precious metals react to this common chemical and will deteriorate over time if exposed to it. Remove your gold or silver rings and bracelets when cleaning with chlorine bleach. And take them off before jumping into the pool or climbing into the hot tub.

- ☐ Although some jewelers recommend cleaning gold or silver jewelry with toothpaste, it's best not to. Some toothpastes contain harsh abrasives that can dull the metal's finish or scratch a stone.

- ☐ Don't soak jewelry with precious stones for more than a few seconds. The water can dissolve the glue that holds the stones in place.

- ☐ Silver reacts to salt, to acid foods like mustard and ketchup, and to sulfur-containing foods like eggs and mayonnaise. Don't use a silver serving piece with any of these foods and clean it right away if it touches them.

Skip the polish when cleaning silver. It's toxic and it smells bad. Instead, Mary Findley and Linda Formichelli recommend this low-tech cleaning approach: Put a sheet of aluminum foil in a plastic or glass bowl and sprinkle with salt and baking soda. Fill the bowl with warm water and add the silver. The tarnish actually migrates to the foil, leaving your silver clean. Dry and buff.

Swish away unreachable grunge. Okay, so you probably won't toss your grandmother's grungy old crystal decanter, but you may banish it to the top shelf, where it's as good as gone. Same with that dirty, narrow-necked coffee carafe. Before you go shopping for new pieces to display in your home, try swishing a mixture of rock salt and vinegar around the inside of these containers. The salt will gently scour the surface while the vinegar will help remove stains, especially lime deposits. For wine stains, try swirling a small amount of warm water, baking soda, and rock salt. Or dissolve a denture-cleaning tablet in the vessel and let it stand overnight. The next morning, rinse with clean warm water.

Cleaning these narrow-necked objects is one thing, but drying them is another challenge. Instead of waiting forever for the thermos, vase, or decanter to dry in your dish rack, drain the water and use the following trick to remove the last of the moisture: Wrap a paper towel around the handle of a wooden spoon so that the towel extends slightly beyond the end. Stick the towel-wrapped spoon into the decanter and let it rest on the bottom overnight. By morning the towel should have absorbed most of the condensation. ◂

Insect Pests
3 Ways to Get Rid of Annoying Bugs in Your House Without Expensive Toxic Pesticides

Shoo away flies with basil. How's this for a great way to get rid of flies *and* guarantee your family fresh pesto throughout the years? Put several basil plants around your kitchen. Flies hate basil, so they'll stay away. Not only will your kitchen be flyless, but it will smell like summer all year long.

Turn away ants with vinegar. Instead of spending big bucks on some toxic insecticide, keep ants away from your household surfaces with vinegar. Fill a clean spray bottle with a 50/50 solution of water and white vinegar. Spray anywhere you see ants infiltrating—along baseboards, on kitchen counters, in moist bathrooms. Unlike poisons, the vinegar is 100 percent harmless, and a quart costs pocket change.

Stop roaches with boric acid. Don't pay upward of 20 bucks for a one-pound (500-gram) can of roach powder at your hardware store, when you can buy the same thing—boric acid—for a fraction of the price. A white powder used as a laundry whitener and disinfectant, borax is also lethal to roaches. You can make your own roach-control powder by mixing equal parts borax and flour, and then sprinkling the mixture where you've seen roaches—along the base of basement walls, in jar lids placed in cabinets (even though it is relatively safe to use around the house, do not place the borax where children or pets can get into it). The starch in the flour attracts the roaches. The mixture sticks to their legs. They track it back to their nests, where it kills them and other roaches. ◂

Personal Care Items
3 Tricks to Keep Hair-Care and Grooming Gear Working Smoothly

Take it easy with curler cleaning.
If you use harsh cleaners on your hair curlers, you risk having those damaging chemicals transfer to your hair. Instead, make your motto "Hair today and hair tomorrow," using this money-saving cleaning technique. For curlers that are submersible in water—plain rollers, Velcro rollers, foam-coated wire sticks—fill your bathroom sink with warm water, mix in a couple teaspoons of your own shampoo or facial cleanser to create suds, and let them soak. (If it's gentle enough for you, it's gentle enough for your curlers.) Gently comb out any hair stuck in the curlers. Then wipe with a rag to remove caked-on films. Rinse and either dry with a clean towel or air-dry.

For stubborn stains, such as hardened setting lotions or gels, mix up a solution of 1/4 cup warm water and 1 tablespoon liquid fabric softener. Gently scrub the solution in with a vegetable brush. Rinse and dry.

For nonsubmersible electric curlers, clean with a rag or brush and the fabric softener solution. Rinse by wiping the curlers with a damp rag, and then dry.

Brush up on hairbrush cleaning.
The first trick with maintaining brushes is to remove the hair often, instead of waiting until it is thickly matted. Every so often, wash them in an economical and effective cleaning solution—2 teaspoons shampoo with 1/4 cup vinegar in a sinkful of warm water. Remove any loose hair, soak the brush for several minutes, and use a wide-toothed comb to remove the remaining hair stuck in the brush (pulling it through each row of tines on the brush). The solution will loosen any built-up oil and dirt, as well as gunked-on hair gels and sprays. Scrub the brush clean using a nailbrush. Rinse with warm, running water. Let the brush air-dry.

Soak razors in mineral oil. Razor manufacturers want you change razors as often as you change shirts, of course, but a simple trick will prolong your razor's life. Pour some mineral oil into a shallow dish and soak it for a few minutes. The mineral oil will halt the corrosion that dulls the cutting edge. When the soaking time is up, dip the corner of a cloth in rubbing alcohol and wipe off the oil. ◁

Controlling Odors

5 Low-Cost Ways to Prevent and Remove Offensive Smells Around the House

Dust away that carpet funk. There's nothing worse than odors trapped in the fibers of a rug or carpet—especially when they're from pet accidents. You may think a professional rug cleaner is the only solution. Think again. Sprinkle baking soda on the odor-causing stain. Let it sit all night, and then vacuum it up the next day. Repeat until the odor is gone.

Skip fancy brand-name fresheners. Chemists are out there in corporate labs right now cooking up the next air freshener scent, while marketers are busy concocting all the selling points to get you to part with your money to have it. But air fresheners don't really freshen the air. They mask smells, and experts say they can actually irritate the lungs. Instead, look for products that actually kill the bacteria that cause odors. Or try the money-saving tricks described below.

Control cooking odors with vinegar. Boil 1/4 cup vinegar per 1 quart (1 liter) water. The rising heat carries the odor-neutralizing vinegar particles to the same surfaces where the smoke and grease landed.

Bleach a foul-smelling garbage can. Scrub the inside with a nylon-bristled brush and this solution: 1 cup bleach, 1 gallon (3.7 liters) water, plus two squirts of dishwashing liquid. Rinse with the garden hose. Air-dry, and sprinkle inexpensive borax in the bottom of the can once it's dry to prevent the growth of odor-causing molds and bacteria.

Use onion and air for a musty basement. In the short term, cut an onion in half and leave it on a plate in your basement. The onion absorbs musty odors. To solve the problem, start by ventilating. Since the musty smell comes from mold and mildew, which thrive in dank, dark environments, you want to get the stale air moving. Open windows and doors, use fans to circulate air, and use dehumidifiers to remove the air's humidity. Next, don protective eyewear and a dust mask, and kill the odor-producing growth with a solution of 2 to 4 tablespoons bleach per 1 quart (1 liter) water. Using a spray bottle, spray any surfaces that won't be harmed by the bleach, such as cinder-block walls and concrete floors. Scrub with a nylon-bristled brush. ◁

SECRET WEAPON

Activated Charcoal

We all know that an open box of baking soda will keep refrigerator odors at bay. But what do you do if you are faced with a strong, persistent, and unpleasant odor in your fridge or freezer? Just head off to the nearest pet store or five-and-ten and buy some fine activated charcoal in the aquarium supplies section. Spread some in a shallow pan and put the pan on a refrigerator or freezer shelf. The charcoal will not harm your food. After about eight hours, put the charcoal in a 350°F (175°C) oven for 20 minutes to reactivate it. By reactivating the charcoal, you can reuse it many times. In a pinch, you can also use cat litter or fresh (unused) ground coffee to absorb fridge odors.

Tools and Supplies

8 Savvy Tips for Using Tools to Best Advantage and Making Them Last a Lifetime

Get the right tool for the job. Charles Cox, a Pennsylvania-based stationary engineer (boiler operator) and freelance handyman, thinks he knows why homeowners shy away from doing their own household repairs. "They either don't know what tool they need or they don't want to buy it," he says. "So they rely on professionals." His example: a leaky faucet. A homeowner fails to free the old, corroded handle from its stem and gives up, calling a plumber and paying more than $100 for the house call. A quick trip to a hardware store, however, and the homeowner could have bought a tool known as a faucet-handle puller for less than $10. This simple screw tool forcefully lifts the frozen handle without scratching its finish. Then, with old parts in hand, the homeowner could have found the right replacement parts at the hardware store. A 25-cent washer might possibly have done the trick. The point? Trust the right tool to save you money.

Spring for a decent set of screwdrivers. Some things are great to keep around generation after generation. An old jackknife. Your grandfather's workbench. Slotted screwdrivers aren't one of them. After prolonged use, flat-head screwdrivers tend to wear down. Their blades grow thin and rounded at the corners. Pretty soon, you're stripping screws and ruining woodwork with slips and gaffs. If they have sentimental value, keep them around for prying open cans of paint. But do yourself a favor and buy a set of new, high-quality screwdrivers—or a screwdriver with interchangeable heads. And if it's too late, and you're stuck trying to remove one of those stripped screws, run a hacksaw blade through the screw slot to make it straighter and deeper.

Save paint longer. Too often, homeowners leave leftover paint in its original can. Labels fall off, cans rust, air leaks in, and the paint goes bad. Instead, store paint in glass jars. Not only can you instantly tell the color of the paint inside, but jars are more airtight than cans. To further tighten the seal—and make sure the lid doesn't stick—wrap a couple of layers of Teflon tape around the jar threads before sealing them.

Clean paintbrushes better—and less often. How many times have you gotten lazy and thrown away a perfectly good paintbrush because you didn't want to face the mess of cleaning it? If you're painting with oil and will be again the next day, you don't have to clean it. Just remove the excess paint from your brushes and rollers and then wrap them tightly in aluminum foil or plastic wrap. This will keep them from drying out. If you're using a water-based paint, and your brush or roller just won't come clean, don't toss it. Many of today's water-based paints contain resins similar to those used in oil-based paints to improve adhesion, gloss, and durability. After cleaning and rinsing the brush or roller in water, try a second rinse in paint thinner or turpentine to completely clean it. Afterward, wash with clean, soapy water to remove the thinner.

Find studs for less. Wall studs, of course. Instead of some expensive stud-finding gadget that may or may not

How I Do It **A Handyman Keeps Tools to an Easy-to-Carry Minimum**

Some people can fix anything. You may or may not be one of them. But if you follow fix-it pros around, you'll quickly learn that efficiency is one of their key traits. They don't waste their energy—and they don't lug around more tools and equipment than they need. Most can get by on a small, broadly useful selection. Handyman Charles Cox is a case in point. He does many of his jobs with five basic tools. Keep these five tools in a plastic tool tray, and you'll be prepared to tackle most minor repairs.

Channel lock pliers

An adjustable wrench that will give you a firm grip on anything from a pipe to a loose nut. Put a little duct tape on the teeth to keep it from scarring metal.

Interchangeable screwdriver

Different sizes and types of heads fit into the end, making this easier to keep up with than a handful of different screwdrivers. It's great for here-and-there jobs (but grab the cordless driver and let the batteries do the work for everything else).

Adjustable wrench

Why try to keep up with a tumbling mess of wrenches, when one adjustable wrench fits all?

16-ounce (500-gram) claw hammer

From tacking up picture hangers to pulling rusty nails from old salvaged wood, the claw hammer is an absolute must.

Continuity tester

The electrician's basic diagnostic tool, a continuity tester is a battery-powered device with a lightbulb, a probe, and an alligator clip. With the power off, you can use this tool to detect shorts in sockets, electrical appliances, and extension cords. If you can do light electrical work, such as replacing a faulty switch, you'll save a bundle. With a little practice, adequate safety precautions, and a continuity tester, you can do it.

work, turn your electric razor on and run it along the wall. You'll hear a change in the vibration as you cross a stud with it.

Don't get stuck on duct tape. Ready for some shocking news? Duct tape is not perfect. Although the manufacturers of duct tape would like you to believe this silvery cloth tape can fix any problem (even remove warts!), the truth behind the hype is that it's not all it's cut out to be. Oh, it's fine in a pinch, but duct tape is almost always a temporary solution. Even the pros who work on heating and air-conditioning systems will tell you it's not the best way to attach ducts. It deteriorates and turns to powder over time. And that's on metal, the surface best suited for duct tape.

When used on glass and plastic, duct tape can peel away within months, especially when exposed to sunlight. Duct tape does not stick well on wood either, and it can destroy fine wood finishes, leaving behind a gummy, hard-to-remove residue. And duct tape should never be used on live wires as a substitute for black electrical tape.

Clean your belt sander. Belts always seem to gum up prematurely, before the sanding surface is worn down. And replacement belts can cost four or five bucks each. Instead of tossing them when they gum up, try this trick: Secure the sander upside down (clamp it or have someone hold it) and press the rubber sole of your shoe to the belt. It will come clean, allowing you to use it much longer. Sales reps will wonder why their sanding belts are gathering dust on the hardware store shelf.

Keep your tools from getting rusty. Moisture in the air invites rust, and if the moist air gets into your toolbox or tool drawer, it corrodes the tools. And if you are like most of us, you store your tools in an often damp garage or basement. One good way to keep the air in your toolbox dry is to drop in some packets of silica gel, sold at hardware stores and craft shops. You can often get them for free in the packing of new products. Once the silica gel becomes saturated, renew the packets by placing them near a lit 60-watt lightbulb for 15 minutes. Another effective moisture absorber that will keep the contents of your toolbox rust-free is a handful of mothballs. You can also use a 1-ounce (30-gram) cube of camphor, sold at local pharmacies. Because camphor loses its effectiveness after about six months, you'll have to replace the cube twice a year. ◄

Hiring Help
4 Tricks for Getting the Best Job for the Money That You Shell Out to Repair People

Hire a qualified electrician. A handyman can be a real help when it comes to tackling small jobs you don't have time to complete, or skilled jobs you just don't feel comfortable attempting. You may even be tempted to give your handyman small wiring jobs or other electrical work. Before you do, however, make sure he is licensed to do electrical work (if local code requires it) and that his work is up to snuff. "You get the wrong guy messing around with your electrical wiring—someone who doesn't know what he's doing—and you're in trouble," says Jim Abbott, owner of Handyman Matters in Toronto, Ontario. The mistakes, which can be dangerous, are hidden behind Sheetrock walls or within electrical panels. Look for red flags, such as light switches and outlets in strange places. "I've seen it," Abbott says. "A guy runs out of wire and puts a switch at eye level or an outlet halfway up the wall."

Ask your handyman for a guarantee. "A lot of handymen give their customers the tailgate warranty," says Jim Abbott. "They drive away in their pickup truck with your cash in pocket, and all you see is their tailgate disappearing. That's it. That's your warranty." Instead, ask them if they'll guarantee their work for up to a year. If they will, get it in writing. If they won't, take their reluctance as a red flag.

Choose your plumber, then your fixtures. If your plumber is charging you by the hour to install new bathroom or kitchen fixtures, here's a sure way to save money. Ask him what brand he likes best. Chances are this will be a common, dependable brand that he's very familiar with. Choose models made by this brand, and he'll install them more efficiently, saving time and money by not having to struggle through detailed instructions about what washers go where and what size wrench he needs to tighten everything. Also, he's more likely to install products correctly if he's already done it countless times before, and that will save you repair costs in the long run.

Shorten that repair visit. Any repairperson who is paid by the hour will happily lounge around your house chatting up a storm or watching you get organized. The clock is ticking, after all, and that kind of work is oh-so-easy. With a little forethought, however, you can make sure that every minute of a repairperson's visit is nose-to-the-grindstone productive.

- Discuss all of the details of the job over the telephone—while the clock *isn't* ticking. This also ensures that the worker will arrive with all of the necessary tools and materials.

- Clear away any obstructions in advance of the repairperson's arrival, and make sure there's proper light for the worker to see by.

- Check the house over for all tasks that this particular repairperson could handle—thus saving you service charges in the future.

- Tell the worker not to bother cleaning up. Cleanup is never done to your specifications anyway, is it? The worker will be out your door in a minimum of time—and your bill will be the minimum as well. ◄

How-To Secrets
4 Little-Known Tricks That Make for a Successful Do-It-Yourself Job

Quiet that slamming screen door. Forget trying to track down a professional handyman, and then paying big bucks for him to drive out and fix your noisy screen door. Here's the easy way to achieve silence of the slams: Apply a few small beads of clear silicone caulk along the jamb in a few places where the door hits. Prop the door open for a few hours to make sure the silicone dries before you close it again.

Keep pictures straight. There's no telling what an interior decorator would charge you to solve the annoying and recurring problem of pictures that won't stay level. Follow this nifty trick and you won't have to find out. Push straight pins into the backside of the frame, one at each bottom corner, and then clip off the heads, leaving about a quarter inch sticking out of the frame. Hang the picture. Straighten it with a level. Gently push the bottom corners so that the pins prick the drywall, securing the frame in place.

Be your own plumber with plastic pipes. You might find it less daunting to do your own plumbing work if you use PVC pipes instead of copper pipes. PVC is cheaper, and there are no torches and soldering involved. All you need are the plastic pipes and glue. Here are a couple of trade secrets for working with PVC:

- Before cutting, measure the length you want, mark it with a pencil, and then wrap tape around the pipe. Using a pencil, follow the edge of the

A Guide to **Money-Saving**
Easy-to-Do Repairs

Avoid paying an electrician $100 for two drops of oil to quiet a rattling fan.

As the owner of Handyman Matters, Jim Abbott has fielded his share of homeowner calls. After a while, he says, you start to see patterns—recurring problems that homeowners could avoid *if they only knew better*. Maybe after reading Abbott's advice, you will know better the next time …

… your bathroom fan starts rattling.

Sure, that rattle is annoying, but even more troublesome is the thought of paying an electrician to come to your house and fix it. Fear not. According to Abbott, many exhaust fans are a snap to repair, a fact that escapes most homeowners, who don't want anything to do with a hardwired electrical fixture. But instead of being hardwired into your ceiling or wall, many fans simply plug into a *box* that's hardwired. That means that if you can stand on a ladder, pop off the fan cover and remove a few screws, you can safely remove the fan. (Be sure to cut power to the fan by flipping the circuit breaker switch before you begin work.) Once you've removed the fan, put a couple drops of oil on the fan shaft. Chances are that will stop the rattling. And you will have avoided paying an electrician 100 bucks for two drops of oil. If not, then take the fan to an electrical supply retailer or home-improvement store and buy a replacement fan that plugs into the same housing. You'll still save money.

… you feel a draft.

Another common caulk-related problem has to do with air leaks. "The way a lot of houses are built these days, you'll have a 2 x 4 wall with a brick veneer on the outside," he explains. "People will caulk around the outside of their windows, which seals the windows to the brick. But the brick is outside the vapor barrier. Brick veneer is designed to breathe. It's even got weep holes to let moisture escape. So caulking the windows to the brick does not tighten up the house." Instead, to stop drafts, caulk gaps around the *inside* of your window frames.

… your kitchen or bathroom caulk goes bad.

Abbott sees it all the time. The silicone caulk around a kitchen sink begins to deteriorate. Water seeps into the fiberboard or plywood beneath the countertop laminate and the counter starts to swell and rot. "The next thing you know, you have to replace the whole countertop." Same goes for the bathroom. If the caulking around the tub or shower fails, water can ruin drywall and, over time, cause dry rot in wood floors and framing. The solution is to prevent expensive damage with a little inexpensive maintenance. Remove the old caulk, clean and completely dry the area, and apply new caulk. "Even if you're not comfortable working with silicone caulk," says Abbot, "paying someone $100 to do the job could save you thousands in the long run."

tape around. Remove the tape, and you're left with your cutting mark.

- Avoid gluing fittings backward. Once the glue dries, the pieces are stuck, and mistakes become do-overs. Try this trick to make everything come out right. After cutting your sections, dry-fit them in place, making sure the fittings face the right way and lengths are correct. When everything looks right, make a mark across both pipe and fitting with a thick colored wax pencil. When you take them apart to apply the glue, you'll be able to line up the pencil marks again quickly and easily for a perfect fit.

Your drill doesn't need fancy attachments. The electric drill is by far the most popular power tool in our homes, and manufacturers sell all kinds of add-ons to help you drill holes that are straighter and of proper depth. Here are three tricks that eliminate the need for these extras:

- To drill a hole to a precise depth, you don't need a special collar to stop the bit. Just mark the depth on the bit with a piece of masking tape.

- To drill a vertically straight hole, you don't need a frame that holds the drill perfectly upright. Just nail two short scraps of wood together at right angles to use as a guide. Just be sure the scraps have square factory-cut edges.

- To drill a horizontally straight hole, again you don't need a frame. Just slip a washer on the bit before you put in the drill chuck. The washer will slide forward or backward if you are not drilling straight. ◂

Bath and Kitchen Improvements

6 Pitfalls to Avoid When You Are Upgrading Your Plumbing and Ceramic Tiles

Check your toilet trap. Some toilet makers cut corners to lower costs. Sometimes they cut curves as well—trap curves. When buying a toilet, make sure the trap (the S-shaped tube underneath the toilet that the water goes down when you flush) is fully glazed. Like the outside of the toilet, the inside of the trap should be shiny and smooth. Otherwise, toilet paper will get caught on the sides of the tube and clog your toilet. Very inexpensive toilets may seem like a bargain—how different could toilets be, after all?—but the unglazed traps will prove that all toilets weren't created equal.

Look for a lifetime faucet warranty. Some manufacturers brag that their kitchen and bath faucets come with lifetime warranties. But it's up to you to read the fine print. Look all the way at the bottom of the page for those tiny asterisked footnotes. There you may find that certain aspects of a faucet—the finish or valves—are covered for only one to five years, not for life. And since valves can total 25 percent of the cost of a faucet, you want to make sure the valves are also covered for life.

Don't fall for a cheap faucet. Hidden beneath the gleaming exterior of kitchen and bath faucets is the truth about how they were made. Cheaper faucets are metal shells covering copper tubes. More expensive faucets are cast brass, which means the brass has been poured into a mold and the faucet is all one piece.

Buying one of the more expensive faucets may save you money in the long run. Eventually water will poke tiny holes in the copper tubes of the cheaper faucets. This can occur very quickly if the water is acidic (lots of chlorine), leading to the need for a new faucet in as few as three years. The cast brass will last much longer. Next time you march down the plumbing fixture aisle, go armed with this insider info, and you'll be better prepared to make a wise purchase.

Check that brass finish. Brass fixtures can make a beautiful addition to your bathroom or kitchen, but looks can be deceiving. Some brass is coated with a lacquer finish that regular cleaning with bathroom chemicals will remove, leaving you with a tarnished brass showerhead. Make sure the product description of the brass fixture mentions PVD (physical vapor disposition). Brass finished using this process means that the coating will not come off and your brass will not tarnish. PVD is a must for exterior door hardware, which is often exposed to corrosive salt air near the coast and acid rain. PVD-finished brass may cost a bit more, but it will maintain its bright good looks a lot longer.

Save money by using porcelain tiles sparingly. Some contractors and tile store sales reps like to push porcelain tile, touting the fact that its through-and-through color consistency means that chips hardly show up. Ceramic tile, on the other hand, features a surface color and a differently colored inner core (usually terra cotta). If it chips, they'll say, the inner color stands out. Of course,

they'll downplay the fact that porcelain tile costs more and that they earn more when they sell it. The benefits of porcelain tile are real, but sometimes unnecessary. Before you buy, think about how much foot traffic a room will get. Hall bathrooms, where guests will be wearing heels and boots, might need porcelain. Bedroom bathrooms, where people walk around with slippers on, might be fine with ceramic.

Test a tile pattern with photocopies. Having trouble visualizing how those fancy tiles will look when installed as a backsplash for your kitchen counter? Or you need to figure out which pattern will work best? You don't want to be disappointed when those decorative tiles that looked so great in the showroom turn out to be just the wrong thing for your kitchen, or to discover that the pattern you envisioned just won't work. To avoid either of these, make color photocopies of the tiles and tape them to the wall. You can rearrange them until you get the right look. ◁

CHOOSING THE
right
Mattress

Mattress sales mean big bucks for retailers. The bedding department for furniture stores is typically one of the highest profit-margin areas. But few high-value consumer products defy quality rankings more than mattresses. One reason is that so much of what makes a mattress comfortable—size, coil type, firmness level—depends on the preferences of the individual. Comparing one model to another just doesn't work. Another reason has to do with the way the industry operates. Bedding manufacturers don't have consistent model names. Store A may sell one manufacturer's top-of-the-line model in a blue damask cover and call it "Joyful," while store B may have the same model covered in green and call it the "Mayflower," while store C may cover that mattress in white satiny ticking and call it the "Crescent."

There are objective criteria, such as material and construction quality, says Missouri author and veteran furniture retailer Michael Fugate. Here's his advice on the four basic types of mattress coil systems:

The Bonnel coil system	The continuous-wire system	Individually wrapped coils	Offset coils
A system of hourglass-shaped coils tied together by thinner spiraling wire. The maximum number of coils in this system, often found in lower-priced name-brand mattresses, is 364 in a full-size mattress.	As the name suggests, this is made from a single wire, often more than 200 yards (180 meters) long. These are most commonly found in Serta mattresses. While the continuous coil tends to be strongest, it does not necessarily offer the most support.	Sometimes known as Marshall or pocketed coils, these are encased in fabric. These are found in Simmons and Sealy mattresses. One advantage: Because they're not connected, one sleeper's movements don't affect another sleeper in the same bed.	Like Bonnel coils, these are hourglass shaped, but the coils are squared off on top and bottom for maximum support. Some Sealy mattresses use this system.

Whatever the type of system, coils should be tempered with heat or electricity for long-lasting springiness. The edge should have a sturdy wire or foam border for stability and to keep the edge firm. The higher the coil count, the more stable the mattress is. Most mattresses feature 300 to 800 coils, with 500 to 800 considered firm. But mattresses with lower coil counts can feel firm if the coil wire is thicker. (Wire thickness is referred to as the wire's gauge. The higher the number, the thinner the wire. Look for a minimum of 14-gauge coil wire and 6-gauge border wire.) While firm, these low-coil-count mattresses can grow lumpy more quickly.

Buying Mattresses
5 Secrets for Getting a Great Deal That Will Give You Many a Good Night's Sleep

Be wary of mattress comfort guarantees. When it comes to buying most things, money-back guarantees are typically a good thing. But do you really want a mattress that someone may have used for several weeks? Straight off the bat, you should know that major bedding manufacturers do not allow retailers to return mattresses just because they didn't feel good. So any retailer offering you the chance to return a mattress after you've given it a test run is almost certainly putting returns back into inventory and selling them as new. Just the thought is enough to keep you up at night.

Buy box spring and mattress in a set. Box springs and mattresses that come in sets are built and fitted for one another. Separate units can cause problems. And since box springs absorb up to 50 percent of the impact, using a well-fitted box spring can prolong the life of your mattress.

Avoid box foundations. Unlike box springs, these plain wooden platforms covered with fabric have no springs. They are usually meant to make a cheap mattress feel firmer and can actually cause the mattress to break down more quickly. Without box springs, the mattress ticking, padding, and other upholstery can wear out more than twice as fast.

Don't assume a firm mattress is best. There's been a change of thinking when it comes to mattresses. Studies show that the long-held belief that firmer mattresses are best for people with back pain may not necessarily be true. Chiropractors say your spine should look the same when you're lying down as it does when you're standing. If you sleep on your side, a too-firm mattress may not have enough give to let your shoulder and hips sink into the mattress. Your body will be unnaturally compressed. Instead, you should look for a mattress designed to conform to the spine's natural curves and to keep the spine in alignment when you lie down. The mattress should also distribute pressure evenly across the body to help circulation, decrease body movement, and minimize the transfer of movement from one sleeping partner to the other.

Skimp on the kids' mattresses. Yes, you read that right. Mattress manufacturers and retailers know how young parents dote on their children. They prey on this tendency to provide "the best that money can buy" by offering high-priced bedding designed expressly for children. Top quality is fine when it comes to car seats, fresh food, and other things directly related to your child's health and safety. But almost any moderately priced bedding will give children proper support. So why buy the most expensive mattress for your six-year-old, when he will eventually outgrow it—if he doesn't destroy it first by bed-wetting or trampolining? ◁

Furniture Fixes

7 Amazingly Easy Tricks for Giving New Life to Your Old Pieces of Furniture

Revive your wicker. Wicker furniture can be a challenge to clean. But that's no reason to pay a professional. Stephen Berne, a Vancouver-based antique chair restorer who is especially knowledgeable about chair caning, Danish cord, and wicker repair, offers these insider tips:

- Use a vacuum cleaner with a brush attachment to lift dust, dirt and lint from within the woven reeds.

- Wipe wicker with a clean cloth moistened with paint thinner (first try a little thinner on an inconspicuous spot to make sure it does not harm the finish). For stubborn stains, lightly rub with a green pot scrubber moistened with paint thinner.

- To bring up the sheen on wicker, apply furniture wax with a clean cloth.

Tighten that sagging chair seat. Like any seasoned craftspeople, furniture restorers have their tricks. Here's one that will save you money the next time your wicker chair seats stretch and droop. First, make sure the chair is made of some natural material, such as rattan or bark (and not paper rush). If so, then turn the chair upside down and wet the bottom for a minute or two by wiping it with a clean sponge dipped in warm water. Once the bottom is soaked (the top should remain dry), then right the chair. When the woven seat dries, it will be tighter.

Repair frayed woven chair seats. If you have a chair with a woven paper rush seat (wicker made of twisted paper), you probably already know that the paper has a tendency to tear in front, where legs constantly rub it. Here's a quick cosmetic fix: Squeeze a bit of white craft glue underneath the torn strands, and tape it with masking tape to hold it in place. When the glue is dry, remove the masking tape, and no one will ever know the strands are broken.

Mask wood furniture scratches. Furniture refinishers would prefer to have your business, but you can save hundreds of dollars by hiding scratches using one of several inexpensive methods. Drop by the hardware store, and pick up a putty pencil or scratch polish. Make sure it matches the color of your wood finish. Apply as directed, and presto! The scratch disappears, not your money.

Follow the antique furniture golden rule. Do as little as possible to change the original construction and finish of your antiques. By stripping a finish and putting on a new finish, you can drastically reduce the value of antique furniture. If a chair is a little loose and creaky or a table's lacquer top is cracking, that's okay.

Protect fussy antiques without the fuss. Contrary to what the makers of those lemon-fresh, spray-on furniture polishes claim, you don't need fancy chemicals to clean and protect wooden chests, desks, tables, and chairs, even if they are your prized possessions. In fact, those products can do more harm than good. "Some sprays have additives that will never come off," says Nancy

Rosebrock, conservation manager at the Biltmore Estate in Asheville, North Carolina. "They crosslink chemically over time and become insoluble. A lot never completely dry, and they attract dirt, darkening the finish." And that, she says, can decrease the value. Instead, Rosebrock suggests a simple regimen of preventive care and cleaning for your wood furniture:

- Protect the wood from moisture. Use coasters, wipe up spills, and avoid cleaning with water.
- Dust regularly with a soft, dry white cloth.
- Wax once a year with a furniture wax, such as Johnson paste wax—but only if the wood's finish is intact. The paste wax, which protects the finish without penetrating the wood, keeps dust from binding with the surface the way car wax makes water bead. Pick a wax that matches the color of the wood (for instance, a lighter wax for maple and a darker one for walnut). If the wood finish is cracked or rubbed away, skip the paste.

Steam out a dent. A dent on a wooden surface can often be fixed by swelling the compressed wood fibers back to their normal size using moisture and heat. Prick the varnish finish of the dented area several times with a fine pin so that moisture can penetrate into the wood. Then cover the dent with a pad of wet cloth, put a metal bottle cap on top of the pad to spread the heat, and apply a clothing iron on a high setting for a few minutes. Be careful not to scorch the finish. Afterward, when the wood is completely dry, fill the pinholes with a thin coat of fresh varnish. ◄

Saving Energy
6 Special Things to Know About How to Reduce Your Consumption of Costly Utilities

Do the math on your home's energy usage. Here's a quick and easy way—without the costly expert advice of a energy consultant—to figure out if you could save money by taking more energy conservation measures. Tally up your fuel and electric bills for the past 12 months. Divide their total by the square footage of your home, not including garages and unheated basements. What do you get? Most homeowners pay 60 to 90 cents per square foot ($6.50 to $9.50 per square meter) per year in fuel and energy costs. If your rate falls within this range, there are many cost-effective ways to dramatically reduce your bills. If your rate is higher than this range, don't waste a moment!

Stop premature bulb burnout. It's as annoying as it is costly to have a ceiling fixture or lamp that needs a new lightbulb every month or two. The lightbulb manufacturers would just as soon you did nothing about it—nothing, that is, except keep buying new bulbs. But premature bulb burnout is a symptom of a bigger problem. The typical 60-watt incandescent bulb lasts 1,000 hours. At 10 hours a day, that's 100 days or a little more than three months. If you notice bulbs burning out well before the estimated life expectancy printed on the bulb carton, you may have a problem. Here are three possible causes, along with quick-and-easy solutions:

- *Poor ventilation.* If attic insulation covers a recessed fixture, it can overheat the fixture, burning out the bulb. The fix: Clear away the insulation to allow the fixture to properly ventilate.

- *Excess wattage.* If you're using a high-wattage bulb in a small, enclosed fixture, such as a lamp globe, the excess heat could snuff the filament. The fix: Remove the bulb and replace it with a lower-wattage one or a compact fluorescent.

- *The shakes.* Vibration, like heat, can make a filament fail sooner than it should. The fix: If your lamp or fixture is in a high traffic area, near a slamming door or on a ceiling beneath a floor that gets constantly trampolined by excited kids, replace the incandescent bulb with a compact fluorescent, which doesn't have a filament.

Cut your electric bill. Saving energy is a hot topic these days, so it's not surprising that marketers have jumped on the bandwagon, trying to lure gullible consumers into buying all sorts of bogus gadgets and other products supposedly meant to save them money. The U.S. Federal Trade Commission recently settled charges against marketers who claimed their "liquid siding" product drastically reduced home energy bills. You *can* save money by conserving energy. And you can do it without a major capital outlay. Here are two surefire ways to cut back on your electric usage and slash monthly bills:

- It's important to know that 20 percent of the average electric bill goes toward lighting. Save $60 a year in electric costs by replacing your five most frequently used incandescent light fixtures with Energy Star bulbs.
- Unplug those rechargeable batteries. Few people realize what a drain battery chargers for cell phones,

laptops, toys, kitchen appliances, and power tools can be. If you have finished charging the item, unplug it. Otherwise, it's just sitting there costing you money.

Reduce heating and cooling costs. Half of your utility bill (electric or gas) goes to heat or cool the home. The easiest and cheapest thing you can do to reduce your heating or cooling bills is to clean or change furnace and air conditioning filters frequently. If you don't, the unit works harder, doesn't cool or heat at full capacity and may cause premature failure. At about $5 for a filter, it doesn't make sense to put it off (some filters can be vacuumed and replaced for no extra charge). Also be sure to close your foundation vents in winter if your home has a crawl space.

Don't use the fireplace. No matter how much your real estate agent may tout the romance and charm of a fireplace in your home, don't ignore this doctor-certified fact: The typical household fireplace chugs pollution into your living areas and sucks heat out—that's right, most draw away more heat than they provide. If someone in your home has asthma or other lung problems, resist the temptation to build a fire. If you can't do without, explore the new high-tech enclosures that are designed to radiate heat and keep fumes out of the house.

Analyze fridge-use claims skeptically. Appliance companies and retail salespeople love to tout the energy-saving advantages of newer, more efficient refrigerators. They claim that the fridge is the biggest energy hog among household appliances. And that the energy efficiency of refrigerators and freezers

Sealing Ducts for **Savings**

According to the U.S. Department of Energy, American homes lose up to 20 percent of the air that moves through their duct systems due to leaks, holes, and poorly connected ducts. And the same holds true for Canadian homes. Not only will faulty ducts make it more difficult to keep the house comfortable (no matter how the thermostat is set), but your utility bills will take a bigger bite out of your paycheck. All the more reason, say the home heating and air-conditioning contractors, to hire them to seal your ducts. But the money you spend on having a contractor work on your ducts might offset any savings you'll see in the future.

Unless the ducts are hard to reach, chances are you can seal them yourself, saving those contractor fees while making your home more comfortable, more energy efficient, and safer. Here's a step-by-step approach, beginning with a few expert tips for recognizing poorly performing ducts.

Signs of duct problems

- ☐ High utility bills in summer and winter.
- ☐ Some rooms are difficult to heat and cool.
- ☐ Stuffy rooms never seem to feel comfortable.
- ☐ Little or no air flows from registers.
- ☐ Air filter gets dirty quickly (needs changing more than once a month, which is a sign of leaks in return ducts).
- ☐ Streaks of dust at registers or duct connections.
- ☐ Lack of insulation on ducts in attic or crawl space.
- ☐ Tangled or kinked flexible ducts in your system.

How to seal ducts

1. Reconnect any disconnected ducts.
2. Seal air leaks using mastic (a gooey, highly effective adhesive that dries to a soft solid) or metal tape. Mastics and tapes should be UL 181 approved. Never use duct tape, which doesn't last nearly as long (see page 118).
3. Make sure connections at vents and registers are well sealed where they meet the floors, walls, and ceiling. Use spray foam to seal the gaps.
4. If your ducts are uninsulated or the insulation is torn or showing gaps, first seal any loose ducts and then add proper insulation.

Insulate attic or crawl-space ducts using material, such as fiberglass batting, rated at least R-6.

has improved dramatically over the past three decades. All true. A typical new refrigerator with automatic defrost and a top-mounted freezer uses less than 500 kilowatt-hours (kWh) per year, whereas a typical model sold in 1973 used more than 1,800 kWh per year. But how many people need to replace a 1973 fridge? Many homeowners with much younger models step onto the appliance showroom floor, urged on by fashion, prestige, boredom—and what they've heard about energy savings.

But you might find the math getting fuzzy when it comes to figuring out just what those savings are. According to the U.S. government's "savings calculator," at recent average national electricity rates ($0.086/kWh), with a midsize, auto-defrost top-freezer model, an Energy Star model would save $7 a year in electricity over another model made from 2001 to 2006. For the same refrigerator made from 1993 to 2001, the average savings would be $32 per year, still not enough to justify buying a new fridge. If your current fridge was made before 1990, the savings are substantial—from $130 to $227 per year. You might have other reasons to buy a new refrigerator—you're remodeling the kitchen or you need a larger fridge—but given the scale of energy savings, it only makes good financial sense to trade in your old fridge if it's truly old. What's a good rule of thumb? Since U.S. efficiency standards first took effect in 1993 (and in 1995 in Canada), requiring new refrigerators and freezers to be more efficient than ever before, it makes sense to upgrade if your refrigerator is a pre-1993 model. Anything younger than that depends on other factors—looks, size, whether you're remodeling or not. If you do upgrade, bear in mind that the most efficient full-size models carry the Energy Star label, meaning they exceed the government standards by 15 percent or more (full-size freezers must exceed government standards by 10 percent and compact refrigerators and freezers by 20 percent). ◀

SECRET WEAPON

Extra Insulation

Since heat rises, a good deal of the heat lost by a house is through the attic. So even though your attic is already insulated with batts or loose fill between the joists, it often pays, especially in older homes, to add another layer of insulation. It doesn't cost a fortune, and it's a job that most homeowners can do themselves, using rolls of fiberglass insulation available at any home center. Run the new insulation over the tops of the joists at right angles to the existing insulation. This covers any gaps in the first layer and insulates the heat escape routes created by the joists. When adding new rolled insulation, work from the eaves toward the center using a piece of plywood as a platform to kneel on. You can cut the insulation using heavy-duty scissors. Three precautions: Use unfaced insulation; if it has facing, slash it every few inches so that it won't trap moisture. Don't block vents in the eaves. And don't cover recessed lighting unless it's marked IC (for insulated ceiling).

Windows Secrets

3 Things You Should Consider If You Have Old Drafty Windows That Are Not Energy Efficient

Think twice before replacing windows. Purchasing replacement windows for your home may not be the money-saving venture that window companies claim that it is. Some companies claim a 35 percent reduction in energy bills. Energy Star, the internationally recognized energy stamp of approval, estimates that Energy Star windows that replace single-pane windows can save homeowners $110 to $400 per year for an average home, depending on the region. That may sound like a lot of money, but when you consider that replacement windows typically cost more than $450 per window ($5,000 to $25,000 per home), the savings just don't add up.

However, Harvey M. Sachs, Ph.D., director of the Buildings Program at the American Council for an Energy-Efficient Economy (ACEEE), says that in most houses, windows account for less than 15 percent of the total heat loss. So even if you replaced all the windows with perfect insulators, you would save at most 15 percent. At those rates, it would take years to recoup the cost of the windows through energy savings. "Getting new windows is really a lifestyle option," says Sachs. New windows may look better, but "it may be more cost effective to do other upgrades."

Make your current windows weather tight. Adding caulk, weather stripping, and a storm-window alternative is often the most cost effective way to fix old windows. Not only will filling gaps stop drafts, making you feel warmer in the winter, but tightening up your house means your furnace or boiler does not have to work as hard to keep your house warm, and your air conditioning doesn't have to work as hard to keep it cool. Here are some low-cost tips for sealing up windows without spending an arm and a leg to replace them:

Caulking. If your windows are a little drafty, easy-to-apply and inexpensive caulk (about $3 per 10-ounce [290–ml] tube) can effectively plug gaps around window frames and sills. For a house with 15 windows, at half a tube per window, the total cost could be less than $25.

Weather stripping. The quality and thickness of foam weather stripping varies (as does the cost, from about $6 to $19 per 20-foot [6-meter] roll). Attach it below the bottom sash, between two sashes and other places to stop those icy wind tunnels. Depending on the type of weather stripping used, the cost to seal 15 windows might run you $90 to $285.

Storm window alternatives. Storm windows aren't that much less expensive than replacement windows (and sometimes they still let in drafts). The least expensive storm-window alternative is the plastic film that seals with a hair dryer. It costs less than $10 per window for the kits (and even less if you buy your own roll of clear plastic and two-sided tape). The drawbacks? You can't open a window if you need to, and you have to reapply them each winter. But the energy savings just may be worth the inconvenience.

Another alternative is window glass film, which is applied directly to the glass. Window film has come a long way in recent years and is no longer associated with bad tinting jobs. It the summer, it reduces solar heat and in the winter it preserves indoor heat. You can get it professionally installed for between $5 and $10 per square foot ($50 to $105 per square meter).

If you do buy windows, get the right ones. If you plan to buy replacement windows, make sure you don't get snookered into buying a cheap window that will have to be replaced again in the near future—or the wrong type of window for your needs. Always look for the Energy Star label. Energy Star is an internationally used designation that government agencies give companies that meet strict energy requirements. Here are six key facts you'll need in order to buy the best windows for your climate conditions:

1. In addition to the Energy Star label, look for the National Fenestration Rating Council label. The NFRC is a nonprofit collaboration of window manufacturers, government agencies, and building trade associations founded to establish a fair, accurate, and credible energy rating system for windows, doors, and skylights. Its label means the window's performance is certified.

2. The lower the U-value, the better the insulation. In colder climates, a U-value of 0.35 or below is recommended. These windows have at least double glazing and a coating that reduces heat transfer through the window.

3. In warm climates, where summertime heat gain is the main concern, look for windows with double glazing and spectrally selective coatings that reduce heat gain. You don't need a U-value below 0.35, so don't pay extra for it.

4. In temperate climates with both heating and cooling seasons, select windows with both low U-values and low solar heat gain coefficiency (SHGC) to maximize energy benefits.

5. Select windows with air leakage ratings of 0.3 cubic feet per minute or less.

6. Window quality means nothing if windows leak around the frame. Look for a reputable, qualified installer. ◀

Energy Conservation *Myths*

You hear a lot on television and in the popular press about energy conservation. Some of it is worthy advice. Some of it is flat wrong. Here are four widely touted energy-saving myths that you should know the full facts about:

> Just having a programmable thermostat won't save you energy. You have to program it properly.

Programmable thermostats save you money

Well, they actually do—but only if you program them for savings. Many people mistakenly think that these computer-chip-driven electronic devices *automatically* calculate efficient temperatures. But they don't. You must program them to lower the thermostat temperature at night or during the day when you're at work. Do that, and you'll save an average of 15 percent on your monthly bills.

Ceiling fans cool a room

They don't cool the room, but they do cool the people in it by creating a wind-chill effect on the skin. That's a good thing, allowing you to raise the temperature of your air conditioner thermostat or turn the AC off altogether. But where people go wrong is leaving those fans on when they leave the room. Instead, treat the fan like a light and turn it off. Otherwise, it will waste electricity.

Computer screen savers save energy

Screen savers prolong the life of your monitor by displaying a moving image to prevent a fixed image from being burned into the phosphor of the screen. But they do nothing to save power. Instead, they burn up electricity. Your computer may have an energy-saving mode. To activate it, go into your operating system software's control panel and explore your computer's power management options.

It takes more energy to turn a computer on than to let it idle

This may or may not be true with a car (depends on how long you idle it), but it's certainly not true with a computer. Shut your computer off at night or when you will be away from it for a long period of time.

Selling Your House

3 Lists of Tricks That Will Help Increase the Value of Your House in the Eyes of Buyers

Boost your curb appeal. You've heard it before—that sprucing up out front can help lure busy buyers into your home. But curb appeal is so important it bears repeating. Here's a step-by-step approach:

1. Walk the perimeter of your house, removing all garbage cans, wood-piles, and leftover building materials (wood, cinder blocks, and bricks).

2. Clean and sweep gutters. Check for roof moss and dry rot.

3. Prune bushes and trees. Remove all dead plants or shrubs. Keep plants from blocking windows. Remember: You can't sell a house if buyers can't see it.

4. Weed and mulch all planting areas.

5. Keep lawn freshly cut, fertilized, and watered.

6. Clear patios and decks of all small items, such as small planters, pots, charcoal, barbecue grills, toys, and tools. (Put them in a shed or storage unit.)

7. Check exterior paint—especially the front door and trim, the first detail a potential buyer will see. Clean, scrape, and repaint if necessary.

Boost your home's interior appeal too. The real estate trend known as staging started in some of the swankest neighborhoods in California and Florida and is spreading across the country. Staging specialists, often combining Realtor know-how with an interior designer's eye, make minor changes to your home in order to appeal to poten-tial buyers. Staging takes the concept of improving your curb appeal inside the home and pushes it even further.

The key principles of staging include decluttering, cleaning, and "neutraliz-ing." "It's not about replacing expensive items like windows and floors. It's about looks," says Kevin Reid Shirley, a Washington, D.C.-based Realtor and staging specialist. "It's about making what you already have irresistible." Statistics show that the work of stagers helps houses move faster and often boosts the selling price.

Stagers might make formal design ideas, recommend outside vendors (painters, haulers, and furniture rentals), oversee the process, and do the final showcasing of the home such as rearranging furni-ture and accessorizing. Some include the fee in their nondiscounted commis-sion rate. Others charge flat or hourly fees in the thousands of dollars.

Save those fees while enjoying the advantages of staged home by using Shirley's advice:

- *Think of your home as a product.* It must be priced right and look better than the other homes in your mar-ketplace in order to be competitive.

- *Prepare to pack early.* When you sell your home, you're going to have to move. When you move, you're going to have to pack. Most of the princi-ples of staging just mean that you're going to pack up some of your things early. If you need room to store extra

6

THINGS YOU SHOULD
know
About Real Estate Agents

Although you can sell or buy a home on your own, it's tricky, and most of us opt to use the services of real estate agents. While these pros can be very helpful in finding the right buyer or locating the perfect house, you have to remember that they are in the game to collect a commission. Here are some things that you should keep in mind when dealing with real estate agents.

1 Licensed real estate agents aren't as qualified as their pay scale might lead you to believe. In California, for example, all you need to get an agent's license is one three-unit college course and a passing grade on the state's three-hour, multiple-choice test.

2 They might not be showing you all the listings, only the ones that pay the highest commission. In the U.S. these days, many listings pay 2.5 percent rather than the traditional 3 percent commission to the buyer's agent. That half percentage point can mean losing $1,500 on a $300,000 home. Make sure your agent is showing you all listings, the ones that pay 3 percent and the ones that pay 2.5 percent.

3 Agents sometimes delay putting a home on the multiple listing service. That way, they can show it to their clients first in an attempt to rake in both the seller's and buyer's commission.

4 Open houses are not a great way to sell houses. But they are a great way for agents to snag new clients. So that open house you're busting your butt over might not be worth the trouble—at least to you. For the same reason, agents include very few details in the ads they run for your house. They want as many people as possible to call. Even if your home doesn't suit the house hunters, the agent now has their names as potential clients.

5 Agents don't always push for the highest price. Sure, they're working for commission, but sometimes a quick and easy sell for $190,000 is better than waiting for $200,000. That $10,000 difference is a lot of money to you ($9,400 when you subtract the total 6 percent commission), but at a 3 percent seller's commission, it comes out to only $300 for the agent.

6 You can back out of the deal. Though it's rare, some sellers change their minds after they've received offers on their homes. Maybe their job situation or their children's school situation changed. Maybe they have reasons for not wanting to sell to a particular buyer (they're going to demolish a beloved home and put up condos). If the offer is equal to or better than the asking price, the agent may claim that you owe the commission anyway, since the buyer has met the terms of the agreement. But there are other conditions that still must be met, such as inspections, appraisals, and obtaining financing. You can use these as grounds to back out.

possessions, use the garage or rent a storage unit.

- *Neutralize your home.* Buyers decide to buy or not to buy a home in a matter of minutes. If they spend even a few moments admiring your personal belongings, such as photographs, heirloom china or tchotchke collections, that's a distraction and invaluable time wasted. "We want them to be able to envision the space with their furnishings and belongings there," Shirley says. "By removing these personal items, you allow potential buyers to imagine their belongings in the space."

- *Clear surfaces.* Remove all unnecessary objects from tabletops, desks, and shelves. Keep decorative objects on the furniture restricted to groups of 1, 3, or 5 items (odd-numbered groups look better). Work extra hard to free up kitchen counter space. Remove messages, magnets, and pictures from the front of the refrigerator. In bathrooms, remove unnecessary items from countertops, tub, shower stall, and commode top. Keep only the most necessary cosmetics, brushes, perfumes, and such in one small group on the counter.

- *Thin out crowded rooms.* Rearrange or remove some of the furniture in your home. Less furniture makes the rooms appear larger.

- *Simplify busy walls.* Take down, reduce, or rearrange pictures and objects on walls.

- *Organize closets.* Pack up and remove all seasonal clothes from your closets. That will make your closets appear bigger. Disorganized closets tell buyers that your home does not have enough storage space.

- *Patch, paint, and clean like crazy.* Spackle wall holes and cracks. Apply a fresh coat of paint to rooms that need it. (Neutral wall colors, such as tan, taupe, beige, and cream, paired with bright white trim, lend a clean, classic, and spacious look to rooms.) Clean carpets and drapes if they need it. Clean windows to invite natural light and enhance views. If an object can't be cleaned or repaired, repaint it or replace it.

Last-Minute Cleanup

When you get the call from your real estate agent that potential buyers are just 15 minutes away, here's an 11-point hit list of last-minute touches.

1. Quickly wash the dishes, or at least put dirty dishes in the dishwasher.

2. Make the beds.

3. Wipe the counters.

4. Empty the garbage.

5. Hide dirty clothes in the washer or dryer.

6. Do a quick vacuum of high-traffic areas.

7. Turn ceiling fans on low.

8. Open all curtains and blinds, unless otherwise advised.

9. Turn on all lights and lamps.

10. Close garage doors.

11. Make sure all toilet lids are down.

- *Forget the potpourri or fresh-baked cookies.* Those common tricks fall flat. The best two fragrances home buyers can smell in your home are Pine-Sol and paint! The perception is that a clean home is a well-maintained home.

- *Decorate dead space.* If you've got unused rooms or finished basement space, help buyers envision how they might use the space. Turn that extra bedroom (the one you use as a closet) into a home office. Set up a desk and computer, even if you have to borrow props or buy them for cheap at a local thrift shop.

Let them see light. If you're selling your home, remember this: What really impresses buyers, at least on a subconscious level, is how bright, airy, and spacious a home is. So here are the secrets for reinforcing this impression:

- Remove a few pieces of furniture from each room and rearrange the remaining furniture for a sparse look.

- Pull two-thirds of the clothes out of every closet and store them away. You want a visitor to peek into the closet and think, Yup, plenty of room in here!

- Open all curtains and blinds, wash all windows, and put high-wattage bulbs in all lamps.

- If you have any dingy, stained, or cracked walls, repair them and repaint in a light color. ◁

Buying a House

2 Simple Secrets That Could Save Thousands When You Are Looking for a New Home

Buy the house before making other major purchases. Salespeople will gnash their teeth when they read this, but hold off on making any major purchases if you're also about to buy a new house. Taking out a loan for a new car, for instance, could radically change your financial picture from the point of view of a mortgage bank. You could be turned down for a mortgage if the bank isn't sure you can handle the payments.

Don't talk about renovations. Your natural, genial nature could cost you thousands of dollars when it comes to buying a house. So for once in your life, turn off the charm. Most people who are selling a home have a lot of themselves invested in the property and they feel better knowing that the next owner will appreciate the abode they're giving up. If you fall into a long-winded conversation with a home's seller about the paneling you want to rip out or the tree you intend to cut down, the offended seller will be less likely to drop his price during negotiations. If you must meet the seller, keep it brief and cordial—but say nothing about your plans for the property. ◁

THE TRUTH ABOUT
vinyl siding

Polyvinyl chloride (PVC) is the most popular siding material. Lots of money and energy on the part of the manufacturers, distributors, and salespeople go toward pushing vinyl siding, as it's commonly known. The marketers prey on the universal homeowner dread of exterior maintenance. Yet while vinyl may be a viable option for some people, it's no miracle product. Listen to what the vinyl salesman says, and then think about what he's leaving out. Here's what he may not be telling you.

Vinyl siding is made from a toxin

While vinyl siding on your house will not likely lead to health problems, PVC is known to cause cancer in humans. Fires in vinyl-clad homes are more dangerous because of the toxic fumes produced by the burning plastic.

Adding vinyl siding is not necessarily a home improvement

Often owners of older homes in need of repair turn to vinyl as a solution. But installing vinyl over wood that is already water damaged can simply mask a minor problem, turning it into a major problem with time. Moisture trapped beneath vinyl will accelerate rot, promote mold and mildew, and invite insect infestations in leftover wood siding and framing. Even in new homes, vinyl siding can act as a moisture trap.

Vinyl siding is not so easy to clean

Over time, vinyl siding grows dingy with dirt and mildew. Marketers often say cleaning it is as easy as spraying it with a pressure-sprayer. But pressure-washing vinyl is a no-no, since the high-powered water can seep in between cracks and get trapped behind the panels, leading to the above-mentioned rot. Power-washing can also rip vinyl panels right off the wall. And you can't freshen vinyl up with a coat of paint. More likely, you'll have to scrub the entire house with warm, soapy water.

Vinyl siding is not maintenance-free

Every siding material requires maintenance. Period. Vinyl installation requires lots of caulk around windows and doors and at corners. Exterior caulk eventually shrinks, cracks, and mildews. Gaps open up, and water enters. Time for maintenance. Also, the vinyl siding pieces are secured to the house by a nail or staple. As the vinyl contracts and expands with the temperature changes, these fasteners can loosen and strips can buckle (especially if they're secured too tightly). High winds can loosen or remove fasteners. Time for maintenance. As vinyl ages, it fades and grows brittle—even more brittle in cold weather—and can crack and shatter when struck by a ball or limb. You can't (or shouldn't) paint faded vinyl. And since vinyl cannot be patched (like wood can), you have to replace an entire panel to fix one crack. All together now: Time for maintenance.

Vinyl siding does not increase an older home's value

More and more people around the country are coming to appreciate historic homes as one-of-a-kind antiques in their own right. As a result, old home values are rising—but not if they have lost their historic charm. While vinyl siding may look like "authentic" wood, installation usually calls for the removal of much of the original wood siding and artistic exterior trim—moldings, scrollwork, gable shingles, and decorative attic vents—that people love.

Vinyl siding will not cut your energy bill

Thin and flimsy, vinyl is not a good insulator. The addition of foam backing beneath the panels will do next to nothing to add energy efficiency to your home. In older homes, experts estimate that if the original wood siding is removed to make room for the new vinyl siding, the net effect would be a loss in energy efficiency.

Vinyl siding will not last forever

The slogan of the siding industry is that "vinyl is final," and its ads imply that vinyl siding is permanent. But don't you believe it. Sure, vinyl will last a long time, a very long time. But vinyl siding is just not as durable as wood or masonry siding. As vinyl starts to noticeably fade and dull, it becomes less attractive. At the same time, the longer you have the siding, the more likely it is to be damaged—accidentally hit by a ball, a branch, a mower or snow blower, strong hail, or wind-blown debris. This means replacing an entire panel with a bright new mismatched panel. At this point, to preserve the value of their property, many homeowners opt for the ultimate act of maintenance: replacing the siding.

The Good Earth

7 Ways to Create a Rich, Fertile Environment for Your Lawn and Plants

Don't bother to test your soil. If you only listened to the "experts" in gardening magazines, you'd fork over some green to a soil lab before you ever forked compost onto your garden. But some gardening professionals think this can be a waste of money. Garden center manager Connie Smith, for example, has never tested soil. In general, she says, if you are diligent about adding compost, manure, and peat to your soil, it will achieve the required pH balance and essential minerals. If you want to learn more about the general nature of soils in your area, the extension agent at a nearby university, or an expert at a local garden center, will tell you what to expect and make recommendations for additions to your soil.

When is testing soil a must? If you're having problems growing a plant that should succeed in your area, especially if your neighbor's plants do well with the same sun exposure, you might have an issue with your soil and a test could help point to a solution. Also, you may want to test your soil first if you plan to dump fertilizer on it every year: You may be wasting money and pouring unnecessary chemicals into your garden when all it needs is a dose of lime or a load of manure.

Get your mulch for free. Mulch is essential stuff for retaining moisture and inhibiting weeds, but the owners of your local garden or home center will be laughing all the way to the bank if you buy it by the bag. Fortunately, arborists and tree trimmers are often looking to give away their wood chips—otherwise, they have to pay a landfill to take them. Call a local arborist and ask if you can get a load of chips dumped in your driveway at the end of the day's work. Many are happy to oblige. Also, check with your town's parks or public-works department, because it often puts wood chips in a publicly available stash where you can load up for free. If you don't have a pickup, place a large piece of sturdy plastic, a painter's drop cloth, or even an old bedsheet in the backseat or trunk of your car, pile the chips inside, then pull it out at home with the help of a friend.

Beware, however, of making mulch from the chips of diseased or insect-infested trees. Always ask about the source of the chips before taking them.

Whack those leaves into instant mulch.

To quickly turn your raked leaves into mulch, dump them into a large trash can and lower your Weed Whacker into it. This process will reduce your leaves to a tenth of their former volume. They'll be easy to pack up and dispose of if that's your wish. But ground-up leaves make excellent mulch too. Your garden store manager will shake his head with dismay when you start passing up the bags of shredded root.

Use compost instead of fertilizer.

North Americans spend literally hundreds of millions of dollars a year on bags of dirt. Sacks of so-called designer soils sell by the truckload each spring. However, you can get all the benefits of these products, as well as expensive fertilizers, by making your own compost. Work the compost into your garden soil before planting, and spread 1/2 inch to 1 inch (1.25 cm to 2.5 cm) compost over the garden every winter after the harvest. Your soil will be more fertile, easier to work, and have better drainage.

Build a simple backyard compost bin.

To compost with lawn trimmings, leaves, and other yard waste, you need a big bin, and big bins equal big bucks if you buy your composter at a garden center or through a catalog. But landscape designer Jennifer Appel has a simple plan for a backyard bin that anyone can build. All you need are a few simple supplies:

- A used wooden pallet, available just for the asking from supermarkets and warehouse outfits
- Two 8-foot 2 x 4 (2.4-meter 38 x 89-cm) studs
- 15 feet (5 meters) of galvanized chicken wire or hardware cloth, 3 feet (91 cm) wide. Choose the finer-mesh hardware cloth if you'll be composting kitchen scraps and other small items.
- A square of breathable landscaping fabric, cut to fit the top of the pallet

Place the pallet on a smooth, level surface near your garden. Saw the 2 x 4s in half, and nail one piece to each corner of the pallet to create four posts. Starting at one corner, staple the wire mesh to the posts, wrapping it around the edge of the pallet to form a box. Instead of stapling the mesh to the final post on the front side of the box, secure it with picture hooks or a twist of picture-frame wire. That way, you can swing open one panel of the mesh for easier access to the compost.

Staple the landscaping fabric over the top of the pallet, and load in your composting materials. Use a mix of carbon-rich waste (sawdust, wood chips, and leaves) and nitrogen-loaded waste (non-meat food scraps, grass clippings, and manure). The open slats in the pallet under the pile will help bring air to the compost from below, reducing odor, but turn the pile with a pitchfork or shovel every week or so to make sure it gets enough oxygen. Within a month, you'll have some nutritious compost ready for the garden, and the marketing mavens at the "designer soil" companies will be going back to the drawing board.

Make a low-cost kitchen composter. You'll be more likely to compost kitchen scraps if you have a composter that's closer to the kitchen sink than that pile way out in the garden. But judging by the glossy gardening catalogs, you'd think you have to spend a pile of money as big as a compost heap to get a good kitchen composter. Instead, head down to a supermarket or home store to pick up a 30-gallon (114-liter) plastic garbage can. To make the can compost-ready, use a power drill with a 1/2-inch (125-mm) bit or a hammer and a large nail to punch holes in it. Starting near the bottom of the garbage can, place the holes 4 inches (10 cm) apart in a ring around the side of the can. Then move up the side of the can 6 inches (15 cm) and drill a new ring of holes. Continue this pattern until you reach the top of the garbage can. Put a few drainage holes in the bottom too. Place the can outside your house in a location convenient to the kitchen and on the way to the garden. Use a bungee cord with hooks at each end to secure the lid against scavenging animals, and turn the contents at least once a week. And throw that gardening catalog, with its expensive composters, into the recycling pile.

Brew your own compost tea. What's compost tea? It's a liquid that's formed by steeping compost in water until the resulting brew is rich in nutrients and beneficial microbes. More versatile to use than compost, the tea can be used to

How I Do It A Nursery Owner's Trick for Preventing Hand-Tool Loss

Indiana gardener and nursery owner Gene Bush has a nifty solution for keeping garden hand tools handy—and preventing them from getting lost in leaves and mulch. Bush mounted an old-fashioned mailbox by the gate to his garden, and he keeps a set of hand tools in it, so they're always ready when he spots a weed that needs digging or a shrub that needs pruning. Bush puts an oiled rag in a zip-sealed plastic bag inside the mailbox, so he can wipe down the tools when he's done with them. Whenever he takes a tool out of the mailbox, he flips up the red flag—this means a tool is out (rather than mail is in), and it reminds him to replace the tool when he's done instead of losing it in the mulch.

feed plants of all kinds, replacing expensive fertilizers. Garden stores will sell it to you by the gallon, and numerous machines can be purchased to brew the tea, but it's easy to make your own with a few basic supplies.

The simplest method is to suspend a cheesecloth bag of rich organic compost in a bucket of water or a watering can for two to three days. Carefully remove the bag and its contents, then use the brew to feed your plants immediately.

You'll get far more microbial growth—and thus more benefit for your garden—if you take a few additional steps. Microorganisms will only grow if they get an adequate supply of oxygen, and an aquarium pump and hose are just the ticket to deliver it. Get a 5-gallon (19-liter) plastic bucket and place it near an outdoor electrical outlet. Attach one end of the plastic hose to the aquarium bubbler, and place the other end in the bottom of the bucket. Fill about one-fifth of the bucket with rich compost. Now fill a second bucket with water and let it stand overnight to let the chlorine in the tap water dissipate. Otherwise the chlorine will kill the microorganisms in the compost. Add the chlorine-free water to the compost, filling the bucket to within 6 inches (15 cm) of its rim. Then add 2 tablespoons unsulfured molasses to the mix as food for the microbes. Turn on the aquarium pump so it bubbles through the mix, and let it brew for two or three days, stirring occasionally. When you're ready to use it, strain the tea through cheesecloth into the second bucket, and return the solids to the compost heap. Apply the tea to plants immediately. ◁

Outdoor Plants
9 Ways to Make the Most of Your Flowering and Foliage Plantings

Don't pay retail for plants. Why pay top dollar to a garden center when you may be able to find plants that are every bit as healthy at other outlets? Arboretums and botanical gardens often hold plant sales, as do neighborhood and high school gardening clubs. Though your local nursery owner won't be happy, your purchases will go toward a good cause.

Give the gift of perennials. You could pay top dollar to give a potted plant to a friend for a birthday or other special occasion. Or you could keep your money and find beautiful plants in your own garden to use as gifts. Many perennials need to be divided every couple of years as they grow. Flowers that grow from bulbs, such as tulips and lilies, are the easiest to divide. After these plants flower, gently lift them from the ground, pull off the little bulbs that have formed alongside the original bulb, and replant these in potting soil. Voilà! A living gift for your best friend.

Ask a neighbor to divide perennials. Although garden centers don't like to talk about it, many of those pricey perennials they stock on their shelves are available for free in your neighbor's garden. Ask if he or she has any perennials that need to be divided—offer to help with the labor in exchange for taking some home for your own garden.

Smaller can be better. Nurseries and garden centers would love to sell you the biggest plant they can, since they can charge top dollar. But if you're buying flowering perennials, choose a 1-quart (1-liter) container of plants over a 1-gallon (3.8-liter) container. Young perennials tend to grow quickly, and within a single season they will catch up in size with those larger plants you could have purchased at a considerably higher cost.

Beware of fast-growing invasive plants. Some common garden varieties may become all too common in the garden if you aren't careful, warns Denver botany professor Greg McArthur. Although garden centers may try to sell you on easy-to-grow plants (knowing that a fast-growing plant makes for a happy customer), some plants spread aggressively and can be very hard to get rid of once they are introduced in a garden. These include ground covers such as periwinkle (*Vinca minor*); flowering plants like fleabane and other asters, broom, forget-me-nots, hollyhocks, verbena, yarrow, and daisies; and other plants such as ferns, mints, and strawberries.

Moreover, some of these plants may leap the garden fence (or, more likely, send roots underneath it) and invade your neighbors' plots or nearby open space.

Such invasive species can seriously alter the local plant environment. Most of these plants have their place in a garden, but make sure to keep them in their place by pulling up shoots wherever you don't want them, or by planting such varieties only in defined areas such as pots, containers, beds bounded by pavement, or raised beds.

"Drought tolerant" doesn't mean "don't water." Beware of the self-appointed xeriscaping expert who says all you need to do is plant the right varieties and then throw away the hose. To get a proper start on life in your garden, drought-tolerant plants need regular watering for the first year after you plant them. After that, as long as you've planted varieties suitable for your zone, these plants should be able to live on the local rainfall in all but exceptional drought conditions.

Wildflower mixes may be wilder than you expect. Seed companies make those boxes or bags of premixed wildflower seeds seem like the answer to all your prayers. Just scatter them on the ground, add water, and a beautiful meadow full of wildflowers will magically appear. But be careful. According to Susan Aldrich-Markham of the Oregon State University extension service, those mixes may contain invasive species that are inappropriate for your area.

Some plants that are considered desirable, decorative varieties in one part of North America may turn into harmful weeds elsewhere, in places with different growing conditions. One researcher planted the seeds from 19 wildflower mix packets, and all 19 contained species that were invasive somewhere in North America. Eight plants were considered noxious weeds in at least one U.S. state or Canadian province.

How do you make sure your wildflower garden is safe and appropriate for your area? The best method is to select packets of seeds for individual wild-flowers, rather than mixes, so you can choose your own blend and be sure what you're planting. If you opt for a seed mix, Aldrich-Markham recommends buying from a local company, because the more widely a mix is distributed, the more likely it is to hold inappropriate seeds for a given area. Make sure the packet lists all of the varieties of seeds it contains, and look up any plants that are unfamiliar. It's a bit more work, but you're better off doing the legwork in advance than planting a meadow from hell.

Squirt rosebushes with this secret formula. Longtime gardener Rita Carey from Squamish, British Columbia, works at a garden center, but that doesn't stop her from recommending this homemade, environmentally friendly spray for rose pests and diseases. Here's her recipe: In an empty 1-gallon (3.8-liter) milk jug, mix 1 1/2 teaspoons baking soda, 1 tablespoon vegetable oil, 1/2 teaspoon liquid dish soap, and 1/2 cup white vinegar. Fill the jug the rest of the way with water and add the mixture to a sprayer. Spray all of the leaves and stems of your roses at least once a week during growing season.

Go low-tech for drip irrigation. For watering flower beds and other plantings, drip irrigation is the best method—it's extremely water-efficient,

and the slow, deep watering is great for plant health. But landscape contractors mentally tote up another boat payment when they sign up for your big drip-irrigation job. Maybe you don't need the expense of a full installed system—here's a simple way to give plants a deep soaking with no expense at all. Save up plastic 2-liter soda bottles and 1-gallon (3.8-liter) milk bottles. Punch a small hole in the bottom of each, then fill each container with water. Stand each bottle next to a plant, and it will slowly release the water. For trees, use 5-gallon (19-liter) collapsible water carriers designed for camping, with their valves set on the slowest drip. With this method, you'll leave the contractor high and dry. And even if you do have a centralized drip-irrigation system, these portable irrigators are extremely useful for watering isolated shrubs, trees, and flowers. ◁

SECRET WEAPON

Stirrup Hoe

Longtime gardener Glenn Deines is a retired blacksmith and welder in the farming town of Platteville, Colorado, and he knows his tools. His favorite device for his home garden is the stirrup hoe, which is just about twice as efficient as a traditional hoe. The stirrup hoe looks like, well, a stirrup attached to a wooden handle. The metal blade digs and cuts in both directions, pushing and pulling, and it's particularly effective in compacted earth, like the paths between garden rows. Since you don't swing a stirrup hoe like a regular hoe, it's great for working in tight spaces between rows—more accurate and less damaging to plants. Also called circle hoes and loop hoes, these tools are easily found at garden and hardware stores.

Container Plants

6 Secrets for Making Your Potted House and Patio Plants Flourish for Less

Don't line pot bottoms with pebbles. Anyone telling you to fill the bottom inch or so of indoor plant containers with pebbles is just trying to sell you a load of fancy stones. It's a waste of money, and it's not good for the plants, says Phil Goodin, head of a Denver-area high school's Plant Lovers Club. Although the conventional wisdom used to be that pebbles or shards of clay pots in a container improved drainage, plant experts now say such stones occupy space the plant roots need and may encourage growth of fungus. Instead, you want a solid column of soil right down to the bottom of the container. If you're worried about soil washing out of a pot's drain hole, cover the hole with a scrap of window screen or a single pot shard before filling the pot with soil.

Try some of those free containers. That fancy-schmancy garden store would just as soon you didn't think about it, but you probably throw away scores of items every year that are perfect for container gardening. Popcorn tins and plastic ice cream buckets make particularly good outdoor flowerpots. All you have to do is drill holes in the bottom of them for drainage. If the exterior of the container is not to your liking, a can of spray paint will change that quickly.

Keep your plants alive when you're away. How do you care for plants while you're away from home? One common solution is to pay someone to water your indoor and outdoor container plants. But you can greatly reduce the need for watering by taking a few steps before you leave home.

- Always use a potting mix with moisture-retaining polymers (or add polymers to the mix). These compounds retain water for later use by thirsty plants.

- When you're headed off on vacation or a work trip, move your plants out of direct sunlight—behind windows with sheer curtains is a great spot.

- Turn down the thermostat in winter to keep the interior of the house cool.

- Move pots and containers close together, so the plants will provide each other with shade and humidity.

- Place sensitive plants inside tents made from white plastic trash bags—place a bag upside down over each plant, using stakes as "tent poles" to keep the plastic off the foliage. Cut a few small holes in the plastic to allow oxygen to reach the plant.

- To conserve water in outdoor containers, move them to a location sheltered from the wind and cluster them together.

- You can also bury potted plants to their rims temporarily and mulch around them.

The neighborhood kid who was counting on making a little extra money won't be happy with these water-saving techniques, but, on the other hand, your lawn will probably still need mowing when you get back.

Salvage your dried-out plants.
If your plants do dry out completely while you are away, you can revive them when you get home by soaking the containers in a tub or kiddie pool. Use warm (not hot) water, and submerge the pots until bubbles stop appearing from the soil. Remove the pot and drain any excess water.

Put an IV drip on that plant. You can pay $100 or more for electronically controlled devices that automatically water your plants while you're away from home. Or you can use the low-tech, inexpensive, and just as effective method recommended by nurse Jennifer James: Hook your plants up to an IV drip. Plastic intravenous solution bags can be refilled with tap water by removing the spike at the mouth of the bag. Hang a bag above a plant and set the dial to slow drip. Only medical professionals can buy intravenous equipment, so ask a friend who works in the field for used bags and feeder lines.

Use a rope to water your plants.
Another solution for watering while you're away takes advantage of the capillary action of natural fibers. Place your potted plants next to a tub of water, then cut natural-fiber clothesline or other rope in lengths that will reach from the tub to each pot. Anchor one end of each cord in the tub with a rock or brick, and coil the other end around the soil atop each pot. Water will flow across the rope to the plants. ◁

Vegetable Gardening
7 Tricks for Growing Incredible Edibles in Your Veggie Patch

Be careful of hardiness zones near borders. Knowing the hardiness zone for your area is critical to choosing the right plants for your gardens and landscaping. These zones are predominantly based on the coldest temperature during winter and on the dates of the first and last frost. The zones are numbered, and plants are generally labeled with these numbers so you'll know which ones are most likely to thrive in your area. But here's a fact that could trip you up if you aren't careful where you buy: Although both Canada and the United States use a numbering system for their zones, the scales are different. For example, the zone for much of northern Montana is 3b, but the same zone over the border in southern Alberta is 4a, even though they share virtually the same climatic conditions. If you shop in the border states or provinces or, even more critically, if you order plants by mail or from the Internet, it's crucial to know which zone system the vendor is using. Otherwise, you might find that your new plants are immigrants with the wrong documentation.

Try vegetables with training wheels. If you're worried that you've got a black thumb, start with green beans, tomatoes, and radishes—and herbs such as basil, rosemary, and thyme. Sure, the experts will get bigger yields, but these can't-miss plants guarantee plenty of luscious fresh vegetables during your first season, and you'll be encouraged to try more vegetables next year.

Jump-start spring with a movable greenhouse. Fancy garden stores will be happy to sell you a spiffy prefabricated greenhouse for starting seedlings or protecting plants from early or late frosts, but it won't come cheap. Fortunately, it's easy to make your own portable shelter for young plants, says longtime gardener Enga Lokey, who lives in sunny Australia but says winters are plenty cold there. All you need to buy is some clear plastic sheeting, four 18-inch (46-cm) lengths of rebar (steel reinforcing rods used for concrete), and some concrete-reinforcing mesh. The mesh looks like wire fencing, typically comes in 5-foot (1.5-meter) widths in rolls or panels, and is available from hardware stores and lumberyards. To cover a garden bed that's 4 feet (1.2 meters) wide, cut the mesh to a 6-foot (1.8-meter) length with wire snips or a pair of bolt cutters. Bend the mesh into an arch form, then anchor it at each corner over the bed by driving the rebar pieces through the mesh like tent stakes, using a hammer or small sledge. Now dig a trench 4 to 5 inches (10 to 13 cm) deep along one side of the resulting tunnel, lay one edge of the plastic sheet in this trench, cover it with soil, and anchor it further with rocks. Pull the plastic over the archway, and anchor it at the ends and on the other long side with rocks, bricks, or a piece of lumber. Use clothespins to gather the loose plastic and keep it from flapping in the wind.

This simple shelter will protect seedlings from cool breezes, keeping the temperature inside several degrees warmer on frosty nights, and it's sturdy enough to resist a snowfall, Lokey says. Always open up the plastic during sunny days or the plants inside will get too hot. When the danger of frost is past, put away the structure or move it to cover some newer seedlings. The same structure can be used to protect plants from frost in the fall, or even to keep producing salad greens all winter. You won't feel like you need to take out a second mortgage to buy a fancy greenhouse.

Protect seedlings with a home-made cloche. The French invented the glass cloche, or bell jar, to protect seedlings from frost. You can buy beautiful cloches today, but why not save your centimes and make them yourself from plastic 2-liter soda bottles or 1-gallon (3.7-liter) milk jugs? Using a sharp knife, carefully slice the entire bottom from the bottle. Place the bottle over the seedling, leaving the cap off for ventilation. Bury the lower edge of the bottle in the soil to anchor it

How I Do It **A Veggie Grower's Surefire Seed Mix**

Nancy Deines has been gardening in eastern Colorado for half a century, and one of her favorite tricks for the vegetable garden is mixing carrot seeds with radish seeds. She spaces the seeds evenly in the row, starting early in the growing season and continuing to plant every few weeks until midsummer. Here's the beauty of it: Radishes are among the quickest vegetables to sprout from seed, and the fast-growing seedlings will mark the row within a week. As the radishes are harvested, they break up the soil next to the maturing carrots, allowing them to grow thicker and deeper. And the carrots will be easier to pull when it comes time to harvest.

Another hint from Nancy: The best-tasting carrots are the ones pulled right after the first frost.

---

in place, or poke a stick into the ground next to the seedling and place the bottle over the stick. With the money you've saved, buy yourself a nice bottle of French wine.

Try this simpler method for supporting tomato plants. Trellises or cages work well enough for holding up tomato vines, but they are not always cheap and you have to find a place to store them. As a result, many commercial growers have adopted the "Florida weave" for supporting tomato plants, and there's no reason home growers shouldn't use it too. To construct the Florida weave, drive a steel fence post or sturdy wooden post at each end of the row of tomato plants and at every second plant between. Now tie polypropylene twine, which doesn't stretch, to the post at one end of the row about 10 inches (25 cm) off the ground. Run the cord to the second stake, and secure it by wrapping it a couple of times around the stake at the same level.

Continue to the end of the row, keeping the cord tight, then return back up the row on the other side of the stakes, securing the cord at each post. The tomato plants' stems should be held between the two taut cords. As the plants grow, add new layers of twine about 10 inches (25 cm) apart. Prune suckers to remove the weight that must be supported and encourage productive growth. You won't need those old tomato cages anymore, but maybe you can make a few bucks by selling them at a yard sale and put it toward seeds for the following season.

Keep those fresh garden vegetables coming in the fall. The grocer starts rubbing his hands with anticipation as the first frosts approach, knowing that home gardeners will soon be forced to return to the veggie aisle in numbers. But you can extend your growing season for weeks if you plant the right vegetables and take a few simple steps as autumn approaches.

Broccoli, cauliflower, peas, spinach, and many other greens can be planted in midsummer for a fall harvest, and root crops such as beets, carrots, parsnips, and turnips will stay fresh in the ground through the fall and into winter. (Mulch over the tops of these plants to prevent the ground from freezing around them.)

To keep plants producing as long as possible, continue to water regularly, keep picking fruit before it goes to seed, don't get lazy about weeding as the summer wanes, and cut back overgrown foliage near the garden so your vegetables get enough sunlight.

Often the first frost of the season is only a warning sign, and if you protect your plants, you'll get another two or three weeks of warm growing weather before regular frosts set in. Cover tender plants with lightweight blankets, sheets, newspapers, or even buckets or tubs. Remove these covers as soon as the temperature rises above freezing the next day. This way, your greengrocer will keep tapping his fingers on the counter and waiting for you to come shopping.

Hang those green tomatoes. If subfreezing weather is forecast and your tomato vines are still loaded down with green fruit, pull the entire plant out of the ground and hang it upside down in a cool, dark place, such as a basement or garage. The fruit will ripen, and you'll enjoy homegrown tomatoes for another couple of weeks while the trucks full of rock-hard out-of-state tomatoes unload at the supermarket. ◁

Your Lawn

6 Tricks to Help You Create a Lush Low-Care Sea of Green in Your Yard

Build up the low yellow spots.
The makers and sellers of pest and fungus treatments would love you to believe that every yellow or dead spot is the result of a sinister invader that can be eliminated with frequent use of their expensive products. But some yellow spots are simply the result of low spots in your lawn, especially if they appear after heavy rain. Grass can suffocate or rot in standing water. Try spreading a layer of compost over the yellow spot to raise it up to the level of the surrounding ground. Within a week or two, new grass will likely sprout to fill the patch.

Quit bagging up grass trimmings.
If you have the kind of mower that shreds grass and drops it right back onto the lawn, you can reduce the recommended amount of lawn fertilizer by at least a third—and possibly even half. The salespeople at your garden center would tear their hair out if they knew you were onto this secret, but a mulching mower will save you having to spread pounds and pounds of chemical fertilizer every year.

Save a bundle on lawn aeration.
It seems that every year a swarm of eager workers roam around the neighborhood posting handbills and ringing doorbells, insisting that you need to aerate your lawn—right now! If you don't keep track, you might do it three or four times a year. Relax. Most lawns only need aerating once a year to improve the drainage and breathability of soil, and it's important to do it at the right time for your area and grass type. Some

grasses do better with aeration at the beginning of the growing season, and some prefer it at the end.

You don't have to pay someone else an arm and a leg to do your aeration. It's not rocket science, and it's no more strenuous than mowing a lawn. Just be sure to mark your sprinkler heads and any buried cables first. Ask several of your neighbors if they'd like to go in on an aeration party, then chip in to rent a machine. You can hire the machines at hardware stores for half a day for about the same amount that you'd pay to have a single lawn aerated. You can take turns using the machine on each of your own lawns, or pay a strapping teenager to do them all in a morning. Either way, you'll come out ahead.

Treat your lawn to a healthy tonic.
You don't have to pay big bucks to the fertilizer makers to spruce up your lawn with a shot of healthy nutrients. Many homeowners have had great success with homemade lawn "tonics" made from simple products that might already be on your pantry shelves. The recipes vary, but most share these common ingredients:

1 can non-light beer

1 can non-diet soda pop

1 cup ammonia

1 cup liquid dish soap

1 cup molasses or corn syrup

1/2 cup mouthwash

What do these ingredients have to do with promoting a healthy lawn? The beer, soda, and molasses stimulate beneficial microbes. The ammonia is a source of nitrates, the main ingredient in most fertilizers. The soap helps spread the solution evenly and bind it to the blades of grass. And the alcohol in mouthwash deters some pests. Mix these ingredients in the reservoir of a 10- or 20-gallon (38- or 76-liter) hose-end sprayer, and apply it to your lawn every three weeks or so. Water well after application. Your lawn will be lusher and need less water, and the big oil companies that supply the raw materials for many fertilizers will have lost another customer.

EXPERT INSTANT ADVICE

Reseeding a Lawn

Whether you've got a small bare patch or half a lawn to reseed, it's best to do it in the late summer or fall, when cool temperatures will give the grass a good start.

1. Rake off any dead grass and debris. Loosen the soil in the bare patch to a depth of 1 inch (2.5 cm). If the grass was killed by dog urine or a chemical spill, douse the area thoroughly with water several times to dilute the harmful chemicals.

2. Spread 2 to 3 inches (5 to 7.6 cm) of compost over the area, then smooth it with the back of a rake so the compost is level with the surrounding soil.

3. Mix the seed with an equal amount of damp sand a day before you sow it. The moisture will jump-start the process of germination. Scatter the seeds evenly with the sand; that way, they'll stay in place on the ground, even on a windy day.

4. Cover the seeds with a thin layer of compost, then water the area gently, being careful not to wash the seeds away.

5. Keep the area moist with a fine spray of water two or three times a day until the seeds germinate, then water regularly along with the rest of your lawn.

How I Do It A Mowing Pro's Guide to Creating a Beautiful Lawn

Yard-maintenance companies will tell you that only their experts know how to mow a lawn beautifully every time. But with these expert mowing techniques recommended by Bill Klutho, gardening guru at the John Deere tractor company, you can have a lawn as smooth as the fairways at Pebble Beach, without paying the "greens fees" demanded by lawn professionals.

☐ *Alternate your mowing route.* Lawns that are mowed the same direction every time develop unsightly stripes that may grow back irregularly. To avoid creating a pattern that lasts all season, alternate mowing one direction across the lawn the first time and then perpendicular to this direction the next time.

☐ *Mow early.* For the best cut, mow in mid to late morning, when it's cool but the morning dew has dried off.

☐ *Take your time.* Don't speed through mowing, because you may miss spots. While you're mowing in a wide-open area, stay in control by keeping your mower on a medium speed setting. Throttle down to lower speeds when you're turning corners and trimming borders for a closer cut.

☐ *Adhere to the one-third rule.* For a healthy lawn, never remove more than one-third of the grass blade at one time.

☐ *Don't cut your grass too short.* Grass about 3 inches (8 cm) tall usually looks better, encourages a deeper root system, and helps prevent weeds from invading.

☐ *Keep your blade sharp.* Sharp lawn mower blades produce a well-manicured lawn, and clean cuts promote better grass health. Use a mill bastard file or a grinding wheel to sharpen the blade, maintaining the blade-surface angle that came from the manufacturer.

☐ *Water infrequently but deeply.* In most parts of North America, lawns need about an inch of water per week during the growing season.

Deter lawn-damaging raccoons. If you wake up in the morning to discover small round holes in your lawn or even large patches of turf mysteriously rolled up, it is probably the work of raccoons or skunks, who visit at night and dig in search of worms, grubs, or other insects that live in your lawn. They are especially likely to show up after a rain, when the water forces their prey close to the surface. Some pest control experts would have you believe that the only viable solutions to this problem are expensive ones: installing a secure or electrified fence, setting out traps, or undertaking an elaborate grub-elimination program with toxic insecticides. But the solution is quite simple. Just go to the store and buy a couple of boxes of moth crystals and sprinkle them over your lawn. This will help persuade the raccoons, who have very sensitive noses, to dine elsewhere. Also, to avoid attracting them, make sure your garbage cans can't be knocked over and have lids that are securely closed, with a bungee cord if necessary.

Dogged by yellow-spotted grass?

If you have a dog and your lawn is covered with yellow or brown circles, the dog's urine may be the culprit. In serious cases, the spots may require reseeding or new sod. The problem is the nitrogen in the urine: Although nitrogen is a key ingredient in most fertilizers, the concentration in undiluted urine is too high for the grass, and it dies from the stress of its own growth. It's a myth that female canine urine contains some substance that causes the die-off. The likely reason female dogs cause more problems is that they tend to urinate all at once on a flat surface, rather than marking as males do, thus concentrating their impact in one spot.

What to do? Some books and websites claim that changing the pH in a dog's urine by altering its diet will reduce the damaging effect of the urine. Veterinarians say, "Hogwash!" Changing the pH content of dog urine has not been shown to affect its impact on grass, and making a dog's food more acidic or alkaline in an effort to change pH can be dangerous, possibly leading to bladder stones or infections. The only way to remedy the problem is to dilute the dog's urine, and there are two ways to do that. The most effective is to pour water on the spot on the grass within 8 hours of a dog urinating on it. Less effective but also helpful is adding water to the dog's diet, through feeding it wet food or moistening dry food with water. The dog will relieve itself more often, but the concentration of nitrogen in the urine will be lower. ◄

Landscaping
7 Little-Known Tricks for Turning an Ordinary Yard into a Dream Setting

Landscape with clipboard and shoe leather. Before hiring a designer or spending a small fortune on new plants, take a walk around your neighborhood with a clipboard and a digital camera, recommends landscape designer Ryan Peif from Greeley, Colorado. Make a checklist of the types of plants you need in your landscaping—flowers, ground covers, shrubs, and such—then take note of the plants you like or dislike in each category around the neighborhood. Equally important, observe what grows well in yards and gardens with the same sun exposure as your own—the soil type and growing conditions in your neighbors' gardens are likely to be very similar to your own. If you see a plant you don't recognize, take a photograph or ask your neighbor for its name. You're not trying to mimic that beautiful garden at the Jones's house down the block—you're picking the best of the best from an entire row of gardens.

Now, armed with your checklist and the photos of plants you might like, head to a garden center and start shopping. The experts there will help—for free—with advice on when to plant each variety, how big they will grow, and how many plants you need to fill a given space. You're well on your way to a beautiful landscape, and without the overhead of a landscape designer.

Use a free landscape consultant. If you go to a residential landscaper and give him carte blanche to come up with a plan for your yard, dollar signs will immediately pop into his eyes. So why not start the process with the services of a free consultant instead? In the United States, the local Cooperative Extension office will provide free pointers and free literature to help you establish the look you want, based on the character of your neighborhood, the climate you live in, and the care required to maintain the plantings and features you want to include in your yard. You can find your local extension office in your phone book's federal government listings, under the Department of Agriculture. Enlist the Cooperative Extension's help in drafting a detailed plan for your yard, and *then* approach a landscaper if you need further professional help. You'll be in much more control of the landscaping budget when you know what you're talking about.

Try the low-tech method for laying out landscaping. Many professional landscapers use specialized computer software to help their clients visualize exactly how their landscaping will look—and to tweak the design until it's just right. But guess who's paying for the fancy computer gear? If you're designing your own landscape, you can use this low-cost way to visualize the outlines of paths, beds, and walls. Buy some brightly colored clothesline or similar lightweight, highly visible cord. Lay the cord along the lines of your paths and beds. Now you can check out the way it looks from different vantage points around your house, deck, and street. It helps to have a partner who can adjust the lines as you make suggestions. When you're happy with the layout, use water-soluble athletic field marking spray (available at many hardware stores) to mark the lines. Place dots every couple of feet along the lines, a couple of inches inside the planned path or bed. Double-check the position from your different viewing points, then paint a solid line. This is where you'll dig.

Scope out new garden centers. Identify the neighboring yards that you admire, and ask the people who live there where they shop for plants and supplies. Then visit the garden center they recommend, but leave your checkbook or credit card at home. Ask lots of questions about your garden's problems and needs without any obvious intention of buying anything. If the staff gives you ample attention and answers your questions coherently and completely, you'll feel happy coming back with your wallet. It's the quality of information the staff provides that marks the main difference between a great garden center and your average home and garden store.

Keep the grass. Your nursery and landscape store would prefer you didn't think about it, but decks, outdoor fountains, and even flower beds are generally more work for the homeowner than simple grass. Decks need resealing periodically, fountains need their water skimmed and filters cleaned, and flower beds require weeding, deadheading, mulching, and more. Square foot for square foot, mowing a regular lawn is a comparative breeze.

Wait and save on plants and supplies. Your garden center sure wishes you'd pay top dollar by stocking up in the spring, when demand is high for plants and supplies. But if you have the space to store items like potting soil, manure, and fertilizer, you'll save a bundle if you buy it in the fall, when merchants are trying to move out their inventory. Planning a big landscaping job for next year? Order your fencing, stones, and other materials in the fall, and store them over the winter for big savings. Bulbs are usually planted in the fall, so they won't be discounted, but this is also usually the best time of year for planting trees, shrubs, and many perennials, and some garden centers may be overstocked on these plants as winter approaches. Landscaping contractors, too, may be eager to squeeze in a final job after most people have stopped thinking about their lawns and gardens—they may be more willing than usual to dicker on price.

Add a simple water feature to your yard. Although a small pond, burbling stream, or splashing fountain is often a highly desirable addition to a landscape, building these features can be expensive and fraught with problems. But there's an easy way to add water and life to your garden that doesn't involve moving parts or a pricey contractor. All it takes is a kids' plastic wading pool, says Indiana nursery owner Gene Bush.

Using Bush's plan, you can use a wading pool to build a self-contained bog that's perfect for water-loving plants such as irises and marsh marigolds.

- Choose a site where the new plants will look natural—the border of a wood or near a pond or ditch, for instance.
- Excavate a hole to the depth and diameter of the kiddie pool. Test the pool's fit in the hole, and remove or add dirt until the pool sits flat on the bottom of the hole and its top rim is level with the ground or lawn.

- Using an awl or a sharp knife, punch holes around the sides of the pool 4 inches (10 cm) below the rim, to allow some drainage during periods of heavy rain. Install the pool in the hole and pack dirt around the sides firmly.
- Now fill the entire pool with a mixture of one half coarse sand and one half peat. Level the surface, then use flat stones or pavers to cover the plastic lip of the pool. Flood the pool with water, and you're done.

It's ideal to construct your kiddie-pool bog in the fall, allowing it to settle over the winter, and make final adjustments or additions in the spring before planting. Any plants that love wet feet will thrive in your new bog, including cow parsnips, irises, creeping Jennie, and many more. To maintain the garden, all you need to do is ensure it stays wet, Bush says. By midsummer you'll have a beautiful new addition to your yard, and you won't have lined the pockets of a landscape designer. ◂

Getting Healthy Plants at a
Discount Center

Garden centers and nurseries would like you to believe you're a fool if you buy plants from discount hardware outfits, supermarkets, and department stores, but in many cases these discounters buy plants from the same distributors as the premium garden centers do. The difference is in what happens after the plants go on display at the store—generally, plants will receive more expert care and constant attention at a garden center, and so they'll stay healthier.

How do you avoid buying a lemon of a lemon tree at a big-box retailer? Fortunately, plants don't have very good poker faces—they show how they're feeling, and if you know what to look for, you can buy healthy plants wherever you shop. So here are five things to watch.

General surroundings

Take a quick look at all of the plants on display. If they generally look good, they're probably getting decent care. If half of them are drooping or brown, head somewhere else, even if the plants you want look healthy.

Roots

If roots are bunched up and growing profusely out of the drainage holes, the plant is pot-bound and likely stressed. Conversely, if the plant lifts easily from the pot, it may have just been repotted, and its roots won't be ready for the garden. With trees or shrubs, the root-ball should feel solid inside the burlap covering.

Overall appearance

The leaves should be green and shiny, not wilting or yellow and brown. The plant should be full and bushy, rather than tall and lean. Stems should be uncracked and scar-free.

Buds

Look for budding rather than flowering plants. Budding plants will transplant easier.

Pests and disease

Inspect the entire plant carefully, especially under the leaves, for any pests or signs of disease.

If the plant passes this entire inspection with flying colors, it likely will thrive in your garden, no matter the pedigree of the purveyor.

Yard Care

6 Maintenance Tricks That Every Home Gardener Should Be Aware Of

Lay off the fertilizer with new plantings. Novice gardeners may be tempted to fertilize newly planted trees or shrubs right away—and unscrupulous fertilizer sellers will egg them on. But fertilizing stresses new plantings severely, because the plants will produce too much stem and foliage growth without the root system to support that growth. Instead, wait several months after planting before applying fertilizer. If everyone knew this, fertilizer company stocks might sink a bit, but plants would be thankful.

Save money on plant-food refills. Those liquid plant-food sprayers that attach to the end of a hose are super-convenient, but they come with a hidden cost. When the bottle of plant food is empty, the manufacturer is betting you'll buy another bottle as a refill … and another … and another, thus padding the company's bottom line. Manufacturers promise a miracle with their liquids, but just because Brand X came in the bottle doesn't mean you can't refill it with the less expensive Brand Y or your favorite recipe for homemade liquid fertilizer. These bottles often carry a warning label that says something like, "Empty bottles cannot be reused." That's because there's an insert in the neck of the bottle specially designed to make a snug fit with the sprayer end. But here's the trick: In most cases it's easy to gently pop out this insert with a screwdriver or a pair of pliers. Now refill the bottle, tap the insert back into place, and hook up the sprayer. If you're careful, you can reuse the same bottle many times.

Here's a good recipe for homemade liquid plant food: Mix 1 tablespoon Epsom salts, 1 teaspoon baking soda, and 1/4 teaspoon ammonia, then add this to 1/2 gallon (2 liters) warm water. Dilute this mix with another gallon (3.7 liters) of water, and spray your plants with this brew once a month. It's also good for houseplants.

Leave branches in place to root out stumps. Digging out the stumps of big shrubs and trees is nasty work, and you might be tempted to dig out the checkbook instead and pay a landscaping company to do the dirty work for you. But if you know one of these pros' favorite secrets, you can leave some green stuff in your wallet. When you have to remove a shrub or tree that has sturdy branches, don't cut it all the way to the ground before digging out the stump. Instead, remove most of the trunk and branches, but leave two or three stout limbs attached to the stump, spaced around the circumference. Now, when you start digging, you can use these branches as levers, giving you major mechanical advantage for working the stump and roots out of the ground.

Steer clear of trees with that "weed and feed." Your local home center might like you to believe that the "weed and feed" mix on sale this week will solve all your lawn problems, but it can cause new problems if you apply it carelessly. Many trees, shrubs, and ornamental plants can be stressed or even killed by such fertilizer, and weed-killer mixes applied to the lawn above their

How to Apply Herbicides Safely

Sometimes you have to use an herbicide to control a virulent weed. But one drop of herbicide on the wrong leaf could kill a plant you love. To reduce this risk as much as possible:

- Always consider every alternative to chemical weed controls before spraying. The best defense against weeds is a healthy garden and lawn, with mulch covering any bare ground or empty spaces.

- Before applying any herbicide, check local restrictions. For example, one popular herbicide ingredient, 2,4-D, has been banned in some localities.

- Spray first thing in the morning or in the evening, when it's cool and there is no wind. Some herbicides (those containing 2,4-D, 2,4-DP, and dicamba or MCPA, MCPP, and dicamba) will turn to vapor and move through the air as the day warms. It's safer to use these chemicals in the evening so the weeds will have more time to absorb them before the temperature rises.

- When you are mixing herbicides, remember that stronger is not necessarily better—it may just be adding cost and putting your other plants at more risk without increasing effectiveness.

- Adjust the nozzle to a medium to coarse spray, and keep the sprayer low to the ground to reduce drift of airborne chemicals.

- Use a 2-foot (60-cm) square of cardboard as a shield to protect your good plants.

- Always wear eye protection and gloves.

root zones. Certain plants are extremely sensitive to mixes that contain dicamba or phenoxy herbicides, including apple, box elder, catalpa, dogwood, forsythia, honey locust, lilac, Siberian elm, and sycamore. Keep the spreader well away from such trees, and treat specific weeds only as needed.

Be careful using weed barrier cloth. Landscaping fabric and other artificial weed barriers are effective options to herbicides—to a point—but they may also cause new problems and still fail to prevent weed growth in the long run. In many cases, it's a shortcut not worth taking, says professional gardener Susan McCausland from Boulder, Colorado. The best place to use barrier cloth is under gravel or rock borders, walkways, and other places where few or no plants are growing.

In garden beds, especially in wet climates, weed barriers may cause numerous problems: They can hold too much moisture, suffocating some plants. They can promote the growth of molds and fungi, and they may cause roots to grow shallower. Moreover, since most people mulch over weed barriers, they soon create a new layer of topsoil as the mulch decomposes, and the weeds that move into this fresh soil will be even harder to remove because their roots will intertwine with the barrier fabric. Even if you don't mulch over the fabric, organic material and seeds will eventually blow in, and weeds will take root.

Plastic barriers are the worst: They block oxygen and moisture from reaching the soil, and they become brittle and disintegrate, making them very difficult to remove. Fabric landscaping or agricultural sheeting is better, because it breathes. The best barriers are those that can be removed each season, so the soil can breathe, or that decompose into the soil, such as burlap or newspaper. Landscapers and garden shops will try to tempt you with this one-stop solution to weeds, but the real way to fight weeds, McCausland says, is to craft healthy soil with compost and mulch and to pull weeds regularly so problems don't get out of control.

Try these homemade hose guides. If you read gardening catalogs, you'd think you're not a good gardener unless you pay for fancy hose guides to keep the hose from wrecking your favorite plants or tipping over lawn furniture as you drag it around the lawn. But it's easy to make your own guides and install them anywhere a hose might snag. To start, buy the required number of 18-inch (46-cm) lengths of rebar. These are available precut at gardening centers. Drive these rods into the soil with a hammer or hand sledge. To prevent injuries, never leave the end of the rebar exposed; instead, cover the bar with one of these attractive choices:

- Paint a PVC pipe, 1 inch (2.5 cm) in diameter, an attractive color or pattern, and cut it just long enough to cover the rebar. The hose will spin the pipe as it rolls past.

- Cut bamboo or copper tubing to the appropriate lengths and use these as rollers.

- Find two ceramic pots that are about 4 inches (10 cm) tall and have a drainage hole in the bottom. Slide the two pots, the first facing down and the second facing up, over the rebar. The two stacked pots will create an hourglass-shaped roller. If the drainage hole is a little too small to fit over the rebar, widen the hole by twisting the rebar into the opening until it slides easily through. ◁

Pest Control

8 Special Tricks for Sending All Those Plant-Eating Critters Packing

Learn more before you spray. Beth Smerek, a bedding plant specialist at a Boulder, Colorado, nursery, advises that most insects are beneficial or neutral to your plants, and when beneficial insects (such as those that eat pests) are killed, a dependency on chemicals is created. Before killing everything that moves the minute you notice some holes in the leaves, bring an affected leaf or picture of the problem to a reputable garden center or an extension agent and find out what is wrong. Then you can choose the treatment that will attack that problem specifically. Smerek adds that it's safer to use chemical treatments on indoor plants, because the indoor environment is completely artificial and contained, and thus the chemicals won't affect creatures other than the target pests.

Kill slugs with beer or coffee. You can buy expensive and toxic slug repellents, but natural methods are cheaper and just as effective. Slugs, it turns out, have a fatal vice: They like beer too much. Fill an empty tuna or cat-food can with beer and bury it in your garden soil up to its rim. Overnight, slugs will move into the beer and drown. You can throw out the entire can in the morning and replace it with a fresh batch. Not a beer drinker? Slugs hate coffee—or at least caffeine—just as much as they like beer. Researchers have found that a solution of 1 percent to 2 percent caffeine will kill slugs. That's much more than the average cup of coffee contains, but coffee still might act as a deterrent. Spray foliage with the brew or sprinkle the grounds around your plants. (Many coffee shops give away grounds to gardeners for free.) If nothing else, coffee grounds make a good addition to the soil, especially for plants that like acidic soils.

Kill slugs with salt. If you're not squeamish, you can deal with slugs you spot in the garden by hand. Sprinkling salt on the critters will kill them, and you can throw them into the trash. Or you can put a board or two on the garden soil, and slugs and snails will take shelter in the damp shade beneath them. Pick up the boards and scrape the creatures into the trash. To make your garden less inviting to slugs and snails, always water it in the morning. If the soil is dry at night, the critters will be less active.

Use newspapers to control earwigs. Frustrate the insecticide salesmen with this no-poison, low-tech solution to earwig control. In the evening, roll up sheets of wet newspaper and lay them around the garden. At sunrise, earwigs will crawl inside the wet pages to take shelter. Collect the papers before they dry out, bugs and all. Don't throw the newspapers into your trash cans, or the earwigs will soon escape and make their way back to the garden. Either burn the papers and bugs, shake the earwigs into a toilet or sink and flush them down the drain, or tie up the papers and bugs tightly inside a plastic bag—with absolutely no openings—and put them in the garbage can.

Don't rely on marigolds to keep pests away. Those cheerful yellow and orange flowers are often sold to gardeners with the promise that they'll deter pests from attacking vegetables, but marigolds' effectiveness against pests is limited. They only work well as a defense against nematodes in the soil, says veteran gardener Beth Smerek. Still, the blossoms are pretty in the garden, so go ahead and plant them. They can't hurt!

Repel aphids with a citrus-rind spray. Soap solutions are usually the recommended method for dealing with aphids. But the makers of insecticidal soaps don't tell you that some of them may harm your plants as much as, or more than, the little bugs. Here's an approach to try before you spray. Ironically, even though aphids love citrus trees, they don't like ground-up citrus rind. Grate the rind of one lemon or orange and combine it with 1 pint (500 ml) boiling water. Let it steep overnight, then strain through a coffee filter to remove the bits of rind. Add the mixture to a spray bottle, and spray the aphids on the leaves of the plants. Make sure to spray underneath the leaves, where many aphids gather. Reapply every four to seven days as long as the aphid problem persists.

Make your own insecticidal soap spray. If citrus spray doesn't work and you need to turn to soap to get rid of aphids, there's no need to buy a commercial product. Add 2 teaspoons liquid dishwashing detergent to 1 pint (500 ml) water to create an insecticidal soap solution. Now, whether you make it at home or buy it at the store, always test the solution on a few leaves before applying it broadly. Spray a few leaves on each species of plant you'll be treating, then wait a day to see if the leaves curl or spot. If not, you can treat the entire affected area. As with the citrus solution, you'll need to spray every four to seven days.

How I Do It An Expert Gardener's Favorite Organic Pest Controls

Although she runs a major garden center, Connie Smith is not a fan of toxic chemical controls for garden pests. The vast majority of pest problems can be corrected with inexpensive organic solutions, Smith says. Here are her four favorites:

☐ *Soap spray.* Great for aphids, mites, and other soft-bodied insects. Choose a commercial variety or brew your own: 2 teaspoons dishwashing liquid, a few drops of vegetable oil, and 1 gallon (3.7 liters) water. Do not use soap sprays in drought or hot weather, or you may damage leaves, and always test them first on a few leaves.

☐ *Horticultural oil sprays.* These smother eggs and developing pests. Use light oils year-round, except in temperatures over 85°F (29°C). Use dormant oils before plants leaf out.

☐ *Sulfur or lime sulfur spray.* Use to control fungus such as powdery mildew and various blights. It's especially effective on fruit trees, berry bushes, and roses. In general, this spray should be applied during the dormant months or very early in the growing season, as buds begin to swell. Do not apply in temperatures over 90°F (32°C), and never use within two weeks of applying horticultural oil.

☐ *Bt (Bacillus thuringiensis).* This is bacteria, usually sold in a spray, that is used as a last organic resort to control caterpillars and some moth larvae. A different form is used to kill mosquito larvae.

Smith says the first three sprays will solve 80 percent of common garden pest problems, with no harmful residues or other long-term issues.

Get rid of grubs and Japanese beetles for good. If you have a problem with grubs eating your grass and plants, chances are you also have a problem with Japanese beetles, because the grubs are most likely the larvae of the beetles. You can solve both problems by just killing the grubs so that they don't develop into beetles. Although gardening outlets are quick to sell fast-acting toxic chemicals to kill the grubs (and a lot of other less harmful insects), there is a perfectly fine natural remedy that will get rid of them for years to come. Called milky spore, it causes the grubs to contract a disease that kills them. Other beneficial organisms are not harmed. The only problem is that you have to be patient. Milky spore is slow acting—after you spread the granules on your lawn, it can take a year or more for the spore to become established in your soil. But once the spore is established, it keeps working for a decade or more. There are reports of a single treatment lasting 40 years. Milky spore is not cheap; a single can of the granules runs about $40, but considering the length of the benefit, it's a real bargain. ◄

Animal Pests

5 Strategies for Making Destructive Four-Legged Visitors Unwelcome in Your Yard

Stink that groundhog out with cat litter. A groundhog (woodchuck) has taken up residence in a burrow that's conveniently next to your backyard garden. The pest control company wants a couple hundred dollars to remove him. Even if the cost doesn't give you pause, then the traps or poisons that some of them use will—particularly if you have kids or pets. What the pest control company won't tell you is that it's easy to stink a groundhog out of his home—for zero cost. Each day when you scoop out the cat boxes in your house, dump that foul-smelling debris down Mr. Groundhog's hole instead of throwing it into the trash can. After a few days of this treatment, the groundhog will pack up and move. Once he's gone, pour rocks into all of the entrances to the burrow so no other animals will decide to move in.

Protect your garden from deer with eggs. A family of deer can wreak havoc on your yard.

They breakfast in vegetable gardens and munch ornamentals and fruit trees at night while you sleep. What to do? Put the shotguns away. Save your money by saying no to high-tech gadgets like strobe lights and noisemakers, expensive repellents, and tall, ugly fences. For a fence to be effective, it must be a full 8 feet (2.4 meters) high—11 inches (28 cm) taller than Shaquille O'Neal. Instead, arm yourself with eggs. Deer hate the taste and smell of raw eggs, which is why many popular commercial repellents feature stinky egg solids as the main ingredient. Here's what you do: Crack half a dozen eggs into 2 quarts (2 liters) water. Mix well, until all the yolks are broken and blended with the water. Sprinkle the raw-egg mixture on the leaves of the plants you want to protect. The mixture should remain effective until the next rain. Reapply after that.

There are other odors that deer don't like: Try hanging cheesecloth bags of stinky socks, deodorant soap, or human hair in the garden. (You can get hair at a salon or barbershop.) The smell may make wary deer steer clear of your garden.

Choose plants to keep deer away. Deer also don't like to brush against certain aromatic plants. So try planting artemisia, lavender, and Russian sage as a natural fence line. Or, if you can't get the deer to stop eating the plants they like, consider replanting with plants that deer dislike. These include such popular plants as begonias, cosmos, daffodils, foxgloves, irises, marigolds, peonies, snapdragons, and zinnias, along with shrubs and trees such as boxwood, holly, juniper, lilac, pine, and spruce.

Fence rabbits out of your veggie patch. Numerous sprays and powders are sold to deter rabbits from the garden, but many of these are not safe for use on garden vegetables. A rabbit-proof fence is the best protection for your vegetable garden. Use chicken wire, and make sure the fence's bottom is buried by at least 6 to 12 inches (15 to 30 cm), otherwise the rabbits will tunnel underneath it. The fence needs to extend at least 30 inches (76 cm) above the ground.

Try other rabbit deterrents. Because a fence is an unattractive addition to many gardens, you may want to try a few low-impact deterrents against voracious bunnies:

- Remove brush piles and other hiding places for rabbits. Clean up spilled birdseed from feeders.
- Post realistic-looking rubber models of snakes or owls in the garden, or cut an old hose into snakelike lengths and coil them among your plants.
- Hang dog hair in cheesecloth bags or distribute it among the plants to frighten away rabbits. Strong-smelling soaps are also said to deter rabbits.
- You can buy coyote or fox urine to spread among plants, fooling rabbits into thinking a predator is nearby.

Remember, rabbits are not dumb bunnies. Eventually they will figure out they're safe from each of these deterrents, so you'll have to mix up your methods to keep them on their toes. ◁

Gardening Tools
7 Easy Ways to Get a Handle On the Tools That You Use to Care for Your Garden

Spritz your tools to repel dirt. The secret weapon against messy tools is the cooking oil spray you keep in the kitchen cabinet. Spray a coat on a shovel or trowel before using it, and clay soil will slide right off. Spray the blades and underside of your lawn mower, and wet grass won't stick to them. Another trick for clean tools? Keep a bucket of sand in the garage or shed, and plunge a spade or hoe into the sand before putting it away. The sand will scrape off any dirt or other mess that has stuck to the blades.

No need for fancy kneepads. Here's a low-cost alternative for gardening kneepads: Use a scrap from an old closed-cell foam camping mat. This will protect your knees just as well as the fancy models in gardening catalogs. It's tough, shock absorbing, and easy to clean with soap and water. If you or your kids don't have an old pad to cut up, check with your local Boy Scout troop or a university outdoor program. The pads get torn and are often replaced. Your garden shop manager will be on his knees begging you for business when he hears about this.

Make tools easy to spot. Don't lose your tools among your flower beds, shrubs, and grass. Exposure to the weather could harm them, and they could pose a danger to passers-by as well. To keep your hand tools from disappearing, paint the handles bright red or orange, making them more visible, a trick dating back to at least the 19th century. A couple of wraps of bright electrical tape will serve the same purpose. Either way, you won't be ringing the cash registers down at the garden center as soon as you might otherwise.

Make a simple tool stand between garage studs. Before investing in a high-priced rack for your garden tools in a shed or garage, look at the walls: If the walls are framed with exposed 2 x 4 (38 x 89 cm) studs, anyone can build a stand for garden tools in a matter of minutes. All you need is some 1 x 4 (19 x 38 cm) pine, some scraps of old 2 x 4, and some nails.

- For long-handled tools—such as shovels and rakes—cut a length of 1 x 4 so that it spans a couple of studs and nail it into place about 36 inches (90 cm) above the floor.
- For shorter-handled tools—an axe, for instance—nail another length of 1 x 4 between two studs about 24 inches (60 cm) above the floor.

- For both sets of tools, nail another 1 x 4 across the bottom of the studs to form a foot piece that will keep the lower end of your tools from sliding out.
- Finally, to help keep the tools upright, cut short blocks of 2 x 4 as spacers and nail them between the 1 x 4s and the garage wall at both the top and bottom. Two blocks in each cavity between studs usually works fine.

Voilà! Slide your hoe or rake behind the 1 x 4s, handle first, and it will be held in place for quick access.

Give trimmings a saucer ride. How do you move weeds, pruned branches, rocks, and the like from your garden? Hoity-toity gardening catalogs would have you believe you need to spend a small fortune on a pushcart. But, in

---

WHAT **LEAF BLOWER MAKERS** DON'T WANT YOU TO KNOW ABOUT Rakes

Your local home center is always eager to sell you the latest "laborsaving" device for lawn and garden maintenance. But few inventions in human history are as useless and obnoxious as the leaf blower. These contraptions are absurd wasters of energy and are so loud they have been banned by many municipalities. They stir up dirt and dust, and can throw rocks at cars and people. Although electric-powered blowers are marginally less disturbing than gas-powered ones, both kinds suffer from one overwhelming negative: They don't work as well as the humble rake, which is more precise, more tenacious, offers exercise to the user, and won't tee off the neighbors by accidentally blowing leaves, grass, and dust onto their lawns.

Next time a salesperson thrusts a leaf blower at you at a garden center, stand proudly and say, "No, thanks. I'm a raker all the way!"

Give Your Lawn Mower a **Tune-Up**

When the lawn mower starts running a bit rough, don't run to a repair shop and pay an exorbitant minimum charge and steep hourly rates. Maybe all you need is a single new spark plug. Even the least handy homeowner can keep his lawn mower in tip-top shape with this simple annual tune-up. Each mower is a little different, and you should consult your owner's manual for the specifics of your machine. But these basics apply to every mower.

☐ Before you work on a lawn mower, always remove the wire going to the spark plug so that there is no way that you can accidentally start the mower.

☐ Clean the underside of the mower thoroughly, scraping off dried-up grass clippings with a putty knife. Unplug any air vents and channels.

☐ Unscrew the spark plug with a deep-socket wrench that fits the hexagonal nut. Install a new plug of the exact same type, being careful not to cross-thread it (setting it in askew, so the threads get damaged as you turn it). Tighten gently.

☐ Unscrew the engine cover and vacuum up any dirt and grass clippings.

☐ Unscrew the oil dipstick and carefully tip the mower onto its side, allowing the dirty oil to drain into a pan, such as an old pie tin. (Some mowers have an oil drain plug that can be removed with a wrench, so the oil can be drained without tilting the mower.) Check the owner's manual for the correct oil type, and pour in new oil until the dipstick reads "full." Clean up any spilled oil with a rag.

☐ Unscrew the air-filter cover, remove the filter, and discard it. Clean the filter area thoroughly with a rag and an old toothbrush. New paper air filters are simply reinserted with the pleated side facing out. Foam filters should be soaked in clean, new motor oil; squeeze out the extra oil onto a rag, then insert the foam filter into the proper position. Replace the cover.

Before storing a mower for the winter

Run it until the gas tank is empty. Disconnect the gas line and, if possible, lift off or unscrew the gas tank and clean it by putting half a cup of fresh gas inside and swishing it vigorously. Do not store gasoline in any container over the winter; always use fresh gas in the spring.

Parts for popular mowers are available at hardware and yard-supplies shops. And you won't pay a repair shop's markup to get them.

addition to their expense, carts and wheelbarrows are heavy and unwieldy, especially on hills. They're often overkill for everyday tasks. The solution? A flying saucer sled. Attach a rope to a handle of one of these round, steel or plastic sleds, and you'll have a sturdy sledge that pulls easily across grass and paths. If you have kids, come winter, this is one garden tool that will still find plenty of use!

Put old golf gear to work in the garden. You can buy all sorts of carts and racks to wheel around the garden with your rakes and trowels. But you can skip right past that page of the gardening catalog if you have an old golf bag on wheels. Long tools fit neatly in the main compartment, and hand tools can be clipped to the outside. The pockets hold seeds, shears, and other smaller items. And if you discover any tees inside one of those pockets, they can be put to use too. Wooden or plastic tees make great color-coded markers for newly seeded gardens.

You can't move the holes off a golf course, but you can borrow the idea for use at home. Take a 10-inch (25-cm) length of PVC pipe that's 1 1/2 inches (38 mm) in diameter and bury it so it stands vertically in the ground at the edge of your vegetable plot. Now you have a caddy to hold your rake, hoe, or shovel at the ready: Just turn the tool upside down and slide its handle into the pipe. Strategically locate these tool caddies around your yard and garden.

Coil a hose without mechanical assistance. You can buy all sorts of hose reels and carts—some of them are so elaborate they look like machines the fire department ought to be operating. If you handle your hose right, you can coil it easily without the fancy gizmos. A hose with longitudinal stripes helps you coil the hose without twists—just keep the stripes running straight as you coil and uncoil. Unkink a hose by pulling one end across the lawn; the weight of the hose will help pull out those twists, and you can judge by the stripes when it's straight. Leave a balky hose in the sun for an hour, and it will be much more pliable and easy to coil.

Inexpensive wall hangers—decorative or plain—make fine places to coil a hose. But if you want to recycle something from home, try these alternatives:

- Cut down an old plastic trash can until you have a tub about 18 inches (46 cm) deep. Punch drainage holes in the base, and coil the hose inside.

- Spin the hose around an old automobile wheel lying flat on the ground. You can dress up the wheel with a coat or two of green or white metal paint to look good in the garden.

- Turn a large old terra-cotta pot upside down and wrap the hose around it.

- To store a hose in winter, drive a stout nail into the wall or a stud in a garage or shed, hang one side of an old bicycle inner tube over the nail, loop the other end through a coiled hose, then pull that end up to hang it over the nail.

Before storing a hose for any length of time, screw the two ends together so that bugs can't nest inside. ◂

WHO'D-A-THUNK-IT
gardening
Aids

Who says you can only use proper tools in the garden? These common household and workshop objects, including a couple of items normally considered candidates for the trash bin, can be put to work as gardening aids in surprising ways.

Kitchen tongs

Take a pair of kitchen tongs outside with you when it's time to trim back any prickly vines, limbs, or rosebushes. The tongs will allow you to hold or bend the branch painlessly while you snip with the other hand.

Sandpaper

Keep a sheet of fine sandpaper or emery cloth handy in your toolshed. When rust appears on your pruning saw blade or some other metal tool, rub it away with a light sanding. Follow up with a light coating of oil—for instance, from a rag carrying a touch of motor oil or olive oil.

Old hose

A length of old garden hose will help you keep tool edges sharp and prevent accidental cuts. Use heavy shears or a utility knife to cut the old hose to the length of the tool edge (on a saw or shovel, for instance). Then slit the hose lengthwise down one side to make an opening for your tool edge. Slide the edge of the tool into the hose, and secure it with twine or a bungee cord.

Ice pick

Speaking of old hose, if a garden hose that's still in use has sprung pinpoint leaks, go to your toolbox and pull out the ice pick. Heat the point of the ice pick over a candle flame until the tip glows, then touch it carefully to the leaky spot on your hose, letting the surface melt and seal.

Carpenter's belt

Adapt your carpenter's belt to the great outdoors. When you're able to carry all of your little gardening implements around your waist—twine, hand tools, measuring tape, and such—you'll save yourself a score of trips to the shed during one day's work.

Soap bar

Before you dig your hands into that soil, scrape your fingernails across a bar of hand soap. The soap that collects under your nails will create a dirt barrier, preventing that embedded, impossible-to-clean rim of dirt underneath. When you wash your hands, the soap barrier will dissolve.

Coffee grounds

Once your coffee grounds have "done their job" inside the house, put them to work outside too. Sprinkle them in your garden, where they will decompose and add nutrients to the soil.

Paper cups

If your seedlings are vanishing from the flower bed overnight, you need a shield to protect them from pests such as cutworms and slugs. Cut the bottom off a paper cup and place the cup over your seedling to keep the hungry critters at bay.

Clothesline

To make a more comfortable grip on your trowel or another garden tool, wrap the handle tightly in cotton clothesline, then cover the clothesline with several wraps of duct tape. Long-term, the bulkier, softer grip will be easier on your hands.

Buying Clothes

11 Strategies for Finding Flattering Garments at a Reasonable Price

Buy next year's attire now. To save loads of money on your clothing purchases, go shopping toward the end of the selling season. For instance, buy your spring and summer duds in July or August rather than in March, when prices are highest. This will mean some planning and forethought—you're going to get most of the wear out of these new clothes *next* summer. But the payoff is enormous.

So when exactly are the selling seasons for clothing? Michael Laimo of Mercury Beach-Maid, a New York City sportswear wholesaler, says that there are two major selling seasons that apply both to men's and women's clothing:

- Spring/summer: March through the end of August.
- Fall/winter: August through February.

However, women's clothing also has "transitional seasons," which are influenced by weather:

- Summer into fall: August through October (dark clothing with short sleeves).
- Winter into spring: March through April (long sleeves and bright colors).

Invest in one great garment. From those slick magazine ads, you might get the idea that you have to spend a mortgage payment on a single outfit if you want to look stylish. Not so, says Los Angeles clothing designer Bobette Stott. Here's the key to controlling your clothing costs: Buy one key piece of high-quality clothing that you will dry clean and fuss over. This garment should last you for years. For a man this item could be a jacket, a good sweater, or a sport coat. For a woman, it could be a great blouse, a jacket or a nice cardigan sweater. Mix and match your high-quality garment with inexpensive, washable clothing that you replace every couple of seasons. With this approach, you will be investing only in one exquisite, showcase piece of clothing—but it will lend its class and style to anything else you wear.

Avoid "one size fits all" clothing. The idea of "one size fits all" clothing sure sounds attractive: You can't go wrong, right? Buy it, and you know it will fit!

Actually, most manufacturers who label their clothing this way are pulling the wool over your eyes. You will usually find this designation on lower-priced clothing, mostly on tops for teenagers. Here's what manufacturers are up to: It's easier—and therefore cheaper—to mass-produce and inventory a garment when it's all in one size. But the only garments that are truly "one size fits all" are some socks, which are made of fabric that's stretchy enough to adapt to a broad range of foot sizes. Otherwise, when you see "one size fits all" on a garment, keep shopping. Look for higher-quality clothing that will last a long time.

Buy online to get deep designer discounts. The clothing market is swamped with garments that vendors need to unload. This is good news for you, because it means you can buy almost any designer clothing online at a big discount. When you shop at a

brick-and-mortar retailer, you are footing the bill for the store's rent, employees' salaries, cushy carpet, and fancy display racks. Online vendors are no-nonsense, product-shipping businesses that do not have all of the overhead and decorative trimmings.

So here's how to get exactly the designer clothing that you want at a fraction of the price: Go to your local department store or boutique. Try on the duds that you like, write down the designer's name, a description of the garment, and the size, then go home. Fire up the computer and conduct an online search for the designer. If the garment you are looking for has been in the stores for just two or three months, you will be able to buy it online for 50 to 75 percent off the retail price.

SECRET WEAPON

RN Number

Garment manufacturers often ship their trendy new styles straight to discount stores at the very same time that they ship them to high-priced department stores, says Stott. The trick is that the manufacturer may package and label the clothing differently for the two stores. How can you tell if the discount-store item is the same, or a cheap knockoff?

Here's the secret: Every piece of clothing is tagged with a code that identifies the garment's manufacturer, no matter what the packaging says. You will see the letters "RN" followed by several numbers on the tag. So jot down the RN number of the garment you like at the department store and see if it matches the number of the garment in the discount store. If the numbers are the same, the manufacturer is the same.

Use these strategies and your clothes will always be on sale. Many of us are programmed to take store pricing at face value. If you see a pair of trousers on the rack priced at $48, well, that's what it's going to cost you to take them home, right? No. The truth is that clothing stores are so desperate to move their merchandise these days that you can take home just about any garment at a discount—if you know how to go about it. Here's how to take advantage of a clothing store's flexible policies:

- Take a full-priced garment to the checkout counter and ask them to hold it for you until it goes on sale. Many stores will accommodate you, and you will be assured that they won't sell out of your size.

- Go ahead and buy the item you want at full price, but keep the receipt in an envelope in your car. Two weeks later, drop into the store with your receipt in hand. If your garment has gone on sale in the meantime, go to the register and ask for credit.

- Make friends with one of the salespeople at your favorite clothing store. This clerk will be able to alert you to upcoming sales, and will keep an eye out for the kind of clothing you like. Selling clothing has become difficult enough that he or she will work like the dickens to get you to buy merchandise.

- If you're making a big purchase at a department store, go ahead and get the extra discount they offer for

WHAT CLOTHING RETAILERS DON'T WANT YOU TO KNOW ABOUT Pricing

You know the shopper's mantra, "Never pay retail," right? In case you've ever doubted this bit of wisdom, here's an inside glimpse of how retail pricing works for clothing.

It's impossible to know precisely what a particular retailer paid for the garments on display, but the pricing process works like this: Say a shirt comes in with a suggested retail price of $60, preprinted on the hang tag. Early in the selling season, the retailer will put that shirt on display for that price. Out of all of the people who end up buying

that shirt, only 10 to 20 percent of the buyers will pay this original price.

Once you factor in sales and coupons, the price of the shirt starts creeping lower and lower. By the end of the selling season, that shirt is marked down to about $20, which is about what the retailer paid for it. But don't feel bad for the retailer—the store's bean counters have their eye on the *average* selling price of the shirt through its entire sales cycle. The retailer is happy if that average hits twice the wholesale price.

So the next time you consider buying clothing that's not on sale, ask yourself: Isn't it worth waiting a month or two if I can get this garment at a 60 or 70 percent discount?

accepting a store credit card. The card will qualify you for future discounts too. But be sure to pay the balance off immediately so you don't have to pay finance charges; store credit cards often have exorbitant interest rates.

Buy classic jeans. When you buy a pair of jeans, put on a pair of blinders so you won't be distracted by all of those trendy styles that involve fading, weird cuts, peculiar colors, and even intentional rips. Manufacturers love it when you fork over cash for this trendy clothing because such jeans go out of style in a heartbeat—and then you have to buy a new pair in whatever the new style is. Instead, buy classic five-pocket blue denim jeans. These will last you for years, and even when they do fade, you won't mind, because they will look totally natural.

Check the nap. Your suit looks funny, but you just can't put your finger on why. Not all manufacturers pay attention to the direction of the nap of fabric—the way the fibers lie—particularly garment makers in developing countries. When you're buying a suit, says Ingrid Johnson, a professor of textiles at the Fashion Institute of Technology in New York City, here's an easy way to test whether the fabric was cut running the same way in both pieces: Run your hand across the fabric in the suit jacket and then in the same direction across the skirt or pants. For instance, you might stroke from top to bottom on a sleeve of the suit jacket and then top to bottom on the skirt. The fabric may feel rough or it may feel smooth—either is okay. But you want to be sure it feels *consistent* on each

piece of the suit. If it doesn't, find another suit.

Color-test duds before buying. When you buy a garment in a store, conduct two quick checks to make sure the coloring in the fabric is high quality: Slip on a pair of sunglasses (the brown-tinted variety work best) to make sure the colors in the clothing still match. Then walk the garment over to a window and check that the colors match in daylight too.

Why bother? Though shoppers rarely hear about it, manufacturers spend a lot of time fretting over a quality issue called metamerism, says Johnson. You see, good manufacturers and retailers make sure that colors of a garment match in all light sources. Here's the problem: A garment may have a few different materials all in the same color—say, a jacket exterior, the cuffs, and the piping. Those different pieces need to all match whether the light source is incandescent, fluorescent, or natural light. If you buy a garment and it doesn't pass this test, you have a right to return it.

Be especially careful when you buy clothing in an off-price outlet. That "bargain" garment could be marked down because it has a serious color problem.

Slip into something old. Open up the yellow pages and jot down the addresses of vintage clothing stores in your area. If you care about the way you dress, it pays to prowl such stores regularly, says Birgit Mueller, an Emmy Award-winning television costume designer. First of all, clothing from the 1950s and 1960s is usually better quality than

5

QUICK FIXES FOR

wardrobe malfunctions

1 Tape up unruly clothing. Slip a few strips of double-stick tape into your purse for use in emergencies. Originally devised for keeping toupees in place, a bit of tape with adhesive on both sides will get you out of any number of dilemmas, says television costume designer Birgit Mueller. If your cleavage is hanging out of your blouse, a couple of strips of double-stick tape will keep your exposure to a minimum. If a button pops off or a hem falls apart, this stuff will secure your clothing until you can have it mended. And if you have to wear a new pair of pants but you haven't had time to hem the cuff yet, two-sided tape will rescue you once again.

You can buy double-stick tape at beauty-supply stores, drugstores, costume houses, wig shops, or in the lingerie sections at department stores. A pack of 50 one-by-three-inch (2.5 x 7.5 cm) strips sells for about $5.

2 Steam that shine away. You've just ironed your dark trousers, and now there are embarrassing shiny spots on the fabric. Don't fret, says clothing designer Bobette Stott. These spots aren't unusual, especially if your garment is made of a wool blend. Here's her cure: Mix 1 ounce (2 tablespoons) distilled white vinegar with 5 ounces (145 ml) water. Dip a clean cloth into the mixture and blot it onto the shiny spots. Then fire up your steam iron and pass it a few inches above the fabric. The steam will help the vinegar break up the shine. Hang the garment to dry, and it's ready to wear.

3 Race against the spot. The more quickly you treat a stain, the better your chances are of removing it. If at all possible, take the garment off immediately and blot at the stain with a paper towel or a clean cloth and try to remove as much of the stain as you can. Then either squirt laundry pretreatment onto the spot and wash it, or take it straight to a dry cleaner.

Remember that heat, like time, is working against you in this race. Never put a stained garment in the dryer, and never store it in a warm area.

4 Blot, don't rub, a stain. Have you ever seen a restaurant patron take a napkin and rub furiously at a stain on her blouse? Big mistake. Rubbing at a stain will only damage the fabric. Instead, moisten the napkin with water and blot at the stain to draw it off. Many people swear by using club soda this way, and the bubbling does provide a little assistance in releasing some new stains.

5 Staple that patch. The quandary is an old one: You start out sewing a patch onto a uniform thinking you have it perfectly situated. But by the time you've stitched its entire perimeter, the patch has somehow contrived to wriggle a few degrees out of kilter. So to keep your patch on an even keel, just staple it to the shirt where you want it, then sew the edges down. When you're done, use a staple remover to straighten the prongs of the staple and pull it out of the fabric.

modern garments. Such classic clothing keeps coming back into style, too, so it's a good investment. You'll be guaranteed a unique outfit—there's zero chance that you'll run into someone else at a party wearing the same dress. Also, vintage clothing is a particular boon for petite people, since clothing was sized much smaller then than it is today.

Shop to hide your bulge. Want to disguise that "spare tire" building up around your midsection? These wardrobe tricks will help:

- Don't wear corduroy, velvet, or any other material with a nap (raised fibers). This adds bulk to your shape and makes you look wider.
- Avoid satin or any other shiny material, which will accentuate bulges.
- No plaids.
- Wear loose, dark fabrics that hang well—preferably silk or high-quality rayon.

Buy wrinkle-free, satin-weave cotton. Nobody wants to go to work in a dress shirt that looks like you've slept in it. Textile expert Ingrid Johnson says that there's actually a special kind of cotton that resists wrinkles—but chances are that a store clerk will have no idea how to identify such a garment for you. Satin-weave cotton, which is more common in women's clothing than men's, feels smooth under your fingertips. But to be sure you're getting satin weave, here's a quick and simple test, says Johnson: Grab a handful of the cotton fabric, squeeze, then let go. Does the fabric hold those wrinkles? If so, that's conventional cotton. Does the fabric spring back relatively wrinkle-free? If so, you've found satin-weave cotton. ◁

Cleaning Clothes
6 Ways to Keep Your Garments Looking Good Longer

Don't clean your clothes out of habit. Many people believe that you should wash a garment every time you wear it. But that's a waste of effort and detergent. When you get home from work, change into your T-shirt and jeans, then evaluate your work duds before you toss them into the hamper. If your clothing passes this five-point check, you can put it on a hanger, air it out for two hours, then return it to your closet:

- *Does it need repair?* Any rips, missing buttons, falling hems, or broken zippers?
- *Does it need a dry cleaner's care?* Tough stains, particularly oily ones, should be taken to the dry cleaner within a day. If you wait weeks, your odds of getting the stain out are reduced dramatically.
- *Does it need to be laundered?* If the garment shows any of the routine smudges and dirt that come out in the wash, drop it into the hamper.
- *Does it pass the sniff test?* Yes, steel yourself and sniff the armpit of that shirt.
- *Does your* body *need to be washed?* If the answer is yes, then chances are the clothes that were hanging on that body need to be washed too.

Lighten up on laundering and soap. Detergent companies don't want you to know this, but most of us are chronically overwashing our clothing. We're wasting time and money (and detergent!), and we're wearing out our clothes faster. In reality, most clothing only needs a touch of spiffing up. Do your regular wash using half the package-recommended amount of detergent, and set the washing machine at the lightest setting. When you have clothes that are truly filthy, use the full measure of detergent and a longer setting.

Ease up on the laundry extras. Household product manufacturers try to sell us all kinds of special washing aids, but clothes don't really need those dryer sheets and that fabric softener. The fabled "static cling" is not as horrible as the TV commercials will have you believe. If you do encounter garments that cling to each other because of static electricity, just dampen your hands and brush them across the material to kill the electrical charge. Towels will absorb water better if they are not doused in fabric softener; cleaning cloths work better without softener too.

Determine how clean your dry cleaner's facility really is. If your clothes come back from the dry cleaner with a funky odor, your first move should be to take off the plastic covering and hang them up in the open—preferably outside on the back porch. There are two possible reasons for this odor, says Brent Newbold, who owned a laundry for more than 20 years and is now chief financial officer for Holy Cow cleaning products:

1. The cleaner didn't dry all of the solvent out of your clothes. Not a big deal. It will evaporate now.

2. The impurities weren't filtered out of the dry-cleaning solvent, and you have dirt from someone else's clothes stinking up your garments. Yuck!

So let your clothes hang in the open for two hours, then give them the sniff test. If they're still stinky after a couple of hours, your problem is with impurities, not solvent. Go to another dry cleaner.

"Clothes should smell clean and fresh if the dry cleaner is running his plant correctly," Newbold says.

Preserve your heirloom gown correctly. The prom or your wedding is a warm memory, and now you want to preserve the gown you wore. Many dry cleaners will gladly charge you $150 to $500 for special protective packaging called "heirlooming." Typically, the gown is thoroughly cleaned and then sealed in plastic and arranged inside a nice, windowed box. But if this service is not done correctly, that precious gown could be ruined. Asking these two questions will help ensure that your gown will be properly protected:

How I Do It A Costume Designer's Stain-Removing Secrets

You don't get to be an Emmy Award-winning costume designer without learning to think quickly on your feet. Here are Birgit Mueller's in-a-pinch fixes for stained clothing:

- ☐ For an oil stain, sprinkle the spot with baby powder, let the powder absorb the oil, then brush the powder off.

- ☐ To clean up a dribble of solid food, makeup, or lipstick, wipe with a piece of velvet. Keep a handkerchief-size square of velvet in your purse for emergencies.

- ☐ Use a piece of white chalk to cover a stain on a white shirt.

- ☐ To remove an ink stain, spray the spot with hair spray, then launder.

- ☐ To remove a red wine stain, blot it with gin, then launder.

- ☐ To remove the odor of sweat from a shirt, mix 1 ounce (30 ml) vodka with 2 ounces (60 ml) water in a squirt bottle and spray it onto the armpits. "We used to use that trick on movie sites in the desert," Mueller says.

- Do you perform this service yourself or do you send it out? If your dry cleaner sends your gown out for servicing, that's actually a good sign. Some specialists in the business really know what they're doing. However, some dry cleaners buy heirlooming kits from suppliers so they can do the job on-site, and some of them may cut corners on preparing your gown.

- Will my gown be vacuum sealed? For long-term protection of the gown, all of the air must be removed from inside the packaging. Otherwise, the garment will turn yellow and deteriorate. If your dry cleaner is doing the work on-premises, ask whether he owns his own vacuum-packing equipment.

Dry-clean your suits less frequently. Your dry cleaner won't tell you this, but most people bring their suits in to be cleaned way too often. New York City fashion coach Susan Sommers often hears clients complain, "My suit looks like hell after only one season." When she asks how often they dry-clean their suits, the answer is inevitably, "Every two or three times I wear it." That cleaning schedule is just too frequent!

If your suit is just a little wrinkled, use a steamer on it to relax the fabric—or have the dry cleaner press it for you. If you get a spot on your suit, try removing it with a disposable fabric-cleaning wipe before you take it to the dry cleaner. Try to dry-clean your suit only once per season. ◁

How Good Is Your Dry Cleaner?

The quality of work varies drastically from one dry cleaner to another. So if you're considering taking your best clothing to an unfamiliar dry cleaner, what assurance do you have that your duds won't be ruined?

Laundry expert Brent Newbold suggests giving him a little audition. When you want to use a new dry cleaner, take him just three items to clean:

- ☐ A cotton shirt.
- ☐ A light-colored linen shirt or blouse.
- ☐ A light-colored silk garment.

These three offer just enough variety for you to evaluate a dry cleaner's work. When you get your clothing back, here's what to look for:

Color.
Did the garments come back their original color, or is there a dull tint to them? If the latter, then the dry cleaner is skimping by not cleaning his filters regularly. You see, a dry cleaner's chemical formula is used again and again. After it's used to remove the impurities from a load of clothing, the dry cleaner runs the chemical through a carbon filter to remove those impurities before it's ready for the next load. When the dry cleaner tries to get too much mileage out of a filter, the impurities build up in the cleaning chemical and leave your clothes looking dull. This will be particularly evident in the light-colored clothing. Also, if your cleaner has too much moisture in his cleaning solvent, it will draw color out of silk garments and fade them.

Fabric feel.
Does the garment look and feel the way it did when you first bought it? If the dry cleaner has correctly added sizing to the garment, it will have a like-new body. Otherwise, it will feel limp—like an old rag. Because it requires more heat than any other fabric, linen is one of the most difficult for a cleaner to "finish" properly with pressing and sizing. A good cleaner also uses special products to keep your silk feeling soft and supple.

Pressing.
Is the pressing neatly done? Each garment should look perfect and ready to wear. A good dry cleaner hires experienced pressers who know a zillion tricks of the trade for giving every garment a clean and crisp look. Rookie employees—or employees with too big a workload—will do a sloppy job. The cotton shirt is a good test of pressing quality because it's a common item that many cleaners do not press well. If you want to throw an extra pressing challenge at the cleaner, turn in a pleated skirt or pleated pants along with the garments listed above. Pleats require extra time and effort, and the cleaner's staff should double-check afterward that the pressing was correctly done.

Buttons.
Are there broken or missing buttons? Good dry cleaners will bend over backward to replace missing or damaged buttons for free—even when the problem is not the cleaners' fault. They will retrieve a loose button from the button trap in their machinery, find a replacement in their in-house supply, or even trek to a garment shop or button supplier to find the right match. If all of those measures failed, Newbold used to offer to change an entire set of buttons on a garment to a new set for free. "A repeat customer is worth his weight in gold. You want people to say, 'Wow!' " he says.

Besides examining the garment, you should also consider the facility's turnaround time. A conscientious dry cleaner will have your clothes done within two hours if you're in a hurry. If you're told the wait is three days, go somewhere else.

Storing Garments

5 Guidelines for Wrinkle-Free Clothes and Orderly Closets

Strip off the plastic bags. Never store your clothing in the plastic bags that come from your dry cleaner. Clothing needs to breathe, and the moisture that gets trapped inside that dry cleaner bag can damage your garments. If you want protection for garments that you put in storage, go to a discount store and buy a breathable cotton garment bag.

Get out-of-season clothes out of your way. One problem with snatching up all of those department-store "bargains" is that your closet gets packed tighter than a tuna can. This is a problem, because your clothes need room to hang freely if you want them to come out of the closet fresh and wrinkle-free. There is one key maneuver for freeing up closet space:

- Find a place where you can hang spillover clothing from your closet. This might be in an empty guest-room closet, a hall closet, or a hanging bar in the laundry room. Every spring and fall, rotate the out-of-season clothing out of your bedroom closet and into your remote closet. Then bring the newly in-season clothing into your bedroom closet.
- If you are rotating your clothing out like this every six months and your clothes are still jam-packed in your everyday closet, rotate them into and out of remote storage four times a year instead of two. Keep only this season's clothing in your bedroom closet. Or keep only one month's worth of clothes in your closet. This

means some clothing hanging in remote storage will actually be in season. That's okay—it will be put in rotation next month.

- Review your everyday clothing needs. If you wear casual clothes five days a week, don't store your fine clothes (suits and sport coats, for instance) in your closet. Put them in the remote location with the out-of-season clothes.

Get rid of clothing you don't wear. As you are rotating your clothing, examine every item. If there's anything you haven't worn in a year—no matter how cute it is, no matter what fond memories it might evoke—get rid of it. You can't afford to have it cluttering up your home. Think hard about your lifestyle. If you are like most of us, you own much more clothing than any one human needs. Buy less and get rid of more. There's no need to open your wallet every time you encounter an incredible bargain.

Know the right ways to keep moths at bay. Unfortunately, the bug-repelling powers of cedar closets and chests are grossly overrated. Sure, a moth will run when it gets a strong whiff of cedar—but we bet you didn't know that that pungent cedar-y smell will peter out after a year or two. Reviving the scent requires sanding off the surface layer of the wood, and almost nobody bothers with that. "When you can no longer smell the cedar, the moths can't either," says textiles professor Johnson. By the same token, if a dry cleaner asks if you want to pay to mothproof garments that are going into storage, tell him, "No, thanks." Dry cleaners mothproof clothing by adding a liquid to the cleaning solvent they use, but the secret is that this treatment only lasts for a month or two.

The better way to store those wool and silk garments? Dry-clean them first, then slide them into mothproof garment bags, which are available for purchase from the dry cleaner, and at some discount stores.

Before storing a garment, clean it. Before you put a wedding dress or a prom dress into storage, dry-clean it. Even if the dress appears perfectly clean, you risk ruining the garment if it hasn't been dry-cleaned. You see, "invisible" stains—such as lemon-lime soda, white wine, even sweat—will turn into yellow or brown spots over time. Such spots, once they develop, are just about impossible to remove.There's another reason for making sure that any clothing is absolutely clean before you stash it away: Moths and carpet beetles are not only attracted to natural fibers such as wool and cotton, but they also salivate when you offer them clothing that is soiled, stained, or sweaty. ◁

10
SPACE-SAVING CLOTHING
storage
Tricks

Is the floor of your closet overrun with shoes? Are you strapped for belt storage? Are you up to your neck in loose scarves or extra ties? You are not alone—just about all of us have amassed so many clothes that we just don't have enough storage space for them. The ultimate solution, of course, is to take an honest look at your wardrobe and get rid of a lot of the items that you never wear. That—and learning to resist the temptation to buy that cute dress or sporty shirt that you don't need—will go a long way toward freeing up some clothing storage space. Still, there are very few among us who would not like to have more places to store our clothes. And manufacturers have been very adept at devising relatively inexpensive aids that will help you squeeze every conceivable bit of clothing storage space out of your homes. Try out these storage tricks, and you'll have that wild closet tamed in no time.

1 Closet them in canvas. When you consider construction costs, adding a closet to your home for a mere $70 is more than reasonable. Visit a storage-gear store in person or online and pick up a freestanding canvas closet, which you can set up in a spare room or basement. This will give your home an extra 3 feet (1 meter) of closet rod, plus storage for folded sweaters as well. The canvas will protect your stored clothes and let them breathe at the same time.

2 Sleep on it. If you'd like to find an extra 15 or 20 cubic feet (0.4 to 0.6 cubic meters) of extra clothing storage space, just take a look under your bed. Container manufacturers have devised a wide variety of clever gizmos for making maximum use of this space, including flat totes that will vacuum-pack bulky comforters, clear vinyl cases for shoes and accessories you want to peruse at a glance, and wide storage boxes with wheels, snap-on lids, or side drawer access.

3 Buy hard-working furniture. When you buy furniture, pick the kind that will perform more than one job—including storing clothing that you can't accommodate in your bedroom. Examples: A daybed with a hinge-up top and storage underneath, or a sofa with hidden drawers below the seat cushions.

4 Show them the door. Add shoe-bag-style organizers to the backs of closet doors and bedroom doors. The typical shoe bag has hooks that fit over the top of the door, draping a couple dozen pockets down the door surface. These are a splendid way of getting shoes off the floor of your closet, of course, but they also provide clever storage for rolled scarves, pantyhose, other accessories, and even kids' toys.

5 Get hooked. In the bathroom, install several hooks on the back of the door for hanging extra towels and robes.

6 Jacket? Rack it. Freestanding coat racks come in handsome designs, and they can turn a small bit of floor space into vertical clothing storage. Park one by the door, in the mudroom, or in the kids' bedrooms. With several hooks for jackets, scarves, and hats, coat racks go a long way toward freeing up space in crowded coat closets.

7 Send them packing. Pull out any suitcases that aren't in current use and fill them with the kind of clothing you don't need day-in and day-out. You'll gain some elbow room in your closet, and your luggage will take up no more space than it did before.

8 Spare the rod. To save closet-rod space, become a fan of the specialty hangers that are available at home stores, discount stores, and organizing stores. Such hangers take up very little rod space, but they can accommodate several skirts, a dozen neckties, a like number of scarves, or a score of belts, for instance.

9 Bin there, stored that. See-through, stacking bins are ideal for storing sweaters, other foldable clothing, and accessories such as handbags and shoes. When you stack such bins, they take up vertical space—but minimal floor space. Since they have transparent sides, you can quickly identify the items that you want. Drawer-type access makes this all the easier.

10 Hang 'em high. Install high shelves in your bedroom to accommodate hats, purses, or small storage bins. A shelf mounted 12 to 18 inches (30 to 46 cm) below the ceiling will be in no one's way, but it will provide a nice "relief valve" for an overstuffed bedroom closet.

Researching Purchases

6 Smart Strategies That'll Mean Less Hassle and Big Savings

Stay on top of fluctuating prices. Major retailers often make a big deal out of their 30-day price guarantees, proclaiming that if the price for a product, like a television or DVD player, drops within 30 days of your purchase, the store will refund the difference in price. But this is a calculated marketing decision. What these retailers don't mention is that they know that few shoppers watch the price *after* they've made their purchase. Not long ago, watching a price meant returning to the store. But thanks to the Internet, you can beat the major retailers at their own game by watching the price online. It should only take a couple of minutes a day. And if the price goes down because of a sale, you'll get some of your green back.

Ask salespeople if they work on commission. Salespeople are legally obligated to tell you the truth about this. And the truth, as they say, can set you free. It works two ways: If you're looking for an honest opinion about a computer or stereo—not just some spiel that will put quick dough in the salesman's pocket—do your research at a retailer whose employees do not work on commission. But sometimes that spiel can mean a deal, since salespeople working on commission usually have the flexibility to slash prices. If they work on commission, ask for a discount—just be wary of the advice that they're giving you.

Sniff out spiffs. Retailers often offer their salespeople "spiffs," or special

How I Do It A Kitchen and Bath Designer's Way of Checking Product Reliability

"When it comes to choosing a brand, it's bewildering," says Jodi Fitzpatrick, a kitchen and bath designer for Home Depot and an associate with the National Kitchen and Bath Association.

"My suggestion? Get the real dirt from a guy with the dirt under his nails: the repairman. Go to an independent, local appliance dealer. First, talk to the salespeople. Next, talk to one of the repairpeople. Then try to figure out who to believe on which brand. Once, when I was shopping for tankless water heaters for one of my clients, I checked with my local bath products distributor, who recommended a certain brand. Then I talked to my favorite plumber, who installs tankless water heaters. He also liked this brand, but he did not like a competing brand because he had had numerous calls about problems with them. Why talk to the installer? Because he or she knows the problems and performance of the product in real-life, local situations. Salespeople, even from a local independent dealer, may be pushing a particular product for a weird reason—like, if they sell 50, the company will send them to Hawaii."

incentives, to sell products that are not selling quickly enough. While commissions might already make salespeople biased toward the more expensive products, spiffs encourage them to sell an unpopular or brand-new (read: no customer feedback) product. If you've done your homework online or by talking to others, you'll figure out in a hurry which ones are being pushed.

You may have more warranty than you think. Salespeople have been known to downplay a manufacturer's warranty if they think they can sell you their own warranty. You're much better off with a warranty that comes from the company, not the store. Ask to see a copy of the manufacturer's warranty, and read over it carefully. You may find that it covers problems for quite a bit longer than the salesperson would have you believe. Refrigerator compressors, the most expensive replacement part on any fridge, often come with a manufacturer's warranty for up to five years.

Skip the extended warranties. Salespeople are good at making two- to five-year warranties sound worth the extra money, but some of these plans can cost you hundreds of dollars! Here's what they don't tell you: Proft margins on electronics are only about 10 percent. Extended warranties are one way that retailers and manufacturers pick up the slack. The repair rate for the first three years of ownership for camcorders, digital cameras, and standard televisions is less than 10 percent. That means 90 percent of the time, all the warranty money goes to the store or makers.

One extended warranty that you might actually go for is one for a laptop computer—laptops have a three-year repair rate of 33 percent. Consider a one- to three-year extension of the standard one-year warranty. Buy the extended warranty from the computer manufacturer, however—this will give you tech support too. Warranties from retailers tend to cover just the hardware, not the tech support.

Have your dealer do the installation. There's always a lot of finger-pointing when something goes wrong with a new appliance. Say the new dishwasher you just spent $500 on doesn't work. The appliance dealer might say it's the installer's fault, while the installer might say it's the retailer's responsibility. You can prevent this kind of hassle by having your retailer also do the installation—most do offer this service. When the same business is both selling and installing your appliances, it's pretty much on the hook for any problems that crop up. ◁

Appliance Care
4 Pro Secrets for Keeping Your Machinery in Tip-Top Shape

Lubricate your icemaker. Finicky automatic icemakers keep many an appliance repairperson in business. If your freezer's icemaker has ground to a halt, try this simple cure before you spend a bundle on a repair call: Remove the ice cube tray and dump out any ice. Buff the tray with a dishtowel until it's perfectly dry. Then give the inside of the tray a light squirt of cooking oil spray. A common reason that icemakers quit producing is that the tray clings to the new ice cubes and can't dump them out. The cooking spray will prevent this bond and will lend no taste whatsoever to your ice.

Unclog your dishwasher. Repairpeople get a good chuckle when you tell them that your dishwasher isn't cleaning as well as it used to. That's because homeowners have a good shot at fixing this problem themselves with this easy, three-minute procedure: Look at the top of the spray arms inside your dishwasher (there are usually two, one at the bottom and one under the upper rack). If mineral deposit or other debris is closing off the holes along the top of the spray arms, they won't clean anymore. Unfasten the clips or screws holding the spray arms in place and put the spray arms in your sink. Unbend a paper clip, insert the end of this stiff wire into each spray hole, and move it around to dislodge the blockage. Rinse the spray arms out under the faucet and return them to duty in your dishwasher. Your dishwasher will now work properly again!

Think *inside* the box. There's hope for cash-strapped appliance owners. Easier access to replacement parts means that if you can get to that broken dryer belt or busted dishwasher spring, you can save on repair bills. Instead of having to drive to the nearest appliance parts dealer, flip through dog-eared manuals and catalogs, and try the patience of a behind-the-counter type who's used to selling to trained technicians who don't ask so many questions, today you can turn to the Internet for parts and advice.

But there's one hitch. Appliance manufacturers have made machines tougher for do-it-yourselfers to get into. "I was out there servicing appliances in the 1970s and '80s," says Wanda Martens, former field technician and major appliance instructor at Dunwoody College of Technology in Minneapolis, Minnesota. "Access has gotten trickier, but appliances are easier to work on once you get in there. Replacing parts is usually a matter of removing a few screws or brackets. The manufacturers build them so that highly paid technicians can fix parts and get out of there."

Many repairs, of course, are too complicated (or potentially dangerous) for homeowners to attempt on their own. The DIY-er has to make that call. You can usually use the Internet to diagnose your problem, find repair manuals (sometimes manuals for similar models give you all you need to know about accessing a machine), and buy parts through mail order. A great place for appliance DIYers to start online is www.repairclinic.com.

Clear a clogged drain tube. It's one of the most common things that go wrong with a fridge. In a typical two-door unit with the freezer at the top, there is a drain tube running from the freezer compartment to an evaporation tray underneath the fridge. You'll find the drain hole on the floor of the freezer compartment, near the back. Its purpose is to drain the runoff that develops when your unit periodically melts its frost to keep itself, as advertised, frost-free. The problem is that algae spores often develop in the tube, blocking it. This causes water to back up on the floor of the freezer, usually forming ice. The solution is simple: Use a turkey baster to force fresh water through it to flush it out. You may have to turn off the fridge to let the ice melt first. The water will run into the tray under the fridge, so empty it. Then pour a teaspoon of ammonia or chlorine bleach into the tube to prevent a recurrence of the algae spores. See—you just saved the cost of a hefty repair bill! ◁

How to Ruin Your Appliances

Appliances eventually wear out. Certain parts simply fail with time. It's inevitable. But appliance abuse and neglect can speed up the breakdown rate of washers, dryers, refrigerators, ranges, and dishwashers, helping keep appliance repairmen busy. Here are some of the most common ways homeowners contribute to appliance demise, along with advice for avoiding these errors.

Washing machine

Repairman's tip:

Never wash anything with heavy metal fasteners.

Some washer parts are easy to replace, but a chipped or cracked inner tub can sound the death knell for your machine. The exposed metal will rust—and keep rusting—and the rust will spot your clothes and linens. The cost of the new tub plus labor to install it makes this repair prohibitively expensive.

Bonus tip: Overloading your washer may not ruin it, but it will create wear and tear on certain parts that glide and spin, making these parts fail prematurely and forcing you to call the repairman or fix it yourself. Be sure to always follow the manufacturer's suggestions for load size.

Clothes dryer

Repairman's tip:

Follow your dryer manual's instructions for proper venting. Replace plastic or vinyl exhaust hoses with rigid or flexible metal venting, making the pathway from the dryer to the outside vent as straight as possible. Clean the lint filter before or after each load. Clean the places in the dryer where lint collects—the back, around the mouth of the lint filter, around the door. Once a year, have a professional clean the interior of your machine.

When the typical 12-pound (5.5-kg) load of laundry comes out of the washer, it contains a half-gallon (2 liters) of water. The dryer's job, of course, is to remove the water. It heats the clothes, converting water to water vapor and forcing it out of the dryer (and the house) through the exhaust vent, along with lint. Dryers are designed to push this lint-laden wet air only so far—between about 40 and 90 feet (12 and 27 meters) when rigid metal pipe is used, but only half that when flexible tubing is used. Every elbow in the pipe (around a corner, up a wall) dramatically cuts down on the maximum distance. Some newer homes have exhaust pipe runs of up to 200 feet (60 meters), making it impossible to adequately vent. So what happens? Your dryer has to work harder to dry your clothes (leading to potential part burnout), moisture problems arise in your home, and lint builds up in the machine and vent pipe. This last consequence is the most serious, because lint is flammable. The U.S. Consumer Product Safety Commission estimates that dryers are the cause of 15,500 fires each year. Lint buildup is a major cause of dryer fires.

Glass-top electric range

Because ranges don't have many moving parts (no motors, no belts), they tend to last a good long while—with one major exception. Damage done to a glass top, which can cost $300 to $400 to replace, makes the repair not worth the money. The most obvious way to break the glass is to bang a heavy pot on it—an impact break. But did you know that improper heating can also crack the glass? Using concave-bottomed pans can trap heat and cause the glass to crack. Using over-sized pots and pans can do the same.

Repairman's tip:

Use flat-bottomed pots and pans and make sure they are not larger than each burner.

Refrigerator

By far the most expensive part on your refrigerator is the compressor, part of the sealed cooling system. The sealed system is often protected under a special five-year warranty, and it should last at least twice that long. But you've got to clean the dust that builds up on the refrigerator's condenser coils, usually located behind a grille on the bottom of the fridge. If not, the compressor will be forced to work harder, and it may eventually overheat. If it fails prematurely—but after the warranty is void—you'll likely have to replace the fridge, since a repair will be too costly.

Bonus tip: A full freezer is more efficient than an empty freezer, which has nothing to hold the cold. An efficient freez-er not only prolongs the life of the compressor—and the fridge itself—but also saves energy. Fill your empty freezer shelves with bag ice, frozen veggies, or even plastic milk jugs filled with water.

Repairman's tip:

Once a year (twice if you have furry pets), snap off the grille and clean the dust from the condens-er coils using a vacuum cleaner and a condenser coil cleaning brush (an under-$10 accessory)— a tapered bottle brush on a plunger-length handle. Gently brush the bottom surface and in between the coils, then vacuum. Repeat until the coils are dust-free. Do not poke at the coils with a vacuum cleaner's hard-plastic crevice tool. That could damage the coils.

Dishwasher

Thanks to rust, dishwashers, like clothes washers, can be ruined by one small nick in the vinyl-coated rack. Once the metal inside begins to rust, you can't stop it. The rust will stain your dishes until you replace either the rack or the machine. Replacing a dish rack can set you back one-quarter the price of a brand-new machine.

Repairman's tip:

Hand-wash skillets, colanders, and other kitchenware with sharp edges. Never force a pan into a too-small space.

Computer Care
6 Slick Tips for Saving Money and Fixing 'Em Yourself

Shave time off the computer repair guy's clock. Here's a little-known secret among techies: The first thing a computer repairperson does when he arrives onsite is to make sure your operating system is updated. If you're like most people, you use Microsoft Windows. You can (and should) update Windows yourself, before the $95-an-hour IT expert arrives. And if you're lucky, updating Windows might even solve the problem you called about. (If a plug-in, such as a digital camera, MP3 player, or printer isn't working, it could be because your drivers are out of date. A Windows update will take care of this.) Think how great you'll feel calling and canceling that appointment!

To update Windows, here's what you do: Once you're logged on to the Internet, open up your computer's Web browser, go to the Tools menu at the top of the page, then click on "Windows Update." You'll immediately be taken to the Microsoft website, which will check to see if your computer needs any upgrades. If so, follow the prompts to download the upgrades. If you have Windows XP, you can have your computer download the upgrades automatically. To do so, click on the "Start" menu in the lower left corner of your screen, click on "Control Panel," click on "Security Center," then turn on "Automatic Upgrades."

For better computer health, get an Apple. Apple computers can be a little more expensive than most PCs. But since only about 2 percent of the population uses Apple's Macintosh computers, very few spyware and virus programs are written to affect them. Virus writers would rather affect 98 percent of the population than Apple's small population. So, if you're having a lot of problems with spyware and viruses, consider buying a Mac next. The peace of mind might be worth the slightly higher cost.

Kick-start a failed Internet connection. If your high-speed Internet service fails to work after a power loss or computer crash, it could be that some of your devices powered up in the wrong order. Instead of calling a computer consultant, save yourself some time and hassle by first trying the following: Shut down the computer. Turn off or unplug your modem, the device that connects you to your cable or phone line. If you have one, turn off or unplug your router, the device that connects the modem and your home network. Wait at least 30 seconds. Now turn everything back on in the following order:

1. Modem—it will send a message to your Internet service provider (ISP) saying you need a new connection.
2. Router—it tells your modem to connect.
3. Computer.

Nine out of ten times, this will fix your connection problem. If it does not, the problem probably has something to do with your Internet service provider, not your computer. At that point, it's time to make a phone call.

Boost your computer's speed without calling a pro. All those software programs that come bundled on your computer take up valuable real estate. They also fight for your computer's resources by constantly searching for updates of themselves, even when you don't have the program open. What the computer companies don't tell you is that when you buy one of their machines, it's already running slower than it should because of all the extra programs. You can free up space and resources by removing all the programs you don't use.

Just deleting the icon on your desktop will not remove the programs—you've got to uninstall them. If you use a Windows XP-based PC, you do this by clicking on the "Start" menu in the lower left corner of your computer screen. Next, click "Control Panel," then "Add or Remove Programs." Scroll down the list of programs and remove the ones you're certain you don't need. The rule of thumb computer technicians use

with clients who want faster machines: If you haven't used a program in a year, you can delete it without worry.

Drain, then recharge, your laptop batteries. Sure, the computer salesman makes it sound like the world will stop turning if you don't buy a second laptop battery. But you can do just fine without an extra, unless you travel frequently. A second battery is bulky and is almost never worth the money. Since batteries drain as they get older—after only a few years, a battery may only reach 95 percent of its original charge—it's best to stick with one battery and keep it healthy. The best way to keep it healthy is to only charge it after it has been fully drained. Leaving your laptop plugged into the wall all the time will actually make it weaker. Before a big trip, when you'll need as much battery power as possible, drain the laptop battery completely (running a CD or DVD is a good way to quickly sap the power), and then recharge it completely.

WHAT SOFTWARE MAKERS DON'T WANT YOU TO KNOW ABOUT Free Spyware

Makers of spyware, that insidious software that secretly gathers information about your Web surfing habits while also slowing down your surfing speed, have become very clever at fooling consumers into downloading their software onto your computer. They've even been

known to advertise spyware as "free spyware blockers." You should only download free spyware blockers from download.com, one of the most trustworthy sites for downloads on the Internet, according to computer technicians. Two of the best free spyware blockers?

Spybot Search and Destroy, and Ad-Aware from Lavasoft.

BUYING APPLIANCES AT
big-box
Home Stores

When you're out to buy a new appliance or power tool, it's only natural to make your local home superstore your first stop. But purchasing a complex mechanical device is not the same as picking up a new faucet or some paint or wallpaper—and you may not be getting quite the same good deal. Here are some things that you should consider before buying that washer or router at a big-box outlet.

These stores don't always have the lowest prices

After entering the appliance-selling game relatively late, retailers like Home Depot and Lowe's don't command the same volume discounts that they do on commodities like lumber and drywall. Nor do appliance manufacturers want to alienate the thousands of mom-and-pop appliance stores across the continent, stores that still offer competitive prices. Consider the potential benefits from buying from a small, local dealer—dependable service, accountability, and supporting the local economy. And if for some reason you buy an appliance from a big-box retailer (maybe you want to purchase everything for your kitchen remodeling in one place), bring the top competitor's lowest price quote with you. Most will match (or beat) that price.

Quality service is not their game

When it comes to large appliances, good service is important. Here's what the big-box stores don't want you to know about how their business models work:

1. They are typically too short-staffed to be able to handle service well (they have to keep those margins up for Wall Street, as well as Bay Street, every quarter!).

2. They provide you with a "customer-service department" rather than simply the "guy in charge."

3. Their organizational structure makes it very difficult to communicate with either your original salesperson or a single customer-service representative. Typically, there's no receptionist. You call in and must navigate your way through a huge phone tree, with no individual employee e-mail or voice-mail boxes for storing messages. Besides, the employees are too busy playing customer pinball to really give you their undivided attention. Think of big-box stores as retailers, period.

Think of big-box stores as retailers, period. If you call in for service, you must negotiate a huge phone tree.

Big-box stores do not have their own installers

When you purchase a large appliance that needs professional installation, it's not store employees coming into your home—they're employees of an installation company that the store has hired on contract. The big-box store acts as the middleman, charging you the installation fee, plus a markup that's usually in the neighborhood of 25 percent. Sometimes these installation companies are start-up outfits that can't generate enough business on their own and need the extra work. The whole setup creates a gap in accountability that can make it hard to solve any problems that crop up.

Buying tools that are exclusive to one retailer is risky

Some brands of power tools are sold at just one retail chain. Rigid power tools, for example, are only available at Home Depot. This can spell trouble for contractors working long distances from their hometowns, and for others who move to an area where there's no branch of that particular store. Without easy access to the store that sells your brand, you might not be able to buy nails or other accessories for your tools. Before you choose a brand, find out where accessories and parts for that brand are available, where repairs are made, and then consider if it's convenient for you.

Power tools that use one kind of battery are a great idea

The battery is typically the priciest part of a new cordless drill, saw, or other power tool. And it's always nice to have a backup battery. Buying multiple tools that use the same battery basically gives you free backup batteries. It also cuts down on the number of battery chargers you have around the house, which reduces clutter and saves you money.

Renting tools can be as expensive as buying them

Renting a power or garden tool can cost nearly as much as buying the same tool new. If you're going to use the tool more than once or twice, it makes sense to buy it. Even if it only takes you an hour to aerate your lawn, you may have to rent the tool for a minimum time period, for instance 24 hours. Instead, if you need expensive lawn tools like lawn mowers or tillers, ask your neighbors if they'd like to go in on buying one.

Upgrade your desktop PC. Computer companies thrive on a marketing strategy known as planned obsolescence—the idea that today's brand-new machine will be out of date in just a few years, thanks to ever-faster processors, bigger hard drives, and more memory. They figure most of their customers would never dream of tinkering with electronics the way they might replace a belt in their vacuum cleaner. But despite the ethereal nature of computer software, many desktop computer hardware parts fit together like high-tech Legos. Instead of buying a brand-new computer for $600 to $1,200, upgrade a few parts. Need more memory? Snap in a random-access memory (RAM) upgrade, which usually costs less than $100. Want to burn DVDs? Buy a DVD burner (another $100 purchase), and add it to one of the empty slots on the computer. This way, you can keep your old keyboard, monitor, and speakers, all of which work perfectly well. ◁

Computer Security
5 Ways to Keep Your Personal Information out of Strangers' Hands

Remember that nothing is free on the Internet. "When you see a pop-up ad for free screen savers, you might think they're cute as a button," explains Ontario-based computer guru Brian Muntz. "They seem innocent enough. But you pay a price: They contaminate your system with spyware. When spyware builds up on your computer, every time you start it up, you have a line of people at your Internet door waiting to collect information about you. It slows down your computer tremendously."

Read that license agreement. To download those "free" screen savers, you must first click a button that says "I accept." Most people click without reading the end-user license agreement (EULA) accompanying it, which is like signing a contract without reading it. Read the EULA, and it will explain (in legalese, of course) that in exchange for the free screen savers, the company will plant spyware on your computer.

Arm your PC with security programs. This is essential: If you're going to have a computer that is hooked up to the Internet, you should have reputable security programs installed on your computer. Spend the extra 25 bucks to get a quality security package. Norton and McAfee are two of the biggest names in computer security software. They each sell bundles that include an antivirus program, a firewall to stop hackers, a spyware blocker, and an e-mail checker (it scans incoming mail for contaminants). You need all these.

Get a router if you have broadband.
"When you use DSL or cable to link directly to the Internet, you're entering what I call the DMZ, the demilitarized zone," says Muntz. "You're a wide-open target," meaning any hacker out there can use scanning software to locate your open Internet protocol (IP) ports and remotely access your computer, accessing personal data or using it to distribute viruses or spam. "That's because you were visible," says Muntz.

Here's the trick. Buy yourself a router, a small modem-looking box that routes data between the cable or phone and a small network of computers. Even if you only have one computer at home—and no plans for creating a network—a $50 router can slam the door on all potential hackers. "If you add a broadband router, and then the router to your modem, you're now invisible. Now when the hacker scans, all he can see is your router, and he can hack that all day long and he's not getting through it, because there are no ports open."

Secure your wireless network.
Many people with more than one computer at home are discovering the benefits of wireless networks (which use routers to link those computers). But there's a big potential problem. "Like anything computer-related, wireless networks are all designed to work right out of the box. So you plug it in, and the next thing you know, you're online and surfing. A lot of users stop right there. They say, 'Beautiful! And I didn't even have to fish any wires through the walls.' But if you can surf, so can anybody else. Any passerby can get onto your network and spread viruses or traffic in child pornography." Some lawyers have even

suggested that homeowners are legally liable for the lack of security on their networks.

Securing the network is simple. You'll find instructions inside the box. Typically, they'll ask you to open your Internet browser and type in a series of numbers (your IP address, which in most cases is 192.168.1.1). This takes you not to a website but to your router settings. Click on the "Wireless" tab, and then click on "Security." Follow the instructions for creating a password, sometimes called a WEP (wired equivalent privacy) key. Choose a password, and voilà, your network is safe. ◁

Cell Phone Service

3 Tips for Outsmarting Cell Phone Companies' Sneaky Tactics

Time your cell-shopping trip carefully. An employee of a major wireless phone service provider let us in on some serious dirt about what goes on in that industry. In exchange for a promise to protect his identity, he revealed some of his company's trade secrets. Here is the first:

The best time to buy a cell phone is at the end of the month. Most phone sales teams have a specific "discount budget" or allotment of money they are allowed to discount in order to close deals. At the end of the month, when sales quotas must be met, salespeople tend to dip more deeply into their discount budgets. Sometimes the budgets themselves shoot up. So bargain for that phone at the end of the month—and don't let them tell you they "can't do any better on the price." What do you say? How about, "I'll sign for two years if you sell this phone to me at this price."

Skip the accessories. Cell phone salespeople typically only make commission off the accessories they sell you, not the phone itself. That's why they seem so insistent that you buy extra chargers and cases. Be a savvy shopper, and only buy accessories that you'll really use (if you don't travel a lot, for instance, a car charger might not be necessary).

Skimp on "replacement" insurance and save your old phone. Cell phone salespeople leap at the opportunity to sign you up for a phone replacement policy at anywhere from $3.99 to $6.99 per month. It doesn't sound like much at the time, especially when compared to the $200 or so they'll quote you for a full-retail replacement phone—but at the end of the year, you've already spent $50 or $100 and have nothing to show for it! Here's a trick for saving money by creating your own insurance policy against loss, breakage, or theft: Save your old phone. Most phone companies will switch your service to the old phone for free, or maybe $50—which is a lot less than $200. ◄

You Can Get Cheaper Cable Service

Cable companies compete fiercely for your dollars. Here are some insider tips for gaining your own competitive edge when it comes to getting the best cable TV and Internet service.

Use your loyalty as leverage

Because of marketing costs, it can cost the cable companies 10 times more to recruit a new customer than to retain an old customer. You can use this bit of advice to your advantage the next time you find yourself dissatisfied with your service. Simply say that you'll take your business elsewhere. Chances are they'll address your problem, and they may even give you a deal on your cable rate.

Start over– with a signing bonus

Since most cable companies don't make you sign a contract, you can cancel your service, often without penalty, and then sign up again the next day to take advantage of sign-up incentives such as reduced fees or six months of free premium channels. Better yet, just call the provider and say you're going elsewhere unless they offer you the new-customer rates.

> You are probably paying for a lot of channels you don't watch. Try a package with fewer channels.

Shop around

If there are multiple cable service providers in your area, call around for the lowest price. If your current provider's price is relatively high, quote the lowest competitor's price (including incentives). Chances are they'll match or beat that price to keep your business.

Ask for the credit you deserve

Every now and again you have trouble with your cable TV or cable-based Internet service, don't you? The next time your cable goes out, don't just settle for restored service. Ask for credit. If you don't have luck with the first customer-service representative, keep asking for a supervisor.

Don't buy services you don't need

All cable companies offer a range of packages with names like basic, standard, and premium, each step up adding more channels and more cost. Take a very close look at the channels offered at each level and compare them to the channels you actually watch. What you are likely to discover is that you are paying for a lot of channels that you never watch. Most people only have at most ten or so channels that they watch regularly.

PRIVATE

part Three

EVERYDAY LIVING

Did you know that the best time to shop at a retail store is two in the afternoon? That you can get the best deal on a car at the end of the month? That the time to lowball a bid on eBay is over a holiday weekend? And if you want to find real bargains at a thrift shop, go in late December or early January? Timing is not the only thing that we've gotten normally tight-lipped insiders to open up about. They've shared a lot of other hush-hush secrets that can save you a ton of money. Discover why you should never, ever write or attach a note when paying a bill. Why mixing business with pleasure will get you ahead at work. Just turn the page to start discovering many, many more rarely disclosed tricks and secrets.

Auto Maintenance

10 Surprising Car-Care Shortcuts That Will Save You Money

Peel off that oil-change reminder sticker. Those quick-oil-change emporiums want you to think that the world will end if you don't change your car's oil every 3,000 miles (4,828 km). They even put stickers in your windshield reminding you to have it serviced. However, most cars do fine driving 7,500 miles (12,000 km) without a change—and some can go twice that. Check your car owner's manual—the manufacturer will give you the real story.

Pump the minimum. Despite what service-station ads want you to believe, very few cars really need expensive, high-octane gasoline. Most conventional automobiles are designed to run perfectly well on the cheapest (87-octane) gas.

Look for a detailer certificate. Detailing a car is just like any other professional service—some people are good at it, some aren't. How do you find a car detailer that's going to get into every crack and crevice and get your auto looking like new? Look for a detailer that has been licensed from a car detailing training facility. While there's no "official" master detailer designation (in other words, it's an unregulated industry) detailers who take the time to go through a certification program are probably better equipped to do a top-notch detail job.

Ignore that tire "dent" warning. If a tire salesman points out dents in the sidewalls of your tires, don't worry—he is just looking to make a quick buck. An unscrupulous tire dealer will tell you these dents are a problem and you need new tires, but in fact, these little concave depressions are more than normal. And they're not really dents—they're where the tire's poly cords are joined together. On the other hand, if you have a tire bulge—a convex lump that's a sign of an impending blowout—that's when it's time to consider forking over the dough for some new tires.

Keep tabs on tire pressure. What's the easiest way *not* to spend a ton of money on your mechanic's bill? Check your tire pressure every month. Reason number one: It's unsafe to have over- or underinflated tires, because the tires can blow out. Other big reasons to watch the pressure, says Lauren J. Fix, owner of Automotive Aspects in Clarence, New York, are that lousy tire pressure will lower your gas mileage, and add wear and tear to your car's brakes and handling systems, and it will also lower your gas mileage. The maximum tire pressure is marked on the sidewall of the tire; many cars also have a more important figure—the suggested tire pressure—marked on the inside of the driver's-side door.

Skip the spray-on wax at the car wash. A few more bucks for a hot wax job (or maybe they call it triple foam, or a sealant, or whatever) at the local car wash seems like such a deal. Does it make your car look better? Absolutely. Problem is, the shine (and additional protection) diminishes after about a week. A better idea would be to save the extra few bucks that the wax costs, and spring for one of those "express" wax jobs most car washes offer. They cost about $30, but they will give you longer-lasting protection.

Catch the wax on the rebound. Car wash owners certainly aren't going to tell you this, but you'll get the hot wax treatment for free at most car washes. How? Prentice St. Clair, president of Detail in Progress, an automotive detailing company in San Diego, says that if your car wash recycles its water—just ask, and you'll find most do—then the spray-on wax that gets applied during other people's car washes will stay in the water supply, and will get transferred onto your car. Just another reason to find an environmentally friendly car wash!

Put your mechanic behind the wheel. Something in the front of your car is squeaking. So you take it to an auto repair shop, you tell them about the squeak, and they throw the car up on the lift. Twenty minutes later, they're telling you that you need pricey new brakes and brake pads. How do they know this if they haven't taken the car for a test drive? One auto service manager we asked says you should get that car off the lift and take it to a different repair shop. A mechanic typically needs to take a car for a spin to diagnose big problems; those that don't are just selling you the most expensive fix to what could be a much smaller problem.

Beware shock absorber shenanigans. Many an unscrupulous mechanic has sprayed oil on a customer's shock absorbers, causing them to appear to be leaking oil. So if your mechanic delivers that kind of grim news to you, take your car to another mechanic for a second—and even third—opinion.

Look for the MAP on the wall. Never heard of the Motorist Assurance Program? Unscrupulous repair shops hope you haven't. The Motorist Assurance Program (MAP) is the first and only agency that accredits car repair shops, ensuring that these shops maintain a standard set of guidelines when diagnosing what is wrong with your car. The MAP guidelines cover exhaust, brakes, ABS, steering and suspension, engine maintenance and performance, HVAC, electrical systems, drivetrain, and transmission. The guidelines are not intended as a diagnostic tool (they won't help the technician locate the problem). However, the program offers peace of mind to the consumer—the knowledge that the repair shop is accredited. It's as close as you're going to get to finding a repair shop that's not out to pick your pocket. ◄

WHAT YOUR **CAR DEALERSHIP** DOESN'T WANT YOU TO KNOW ABOUT Maintenance

When you drive your new car off the lot, chances are your dealer will have given you a service schedule for your car. The manager of a New York-area auto-maintenance shop confesses that that schedule is the biggest "hose job" in the business. The dealer is trying to scare you into believing that your car needs all sorts of preventive maintenance work, and that it all has to be done at the dealership.

The only service maintenance schedule worth following is the one that comes from the car manufacturer; you'll find it in the vehicle's manual. This service schedule is a heck of a lot more conservative than the one your dealer has prescribed. We know of one woman whose dealer's service schedule said that she needed—all within the first year—an oil and filter change, a tire rotation, a brake system check, an air system check, and a transaxle service. In addition, the dealer said that an engine oil flush, fuel system service, four-wheel alignment, tire balance, and wiper blade replacement were all required. The total cost for this dealer service schedule? More than $600. What, exactly, did the manufacturer recommend after a year? Changing the oil filter, rotating the tires, and just checking everything else. Total cost? About $70.

Road Safety
6 Tips to Surviving the Most Dangerous Driving Situations

Stop your car from hydroplaning. Hydroplaning occurs when your car tires are driving on water, rather than directly on the pavement—usually when you're driving quickly and you suddenly drive through a deep puddle. If it's raining hard enough, you don't even need to drive through a puddle to hydroplane—it can happen anywhere on the road. This is a pretty dangerous condition; it's very easy to lose control of the vehicle. If it happens to you, *don't brake*—just let the car coast until the hydroplaning subsides (and if you're driving a manual transmission car, you'll want to engage the clutch).

Survive skids on ice and snow. Don't have a panic attack. Don't hit the brakes. Take your foot off the gas, and steer in the direction that you are skidding. If you must hit the brakes, apply steady but gentle pressure, but do not pump them or allow them to lock. The brakes will likely make some noise, but you should be back in control in no time.

Sit back to sidestep air-bag injury. Who's at highest risk for being injured by the air bags that are supposed to protect us? According to the Michigan State Police, it's drivers who sit too close to the steering wheel. Sit back in your seat, rather than hunched over, put at least 10 inches (25 cm) between yourself and the steering wheel—and, of course, always wear your seat belt.

Minimize the impact if the worst is inevitable. So a vehicle is coming toward you; maybe the driver is distracted (or even worse, asleep at the wheel). What should you do? Make sure your headlights are on—bright oncoming lights will get the driver's attention—and that you're driving as close to the right side of your lane (away from the oncoming lane) as you can. If the car is in your lane and it's not moving, don't play chicken with it. Slow down so that you minimize the force of an inevitable crash, then veer off the road to the right (not left, into the

Car Emergency Kit Checklist

Here are 15 things that'll get you out of most car-related jams. Keep them in your trunk or glove compartment so that they are always handy.

- ☐ Maps
- ☐ First-aid kit
- ☐ Flares or emergency lights
- ☐ Jumper cables
- ☐ Paper towels
- ☐ Flashlight, portable flashing light, and extra batteries
- ☐ Energy bars (or other nonperishable food)
- ☐ Drinking water
- ☐ Matches and emergency candles
- ☐ Brightly colored flag, banner, or "help" sign

In the winter, add these, if appropriate for your climate:

- ☐ Cat litter, sand, or salt (provides good traction in the snow)
- ☐ Snow shovel
- ☐ Ice scraper/windshield brush
- ☐ Extra clothing and shoes, particularly warm jackets, hats, and gloves
- ☐ Windshield wiper fluid and/or deicing fluid
- ☐ Gas-line antifreeze

oncoming lane). If it looks like you'll hit a street sign or another obstacle, so be it—at least it's not another moving vehicle traveling at top speed. Just try not to hit that obstacle head-on; see if you can maneuver your vehicle so that you hit it at an angle instead.

Don't swerve with deer. Most deer-car collisions happen in the fall, between the hours of 6 p.m. and midnight, say the Michigan State Police troopers. If it's dark out, the easiest way to spot deer is to drive with your high-beam lights on—they illuminate the animals' eyes. If you see a deer in your path, it's rarely prudent to swerve: It's better to strike a deer than another car, or a telephone pole or something else that can cause even more damage to you and your vehicle.

Stay calm if you get stranded in the snow. Avoid overexertion and overexposure to the cold. If you can't shovel your vehicle out of the snow—or if there are blizzard conditions—stay inside the car. Don't leave the car unless help is visible within about 100 yards (90 meters). Turn on flashing lights or set up flares. In daylight, tie a brightly colored cloth to the antenna to make your car more visible. Run the engine for about 10 minutes every hour to provide heat without burning too much fuel. For safety, make sure the tailpipe is free of snow and crack a window on the side away from the wind. Bundle up in a blanket; sharing it with another person gives extra warmth. Don't fall asleep; take turns sleeping if there is more than one person in the car. These tips come from the Canadian Centre for Occupational Health and Safety. ◁

Driving Violations
5 Tricks to Avoiding (and Getting Out of) Traffic Tickets for Speeding

Understand that your car says a lot about you. Most officers decide whether you're getting a ticket or a warning before they even approach your vehicle. A good rule of thumb is to keep your car maintained in such a way that you wouldn't be embarrassed to drive it to a job interview. Keep it clean, decluttered, and free of bumper stickers that are anti-police or pro-violence. Forgo aftermarket add-ons like spoilers, tinted windows, and neon undercarriage lights. You want to say "I'm responsible and law-abiding," not "I hate the police, I speed all the time, and I'm trying to hide something from you."

Wave at the hidden police cruiser. So you were driving down the road a little faster than you should have been, and you spot a police cruiser lurking behind some shrubbery. One former police officer says that the smartest thing that you can do right then is to wave at the officer. Why? He will either think that you know each other and wave back, or will think that you're acknowledging that you were driving too fast, and are letting him know that you're slowing down. Either way, you drastically reduce your chance of getting a ticket.

Never admit that you were speeding. If you do get pulled over, says one former police officer, never acknowledge that you were, in fact, speeding. You don't want to give the police any ammunition to use against you, should you contest your ticket in traffic court. When the officer tells you that you are speeding, giving a brief, noncommittal response like, "I see" or "I was not aware of my speed" is the way to go. (Asking sarcastic questions like, "What's the problem, Officer?" won't help your case!) Secret sources who have dodged more than one speeding ticket in their lives also advise that you just get through the meeting with the police as quickly and politely as you possibly can. You don't want them to remember anything about you, except that you were nice and did what you were told. Why? Read on.

Plead not guilty, and defer your court date as often as you can. The more time you put between your speeding encounter and your court date, the better, advise some ticket dodgers we know. Imagine how many people an officer pulls over in a month. How many of them do you think he'll remember two or even six months from now, especially if you take your ticket quietly and move on? The more continuances you can reasonably request, the more time you have to collect your evidence and prepare your defense—and the less specific that officer's recollection of you will be. Getting a continuance also increases the probability that the ticketing officer retires, transfers to another department, or just doesn't show up for your court date. In almost all of these extenuating situations, the case against you will be dropped.

Know the tactics that can get your ticket dismissed. There are dozens of ways to have your traffic violations reduced or dismissed—opportunities vary from region to region, so check to see if these apply in your state or province. Here is just a sampling:

POI Software

For those who have GPS navigation systems in their cars, here's an added bonus: You can download additional Points-of-Interest (POI) software onto your gizmo that will tell you when you're approaching stoplights that are hooked up to traffic cameras. You'll find links to this software on the GPS manufacturers' home pages.

- The issuing officer does not show for your court date.

- Two officers were in the patrol car when you received your ticket, and only one shows for the court date. In many jurisdictions, both need to be present to recount their testimony firsthand.

- A factual error on the ticket itself (your license plate number, name, date, or other inarguable fact is incorrect) may get you off the hook.

- There is no correct speed limit sign posted within a reasonable distance of where you were pulled over (in the U.S. this distance varies by state, but is usually about 1/4 mile). ◄

Buying a Car

6 Tricks for Beating Car Salespeople at Their Own Game When Purchasing a Vehicle

Realize that "certified" doesn't mean squat. You'll never get a used-car dealer to admit this, but the term "certified pre-owned" is virtually meaningless—it's nothing more than a marketing come-on. In fact, one auto expert said he's seen "certified" cars with bald tires and bad brakes. He said the "certified" tag just means someone went through a checklist in the garage before putting the car back out on the lot. Many times, a dealer selling a certified used car offers a long-term guarantee, which is good, but unless that guarantee covers everything—and we mean everything—chances are you're just buying a regular old used car with some problems. Before you buy that car, take it to your own mechanic for a careful going-over and let him certify it for you.

Know your extended-warranty options. After jacked-up financing rates, car dealers' biggest profit generators are extended warranties. Before you sign on the dotted line, know that there are other warranty options out there: The Internet can be a saving grace for consumers, with plenty of websites (such as www.warrantydirect.com) offering policies that beat or exceed the ones being offered by the dealer. Again, you may not buy your warranty over the Internet, but just knowing what your pricing options are will give you leverage with the dealer.

Don't fall for dealer sealer. Don't let a car salesman sell you on the protection programs that promise to keep your car looking shiny and new for years to come. Why? It's nothing but a big scam. "They charge anywhere from $300 to $1,500 to throw some stuff on the car, and they'll dazzle you with phrases like 'polymer paint sealant,'" says detailer Prentice St. Clair. "This adds very little value to your car." St. Clair says many of these treatments are guaranteed for five years, when in fact even the best sealants will only last 6 to 12 months. The dealerships are simply banking on the fact you'll never come back in to touch up any mischievous markings that appear on your car.

EXPERT INSTANT ADVICE

Specificity Saves You Money

Ever wonder just what happens when the car salesman tells you he has to "go speak to the manager"? One car dealer who asked us not to reveal his name explained exactly what happens: They spend their time formulating a strategy to sell you a car for maximum profit.

This same expert disclosed the very best way to buy a new car for the lowest price. It's almost too obvious, but he swears virtually no one does it: Know exactly which car you want to buy, including model, options, and color. Then go to five different dealers and tell them what you want. Tell each dealer that you're going to four competitors, and that you'll be back the next day and you want to hear his best price—no nonsense, no sales games, just the price. Our source promises that this is the shortest, quickest way to find a good deal.

How I Do It   A Travel Pro Tells Why He Always Rents the Smallest Car Possible

At many popular vacation destinations, they don't stock enough compact and economy cars to fill the needs of everyone who wants to save a few bucks by renting a smaller automobile. This can work out to your advantage.

Let's say you're headed to a big-time tourist mecca, like Las Vegas or Disney World. According to Peter Wu, a frequent traveler (and former chief purser of a major airline), your best bet is to book the smallest car possible. Chances are you're not the only one looking to save a buck; therefore, the smallest cars will likely be the first ones off the lot. If all of the smaller cars are gone by the time you arrive at the rental office, the company will give you a free upgrade.

What if your ploy doesn't work and the car rental agency hasn't run out of the tiny cars? Don't feel bad, says Wu. If you really want a larger car, just tell the counter representative that you have changed your mind and will pay the higher rate. Upgrading to a larger car is much easier than switching from a midsize rental car to an economy model.

Carefully study the fine print of such protection agreements too. "For instance, some dealerships will tell you that bird droppings won't cut through the polymers," St. Clair says. "And then you read the fine print about exclusions, and it says, 'Bird droppings not covered.'"

Pass on rust-proofing. When your car salesman offers to sell you rust protection for your new car, take a pass. Cars are made so well nowadays that this protection is an out-and-out waste of your money. Stick to your guns—don't let his warnings and worries about road salt rattle you.

Check out the tire specs. The salespeople won't mention it, but some new cars are being sold these days with "performance" tires that are designed to give the car better handling on dry roads at super-high speeds—speeds the car can't even reach. Such tires can cost twice as much as conventional tires, and often

come with no warranties whatsoever. Because the cost of these tires is rolled into the sticker price of your new car, you might not realize what you've ended up with until a few years later, when you have to replace those pricey tires. So research what the options really are for tires on the model you want to buy.

Buy your car in September. This is the time of year when the next model year cars are being rolled out. Dealers are anxious to liquidate the older new cars, and you can get a real deal. Visit the dealership on a weekday, preferably toward the end of the month (see next page). ◁

Bargaining Car Price
8 Ploys for Buying the Car You Want (Almost) Hassle-Free for the Best Price

Ignore the multiple-rebate ploy. Those car ads in your newspaper are there for one reason and one reason only—to get you into the showroom. And while there are many laws concerning truth in advertising, car dealers get around them by not telling the *whole* truth in advertising. For instance, one car dealer confesses that many of its ads list *all* the rebates you're eligible for—but what the ads don't tell you is that you're only going to be allowed to cash in on one of them. Misleading? Certainly. Illegal? Hardly.

Arrive armed with the car's invoice price. Edmunds.com is the last website that your car salesperson would ever want you to visit. It's a buyer's best Internet source for finding the invoice price (the price the dealer pays) on a new car. At www.edmunds.com, you choose the make, year, and model, and basically build your car with the option package that you're looking for. A few minutes later, you'll have the invoice price and the manufacturer's suggested retail price. Another cool feature on Edmunds.com is the True Market Value, "what others are paying," price, which clues you in on the amount (typically somewhere between retail and invoice) that customers in your area are paying for the same automobile. In Canada, you can try www.carcost canada.com for similar advice, but you'll have to pay a $40 membership.

Go car shopping at the end of the month. It sounds like one of those urban legends, but it's not—car dealers will be more aggressive on the last day

of the month, and this can work in your favor. Virtually all car dealerships have monthly quotas, and if quotas aren't being met, the last business day of the month—and the few days preceding—are the days when the car salesmen are really looking to move their cars off the lot.

So how do you know if the salesmen are scrambling for those sales quotas? Glance around the showroom. If they're nervously scrambling around the room, chances are they are scrambling for sales. While you're not going to get a car for free, just knowing there's a little pressure on the sales force should allow you more room to negotiate.

Order up a discount. Car dealers will never tell you this, but they'd much prefer to sell you a car off their lots (thus clearing out inventory) rather than special-ordering one for you. You can use this fact to your benefit. Tell salespeople that you want to order a base-model car that doesn't have all of the expensive options of the showroom vehicles. They'll likely be more willing to roll back the price of a luxury-packaged car if you agree to take current stock off their hands.

Don't mention your trade-in. New-car dealers love hearing that you want to trade your old car in when you purchase the new model. Why? Because the more variables that they can work into the equation, the easier it is for them to play the smoke-and-mirrors game with the price of that new car. It's a much better idea to negotiate the price on the new car and then, at the last moment, tell them you're interested in trading in your old car. Make it two separate transactions so they can't use "fuzzy math" to confuse you. Of course, no dealer is going to give you more than wholesale value for your trade-in, so unless you've got a real junker, it's almost always better to sell your old car yourself.

Pick apart that trade-in deal.

Sometimes a car dealer will promise you a generous trade-in allowance on your old car, and then neglect to mention that he is jacking up the cost of the new one. The cost of your new car should be the same whether or not you're trading in an old one; to be as prepared as possible, find out how much other dealers are asking for the new car. You should also ask the dealer whether his advertised generous trade-in offer applies to all used cars, no matter how much wear and tear they have. Also, ask whether his special offers apply exclusively to in-stock vehicles, or to those with the most expensive options packages.

Never pay more than $500 over invoice.

You've done your research on the car's invoice price—now use this knowledge to your advantage. If a car isn't the hottest new thing (meaning, the demand outweighs the supply), you should never have to pay any more than $500 over the invoice price. It's just that simple. The salesman won't be happy, and the sales manager won't be happy, but know this—they'd rather sell you the car and make $500 than not sell you

WHAT CAR DEALERS DON'T WANT YOU TO KNOW ABOUT Loans

Car dealers who lure you into the showroom with the promise of a low-interest car loan hope that you won't take a second look at their paperwork. However, there are a number of factors that could mean the "deal of the century" is not so generous after all. Here are some questions to ask that will expose car-dealer double-talk:

- Does the loan require an enormous down payment or a "balloon payment" at the end?
- Is the price of the car higher for people who accept low-interest financing?

- Are you given an unusually short period of time to pay the loan off–say, just a couple of years?
- Will you be required to buy extras that you don't want, such as an extended warranty?
- Will you have to give up the rebate offered by the automaker?

Before you go anywhere near that finance officer's desk, though, know your credit score, and be armed with the interest rates that you qualify for. You can order a free copy of your credit report in the U.S. at www.freecreditreport.com and in Canada at www.equifax.com. At www.bankrate.com, you can research the going rates for auto financing in your area.

the car, especially if that car has been sitting on the lot for a month or two. So go armed with the invoice price, and get the best price possible on the car.

Make them an offer they can't refuse. The second-to-last thing any car dealer wants to do is lose money on a sale. So what's the last thing he wants to do? Leave inventory sitting on the lot, says an anonymous New Jersey car dealer. This has a direct correlation to the amount of "holdback" money that the dealership gets from the automaker. "Holdback" is money meant to offset the costs of keeping the car on the lot, usually distributed in the form of interest payments. The more quickly a dealership moves cars, the more of the holdback money it gets to keep. But as months wear on and cars sit on the lot, the holdback money disappears and the dealership is left holding the bag. Oftentimes, just to move inventory, the dealer will sell cars for less than he paid for them. While there's no surefire way to know how long the dealer has had your preferred car in inventory, it's safe to bet that as the new model year's cars are coming in, last year's models are primed for sale. So make an offer that's a little below invoice, and see what happens. You may end up pleasantly surprised. ◁

Auto Insurance
4 Tips for Getting Good Coverage and Low Premiums on Your Car Insurance

Keep your credit score healthy. Clean up that credit score before shopping for auto insurance. Why? According to Loretta Worters, vice president of the Insurance Information Institute, drivers with long, stable credit histories are less likely to be involved in accidents. People who are lax with their financial affairs, according to the folks who study insurance data, are statistically more likely to file an insurance claim, so the insurance companies consider them to be a higher risk. It may sound like comparing apples to oranges, but the fact remains, this is one method insurance companies employ when determining your auto insurance rate.

Don't let your insurance lapse. Don't fall into the trap those car insurance companies have set up for you—namely, the trap of "I'm not driving my car right now so I don't need insurance." Even if you won't be driving your car for an extended period of time—say, you're traveling overseas for several months or health issues prevent you from getting behind the wheel—it's always better to strip down your insurance to the bare minimum than to cancel it outright. Why? Because car insurers like to see someone insured for 36 consecutive months. So if you let it lapse, you'll be starting from scratch, which means higher premiums and a tougher time landing a policy. That's why you're better off calling your insurance agent and whittling down the coverage to just the bare minimum. This way, you'll maintain your 36-month standing and find it a piece of cake to bring your insurance back up to its previous levels when you finally do get back behind the wheel.

Set up your own car insurance. Your insurance agent chuckles every time you renew collision and comprehensive insurance for a car that's more than five years old. If your car is only worth a couple thousand dollars, it makes better economic sense to lower your insurance premiums and put the cash you save into an account. If you have an accident or your car is vandalized, use your own cash to repair or replace it. Ask your insurance agent how much your premiums will drop if you raise your deductibles or eliminate collision and comprehensive altogether. (Collision covers damage from accidents, and comprehensive covers theft and other damage.) Coverage that once made sense for a brand-new car isn't advisable for an old clunker.

Caught cardless? Call your agent. A phone call to your insurance agent might just get you out of a pickle, under certain circumstances. Consider this scenario: You get pulled over by a police officer, and for the life of you, you can't find your insurance card. With a little luck, however, you won't get stuck with a $200 ticket for failing to produce your documents, says Lloyd Bezar, an Allstate agent in Pennington, New Jersey. Simply ask the officer if you can call your insurance agent and have her vouch for you. In most cases, assuming you actually do have the insurance, the officer will let you go without writing you a ticket. (That said, you're on your own if you were speeding too.) ◁

Recreational Vehicles
4 Travel Strategies That Every RVer Should Know

Land on free parking. Don't be gouged every night for RV campsite parking fees—you really only need to stop at a campsite when you need to dump your waste or pick up water. On the nights when you don't need a hookup, stop by a Wal-Mart or a Sam's Club; both will let you stay in their parking lots after hours for free. Churches, too, usually don't mind RVs in their parking lots, as long as you're gone by the time services start in the morning.

Get a tax break on your RV. Still on the fence about making the leap and buying an RV? Well, maybe this will swing you: If you pay taxes in the U.S. and you finance your purchase, you can write off the interest payments much in the same way you'd write off the mortgage interest on a second home. As long as you use the RV as security for the loan and as long as the RV has sleeping, toilet, and kitchen quarters, you're all set.

Make sure your RV isn't a heavyweight. Plenty of RV makers are building motor homes that are dangerously close to maximum capacity. In other words, each RV comes with a maximum weight the entire rig should carry, and if it's already close to that weight and you haven't even added your family of four or filled the water tank—watch out! Way too many buyers and renters overlook this crucial fact.

Watch out for water damage. Bruce Powell of Pappy's Motorhome Rentals in Salt Lake City, Utah, offers his professional advice on how to avoid buying an RV with water damage: Even if the RV looks pristine, bring it over to another RV dealer and have him check it out. The main thing to look out for is water damage that came in through the roof and settled back behind the walls. Water behind the walls will lead to wood rot, which leads to big bucks and big headaches. ◂

Keeping Pesky Pests Away

Give mice the rough treatment. Rodents can gain entry to your RV through the access slots where you hook up a cable or hose. To keep these critters on the outside, wrap the cable or hose in a bit of steel wool before you connect it, making sure the material fills the surrounding gap. Any mousie trying to enter your vehicle will scrub that plan.

Hate those love bugs? RV drivers who visit the southeastern United States know about the love bug problem. These creatures seem to make a beeline for the highways, only to plaster themselves across the forward-facing surfaces of your vehicle. To make matters worse, the acid in those crushed bug bodies will eat through the finish. The solution: Apply a light coating of baby oil to the vulnerable surfaces of your RV. When you stop for the night, your love bug "collection" will be easy to hose right off.

Secure the perimeter. Buy a gallon jug of pump-up bug spray at a discount store and keep it in your RV. When you set up camp, spray around any spots where the local bugs might gain access to your vehicle—the stabilizer jacks and the tires, for instance.

Motorcycles

6 Tricks to Make Two-Wheelin' a Breeze

Make yourself easy to see. If you ride a motorcycle, you have to put extra effort into being seen—your life depends on it. During the day, ride your motorcycle with the high-beam headlight on. Check the alignment of your headlight and running lights to make sure motorists can easily see them. Many headlights are pointed too far down. Replace weak brake lights with bold halogen lights that will command attention. Adding side lights and reflective devices to your cycle and clothing will reduce the odds of getting smacked by another vehicle in an intersection at night. Also, if your cycle is dark-colored, customize it with a touch of contrasting light color to increase your visibility.

Beware of oil slicks at tollbooths. When you're riding long-distance on your motorcycle, remember that tollbooths are one of the most treacherous locations you will encounter. There are fewer spots on the road that are more likely to be slimy with oil—a tricky obstacle for two-wheeled vehicles. So enter and leave a tollbooth very slowly, and stick to the left tire track to get clean pavement as you pay your "dues." Warn your passenger that tollbooths are a lousy place to make sudden weight-shifts.

Let the postman carry your luggage. If you take your motorcycle on long trips, you know how important it is to pack sparingly, no matter how commodious your saddlebags seem to be. Well, shipping and mailing companies can be your best friend in this respect. Learn the locations of the shipping stores and post offices along your route. Mail ahead to yourself bulky items such as fresh laundry and gifts for people you're going to visit. Mail home your dirty clothes, purchases, and gear you don't need anymore.

Prevent your visor from fogging up. Try this trick from veteran cyclists: Put a drop of dishwashing liquid on the inside of the visor, rub it all around until you can't see it, and wipe off any excess. No more misty visor!

Cleaning marked-up chrome. How do you get those "indelible" boot marks off your chrome exhaust pipe? Pull on rubber gloves and dampen a cleaning rag with oven cleaner. Mask off nearby parts of your motorcycle, then smear the oven cleaner onto the marked-up exhaust pipe; let it sit for 10 minutes. Scrape most of the oven cleaner off with a flat piece of wood or similar non-scratching device. Rinse with a clean, wet rag, and add wax for protection.

Fast, easy spoke cleaning. Cleaning spoked wheels is one of the more annoying motorcycle maintenance chores. Here's how to keep the hassle to a minimum. Buy three bottle brushes and use a separate brush for each of these tasks:

- Clean the spokes with a car-washing solution.
- Apply a car wax according to the package directions.
- Polish the wax.

Hang the brushes side by side in your garage. Put a masking-tape label on each so you can tell them apart at a

General Savings

8 Ways You Can Always Be at the Top of Your Game When It Comes to Finding Bargains

Watch the economic news. Toward the end of the year, pay special attention to the financial section of your newspaper or stories on the evening news about the economy. The retail industry will never tell you when business is slow—store managers *hate* for you to have this information. But the media will certainly let you know. If media forecasts are saying that holiday sales will be sluggish, you can bet that stores will start discounting their merchandise during the fall shopping season. Head to the store and take advantage of discounted merchandise. If you learn on the news the day after Christmas that the shopping season indeed turned out to be disappointing for retailers, plan to head to the store and stock up on bargains, since prices will *really* be slashed.

Check your junk mail. Day in and day out, your mail brings into your home all sorts of offers for cheaper versions of services you purchase each month, such as your cable television and cell phone. Don't just drop these solicitations into the recycling bin—use them to your advantage, urges Jeffrey Strain, a frugality guru and the founder of savingsadvice.com. When a great offer shows up in your mail, call up your current service provider and explain that you're considering switching to the competitor. Read the competitor's offer over the phone and ask whether your existing provider can match this deal. Most of the time, you'll be able to save money with one quick call. When Strain made one of these calls to his mother's cable television provider, the discount he grabbed saved his mom $230 over the next six months!

Become a pro at shopping. An ancient lost art will put thousands of dollars into your pocket every year. Here's what to do: Establish a specific price in your mind—let's say $20—and anytime you're going to buy an item that costs more than this amount, first thoroughly educate yourself about the product, urges Alan Zell, a retail expert in Portland, Oregon, who calls himself "the ambassador of selling." Long ago, shoppers researched the difference between quality brands and poorly made brands. They learned to recognize high prices and bargains. They thought long and hard over their purchases before they put their money on the counter. Shopping carefully like this has become a lost art nowadays, and that's how businesses like it! Stores are more than happy for you to simply grab whichever item is convenient, since you often give them more of your money than you would if you took a little time to make a well-informed purchase. Remember: Stores are professionals at selling you stuff. Level the playing field by becoming a pro at shopping. Once the price passes $20, give all purchases your full attention.

Use credit to your advantage. If your credit card doesn't offer rebates or other incentives, take out a pair of scissors and cut it up, then sign up for one that does. Credit card companies have so thoroughly blanketed the country with their cards—and pleas in the mail for even more people to get them—that they're desperate for your business. Use this inside information to your advantage. Many credit card companies are offering incentives for you to use their cards nowadays. One card may offer you a small discount or rebate when you use it to buy gasoline or groceries. Others may let you earn money toward a new vehicle, discounts on air travel, or discounts for tickets to major amusement parks. If you see an offer for a credit card that provides discounts on items you plan on buying anyway, sign up for it. Then every time you make a purchase, put it on the credit card so you can rack up the benefits. However, remember that these incentives are bait—the credit card companies are trying to lure you into giving them more money than you'll save. Avoid these sneaky traps by paying off your balance every month so that you aren't hit with finance charges and late fees. And avoid cards with a high annual fee, because they eat into your benefits.

Pay some bills in big chunks. Are you still paying bills every month? Put your checkbook away so you can save your time—and money. Many of the service companies you pay regularly, such as your insurance or lawn maintenance, may charge you a lower fee if you pay every six months or annually rather than monthly. Always ask the service provider if you can lower your charge by paying in big chunks once or twice a year. If you can get a discount this way, take it! Not only will you save money on the service, but you'll save time and money on filling out checks and buying postage stamps.

Plan ahead and buy off-season. When it's hot, people want to buy window air conditioners and barbecue grills. When it's cold, they want sweaters and winter coats. And businesses charge a lot of money for these items because demand is so high. Instead of shopping with the herd, make your purchases at times when demand is low so *you* hold the upper hand. The shopkeepers will be happy to offer you a bargain just so you'll take the merchandise off their shelves. This will require you to look a little farther down the road when planning your purchases, and also know when stores are eager to reduce their inventory. If your air conditioner or grill is on its last legs, buy a replacement during the early fall. New models of big appliances such as stoves tend to arrive in stores in early fall too. Store managers will give you a great deal on *last* year's model, since they just want it out of the showroom.

Learn the skill of negotiation. In plenty of locales around the world, the price tag on an item is merely the starting point—you then discuss a more reasonable price with the store owner. Make haggling a regular part of your shopping

experience, urge Toronto-based Anna Wallner and Kristina Matisic, bargain-hunting hosts of the TV show *The Shopping Bags* and authors of *The Shopping Bags: Tips, Tricks, and Inside Information to Make You a Savvy Shopper*. You'll be astounded how often retailers will give a discount in order to make a sale, they say. Look for a small imperfection in the item—perhaps a bouquet of flowers looks less than fresh—and ask for a discount. However, never name the discount you'd like. Just ask for a better price and let the salesperson toss out a figure. When *you* name the price, you may be offering a figure that's higher than the salesperson would suggest.

Stock up on gifts. A steady stream of coworkers, acquaintances, and distant relatives will always be having birthdays. That's just a fact of life. And when you suddenly remember that a birthday is coming up in a few days, you'll probably buy a knickknack or gewgaw that's too expensive just because it's convenient. That's often a fact of life too—but it doesn't have to be. Instead, always be on the lookout for bargains on items that would make a neat gift when you want to give someone *something* but it doesn't have to be perfect. Try a candle in a nice candleholder, or a funny gift book from the rack at the front of the bookstore, or a silicone spatula or other new-fangled kitchen implement. Tuck these into the back of your closet. When a birthday pops up, pull an item from your stash, wrap it up, and pat yourself on the back for your thrifty thoughtfulness. ◄

Special Savings Tricks

8 Secret Ways a Little Ingenuity Can Help You Cut Your Money Outflow

Form a "hand-me-down" club.
Children's clothing stores have a great racket going: Since kids grow so fast, their clothes quickly become unwearable even though they still look nice. So parents have to buy a constant stream of new apparel just to keep up with their growing kids. Instead of enriching the coffers of your local kids' clothing store, organize a club of parents from your child's school or day care to exchange hand-me-down clothing. Twice a year, in the fall and spring, everyone can bring in the clothing that's still in good condition but no longer fits, and you can quickly assemble a new wardrobe for your child while getting rid of items you no longer need. Just make sure a wide range of ages is represented at the gathering, rather than only kids in one grade. That way you'll always have bigger clothes working their way into your trading system.

Get socks of one color. Always buy the same color and style of socks for your child—preferably white, since you can bleach them when they're stained. Since socks invariably vanish, when you lose one of a pair, you can simply pair it up with another, because they're all identical. You'll never be stuck with an "orphaned" sock that has no match. Just imagine how the clothing manufacturers will grit their teeth as you stroll right by that display stand of socks in every imaginable color and texture.

Get the most at the gas pump.
When gas prices soar, every extra block you drive to find bargains puts more money into the pockets of big oil com-
panies. But you can do your bit to get back at these giant corporations with one simple step: Fill up your car during the morning or late evening. Gasoline becomes denser when the temperature is cool. Since the gas pump only measures the *volume* of the gas you put into your car, when the gas is denser, you get a greater quantity for each gallon (or liter) that the gas pump measures. You'll get more distance for your buck than you would if you filled up at noon, when the temperature is higher.

Take a job for a discount. If you're looking for a part-time job, fill out applications at stores where you frequently make purchases, such as clothing stores or sporting-goods shops, which give their employees a discount. If you have teenagers in your home who are ready for a job, encourage them to work at your family's favorite stores with employee discounts too. Not only will you benefit from the discount, you'll also gain access to a new world of inside information on upcoming sales!

Skip the premium channel. If you pay for a premium movie channel just to watch a particular original series, you can bet that some cable bigwigs are getting a laugh over how much they're charging you for a few hours of entertainment. Call your cable company today to cancel your subscription to the channel. These series typically only contain 12 or so episodes per season, and you then have to wait for many months—or even years—before the next season begins. All the while, you're paying those bloated fees to the cable company. Instead, ask a friend who pays for the cable channel to tape the show for you (this is really a small favor to ask of a friend, don't you think?) or just wait a few months and rent the whole season for about $20 when it comes out on DVD. Or, even better, go the to library, take it out, and view it for free.

Turn your back on the vending machines. Want to get a $250 raise for the coming year? Stop buying your sodas and snacks from the vending machine at work. If every day you only brought in one soda and a resealable plastic bag of chips (refilled from a big store-bought bag), you could save $1 each day. If your worksite has a refrigerator, store your sodas and cold snacks there. If not, just bring them in a tiny cooler. Quit being a sucker for vending machines that are more about convenience than they are about product.

Help your friend move. Always help friends pack their belongings and load the truck when they're moving—this simple favor can save you big money. When people are loading their households into boxes, they usually find items that they no longer need or don't want to bother packing and unpacking. As a result, you can bring home hundreds of dollars' worth of spices, frozen food, videos and DVDs, books, toys, furniture, and other handy household items. Best of all, at the end of the day your friends will still think you've done *them* a favor!

Get a reporter's help. Companies live in absolute dread of looking like "the bad guys" in newspaper or TV news stories. If you have tapped out all of the possible ways to air a consumer complaint within the offending company, contact the consumer reporter at your local newspaper or television station. Reporters love "little guy vs. unscrupulous company" stories. Once they make an inquiry, your consumer problem will probably be solved very quickly. ◄

WHAT RETAIL STORES DON'T WANT YOU TO KNOW ABOUT Gift Cards

If a salesclerk tells you that your gift card has expired, don't take it lying down. Retail stores don't exactly advertise this fact, but many gift cards have an "expiration" date on them. They're hoping that the $30 gift card you got for your birthday will languish in your dresser drawer for a year and then they'll get to keep the money. Check your state's or province's consumer laws. In some places, such expiration policies aren't allowed (California, for instance), and in others a generous time frame is mandated (in Massachusetts, it's seven years). Act quickly and complain up the chain of command at the store. If your gift card just expired recently, you're more likely to get your money back.

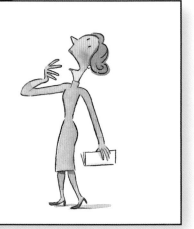

Grocery Savings

9 Tricks for Getting the Best Quantity and Quality When You Go Shopping for Food

Food-shop just once a week. If you're hooked on impromptu food shopping, break that expensive habit right now. Attach a magnet-backed notepad and pen to your refrigerator, and the moment a food container runs empty and you need to replace it, add it to your list. This simple discipline will have a major impact on your family budget. When you don't keep a list, you're likely to drop into the store for one item here, and two items there. Instead, establish a time each week that you can go to the store when you have time to focus on your shopping and you aren't in a rush. Be sure to take your list with you on your way out the door. Supermarket managers love it when you don't keep a list, for several reasons. First, the more times you go into the store, the more chances you'll have of picking up unnecessary items on impulse. Also, when you buy goods on the spur of the moment, you're more likely to pay full price for them, since you didn't have time to look for a sale or wait for one to arrive. In addition, the more trips you make to the store, the more gas you burn, which adds an invisible cost to your groceries.

Get the smallest carrier possible. If you're going to the supermarket to buy only one item, refrain from getting a basket. If you're only buying three items, get a basket, not a cart. Only get a cart if you're picking up a bunch of items. When you venture into the store knowing you're going to have to carry your purchases up to the counter, you probably won't make impulse buys. Since you've already scouted out the bargains in the sales ads and made a list of the items you need, you shouldn't be buying more stuff anyway, right?

Look for "limited purchase" signs. When you see a sign in the supermarket or clothing store that advertises a low price—but only lets you buy a few items at this price—take advantage of the deal. You may never see this product at a price this low again. When a store sets these limits, it's a sign that it's selling the products at, or even below, the price that it paid for them, says Eugene Fram, Ph.D., a professor of marketing at the Rochester Institute of Technology. Stores don't set limits because they're worried that customers will pile their carts high with the discounted items—they're fearful that owners of smaller mom-and-pop stores will buy out the inventory and resell it at a higher price in their own stores. So mom and pop may be out of luck when these limited offers come around—but it'll be your lucky day.

Know prices of one dozen products. Buy a small spiral-bound notebook, and look through your refrigerator, freezer, and pantry for the 12 products you buy most often. For many people, this list will include sodas, milk, juice, and bread. Give each item its own page and write its name at the top of the page. Take your notebook to the store whenever you shop, and each time you buy the item, jot down the price. And each time you see the item listed in a supermarket sale circular, note the price in your notebook too. It won't take long for you to become aware of when you should stock up on bargains and when you should wait for a sale. As savvy shoppers have learned through their adventures in bargain-finding, you *have* to know the difference between great prices and expensive markups in order to save money. Although a large supermarket may contain 30,000 items, just being able to find your top 12 items at a discount will save you big money. One frugality expert shared this information with us: By simply stocking up on chicken breasts *only* when they're on sale—rather than paying the going price every week—she saves $325 every year.

Watch the register. The checker at the supermarket will want to discuss the weather or make other small talk with you as she rings up your purchases. She may or may not have been trained to do that to help the store

make more money from you, but either way, this distraction can certainly do it. Politely respond that you need to pay attention to something else instead—and keep your eyes trained like a hawk on the register readout. Cash registers aren't always updated with the latest sales prices on items, and some stores pledge to give customers an item free if the register rings up the wrong price. Since you've done your homework and know *exactly* how much the items should cost, alert the clerk if any wrong prices come up. If the store has a generous mistake-finding policy, your moment of attention has earned you a free item. But even if you don't get the product free, at the very least you're ensured that you're getting the low price that you took the time to find.

Check your discount card carefully. Many supermarkets offer discount cards so you can save money on certain products. Often these cards come in the form of tiny plastic rectangles that go on your key chain, which the clerk passes over the register scanner. Be careful when you hand your key chain to the clerk if more than one store's discount card is attached to it. If the clerk scans the wrong card, the machine may still beep as if it's going to give you the discount—but it never does. Hold the right card between your fingertips as you hand your key chain over at the checkout counter,

How I Do It **A Bargain Hunter Tracks Sales Patterns**

You don't have to monitor the constant pricing activities at all the supermarkets in your town to save on groceries, says Stephanie Nelson, a bargain-finding author and founder of couponmom.com. All the sales will ultimately come to each store, she says, and running back and forth between stores eats up your precious time and expensive gasoline. However, develop a fundamental understanding of the store's sales programs. Choose a store that doubles or triples the value of the coupons you use. If the store offers a special membership card so you can save money, use it. Read the store's advertising section in your newspaper each week for upcoming sales. When you see a great sale on an item, buy a six-week supply so you'll have enough to last you until the item goes on sale again.

and watch the register to make sure that it's displaying your discounts.

Hit the farmers' market late in the day. Farmers' markets are great places to buy fruits and vegetables—the produce is fresher because it's grown close to your home. And when you show up at the right time, you can take home your favorite fruits and veggies at a steep discount. Late in the day, sellers are faced with the prospect of having to cart home or throw away unsold merchandise. They hate having to do that. So they're likely to sell you their remaining items at a reduced price so they won't have to figure out what to do with them. To find your nearest farmers' market, visit the U.S. Department of Agriculture's website at www.ams.usda.gov/farmersmarkets. In Canada, search for "farmers' markets" and your province's name.

Do it yourself to save money. Food companies like you to think they're doing you a favor by offering bags of prewashed salad and individual servings of soup. Actually, they're just looking for a way to charge you more money. Buy individual salad components instead of bagged salads, and soup, oatmeal, cereal, and other foods in regular-sized containers instead of tiny ones. Washing the salad or dividing the food into multiple bowls only takes a few seconds, and you won't be paying extra money for conveniences that you don't really need.

Keep your beer in the dark. If you're a big beer drinker, you can save a bundle by taking a tip from wine connoisseurs. Create a "beer cellar." Find a cool, dark spot where you can leave cases of beer without moving them—under these conditions, beer will stay fresh for six months. Watch for the summer sales, when you can buy in bulk and get the best discounts on your favorite brands. The convenience store manager—the one who has been charging you those outlandish markups on six-packs—will just weep when he sees his bottom line. ◄

Using Coupons
4 Special Ways to Get the Most from Your Coupons When You Go Grocery Shopping

Get more coupons. Coupons are a great way to gradually save big money on your grocery bills each year. So why stop with getting only one set of coupons from the Sunday newspaper or door-to-door packets when you can get two, three, or even more bundles of coupon circulars? Ask your friends and family if they receive the coupons but don't use them. If so, ask for them. In addition, swing by the supermarket late on Sunday evening. They may let you buy any leftover newspapers at a steep discount. If your main source of coupons is flyers in the supermarket itself or the website of the supermarket chain, you can pick up or print out as many coupons as you want.

Combine your savings. You'll never get your grocery store manager to volunteer this information, but when you use your coupons on items that are also on sale, you may get the merchandise for just a few cents—or even free. Most items in a supermarket will go on sale every six weeks or less, says Stephanie Nelson, known as the Savings Mom on ABC News' *Good Morning America*. Looking at the store's weekly advertisement in your local paper is a good way to find these sales. When you find an item that's on sale, review your coupon file to see if you have a coupon to lower the cost even further. If this is a store that doubles or even triples your coupons, you may have just found a free product. When you find a great bargain, stock up on it so you'll have enough to last until it's on sale again.

Watch for the bonus coupons. A lot goes on as you leave the checkout counter—you're paying, grabbing your receipt, and preparing to wheel your bargain-laden cart to your car. But don't forget one more slip of paper: Many checkout lines have a machine that spits out

WHAT GROCERY STORES DON'T WANT YOU TO KNOW ABOUT Product Placement

While you're wheeling your cart down the aisles, do plenty of stooping down low and reaching up high. Food makers may pay extra to stores to have their products stocked at eye level so consumers see them easily. And guess who pays the extra cost so these foods can have prime real estate in the supermarket? That's right—you. Supermarket managers cross their fingers and hope you'll drift through the store with your gaze firmly at eye level. So be sure to look up and down. The items stacked on the highest and lowest shelves will probably be better deals.

coupons for items you might be interested in on your next trip to the store, based on the products you've bought on this trip. It's easy to ignore these coupons in the hustle and bustle of the checkout stand. When the coupon emerges from the machine, tuck it into your purse or pocket rather than putting it into a bag of groceries, where it will likely get lost.

Organize your coupons with coupon mom.com. Stephanie Nelson hates the thought that grocery manufacturers offer consumers *$318 billion* in coupons each year, but we don't make use of 99 percent of these savings. So she's created a tool to help you grab thousands of dollars of this bounty each year.

Most people find coupons too hard to use, since hundreds of them are jammed in random order into circulars in your Sunday paper with no organization by name or product type. It's a chore to hunt through piles of coupons to find just the one you need. Her tool quickly and easily solves these problems for American bargain hunters. You'll find it on her website, www.couponmom.com. Founded in 2001, the site offers a feature she calls the Virtual Coupon Organizer. To use it, you must first start saving the coupon circulars from your Sunday paper or other source. Write the date on them—along with an S or a V, which stands for SmartSaver or Valassis, the two companies that produce these circulars—and stick them into their own section in an accordion file. Before you go grocery shopping the next time, call up the virtual coupon tool on the website and select your state from a menu (this feature works for 44 states). The site will then tell you *all* the products with coupons that have run in your

newspaper that are still valid. If you need kitty litter, simply search down the list of hundreds—or even thousands—of items to see if there's a coupon for kitty litter. If there is, you'll see the date that this coupon appeared in your newspaper, and which of the two circulars contained it. Go to that circular in your accordion file and pick out the coupon with ease.

Along with this ultra-cool money-saving tool, the site also has a feature that allows you to choose your state, then see a list of dozens of *other* great discounts at particular supermarket chains and drugstores in your area that don't even require a coupon.

In Canada, you can go to www.frugal shopper.ca, which partners with some of the country's largest retailers and has coupons featured in store flyers listed by province. Or visit www.save.ca to select coupons for your favorite brands. Just specify your province and click on the coupons you want to receive. They will be mailed to you free of charge the next business day. ◄

Retail Shopping
11 Secrets That Renegade Shoppers Use When Buying General Merchandise

Speak your mind. You needed to find out if the pair of jeans you admired on your friend were available in your size—but the 20-something store clerk was too engrossed in her cell-phone conversation to help you. Don't handle the situation by vowing never to go to the store again. If you're steamed over any issue in a store, from an encounter with a rude or unhelpful salesperson to shoddy merchandise—use the situation to your advantage. Store managers want their customers to return, and they have a lot of leeway to give you a special offer when you're disgruntled to make you happy with the store again. Ask for a refund or a discount, store credit, or some other type of incentive on your next purchase.

Don't be afraid to ask for a discount. Similarly, forget about feeling embarrassed or uncomfortable when you call a company and threaten to take your business elsewhere if it won't offer you a discount. This call might be the best conversation the customer-service representative has had all day! Many customer-service reps get bonuses for keeping customers who are thinking about leaving, says frugal-living advisor Jeffrey Strain. That's because it costs companies a lot of money to bring in new customers, and many are happy to offer a discount to keep you from canceling the service. So make that call—the company's representative should be happy to work with you to offer you a deal, and a few minutes on the phone can put hundreds of dollars back into your pocket.

Follow the return policy. Before you fork over $100 at the mega-electronics store for a portable DVD player for your kids to watch in the car, visit the customer service desk and read the fine print about the store's return policy. If you don't, you could get stuck with a bad purchase. Stores often require you to follow complicated directions in order to return a product. You may need to provide the receipt and all of the item's original packaging to get a refund or replacement item. So be sure to review the return policy before you leave the store to cut down on confusion later. When you get home from shopping, take your receipt out of the shopping bag and stash it in a special folder in your desk drawer. Then stow the item's box and other packaging in the original shopping bag in the back of your closet until the period of time in which you can return it has passed. If you become dissatisfied with the item, you can quickly reassemble all the elements you need to return it to the store.

Show up at the right time. The more information you have about a store and its products, the more chance you'll have of finding a great bargain. And when, exactly, is the best time of day to find the inside scoop on a store's merchandise? About 2 p.m., says Anne Obarski, a St. Charles, Missouri, consultant who advises businesses on how to provide good customer service. At this point in the day, the morning shift is still working and the evening staffers are just starting their shift. Avoid hitting stores during the first 45 minutes after they open—the few workers are still busy getting the store ready for the day. Late in the evening, they're often more interested in closing up the shop than helping you with your purchase.

Write a nice letter to get freebies. Wouldn't it be nice if manufacturers filled your mailbox with free cosmetics and other products? They're happy to do so; all you have to do is say something nice to them. Manufacturers get lots of letters from customers complaining about items, and it makes their day when they get a letter *complimenting* their products. If you use a product often and really enjoy it, write a letter to the manufacturer, recommends Donna Montaldo, the coupon and bargain expert at about.com. She's written letters to show her support for her favorite cosmetics, and by doing so, she says, "you can usually get a ton of coupons in the mail." Find the mailing address of the company on the product's package or on the company's website. Make sure you mention the exact name of the product you enjoy and how long you've been using it when you write the letter. Apply a stamp, cross your fingers, and wait for those coupons as a thank-you for your letter.

Act promptly on rebates. Many manufacturers offer rebates on their products, from toothpaste to televisions. These can put $20—or even more— back into your pocket. But companies don't always make the rebate process easy, and when you don't follow their rules, you probably won't get your money. After all, they count on a certain percentage of their customers failing to apply for the money. Since you often need to mail in a receipt to claim your rebate, ask for a duplicate of the receipt at the checkout counter. This way you'll have a backup copy in case the company loses the one you send in or you need to

WHAT WAREHOUSE STORES DON'T WANT YOU TO KNOW ABOUT Prices

Managers of warehouse stores—those no-frills stockrooms with bare concrete floors and pallets stacked high with bulk goods—want you to think these stores offer the best bargains you'll find. That's not really true. These stores *do* tend to offer better deals than you'd get if you simply filled your cart at the grocery store without comparison shopping and seeking out bargains, says Jonni McCoy, founder of miserlymoms.com. However, now that you have the inside scoop on finding bargains, you're not just an average shopper anymore. You can find better deals on many items than the prices that warehouses offer. When you use coupons and wait to buy items when they're on sale, you'll generally get your household goods more cheaply at the supermarket (she's made spreadsheets to prove this!) You can save 50 percent or more on cereal, meat, toilet paper, paper towels, and many other staples when they're discounted at the supermarket versus the warehouse store. Plus, at the supermarket you don't have to pay an annual membership fee, which takes away some of the value you gain at the warehouse store.

Annette Economides, a Phoenix-based bargain finder, publishes "The Home *Economiser* Newsletter." She knows virtually every trick in the book when it comes to saving money. But she doesn't always have time to use every trick. When she needs to go shopping but is in a time crunch, she'll run down her shopping list and look through the newspaper sales circulars from several stores to find the cheapest prices. Often these are the loss leaders, or absurdly low-priced items that stores set out solely to bring in customers. Once she finds the lowest prices for as many items as possible, she'll head off to one store that has a policy of matching its competitors' prices. When she pulls her cart up to the register, she pulls out her advertising flyers and shows the clerk the low price that the store needs to match on each item. This way, she reaps the benefits of sales all around town—but only has to expend time and gasoline shopping at one place.

return the item because it's defective. As soon as you get home from the store, immediately send off for the rebate. You often have to fill out a form and include the proof of purchase—which is often found on the package—along with the receipt. If you don't stuff all these bits of paper into an envelope right away and mail it to the manufacturer, odds are good that you'll lose one of these crucial elements, and your rebate will slip away.

Befriend the store's staff. You have your eye on a particular backpack that you're planning to buy before your hiking trip later in the summer, but it's not on sale now. Engage the salesperson—or even better, the store manager—in a little chitchat to establish a friendly atmosphere, then ask if the item will be on sale anytime soon. You're not just a run-of-the-mill customer anymore—you're a person about to reel in some inside scoop. Since you have a casual banter going, the staffer may share some inside info on upcoming sales that the other shoppers don't know about. Next weekend, or even a few months from now, you may be able to stroll back in and snag the backpack at a 20 percent discount.

Take advantage of loss leaders. Stores often advertise products at a super-low price just to bring you into the store. They may lose money on these loss leaders, but they'll make even more money because they're using the bargains to lure customers toward other items in the store that are marked up in price. When you head into the store to buy one of these great bargains, just buy the loss leader, turn right around, pay for it, and leave. When you buy other things, you're almost guaranteed to blow any money you've saved on the bargain.

Check out new apparel thoroughly. Clothing retailers are perfectly happy when you take home damaged goods and decide, later, that complaining is not worth the bother. But think about it: There's a good chance that some other customer has tried on the garment that you're thinking of buying. Sometimes a hurrying shopper will get a foot caught in a hem and rip it. Some unscrupulous shoppers will even snip off the extra buttons from a garment while they're in the fitting room. So before you head for the cash register, check that a new garment's hems, extra buttons, fasteners, and other details are intact and operating correctly.

Beware "sales" bins. When you're cruising through a department store, you find all of the display racks in impeccable order—until you come across a bin of items dumped in a disheveled heap. Your immediate reaction is, Oh boy, steeply discounted items! That's just what the store manager wants you to think. Hold on to your wallet and check the prices carefully. An unkempt display does not necessarily mean a good deal.

Use coupons for bargains. Coupons are not just for groceries. Department store ads in newspapers often have coupons for 10 to 20 percent off in certain departments or for certain kinds of clothing. Combine that with a sale, and you can snap up some dazzling duds at truly bargain basement prices. If you have a store credit card, check the inserts that come with your bill. You may find a coupon or two tucked in there to lure you back to the store. And stores often have special sales offering an extra 10 to 20 percent off for using their credit card. ◄❙

Shopping Alternatives

6 Tricks for Finding the Best Bargains at Yard Sales, Outlet Stores, and Thrifts

Plan your yard sale attack. One of the penny pinching-est people on the planet revealed to us her personal game plan for scooping up scores of cents-on-the-dollar yard sale bargains in a single weekend. Now you know too: Go to a nearby convenience store and pick up a street map that covers all the residential neighborhoods in your town or city. When your Friday newspaper arrives on your doorstep—with its classified section brimming with ads for garage sales—plan your attack. Circle the ones that fall within pricier neighborhoods, and use your map to list the order in which you'll hit each sale. Homes in more expensive areas of town tend to offer more upscale goods, says Shelley Kincaid, author of *The Garage Sale Decorator's Bible* and host of a home-décor-on-a-budget TV show in Colorado. She should know: She says she goes to dozens of yard sales *each weekend*. By carefully planning your route to all these sales, you'll cut down on wasted miles driving back and forth. When you spend $5 or $10 less on gasoline, the bargains you'll find become even better deals. To *really* cut down on driving time, look for community sales, in which dozens of households in a neighborhood or subdivision are selling their items at the same time.

Equip yourself for yard sales. Finding great deals at yard sales depends on speed—so you can find the good items before other shoppers get to them—and a discerning eye that lets

Break the Secret Yard Sale Code

The most experienced yard sale shoppers can hit sales early by understanding a subtle code embedded in the classified ads. By mastering this code-speak, you, too, will be able to zoom directly to all the sales that offer the particular items that you want.

- At a *moving sale,* you'll find household items that are useful, but that the soon-to-be-moving owner can't move or won't bother bringing—think plants, lawn mowers, and gallons of paint.

- An *estate sale* is likely to showcase items from an older person who has passed away, such as antiques and vintage collectibles.

- The contents at a *divorce sale* will vary according to which member of the split-up couple is hosting the sale. If the man is doing the selling, expect to find items such as appliances, dishes, and women's clothing. If the woman is hosting the sale, look for sports memorabilia and power tools. Divorce sales are particularly good places to find a bargain—sellers are inclined to sell stuff for a song, since they just want the merchandise out of their lives, says yard sale expert Shelley Kincaid.

you pick out the quality merchandise from the junk you don't want. Load up a fanny pack with the following weapons so you can move quickly from sale to sale and pounce when you find a great deal:

- *Small bills and coins.* Your debit and credit cards are no good in the yard sale world, and sellers may not want to take checks either. You don't want to lose that beautiful lamp because you ran out of cash.

- *A tape measure.* From curtains to couches and from mirrors to mini-blinds, you need to know if certain items will fit in your home before you buy them. Know what sizes you're looking for before you take off for the yard sales, and measure these sorts of objects at the sale before you purchase them. If you forget your tape measure, you can also use a dollar bill to check sizes—it's six inches long.

- *A magnifying glass.* Quickly check for dents, loose threads, and other imperfections before you shell out any cash.

- *A map.* When you finish at one sale, it's time to make a beeline for the next one.

To call it your own, take a piece home. It's nothing short of a tragedy: You find a beautiful chest of drawers late in the day after you've spent most of your money on garage-sale bargains, and you don't have enough cash left to buy this new treasure. Sure, you could give the owner a few dollars as a deposit, but who's to say he won't go ahead and sell the chest of drawers to some other buyer who happens to have cash on the barrelhead? Here's a crafty trick gleaned from one of the world's best bargain hunters: Give the owner as much money as you can for a deposit. Then, before leaving to get the rest of the money, take a drawer with you. No other shopper will be willing to buy the incomplete chest, so you're assured that it will be waiting for you when you return. Top-drawer advice!

Plug into irregulars at outlet malls. A salesperson at a regular retail store would *never* steer you away from a full-priced pair of jeans and suggest you buy a slightly damaged version for a 30 percent discount. But that's exactly the sort of offer you'll find at an outlet mall. On your next shopping trip, skip the retail mall and head for the nearest outlet mall. Many clothing chains operate stores in outlet malls that offer merchandise for a lower price than you'd find at a regular retail mall. Some of the best bargains you'll find in outlet stores are items with tiny irregularities. These imperfections may be so small that you can't even find them! Ask the store manager to show you the section containing irregular items. Once you pick the item you want, ask the manager for his or her opinion on whether the defect will significantly decrease the usefulness or life span of the item. Odds are good that it won't. At outlets, you do have to be careful of brand-name merchandise that is made specifically for outlets and is of a lower quality than the brands' department store merchandise. So inspect items carefully for workmanship, fabric quality, and such.

Buy slightly vintage bread. It probably takes your family a few days to finish a loaf of bread—so what's one more day? Steer your cart right past the bread aisle in the supermarket, and buy your bread and other baked goods from your nearest day-old-bread outlet. This is where bread, rolls, and other bakery items go when they don't sell quickly in the supermarket, and these bread thrift stores offer the products at a very steep discount. When you get them home, just pop them into the freezer and take out a few pieces as you need them. Bread freezes very well.

Shop at year's end at thrift shops. Secondhand outlets run by charities such as Goodwill Industries or the Salvation Army would like your business year-round—and shopping there frequently is a good idea, since you can get clothes and other household items for a fraction of what you'd pay in retail stores. But there's a special two-month period during the year when you'll find an extra-large variety of bargain merchandise: December and January. Crowds of people flock to these stores to drop off their donations at the end of the year for tax purposes, and you'll find that the extra assortment of goodies on the shelves lasts even into the new year. If you only go to these stores once during the year, this is the time to visit! ◁

WHAT HOUSEHOLD PRODUCT MAKERS DON'T WANT YOU TO KNOW ABOUT Amounts

Even though labels tell you to pour a cupful of detergent into your washing machine, squirt the cleaner into the reservoir in your dishwasher until it's full, or add a level scoop of coffee into your coffeemaker—you don't *have* to use this much. Manufacturers are in business to make money, and the more times you return to the store to replace their products, the more money they make. Experiment by using a little less—pour out a quarter-cup less laundry detergent. Keep your toothbrush an extra week beyond what the package recommends. Squirt only half as much cleaner into your toilet bowl. You'll find that you can cut back on many household products without seeing a difference in results—and all those bottles, jars, and tubes of product will last longer!

Buying Online
5 Little-Known Ways to Safely Get Those Great Savings Available in Cyberspace

Buy from auction sites on holiday weekends. When you bid on items on the eBay auction website, you will always see when the bidding will end. Watch for items for which the bidding will close at a time when most people are away from their computers, says Steve Economides. (The aptly named bargain guru is operator of americascheapestfamily.com with his wife, Annette.) If bidding stops at 9 p.m. on July 4, or 8 a.m. Christmas morning, few people will be adding bids and running up the price at the last minute. You can sneak in at the closing seconds, place your bid, and claim the item for yourself.

Be creative with your spelling. If you're looking for a particular item on an auction site—say, an Armani suit—try searching for it under a few misspellings, say bargain hunters Anna

Wallner and Kristina Matisic. Sellers who aren't good spellers may be offering the suits as Aramani or Armane, for example. Since most people searching through the site would only look for the suit under its proper spelling, you'd be competing with fewer shoppers when you cast your bid.

Look for a reputable rating. When considering whether to buy an item on eBay, consider the seller's rating. Unscrupulous folks hiding behind a pseudonym online may take your money and never send you the product. However, people who buy merchandise over the site can rate sellers based on criteria such as whether the item was described accurately, whether it arrived on time, and if it showed up undamaged. Steer clear of sellers with less than a 98 percent positive rating, Annette Economides warns. Your risk of having an unhappy transaction goes up as the seller's approval rating drops. If you're tempted to buy an item but the seller's reputation seems questionable, send the person an e-mail asking about the product. If you receive a thoughtful response in a timely manner, this is a good sign that you're dealing with an honest individual.

Let the Web shop for you. A number of websites have sprung up in recent years that will hunt down bargains for you. Before you start driving from store to store to compare prices on electronics, appliances, clothing, or other household goods, first visit several shopping comparison sites to get a sense of what a bargain price for the item looks like. In 2006, *Consumer Reports* magazine investigated six of these sites: froogle.com, nextag.com, pricegrabber.com, shopping.com, shopzilla.com, and shopping.yahoo.com. The magazine found that Yahoo and Froogle displayed the lowest prices. But search for your desired item at more than one of these sites to make sure you find plenty of options. Be sure to find out what the shipping and handling charges will be from each source so you're comparing the full cost from all the potential sellers.

Google those online vendors. Check the reputation of any company you buy from over the Internet. There are swarms of companies willing to sell you merchandise online, some of them reputable name brands and some of them fly-by-night shysters. Such companies would be embarrassed to have you do this, but go to your favorite Internet search engine and enter the company's name. You will probably be able to click your way to a forum where other customers air their opinions of the service they received. Another check to make: On the company's website, make sure there's a phone number and an address—signs of the company's stability. Make sure the address and phone number are accurate by checking them in the business listings of a standard directory search site such as 411.com, WhitePages.com, or superpages.com. You might also want to call the phone number. Be especially wary of doing business with websites that have offices that are based in other countries, since they are harder to check and you'll have fewer alternatives if your deal goes awry. ◁

Online auction sites are a great place to find bargains—but they're also cyber-hangouts for very sneaky crooks. Plenty of fraudulent folks will advertise cool merchandise at tantalizing prices, then take your money and run as soon as you pay them. These scams are especially painful when you're trying to buy big-ticket items that cost thousands of dollars. On smaller purchases, you may be protected from online fraud; for instance, when you use eBay, the site protects you up to $175, and when you use the PayPal method of paying, it may protect you up to $1,000.

To protect yourself on larger purchases, arrange to pay the seller through an escrow account. An escrow service will hold your payment until you verify that you've received the merchandise, then it will turn the money over to the seller. This way your money's in neutral hands until you're happy with your purchase.

But not every escrow service is safe. Plenty of services exist only to scam you. Here's how to protect yourself:

- Some of these scammers work hand-in-hand with fraudulent sellers to rip you off. As a result, eBay endorses escrow.com.

- If you choose to use a different service, be wary of any escrow providers that the seller suggests.

- Steer clear of escrow services that don't list their address and phone number on their websites, or services that have misspellings or odd language on their sites.

- Call the phone number to see if someone answers.

- Also, services should be licensed and bonded; verify this information with a state or provincial consumer-protection agency in the state or jurisdiction in which the company is located.

Auction Strategies
6 Best Bets for Getting the Best Bargains When Buying by Bidding

Check out storage-unit auctions. Check your newspaper classifieds for storage facility auctions, and visit your local storage companies to ask if they have any upcoming auctions scheduled. People keep all sorts of valuable items in storage facilities: seasonal sporting equipment, collectible comic books, china dishes, and other cool stuff. However, they don't always pay their monthly fees! When this happens, managers regularly sell off the contents of abandoned storage units to the highest bidder—which could allow you to bring home great bargains.

Know your auctioneer. At an auction, the auctioneer's obligation is to make money for the people selling the merchandise, says Gary Peterson, president of the Auctioneers Association of Canada and the auctioneer with Hudson Auctions in Hudson, Quebec. However, the auctioneer wants *you* to leave satisfied with your purchases too. Strike up a conversation with the auctioneer before the sale begins. Mention the items you're interested in buying and ask the auctioneer if he knows any helpful information about the items, such as their age, condition, and value. Once you get to know an auctioneer—particularly if you're a regular at auctions in your area—he can help you out in a number of ways, Peterson says. An auctioneer may choose to "ignore" your bid if he thinks you're trying to pay too much for the item. Or if he notices that you're not paying attention to an item that you'd probably be interested in, he may mention during his high-speed patter that you should consider bidding. By having

a good rapport with the auctioneer, you'll notice these helpful little signals.

Bid reasonably. If you're going to toss out the first bid at an auction, start with a low price, but not a price that would be a "steal" for the item, says auctioneer Peterson. For example, if you think the item is worth $1,000, don't start your bidding at $5. Offer $100 or $200 instead. The auctioneer needs to make money for the seller hosting the auction, and if certain items aren't going to fetch a reasonable price, the auctioneer can halt the bidding. If few people were going to bid against you anyway, your excessive bargaining just lost you the prize!

Set your limit ahead of time. Before bidding begins on an item—whether it's an in-person or online auction—write down on a piece of paper how much you're willing to spend, then add an extra 10 percent. During a heated exchange of bids, most people lose their ability to stick to a reasonable price. Once you reach your limit, and then the added wiggle room you've allowed yourself, stop bidding. Don't go a dime higher. Let the winning bidder realize with dismay that she's just paid too much on an item, and save your money to win on an auction bid another day.

Avoid publications promising big savings at auctions. Government auctions that sell property such as seized vehicles and foreclosed homes can be places to find decent bargains. However, pay no heed to advertisements that want to sell you guides on finding auctions that sell this type of property for next to nothing. For starters, you may be charged for more guides than you really want, according to the Federal Trade Commission. At around $50 a pop, these get expensive quickly. Another reason to skip these is that they only provide information that you could easily find on your own. Finally, they tend to exaggerate the deals you'll encounter. Don't get your hopes up *too* much about the savings you'll find at these auctions. Plenty of people know about them and show up to bid on worthy sales. If indeed you find a car for a few hundred dollars, or a house for a few thousand, they're going to be very questionable in value. Instead of purchasing one of these guides, visit your local city hall, which may have information about upcoming auctions. Or find auctions on the Internet by searching for the words "government auctions" and looking at sites ending with ".gov" in the search results in the U.S. In Canada, the Public Works and Government Services Canada website is a good one to access at www.pwgsc.gc.ca. It provides a list of Crown Assets that are on the auction block; to view featured items go to crownassets.pwgsc.gc.ca.

Seek out auctioned furniture deals. When home interiors retailers receive a truckload of products, if one box inside the truck is damaged or open, they will typically refuse the entire truckload, not just the one box. Instead of having the shipping company return all the products, the manufacturer of the products often sells the truckload of refused goods to the shipping company. The shipping company then auctions it off for pennies on the dollar. Most of the material is perfectly fine, and the auctions are open to the public. Contact the major shipping company in your area and ask about these auctions. You can save a lot of money. ◁

When Shopping for Anything, Free Is the Best Price

EXPERT INSTANT ADVICE

Whenever you need to buy anything, always work your way up the "shopping hierarchy" from the cheapest to most expensive to find the best deal, urge Steve and Annette Economides, authors of the book *America's Cheapest Family Gets You Right on the Money.* Here's how the hierarchy works:

- First, try to borrow the item from a friend or neighbor. If you only need to cut down a few trees, *borrowing* a chain saw makes a lot more sense than buying one.

- Can't borrow it? Try to get it *free.* Websites such as craigslist.org or freecycle.org will identify all sorts of useful items that people in your area are giving away free. Steve is well on his way to collecting thousands of free bricks he wants for building a walkway—instead of paying hundreds of dollars for new bricks.

- If you can't get things free, buy a *slightly damaged* version. A new washing machine may have a small scratch on the side but will still work perfectly fine.

- If a dinged version isn't available, then shop around for a store offering the item at a *discount.*

- Finally, if you can't get the item free or cheap, only then should you pay full price. But odds are very good that you'll find what you're looking for long before you have to settle for the most expensive option.

Budget and Savings
6 Easy Ways to Keep More Cash in Your Pocket

Keep a slush fund handy.
Something—be it a car repair, an emergency root canal, or a job layoff—always comes up to throw you off your monthly budget. To keep these incidents from running you into debt, you need to have an emergency stash in an easily accessible account, preferably a money market account (they earn a little more interest than regular savings accounts).

But how much is enough to get you out of a bind? Easy. Track all of your spending for a month (including everything from your mortgage payment to lunch at the deli), and multiply that monthly total by three. That three-month operating budget is a scary number, eh? Well, this is the minimum you should have on hand in case the roof caves in (literally or figuratively) and you need some dough to get you through the rough spots. And don't worry if this money isn't accruing the big interest; it's there for emergencies.

Ditch the ATM card. We're always making impulse purchases, from a pack of gum at the supermarket checkout line to that new Van Halen-meets-bluegrass CD. How can you stop your bank account from hemorrhaging? Take a page from the old-timers and shred your ATM card. It's just too easy to take out $100 at the local 7-Eleven when you're jonesing for a Snickers bar at 2 a.m. Instead, figure out how much cash you'll need each week for your regular, cash-based purchases (things like lunch at the cafeteria and your daily cup of coffee), head on over to the bank teller's window, and get your walking-around money for the week. With a finite amount of cash, you'll start to think twice before those spur-of-the-moment spending sprees.

Unionize your money. There's a better place than a bank to park your dough for your checking account needs, and if you want to take out a home equity loan, there's a better place to get that as well. It's called a credit union, and it acts much the same as a bank, but it has better loan and savings rates. Here's how they work: A credit union is a cooperative venture that doesn't have to make profits for clamoring stockholders. The people who do business with the credit union—you, with your checking accounts and loans—more or less "own" the credit union. Many credit unions now offer the same services as banks, including debit cards and online banking. You can find a credit union at the Credit Union National Association's website, www.cuna.org. It has a searchable list of credit unions broken down by state, and eligibility criteria. In Canada, try the site cucentral.ca, run by the Credit Union Central of Canada.

Put yourself on your payroll. There comes a time every month when the bills start piling up and you force yourself to sit down and write out all the checks. Well, there's one more check you should be writing—one to yourself. Jay Fine, a longtime financial planner based in Monroe, New Jersey, offers this easy way to put your retirement planning into high gear. "Put yourself on the payroll," he says. "Every month—or even better, every paycheck—make sure you set an amount aside for investment. A good number would be about 6 percent. Anything more would be great. If you have to, you can even write yourself a check to deposit or send to another account. But just as you

pay your mortgage and your electric bill without fail, now you'll be making sure to pay yourself as well."

SECRET WEAPON

Budget Formula

So you diligently track your income and every expense that you have. But how do you know if you're spending reasonable amounts of money on things like housing, debt, and groceries? Follow these parameters offered by E. Kim Dignum, a financial planner in Fort Worth, Texas, courtesy of CNNmoney.com (all figures are percentages of your gross household income):

30 percent: Housing and debt (mortgage/rent, credit cards, auto loans, student loans, etc.)

26 percent: Living expenses (food, clothing, utilities, transportation, medical, entertainment)

25 percent: Taxes (federal, state, local, and property; FICA and Medicare or CPP in Canada)

15 percent: Savings and retirement (401(k), stocks, mutual funds, college savings, RRSP in Canada, etc.)

4 percent: Insurance (life, health, disability, auto, homeowners, etc.)

Make, and stick to, a budget. Budgets are the first steps to gaining some financial order in your home. Stanley Kershman, an author, lawyer, and creator of the website www.debtonadiet.com, has a six-step plan to accomplishing just that:

1. Don't attempt to do your entire budget in one sitting. Take a few days, breaking the work down into manageable pieces.

2. Gather up all of your income information, including salaries, interest, and gifts.

Easy Financial Rules of Thumb

Concerned about how much you're spending, how much you should be saving, and how much house you can afford? Use these easy equations to determine how financially healthy you are:

- The **price of your home** should not be more than 2.5 times your annual gross household income.

- Your **total monthly debt payments** (including mortgage, student loans, car, and credit card payments) should not be more than 35 percent of your monthly gross income. Some mortgage brokers will stretch this ratio up to 40 percent, but that leaves you very little budgetary wiggle room.

- To **retire comfortably**, your nest egg should be about 20 times what you want your annual income to be. If you anticipate needing about $75,000 a year to live on when you retire, you'll need to save a nest egg of about $1.5 million. Of course, this will vary if you retire early or continue to work longer than usual.

3. Next, gather up all of your expense information. Do this thoroughly, even if it takes three days, a week, or a month. Make sure you're not missing anything.

4. Using a budget worksheet—the free one on debtonadiet.com or one you mock up on your own—add up all of the totals for the income and outflow.

5. Figure out where you can do some fine-tuning, either to pay down your debt or increase your savings goals. However, above all, make sure you're making as much money as you're spending. Stay out of the red.

6. Redo the budget with the new totals, and post it around your house, lest you forget you are now living within the cozy confines of a household budget.

Divvy up any unexpected income. When you have a windfall—a bonus, gift, or extra cash for extra work—use the rule of thirds to determine how to use it:

- *One third for the past.* Use one third to pay down debt you owe.

- *One third for the future.* Put a second third immediately into some sort of savings or investment.

- *One third for the present.* Use the final third to make a home or personal improvement or purchase you want.

If you follow this rule, you'll see your debt shrink and your savings grow, and you won't feel deprived. ◂

Credit Cards

8 Little-Known Tidbits That Will Help Get You Out of Debt Fast

Pay down the expensive debt first.
Let's say you have $5,000 of debt built up on a high-interest-rate credit card (perhaps 18 percent) and you also have a $50,000 home equity loan at 8 percent interest. You only have so much money to devote to paying down loans each month, so which of these debts should get priority? First pay down the high-interest-rate debt, even if it's the least amount of money you owe, say financial planners. If you must, just pay the minimum on the home equity loan while you aggressively eliminate the credit card debt. You'll save a lot of interest in the long run.

Drowning in debt? Ask for a life raft. Here's something that you'll never hear from a Visa or AmEx customer service rep: If you owe so much money on your credit cards that you're seriously considering bankruptcy, chances are the credit card companies will strike a deal with you. In most cases, a very good deal. Here's what you have to do, according to Howard Dvorkin of Consolidated Credit Counseling Services in Fort Lauderdale, Florida, and author of *Credit Hell: How to Dig Out of Debt*.

Start calling the phone numbers on the backs of your credit cards. When you explain your situation to a credit supervisor, you do nothing but tell the truth: You are considering filing bankruptcy. The B-word is one that the credit card companies hate to hear. If you did declare bankruptcy, credit card companies would usually be left holding the bag. (While bankruptcy may sound like an attractive way to get out of your financial predicament, keep in mind

that it seriously blemishes your personal financial record.) Tell them that if they want to see any money, they should make you an offer you can't refuse. In many cases, according to Dvorkin, the credit card company will make a deal with you then and there—it may slash what you owe by as much as 50 percent. Other options it may give you include rejiggering the monthly payment plan or eliminating future interest on your account. From the credit card company's point of view, it's better to get something instead of nothing.

Pay credit card bills twice a month.
Credit card companies will never offer you this brilliant idea, but it's yours

SECRET WEAPON

Prosper.com

Tired of paying 20 percent interest on your credit cards? Get a "prosperous" personal loan. In the U.S., a new website, Prosper.com, allows you to borrow money from regular folks, at interest rates that *you* determine. How does it work? Simple. Go to www.prosper.com, sign up, and type in the loan amount you need, along with the interest rate that you are willing to pay. Prosper will review your financial situation, and then lenders will bid on your proposal, and a match is eventually made. Prosper.com acts as the mediator and takes a small percentage of the deal—a one-time 1 percent charge from the borrower, as well as a 0.5 percent annual service fee from the lender. Backed by Accel Partners, Benchmark Capital, Fidelity Ventures, and Omidyar Network, Prosper had already done more than $20 million of business as of late 2006. Loans for first-time users range from $100 to $25,000.

right now. If you owe a lot on high-interest-rate credit cards, make a payment every two weeks instead of once a month, even if you're just paying the minimum amount due. Why? Because this will cut into the interest as it accrues. It may not seem like much, but over time, you'll save a bundle.

Pay credit card bills immediately. While it's wonderful that credit card companies give you a grace period before interest accrues on your balance, keep in mind that the longer you wait to make your payment, the more interest accrues on your previous debt. So don't file that bill away for later—pay it at your first opportunity.

Resist pre-approved credit card offers. Credit card companies know how to ensnare new customers: Keep up that barrage of offers. Once you take the bait on a card and they have you, chances are you're going to run up some debt. Here's a way to resist temptation: Stop receiving them. That's right—you can opt out of receiving credit card offers. There are two ways to do it:

- The first one you can do on the Internet, at www.optoutprescreen .com. When you get to the site, which is the only official site that credit rating companies will use for this service, you'll find three choices. You can stop receiving offers forever, for five years, or if you had previously "opted out," you can opt back in. Your information and preferences go directly to all of the major credit rating companies.
- If sending this information over the Internet still spooks you, you can call 888-567-8688 and accomplish the same thing.

Canada does not have one central service like this, but if you receive a lot of solicitations from one or two companies, you can call them and ask them to remove your name from their mailing list.

Use good penmanship. Here's another easy way to avoid credit card late fees: Write legibly, because it's perfectly legal for credit card companies to hold, reroute, and otherwise stall payments that they say they can't read. They can do this for five days without having to contact you. If your payment due date passes in the meantime, tough luck.

Stop writing notes. Don't write notes to your credit card company and enclose them with your payment. Why? Those companies are allowed to take the notes, along with the bills and checks to which you attached the note, and reroute them back and forth to different departments for up to five days. As a result, you may miss your payment deadline. It will also give the credit card companies another few days to suck some interest charges out of you. Even a small notation on your bill means your bill is being redirected and, quite possibly, late.

Can those yearly credit card fees. Want that annual credit card fee waived? As with many things in life, you may just get your way if you ask. Simply dial up the number on the back of the card, and tell the representative that you don't want to pay the fee any longer, and you'll switch to a different credit card if you have to. One credit counselor says that most of the time, the first customer service rep on the line will have the authority to waive or discount the fee. If you routinely carry a balance, it's likely that you'll get your way. ◂

Lower Your Bills

11 Ways to Pay Less for Cable, Groceries, and Phone Service

Get 4-1-1 for F-R-E-E. Here's a way to sidestep the directory assistance charge on your phone bill, which can cost 75 cents to a dollar per request: Call 800-FREE-411. It's completely free, though you may sometimes hear a brief commercial. You can access this service from both your landline and cell phone. This does not apply in Canada—although you can use websites to get phone numbers, including whitepages.ca, canada411.ca, and 411.ca. In the U.S., you can get phone numbers online at anywho.com, switchboard.com, superpages.com, and many other sites.

Cut those cable bills. Cable and satellite TV companies won't yell from the treetops, "You're paying too much for your service!" but almost all of them are open to negotiating your service rates Here's how you do it. Call the "billing inquiries" number on your bill. When you get a human on the phone, tell him or her that you've been receiving offers from satellite or cable (whichever one you don't have) and that you're being offered a significantly better deal. It helps if you actually have a real offer in hand. Chances are, this operator will pass you along to a different department. Tell this

---

WHAT YOUR BANK DOESN'T WANT YOU TO KNOW ABOUT Fees

You can negotiate the fees that banks and credit card companies charge you for their services. Try these:

- ☐ Overdrafted on your account? "Insufficient funds" fees on checks start at around $25, and go up from there. If you've been an otherwise good customer and ask, this fee can usually be waived. All you have to do is call the number on your statement or credit card—no crying or pleading necessary.

- ☐ If you're going through a major bank to secure a mortgage, virtually all the fees are subject to discussion, most notably the notion of "points," which is an extra percentage or two you pay up front to secure the loan. Appraisal fees of the property you're purchasing are also often waived. Just ask the bank manager for a face-to-face meeting, point out the fees, and politely ask if they can be waived. The fees are negotiable, and there's a lot of competition for your business—so there's a good chance the bank manager will comply. Just because a host of other people blindly pay them, that doesn't mean you have to.

- ☐ Credit card issuers love sticking you with late fees, even for your first offense. But a phone call to the customer service number listed on the back of your card will more often than not result in the fee being waived without any red tape, provided you've been a good customer up to that point.

next person that you're happy with your service, but the price differential has you thinking about switching. Ask if he can offer a similar price. You will almost be certainly offered a price break.

Keep your eye on the cash register. Don't "check out" mentally at the checkout counter—it may cost you! You might think that modern scanner systems don't make mistakes. However, studies show that discrepancies between the sticker price and the scanned price happen in about 5 percent of all cash register transactions. Speak up if you see an error—many stores will even credit you the full value of the item if you point out price mistakes.

Study your grocery store's sales patterns. They might not admit to this, but many supermarket chains put foods on sale at regular intervals—for example, a certain ice cream might go half-price once every four weeks. Other foods that regularly go on sale include breads, orange juice, soda, spaghetti sauce, apples, lettuce, shrimp, chicken breasts, yogurt, and cereal. Once you become aware of the patterns, you should never have to buy these products at full price again!

Seek out savings "triple plays." While most retailers limit you to one discount at a time on a product, grocery stores allow you to apply multiple discounts at the same time on a product. It's rare, but every now and then a store will have a sale on a food product that you love, that you happen to have a coupon for, at a time in which the store is offering double- or triple-coupon discounts. At moments like these, stock up—you'll be getting a favorite food nearly for free! This strategy works well for yogurt, bread, ice cream, and frozen prepared foods (items for which discount coupons are often available).

Go directly to the source for coupons. Pretty much every national brand has a website, and many of them provide printable coupons, rebates, and

---

WHAT MANUFACTURERS DON'T WANT YOU TO KNOW ABOUT Refunds

The dirty secret of companies that offer refunds is that many if not most of the people who buy an item with a refund offer don't actually bother to claim it—or they make some mistake that disqualifies their claim. Claiming a refund takes time and patience, but if you're buying something that you would buy anyway, applying for a refund puts money back in your pocket—and in the case of big-ticket items, it can be significant amount. To make the most of refunds, keep these points keep in mind:

☐ Apply for the refund as soon as you get home. The longer you wait, the less likely you are to do it. The expiration dates can be very short.

☐ Remove the product code or other part of the package designated as the proof of purchase. Fill out the refund form, photocopy it, and mail it. Be sure to include the proof of purchase, a copy of the receipt, and anything else that is required. Send exactly what is specified or you'll be disqualified.

☐ Keep a log of refunds that you have requested, listing the item, the company, the amount due, and the date you mailed it.

other special offers (sometimes including free samples). Our best strategy: Look at your local grocery store's current sales flyer, and find what products are on sale and that you need. Next, go to the website of the product and see if there is a coupon available! The result: huge savings (as a test, we just did this, and discovered we could buy cans of tuna for 25 cents each!).

If you cook, plant herbs—not vegetables—in your garden. Fresh herbs bought at a grocery store are incredibly expensive, no matter what time of year. Serious cooks can save a small fortune if they can harvest basil, oregano, thyme, mint, and rosemary from their own gardens. However, you won't see the same cost benefit with vegetables. The week your zucchini harvest comes in is usually the same week that it comes in at local farms—meaning the grocery store will be selling them at a deep discount.

Don't double-buy long-distance service. For people with both home and cell phone services, it's highly wasteful to pay for expensive national calling plans for both. Choose the most cost-efficient or convenient service for your long-distance calls, and use the other service for local calls only. Or skip long distance on both if you use an Internet phone service.

Upgrade to a digital cable box. Even if you don't have a new television, this can pay. Most televisions sold today are high-definition sets that require an upgraded, digital cable signal to deliver a great picture. To keep customers loyal, many cable companies will let you exchange your old cable box for a digital box, for free. The benefit? Many more channels at no extra charge.

Get free telephone service over the Internet. Phone companies don't want you to know this, but if you have broadband Internet service, then you can use your computer as a telephone at no charge! All you need is a headset with a microphone or an inexpensive telephone that connects to a USB port on your computer and some free software that you can download in minutes. Skype (www.skype.com) is the best-known Internet phone service—it allows you to call any other similarly equipped computer around the world for free. And if you want to use Skype to call regular phones in the U.S. and Canada, it's just a modest annual fee, far less than the cost of one month of typical phone service. Calls to most countries overseas cost only pennies a minute.

Cash in on store courtesy cards. Sometimes called club or thank-you cards, store courtesy cards have proliferated in recent years. There's not a major drugstore or supermarket chain that doesn't offer one now. And even some big-box electronics stores have their own version. The stores offer the cards because they want to make you a regular shopper, and some consumers are suspicious about the cards—especially if there is a fee associated with them. But today most of the cards are free, and the savings can be significant, and there is no limit to how many stores you can have a card from. Some cards work by giving you a coupon rebate, say $5 off future purchases once you buy $100's worth of goods. Others give you a reduced price on certain items when you flash the card. Either way, you win, provided you regularly comparison-shop and make sure that you are not paying any more than you would at another store. So fill your key chain up with these little money-saving tags. ◁

Stocks and Investments
3 Questions to Ask Yourself to Determine If You Have the Right Broker

Have you researched him? Here's a secret tip to determining if your stockbroker is legit: All of the complaints filed against him, and all the settlements he's been involved in, are public knowledge and easy to find. In the U.S., all you have to do is look your broker up on the National Association of Securities Dealers' website, www.nasdbrokercheck.com. The site will list your prospective broker's employment history, plus either the nasty details of the broker's professional career or a clean bill of financial health. (You can also call 800-289-9999 to get the same information.) In Canada, find your provincial securities commission through the Canadian Securities Administrators site, csa-acvs.ca, and contact them to check a broker's references or to see if complaints have been filed.

Is he pushy? One broker who asked not to be named said that you should start worrying if your broker is pushing a particular stock, especially one that has been in the dumps recently. Unscrupulous brokerage houses sometimes engage in what's known as a pump-and-dump scheme: They highly recommend a stock to their customers, the price rises as those customers buy it up, and the brokers quickly sell their own shares of the stock behind the scenes, pocketing bucketloads of cash. It's ugly, and it's illegal, but it happens.

Does he crow about his "hot tips"? Keep this in mind next time your broker tells you about some "undiscovered gem" of a stock: It's almost certainly not "undiscovered." The odds of any one Wall Streeter knowing something the rest of them don't know are between slim and none. By the time the "secret" reaches you, chances are that the Wall Street highfliers have already made their move on the stock, leaving latecomers little chance of making a profit. ◁

SECRET WEAPON

Free Cash Flow Multiple

Want to know the secret to picking successful stocks? The "free cash flow multiple" is a measure that top Wall Street analysts use when trying to determine the health of any one particular stock. The number measures how much cash a company generates after it's finished paying its bills, including reinvesting capital back into its business.

To figure out what a stock's free cash flow multiple is, do this: Subtract a company's capital expenditures from its cash flow from operations. This information can easily be found on the face of a cash flow statement (which can be found at Yahoo!, Google, or tons of other Internet financial sites). That's free cash flow. Next, divide that free cash flow figure by how many diluted shares the company has outstanding (also found on any number of financial websites). This will give you the free cash flow multiple. You can feel pretty good about buying stock in a company at 12 times the current year's free cash flow, and very good at 10 times. The lower the multiple, the more attractive the company is. Don't like to do math? Your broker should be able to get you the free cash flow number very easily.

Investment Cautions
2 Traps to Avoid in the Pursuit of Quick Wealth

Be aware of investment scams. The moment you get a few extra dollars in your pocket, investment advice starts leaping at you from every corner of your life—from a favorite uncle, from coworkers, from strangers on the telephone, from unsolicited e-mails, and from magazine ads. Greet all unsolicited investment suggestions with an enormous amount of skepticism. Here are seven signs of a possible investment scam trying to pluck dollars out of your wallet.

- A promise that there's no risk
- A promise that you'll make lots of money quickly
- A promise of tax sheltering in an "offshore" investment
- An offer of offbeat investment "opportunities" such as oil leases, artwork, coins, or jewels
- A woeful story from a stranger who wants your help in accessing a large bank account or other funds
- An investment based on information that, supposedly, no one else has access to
- An investment plan that asks you to recruit other investors

Think twice before becoming a day trader. It sounds like the ideal life. Rather than reporting to an office or waiting on tables every day, you're going to sit at a computer at home in your pajamas, making quick buy-and-sell stock decisions and racking up bucketloads of cash. Well, hold on to your wallet, hotshot. Here's a reality check.

- *Don't bet the farm.* The harsh reality: Most day traders lose money big-time. So never, never, never day-trade with money you need for routine living—tuition money, retirement funds, money you need to cover household bills, and the like.

- *Understand the expenses.* Many day traders have to pay the company they're affiliated with enormous commissions in exchange for training and equipment. They work with borrowed ("on margin") money and can quickly ring up mountains of debt. Given the hefty expenses, have a clear idea of what it takes to turn a profit in this scenario.

- *"Easy" is a myth.* Day trading requires that you be glued to a computer all day, every moment, monitoring prices and trends. Done right, this is hard and gut-wrenching work. Anyone who tells you otherwise is scamming you.

- *Consider the source.* Once you become known as a day trader, you will be barraged with hot "insider" advice, primarily from people who are trying to drive up their own investments. Don't act on advice if you aren't sure of the source.

- *Check out that class.* You may have been invited to find out about day trading at a special class or seminar. Find out whether the instructor will benefit if you decide to become a day trader. If so, the information provided in the class might be seriously skewed. ◄

6
SECRETS TO
boosting
Your Credit Score

In our modern society, where most people pay for all their major purchases—from houses to appliances and cars—with loans, your credit rating is extremely important. The better it is, the more likely you are to get a good loan rate, and a few points' difference in your rate can add up to a substantial amount of money over the life of a car loan or a house mortgage. Here are some inside tips on keeping your credit rating in tip-top shape.

1 Ask for leniency

The quickest path to a low credit score is making late payments on obligations such as your credit card, mortgage, or car payment. But if you're coming up short this month and have been a good loan customer up to this point, there's an easy solution: Call the lender and ask for an extension. Or ask if you may make a smaller payment this month. If you have a good track record, chances are you'll get a free pass and be able to keep your credit rating high. But keep in mind that this is a one-time maneuver designed to give you a little breathing room. You can't call up month after month and expect to receive an extension from your lender.

2 Limit the number of credit cards you apply for

Want to watch your credit score go into a downward spiral? Never apply for more than two credit cards at any one time, says Stanley Kershman, a lawyer, author, and financial whiz based in Ottawa, Ontario. If a credit bureau sees that you have applied for three or more cards in a short period of time, the company will probably assume you're in desperate need of cash—and desperate people do not make good credit risks. An even worse scenario, says Kershman: The credit bureaus think your identity has been stolen, which would also send your credit rating down the tubes.

3 Shred your financial statements

The one surefire way to see your credit rating head south is to get your identity stolen. Not only will it ruin your credit rating, but it's going to take a lot of time, effort, and aspirin to restore your previously sterling credit rating.

So how do you avoid this mess in the first place? Don't throw your mail away—shred it. This includes bank statements, credit card bills, and anything with financial information on it. Shredders range in price from about $30, for the most basic model, to more than $1,000 for one that turns your important financial documents into dust. In truth, a simple shredder is all you need. That's because crooks—the bums that they are—always take the easiest route. It's a lot easier to read a bank statement that was ripped in half as opposed to one that was shredded into 50 pieces.

4 Don't be ruined by late payments

Did you know that if you miss a deadline on your car or credit card payment, your *other* lenders can jack your rate up to the default rate? This clause is called "universal default," and you want to avoid it at all costs. If you read the fine print on your credit card agreement, you'll read all about it. In a nutshell: If you are more than 30 days late on any payment, all of your credit card lenders earn the right to treat you like a financial pariah. Your low 0 percent or 3 percent credit card deal can skyrocket to a default of 20 percent or 30 percent. Remember, the credit ratings and reports will be seen by anyone who's holding your credit, and if you're making late payments for one credit card, you can be sure your other credit card companies are going to find out. Be sure to make your payments like clockwork.

5 Watch your credit account online

Identity theft is a multibillion-dollar business now, and hordes of thieves are hoping you won't do this. But if you check your account on the Internet religiously, you'll spot any criminal spending quickly and you'll be able to take action. Check your hard-copy statement or go to your credit card company's website for information on how to get online access to your account.

6 Never use a P.O. box

Oddly enough, using a post office box can harm your credit rating. When credit rating companies see that your bills are headed for a P.O. box, they worry that you have either lost your home or that someone has stolen your identity. Both scenarios raise a red flag.

Insurance

6 Secrets to Buying the Right Policies for You and Your Family

Don't buy worthless disability insurance. Some disability insurance is what's known as gainful occupation coverage. This kind of coverage means that if it's possible for you to work at *any* job you're qualified for—for example, as a fry cook at Burger King—no insurance dough for you. Don't buy this kind of coverage. Instead, ask your insurance agent for either an "own occupation" policy or an "income replacement" policy. The former will pay out if you're prevented from doing the job you have—for instance, if a writer loses his ability to type, the insurance will pay the claim. He'll continue to get paid even if he changes careers and goes back to work. An "income replacement" policy will continue to pay benefits to that writer, but will cut his benefits should he decide to go back into the workforce and pursue another career. These two kinds of policies make a lot of sense considering that, according to the U.S. Social Security Administration, 30 percent of Americans between the ages of 18 and 35 will one day be forced out of the workforce for a long-term disability.

Don't get canceled; get renewed. Disability insurance doesn't come cheap, so don't let the insurance companies talk you into making it even more expensive down the road. It's better to put a little more money into the policy up front and get what's known as a noncancelable and guaranteed renewable policy. This covers you in virtually any situation. Changing your profession from accountant to javelin catcher? They still can't cancel you, and must renew you. The other two types of disability insurance—plain old "guaranteed renewable" and "conditionally renewable"—have major disadvantages. The "guaranteed renewable" policy may be just that, but it allows the insurance company the flexibility to make changes to the policy, and "conditionally renewable" means, well, don't expect to get renewed once the company finds out you're catching javelins for a living.

Get your long-term-care insurance now. Even if you're only 35, signing up for this fast-growing segment of the insurance industry is a smart move. Why? Because your premiums will be very low, and as a result, you'll save money over time. Long-term-care insurance covers you in the event of disability or prolonged illness. The insurance can grant you all sorts of protection, such as covering nursing home costs and in-home health care. The trick here, though, is that very few young people think that far enough in advance. By the time they are senior citizens, the monthly premiums can be too much to bear.

Factor inflation into your long-term plans. So you're smart and got your long-term-care insurance now—great. But don't let the insurance companies snooker you down the road. Make sure inflation, and your own advancing age, don't get you in the end. Today's $5,000-a-month coverage might just be pocket change in 50 years. So when you buy your policy, you'll be faced with two choices for combating inflation—you can either choose to buy more coverage at a later date, or choose to have the insurance company automatically increase your coverage each year in step with inflation. Bet on the latter, because if you have to buy added insurance down the road to keep up with inflation, you're going to be charged a price in relation to your current age.

If it's not excluded, it's included.

Here's something you need to know when it comes to your insurance, especially homeowners' policies: Unless the policy specifically excludes something from coverage, the insurance company has to cover it. Let's use a wildly hypothetical example to explore this. Say aliens from planet Xenon land in your living room and demand your self-cleaning oven. They claim they need it to get back to their homeland. Because they have their laser guns pointed at your dog, you allow them to take the oven. Now you need a new oven, so you call your insurance company to file a claim. "Aliens stole my oven," you'll say. "Sorry," the insurance agent will then say, "but you're not covered for alien thievery." Well, guess what? You are. And you can tell that drone on the other end that if it isn't excluded, then it's included.

Become a loyal customer. Here's something not all home insurance agents are telling you up front: If you give your insurance company your business over an extended period of time, you may be eligible for a loyalty discount. In fact, the Insurance Information Institute claims many home insurers will reduce your premiums by 5 percent if you've been with the company for three to five years, and up to 10 percent after you've been a customer for six years. The only way to find out about these loyalty programs is by asking. ◂

WHAT YOUR INSURANCE AGENT DOESN'T WANT YOU TO KNOW ABOUT Riders

You really don't need all of those life insurance riders (extra benefits for more money) that you have attached to your policy. For most people, a typical, basic life insurance policy—be it term or whole life—is all you really need. Here are some that you may have that you can get rid of:

☐ Accidental death and dismemberment, better known to Billy Wilder fans as "double indemnity," is not necessary. Should you die in any "accidental" manner, this rider doubles the payout. For a $100,000 policy, expect to pay an extra $10 to $12 per month. That's not much now, but it adds up over time. And the chances of your dying in an accident are—knock on wood—slim.

☐ You can also forget about the "waiver of premium" rider. This rider, for about 8 to 10 percent of your yearly insurance payment, would have the insurance company continue to pay your premiums should you become disabled. If you're concerned about this, just buy disability insurance.

☐ A spousal rider allows your spouse (and children) to get term life insurance after you die if you had whole life insurance. This is useless, because kids generally don't need life insurance and your spouse could probably do better shopping for a new policy.

Taxes and Estate Planning
8 Tips to Surviving Tax Returns, Audits, Wills, and Probate

Don't do your own taxes. It may sound like we're advertising for H&R Block, but it's really worth it to pay someone a couple hundred dollars to prepare your taxes for you. Why? "What people don't understand is that nearly 80 percent of the IRS hit list—returns that are audited—are self-prepared," advises Dan Friebis, EA, ATA, ATP, a tax professional in Port Orange, Florida, with 28 years of experience. This number is staggeringly large because "people don't really know how to use [tax-preparation] software," he says, and get overly eager to pad their returns as they watch the amount in the "refund" box grow. In the process, they make trouble for themselves because the IRS has its own averages for what people of certain professions, in certain areas of the country, should reasonably claim as deductions. (To give you an idea of how low audit rates are for those who use professional tax services: Over the past seven years, Friebis has prepared over 13,000 returns, only two of which were audited. In the end, neither of those two audited parties ended up having to pay the IRS any extra money.)

Don't donate your car. As you've probably heard on the radio and from your tax professional, donating a car is tax-deductible—but that doesn't mean that it's a smart idea You'll probably be able to pocket a lot more money by selling it to a used-car dealer. Let's say you're in the 25-percent tax bracket, and you have an old junker that the Kelley Blue Book—the bible of used-car pricing—says is worth $2,000. You can deduct 25 percent off your taxes—$500—if you donate the car. If you're keen to have the car benefit those less fortunate, donate a chunk of the cash you got from selling the car.

Don't file a Schedule C, if possible. The "single-highest audit risk, bar none, is a person who's self-employed and files a Schedule C/sole proprietor form," says Friebis. By filing as a sole proprietor, you have about a one-in-three chance of getting an audit letter from the IRS, because the IRS has something similar to a points system about how your return should measure up regionally and nationally, and if you're even a little bit out of these parameters, watch out. You're much better off making your sole proprietorship an S corporation or a limited liability company, if you qualify and if you will earn enough to make the paperwork worthwhile. Changing your business to one of these lowers your risk of being audited to about 1 in 1,000, depending on region (and if you file as an S corporation, your personal assets are also protected if your business is ever sued). If you're starting your own business, Friebis advises, your first visit should be to an accountant, not a lawyer.

If you do **get audited, seek professional help.** Even if you prepare your tax returns yourself, don't face the IRS without a professional in your corner. The IRS "is hoping that you pay just out of fear" of being audited in the first place without even fighting the audit, confesses an anonymous tax professional. And don't just pick a random pro out of the phone book—get a recommendation from someone you know who has had success with that preparer. Another thing: Look for someone with the letters "EA," which stands for "enrolled agent," after her name. EAs have licenses to practice before the IRS and their specialty is strictly tax law; CPAs may be good number crunchers, but relatively few are well versed in tax codes, or in dealing with government auditors.

Eat, drink ... and deduct? A tax pro we talked to was more than happy to dish, no pun intended, on little-known deductions. Our favorite? If a husband and wife own their own business together, any meals that they eat together at which they discuss business are *100 percent deductible*, not limited to the entertainment deduction, which is only 50 percent allowable. (Who *doesn't* discuss work with his spouse over dinner, even if he doesn't work with her?) By the same token, if you work for someone else and have lunch

Public Records

There's a good reason why you better behave yourself during divorce or other court proceedings. A tax pro who didn't want us to use his name offered this shocking revelation: IRS auditors are literally hunting for tax dodgers on a regular basis, and it's very easy for them to find you. Auditors first check the newspapers for recent court cases, especially granted divorces, and then they go straight to the depositions. Divorce cases are fertile grounds for finding folks who have been cheating the government. Why? Think about all the he-said, she-said accusations that go on when warring spouses are trying to divide their assets and battle for custody. Everything you say during these proceedings is part of public record. Accusing your ex of declaring less income than she made, or hiding a million dollars in blackjack winnings under the mattress, will get you *both* audited faster than you can say "ex-wife." For your sake, if not for hers, keep your mouth shut about your financial status in court and make an attempt to be reasonable with each other.

with a coworker or your boss, and you buy yours and he buys his, your meal is deductible. It's called a "corporate meeting meal" deduction. Finally, say you're on a deadline at work and can't get out for lunch. If you order in and eat that meal at your desk while you're working, this "meal on premises" is also 100 percent deductible. The key to taking these deductions is to document carefully, and save your receipts.

Put your trust in trusts. Everyone needs a will, but most folks need much more than that. In the U.S., options you should consider:

- A revocable living trust keeps all of your assets (except, in most cases, your principal residence) under one umbrella. You put your name on the trust and name a beneficiary; when you die, the assets all transfer to the beneficiary, bypassing probate altogether. If you don't have this trust, a probate lawyer can take up to 3 percent in fees off the top "just because he can," says one estate pro, and your assets could be tied up in the courts for up to a year and be subject to estate tax. If your assets are in the trust, the lawyer (and the government, if your estate is under the maximum net assets allowable) would get zilch.

- A pour-over will is a part of the revocable living trust that takes precedence over any prior wills and directs where and how your assets will be distributed. You should retitle all of your assets, with the possible exception of your principal residence, into the trust; any assets that you forgot to mention or retitle (or didn't know about) would be automatically assumed part of the trust and would avoid probate.

- An AB trust protects your assets in the event that your estate is valued at more than the estate taxable maximum. Let's say that your family fortune is valued at $4 million, and the maximum estate tax exclusion allowed before taxing it is $2 million. An AB trust is one in which you can divide the money equally among spouses. Say you and your husband adopt an AB trust, which separates $2 million of your $4 million estate into the surviving spouse and a trust in the name of the other spouse, which the surviving spouse has the use of for health and welfare. When a surviving spouse dies, the trust of the spouse who predeceased goes directly to the ultimate beneficiary. The last surviving spouse has use of his or her deceased spouse's money, but these assets do not have to be included in the surviving spouse's estate. When managed properly, you can eliminate most of your estate tax this way. Consult your tax professional for specific advice.

Change personal debt to a home equity loan. A distressing number of people pay high interest rates for the personal debt they carry (credit card balances are a prime example), and sadly those fees are not deductible on your taxes. If you must have personal debt, cover it all with a home equity loan. Home equity loans, which are based on the value you have already accumulated in your house, generally come with lower interest rates. The bonus: For home equity loans up to $100,000, you can deduct the interest. Be disciplined with your home equity loan, however. If you're going to use it to wipe out your other personal debt, make sure the term of the loan lasts no longer than the original debt would have. If you prolong the payments, a home equity loan might not save you money after all.

Deduct your charity mileage. Log the miles that you drive while helping a charitable organization. For instance, when the Boy Scouts hold a holiday food drive and you drive all of those goods to a homeless shelter for them, you can deduct that mileage on your taxes. Go to the IRS website (www.irs.gov) to find the current cents-per-mile rate it allows for charitable driving—it's lower than the business mileage deduction, but a savings nevertheless. ◁

Retirement

3 Clever Moves for Your Career Endgame

Play catch-up. Maybe during your first few decades of work, you failed to see the wisdom of socking away cash for retirement when there were so many more fun things to do with it. If you're now age 50-plus, retirement is just around the corner and some age-old bits if investing advice apply to you in spades:

- It's never too late to save.
- Contribute the maximum allowable to your IRA or 401(k).

The good news is that U.S. taxpayers who are age 50 and up are allowed to contribute more into these tax-deferred accounts than other folks. For the year 2007, for instance, most workers were allowed to put as much as $15,500 into their 401(k) accounts. The 50-and-older crowd was allowed an extra $5,000. So start playing catch-up—it's time to mend those wanton ways.

Roll over, play smart. Many people in the first couple of decades of their careers change jobs every few years. If they have a 401(k) with the former employer, they often take the cash out of the account and pay the early withdrawal penalty. Big, big mistake. There's no wiser savings plan available to you than funds that are allowed to grow tax-free. So when you leave an employer, roll your 401(k) savings into an IRA, where your cash will grow with similar protection. You'll be so glad you make it a career-long habit—just ask anyone nearing retirement age.

Delays pay—up to a point. Everyone's retirement needs are different, but if you qualify for Social Security in the United States, waiting to file will put more money into your pocket—up to a certain point, anyway. For one thing, for every year that you delay retirement, that's an extra year of earnings from the work you do—and higher lifetime earnings can translate into a larger Social Security payout. On top of that, for every year that you delay retirement, the Social Security folks will permanently increase the benefit that you receive when you do eventually retire. These benefits stop increasing when you hit age 70, however—so that becomes a magic number for you. Once you reach age 70, there's no longer a reason *not* to file for benefits. And if you want to, you can keep working without penalty.

Even if you've decided to delay retirement, sign up for Medicare—the U.S. health plan for older people—before your 65th birthday. Unless you are still covered by insurance at your or your spouse's employer, delaying will usually actually cost you more. ◁

Getting Hired

9 Inside Tips on What to Do and What Not to Do When You Are Looking for a Job

Sweep the Internet for your own name. They won't ask your permission, but you can bet that prospective employers will punch you up on Internet search engines to find out every juicy little detail of your life that's posted online. Googling applicants is standard practice now, human resources directors confide, but they don't exactly broadcast that fact to the general public.

Actually, getting googled is a positive sign, because it means a company is interested in you. But it also means that just about everything you've ever "shared" in cyberspace is available for them to see and judge you by. Fair? Probably not. But it's a job-hunting reality these days.

Your first countermove is to do a Net search on yourself to see if any surprises are lurking out there. Then run through all the sites you have posted to—chat groups, discussion forums, friends' blogs or home pages, your own blog or home page, and social networking sites like MySpace or Facebook. If you find something you'd rather not have come up at a job interview—beer-soaked beach party photos, say, or an angry tirade you once wrote about the very industry you're trying to land a job in—see what you can do to make them disappear. Ask your friends to take those party photos off their sites, and see if more formal sites offer a "private access" option for archived material.

You might be stuck with having some embarrassing material stay posted, but at least you'll be aware of what your prospective employer may have seen. That way, you'll be better able to deal with it if it comes up. And from now on, remember the 21st-century version of your grandmother's advice: Never post anything on the Internet that you would not want to discuss at a job interview.

Give your letter the stamp of character. Here's a secret straight out of the human resources office: You are being judged even before your résumé is opened. Did you use stationery from your current employer to try to find your next job? Did you run your letter through the company mail meter? If so, the HR person receiving your letter is going to make some instant judgments about your character—and drop your résumé in the "round file."

Instead, make sure the first correspondence you send to your future employer screams, "This is special!" Choose an attractive envelope, and interesting stamps. Always—without fail!—address it to a specific person, such as the head of human resources, the personnel director, or the person in charge of the area you're applying to. Use that person's name on the envelope, not just a title. Spell it right. And don't just scribble your return address any old way. If you don't have a personal address sticker you're proud of, print your name and address in lettering that says, "I am somebody!" Yes, you want your communication to be businesslike, but you also want to make an impression. The best résumé in the world won't do you any good if it doesn't get opened.

Use e-mail like a professional. Applying by e-mail? Keep in mind that the person reading it will notice things that you don't.

- Rule #1 is to show some professionalism. Will an e-mail address like yugogirrrl@yahoo.whatever be the first thing your prospective employer sees? That's pretty far down the professionalism scale. So are jokey instant messenger screen names. So are sign-offs without enough contact information because you're assuming they'll just hit "Reply" to get back to you. Solution: Set up a separate e-mail account just for job searching.

- Another thing they're looking at right away is your spelling and grammar. Forget about the quick-typing culture that's connected with casual e-mail. Proof your cover letter and your attached résumé. HR types are unanimous on this: If they see typos and sloppy grammar, you won't be considered even if your résumé is CEO caliber. Their thinking is that if you don't care enough to check for errors, you won't be much of an employee.

- Also, remember that sending your correspondence to a specific person, by name, is even more important when you're applying by e-mail than by regular mail. You can usually find out the name of a human resources person, as well as his or her e-mail address, by checking the company's website. If you can't find that information online, there are reference volumes at your local library that provide data on companies, such as the Harris directory.

Surprise: HR's on the phone! There's a trend among human resources hirers you should be aware of: They're likely to hit applicants with an unexpected phone call as the first step in the interview process. It's nothing to get panicky about. It's just that they've read your cover letter and résumé, checked your references, and looked you up on the Internet, and now they want to learn more about you before committing to an in-person interview. So be prepared for that phone call, and keep any notes or talking points you think you may need by the telephone, or otherwise handy.

One extra piece of advice: If they've caught you at a bad time, it's okay to say so. It's much better to arrange a call back in an hour than try to make a good impression while the kids are screaming, dinner is boiling over on the stove, and dogs are barking. And a little extra time to collect your thoughts won't hurt, either.

Tout skills and strengths, not hopes and dreams. One of the most common résumé formats calls for placing an "objective" at the top of the first page. Something like,

"Experienced widget designer seeks new challenges within an innovative organization," blah, blah, blah. Your potential employer would never be this blunt, but in truth he doesn't care what your hopes and ambitions are. He wants to know what skills, talents, and traits you have that will benefit his company. So craft a concise, one- or two-sentence "positioning statement" at the top of your résumé instead. This feature in particular should be tailor-made for every prospective employer you write to.

Leap on job prospects immediately. Have every element of your personal presentation ready to spring into action on a moment's notice—particularly a polished résumé, work samples, and a list of references. If you see a classified ad for the ideal job in the weekend newspaper, you want your materials on a hiring manager's desk on Monday morning. Why? The inside secret is that companies typically pluck the best prospects out of the first batch of applicants and give them the most consideration. This may not be scientifically wise on their part, but it's human nature. If you respond immediately, you could be getting called in for a job interview while other applicants are still dusting off their out-of-date résumés.

Respect your friendly recruiter. Many a job opportunity is lost because the applicant doesn't realize what the hiring team in the company knows only too well. Which is: The human resources staff "recruiter" has as much say about whether you get hired as the department head with the vacancy. Often your first interview is with this personnel department staffer. Treat it as the real thing, not a preliminary formality, or you may never get that second interview.

"If I'm the HR recruiter and I sense you're talking down to me or dismissing me in your mind, you're not going to get past me," says Dale Kurow, a New York career coach and former human resources director, who is author of the e-book *Surefire Networking Tips*. "I'm reading your personality and looking for a cultural fit with the company, so an arrogant attitude is not what you want to have coming across."

True, the HR gatekeeper usually doesn't have the expertise to grade your technical capacity, but you need to see this as a communications challenge. "I always made sure that I knew enough about things like systems and applications programming, for example, to ask intelligent questions," Kurow says. "Applicants who really know their stuff are able to frame their knowledge in a way that even a six-year-old can understand."

Take The Lunch seriously. So, the hiring manager and two other company Ms. or Mr. Bigs invited you to lunch? What a nice, friendly gesture. And they'll do everything in their power to encourage you to think that's all it is. Don't believe it for a minute. Their motive is to evaluate you in a social setting. For some jobs—especially higher-level ones—The Lunch is the part of the interviewing process where you need to show that you have good casual communication skills, that you fit into the corporate culture, and that you can represent the company to outsiders gracefully and confidently.

How to Ace That Job Interview

There's so much advice floating around on how to handle job interviews that you'd probably make a fool of yourself if you tried to follow it all. Stick to the following simple tips and you'll do fine:

- **Rehearse the interview.** Have a friend play the role of interviewer and practice answering questions. It may seem silly at first, but you'll learn a lot. Some career coaches even suggest interviewing for jobs you don't really want just to get used to it.

- **Do a dry run to the interview site.** The surest way to get to your interview on time is to make the same trip the day before. See how long it takes to get there, notice the traffic, figure out where to park, and time the walk from the parking lot (or public transportation stop) to the building.

- **Dress like you care about the position.** Err on the side of conservatism. For most professional or office jobs, that means suits for men or women—even if a suit isn't "you." You're not making a fashion statement; you're showing them that the job is important to you.

- **Impress the receptionist.** He or she might be asked their opinion of you. "I know people who didn't get the job because they were rude to the receptionist," says Alison Doyle, a veteran human resources professional.

- **Stride confidently as you enter.** The biggest impression you make is visual, not verbal, and it comes in the first 10 seconds. So don't walk in chewing gum or finishing off your Diet Coke. Smile, walk into the room purposefully, and shake hands firmly.

- **Refuse the coffee.** Or the soft drink. Or the glass of water. You don't want to be worrying about spilling, or wondering where to put an empty cup.

- **Bring only what you need.** Some notes or work samples might help your cause. Shuffling through piles of folders definitely won't.

- **Turn off the cell phone.** Better yet, leave it in the car.

Are you up to it? Of course you are. You wouldn't have made it this far if you didn't have plenty on the ball. But get the details down. Arrive on time (yes, they're watching for that). It's okay to order a pre-meal drink if they do; it's also okay not to. They invited you, so let them pay. Turn off your cell phone, your BlackBerry, and anything else that can be turned off. You're not impressing anybody about how busy you are by taking calls or messages during lunch. Don't order the most expensive thing on the menu, but don't be a killjoy by saying something like, "I think I'll just have a small salad today." Order something you know and like. Show them you can enjoy yourself and be a pro at the same time.

Finally, feel free to cheat by scoping out the restaurant in advance. Check out the menu, the wine list, the service staff, the bathroom location, and the dominant attire among the clientele—anything that will help you feel more at ease is a definite plus.

Check your personal life at the door. In a job interview, focus on professional issues and avoid personal matters altogether. If you blather on about your childhood or your marriage, the interviewer will assume that personal issues will intrude upon your work life as well. This will leave you with plenty of "personal time," all right—and no job. ◁

Maximizing Compensation

5 Important Things to Keep in Mind When You Are Negotiating Salary or Benefit Matters

Pin down the benefits before saying yes. Don't accept a job offer without being clear about the benefits package you'll be getting, even if you're happy with the salary offer. Sometimes a company can meet your salary requirement only because they are seriously skimping on the benefits package, though of course they won't tell you that unless you ask. Remember that your compensation is a package, not just a salary. Employee benefits can make up as much as 40 percent of that package. If you have to pay all of your medical insurance premiums and shell out $300 a month for parking, that so-called acceptable salary is in effect reduced considerably.

Never lowball yourself. When you offer to work at a low salary or inadequate benefits, you're probably assuming that the hiring manager thinks you're eager to work and a good team player. And you hope you'll be rewarded down the road. Forget it. What he or she is actually thinking is, We can get away with paying this sucker less than others. And chances are they'll keep thinking that for years to come no matter how good a job you do. Greed is not an issue in a salary negotiation. You are expected to ask for the salary (or raise, or benefits package) you think you deserve. Then you negotiate from there. You are not scoring points by lowballing yourself. You're only undermining your position.

Sympathy is not a factor. The man or woman on the other side of the desk will probably nod with sympathy when you say you need a better medical plan or more money because your child is sick. But that doesn't mean you're going to get it. The only thing on his or her mind is negotiating in the best interests of the company. Push for what you deserve (based on your qualifications), not what you "need" (based on your family situation). Convincing the company that it needs you and that you've earned what you're asking for will get you much further than any personal plea.

Money isn't everything. If your raise request is turned down, you may be able to get the equivalent of what you were asking for in better benefits. That could be some combination of a pension hike, more vacation time, broader medical coverage, or a more flexible schedule. But even though your boss may be willing to boost your benefits, he or she probably won't bring it up. That's your job. In fact, you should go into your raise negotiation with a backup benefits request ready.

Getting a raise takes time. Getting a salary increase, especially a merit raise, is rarely something you can just ask for and expect to receive. You have to build up to it. You not only have to do your own basic job well, but you need to take on more responsibilities and get a reputation as a person who can get things done. When you do ask for an increase, have a list of your accomplishments—and documentation to back them up—and know how they connect to the bottom line (sales increased, costs reduced, problems solved, processes speeded up). And another thing: Never give an ultimatum, threat-

Understanding a Company's Benefits Package

The benefits package confuses most employees, and the companies like it that way because it leaves you at their mercy. Here's a checklist that will clear the fog:

- **Start date.** Do you get the benefits right away or after a trial period?
- **Medical plan.** Does it cover pre-existing conditions? If not, what qualifies as a pre-existing condition? Is there a waiting period? Is your family covered? Is your unmarried partner covered? Will you have to pay some of the premium? How much?
- **Retirement/pension.** What program does it fall under? Does the company contribute all, some, or none? Are you required to contribute? How much? How much will you get upon retirement?
- **Vacation.** How many days? At what rate does vacation time increase with tenure? Are your vacations paid? Do you lose vacation time if you don't take it? When are you eligible for vacation time? Can you split it up?
- **Holidays.** What are they? Do you get your birthday off? Will you be asked to work on some holidays?
- **Life insurance.** Is it provided? How much? Do you have to pay?
- **Disability coverage.** Does the company offer coverage if you can't work? Is it long-term or just short-term?
- **Education/vocational training.** Does the company pay for work-related classes?
- **Day care.** Is it offered? Is it on-site? Is it free?
- **Parking.** Does it exist? Is it free?

ening to leave if you don't get the raise. Your boss may surprise you and accept. If you're that dissatisfied, start quietly looking for another job while you still have the current one to support you. ◄

Getting Ahead
9 Secrets for Honing That Competitive Edge and Advancing Your Career

Recruit yourself a mentor. You learned your work skills with the help of at least one experienced teacher. Learn your career advancement skills the same way, and you'll leave the lone rangers behind. "I can't stress enough the value of having a mentor in your job, especially when you're new and trying to get the lay of the land," says career coach Kurow. "A mentor will offer advice, act as a sounding board, give you professional support, and provide that objective feedback which is so crucial."

There's nothing formal about a mentor-mentored relationship. Once you've done some people-watching in the workplace and found somebody you might want to enlist as your mentor, simply ingratiate yourself with that person. First offer help. For example, you might mention that you're interested in a project she or he is working on, and you'd like to assist if possible to gain experience. Then offer friendliness.

If you're graceful about it and the person turns out to be a good choice, things will work out better than you may have thought. "It's not like you're being manipulative and going in with a hidden agenda," Kurow says. "If the person is sharp enough to have become a success in the company, they'll know what you're up to. They'll usually appreciate it that you chose them as a mentor."

A secret source of power. The pipeline to valuable information in a typical workplace runs through the administrative support staff. Administrative assistants and receptionists know this, but most of your coworkers are too busy feeling superior to give them the time of day. So get a leg up on the competition by making sure you're friendly, helpful, and respectful to all different kinds of people, up and down the ladder. To get ahead, you need informal as well as formal sources of information. And trust us, good administrative assistants know what's going on. The best ones know what's happening before it happens. So make it a habit to always say good morning, and occasionally ask, "What's new?" You might get an answer.

Another reason for respecting the clerical help: self-defense. "Law offices and accounting firms are full of people who won't even look at receptionists or secretaries," says Susan RoAne, a California personal communications consultant and author of *The Secrets of Savvy Networking*. "What a foolish mistake. Who's in a better position to botch up your stuff intentionally than they are?"

Solve future problems now. Figure out what your company's future problems will be within your area of responsibility, and create innovative solutions that will nip them in the bud. Missy Cohen-Fyffe has an example. She is president of Babe Ease in Pelham, New Hampshire, which creates and distributes baby products. The company requires a complex system for storing and shipping its goods. One day one of her workers asked her, "Do you mind if I come up with a different organizational system?" Without being asked to, the worker devised an amazing system for keeping the back office more organized in respect to reordering supplies and goods. Need we say she got a hefty merit increase?

Stop fixating on the time clock.

Managers don't expect you to be a slave for the company. In fact, most respect people who value and guard their private time. But if you consistently put in the bare minimum time required at work, or fixate on getting every last half-day of time off possible, or take every single minute of each day's lunch time no matter what deadlines are looming, you send a clear statement to your managers that what comes first is you, not your work. The better approach: Show passion for your work, and as it ebbs and flows, adjust your schedule to get things done. More than anything, managers love a worker they can depend on. Show you can be trusted and are flexible, and the free time will take care of itself.

Stay up on popular technology.

An estimated 80 percent of jobs in modern cultures involve daily use of a computer. In fact, for many people, computer proficiency is vital to workplace success. So go out of your way to learn and practice the computer skills you need to thrive at work. Then go the

---

WHAT YOUR WORKPLACE COMPETITORS DON'T WANT YOU TO KNOW ABOUT Promotions

- **Your work skills are not enough.** If you don't communicate well, promote yourself, establish alliances, fit in with the company culture, and stay informed about what's going outside your workstation or cubicle, somebody with less talent is going to pass you by on her way up the ladder.

- **It's a small world after all.** While you stick to your own kind, your rivals are connecting with every conceivable kind of human being. They're taking advantage of today's workplace diversity to expand their cultural horizons—and their contacts. Who's better positioned for advancement in a globalized market?

- **The action's outside too.** You may focus on the in-house environment, but your workplace competitors have joined professional associations, established links to colleagues in other companies, and befriended vendors and suppliers who flit from company to company like pollinating bees. Your competitors know that sometimes the best information about the company where you work comes from the outside.

- **Red tape is for cutting.** Your rivals are delighted that you work hard to be a regulation-respecting "loyal" employee who sees that those around him toe the line. Because while you're creating red tape, they're cutting it. And guess what? The can-do person gets promoted before the can't-do person.

next step and monitor what's hot in terms of electronic gear, software, and websites. No work manual will tell you this, but people who are savvy about technology often move ahead faster than people who don't care much about it.

Learn how to write power-packed e-mails. For such a common mode of workplace communication, intra-office e-mails as a rule are terribly written. What easier way to stand out from the crowd than to consistently send sharp, welcome electronic messages? Just do the following:

- *Hone your subject line.* The key is to be specific, not necessarily short. Instead of giving your e-mail the name "Byrne project," call it "Byrne project: new deadline for phase 2." Your e-mail is already more interesting than most.

- *Don't bury the lead.* If you want to annoy people, make them read three paragraphs before you get to the point. If you want to rise in the company, state your purpose in the first sentence or two and then get to the why and how of it.

- *End with an action request.* Example: "I will call you on Monday at 10 a.m. to follow up on this." Or: "When can we get this done?" Otherwise, nothing is likely to happen.

- *Be human.* Decent people who would never dream of being cold and abrupt in person often come off that way in their e-mails. Being businesslike doesn't have to mean being impersonal. Remember that the sender and receiver are both human beings.

- *Proof your e-mail.* It's worth repeating. Just one misspelling, grammatical error, or typo makes you look foolish. It also makes you look disrespectful to the recipient. Sending clean e-mails automatically lifts you above the sloppy crowd.

- *Behave yourself.* Irony doesn't work in e-mails. Neither do sensitive subjects, such as sex, race, religion, and politics. Stay away from them, because every message you send is being judged.

- *Stop cc-ing everybody.* All you're doing is making all involved feel less important.

- *Pick up the phone.* If you have to spend more than five minutes on an e-mail message, call instead. It's easier to explain things on the phone, and you can always follow up with a shorter e-mail.

How I Do It A Human Resource Director's Self-Promotion Strategy

Before career coach Dale Kurow starting helping others get hired and promoted, she was doing the hiring and promoting herself as a human resources staffer at a major company. It was there she learned a key trick:

"I once had a boss who was trying to get me fired, but it had more to do with his problems with his own boss than my performance. I knew I was doing a good job, so I asked other directors and people I worked with to let him know that. They did, and everything turned out fine."

The moral of the story: Don't wait until there's trouble. Have others toot your horn for you when the occasion arises.

"If somebody tells you that you're doing a fine job, ask them if they wouldn't mind passing that word along to the boss," Kurow says. "It's a way to shine your light, but more effective because somebody else is doing the shining for you. And most of the time they're very happy to pick up the phone or send a memo or e-mail on your behalf. All you have to do is ask."

Read the trades. Every industry has newsletters, magazines, and websites that are devoted to it. Subscribe to the ones relevant to your work. You'll learn about trends, the competition, key vendors, government actions, even your own company. There are two benefits: First, you'll be smarter about your job. Second, you'll impress and help your managers and coworkers with your expertise.

Managers, learn to manage "sideways" and "up." Most managers focus their time and energy on the people they oversee. But there are two other constituencies you need to manage as well: your peers (that is, managers at the same level as you), and your bosses. Often, these two groups are harder to win over than your employees! But work hard at it anyway. When your peers respect you, and bosses appreciate the way you communicate and assist them, you greatly increase your value to the company.

Never let your manager be surprised. It's one of the unstated rules of workplace survival: Don't let your boss learn about bad news, angry customers, accidents, or even positive developments from anyone but you. There is nothing worse for a boss than not knowing about something significant in her area of responsibility—and then finding out about it from an angry superior or a cutthroat peer. Make it a policy to let your boss know quickly about everything noteworthy that is going on—good *or* bad. She will be grateful for the candor. ◁

Office Politics

4 Tricks for Dealing with the Wide Variety of Human Interactions You Encounter in the Workplace

Learn to love office politics. Hard workers may hate to hear this, but "keeping your nose to the grindstone"—that is, concentrating on nothing but the job at hand—is a strategy for failure. You may think it's admirable to stay away from office politics, but all that really means is you're limiting your potential. "Office politics" is just a term for the range of human interactions that go on in any workplace.

"Being involved in office politics doesn't have to be something cold and calculating," says communications skills counselor Susan RoAne. "It's just being savvy, alert, aware of what's going on around you, and it's ultimately a means for doing a better job and having a more successful career."

So the most important tip concerning office politics is this: Embrace it. Get good at it. How? By doing what real politicians do—form strategic alliances. Establish relationships with some peers, some superiors, and some below you in the hierarchy. Go out of your way to help a person you like or respect, or somebody who has something to offer. Then ask her to help you. That may lead to a second link with somebody else as well. If not, create a second on your own, then a third.

Cultivate these work relationships. No matter how dedicated an employee you are, at some point you are going to need people to back you up. And no matter how well you do your job, you're going to need allies to help you up the ladder.

That's why you need to be involved in office politics.

Mix business with pleasure. The advice you usually get is to keep your social life separate from your work life. Balderdash! Make sure that you *do* have a social life at work. Not only are office friendships natural, they're also essential if you want to shine. Friends make for loyal allies, honest advisers, information sources, and links to other allies, advisers, and sources. So by all means, cultivate friendships at work.

But don't limit your socializing to individual relationships. Never miss the company picnic or Christmas party. Even if you'd rather stay home and watch the paint dry, lighten up and attend anyway. Such events are priceless opportunities for making the connections you seek in the comfort of a social context. Remember, RoAne says, it's as much about who knows you as it is about who you know.

"You need to have a presence in your job, a visibility," she says. "Socializing lets people get to know who you are and what you do."

Keep an eye on fellow workers. You'll never find this in the employees' manual, but the most useful habit you can develop at work is to carefully observe your coworkers' actions and behavior. And the best time to do it is when they don't know you're watching. Start looking from the first day on the job and don't stop until you get your

- **You're involved in office politics whether you realize it or not.** As knowledgeable personnel staffers like to put it, anytime more than two people are present in a work environment, office politics rage. If you're not an active participant, then you're a passive victim. That's why your rivals love it when you insist on "staying out of it." They know they can eat you for lunch.

- **Staying aloof gives you a bad rep, not a good one.** By refusing to play the office politics game, you do not come across as morally superior. And you are not impressing higher-ups. You are perceived instead as lacking in social skills, short on savvy, and not the kind of "people person" deserving of promotion.

- **Management actually approves of office politics.** Management likes engaged, action-oriented workers—in other words, office politics' primary participants. Management likes the creative ideas that arise from employee interaction, even if the motive is self-interest. Management likes the stability that results from in-house social relationships, since studies show that employees who socialize at the office are less likely to leave. In fact, management likes office politics so much that it watches to see who swims best in the office politics pool.

- **"Negative campaigning" is for losers.** There's certainly no shortage of would-be career climbers who turn to backstabbing and bad-mouthing because they think that's what office politics consists of. Smart office politicians love it when rivals do things like that, because they know it will backfire. Sure, a well-timed backstabbing of a fellow worker pays off on occasion, but in the long run that kind of negative behavior is a career killer. A good office politician makes alliances, not enemies.

gold watch. Watch everybody—colleagues, subordinates, and superiors. Watch them at meetings, at parties, at lunch, and during the workaday routine. Eavesdrop when you can (without being sneaky, of course). Observe body language. Use small talk to probe.

Here are some of the things you're looking for when you're new: Who takes lunch together? Who does what at lunch (cafeteria, brown bag, catering truck, restaurants, a gym or a jog)? Who commutes together? Who laughs at whose jokes? Who supports whom at meetings? Who comes early? Who stays late? Learn your fellow employees' individual interests, their status in the office, their family situations, and their hobbies. Notice how they talk and the tone of voice they use. Discern their values and their lifestyle.

You care about all this information because it constitutes the workplace culture in which you are performing. It is the raw material of your success. You will be able to make better decisions.

You will see opportunities you otherwise may have missed, and you will be able to act on those opportunities more efficiently.

Example: Your surveillance reveals that Mary in IT is an avid collector of dolls. A month later you run across an article on a famous person who is a doll collector, so you pass it along to her, saying you thought she might be interested. Another month later you need some quick help from IT on a project. You have a casual contact there, don't you?

That's just a little thing, maybe, but if you make a true effort to observe constantly, you'll multiply it by a factor of thousands.

Are you practicing office politics by doing this? Of course. Are you spying? Not really, because you're not seeking information to use against them. You're seeking information in order to work with them—albeit for your own benefit. Besides, a lot of them are watching you too.

Hear it through the grapevine.

As a source of factual information, the company grapevine is by definition unreliable, since rumors aren't facts. But as a barometer of workplace mood, it's essential. And as an indicator of what the future may hold, it's priceless. There's a reason for the grapevine's value that you're not supposed to know about: Management uses the grapevine to float ideas, to test employee reactions to possible new policies, or to slowly break the news of upcoming layoffs. You can't afford to ignore the grapevine.

Find out who the grapevine perpetrators are. Instead of shunning them as hopeless gossips, cultivate them as sources. Don't take their word at face value, of course, but register it and follow up. Remember that informal information is as valuable as formal information in the world of office politics. And in many cases, knowing that the top brass is monitoring your reactions to the rumors, you can make sure you respond in ways that make you look good. ◀

Legal Problems

3 Secrets for Handling Difficulties Arising from Harassment and Discrimination on the Job

After complaining, stick it out. Once you complain in writing that you've been a victim of harassment on the job, management and their attorneys are secretly afraid of one thing above all else—that you will also sue them for "retaliation." That's because they are not allowed to punish you for filing a claim against them. In fact, if you can prove that they disciplined you unfairly, you're more likely to win an award on those grounds than on the original harassment suit. So look for and document post-complaint actions that smack of retaliation. Your lawyer would love to file such a suit, and their lawyer shudders at the thought.

But that doesn't mean they won't go after you in more subtle ways. You may find yourself getting assignments you despise, loaded down with paperwork, or otherwise made uncomfortable. Their secret goal is to get you to quit. Don't. Because once the company can claim you "abandoned" your job— which you technically have if you quit—your harassment case immediately becomes so weak that lawyers are unlikely to take it.

You have little to lose. Employers have spread the word that trying to win harassment or discrimination cases against them is a losing proposition. They've been pretty successful at making employees think that there's little chance of winning, and less chance of collecting a worthwhile amount. What they don't want getting out is the truth, which is that you really can't lose in most cases. "If you win the suit, they have to pay your attorneys' fees," says Charles Joseph, a labor lawyer with Joseph & Herzfeld. "But if you lose the suit, there is a slim-to-none chance that you have to pay theirs."

How to Document Discrimination on the Job

- **Keep a record.** Start a diary at the first hint of discriminatory behavior or harassment. Write down the date, time, and place, along with who did what and who witnessed it. Example: "On June 30, 2007, in the coffee room Jack Pigg, my supervisor, called me an old fogy and said he resented having to work with geezers. My coworkers Jane Doe and Tom Katt were in the room and heard him."

- **Collect evidence.** Make sure you keep the evidence, even if it doesn't amount to much on its own. A note or memo with an ethnic slur, for example, that possibly refers to you goes into your discrimination case file. If the offense is public, such as a racist or sexist cartoon posted in the rest room, you have the legal right to take it down and copy it, or even keep it in your file. Remember that you're amassing evidence, not necessarily finding a smoking gun.

- **Skip the tape recorder.** Don't tape conversations with the discriminator or harasser unless you know for sure that it will produce a smoking gun otherwise not available. Even if you live in a state or province where it's legal to tape without the other's consent, don't do it. Labor lawyers say it hurts you with jurors, who tend to see "tapers" as unethical.

And if your case is solid, the judgment in your favor could involve a considerable amount of money. After all, discrimination and harassment are odious practices. "They do not want you to know that punitive damages are not as uncommon as people are led to believe," Joseph says.

It is true, of course, that it's pointless to pursue legal action when you have little chance of winning. But the strength of your case is for your lawyer to decide, not theirs.

Get counseling. There's a little-known fact of legal life that company lawyers hope like heck will never come up. It's not uncommon for victims of discrimination, harassment, or other illegal on-the-job practices to suffer from depression or other harmful mental conditions. But it's also not uncommon for victims to shun counseling, or at least put it off until their cases are resolved. That's a mistake. Besides providing the help you need, seeking professional care can help your legal cause. "Seeking counseling from a mental health professional can increase your award at trial," Joseph says. ◂

Getting Fired
8 Things You Should Consider Doing If You Are Unexpectedly Booted Out of Your Job

Ask for a good letter of reference. How crazy is it to ask somebody who just fired you to provide a reference letter for your next job? Not crazy at all, really. In fact, you should bring up the subject before you empty out your desk or locker and head home, says Alison Doyle, a job search expert at about.com. It will go a long way toward diffusing your worries about how this stain on your résumé will go over with prospective employers.

What are your chances of getting a positive reference under the circumstances? Better than you think, Doyle says. "It's something you can negotiate," she says. "If they won't offer a letter, you can ask for a good verbal reference if they're contacted. Or they might agree to just verify your period of employment and salary, with no reference good or bad."

At the very worst, you'll find out if they're going to give you a negative reference when future prospective employers give them a call. At least you'll know what you'll be dealing with. But there's some inside information involved that helps your cause. Unless you've been fired for punching a coworker or something equally unforgivable, many if not most companies are loath to say anything negative about a former employee. "They don't want to raise possible legal issues that can result form giving somebody a bad reference," Doyle says.

Or get a reference from a friendly manager. Whoever fired you may not appreciate it if somebody else in the company agrees to put in a good word for you with a potential new employer. But there's nothing they can do about it. If the company itself won't give you a reference letter, seek out another high-ranking staffer—a supervisor, a manager in another department with whom you worked often and well, or a respected veteran. Even if that person cannot go on the record with a formal letter on your behalf, he or she may agree to be listed as a reference and speak well of you when called. That will certainly water down the negativity when you're dealing with a prospective new employer.

Quit before you're fired. You remember the old cliché: "You can't fire me, because I quit!" In the movies, the characters say things like that to save their pride. But in real life, quitting before it comes down to an unpleasant firing makes sense if you're truly dissatisfied with your job situation.

Because your boss may know something you don't—that your job performance really has been suffering. The real forbidden knowledge in this case may be something you're keeping from yourself: Which is that deep inside, you know you're dragging because, frankly put, you hate your job. You may even unconsciously want to be fired.

If that's the case, the solution is to start looking for another job right now. Don't just up and quit; the best time to look for a new job is when you already have one. You have the security of a paycheck coming in, and you're out there in the workaday world with all its connections and energy instead of making phone calls from your kitchen table. Don't feel guilty about looking while you're working; you'll probably be doing your current job better with the new energy fueled by your decision. Just take advantage of your lunches and off hours to job-search. Use private e-mail, and check your home phone messages. And be up-front with prospective employers about your current situation.

Do tell your current boss about your plans, but not right away. First decide what it is that you're really looking for. Then get some résumés out there and wait until you've had some bites and prospects before breaking the news that you're "looking." The boss may be hurt or angry, but he or she may also be relieved that the situation is moving toward a solution that won't include a firing.

If you're leaving, ask for a promotion. Here's a variation on your pre-emptive dodge-the-axe strategy. After some soul-searching, you decide that you're so dissatisfied with your job that quitting is the best solution. Your next move is to march straight into the boss's office—not to tell him or her that you're leaving but to air your grievances. "Don't show your cards by revealing your plans to quit," says Karen Schaffer, a Halifax, Nova Scotia, career coach and author of *The Job of Your Life: Four Groundbreaking Steps for Getting the Work You Want.* "Instead, roll the dice, tell them how you feel, tell them what you want, and ask them what their plans really are for you."

Why bother if you're quitting anyway? Because that's the best time to do it. "You go in feeling liberated, with nothing to lose," Schaffer says. "At least you're creating parameters about what you want." In other words, just voicing your desires provides a context when you do give notice, and will even help make things clear in your own mind as you look for a new job.

But beware: You may get what you want and end up not quitting after all. "Sometimes management has no idea that you have a problem with your job," Schaffer says. "If you're valued, they may try to accommodate your concerns." And if you're not valued enough for them to do that, then you know your decision to leave was the right one.

Turn getting fired into a positive future job asset. The moment of truth has come, when the hiring manager asks about your termination from your previous job. You can handle it if you know what the interviewer is really thinking: He doesn't want to be judge and jury. Nor is he interested in rescuing your career. He just wants to know if there's a problem or not.

Don't plead your case. Don't try to defend yourself with detailed complaints about what "they" did to you. Don't act morose, angry, repentant, or bitter. Don't bad-mouth anybody. All you're accomplishing with defensive behavior is convincing your would-be next employer that this thing is still festering.

Do this instead, says Karen Schaffer, the Halifax career coach: Use a general, big-picture description of the situation, like "bad fit," "unfortunate situation," or "unresolved conflicts." Then, in two or

WHAT **COMPANY LAWYERS** DON'T WANT YOU TO KNOW ABOUT Overtime Pay

Some salaried employees classified by their employers as "exempt"—that is, not eligible for overtime pay because their work doesn't fit into a schedule—are not really exempt under U.S. federal labor laws (most provinces in Canada have similar laws; check on your provincial government's website under "Hours of Work and Overtime Pay" for specific details). They are entitled to time-and-a-half for every hour over 40 in a week, even if they don't know it.

It doesn't matter if you're the one who volunteered to work overtime. If they let you do it, they have to pay you extra.

If you work 35 hours one week and 45 the next, it doesn't average out. You're owed time-and-a-half for those extra five hours in the second week.

Automatic clocking-out doesn't deprive you of overtime pay. If you work extra hours during lunch or after your shift, you must be paid time-and-a-half for that time no matter what the time clock says.

If you're required to arrive early to "prepare" for work, you're owed for that time, and you get time-and-a-half for it if it brings your weekly hours past 40.

You can collect three years' worth of back pay if you weren't properly compensated for overtime work. Executives, professionals, and most white-collar staffers who work independently are exempt; if you are otherwise, check with a labor lawyer on your status. You may have money coming to you.

three sentences, show that you've dealt with it, understood it, put it behind you, and moved on. Say something like this: "It was one of those unfortunate situations that had to end in a separation, and they moved before I did. I realize now that I should have taken some action on my own instead of letting things fester, but I've learned from the experience."

"Put a positive but still realistic spin on it," says Schaffer. "If you convince them that you 'own' the situation, management will usually accept that."

Call the unemployment office immediately. You were fired, but you managed to walk away from your old job with several weeks' or months' worth of severance pay. So it will be quite a while before you need to bother with calling the unemployment office, right? Wrong. You may be shocked to learn that, in the U.S., many states ignore severance pay as just another benefit of your old job, and they're willing to send you an unemployment check even during the period that you are covered by the cash payout from your former employer. Call your state's unemployment office to get the particulars. When your unemployment checks start arriving might depend, for instance, on whether you took a lump-sum severance payment from your old job or if it's paid out over time like a continuing salary. In any case, register immediately with your unemployment office so you do not miss any funds that you are entitled to. Some states don't pay benefits for the first week in which you qualify for unemployment. Also, it typically takes a few weeks for your first unemployment check to arrive. So you want the clock on your case to start ticking right away.

Make your case anyway. Maybe something untoward happened at work, and the bosses told you that you were fired "for cause." So surely you could never qualify for unemployment funds, a benefit reserved for workers who lose their jobs through no fault of their own? No, don't make this assumption if you live in the U.S. The laws vary from state to state for deciding who qualifies for unemployment. You may be surprised to find a sympathetic ear at the unemployment office when you describe the circumstances of your firing. If you actually resigned from your job and weren't technically fired, you might be able to persuade the state that there were compelling reasons you felt pressured to quit. Even if you are turned down initially by the state unemployment office, you will probably be offered a chance to make your case in person at a hearing.

Ashamed? Get over it. As smart and talented as you are, you might never have imagined that you would be without work for an extended period of time. What's more, the idea of filing for unemployment benefits makes you feel uneasy—as if you're accepting handouts when you're not actually destitute. Get past that mental block. If your car or home got damaged, you would accept the insurance money. Unemployment benefits are just an insurance program that happens to be run by the government. You deserve the money, so take it. ◂

Home Security
7 Shockingly Simple Tips to Put Prowlers Out of Business

Secure your door. Locksmiths will probably quote you a hefty fee to "burglar-proof" your front door. You can accomplish the same thing by spending a few bucks on a good dead-bolt lock, a few pennies on the right screws, and a few minutes with a screwdriver. The secret is a strong strike plate, which is the metal square that the bolt fits into when you lock up. Make sure the dead-bolt kit that you buy has a strike plate with four screw holes rather than just two; it's twice as strong that way. If the screws that come with the set are tiny, replace them with four 3-inch (7.6-cm) screws, which will go deep into the hard wood of the door frame and hold fast. You want your strike plate attached to the hard wood on the door frame, not just to the decorative trim that surrounds the door. That way, anybody intent on breaking into your home cannot kick in your dead-bolted door—the strike plate won't give. Do this with all your doors (back, side, garage) and you've eliminated a burglar's favorite points of entry.

Secure a window the easy way. Security specialists want you to believe that barred windows are the only safe windows. True, putting bars on all your windows will keep intruders out, no question about it. What those installers won't mention is that burglars usually look for open—not bar-less—windows. (Drive around any residential area for a few minutes and you'll be amazed at how many windows are left open.) Just by closing and latching your windows, security experts say, you make your home significantly less likely to be burglarized.

But latches are not locks, and they can be forced. Solve that problem by driving a long, fat screw into each of the two tracks that the window slides along (either up or sideways) to open. That way, even if the latch is broken, the window will be blocked before it can slide totally open. Position the screw so that it allows the window to open no more than 4 inches (10 cm)—enough for ventilation, but not enough room for a probing hand to remove the screw.

If the window simply opens inward instead of sliding up or sideways, install extra mini-dead bolts or simply hammer in strong, 3-inch (7.6-cm) nails on both sides of the frame and bend them to block the window's inward path. Such simple "secondary blocking devices," as they're known among security folks, aren't exactly at the Fort Knox level of security, but they deter burglars, who hate struggling with stubborn windows.

Adopt a pooch. If you don't have young children in the house, adopt a *big* pooch—they're one of the best burglar deterrents around. Good watchdog choices include Doberman pinschers, huskies, Great Danes, German shepherds, and retrievers. If you're not able to care for a dog or if they're not allowed in your building, it still doesn't hurt to get a tape recording of a dog barking to play every now and again (and have it running on your answering machine's

WHAT **BURGLARS** DON'T WANT YOU TO KNOW ABOUT Break-Ins

- ☐ They prefer to break in during the day. While most people fret about night prowlers, competent burglars look for open windows in the morning or afternoon, when most folks are out of the house.

- ☐ They hate barking dogs. Even a small pooch will help protect your home, as long as he makes a lot of noise when strangers come by. Big, mean-looking dogs are even more effective. Don't forget the prominent, menacing "Beware of Dog" sign either.

- ☐ They'll come right up to your front door and knock. What better way to find out if anybody's home? As long as they look like they have some reason to be there, they don't attract suspicion. If there's no answer, they can look for your hidden key or an open window—or just kick in your front door if you don't use a strong dead-bolt lock.

- ☐ They don't care if your income is modest. Don't think you're safe because you're not swimming in jewelry or valuable art. Burglars are usually looking for quick cash, not the big score. Criminals break in because they want small, easy-to-grab and easy-to-sell items—like laptops, video players, watches, CDs, and small electronic devices.

outgoing message). Consider posting "Beware of Dog" signs.

Resist a pricey monitoring alarm system. If home security vendors can't scare you into signing up for an expensive monitoring system that you don't need, they may try an appeal to your pocketbook. After all, everybody knows you get an insurance discount when you buy the top-of-the-line home security package. What "everybody" may not know is that the insurance discount you get is peanuts compared to the yearly fees you'll be paying for the monitoring system. Stick with the basic package of alarms and signs. On the other hand, experts do recommend that you consider a monitoring service if fire is a big concern—for example, if you live in a high-fire-risk area such as brushy foothills. The police may not get there in time to catch a thief, but firefighters will certainly be welcome if your system is set up to trigger a call at the first sign of a fire.

Get this important alarm protection. An anonymous stalking victim offers this advice to people who fear for their safety: If you have a home alarm system, always opt for the "phone line cut" service, which can detect whether an intruder has cut your phone line. It automatically sends police to your house, even though you're not able to call them yourself.

Give your neighbor that spare key. You'll hear a thousand different ideas on the best hiding place for your spare home key, but you'll seldom hear the only one that counts: "Nowhere." You'll never find a spot that a burglar hasn't thought of. Instead, give that key to a neighbor. That solves a number of problems (besides getting in when you've locked yourself out). If you're expecting service people while you're away, a neighbor can let them in and see them out. A key exchange also establishes a mutual trust with your neighbor that is an important security strategy in and of itself. When you're away, have neighbors keep an eye on your home, gather mail and newspapers, watch for strangers, and even park their car in your driveway from time to time to simulate occupancy. You should have a pact of mutual protection that kicks in when one of you isn't home. Tell them what days you'll be gone, who will come by in your absence, who they can let in, and how they can reach you if they encounter anything suspicious.

Watch the foliage. Overgrown shrubbery and high hedges around the perimeter of your house provide as much privacy for burglars as they do for you. Trim foliage in your foundation plantings often so that it can't camouflage a burglar's activities from the view of neighbors and passersby. Think twice before installing a tall privacy fence or planting a tall hedge. You may just be inviting an intruder to take advantage of the cover they provide. Also check out large trees near your house and prune branches if they provide ready access to second-floor windows or a balcony. The same is true of trellises on the side of your house that make an inviting ladder for a burglar. Another thing to keep in mind is that basement windows are often obscured by shrubbery, making them a favorite access point for burglars, especially because they lead to an area of the house that is often not occupied. Keep these windows locked whenever possible. ◂

Personal Security
4 Little-Known Safety Tips That Can Save Your Life

Don't look like a target. You know the cliché: "It can happen to anybody." But criminologists know something else—that bad things are more likely to happen to those who make themselves more attractive to muggers. How? By walking along looking lost, distracted, or vulnerable. Don't be like them. Stay aware of your surroundings and adopt purposeful, assertive body language that projects confidence. That doesn't mean that you should try to come off as tough or threatening. Just don't act like a potential victim.

"There's really no such thing as 'random' street crime," says Jon French, a security consultant who works with U.S. companies doing business in Mexico. "The muggers go after who they perceive to be the easiest targets. If your body language says 'Don't mess with me,' you're less likely to get mugged."

Know your enemy. The politically correct message you hear is that you shouldn't stereotype criminals—they could be anyone. But if you could be a fly on the wall when cops and security pros are chatting it up, you'd know that there is one category of human beings responsible for the overwhelming majority of violent crimes: young men. "It's almost always young males who are the perpetrators," says personal security guru Chris McGoey. True, the proper public posture is to avoid stereotyping, and in most cases that's good advice. But not when it comes to protecting yourself from muggers, robbers, and thieves. It's not that all young men are criminals, it's that most criminals are young men. Just exercise caution when unknown males in their teens and 20s cross your path in vulnerable situations.

"You have to use common sense," McGoey says. "If you're getting gas at night or running into a convenience store and you see young guys loitering, don't go that way. If you're walking through a parking lot, be suspicious of young men hanging out in parked cars."

Don't bring your stalkers home with you. If somebody is following you, your natural instinct may be to get home as quickly as you can and lock the doors. After all, that's what they do in the movies, isn't it? In truth, though, heading for home is a bad idea—you don't want your stalker to know where you live.

"If you are being followed, never lead the person back to your home," the U.S. State Department instructs its overseas diplomats. "Do not stop or get out of the car. Drive to the nearest public place." There you'll be safe and can take your next action, which is to call the police. If you think you're being stalked while on foot, don't wait to be sure. Use your cell phone to call the police immediately. No phone around? "If you're in danger, try to attract attention," advises the Citizens for Crime Awareness, a nonprofit crime prevention organization in Winnipeg, Manitoba. "Scream, run, and yell if you are able."

Repel a potential rapist. You've been attacked by a rapist; sexual assault might be imminent. What's your best plan of attack? According to the Hingham, Massachusetts, police department, your best defense is your common sense. Your goal isn't to fight the rapist, but to make an opportunity to escape from him. This can be done passively by claiming to be pregnant, sick, or having a sexually transmitted disease. You can also try to discourage him by saying that a friend or family member is on the way over.

The website www.safetyforwomen.com says that using items on your person, or in your immediate environment, can be your key to surviving violent confrontations. You can use the most mundane things to defend yourself, including glass bottles, hair spray (throw the can at your attacker, or spray him in the eyes), silverware, sand, bricks, even furniture. ◄

Telephone Tricks and Tips

6 Secret Techniques for Stopping Eavesdroppers and Unwanted Calls

Know how to recognize if someone has tapped your phone. Maybe you're involved in a court case, or work for a high-profile company. Truth is, there are some folks who are often the targets of covert eavesdropping, even in their own home. Signs that someone is eavesdropping on your telephone calls include:

- Strange sounds coming from your phone, like static, squealing, or scratching noises; sounds that come from the phone when it's hung up; volume changes or other odd noises.

- Interference on your home or car radio.

- A telephone repairman shows up when nothing is wrong with your service, or no one called him.

- Friends or business associates know things you didn't tell them—like secret meetings, trade secrets, even personal information that they'd have no way of knowing otherwise.

Block the call-waiting service. Call-waiting can be a problem if you have to make a very important phone call and don't want to be interrupted by telemarketers or Aunt Mabel while you're on the line. Before you make your call, dialing *70 will block call-waiting—anyone calling your number will get a busy signal. This trick is only good for a single phone call; you have to repeat *70 whenever you want to use it. This number might vary depending on your region; check your local phone book for specific information.

Know how tricksters can circumvent your caller ID service. It's quite easy for unwanted callers to get around your caller ID system. They can buy a device or service to install on their phone that will block their number on any caller ID system, or dial *67 before dialing your number. Another trick, which can be done from virtually any phone, says one private investigator, is for the sneak to dial the operator and tell her that he's having trouble getting through to your line. Then the operator will dial the number for him, in which case the original caller's number won't be listed. Your best line of defense? Don't pick up the phone when there's anything other than a familiar name on your caller ID.

Reject unknown callers. Your phone keeps ringing, but all of the numbers are coming up as "private" or "unknown," so you don't want to answer—how annoying! There's a way to keep those calls from getting through to your line in the first place. Dialing up a service called "anonymous call rejection" from your phone means that callers who block their numbers will get a recorded message saying that your line doesn't accept unidentified callers. The way to turn on this call rejection is usually dialing *77 from your phone; turning it off is usually *87. Consult your local phone company for specific advice; there might also be a charge for this service.

Cut off those pitchmen. Reduce the number of telemarketer phone calls by signing up for the National Do Not Call Registry. When you do, most of these annoying pitchmen will be forced to bother someone else. (However, some groups—charities and political outfits, for instance—are exempt.) Sign up by calling 888-382-1222 or visit

www.donotcall.gov on the Internet. When a telemarketer does get through to you, tell him to put you on his "do not call" list. In Canada, residents can ask for a registration number when they tell a telemarketer to add them to the "do not call" list, and they can use this number if they need to file a complaint in the future.

Weed out nonurgent phone calls. If you are constantly being interrupted by a ringing telephone, wean some of your contacts off voice communication and onto e-mail communication. After all, you can respond to e-mails on your own schedule rather than the sender's, it's easier to save e-mails than it is to take notes over the phone, and you can easily delete inconsequential e-mails without offending the sender. Tell frequent, nonurgent callers, "I'm late for an appointment—would you please send me an e-mail on that?" Emphasize to colleagues that e-mail is the best way to get your full attention. Also, have a separate set of business cards printed up with nothing but your name, title, company, and e-mail address. ◂

Identity Theft
8 Surefire Ways to Protect Yourself from Prying Thieves

Guard your Social Security number like the crown jewels. Many businesses act like it's their right to demand your Social Security number whenever they feel like it. It's not. In most cases, even when some form or employee tells you it's "required," it usually isn't. Be *very* selective about who you give this number to, because a Social Security number (or a Social Insurance Number in Canada) is the holy grail for identity thieves. Once they've got yours, they can commit crimes in your name and get rich at your expense.

"Companies are always asking for unnecessary information," says Linda Foley, executive director of the Identity Theft Resource Center, a San Diego-based nonprofit organization that helps identity theft victims. "Your vet doesn't need your Social Security number. The airline doesn't need it to find your lost luggage. The self-storage place doesn't need it to rent you space."

If such businesses ask you for it, simply refuse or offer to supply another identifying number instead, such as your driver's license number. When sweepstakes or contest forms ask for your Social Security number, it's usually to get you on a company's marketing lists. Write in the space that you'll provide the number if you win. Work- and tax-related dealings usually do require your Social Security number, as do credit checks. That's legitimate. But even then, hold out until you're convinced it's necessary. For example, when filling out a job application, ask if for security reasons you can withhold your number until you are offered the job.

Leave your cards at home. Health-care providers like doctors and pharmacies have you convinced that you've got to have original ID cards with you to use their services. Not true. To start with, never carry around your Social Security card. Memorize the number and keep the actual card at home, or in a safe-deposit box. And don't carry around any other identification card that includes your Social Security number. If you lose your purse or wallet, you're better protected against identity theft.

But what about your Medicare card and other health insurance cards? Don't you need to keep them on your person in case of emergency? Yes and no—you don't need to carry originals, and again, you need to protect your Social Security number. So here's what you do: Copy both sides of your insurance card, and cut the copy down to wallet size. Snip the last four digits of your Social Security number off the copy—it's like a PIN code, personally identifying you. Without these last four numbers, an identity thief can't do a thing. On a third piece of paper, write down the name and phone numbers of two or more trusted friends as medical contacts. Keep all three of those card-size pieces of paper in your purse or wallet instead of your Medicare card. Give the four missing digits to those two or more trusted friends, along with any pertinent medical information about you—medications you're allergic to, drugs you're taking, and conditions you have. Now, if you have a medical emergency, even if you're unconscious,

Identity theft experts such as Frank Abagnale, Jr., the reformed con man upon whom the movie *Catch Me If You Can* was based, strongly recommend shredding bank notices, credit card offers, or any other documents with potentially vulnerable information on them before you throw them away. And they insist that you use a crosscut shredder—the kind that turns paper into confetti—so identity thieves can't fit the pieces together like a jigsaw puzzle. But one elderly lady convinced an Identity Theft Resource Center caseworker that a simpler, cheaper way to render documents useless to identity thieves works just as well.

"What I do is tear up the papers and put them in a large mixing bowl," she said during a question-and-answer session after an identity theft prevention talk. "Then I pour boiling water over them and leave them overnight. In the morning, there's nothing but pulp."

---

the hospital personnel have a copy of your Medicare card, a contact to confirm your Social Security number, and access to crucial medical information. That could save your life.

In Canada, you have to pay for medical services if you don't have your original card with you, although you will be reimbursed for most of the costs.

Get updated. Software companies may not like you to use "borrowed" or otherwise illicitly installed computer privacy protection programs, but hackers love it when you do. That's because unlicensed spyware and firewall protection isn't eligible for free software updates. There's a reason all those updates are offered: Identity thieves are constantly finding ways around existing software to get into hard drives to steal your passwords and financial data. Using non-updated protective software is like taking last year's flu vaccine. It won't work. For extra protection, put password protection on files that contain sensitive personal information, like your credit card or bank account numbers. Just click the help button on your computer and follow the instructions.

Check for credit trouble without paying. Companies that charge $50 to $120 a year to monitor your credit rating won't go out of their way to tell you, but if you live in the United States, you have free access to your credit reports. By law (as of 2005), each of the three licensed credit bureaus must provide you with one free report each year if you request it. Stagger your requests and you can review your credit standing every four months, which is usually often enough to make sure an identity thief hasn't run up unpaid bills in your name. What's more, you're entitled to a free report right away if you've been denied credit, or if you suspect you've been a victim of identity theft.

To order a free credit report, go to www.annualcreditreport.com—this is the only site, besides the credit bureaus' sites, that is authorized to process credit report requests. (There's no similar site in Canada.) If you prefer, you can contact the individual credit bureaus directly at:

- Equifax, www.equifax.com, 800-685-1111 (or in Canada, www.equifax.ca, 800-465-7166)

- Experian, www.experian.com, 888-397-3742 (or www.creditbureau.ca, 800-646-5876)

- TransUnion, www.transunion.com, 800-916-8800 (or www.transunion.ca, 800-646-5876)

Whether you order your report online or by phone, you will have to give your Social Security number.

If you spot an irregularity on one of your credit reports, ask the credit-reporting company to place a fraud alert on your report right away. This means that any company reviewing your report must check with you personally before issuing credit in your name. Each credit-reporting company is required to notify the other two credit bureaus, but they aren't always prompt about it. Call the other two agencies yourself to make sure the fraud alert is applied to all three reports. You will probably get a recording that will ask for personal information to verify your identity. It is okay, in this case, to give out your Social Security number.

Trash the junk mail. Most of your junk mail problem will disappear when you "opt" yourself out of marketing offers originating with companies you're already doing business with. It's a little tricky, but you can do it. Look for small print in the bills between May and July, when the companies are required to inform you how to stop receiving pitches. Then you have to send in the request, and usually to a different P.O. box than where you send payments. That's simply to make it harder for you. "They don't want you to opt out," says Foley. "They want to keep sending you offers." (To learn more about opting out of pre-approved credit card offers, see page 234.)

Get your identity back ... without paying for it. If you've been a victim of identity theft, you may be on the hook for a lot of lawyer's or restoration service fees to fix the problem. But did you know that there are free services that will help you get your good name back and your true credit record restored? Believe it or not, your best first step is to contact the U.S. Federal Trade Commission (www.consumer .gov/idtheft). This government agency is set up to walk you through the process of recovering your identity with simple, clear instructions; its website includes a link to a useful PDF: "What to Do If Your Personal Information Has Been Compromised." Yes, you'll have some paperwork to fill out, but you'll have to do that even if you pay a restoration service to help you. On the FTC site, you'll learn exactly how to close accounts that may have been tampered with or opened fraudulently in your name, file a police report, and file a complaint with the FTC. If your problem requires ongoing help, the Identity Theft Resource Center (www.idtheft center.org) can assist you.

In Canada, your best bet for reporting identity theft is to call the Canadian Anti-Fraud Centre's PhoneBusters (888-495-8501), your bank, the local police, and the three credit bureaus (opposite page).

Choose a hack-resistant online password. Just as you wouldn't give your ATM code to a stranger, it's just as important to protect your online passwords—otherwise, computer hackers could have access to your medical and financial records, e-mail account, even your credit card information. Here are a few ways to choose passwords that no one will ever guess:

- Birthdays, kids' names, anniversaries—forget it. These are the first bits of data that thieves and hackers go to when trying to break into your accounts.

- Don't think that spelling your spouse's name (or any other easy password) backward will work either. Hackers have programs that will detect words spelled out backward and forward.

- Don't use one password for all of your accounts. If online thieves happen upon just one, you're in big trouble.

- Your best plan of action: Choose passwords that have both letters and numbers. Pick a password that's not even a real word—just jumble up some letters and numbers. And change your password frequently.

Be wary of clicking on a link in an e-mail. If you receive an e-mail from your bank, broker, or some other business that you regularly deal with, be aware that the e-mail may not have come from the business in question. It may be a trap designed by an identity thief to get you to click on a link. Instead of taking you to the business, that link will take you to a phony website, cleverly designed to look like the real thing. There the thief will try to extract as much information as he can from you, such as your password, your Social Security number, and your mother's maiden name. If you do get an e-mail from a financial institution, never click on a link in the message. Instead, call the branch you normally deal with and speak with a customer representative. Or if you bank online, go directly to the website by typing the name in your browser. ◄

Auto Theft
4 Ways to Deter Potential Car Thieves and Carjackers

Use a steering-wheel locking device. Any car-alarm vendor will want to sell you the latest high-tech device, like hidden "kill switches" that automatically cut off the ignition, engine, and fuel supply so even the most skilled hotwire pro can't start your car, let alone steal it. But think about it: For the gizmo to work, the bad guy has to already be in your car. Do you really want that? Instead of the kill switch, use an easily installable mechanical device that locks to the steering wheel or steering column. Until you unlock it, nobody can turn the steering wheel, which means nobody can drive the car away. But best of all, these clubs, collars, or J-bars are highly visible, so they act as a deterrent. If car thieves spy a good auto theft device, they're likely to look for another car to steal.

Park using this special trick. Here's how to park so that it's harder for thieves to make off with your vehicle. On the street, park between two other cars (practice that parallel parking!) and turn your wheels toward the curb. Thieves are looking for fast getaways, and the last thing they want to do is waste time maneuvering out of a tight spot. Take your ticket with you when you park in a parking garage—and never leave the ticket in plain sight on your dashboard. Auto thieves look for those tickets so they can take your car out of the garage without having to stop and explain to the attendant how they lost your ticket. If your home has a garage, always use it. A car sitting out on a residential street is an inviting target, even if it's locked. Finally, the more light and traffic around, the safer the parking place. Car thieves hate audiences.

Pay attention to prevent carjacking. Carjacking is a violent crime in which the thieves physically overpower you to take your car—and sometimes you with it.

"Carjackers, like street robbers, depend on the element of surprise," explains security guru McGoey. "I interview victims all the time, and they usually say they never saw the guy coming until he appeared at the car door." Your first line of defense against carjacking (and most other street crime) is to be aware of your environment at all times, and hyper-aware at key times. This means not chatting on your cell phone as you walk around, not dawdling before getting into or out of your car, not putting on makeup before getting out of the car. If you're like most people, you do things like that all the time.

"People go out of their homes and they're immediately in la-la land, just oblivious to the world around them," McGoey says. "If you just pay attention to your environment, your chances of being victimized are drastically reduced."

Here are a few strategies to remember:

- Be especially careful when you are approaching or leaving your automobile. Don't park in deserted spots, in areas with obstructed vision (because of trees and walls), near a big van with no windows, or near somebody who's just sitting inside a nearby car.

- Once you park, look around again, scan the area, ready to drive away if anybody approaches. Then get out, lock up quickly, and walk away.

- Reverse the strategy coming back to the car. Never turn your back to load groceries, kids, or anything else. Make it a habit to start your car and drive away quickly. Keep your antennae up in unusual situations. Are you bumped in traffic by a car with a young male inside who gets out to "help"? High alert! This is a common carjacking ploy.

Survive a carjacking. If you're confronted by an armed carjacker, don't resist. Give up your keys, and hand over the money if it's demanded. Don't argue, fight, or chase the robber. These people have no qualms about hurting you. However, never agree to be kidnapped if you can avoid it. Wherever they take you will probably be more dangerous than where they are confronting you. If you're still outside the car, drop the car keys and run for help if you can, screaming all the way. If you're forced to drive, you have to assess the situation and the degree of danger. Consider crashing your car intentionally near a busy intersection to attract attention. ◀▮

Disaster Kit

Is your family ready if disaster strikes? The American Red Cross recommends that every family prepare a disaster supplies kit that could sustain you for three days in case of an emergency. The following supplies should be kept in an easy-to-carry container, like a duffel bag or a small plastic trash can:

• Flashlight and extra batteries

• Battery-powered radio and batteries (or a hand-crank powered radio)

• Plastic sheeting and duct tape

• Water (a three-day supply of one gallon (3.7 liters) per person, per day)

• Nonperishable food that's compact and lightweight (granola bars, peanut butter, crackers, trail mix, etc.)

• First-aid kit

• Sanitary supplies (toilet paper, soap, personal hygiene items)

• At least one complete change of clothing and footwear per family member

• Blankets or sleeping bags

• Miscellaneous items like medication, baby supplies, and important family documents (keep the latter in a waterproof container)

You'll find a more detailed checklist at www.redcross.org (click the "Get Prepared" link, then go to "Be Prepared At … Home").

Getting Legal Advice

4 Secrets for Obtaining Help with Legal Problems Without Paying a Fortune

Start with free legal advice. Can you imagine an attorney telling you, "You don't need to pay for my legal help to solve your problem"? No. But a lot of people needing legal help should hear that. For a lot of legal situations, it makes sense to aim your first call at any one of a myriad of free legal services. That applies especially if you're over 60 in the U.S., because most states have senior legal hotlines that let you talk to an attorney over the phone at no charge. The hotline staff will also review documents for you, prepare letters, and get you whatever legal forms you may need. And if they can't do it all, they may refer you to some other free legal service that can. You'll find a list of these senior legal hotlines, complete with phone numbers, at the federal Administration on Aging website. Just go to www.aoa.gov and search for "legal hotlines." If you're not an Internet person, call 202-619-0724. There are no similar hotlines in Canada, but the government website www.seniors.gc.ca has a legal matters section that will take you to many helpful local links.

Younger folks have other options. If the problem is with a company or public utility, contact the company's consumer service (or complaint) department. They usually don't want legal hassles any more than you do, so you might be able to work something out. Government agencies provide some legal services for consumers; start by calling your state or provincial attorney general's office and asking for the consumer protection department. If your problem is with a regulated industry—say a bank, an insurance company, or a health care provider—look in the yellow pages under your state government for the agency in charge, such as the "Insurance Commission." At the very least, the phone call will glean some additional information, and you might even find a solution.

Check out community groups that make it their business to help people in legal trouble. Civil rights organizations, women's groups, immigrant centers, and a lot of other volunteer agencies will help you out in certain situations. If you're going to search the yellow pages for a lawyer anyway, consider trying one of the free advice services first.

Get your legal advice à la carte. The legal profession may have you convinced that seeking its help involves a major full-time commitment. You must "retain" a lawyer, they say, so he or she can "represent" you and "handle" your case. Well, we'll let you in on a secret: You don't have to do anything of the kind. Instead, think of a lawyer as the legal version of an electrician.

"Just because you need to consult with a lawyer from time to time does not mean you need to retain a lawyer," says Birmingham, Alabama, attorney and divorce mediator Lee Borden, who runs divorceinfo.com. "Just pay for the specific service you need."

Take a simple, uncontested divorce, for example. You can probably handle most of it yourself, but you may need a professional to, say, determine the true value of your spouse's retirement accounts, or to review a particularly confusing document. If that's the case, call your lawyer,

How to Size Up a Lawyer

It's not easy to judge the skills of a potential legal advocate. The reason you're there in the first place is that he or she knows so much more than you do about the subject matter. Intuition and good character judgment help, but so does a list of specific questions. There are no correct answers, but productive questions planned in advance will give you much more to go on than trying to wing a conversation. Try these:

- Do I need an attorney?
- What area of law do you have the most experience in?
- Have you handled matters like mine before?
- What have been the results of similar cases you've been involved in?
- What are the possible outcomes of my case?
- What are the alternative approaches for pursuing my case?
- How long will the case take?
- What are the chances of a settlement instead of a verdict?
- How will you keep me informed of progress?
- How much control will I have to give up to you over the decisions in my case?
- Is mediation or arbitration an option?
- Will you be working on my case personally?
- What are your exact rates and how are they determined?
- How often will I be billed?
- How do you charge for expenses?
- Who else in the office will be working on my case?
- Are there things I can do on my own to help things along, or to save me money?
- What's a ballpark figure for total cost?
- Can I meet any paralegals, junior attorneys, or support staff who will be involved in my case?
- If I am dissatisfied with how things are going, can I "fire" you?

ask how much it will cost you to have that (and only that) done, and proceed accordingly.

This pick-and-choose approach—or "unbundling," as it's sometimes called in divorce cases—has two big advantages for you. It saves a ton of money and keeps you in control of your own case. The help is there when you need it, but you're still making the decisions—in a divorce case, for instance, what issues to negotiate and whether you will discuss things with your spouse (something a retained lawyer usually won't let you do). Obviously, you'll need to dive in and retain full-time legal help if you're dealing with a bitter, adversarial divorce or more serious legal problems, such as criminal charges. Otherwise, don't shun legal advice just because you think you'll get deeply obligated to a lawyer's services. Approach it like conveyor-belt sushi—just grab what you need.

Watch out for additional costs. When you do hire a lawyer, be aware that you may face a lot of unexpected charges. Here are some things to keep in mind:

- You can be charged for telephone calls. Time is money, and phone calls take time. So the meter might be running, no matter who initiates the phone call. That's why legal consumer advocates like lawyers.com suggest you make sure any call to your lawyer is really necessary. If you can get the needed information from an administrative assistant, you'll save money.
- They charge for travel time and transportation costs—even if they're just going across the street. So your lawyer's offer to "drop by" your home or office to discuss your case may be a considerate gesture, but it's seldom a cost-free one.
- The hired help costs money too. Every time a paralegal looks something up in the law library or an administrative assistant types up a document, that's time spent on your case. You can be charged for it.
- Billing rates vary according to the rank of the attorney doing the work. Partners in the firm naturally cost the most. That doesn't mean you're wasting money, though. More experienced partners may resolve your case faster.
- Each time you're billed, you are supposed to get an itemized bill. Insist on it. You can learn where you're needlessly and unknowingly running up expenses. Then you can adjust your interaction with your lawyer accordingly to save money on the next bill.

Beware of ambulance chasers. In a lawyer, initiative and a go-get-'em attitude are not necessarily a good thing—these qualities may mask a serious ethical lapse. Let's say you have been in an accident. If a lawyer you've never met approaches you, already knows about your problem, and offers legal services, say no. This is ambulance chasing, even if there's no ambulance and no physical chasing. Does that mean this person is a "bad" lawyer? It doesn't matter. In most areas, such unsolicited contact violates the normal standards of professional conduct. A lawyer who has no qualms about breaking the rules is not somebody you want acting in your name. ◁

Divorce Cases

5 Ways to Keep the Pain to a Minimum When a Breakup Is Inevitable

Have a kinder, gentler split-up.
Judges, lawyers, therapists, and just about everybody else involved in marital issues tend to see divorce as a knock-down, drag-out battle. They're all wrong. "Despite the common cultural assumption that people going through a divorce have to fight about it, most people end their marriages with dignity and quietly move on with their lives," says attorney Lee Borden. "A cooperative, uncontested divorce is not only a good idea, it's the way most people do it."

So once you decide to split up, the first person you should talk to is not your lawyer but your soon-to-be ex-spouse. The conference agenda: Can we do this together? Can we agree now on the big issues and work out the details as we go along? Can we talk about who needs to end up with what, about where the children are going to live, about who's going to pay how much for their support? If so, what might have been World War III turns into a simple signing ceremony.

Warning: Divorce professionals may try to steer you and your spouse away from the peaceful path. "It's not that they're trying to stir up trouble," Borden says. "They spend most of their time with the nastiest adversarial cases, so that's the way they think divorce has to be."

If your spouse is reluctant to try the cooperative approach, trot out the following facts about contested divorces: They take much longer, they are infinitely more expensive, they create more problems than they solve, and they leave the two of you permanent adversaries.

That can make for a lifetime of tension-packed encounters at your children's school performances, graduations, weddings, and grandchildren's birthdays.

"You don't have to like each other a whole lot," Borden says. "Just be smart enough not to get caught up in all that adversarial stuff if you don't have to."

Keep relatives on the sidelines.
Why do relatives who never gave a moment's thought to your marriage suddenly present themselves as indispensable guides as soon as you start down the road to divorce? Because, they tell you, they "have your best inter-

ests at heart." Because they "know how you feel." Because they "know a good lawyer/counselor/detective/psychic" you simply must see. Because, some will say, they've "been there." And because, all will say, they knew all along what a rat that no-good spouse of yours is.

The only thing they don't seem to know is that this is your divorce and yours alone. You and only you must control it. No matter how well intentioned or well informed your family members are, it is almost always best to accept their emotional support but keep them away from the action.

Sure, go ahead and listen—to your wise uncle, to your parents, to your sisters, and cousins and aunts. Listen to your stylist, to your mail carrier, to your child's soccer coach, to the kid who prepares your morning latte. Then make your own decisions. Your family and your friends can be cheerleaders, but they can't play on your divorce team.

Look beyond a 50-50 split. The idea that splitting everything down the middle is the only fair way to divide marital assets is so entrenched that few people question it. After all, isn't marriage a 50-50 proposition? And don't community property jurisdictions, like Texas, California, and all Canadian provinces, call for a 50-50 split of material assets acquired by either spouse during the marriage? Well yes, but most states are not community property states. The judge's task in those states is to treat both spouses fairly, to "do equity" as the law puts it, and not necessarily to split everything in two. And even in community property states, fairness can take precedence over arithmetic if both parties are willing.

Your lesson in all this, if you're getting divorced, is to avoid getting hung up on some perfect 50-50 solution. Look at the big picture: Are you getting what you want and need, in an overall package that strikes you as fair? That's your goal. That's especially true when it comes to individual assets. A judge, for example, may have a reason for awarding the house to your spouse. Perhaps it was your spouse's father who gave it to the two of you in the first place. Unfair? Not if you weren't planning on living in the house anyway, and you get something else you wanted more. Focus on what you want, not what the calculator says you should have.

Don't let lawyers run wild with the case. Divorce lawyers tend to be set in their ways, going about things as they've been trained to do, which is not necessarily the best way for your particular case. As a result, costs skyrocket, squabbles proliferate, and the case drags on.

That's why neutral divorce law experts advise you to keep control of the proceedings and not let the lawyers turn it into a bigger case than it already is. How? Mostly by doing on your own those things you can do more quickly, more efficiently, and light-years more economically than your lawyer.

For example, both sides in a contested divorce need to know who owns what so that the assets can be divided fairly. Your lawyer is well trained to use the legally intricate "discovery" process to extract this information from your spouse's lawyer, who is just as well trained in finding ways not to provide it. The two of them can go round and round for months, racking up billable hours without much information changing hands. Better for you and your spouse to sit down together like adults and get it done in a day or two. All it takes is a realization that both of you gain—financially and emotionally—from sharing this information, which eventually is going to come out anyway.

Of course, if the two of you hate each other so much by now that you're incapable of communicating like adults, this won't work. It also won't work if one spouse—typically the man, even in this day and age—holds the lion's share of the information about family finances. He may just sit there with folded arms, offering you nothing. And finally, your lawyer may warn you against talking to your spouse under any circumstances until the case is concluded. We would never advise disobeying your legal counsel, but we will tell you what experts say off the record: Most divorce attorneys are secretly grateful when their clients work anything out on their own.

Be wary of potential financial traps. No matter how friendly your divorce is, when it comes to financial matters and divvying up property, it pays to question not only the motives of the other party but also your own. Here are three traps you should avoid falling into:

- *Your spouse has no intention of paying that debt.* No wonder your spouse generously offered to assume the $35,000 joint loan debt in exchange for your letting him have the paid-for Range Rover. He already knew he was going to file for bankruptcy or simply default on the debt. And what can you do about it? File an enforcement petition, perhaps, but that's not going to get you the vehicle back, or

How to Develop a Winning Divorce Strategy

Alabama attorney Lee Borden has spent most of his waking hours helping good people through bad (and not so bad) divorces. Over the years, he's uncovered one golden piece of expert advice for taking control of your divorce so you can come through the ordeal sane, satisfied, and successful. Think strategically, he says. Not emotionally. Not vindictively. Just strategically. Thinking strategically isn't all that hard once you decide to do it. Just ask yourself three questions whenever any issue arises during the proceedings:

- **How much is this issue really worth to me?** "It's the most frequent mistake I see people make in divorce," Borden says. "They lay down the gauntlet on some issue, argue about it, and pay their lawyer thousands of dollars to fight for it—all without stopping to think if it's really worth it to them." Strategic thinkers evaluate their goals.

- **How likely is it that I'll win this battle?** Even if you do decide an asset or arrangement is worth fighting for, it makes no sense to press the issue if you're going to lose anyway. Yet, Borden says, divorcing men and women constantly ignore their lawyers' warning and fight tooth and nail for something they're never going to get. Strategic thinkers choose their battles realistically.

- **What is it costing me to fight about this thing?** Here your lawyer probably won't help much. You're the one who has to decide whether you're going to spend more on attorney fees and other costs (such as witnesses, filings, transportation, phone calls, and such) than the item is worth. Strategic thinkers care about coming out ahead, not just winning battles.

pay the debt. Lesson: Never exchange a solid asset for a debt payment unless you're sure that the debt is going to get paid. You're better off taking on your share of the debt while claiming your share of the assets.

- *There's a looming tax burden.* Future taxes are a big-money item that even divorce judges and lawyers often overlook and your spouse might "forget" to mention. So one spouse who thinks he or she did pretty well ends up getting a nasty surprise months or years after the divorce when a humongous tax bill falls right on his or her lap. Make sure you or your lawyer or your accountant considers the tax implications of any asset you're claiming or conceding. You don't want to get hit down the road with something like a capital-gains tax on the sale of property that you didn't even get to keep.

- *Your spouse is not moved by your generosity.* But she or he is more than happy to take advantage of it. This is one of the more heartbreaking mistakes divorced people make. One spouse, still carrying a torch, believes that by being nice and giving up more than necessary, the other spouse will be wooed back to give the marriage another go. It almost never works. You end up just as divorced, but worse off financially than you should be, and more bitter than you would have been. Being civil and cooperative is laudable. Letting yourself get taken advantage of isn't. ◀

Child Custody
3 Unexpected Suggestions for a Clearheaded Custody Arrangement That Benefits the Child

Don't listen to what your kids say they want. Yes, you read that right. It may seem counterintuitive to play down the children's expressed desires at a time when you're fighting for their best interests, but it's the big picture that matters. Many a child-custody arrangement turns unnecessarily complicated because one or both of the separating parents goes out of their way to accommodate little Brittany's Friday-night sleepovers or Jimmy Joe's absolutely nonnegotiable need to take his tae kwon do lessons from the same Mr. Mathers that he started with. But a year from now, Brittany may completely lose interest in those sleepovers, and Mr. Mathers may take a position with an accounting firm on the other side of the continent. Your kids are going to change, their schedules are going to change, and your own situations are going to change. That's true for parents and children in any family situation.

So don't spend time, money, and emotional energy bickering over scheduling details. Focus on the broad outlines of a custody arrangement that works for both parents and places the children where it's best for them to be. Your concern should be with nurturing the best family relationships possible under the new circumstances, not with which parent lives closest to the coolest video game store in town.

Think twice about keeping the house. Your lawyer will promise to fight tooth and nail for you to keep the family house, a prime spoil of the divorce wars. But the same lawyer who will lead you into battle also knows something else—down the road that dear, memory-filled house may be more of a burden than an asset.

So consider at the outset what your situation might be like. Here's a typical one: You're going to be a single mother. You won the house in your settlement, but your income is going to be less than what it was when the two of you brought home money. Still, the house payments, maintenance costs, and property taxes won't go down. You may, in short, be putting yourself into a situation where you're "house poor." Yes, the kids get to live in the house they've always known. But will their—and your—quality of life suffer as you scramble to pay for it?

Living below the standards of your own neighborhood is a tough position for a single parent to be in. And it's tough on the kids too. They know what's going on. They know their friends and neighbors have better toys, better clothes, and better cars. They know that each time they're invited on a ski trip, they probably can't go. They're aware that the family attends big barbecues at the neighbors' houses but such events are never held at their own house.

If it's realistic to keep the house, go for it. But if it's not, bite the bullet, take more cash instead, and start your new life in a financially comfortable situation. Your children will adjust, and they'll feel a lot better about it once you and they take that nice vacation you wouldn't have been able to afford otherwise.

Forget the win-at-all-costs approach. What you think is best for your child may not be worth fighting for.

What's more, the priority in custody negotiations should often be what's best for the parents, not the children. Yes, that's a shocking thing to say, which is why experienced family law professionals are reluctant to warn you. But consider: A sane parent will realize at some point that spending $50,000 in legal fees to come out of the divorce in possession of a $30,000 retirement plan makes no sense. He or she will give up that particular fight, and wisely so. But if the issue has to do with child custody—say, whether the seven-year-old will split time with his parents 50-50 on a weekly changeover or a monthly changeover—parents will spend their last dollar and sacrifice any remaining vestige of goodwill with the other spouse to get what they want.

"It's not unusual for a parent who cannot afford it to spend $100,000 arguing over a child custody issue," says divorce mediator Lee Borden. "In their mind, cost is no object in protecting their child from this ex who grows increasingly evil as the fight progresses. They lose contact with reality."

That's self-defeating. For one thing, that $100,000 can put your child through college. Also, the fight itself becomes the focus, rather than the child's welfare. You may be spending more energy on "winning" than on being a good parent. And perhaps most important, the fight is poisoning what's left of your relationship with your spouse. That relationship still matters. The two of you are going to be parents together as long as both of you live. That hasn't changed.

If you want what's best for your child, seek peace. That matters more than the actual custody arrangement. "Children don't seem to mind even a seemingly inconvenient arrangement as long as Mom and Dad aren't fighting," Borden says. "If Mom and Dad are fighting, I'm not sure any arrangement is going to be good for them." ◀

Wills and Living Wills
5 Things to Keep in Mind When You Prepare These Two End-of-Life Documents

Don't fear going to probate court. Television dramas and certain elements of the legal profession have given probate—the court proceeding where a dead person's will is carried out—a reputation as an expensive, uncomfortable nightmare. That's a bad rap, says Michael Palermo, an estate planning lawyer in Lexington, Kentucky. "Probate is not that big a deal in most places," he says. "In some states, the process is so expedited you may not need a lawyer or even have to go to probate court."

So if it falls on you to handle things after a relative dies, consider going down to the county courthouse without paying for a lawyer and filling out some papers yourself to get the procedure started. The papers will have a name like "Petition for Probate of Will." Follow instructions, ask what you need to do next, and see if you think you can handle it. Many times you can, Palermo says.

You probably *will* need a lawyer if:

- The deceased lived in the "difficult" probate states of California or Florida.
- There's fighting going on among interested survivors.
- There's any kind of unusual complication.

Even then, Palermo advises, hire your lawyer by the hour. "Don't agree to pay a fixed percentage," he says. "That could cost you thousands of dollars for the handling of what are really some very simple tasks."

Read a will carefully before signing it. Yes, that may be the most ignored piece of advice ever given. After all, aren't we paying lawyers so we don't have to read 75 paragraphs of mumbo jumbo? But here's the reason it's especially important to go through your will before signing it: Although it's not the image law firms like to project, wills are put together from form documents. In other words, your last will and testament is essentially a re-tweaked version of somebody else's last will and testament. With all of that cutting and pasting going on, incorrect information can and does sneak into (or fall out of) the final printout. One lawyer tells of a will that was almost signed even though it had the wrong name throughout. So look it over and don't be shy about chirping up if you see a problem.

Explore what a will won't cover. It's convenient to think that a good will takes care of everything, but it doesn't. Though many a will-maker or heir isn't aware of it, a will only arranges for the transfer of assets that aren't already spoken for in some other way. In fact, a common estate-planning blunder is assuming that the will "trumps" previous arrangements. You can avoid a lot of spats and misunderstandings if you make an inventory of all the "out of probate" money or property you have—that is, assets that automatically go to somebody upon your death regardless of what the will says.

Example: You named Son #2 the beneficiary of your retirement plan when you first opened it, oh, so many years ago. That money still goes to Son #2 even if

your will says Son #3 "gets everything." Or if you own your house together with your wife, the terms of your "joint tenancy" agreement probably stipulate that she retains full ownership of the house upon your death, even if you froze her out of the will. Along the same lines, your life insurance beneficiary gets the life insurance money no matter what. And most of the time, the fact that you divorced that beneficiary decades ago doesn't change things. Of course, you can always change beneficiaries and restructure your house ownership or joint checking accounts.

A good time to think of these things is when you're having your will drawn up. The point here, though, is that the will itself doesn't take care of "out of probate" assets. So it's a good idea to put together a document listing these assets, noting who gets what when you die, and keeping it with your will. You could be saving all your heirs from confusion, and some of them from disappointment.

Give broad guidelines in a living will. The common advice to "be as specific as possible" when putting together any legal document isn't necessarily the best way to go with a living will. If you try to leave detailed, maddeningly precise instructions on what to do in every possible medical situation when you're unconscious or otherwise incapacitated, you're going to leave some things out. Even with the very specific situations you address, it's impossible to be sure that the actual circumstances will turn out to be exactly what you had in mind. Doctors and family members will still have no idea what to do—as if you had no living will at all.

So instead of a precise list, consider the *Pirates of the Caribbean* approach—guidelines instead of rules. Communicate a broad set of thoughts and convictions about the kind of care you want in extreme circumstances, and under what general conditions (if any) you should be taken off life support. Designate a substitute decision maker—often referred to in legal terms as a "trustee" or, in much of Canada, an "attorney"—to carry out your desires if you're unable to do so. For example, if you leave instructions that in case of debilitating Alzheimer's disease, you want to be set up at the St. Mary's extended-care facility in Room 12B with roast beef for dinner on Tuesday nights, that would seem to outline a clear course of action. But what if putting you in that particular place turns out to be the third-best choice of facilities for your condition? More important, what if your finances by then strain under the expense? Better to instruct a decision maker to, say, "arrange for the most appropriate care without creating a significant drain on the family finances." (Your lawyer, of course, will help find the best language to express your thoughts.)

In other words, leave your decision maker with some discretion. That will make it more likely—not less—that your true wishes will be carried out.

Your spouse may not be the best living-will decision maker. No matter what anybody might assume, your spouse (or another very emotionally close relative) is not necessarily the best person to carry out the instructions in your living will. Let's say you're a woman who's considering designating your husband as your decision maker because, after all, "he loves me the most." But the very fact that he loves you the most may make the decision making more difficult for him. The inevitably heightened emotions in a medical emergency or a pull-the-plug situation can obviously interfere with the one thing needed most at such a time—clear thinking. That's not to say that your spouse is ineligible to be your decision maker. Many spouses fill the role just fine. But there's nothing automatic about it. Choose the most qualified, responsible, loyal, and clearheaded person, whether you're married to this person or not.

And guess what? Your spouse may not even want the job. "Some view it as a burden they'd rather not have placed on them," says Brian Babcock of the large Canadian law firm Weiler, Maloney, Nelson in Thunder Bay, Ontario. "They know they're going to be too emotionally distraught to think rationally if the time comes, so they'd just as soon you selected another family member or a close friend." But under no circumstances should you try to spare your spouse's feelings by keeping secret your selection of another person to carry out the directive in your living will. The decision maker should consult with your spouse, after all. Also, not discussing your decision with your spouse can lay the groundwork for chaos at the worst possible time.

"We've had cases in which the spouse thinks they have the power and are giving instructions on the spot at the hospital, and then the true designated decision maker shows up with the directive," attorney Babcock says. "That causes a great deal of confusion with the medical staff." ◁

part Four

FAMILY AND FUN

Marriage counselors—and certainly not romance novelists— won't tell you this, but mutual respect is more important than love for a happy marriage. Or that most marital spats never reach resolution, and often it's best just to drop it. Be ready to reverse some other long-cherished beliefs: The best parenting policy for sibling scuffles is hands off. Giving your teen a checking account is a smart move. It's cheaper to host a sit-down dinner than a buffet. "Sold out" tickets to a live event are rarely really completely sold out. Also, discover the first thing you should do when you enter a casino, the best source of instant advice when traveling, the best seat in a restaurant, and a lot of other secrets that experts are loath to reveal.

Love and Marriage

4 Easy Ways to Make Romance and Attachment Last

Shop for the right spouse. Did you know that there's actually a formula that predicts whether a marriage will succeed? Beatty Cohan, a psychotherapist in Sarasota, Florida, and coauthor of *For Better, for Worse, Forever: Discover the Path to Lasting Love*, offers these predictors for a successful marriage:

- *Look to the parents.* Check out your beloved's family background, particularly the parents' relationship, to get a good idea of the behavior he's been exposed to. What we learned as kids we often play out as adults.

- *Turn investigator.* Are there signs of alcoholism or other forms of addiction in the family? Be careful—there's often a genetic link. Also watch for a family history of depression or excessive anxiety.

- *Listen carefully.* Identify how your potential partner communicates. Also pay attention to how he or she handles sticky situations and painful emotions.

- *Is there compromise?* If you're forever giving in, then you've got a problem. Compromise is one of the key elements of a healthy relationship.

- *Is there true intimacy?* We're not talking sex here, but the kind of intimacy that comes when he can clean up the vomit when you have the flu; when she invites your mother for Christmas even though she can't stand the woman; when he has a hot bath and glass of wine waiting for you after what he knows was a difficult day.

Don't just tell her you love her—show her. Karen Sherman, Ph.D., author of *Marriage Magic! Find It, Keep It, Make It Last*, offers these hints on little ways you can show your mate how much you love him or her:

- Surprise your partner with her favorite dessert.
- While he's showering, draw a heart or a sexy note in the steamed-up glass.
- Give him a foot or back massage—without him having to ask for it.
- Leave a sexy voice mail, saying, "I'm thinking about you" in a low voice.
- Tuck a sexy note into his briefcase or text it to her cell phone.

Light the Sabbath candles together. Not Jewish? No problem. A study conducted by researchers at Syracuse University finds that couples who participate in and value religious rituals, particularly holiday rituals, seem to have stronger marriages.

Take some "alone time" away from the kids. One of the toughest times in a marriage is when you have young children. Finding alone time (okay, time for whoopee) takes creativity. So how about these creative tips culled from young parents we know?

- *Keep 'em occupied.* If the kids are old enough to play alone in the fenced backyard, throw 99 pennies out there and tell them whoever finds 100 pennies first wins a prize.
- *Invest in hardware.* That would be a lock. For your bedroom door.
- *Set the alarm.* Wake up at 3 a.m., make love, go back to sleep.
- *Hire a babysitter.* Only this babysitter takes the kids *out* of the house while you and your partner steal some much-needed alone time.
- *Take advantage of naptime.* Who says you have to do the laundry while your two-year-old naps? ◂▮

WHAT YOUR MARRIAGE COUNSELOR DOESN'T WANT YOU TO KNOW ABOUT Compatibility

If you knew these things, you wouldn't need a marriage counselor, would you? This insider info comes from psychologist Karen Sherman and from psychotherapist Wendy Allen, Ph.D., author of *How to Survive the Crisis of an Affair*.

- ☐ Sixty-nine percent of all arguments between you and your partner will never be resolved. So don't try so hard.
- ☐ A couple that doesn't fight is in trouble.
- ☐ Having a "good enough" marriage is the most couples can expect and is actually quite an accomplishment.
- ☐ Letting go is sometimes better than discussing everything to death.
- ☐ Respect, not sex or money, is the most important factor in a happy marriage.
- ☐ There are marital breaches worse than an affair.
- ☐ A therapist cannot teach, train, or guide you to "be happy." That is not a reasonable outcome to expect from therapy.

In short, there's no way you're going to be compatible all the time.

Kids and Teens

12 Keys to Raising Healthy, Responsible Children

Get the TV out of the bedroom. Studies find that kids who have televisions in their bedrooms are more likely to be overweight. But here are other crucial reasons for ditching the tube: When a TV is in a child's bedroom, you have no control over what he's watching, nor do you have any opportunities for family bonding time—when everyone piles onto the couch to watch a favorite show.

Get them used to doing chores from a young age. We know one parent who still makes her high school daughter's lunch every day. Don't find yourself in this situation! By the time your two-year-old begins talking, he's old enough to start helping around the house. Here are some age-appropriate chores to give your kids to teach them responsibility, and how a household is run:

- *Two to four years old.* Ask them to put toys away, help to set the table, and put dirty laundry in the laundry basket.

- *Five to seven years old.* They should begin emptying the dishwasher (at least putting the silverware away), setting and clearing the table, emptying trash baskets, and doing light yard work with your guidance (like pulling weeds).

- *Eight to ten years old.* Kids should be changing sheets, dusting, vacuuming, putting away laundry, and bringing groceries into the house.

- *Eleven and up.* They're ready for almost any tasks that you can throw at them. This might include cleaning bathrooms, mopping floors, washing and folding laundry, putting away groceries, and simple meal preparation.

Teach them how checking accounts work. If you really want to teach your teen about money, then stop handing over the credit card and the "allowance." Instead, put your kid on a budget, open a checking account for him or her, and let your teen *really* learn to manage money. Tell your kid that all clothing, movies, entertainment, fast food, and cell phone bills come out of his or her checking account (which you fund). If your son or daughter has a job, then cut

How I Do It A Parenting Expert Gets a Child to Behave at a Restaurant

You *can* eat out in a sit-down restaurant with children. Just follow these tips from Stacy DeBroff:

- ☐ Pick the right restaurant. Chain restaurants are great because they're used to serving families and they're trained to turn over tables fast, meaning you'll get your order in and get fed in a hurry.

- ☐ Get a booth. It provides the all-important buffer zone between your family and the rest of the restaurant.

- ☐ Reward kids for good behavior. To get your kids to behave during the meal, tell them you'll take them out for ice cream afterward. Don't offer dessert *at* the restaurant—it just adds to the sitting time.

- ☐ Bring a "restaurant kit." This would be a bag filled with crayons and paper, small puzzles, Legos (depending on age of child), even a Game Boy or other handheld electronic game (hey, whatever works!).

back the amount you're funding by the amount they're making. Just make sure you also set up a savings account for your teen and insist that at least one-third of any savings or money from you be socked away.

Don't interfere with sibling scuffles. Stay out of fights between siblings unless bloodshed is imminent, recommends Stacy M. DeBroff, author of *The Mom Book*, a compilation of tips for moms from moms. She notes that fighting actually teaches siblings valuable skills such as assertion, managing anger, and compromise. If ignoring a fight doesn't work, send them to separate rooms until they cool off.

Limit choices. An inexperienced parent will ask a four-year-old, "What do you want to wear today?" Uh-oh. Offering such an open-ended choice just ensures you'll wind up with a little girl wearing black tights, a pink tutu, and a sequined top that reads "I'm Hot." Instead, pull out two outfits and ask which she wants to wear. The same goes with food. "Hamburger or spaghetti?" replaces "What would you like for dinner?"

Talk about sex. Get over your embarrassment and let your teen know that he can talk to you about sex without fear of lectures or retribution. The reality is that 85 percent of North American teens have had sex by the age of 19. Open discussions at least ensure that the sex they're having is safe, and may even convince your teen to hold off a while longer.

Monitor your teen's driving speed. If your teenager has a lead-footed tendency, step in and address it. A University of Florida study found that teenagers who break the speed limit are more likely to gamble, use drugs, and drink alcohol than those who don't.

Think of speeding as an early warning sign of worse to come.

Get your teen in the spirit to worship. Encourage your son or daughter to get involved in some sort of religious or spiritual organization. Why? Researchers who tracked 1,182 adolescents from 7th through 10th grade found those who thought religion was important were much less likely to smoke, drink, and use marijuana.

SECRET WEAPON

Dinner

Forget all that psychological baloney about what makes for a healthy child—a box of Hamburger Helper can be your best tool. Studies find that simply sharing a meal as a family helps groom kids who do better at school, have better relationships with their friends, and are less likely to do drugs or become depressed.

Moms, get closer. If you think you're not necessary now that your kid is driving, think again. A large government study finds that the closer Mom is to her teenager, the less likely teens are to start having sex. Some ideas: Set a weekly date for breakfast, lunch, or dinner. Have a mother-kid weekend away a couple of times a year. Start an activity that you can do with your teen, such as tennis, jogging, or even performing together in the local theater. Begin a marathon gin rummy game that goes on until one of you hits 100,000 points (or goes to college). And in the midst of all of this, say the researchers who conducted the study, slip in a few comments about the importance of education—it also helps.

Ban tattoos. So you gave in to the double ear piercing, but when it comes to tattoos for your adolescent, just say no. When researchers studied more than 6,000 junior and high school students, they found those with tattoos and body piercings were more likely to smoke cigarettes or marijuana, go on drinking binges, have premarital sex, get into serious fights, join gangs, skip school, and get poor grades. If your kid is asking for a tattoo, take it as a canary-in-the-mine kind of warning and sit down for a heart-to-heart.

Set your expectations high. Just because you drank and smoked pot in high school, don't think it's reasonable for your kid to follow suit. If you vocalize the expectation that *your* child will *not* drink or do drugs when in high school—and make that expectation known to your teen—you reduce the risk that your child will engage in such behavior.

Visualize the future with your kids. It's never too early to begin talking to your child about his or her future. By age 10, kids are old enough to start looking ahead and figure out the value of an education (for instance, "I go to school so I can go to college so I can get a good job so I can afford that vacation in Aruba"). Why bother? Because studies find that teens who can visualize themselves with a future are less likely to do those things that destroy a future, such as engaging in sex, drinking, drugs, and crime. ◁

7 TIPS ON RAISING
financially savvy Kids

We've all heard horror stories about kids who go off to college with shiny new credit cards and run up mountains of debt over the first several months. That won't happen to your kids, thanks to these tips from Syble Solomon, the creator of Money Habitudes, a deck of cards used by educators and counselors to identify financial issues in relationships:

1 **Show them money going in, not just out.** If your kids only see you withdrawing those $20 bills from the ATM, they're going to think machines hand out money. Make sure they also see you depositing funds.

2 **Teach them to set goals and save for them.** Label a jar with a set amount of money to be used for something specific. Start small—say, $5 to buy some ice cream and sprinkles. Collect $5 worth of change in the jar and count it out before buying the treat. Keep this money separate when you go to the store, so your child can buy the ice cream himself with the cash.

3 **Differentiate between wanting and needing.** You *need* shoes, but you *want* the trendiest brand. You *need* food, but you *want* to eat out. Apply this rule to anything you buy and to any of their requests for "stuff."

4 **Make choices, not sacrifices.** Instead of saying, "We can't afford that," "That's too expensive," or just saying no, substitute a comment that expresses an intentional choice. Examples: "I want to stay home and visit state parks this year so we can save for a special vacation next year." "I choose to bring my coffee [or water, or soda] with me and not buy it at the convenience store so I can save that money for more important things." Instead of feeling that "no" means sacrifice, scarcity, or embarrassment, children learn that life is about making choices.

5 **Show them you're planning for the future.** In addition to using a change jar to save for special treats, let your kids hear you talk about saving for a new roof, paying off the car, putting money aside to celebrate a birthday, saving for their education, and paying bills on time.

6 **Give to others.** Along with that jar for ice cream, label another jar for charity. Make sure your children put a fixed percentage of their earnings and allowance in it. And make sure they see you giving to others, whether it's tithing to the church, writing a check to a nonprofit, or volunteering for a charitable cause.

7 **Turn off the shopping channel.** Keep TV time to a minimum to avoid the "buy me" ads that dominate. Also point out the marketing tricks that advertisers use, and make sure your kids understand how they try to sell.

Parents and Siblings
5 Secrets to Getting Along Well with Your Relatives

Involve your dad in your life. As we get older, most of our dads tend to blend more and more into the wallpaper. Instead of leaving him to molt into the easy chair while you and your mom chatter like 13-year-olds, find ways to involve him, says Tina B. Tessina, Ph.D., a licensed California psychotherapist and author of *It Ends with You: Grow Up and Out of Dysfunction*. For instance, ask him to flex his handyman muscles by fixing that loose shelf, or ask if he'll give you an opinion on that weird noise in your car.

Digitize, then share the memories. Forget photo albums. Today's memories have gone high-tech, with DVDs and home movies produced on your home computer. So get out your camcorder and start filming, particularly those older relatives who may not be with you much longer. When they do pass on, make copies and send one to each family member.

Make the trust a living one. Probate lawyers won't like that we shared this tip from Kraig Kast, CEO of Atherton Trust in Redwood Shores, California: You need to set up a living trust *now*. Having a living trust ensures that when you die, your financial wishes are immediately carried out without the cost or delay

---

WHAT YOUR PSYCHOTHERAPIST DOESN'T WANT YOU TO KNOW ABOUT Family Stress

You can deal with stressful family situations without seeing a shrink. How do you show grace under pressure? California psychotherapist Tina B. Tessina offers these insider's techniques:

- ☐ **Put it in perspective.** Will what they're saying or doing be important in an hour or two? A day from now? Most won't.

- ☐ **Rise above it.** Next time you are totally fed up with your mother, remind yourself of all of the tough times she has experienced.

- ☐ **Cut yourself a break.** If your mother upsets you by bringing up that failed first marriage again, don't beat yourself up for getting tense about it. Your reaction is normal. It's what you do about it that counts.

- ☐ **Take a time-out.** If you can't send your uncle Richie to time-out when he's had one vodka martini too many, at least you can send yourself there. Take a walk or go shopping.

- ☐ **Keep your mouth shut.** One of the most powerful tools you have is silence. Use it!

- ☐ **Pretend they don't belong to you.** If your in-laws are obnoxious, pretend they're your friend's parents. You wouldn't snap and say something you'd regret to your friend's parents, would you?

associated with probating a will or intestate (no will) estate.

Practice saying no to relatives.
Always find yourself saying yes when your sister asks for money? Then practice ten ways to say no in front of the mirror before you see her. Here's a couple to get you started: "No, I can't. All my money is tied up in retirement accounts and I can't take it out without paying a penalty"; "No, sorry, but I'm going back to school to get my master's and I need every cent"; "I'd really like to, but our water heater just burst and we have to recarpet the basement."

Learn your family's health history.
We know, we know, you don't want to hear another single word about your dad's chest pains, your mom's high cholesterol numbers, or your brother's arthritic knee. But there are good reasons to listen to them besides being a good offspring or sibling and lending a sympathetic ear. As a matter of fact, it's not a bad idea to pursue information on the health of all your extended family members even further by asking about chronic conditions that affected your grandparents, aunts and uncles, and even nieces, nephews, and cousins. Compiling a family medical history will give you and your kin insight into the various diseases and conditions that are common in your family. It can be helpful to doctors in diagnosing a medical condition, determining what medical tests to run and preventive measures to take, and calculating the risk you, your children, and other relatives have of certain diseases. Among the major diseases that the Mayo Clinic recommends that you ask about are heart disease, stroke, cancer, depression, diabetes, Alzheimer's, obesity, blindness, and deafness. Find out the age the conditions were diagnosed and if they were treated successfully. Allergies, asthma, migraines, and frequent colds are other conditions that families may share as well as problems with infertility, miscarriages, birth defects, and learning disabilities. ◁

Dos and Don'ts on Fitting In with His (or Her) Family

So you just got married and you've got a whole second family. Here's how to survive the transition and thrive long-term, courtesy of psychotherapist Tina B. Tessina:

DO understand how your spouse relates to his or her parents.

DON'T assume that family relationship will resemble the one in your family.

DO take the time to get to know your in-laws—if you're separated by distance, write or e-mail each other.

DON'T take offense easily—you may just not understand the family dynamic.

DO check with your partner about family customs. Will his mother expect a hostess gift? A thank-you note? What do they like to eat? What's their sense of humor like? Can you talk about politics or religion in front of them?

DON'T criticize your partner's family. Rather, ask for explanations of things you don't understand.

DO be polite and friendly—use your most charming ways around your in-laws.

DON'T assume they understand how you feel—they may not have a clue. Along those lines, don't take their comments and reactions personally. You may not understand them as they were meant.

DO think about what will work best for you and your partner before you try to please your partner's family.

DON'T ignore your partner while you're with your family. You can talk to your sister, but make sure you check in with each other frequently.

DON'T hesitate to ask your spouse how it went when it's over. A "debriefing" can help both of you.

DO consider doing something that's time-limited and easier. If you go to dinner in a restaurant, everyone might be a bit better behaved.

Family Pets

7 Hints for Keeping Your Four-Legged Family Members Happy and Healthy

Vacation with your pets. This tip isn't going to make the local kennel happy, but Spot and Fifi don't have to be boarded while you go on vacation. Plan ahead and find one of the many pet-friendly hotels that have sprung up, suggests Dr. Kim Langholz, a community practice veterinarian at Iowa State University in Ames. Just think through the details, she says. And plan early, since it could take six to eight months to get all your paperwork in order before traveling to some locations abroad. Other things to consider:

- What, if any, health papers do you need for your pet, including vaccinations? Take your pet in for an annual checkup and ask the veterinarian which shots need to be updated.

- If you're traveling by plane, where will the airline put your pet? Can you carry him in the passenger cabin, in a carrier, or must he travel in cargo? If it's the latter, make sure the cargo area is pressurized; while typical on larger planes, it's not always available on smaller commuter flights.

- Make sure the contact information on your pet's ID tags is current, including your cell phone number.

- If you haven't already, have a microchip implanted in your dog or cat. If she runs off while you're away and someone finds her, the microchip contains information that will get her back into your arms.

- Check the legal requirements at your destination. Some municipalities won't allow pit bulls or ferrets, for instance.

Pack for your pooches and kitties. If you're taking Fido to your mother's for Christmas, make sure you take all the necessary accoutrements, says Langholz, including:

- A health certificate, along with information about vaccines, medications, and your vet's telephone number. In fact, why not just ask your vet for a copy of the past two years of your pet's medical records?

- Enough medication for the entire trip. Make sure this is in your carry-on bag.

- Your pet's regular food, unless you're sure you can find it at your destination. Switching food abruptly could give your pet diarrhea—not exactly the best way to endear yourself to Aunt Mabel.

How I Do It A Vet's Guide to Brushing a Cat's Teeth

Given a study that found cats with oral disease are five times more likely to test positive for feline leukemia and feline immunodeficiency virus (FIV), tooth brushing is no joke. Here's how James Richards, D.V.M., head of Cornell University's Feline Health Center, recommends you do it.

- [ ] Ideally, start with a kitten or very young cat. The "old dogs/new tricks" adage is just as true of kitties.
- [ ] Help your cat feel comfortable with having her mouth touched by gently placing your finger in her mouth or on her teeth when she's on your lap or while you're petting her.
- [ ] Try putting your cat's favorite foods (such as water from a can of tuna) on the toothbrush and letting her get used to it before attempting to brush.
- [ ] Always offer a special treat after tooth brushing, one that isn't available at any other time.

- Pet favorites, including toys, bedding, and kitty litter. Some people even take along tap water from home!
- A first-aid kit for your pet, available in most pet stores.

Distract them for nail clipping with peanut butter. Nobody enjoys clipping a pet's toenails, but it's a must if you want to save your floors, clothes, and furniture. Kayce O'Brien, a project manager at Johnson & Wales University in Denver, found a way that works for Finnegan, her two-year-old Lab-retriever mix. She smears natural peanut butter on the lower part of her refrigerator (stay away from chunky), and as Finnegan licks away at the luscious treat, she quickly lifts his paws and clips away. This also works, she says, for ear cleaning and fur brushing.

Show your cat who's boss. To do that, you need to do some serious training to make sure your cat doesn't

destroy your house. Amy Osete, vice president of marketing for pet products manufacturer Bamboo, suggests the following:

- Get a scratching post covered with sisal rope, corrugated cardboard, or carpet turned wrong side out (if you have the same stuff on both the scratching post and the floor, your cat may think scratching on the floor carpet is okay).
- Spread a paste of cayenne pepper mixed with water or dried orange or lemon peel with water on electrical cords to keep kitty from chewing them.
- Temporarily cover counters and furniture with double-sided tape so that kitty learns not to jump up or curl up on them.

Let someone else handle the mess. Tired of arguing over whose turn it is to scoop up the backyard poop? Just hire it out. Today even the smallest town has at least one poop-scooper for hire.

Give your cat a sense of the outdoors. Even though Buttercup is an indoor cat, she can still get a taste of the outdoor life. What about giving her free rein on the screened porch? Or you could purchase a large dog crate and pad it with soft pillows for sunny afternoons in the backyard. And, of course, you can always put her on a leash. If you want to try walking your cat (and yes, many people do), Belinda Mager, spokesperson for the Humane Society of the United States, recommends the following:

- Use a harness, not a collar.
- Begin the training in the house, when she's hungry. Why the hunger? You'll be using treats as an incentive.
- Start by putting her on the leash for one minute, then increase the time during each training session.
- Once she's comfortable on the leash in the house, it's time to venture outside.
- Stay in the yard and don't go far. This also reduces the risk that you'll run into dogs and other animals.

You can have a pet if you are allergic. Don't instantly blame your pet for all your bouts of sneezing and watery eyes. Sure, you may have a reaction when you are around the cat, but many if not most allergy sufferers are sensitive to more than one allergen. If you react to animal dander, chances are good that you are also sensitive to other common allergens such as dust, cigarette smoke, and pollen or any combination of them. And the effects of these allergens are cumulative. So before you go bundling

the family pet off to a shelter, try lowering the overall allergen level in your house. Basically this means controlling dust by cleaning thoroughly and frequently, keeping out pollen by closing windows and running the air conditioning during peak seasons, and by banning smoking inside the house. Consult with your doctor about allergy shots, antihistamines, and other treatments that may reduce your reaction to dander and other allergens.

To specifically reduce allergy symptoms from a pet—provided they are "simply miserable but not life-threatening"—here are some suggestions from the Humane Society of the United States that may let you keep that furry creature that has won your heart:

- Make your bedroom an allergy-free retreat that the animal is never allowed to go into. Install a high-efficiency HEPA air cleaner. Put impermeable covers on mattresses and pillows to keep them from picking up dander brought in on clothes.
- Use HEPA air cleaners throughout the house and cut back on dander-collecting fabric furnishings such as curtains and carpets.
- Vacuum frequently using a HEPA-filter machine or a microfilter bag. Launder slipcovers, pillow covers, and pet bedding regularly.
- Bathe your pet weekly. It's more effective than any dander-control spray. Even cats can be trained to tolerate bathing.
- Some but by no means all allergy sufferers are less irritated by animals with constantly growing hair, such as poodles and bichon frises, so you might want to consider one for your next pet. ◁

OWNING A PET
turtle or Tortoise

Okay, maybe it's not everyone's choice for the ideal pet. However, turtles don't bark, scratch, or pee on your Persian rug. Here's what you need to know about owning one, says Susan M. Tellem, a representative for American Tortoise Rescue:

Water Turtles (Red-Eared Sliders or Cooters)

What to buy Choose a healthy turtle at least four inches in length. Any smaller and the person selling it to you is breaking the law.

What to look for Clear eyes and energy. A runny nose or swollen eyes means you're getting a sick turtle, one likely to carry salmonella.

Where they live In a pond. Tanks are cruel for these creatures used to traveling from pond to pond in the wild. They need a safe area, protected from predators like raccoons and dogs. Electric fencing is a good option, or a screened cover over the pond.

What to feed them They're carnivores, so live food like feeder fish as well as prepared turtle food is the way to go.

Where they go These turtles hibernate underwater all winter and need protection from predators during this time.

Tortoises and Land Turtles

Where to buy them Not at the pet store—these typically come from the wild. There are lots of rescue chapters around the country that can help you find the right tortoise.

What kind to buy One that meshes with your household. Smaller ones include Russians or box turtles. Both hibernate and like cooler weather. Larger ones include desert, leopard, or sulcata tortoises. They're vegetarians. If you get a desert tortoise, and live in the U.S., many states require a permit, because they're endangered. For that reason, they're not allowed on the East Coast. Also know that sulcatas can grow to 200 pounds, so you'll need at least a fenced half-acre.

What to feed them Box turtles are carnivores. Snails and worms work, along with some greenery. The larger tortoises are vegetarian.

Dating and Relationships

5 Ways to Better Your Luck in Love

Online, leave some things to the imagination. If you are dating on the Internet, don't put anything on your site that you wouldn't want up in a PowerPoint presentation given to your coworkers. That's because, office etiquette experts say, that is essentially what you are doing when you post information on a dating site. Your boss doesn't need to know that midnight skinny-dipping is your favorite pastime. Plus, work aside, dating experts say that the people who have the most success with online dating are the ones who use some discretion.

Embrace chivalry on a first date. No matter who asked whom out on that first date, etiquette experts say a man should *always* foot the bill (for same-sex couples, the asker buys). Here's a trick: If you are a woman on a first date and the guy doesn't reach for the check, take a trip to the powder room. If he doesn't pay while you're gone, offer to split the check. If he allows that, find yourself another knight.

Tread carefully with office romance. Twenty percent of us meet our mates at work, says Robin Bond, a workplace etiquette expert and employment attorney in Wayne, Pennsylvania. Because there's nothing other than *American Idol* to talk about at the water cooler, the news about your office romance will spread like wildfire, and the relationship could be quickly construed as inappropriate. To handle an office romance professionally, keep the following rules in mind:

- Most important: *Do not* speak to anyone in Human Resources about the romance. "Despite what the company might tell you about HR being your friend, they are not—do not trust anyone in HR," says Bond.

- Make sure you like the coworker enough to take a risk. If it is just a fling and the person has no potential as the love of your life, end it.

- Assess how much you like the person by hanging out with him or her at group lunches or happy hours.

- Be certain the person likes you back. People are quick to cry sexual harassment these days, so be sure your advances are wanted, Bond says.

Set the mood with food. If you are preparing a romantic meal for the one you love (or really like), certain foods can make the evening more pleasurable for both of you … without your date suspecting a thing.

- *A game animal.* According to historical theory, if you eat a wild animal, you take on some of its wildness. Given that your beloved is not a vegetarian, of course, make something like a wild game hen or roasted duck.

- *Oysters.* Used in ancient times in lieu of Viagra, oysters contain zinc, which is stored in the prostate and is thought to prolong sexual pleasure in men. Enough said.

- *Wine.* This one is a no-brainer when it comes to romance. But keep Shakespeare's words of moderation in mind: "Liquor provoketh the desire but taketh away the performance."

- *Chocolate.* This popular food contains a chemical called phenylethylamine, a compound that the body naturally produces when a person is in love. Your date may instantly feel more amorous toward you after a bite (or a bar).

In love with your friend's ex? Be careful. Most etiquette experts agree that a friend's former boyfriend, husband, girlfriend, or wife is totally off-limits. If you truly feel this ex is your soul mate, there are a few things you can try that may still salvage your friendship. For one, out of respect for the failed relationship and both parties who were in it, wait an appropriate amount of time before you dive in (the rule of thumb for relationship mourning is three months for every year the couple was together up to a maximum of a year or so). Second, if you ask your friend—asking is imperative—and he or she gives you the go-ahead, you are closer to the green light. If your friend was the one who did the breaking up, you are even closer. If your friend is now happily recoupled, you are as good as home free. ◁

SECRET WEAPON

A Bright Tie

At social gatherings where you are likely to meet potential dating partners, wear some distinctive article of clothing or jewelry. It not only makes you stand out from the crowd, but also offers anyone interested in you an excuse to start a conversation. For a man it might be a bright red or unusually patterned tie, while a woman might try distinctive earrings, a necklace, or an embroidered vest or belt.

Parties and Entertaining
7 Ways to Be the Perfect Host (and Guest)

Dress your event up by serving mixed drinks. Most people think that wine is cheaper than liquor. The truth is, serving mixed drinks instead of wine will actually *save* you money on your booze tab. "A bottle of wine yields only five glasses, which will serve only three to five guests at best," says Denise Vivaldo, author of *Do It for Less! Parties*. At an average cost of $15 a bottle, a fairly decent wine adds up if you're having a lot of people over.

Here are a few less expensive (and perhaps more festive) options: For easy, frothy daiquiris, mix a liter of rum with frozen limeade; for a new twist on the classic Cape Codder, combine sparkling cranberry juice with a liter of vodka. (Use one part liquor to three parts juice for both cocktails.) You will get about 30 cocktails out of a liter of liquor, which costs roughly the same as a bottle of wine.

If you don't want to spend the night with a cocktail shaker in your hand, opt for a champagne punch so that guests can serve themselves. A punch made of inexpensive sparkling wine, fruit juice, and soda is cheap, easy, and a real crowd pleaser. Here's how you do it: In a punch bowl, combine a bottle of sparkling wine or champagne with a 12-ounce (355-ml) can of frozen juice and two 12-ounce (355-ml) cans of a light-colored soda such as ginger ale or Sprite. Stir and serve!

Not a drinker? Fake it. Here's the scenario: You don't drink, but you're at a party and you're being pressured to booze it up. Why not ask the bartender for a virgin drink that looks alcoholic?

You can order a soda and ask the bartender to put some fruit and a stirrer in it. If someone asks, just say it's a gin and tonic if you are drinking Sprite, or get a Coke and say that it has rum or whiskey in it. If you are at a barbecue and people are drinking beer out of bottles or cans, dump the beer out in the bathroom and fill it with water. Not comfortable with the drinking façade? It's perfectly acceptable to be firm about refusing liquor.

Rent the dishes yourself. If you're hosting a catered party, ask the catering company to itemize all charges. When you get the figure you'll be charged for such accessories as dishware, silverware, and tablecloths, use it to do some comparison shopping. Chances are, the caterer is renting these accoutrements himself and is just marking up the rental fees. Call several party suppliers in the phone book to see if you can beat the figure your caterer is charging you. The caterer may stamp his feet, but you're in charge.

Keep your pipes clean. Nothing will kill the mood of a great party faster than a backed-up toilet. It's one of those aspects of party planning that no one really talks about, but it should not be overlooked. If you're hosting a sizeable event at your home, prepare for a potential septic challenge by having all toilets that partygoers will use professionally snaked right before the event. It's better to spend $40 ahead of time than risk the embarrassment and expense of an emergency call to the plumber in the middle of your party.

How I Do It An Etiquette Expert Hosts a Fun, Sophisticated Evening

An inventive host will go the extra mile to inject some fun into a party to help people mingle and have a fabulous time, says Liz Scofield, an etiquette instructor at Lehigh University.

"One year, my husband and I gave people secret tasks they had to accomplish throughout the evening," she confesses. "For instance, one person had the task of finding out how old I was. Another guest had the task of making someone tell a dirty joke. And to accomplish their tasks, guests couldn't flat-out ask someone her age or to tell a dirty joke—they had to somehow convince the other person that it was the perfect time for a dirty joke or for an age revelation.

"It was on a sophisticated yet lighthearted level, and it was absolutely wonderful. People were on their toes and on the alert for the tasks. We had prizes at the end of the night for people who completed their tasks—it was a magnificent success. I think communication games like this can really make people interact and have a great time at a party."

Play musical plates. Worried that your party guests will clean out your buffet? Use smaller, 9-inch (23-cm) plates instead of the standard 12-inch (30-cm) size. By shrinking the size of the plates, you will trick your guests into thinking that they're putting more food away than they are. On the flip side, if your dinner is winding down and you don't want leftovers, switch over to larger, 12- or 14-inch (30- or 36-cm) plates and hope that your guests pile them high!

Celebrate diversity at your party. Here's a tip that will not only make you look like a hero for celebrating everyone's cultural background, it will save you from having to make all the food yourself: "To make everyone feel included, request that each person bring a menu item that is representative of his or her religion or cultural background," says Liz Ngonzi, president of Amazing Taste, an event-planning firm in South Orange, New Jersey. For an added bonus, ask them to send you the recipe in advance so you can create a multicultural holiday cookbook for your guests.

Make just one outstanding dish. When you are trying to be the perfect host or hostess, there is a natural tendency to overdo it, to try too hard. And when it comes to a formal sit-down dinner or even a buffet, you want every course or dish to be extra special and perfect. In the process, you can not only bust your budget but also drive yourself into a frenzy. Well, the solution is simple: Make one dish the star of the meal and spend your extra effort and money on that one course. As a matter of fact, if the other parts of the meal are straightforward and simple—but made with fresh, tasty ingredients—they will set off the prize dish rather than compete with it, letting it shine like a diva with a fine but unobtrusive supporting cast. And you'll garner more compliments. ◁

Tying the Knot

7 Special Tips from Seasoned Wedding Coordinators

Hire a wedding coordinator to save you time and money. Most brides think that hiring a wedding coordinator will break their budget. It's a little-known fact that wedding coordinators can actually *save* you money after you get all the discounts and perks they have arranged with partner vendors, says Sharon Naylor, who has written 30 wedding books including *1000 Best Secrets for Your Perfect Wedding*. But use caution when selecting a planner: Anyone can call herself a "wedding planner." Look for someone who is certified by organizations such as the American Academy of Wedding Professionals or the Association of Bridal Consultants (www.bridalassn.com) who have consultants throughout North America.

Read the fine print on your contract. Caterers bank on the fact that most clients won't read their contracts carefully. Read yours, and then read it again, because they often charge you for things that you don't know you're being charged for: They might have a minimum number of guests they'll serve (i.e., you will be charged for 100 people even if only 75 show up), a per-slice cake-cutting fee, or overtime for waitstaff who stay late (whether you ask them to or not). These fees are often not added until the final invoice, so make sure you get a breakdown of all extra costs before the big day.

Skip the custom-printed invitations. Here's a secret: Most people couldn't care less about other couples' wedding invitations. Your guests will probably never even notice the scalloped edges and silver ink that cost you an extra $2 per print. Therefore, they probably also won't know if you've made your invitations yourselves. Instead of ordering them custom made, use invitation software such as www.mountaincow.com's Printing Press—your whole set of invites will only cost about $40. Although they are the enemy of wedding invitation designers, invitation software packages offer modern fonts and graphics, and they are easy to use.

Book a budding musical talent. If you have always dreamed of having a live string quartet at your wedding but can't afford their fees, hire music students. Your guests don't have to know that the musicians are still perfecting their talents. A local performing arts school, university, or music school will be able to recommend some students; you may also find performers' contact

SECRET WEAPON

Credit Card

Even if you have a million dollars in the bank, experts will tell you to pay for everything related to your wedding and reception with a credit card. This will protect you should anything go wrong with your vendors. If the first-rate photographer you booked gets hit by a bus the day before the wedding and you put the deposit on a credit card, your money will be refunded. If you had paid with cash, your money would have gone down with the photographer. Your credit card is like a free wedding insurance policy in your wallet, so use it.

information on bulletin boards at music stores. To avoid disaster, hold a brief audition for your musicians before you hire them, or ask for permission to observe them at another gig.

Focus your flowers. This nugget comes straight from a former florist: "The cost of flowers is minimal—it's the labor it takes to arrange them that costs so much," says Deb McCoy, president of the American Academy of Wedding Professionals. "To save money on flowers, put your money into your bridal party flowers and go with nonfloral table centerpieces at your reception." The flowers in the bride's bouquet and on your mom, dad, bridesmaids, and other relatives are the flowers that will forever be in your photos, so that's where you want to invest. Rather than having floral centerpieces, McCoy suggests something you can make yourself: "Put beautiful, tall candles on the tables and surround them with glass pebbles, or float votive candles in water." You will save a ton of money.

Cut to the cake. Plan to cut your cake and toss your bouquet early in the night. Your wedding guests will never know you've done this to let your photographer and videographer leave early, and it will cut down on the per-hour costs. Plus, after the professional photographers leave, your guests will be more likely to start snapping pictures with the inexpensive, throwaway cameras on their tables (if you provide them).

Don't hire a hat-switching photographer. No matter how fabulous your friend is at shooting photos for CNN, and no matter how hard he tries to convince you that he can transfer that skill to your wedding for decent price, *do not*

hire him to save a few bucks on your wedding photos. "Shooting news photography and wedding photography are two totally different skills," McCoy says. "A wedding is a scripted event, and if you go with someone who isn't a seasoned wedding photographer, I guarantee he or she will miss 50 percent of the high points." Think about it this way: Would you rather have 20 beautiful photos of the happiest day of your life or 200 blurry ones?

"Photography is the one thing you can't put a price on—I call it the bite-the-bullet component of a wedding," McCoy says. "Most of the complaints I get from people are about the photography, and the reason I get these complaints is that they shopped quantity instead of quality." Talented wedding photographers are hard to come by, so you are probably going to have to spend a little more than you planned to get a good one. ◁

Caterer Confidential
6 Classy Ways to Serve a Crowd for Less

Check out your caterer at an event. You've found a catering service that you like, and you are ready to go with it, but there are still some lingering doubts in the back of your mind. After all, this is a very special occasion; otherwise you wouldn't be hiring a caterer. You can and should always ask for references, but you can't be sure that you aren't just getting friends of the caterer, who are not going to bad-mouth him. So how do you make sure this particular caterer can do the job you want? Ask the caterer to arrange for you to visit another function he is handling so that you can observe firsthand how he and his staff perform. Be sure to dress properly for the occasion, as if you were an invited guest, and don't overstay your welcome. You can pretty much gauge how well the caterer is doing in a half-hour or so.

Take a seat and save. "Most people are under the impression that buffets are cheaper than sit-down dinners, but that is absolutely not the case," says McCoy. Although some catering companies tell their clients otherwise, the buffet actually requires more food and labor. When you have a sit-down dinner, she says, chefs are exacting in their quantities. They say, "Okay, there are six ounces of meat, five ounces of potatoes, and four ounces of peas on each plate." This helps keep food costs under control. When they put buffets together, they have to plan for guests returning again and again, so they have to make a lot more food. Plus, buffets require constant maintenance—servers have to be there to replenish the food, and keep the area tidy. And you also need people to wait tables to serve drinks and such, which requires hiring nearly double the staff.

The cheapest way to go? Have a sit-down dinner—packaged. "Every hotel, club, and catering facility offers packages where you can get a sit-down dinner including everything from your appetizer to your salad to your champagne toast. Of course, they vary in price depending on the items you choose, but it is your best value," McCoy says.

Serve surf and turf. Even though it may sound more expensive to serve each guest a combination plate, chefs say combo platters can cost up to 40 percent less than dinners at which guests have a choice of seafood, chicken, or beef. The savings come from the planning that goes along with combination platters—the chef knows exactly how much food to buy. No need to get extras in case guests change their minds on site. So go ahead, serve surf and turf—you'll save money, but your guests will think you just won the lottery.

Order up extra bartenders. Caterers will tell you that one or two bartenders will be enough to staff your wedding reception, but unless you want 200 people standing in line for drinks all night, it won't be. Most catering companies will assign one bartender to every 75 guests, but wedding planners in the know say that you should specify in your contract that you want one bartender for every 50 guests during the cocktail hour (when guests will do most of their imbibing), with one bartender for every 75 guests during the dinner hour. It will cost a little extra, but it will prevent your reception from looking like a cafeteria line.

Buy booze by the head, not by the drink. Even if most of your wedding guests are nondrinkers, don't let the caterer talk you into paying by the drink. The secret about teetotalers is that many actually do imbibe when the liquor is free, and what's free for them costs you about $7.50 per cocktail.

"I was pulled into this trap when I planned my stepdaughter's wedding a few years ago," says McCoy. "Because most of the people in my family don't drink much, the catering director persuaded me to pay for the liquor by the glass. It ended up that the liquor bill was more than the food bill." It is almost always cheaper to buy liquor by the head. Caterers "may charge you $20 per head for a four-hour event where guests can drink as much as they want," McCoy says. "With a per-head liquor contract, there will be no surprises when it comes to paying the bill."

Spring for top-shelf stuff. People will remember whether they had Grey Goose or Banker's Club vodka at your celebration, so you may want to spend a little extra for the brand-name booze. Here's the thing: The price discrepancy between shelf and *top*-shelf liquor is only a few dollars per head, but it can make a significant difference in how classy your event is, and how happy your guests are. For 200 people, the cost will only be a few hundred dollars extra. ◁

Your catering director will try to talk you into courses that you just don't need in your meal, warns wedding specialist Deb McCoy. Both an appetizer before your meal, and an extra dessert before the wedding cake, are unnecessary. Skipping them could save you thousands of dollars.

With regard to the appetizer, if you serve hors d'oeuvres during your cocktail hour, no one will be chomping at the bit for an extra course before the entrée. In fact, they will probably be bursting with the mini quiches and cocktail shrimp they just chowed with their vodka tonics. When everyone is seated, jump right to the salad.

Your caterer will also try to tell you that wedding cake is just there for show, and that no one will eat it. Not true. It *is* true that your guests may not eat their cake because they just ate a bowl of cherries jubilee that cost you an extra $5 to $6 per head. Instead of spending the extra money on the extra dessert, spend half of it—$2 or $3 per head—on upgrading the wedding cake. Splurge on a cannoli cream cake, or one with raspberry filling. The last taste your guests will have in their mouths will be a delicious one.

Dinner Parties
5 Secret Ingredients for a Great Evening

Bring a nonedible hostess gift.
The key to choosing the perfect hostess gift: Choose something that will please the hostess without disrupting the flow of the party, says etiquette instructor Liz Scofield. Don't bring flowers—she'll have to leave her guests and go searching for a vase. Don't bring a dessert—she probably already has every crumb of the meal planned out, and she'll feel obligated to serve what you brought in addition to what she already had planned. Instead, present her with something fresh and delightful, such as homemade chocolate, gourmet teas, cocktail napkins, or candles. Better yet, send something ahead of time that will add to the festivities, such as a floral arrangement.

If you are on the receiving end of a disruptive hostess gift, tell the gift giver, "This is great—I will save it for the next special occasion when it can be appreciated on its own."

Pinch pennies with pasta. Pasta will stretch a dinner like no other food—both in terms of cost and quantity, says catering expert Vivaldo. One cooked pound of pasta mixed with grilled vegetables and chicken will serve six to eight guests for just $5 or $10. Compare that to $50 and up for a leg of lamb or other higher-end meat dishes. To hide the fact that you have chosen pasta to cut costs, give your dinner party an Italian theme. Serve Italian wine and bread, throw some red-and-white-checked tablecloths on your tables, and make a tiramisu (or other Italian dessert) to top it off.

Dine with both ying and yang. You may think a dozen guests with similar interests equals one successful dinner party. Not so—the secret to a rollicking evening is usually a quirky collection of opposites. If you want a dynamic, delightful dinner, mix it up a bit. Invite both your conservative neighbor and your bohemian brother-in-law, for starters, and see what happens.

Don't get stuck with the blowhard. If you find yourself stuck at a party with the most boring blowhard you've ever met, excuse yourself to get a drink refill and offer to get him something as well. If he says no to the drink, you are off the hook and can depart with grace. If he says yes, it's still okay if you get the drink, hand it over, and then walk away. Another way to escape? Introduce chatty Charlie to a passing friend and remark on the interest or hobby they might have in common. Then leave.

Master the art of the empty invitation. Learn when to give an empty invitation and learn when an invitation is empty, Scofield says. Few people would admit to giving one, but there are some invitations that are offered purely out of social grace, not out of a genuine desire to see someone again. These "empty invitations" are particularly prevalent at the close of a social event such as a dinner party. "For instance, if you just met someone at a dinner party and they offer to let you stay at their home the next time you come into town, that's an empty invitation," she says. "If you tried to take the person up on it, they would likely tell you their house was full that weekend."

Similar to the empty invitation is the empty parting comment, such as "Let's have lunch" or "I'll call you." These comments really mean, "I like you as a person, but I probably won't call." To avoid confusion, if you are the one giving the empty invitation or parting comment, substitute it with a more general phrase, such as "It was good to see you." ◄

Psst ... Table Manners Still Matter!

If you think people don't care about etiquette at the table as much as they used to, think again. One soup slurp or tooth pick is all it takes to turn some people off. So to stay on your toes, here is a quick—and necessary—table manners refresher course from Louise Fox of the Etiquette Ladies, Canada's Etiquette Experts:

- ☐ If you are the recipient of a toast, keep your glass at arm's length—never drink from it. Instead, simply nod your head and graciously say, "Thank you."
- ☐ Never take your cocktail to the dinner table.
- ☐ Allow your food to cool on its own—never blow on anything.
- ☐ If you wear lipstick, keep it off your plate and napkin by blotting it as soon as you apply it.
- ☐ Your napkin is there for you to dab your mouth *only*. Do not use it to wipe off lipstick or (God forbid) blow your nose.
- ☐ Keep your elbows off the table at all times.
- ☐ Don't put your purse, keys, sunglasses, or eyeglasses on the table.
- ☐ Take food out of your mouth the way it went in. If a piece of steak fat went into your mouth with a fork, spit it out onto the fork.
- ☐ Remove an olive pit with your thumb and index finger.
- ☐ Taste everything on your plate before you add salt or pepper.
- ☐ Leave your plate where it is when you are finished with your meal—don't push it away from you.

You'll find even more good-behavior tips at www.etiquette ladies.com.

Class Reunions
5 Time- and Money-Saving Tips for Your Stroll Down Memory Lane

Reunite by sunlight. The caterer may try to talk you into a dinner reunion, but a daytime meal will save a bundle on your reunion (or just about any big event). Daytime meals—breakfast, brunch, and lunch—cost a lot less than evening meals because these foods typically cost less, people expect smaller portions, and you can get away with serving less alcohol. At a daytime outdoor reunion, you can organize games like horseshoes and volleyball that will break the ice and encourage people to interact. Daytime events such as picnics or barbecues are also more casual; for example, you can get away with plastic plates rather than fancy, rented china.

Trick former classmates into pitching in. Sure, it may have seemed like a great idea to run for class president when you were 17, but 10 or 20 years later, you're stuck planning your high school reunion—a *big* responsibility. To figure out how much of this work you're able to delegate to others, survey the group and see if anyone is in the event-planning business. Ask these event planners if they can arrange for a discounted (or free) venue, photographer, or caterer, says Ngonzi. In exchange for your much appreciated discounts, offer to advertise the businesses prominently at the reunion.

Ask attendees for their two cents. Whether you are planning a high school reunion, coworker reunion, or family reunion, one of the best things you can do is to ask attendees for suggestions. Even if you never use their ideas, people love to think that they had a role in creating a fabulous event. Try emailing attendees a survey a few weeks (or months) before the event to ask what their thoughts are on games, activities, and themes. Then you can use the innovative ideas and ignore the lame ones.

How to Make a Memorable Entrance

Psychologists say most people form impressions of others within the first four minutes of meeting them, and 80 percent of those first impressions are based on nonverbal behavior. Making a dignified entrance at an event might just be more important than the conversations you have later.

When you make your entrance, the best way to draw attention to yourself in a tasteful way is being attractive, charming, witty, and memorable, says Scofield, the etiquette teacher. To turn heads and leave good impressions, pay attention to:

- **Your walk.** As you enter, walk with confidence, but not arrogance. Keep your head up, your shoulders back and down, and smile. No swaggering!

- **Your clothes.** Your clothes should be stunning without being over the top—fashionable without revealing too much skin.

- **Your placement.** When you first pass through the door, pause, step to the right, and survey the crowd. People watch the front door, so you'll be in plain view.

- **Your sociability.** Do not make a beeline for safety nets such as the bar, food, or people you already know. Instead, move from group to group and introduce yourself. If you are confident and friendly, people will naturally be attracted to you.

Spark a prom déjà vu. For a great high school reunion favor, create a replica of the champagne flute you got at your junior prom. It's a little-known fact that giving out these flutes can also save your event organizers some money! If you request that guests drink all alcoholic beverages out of the flutes, you will cut down on alcohol consumption (those flutes don't hold much in the way of beer or cocktails). Also, if your high school reunion is being held in a public place, the flutes will deter reunion crashers on the prowl for free drinks.

Find an affordable reunion space. Looking for a place to hold your class reunion? Renting a hall, a dining room at a restaurant, or a conference room at a hotel can be an expensive proposition. And if you are the chief organizer, you not only have to make an upfront down payment on the space but also have to nudge your former classmates into paying their fair share. And to be quite frank, many of your classmates are probably deadbeats—they think they've done their part just by showing up. But finding affordable space is really not that difficult.

- First off, chances are at least one of your former classmates has gone into the restaurant, bar, or hotel business and would be more than willing to offer a special deal, especially if he or she is the owner or manager.
- If that doesn't pan out, talk to the administrators at the school itself to see if there is any way to make an arrangement to use the school gym, cafeteria, or even the schoolyard if you're thinking of a warm-weather gathering. Colleges, eager to endear themselves to future donors among their alumni, are more likely to offer

a venue; just call the alumni affairs office at your college.

- For outdoor get-togethers, check the parks department for available space; some even have pavilions you can rent for a moderate fee.
- If you end up having to go to a commercial source, make bars, not restaurants, your first choice. Bars often have large back rooms that they will rent out inexpensively. ◁

Plan a Big Event from Your Laptop

Party and event planners don't tell people about event-planning software packages. That's because many of them use such software themselves and fear that if the secret gets out, they'll lose business. Instead of hiring a party planner or wedding coordinator, you can spend the $75 to $200 for software and do it yourself. Here are just a few good packages:

☐ **Mountain Cow's Printing Press.** Printing Press is an invitation software package that helps you design and print perfect invitations or "save the date" cards. Features modern fonts and graphics. Available at www.mountaincow.com.

☐ **My Wedding Companion CD.** The longest-selling wedding planning software on the market, My Wedding Companion organizes every aspect of your wedding, from the registry and seating chart to your honeymoon. Available from Amazon.com or Amazon.ca.

☐ **B'nai Mitzvah.** This bar and bat mitzvah planning software can also be used for planning other types of parties and events. Can be purchased at www.castlecomputer.com.

☐ **Reunion Planner Software.** Helps you organize a reunion celebration; keeps tabs on your budget, contact information, name tags, and seat assignments. Available at www.reunionplanner.com.

☐ **The Ultimate Wine and Cheese Pairing Guide.** Never be confused about wine again. This software has lists of the most popular white, red, and dessert wines, as well as classic food pairing matches for each. Available from Amazon.com or Amazon.ca.

Dining Out

6 Tricks for Having a Memorable Meal When You Eat Out at a Restaurant

Fine-tune restaurant recommendations. Hotel concierges are all too happy to recommend a restaurant to a stranger in town. What many don't want you to know is that they get referral fees in exchange for steering customers to certain eateries. That doesn't mean the place they pitch won't be good, because they do want you to be happy. But it does mean it may not be the best choice for what you had in mind. So ask some specific questions about the food, prices, and atmosphere. Kids welcome or romantic? Quiet or lots of music? Local style or haute cuisine?

Get a second opinion about restaurants. Your concierge isn't the only source of restaurant tips when you're out of town. The hotel teems with savvy locals. But remember about different strokes for different folks. If you're looking for upscale dining, hotel waiters may be plugged into the scene. But asking most other hotel staffers could backfire; they probably can't afford to frequent such places and don't want to be reminded of it. Hotel bar customers are a better bet. Even if they're from out of town themselves, they often have experiences to share. But if it's 100 percent local food and atmosphere you're after, the staff is a gold mine of advice. "Where do the locals eat?" is a question that can lead to unexpected pleasures.

Watch out for terms indicating fat. The folks who write restaurant menus are trying their darndest to sound enticing while dancing around the fact that many of their offerings are dripping with hidden fat—much of it the artery-clogging kind. You probably already know that words such as *creamy, breaded, buttery, crisp, pan-fried, cheese sauce,* and *stuffed* are indicators of fat—often saturated or trans fat. Other words to look out for are not as obvious: *Thermidor, Newburg, Parmesan,* and *scalloped.* But it's the foreign words that can really fool. For example, the innocent-sounding *au gratin* added to oysters or whitefish turns a lean, heart-healthy food into a plate of saturated fat.

Also from the French we get *au lait, à la mode, au fromage,* and *sautéed*—meaning, respectively, "with milk," "with ice cream," "with cheese" and "pan-fried in fat." On an Italian menu, beware of *Alfredo, carbonara, saltimbocca, parmigiana, lasagna,* and *manicotti,* which indicate heavy amounts of cream and cheese. (On the positive side, *griglia* indicates a heart-healthy grilled approach.)

In a Mexican restaurant, watch out for *chimichanga* (a fried burrito), *chalupas* (small deep-fried tortillas), *milanesa* (breaded and fried), and *con queso* (with cheese). *Relleno* means stuffed, which is always risky. For example, a chile relleno is actually a breaded chile pepper deep-fried in oil or lard and stuffed with cheese. Not what cardiologists recommend.

Rule of thumb: If you can't translate a menu word into a specific English word yourself, ask your waiter what it means, exactly. Better to appear unworldly than walk away less healthy.

Forge an alliance with your waiter. A discreet, professional waiter would never mention it, but the truth is that most of the foul-ups at a restaurant are not the waiter's fault. He or she is only the most visible link in a chain that includes chefs, sous-chefs, line cooks, prep staff, bussers, cleanup crew, hosts, managers, and owners. It's not the waiter who overcooked your veal, or forgot to hold the onions, or sat you at the table by the restrooms. But most customers will jump all over the waiter when things go wrong.

That's a mistake. The waiter is on your side. Nobody has more at stake in your satisfaction. So let your waiter know early on that you consider him or her your ally, not those others. Don't say, "Waiter, you brought me the wrong dressing." Say, "They put the wrong dressing on this, didn't they?" Even if the first statement is truer than the second, your server will appreciate your sympathetic approach and take better care of you.

Make dinner conversation interesting. If conversation makes the meal, avoid making a common mistake when you're dining with another person, or several others. Somewhere along the line it became common wisdom that the key to being a good dinner partner is to keep the conversation focused on the person you're with, and then "be a good listener." So now, who knows how many restaurant meals consist of one diner having to answer 75 questions before she or he has buttered the first roll. "Yes, you do have to listen," says Susan RoAne, a California business networking consultant and author of *What Do I Say Next?* and *How to Work a Room.* "But if all you do is ask questions, I'm going to clam up and my attitude becomes, 'What's it to ya?' "

Instead of grilling the person across the table from you, bring something to the party yourself. Good conversation strikes a balance between giving and

How I Do It A Restaurant Manager's Tip on a Great Seat

Karen Beban, the manager of a northern California seaside restaurant and a frequent restaurant customer, has a favorite way to enjoy great service while having a wonderful time when she dines out. "Eat at the bar," she says. "I recently read a complaint from a woman who felt she was getting the single-woman treatment when the host suggested she eat at the bar. Wrong. Eating at the bar is more fun, whether you're single or a couple."

By way of example, Beban relates a recent dining experience: "A friend and I tried a fairly new restaurant in Sausalito with a good reputation. We sat at the bar, of course. Carol immediately learned the bartender's name, and we asked him about the new chef. Connection made. We ordered martinis before lunch, asking him to suggest an appetizer. Rapport established. We let him suggest the glass of wine with our entrée—pinot grigio for her, zinfandel for me."

At the bar, there's a more open camaraderie with the diners and drinkers around you, not to mention having your "waiter" standing right there the whole time. "Besides having a great time, we got extra scallops and our wineglasses refilled at no charge," says Beban. "When we go back, we'll make it a point to remember the bartender's name and ask him about the vacation he told us he was about to take. And he'll remember the large tip we left, and how much fun we were."

Beban offers a few cautions for maximum bar dining pleasure. Don't sit at the bar with a large party. A bartender counts on turnover for tips, and that can't happen if diners take up all the seats. Don't sit at the bar if all you're having is herbal tea and salad. And if you're out with the kids, stick to the main restaurant floor. Bars are for adults.

receiving. "Naturally you want to show you're interested in your dinner partner," RoAne says. "But you want to be interesting too."

Don't nitpick; relax and enjoy.
Anyone who works the floor of a restaurant knows something you don't, but should: It's not the food that determines whether a customer has a good time, and it's not the service. The biggest factor is the attitude of the customer himself. Sure, a high-priced entrée that disappoints, or a Simon Cowell wannabe as a waiter, can ruin your evening. But more often than not, waiters say in private, disgruntled customers walk into the restaurant poised for battle and ready to have a bad time. They usually find it.

So here's a tip for your dining pleasure: Relax and have a good time. Don't make a big deal out of small things. If there's a piece of cork floating in your wine, you can raise a stink, alienate the serving staff, and poison the atmosphere for the rest of the evening. Or you can just take the piece of cork out. The wine's still fine. Leave the nitpicking to the professional restaurant reviewers. They get paid for finding problems. You, on the other hand, are paying. So decide to have a good time. No restaurant's perfect, and it doesn't have to be for you to enjoy it. ◁

Wine Secrets

4 Things to Consider When You Order Wine with Your Meal

Order wine by the bottle.
Restaurants love it when you order your wine by the glass. That's because they make more money per bottle that way, and you usually end up paying more per sip. How? Do the math. You and your date each order a glass of wine, typically five ounces. So far, so good. You liked it, so you each order another glass. You've now probably paid a few dollars more than what a bottle costs, and if you had bought a bottle, there'd still be another glass left—which you don't have. So unless you're purposefully tasting around— that is, trying different wines, a glass at a time—or you're sure you'll each order only one glass, buy a bottle. It's a better bargain and more fun to boot.

Serve your own wine. Do you really need your waiter controlling the wine bottle all meal long and refilling your glass every time you take a sip? Before you answer, be aware that the motive isn't entirely good service. As often as not, all that fussing and pouring is mostly about pushing the wine at you so you'll drink more and order more. So unless you honestly enjoy the extra attention, take control of your own consumption by telling your waiter after the wine is first served that you'll be pouring for yourself throughout the meal. After all, it's pretty easy to do.

BYOB (bring your own burgundy).
Restaurants in the U.S. aren't crazy about customers toting in a bottle of wine to drink with their meals, and the industry as a whole has fostered the impression that you can't do it. But in fact most restaurants in all price ranges will let you bring your own bottle, but they'll charge a "corkage fee." That fee might be $10 per bottle or it might be $50 or more. Not only does corkage vary from restaurant to restaurant, it sometimes varies from table to table in any one restaurant. At the end of the day, they can charge whatever they want.

So call ahead, let them know what you're bringing with you and ask about the corkage fee. That way you get a fee nailed down in advance, and they usually appreciate the heads-up. If you plan to drink a second bottle, consider buying that one from the house. Sometimes when you do that, the corkage fee on the first one goes down or even gets waived. In several Canadian provinces—like Quebec and Ontario—some restaurants are designated "Bring Your Own Wine" establishments and customers are encouraged to bring their own. Wineglasses are supplied free of charge and no "corkage fees" are applied. However, waiters expect a better tip for these services.

Doggie-bag that merlot, please.
Hesitant about ordering that second bottle of wine because you're not sure the two of you can finish it? Go ahead. In the United States, it's perfectly legal in most states to take the unfinished portion home with you, properly sealed and bagged by the restaurant staff. Problem is, "recorking" is not something restaurants are in the habit of suggesting, and most diners are unaware that such a thing exists. But now you know, so get that wine to go. ◄

HOW TO ORDER
wine
Without Worry

Nearly everyone knows by now that rules about wine were meant to be broken. Some white wines go well with meat and some reds with poultry and seafood dishes. But it's still important to wait until everyone has decided on a main course before selecting wine in order to get one that goes well with everything. Here are some tips on handling the wine-ordering ritual.

- ☐ If you know which wine you want, order it. If you don't, tell the waiter or wine steward how much you want to spend and have him or her recommend one. Then accept the recommendation gladly, knowing your chances of enjoying the wine are better than if you'd taken a shot in the dark.

- ☐ Take advantage of the wine list—not just to find a bottle to order but to point to your choice if you can't pronounce the name. The waiter will nod knowingly and say the name perfectly. And then you *still* won't be able to pronounce it, but it doesn't matter. Your only job is to drink it.

- ☐ If you chose your wine off the list, check the label when the bottle comes to make sure you're getting what you ordered. That includes the year. A 2001 might cost a lot more than the 2003 you asked for, but if you drink it, you can be charged the higher price.

- ☐ When the waiter pulls out the cork and then puts it down in front of you, stick it in your ear and say, "Sounds good." Are we kidding? Yes. But it's no more ridiculous than the cork-smelling routine that some folks feel obliged to perform. All you need to do is make sure the cork's not moldy or decaying. If it's moist on the bottom, that's good; it means the wine was stored correctly. Otherwise forget about it. It's just a cork.

- ☐ If you ordered, you'll get a splash in your glass to taste. Relax. It's not a test. If the wine's gone bad, you'll know. First look: You don't want brown or cloudy. Then smell and taste. Remember, you're not judging at a wine tasting. You just want to be sure the wine hasn't oxidized (turned vinegary) and the cork didn't go bad (musty taste). If it's bad, don't be shy about telling the server. Suggest the server taste it to confirm. Trust us, he or she won't take it personally.

- ☐ Tell the server out loud that the wine's okay. Something like, "Nice wine, thanks for the suggestion" will work fine. He appreciates the verbal confirmation, because it's like a contract that you agree to pay for the bottle.

Having a Drink

5 Tricks for Getting on the Barkeep's Good Side When Out for a Quick One with Colleagues

How to get a free drink. You won't see a sign on the wall announcing it, but a bartender has some (limited) leeway to offer a round on the house. There's no guarantee that you'll get one, but these "buybacks" go to customers who (1) have been ordering multiple rounds, (2) have been tipping well, and (3) aren't acting like jerks. But even if you qualify on all three counts, you have to help the barkeep know it.

First, if the bar's crowded, the bartender's more likely to connect you to what you've been buying if you (and your party, if there is one) order the same drink each round. A bartender may not always remember a face or name, but will always remember making a manhattan and a whiskey sour on the same ticket four times.

Second, unless you're a known regular, tip as you go—in cash, even if you're on a tab, and even if you'll be paying with a credit card. That puts your tipping on record, and servers prefer tips in cash anyway.

Finally, go out of your way to ingratiate yourself with the bartender. Thank him or her for the attention, hand out a compliment on the drink preparation, or (if it's not too busy) strike up a light conversation. Sympathize subtly with the beleaguered bartender, sharing in the eye-rolling over obnoxious customers. The idea is to establish your non-jerk credentials.

How to get another free drink. Always tip your usual amount on the free round. Most bar customers don't, thinking free means completely costless. That drives bartenders crazy. You still come out ahead when you tip your buyback, and you greatly increase your chances of getting another one.

How to get to the front of the line. What do you do when you need to order directly from the bar but it's already crowded with patrons waiting to do the same thing? Try politely asking if they'd mind if you went first. Tell them why you need to go ahead of them, and you'll be surprised at how often they'll step aside, says Susan RoAne.

Maybe your husband spilled his drink back at the table and is very upset about it. Maybe the movie you're going to starts in 20 minutes. Maybe the babysitter has to go home and you barely have time for a nightcap. Maybe you really have to go to the bathroom but your table is waiting for you to bring the drinks first. "If you give a reason for your request, reasonable people will usually accept it," RoAne says. "Most people are actually very nice."

One caveat, though. It helps if the reason you give is actually the truth. Otherwise, you'll have to carry a guilty conscience back to the table along with the drinks.

Be decisive when ordering. Cocktail waitresses and bartenders frequently encounter the type of customer who comes into the bar presumably to have a drink but then acts completely stumped when asked what he or she wants. If that's you, then you should know your server's secret thoughts: This table is going to waste a lot of my time, so I'm staying away from it as much as I can. Since being ignored is exactly what you don't want, make sure you have something to say to your server as soon you sit down. One way to do that is to think about what you'll have well before you reach the place. You can browse through a bartender's guide or poke around the Internet for ideas. If you're still clueless when the moment of truth arrives, order what somebody else in your party is ordering. If that's not an option, tell your server you'll start off with a soda water for now. That "for now" is a signal for your server to come back soon, and buys you time to make a decision.

Think like a bartender. To competent mixologists, the bar area is their personal fiefdom, over which they exercise absolute authority. It is not a democracy, and it is not always fair. Once you realize this mind-set, you'll get better service. "The bartender decides who is served and when," says Karen Beban. "If you feel you've been slighted, don't make an issue out of it if you want to drink at all." Show some patience, don't take things personally, tip, and you'll soon break through the service barrier and will usually be treated well.

The bartender has a lot to consider that is not always obvious to you. For example, pushy twenty-somethings may be passed over at first. That's not because the bartender thinks they're jerks; if that were the case, they'd be served quickly so they'll go away sooner. The bartender is more likely buying time to figure out if they're too drunk to be served. Or a male bartender may serve some lovely lady ahead of you. There's a good reason for that, according to Beban: "He's a man and he can't help it."

The point is that when you sit down at a bar, you've entered into a bartender's unique domain. Take a few minutes to absorb the vibes, reserving judgment until you have a take on where the bartender's coming from—his or her quirks, concerns, and competence. You'll usually avoid a lot of unnecessary anxiety that way. ◂

Movies

5 Secrets for Having a Great Time When You Go Out to See a Hit on the Silver Screen

Buy your movie tickets in advance. On a typical Friday night hundreds of people line up for tickets to some huge blockbuster that everybody wants to see at once. Half of them are in the ticket-holders line by mistake, and the other half have no guarantee the darn thing won't be sold out before they reach the ticket seller. But others just walk up to a machine, swipe their credit card, grab the tickets that pop out, and walk right in. That's because they're the ones who knew enough to buy their movie tickets in advance online or over the phone.

Most people don't yet realize that in some cases it makes no more sense to wander ticketless into a movie complex than it does to show up at a visiting performance of the Bolshoi Ballet and hope to get in. You might, but you'll more likely find yourself all dressed up with nowhere to go. Moviegoing has changed, and the planned evening out, complete with advance tickets, is more and more the way to go. The online buyer who takes advantage of that today is way ahead of the clueless masses who will follow tomorrow—and wait in line in the meantime.

The two main sources for online tickets are MovieTickets.com and Fandango.com. They sell tickets at the same price as the theater box office, but charge a fee of $1 or $1.50 per ticket. That's worth it if:

- It's the opening weekend or early in the run of a major release, such as *Superman Returns Yet Again* or *Son of Titanic*. Tickets for these block-busters (the real ones, not the names we just made up) are often available several weeks in advance.
- It's a Friday or Saturday night in a major and always crowded theater complex.
- You have an evening planned around a major new movie across town and you don't want to risk any surprises.

Register at both online ticket sellers. Both major online movie-ticket sellers—MovieTickets.com and Fandango.com—make purchases easy, displaying info about what's playing where in your area and then taking you through a quick and simple point-and-click process to buy the tickets. But you'll often find that you can't get tickets for the movie you want to see. That's because of a quirk in their operations that they don't tell you about, namely that each has exclusive arrangements with the movie theater chains. So if the movie you want is playing at, say, an AMC theater, you need to purchase it at MovieTickets.com. But if it's showing at a Regal theater, only Fandango.com will offer it.

Once you know this, the way around it is obvious. Just punch up the other service if you strike out at the first one. Of course, neither is going to say, "Please see our competitor for tickets to this movie." So it makes sense to be registered at both sites, registration being a simple matter of giving them basic information such as your name, age, and credit card number.

Sidestep all of those pre-movie ads. Plenty of moviegoers are convinced that the very idea of a theater running soft drink and credit card commercials before a movie portends the decline of civilization as we know it. Alas, the ads probably aren't going away anytime soon. A captive audience of mostly young adults with nothing to do but stare at the screen is too mouthwatering for advertisers, and the exhibitors need cash any way they can get it. But you can cheat the system in three ways.

The first is simply to frequent movie theaters that don't show ads. And yes, there is such an animal. Some upscale theaters proudly announce they don't run commercials—it's part of their package of extras that lets them charge $2 to $6 more per ticket. More economically, seek out smaller or older theaters that never did run ads and still don't. Call ahead to find out.

Another ploy is to time your arrival to a minute or two before the true,

Movie Clubs

The online sellers don't promote it—or even tell you about it—but you can avoid paying the extra $1 or $1.50 ticket fee if you've joined the clubs that the theater chains sponsor. For example, if you're a member of AMC's Movie Watchers club, there's a place to punch in your membership number at MovieTickets.com. Do it and you won't be charged the fee.

These clubs, by the way, are free and worth joining. "They're like frequent-flier programs for moviegoers," says Ross Melnick, cofounder of Cinema Treasures, an organization dedicated to saving old movie houses. "They want to reward brand loyalty, so the premiums are pretty good—like free tickets and free popcorn and drinks on certain days."

announced showtime. If you're just going to be sitting there chomping on popcorn and waiting, why not chomp and wait in the lobby, watching people instead of commercials? This strategy works best in uncrowded theaters; otherwise, you might end up in the front row.

The most rebellious response to commercials is to ignore them. The no-talking rule is sacred in a movie theater, but it doesn't kick in until the lights go down. These days, most of the advertising is packaged into what's euphemistically called "pre-show entertainment," which generally runs with the lights on. So chat away until the lights dim for the trailers. Talk about how much you hate ads in movie theaters.

Snack before or after the show. The food they sell you at the movies is expensive, messy, unhealthy, and only available at the end of a long wait while the kids behind the counter move in slow motion. The theaters constantly try new tricks to keep us spending $14 for junk we'd never buy anywhere else, but they ignore the solution that will work best. Are you ready for a radical new approach to dealing with movie food? Here it is: Just don't eat the stuff. Have a nice meal before or after the show instead.

Most of us eat popcorn and candy at the movies despite the hassles because … well, we've always eaten popcorn and candy at the movies. But it wasn't always thus. "You know, for a long time there was no food, because the movie palaces didn't want their rugs and tapestries and upholstery ruined by gum and chocolate and spilled drinks," says Ross Melnick. "You really didn't have much food in the better theaters until after World War II." So consider boycotting the snack bar as an act of nostalgia for the golden age of cinema.

Try a drive-in theater for a change. Few moviegoers realize that the number of drive-in theaters is actually increasing, and everybody connected to the walk-in movie business would prefer that they never realize it. That's because drive-in picture shows make for a great alternative, offering everything a standard theater offers except matinees. And they do it without a lot of the problems of the megaplexes. To wit:

- *High ticket prices?* Drive-ins generally charge only $5 to $8 dollars per person, and you almost always get a double feature.

- *Parking hassles?* By definition, you don't pay extra for parking at a drive-in. And once you park, you're already in your seat.

- *Expensive snack foods?* Drive-ins are the only movie venues where you can pack in anything you want. Carry in a rack of lamb with mint jelly and a few bottles of pinot noir, if you like. As long as the driver doesn't drink the wine, it's perfectly fine. And if you don't want to bring your own, a drive-in's food selection is usually much more ample than what a walk-in offers.

- *Poor sound?* Those tinny speakers you hang on the window are relics of the past. Instead, you tune into a low-frequency station on your car radio. If your speakers are decent, the sound is wonderful.

- *Talkers?* The only ones you have to worry about are right there in the car with you.

- *Antiseptic atmosphere?* Are you kidding? Parked under the stars enjoying a big-screen movie with your family or friends in the private comfort of your automobile? That's as good as it gets. ◁

WHAT MOVIE THEATERS DON'T WANT YOU TO KNOW ABOUT DVDs

All the hype surrounding the release of a blockbuster movie is designed to get you to rush out to your local multiplex as soon as possible. But unless you just have to be the first on your block to see the latest multimillion-dollar production from Hollywood, it pays to be a little patient. The time between a film's release in the theaters and its release on DVD is growing shorter and shorter. It used to be six months, but recently it has dropped to a matter of a few weeks. And indeed, some movie companies are talking about releasing them simultaneously, since the filmmakers now make much more money from DVD sales and rentals than from theaters. If a movie is really good, it will be just as enjoyable to watch at home in a few weeks as in a theater now. This is especially true now that more and more homes have large-screen televisions that show off those spectacular special effects as well as the downsized screens at the multiplex. And if you miss the theater experience, just hook your TV audio to your stereo, make some popcorn, turn down the lights, and settle down. By the way, new blockbuster DVDs are often discounted heavily (to less than the cost of two movie tickets) during the first week of their release at outlets like Best Buy and Circuit City. Go on Tuesday—the day of the week when DVDs are released.

Live Events
5 Ways to Live It Up and Make the Most of Special and Pricey Live Entertainment

How to get tickets when they're "sold out." Never take it literally when it's announced that there are no more tickets left for a major concert, show, or sporting event. "Nothing's ever really sold out," says Kenneth Dotson, chief marketing officer at TicketsNow. " 'Sold out' just means that face-value tickets at the box office are gone. There are always tickets available for any hot event." And he should know. His is one of a growing number of reputable online ticket brokering sites that hook up ticket-seekers with licensed ticket resellers. And most of the time there are tickets to be had right up to the last minute. Just go to the site, see what's still there, and buy the ticket right then and there. The cost? Don't ask. But a lot of sold-out concerts are once-in-a-lifetime events that you might be willing to splurge on. For example, as we've been hearing since 1972, the next Rolling Stones tour will probably be their last one.

Get a good seat by paying more. The cruelest deception foisted on the public is that good seats for big-time concerts or sporting events are available at the box office if you jump on them fast enough. Forget it. The bigger a show is, the less likely it is that any significant number of decent seats are going to be sold through the standard channels. They all go to promoters, advertisers, underwriters, sponsors, and a host of other insiders with enough pull to get first shot at big blocks of tickets. In other words, you didn't miss out on the good seats; they were never there in the first place.

But that doesn't mean you can't get your hands on them. You can, on what's called the "secondary market." While most regular folks assume they're doomed to the nosebleed section, the smart ones are snapping up the choice location tickets that the insiders turned around and unloaded to licensed resellers. Those prime tickets are sitting there at online ticket broker sites, waiting for you to point, click, and buy. You'll pay considerably more than what's printed on the ticket, of course, but that price was an illusion to start with. These days, face value has given way to market value. That has created controversy, but right now it's the way it is. At least you can be assured that what you're paying for good seats is exactly what they're worth on the free market.

So if your team looks like it could make it to the World Series, or Coldplay's coming to town, ignore what the ads say and go directly to a reputable online ticket brokering site like TicketsNow that guarantees you're not being sold fraudulent or stolen tickets. You'll be in a privileged position, because the entertainment and sports industries still maintain the farce that tickets in the 21st century are sold like they were in the 20th. No ad says, "Good seats available on the secondary market." But for major events, that's the only place they're available.

Get loads of free info at ticket sites. Broker websites help their customers pick and choose by displaying all kinds of information and graphics about the concerts, shows, and sporting events they offer tickets for. For example, they'll have seating charts of major venues across the continent, and schedules of upcoming events. The displays are ostensibly for paying customers, but it turns out you don't have to be one to gain access to them. Just Google up online ticket brokers, find a site with good information, and find out all you need to know.

Phone in your order and get special info. Ticket brokers like you to do your shopping online, because there's virtually no labor cost involved. So they don't shout too loud about the call-in service they might also offer that lets you do your purchasing over the phone. This is worth taking advantage of, and it's not just for the Internet-challenged. TicketsNow, for example, has more than 100 "customer care representatives" available who can often give you something that the site alone might not—answers to your personal questions. Which is the shady side of the venue? What are the bathrooms like? Do they sell Coke or Pepsi? And, of course, they can sell you the tickets. The site will probably have an 800 number in plain view, but the "Contact Us" button might give you more direct access to the customer service phone connection.

Plan ahead and sell those unused season tickets. Do you own the right to season tickets that have been in your family for decades? Wouldn't it be a tragedy to have to give them up because of soaring prices? That particular tragedy is happening a lot these days, but you can avoid it thanks to the secondary market. Here's how:

Unless you're a mega-fanatic with no work schedule and a thermonuclear passion for your home team, you probably won't be attending all 81 baseball home games, or all 41 basketball or hockey home games. In fact, if you're typical, you probably spend stressful hours arranging to give away the ones you can't use. So go ahead and get your season tickets, check the schedule and plan the games you'll be going to. Then check the Internet for a licensed ticket reseller who will buy the rest en masse. True, you can't anticipate those unexpected great mid-season matchups, and you do run the risk of later wishing you had some tickets back.

But consider the payoff: In one stroke, you've kept the season tickets in the family, drastically reduced your total cost, removed the headache of constantly dealing with extra tickets, and still guaranteed yourself entry to most of the games you'll want to see. Not bad when you think about it. And you've done nothing involved with scalping, as long as you sell your ducats at face value to a legitimate licensed reseller, who must follow state or provincial laws. ◁

6 FREE LIVE
performances
You'll Enjoy

There's a good reason live entertainment seems so outrageously expensive these days: It is. But if you can accept the radical notion that there's solid entertainment to be had without megabuck superstars, you can live it up for free. Start with these ideas:

1 Art openings

The best entertainment bargain on the planet. Free admission, free wine, free hors d'oeuvres, free people-watching, and free mingling with the artist, who is obligated to be nice to you. You might even like the paintings or other art.

2 Free concerts in the park

Instead of passing by these things as you usually do, plop yourself down on the grass as close to the musicians as possible, and get into the sounds. Let yourself go. The players are usually pretty good, or the city wouldn't let them be there. If the music's not your bag and you get bored, watch the drummer if there is one. See if you can follow what he or she is doing.

3 Community theater

Human beings will travel thousands of miles and spend hundreds of dollars to see a Broadway play. Why not try walking a few blocks to see amateurs or semi-pros do basically the same thing—but from closer up? Ask about being a volunteer usher. Free admission is your pay.

4 Open-mike night

Small venues have them on off nights, where anybody can get up there and sing or play or do a comedy routine. Don't smirk. A lot of artists started their careers this way—performers that people now pay $500 to see from 45 yards away in a football stadium. And if some poor deluded wannabe is really awful, that, too, can be entertaining.

5 Author readings

You read the book, now hear the writer. Or the other way around. Big-time and semi-big-time writers often make the rounds to local bookstores to read from their work, sign books, and schmooze with readers. Check the bulletin boards at your area's bookstore or those piles of flyers at the checkout counter. Contrary to movie-comedy stereotype, authors are usually not boring.

6 (Very) small-time sports

True lovers of baseball or any other sport can re-create a no-cost version of major-league spectator pleasure by grabbing a free bleacher spot at a muni-league, high school, or even Little League game. Pick a team to root for (or allow one to pick you). Return a few times, and you'll find yourself experiencing the same thrills and emotions that would cost you two days' salary at the pro stadiums. It ain't the New York Yankees, but as Shakespeare should have said, "The game's the thing."

Casino Games

12 Secrets for Enjoying Gaming and Limiting Your Losses Against the Unfriendly Odds

Be a high roller—for a few minutes. When you enter a casino and start playing for the first time, make your initial bets higher than what you would normally use as a minimum bet. The pit boss assumes that this is your usual betting pattern, and will use it to calculate your comp eligibility—that is, what kind of freebies the house might offer. Not surprisingly, the hotel's generosity when it comes to meal and room discounts is a direct function of how much it thinks you're going to bet per hour. You can always settle into your more modest wagering habits as time goes by. The pit bosses rarely have time to check in on you later.

Check the odds on video poker machines. Casinos don't make it obvious which video poker machines pay off better. So every day a good percentage of push-button suckers are feeding extra coins to the house without knowing it. Avoid being one of them by taking a look at the payoff chart that's right there on the machine. Almost all will range from a high payoff of 250-1 for a royal flush down to even money (1-1) for jacks or better. What you want to notice are the two payoffs right in the middle. If a full house pays 9-1 and a flush 6-1, you're in the right place. It's what the pros call a "full pay" machine.

But a lot of them (and all of them in some states or provinces) will pay just 8-1 for a full house and 5-1 for a flush. That means that when you insert a silver dollar and then get lucky enough to punch up a boat—say, three queens and two 8s—the full-pay machine will drop 9 silver dollars

into your tray and the short-pay machine just 8. No big deal? Well, over the long run it's a very big deal, upping the house's advantage by a significant 2.2 percent. Why give away your money?

Cough up the coins now instead of later. It may seem like you're extending your chances of winning—or at least getting to play longer—when you drop in only a single coin with each hand in video poker. That's just what they want you to believe. The truth is, by putting in the full number of coins with each hand, which is usually five, you increase your chances of being ahead in the long run by a full 12 percent.

Here's why: When you play five coins instead of one, you of course get the same proportional payoff each time you win. For example, if you put in one coin and hit a flush, you get five coins back. If you had put in 5 coins, you would have received 25 coins back. It's like having made five flushes at a time.

Obviously, that comes out as a wash because you also lose five times as much when you pull bust hands. Where the advantage comes in is with an extra-high payoff for that fifth coin with the best hand you can get—a royal flush. The payoff for a royal flush—a straight from the 10 to the ace, all of one suit—is 250-1. (If it's less, don't play that machine.) It stays that way with the first four coins you play. That is, you'll get 500 back if you bet two, 750 back if you bet three, and 1,000 back if you bet four. But if you bet five, the payback jumps to 4,000, the equivalent of 800-1, if you're using a full-pay machine, as you should be. And if you play video poker long enough, you will get a royal flush with any luck. By betting five, you can milk that magic moment to the max.

Never take the craps dealer's suggestion. "The bets to stay away from at the craps table are the ones the dealers try to get you to make," says Bill Burton, author of *1,000 Best Casino Gambling Secrets* and the gambling expert at About.com. "When they encourage you to make certain bets, it's not because they care about you." What they care about is steering you toward the "side" or "proposition" bets where the house has the biggest advantage. These are the bets you place in the middle of the table that usually have to do with what will happen on the next roll of the dice rather than whether the shooter will make the point or not. They're sucker bets—easy, fun, and the surest of losers over a short time.

WHAT THE CASINOS DON'T WANT YOU TO KNOW ABOUT Your Odds

- There's a difference between the true odds of your winning any particular bet and the odds the casino actually uses to pay you if you do win. That difference is always in the casino's favor and it's the reason casino owners (always a government agency in Canada) are rich and you're not.

- Because of the house edge, the casino will always win in the long run, no matter how smart you are, how good you think your system is, or how lucky you are. The Las Vegas strip is paved with the losses of innocent fun-seekers who don't know that.

- Some of the games have a much smaller house advantage than others, so your chances of walking away a

winner after playing them are higher. This assumes, however, that you play the best strategy and that you're able to walk away while ahead.

- If gamblers only played blackjack, mini-baccarat, pai-gow poker, live poker, the sports book, and bingo, they'd lose a lot less money. Those are games with a house edge of less than 3 percent.

- The casino loves to see you playing games like Caribbean Stud Poker, Let It Ride, Red Dog, single-deck 21, and those undignified spectacles like the Big Wheel or Wheel of Fortune. The house edge on these is astronomical.

- Playing keno is the equivalent of making a charity donation to the casino ownership. Yes, the young keno ladies are

friendly and they need the tips. And yes, it's simple and kind of fun to try to divine some numbers while you're at the coffee shop or buffet or bar. Just be aware that the house advantage in keno can run as high as 50 percent. You're better off playing the state or provincial lottery—it's essentially the same game, but at least you're donating your money to the public good instead of business magnates.

The side bets on a craps table suck away cash that would be better placed on the pass line, where you have a decent chance of coming out ahead. On this basic and better bet, you're simply going with the shooter, hoping he or she will roll anything but a 2, 3, or 12 on the first toss of the dice. If it's a 7 or 11, you win. If it's anything else (4, 5, 6, 8, 9, 10) you win if the shooter repeats that number before rolling a 7. It pays even money, and at 1.41 percent, the house advantage is relatively low.

But the friendly men or women who run the table—called dealers even though they don't deal any cards—will hype plays such as the Big 6 or Big 8. These are side bets that wait for you in a corner of the layout like a black widow spider. Put $6 on the Big 8 and if an 8 is rolled before a 7, you win $6. Put the same $6 on 8 over at the "place" area—for all practical purposes the same bet—and you win $7. How unfair is that? So unfair that in Atlantic City, Big 6 and Big 8 are outlawed.

Rule of thumb: Avoid any bet a dealer wants you to make. "That's especially true for craps, where there are about 40 possible bets, a few of them with decent odds and all the rest terrible," Burton says. "But it also applies to games like Let It Ride and Caribbean Stud."

Getting odds better than most at craps. Talk about forbidden knowledge! There's a bet you can make at the craps table that offers the most favorable odds in the entire casino, but it doesn't even appear on the table layout. That's right—no marked area to place the bet in, no mention of it anywhere, and, you can be sure, no information about it forthcoming from the dealers. It's called the "odds bet" and it's the only play available that actually pays in proportion to the risk, with no house advantage at all.

You are eligible to make an odds bet if you have a bet on the pass line, gambling that the shooter will make the "point" by rolling that number again before rolling a 7. If you have $5 on the pass line, you can put up $5 more as an odds bet, or $10 if the casino offers "double odds." You do this by placing the chips a few finger widths directly behind your pass line bet, outside the back line of the pass bet area.

How much you get if you win depends on what the point number is, but it's always better than the even money pass line payoff. If the point number is 6 or 8, the payoff for an odds bet is 6-5. So if you bet $5 on the pass line and added on a $10 "double odds" bet, your payoff is $5 for the pass bet and $12 for the double odds bet. You invested $15 and got that $15 back plus $17 more.

If the point made is a 5 or 9, the payoff is slightly better at 3-2. The odds-bet payoff when the shooter makes a point of 4 or 10 is the highest at 2-1. That's because there are fewer possible rolls of the two dice that can add up to a 4 or 10.

Choose the crowded roulette table. Roulette's not a game you're likely to win at. The house edge is simply too big. But hey, it's so much fun that folks are going to go for some spins anyway. What's the point of hitting a casino if you can't whoop it up and high-five your fellow players around the wheel, with free drinks to boot? So go ahead and play. But play slow.

Why? Because the more time between spins, the longer it will take for you to lose your money. That sounds negative, but the unvarnished truth is that only the house wins at roulette over the long haul. So what you want to do is shorten the haul—not in time spent at the table but in the number of spins that take place in that time, and therefore the amount of your hard-earned money you're risking.

You can't slow the pace on your own, of course, no matter how much you pretend to fumble in your pocket for chips or act distracted. Instead, choose the most crowded roulette table in the room. At a full table, it takes up to three minutes between spins of the wheel. Now, full tables look like something the casino prefers, with more money riding on each spin. But the house actually doesn't care for full tables, precisely because they result in the slower play you the customer are looking for. They're likely to suggest some move to a less crowded table, or open up a new one in hopes of evening things out. But stay put. At the full table, you'll have more fun, lose less money, take just as many free drinks, and maybe—just maybe—get lucky and win.

Seek out the single-zero roulette tables. They're not everywhere, and even where they do exist, the casino wants you on the double-zero table. However, the smart roulette player will stick with the lonely 0.

The reason is simple. A typical roulette table has 38 numbers—1 through 36, plus a zero and a double zero. Your chances of hitting one are 37-1, but the payoff is only 35 to one. A single-zero table also pays 35-1, but your true odds

are better at 36-1, because there are only 37 numbers. That slight difference shifts the house edge downward significantly. You'll still lose in the long run, but not as fast.

Watch the odds at blackjack. Cruise the Vegas strip and you'll see a growing number of places shouting the wonderful news that they pay 6-5 for a natural blackjack. That means if you're dealt an ace along with a 10 or face card at the blackjack table, you immediately win $6 for every $5 you put up. Not bad, huh?

Actually, it's terrible. Because throughout modern gaming history, a natural blackjack has paid 3-2 just about everywhere in the United States and Canada, and it still does in most casinos. If math wasn't your best subject, take our word for it that a 3-2 payoff is much better for you than 6-5. So much better, in fact, that the shift to a 6-5 natural blackjack payoff ups the casino's advantage by so much that it turns a fairly customer-friendly game into a bad proposition. So before you sit down at a blackjack table, make sure that natural blackjack pays 3–2. If there's no indication, ask the dealer what the payoff is. If it's 6-5, go somewhere else.

But don't go to the video blackjack machines. They're even more likely to short-change you in their natural black-jack payoffs, sometimes going even lower than 6-4 down to even money. So unless you find machines that pay 3-2, forget about video blackjack.

Consider the difference: If you have a $50 bet up and get dealt an ace and a king, you'll win $75 at an honest 3-2 table, but only $60 at a 6-5 table and a piddling $50 at an even-money machine. The casino counts on hordes of clueless gamblers not knowing or caring about the difference. But from now on you're not one of them.

Don't go by what you see on TV poker tournaments. Seasoned veterans of the casino poker rooms love the televised poker tournament fad more than they'll ever let on to you. That's because they know that television-educated players are usually easy marks. Inspired by the Joe Hachems and Chris Moneymakers they see on ESPN2, they rush to the table full of enthusiasm … and soon leave it with no money. Here's what the table vets know that television-educated players don't: Casino poker isn't like television poker.

So keep two things in mind. Unless you're well off enough to qualify for a *Forbes* magazine listing, you'll probably be playing with a limit that's too low to bluff anybody out the way they do on TV. And unlike TV tournaments, your game won't be edited so that all the hands are fascinating or decisive. Casino games are more like arduous grinds that reward stamina, patience, and most of all, knowledge.

That doesn't mean you shouldn't play. Poker is a fun challenge, and unlike most casino games, a certain percentage of customers have to be winners, since they're playing against other customers instead of the house. Remember, though, that the winners aren't the ones who pull off spectacular stunts, but the ones who have mastered the odds so they know the right move to make in all situations. You can't learn that from TV. You need a book to learn the percentages from, and lots of practice.

Player's Card

The first thing you do when you walk into a casino is go straight to the players club and ask for a player's card. Do this even if you're planning on staying for three minutes, and even if you don't intend to come back for 15 years. This card is free money. It's your ticket to all kinds of hotel discounts, and even comped rooms and meals. But about half of casino gamblers ignore it, either because they can't be bothered or don't know about it. Once that card's in your possession, take advantage of it:

Flash it. When you approach a table to play, give your card to the dealer or directly to the pit boss. They'll use it to enter your playing time and estimated total bets into the computer.

Insert it. Don't play the slots or any other machine game without inserting your card in the indicated place and making sure a light indicates it's been accepted. You'll get "credit" for your betting.

Ask. If you've been playing more or less steadily for much of the day, ask for a casino host and see if the casino will comp you a meal or offer you a gift shop discount. They won't think you're being presumptuous. If the answer's no, they'll probably indicate how much more you need to play to be eligible. Unless you're a high roller, the casino isn't going to come up to you and say, "Gosh, you've been a good customer—let us buy you dinner." You have to ask.

Take a shot. Before you pay your bill and go home, ask the casino host if you've played enough to get a break on the room rate. If you put in your time at the tables, you just might get it.

Try again. When you make a reservation at a casino hotel that you've played at before, give them your card number and ask them to review your play record. See if you can get your room comped (that is, free) or at least get in at the "casino rate," which is usually a healthy discount.

Understand that player's cards won't jinx you. One of the myths in Atlantic City and Las Vegas is that players who use their casino-issued gaming cards (see Secret Weapon box) to play the slots are at a disadvantage. As you may know, the cards are used to track your play, and then the casinos are able to offer you deals and discounts in order to keep you in the casino, and get you back to the gaming floor. The prevailing theory is that if you're doing too well at the slots, the machine and the card will recognize this, and your three cherries will turn into a bunch of blank spaces. Don't believe it. According to one casino executive, slots are always 100 percent random; if they weren't, these gaming meccas would quickly lose their licenses.

Use your player's card, no matter how little money you're gambling with. Even $100 poured into a slot machine will garner you freebies in the mail, from free meals to free money.

Bump your bet up at just the right moment. It's easy to rack up points for free meals, rooms, or entertainment on your casino card when you're playing the slots. It's much harder when you sit down at any of the gaming tables, like blackjack or poker. As a general rule, expect to have to play $25 hands for about four hours over the course of your trip to start to see the free offers come your way. There's a way to beat that system, according to one casino executive: Bump up your bets when you see the pit boss come around. His job is to track who's betting what. So if you're betting 10 bucks a hand, and you see the pen and pad coming your way, bump your bet. The higher the better. This way, it will appear you're a high roller when, in fact, you're just taking advantage of your good timing.

Negotiate your "comp" points. Casino executives won't ever tell you this, but it's possible to get casino points on your card just by asking. Virtually all casinos run their comp programs the same way: With frequent play, you accumulate "points" on your comp card, and your points are then converted to free perks. Well, mid- to top-level casino employees—basically, everyone in the casino who is not a dealer—have discretionary "banks" of points they can dole out to players. So if you're looking for a free room, it's worth asking the pit boss if he could spare some points for you. And after you get that free room? Lounge around and hit the nickel slots. They won't know what hit them. ◂

Family Outings

3 Savvy Ways to Make a Day with the Kids an Enjoyable Treat for All

Prep for the fest. Plopping your family into the midst of a daylong festival, carnival, or amusement park can be tricky indeed. Opportunities abound for the kids to get cranky and dispirited, all while money is flowing out of your wallet like a river of green. A little advance preparation will make all the difference:

- Get a map of the festival grounds and an event schedule in advance. Plot out strategies for parking, a walking route through the attractions, and top-priority activities. Make a mental note of the bathroom and food stall locations.

- If you're arriving at an amusement park right at opening time, make a beeline for a favorite ride at a part of the park that's farthest from the main entrance. You will be able to start the day by taking your favorite ride several times before any line at all builds up.

- If your chosen venue will allow it, pack along parent-approved snack foods and a bottle of water for each person. Because provisions are typically outrageously overpriced at festivals and amusement parks, this will seriously reduce the cost of the trip and will ensure that the day is not a complete nutritional disaster.

- Have a plan for killing small amounts of time. Take along books or small games to entertain the kids during waiting times—while standing in line, for instance, or to occupy five-year-old Susie while ten-year-old Zack gets to go on the roller coaster.

- Some valuable survival items to pack: hats, sunglasses, sunscreen, camera, a lightweight picnic blanket, disposable wipes, and a change of clothes.

Picky kids? Let them plan. Ever feel like you can do nothing right—in the minds of your kids, anyway? If choice of family activities is a constant sore point among your children, try this tactic: Let your kids plan the family outing once in a while. You can set broad parameters—budget, distance, time frame, and such—and leave the rest to your children to plot out. The planning will be a great life lesson for the kids, and if the outing is not completely to their liking, they will only have themselves to blame.

Take Harry Potter along for the ride. Anytime a family trip requires an hour or more of driving, you're confronted with the age-old quandary: how to entertain the kids. Books and puzzles will only take you so far. Same goes for cow-counting or license plate games. Giving them unlimited Game Boy time doesn't feel responsible. And just letting them scream and shout will give you a migraine. One of the best solutions around: books on tape. An engaging children's story will keep the kids quiet for hours on end. The story becomes a shared family experience—something you can all talk about over lunch. Best of all: Your local library has a mountain of recorded books that you have access to for free—enough variety to appeal to every taste, from Winnie the Pooh to Star Trek to Sherlock Holmes. ◄

Planning Your Trip

5 Things You Should Know About Getting the Best Travel Bargains

Go directly to the airline. There was a time not so long ago when, if you wanted to book a flight, you had two choices: Either book directly with the airline, or book through a travel agent. Then came the Internet, and airline pricing became a much more competitive game. Prices on Internet travel sites offer some pretty great deals, and now the airlines themselves have taken back the game. In many cases, the airlines can meet or beat the rates on the most popular websites. Always check those airline websites or to give them a call on their 800 numbers—you may be surprised.

World traveler? Talk to an agent. If you think all travel agents charge more for airline tickets than the airlines themselves, think again—especially when it comes to around-the-world travel. And while airline consortiums offer these tickets, it's almost always best to go through a third party. "For a myriad of complex reasons, you'll typically find the lowest rates for this type of travel through travel agents," says Edward Hasbrouck, author of *The Practical Nomad: How to Travel Around the World.* He says tickets purchased through airlines could be twice the price offered by travel agents who specialize in these global adventures. Hasbrouck says the main reason for this is the regulation of international airfares.

Talk the hotel manager's prices down. Here's something the big hotel chains will never advertise: You can negotiate with them. There's always someone in the hotel who is authorized to cut a deal, and doing so is easy. Just tell them you'd love to stay there, but their price is high and you'll probably end up staying somewhere else. If there are empty rooms in the hotel, you can bet you'll get a deal. Another surefire way to get a better rate is to ask, "Is there a lower rate I qualify for?" The hotel manager could, on the sly, give you the military rate, or the friends and family rate, or any other "special" rate he has. In the end, hotel managers prefer selling you a heavily discounted room to leaving it empty.

Know your ABCs. Hurricanes not only do major damage, but they also scare the heck out of tourists. So what to do? The best place for a Caribbean vacation are the ABC islands: namely, Aruba, Bonaire, and Curaçao. They all lie outside the path that hurricanes have been following for hundreds of years. So next time you book that summer getaway, be sure to sneak a peek at these less-traveled gems.

Buy now, visit Cinderella's Castle later. You know that a vacation to the Magic Kingdom is in your future, but you just haven't decided precisely when yet. A never-expiring pass might be just the ticket for you. A seven-day park-hopper pass costs about $250 (at the time of this writing) and expires after two weeks. But for an extra $75 or so, you can get a pass that doesn't expire. This is a good idea because it allows you to get some of your travel arrangements out of the way now; you can work on the scheduling later. Also, Disney ticket prices go up every single year. If you know you'll be heading down there eventually, you could spend now and save big later. ◁

Cabdrivers

Mark Zwick, one of the partners of PhillyTrips.com, takes at least four big trips a year to destinations all over the United States and Canada. You would think he'd go broke buying guidebooks, but he doesn't.

"I always depend on the taxi drivers," Zwick says. "They always know the places to go, the things to see."

As an added bonus, many taxi drivers work in tandem (and on the sly) with restaurants, bars, and nightclubs. Many times a taxi driver will have special coupons for his favorite places, and he'll be more than happy to let you have them. Why? Because he gets a kickback from the establishments.

So let those taxi drivers take you to some places where they get a little something extra, because most of the time you'll be getting something extra as well in the form of discounted meals or drinks.

Using the Web
6 Ways to "Net" a Great Trip by Making the Most of Travel Websites

Search solo even for a group. Airline search engines mess with your head a little when it comes to booking your family's travel. Consider: If you're booking a flight for you, your spouse, and your cousin Larry, you're going to type "3" when the site asks you how many tickets you want to buy. The truth is, sometimes you'll get a cheaper rate by booking seats individually, because single seats can easily go unsold (especially middle seats in the back of the plane). Airlines jump at the chance to get rid of them. See what happens when you book seats individually.

Discount airlines are not on big travel sites. The main travel websites like Expedia, Orbitz, and Travelocity

don't carry JetBlue or Southwest Airlines tickets in the U.S., or Zoom in Canada. Why? Those low-cost airlines never release their inventory to the online travel superstores. Quite frequently, their fares are less expensive than those of other carriers. No matter how many comprehensive travel sites you may visit, make sure you check their prices against those offered by JetBlue and Southwest or Zoom before you buy.

Trash your cookies. You're shopping for a flight on the Web and the flight prices seem to keep going up, not down. Why is that? Many Internet sites install "cookies" on your computer when you visit. A "cookie" is a collection of information that will almost certainly include your user name and the date and time you visited the site. Sometimes travel websites use this information to increase their prices if you repeatedly run the same searches for airlines or hotels. If you price a flight, and go back to the site a few hours later only to find that the price has increased, it's probably a cookie at work.

Before you buy a ticket, erase the cookies from your computer. This is easy—methods vary by browser, but you can usually do it by going to "Tools" at the top of your browser and selecting "Internet Options."

Check out this website for travel pros. So you've checked the airline for price quotes, done the requisite Internet searches at Orbitz, Expedia, Travelocity, and the rest, but still you remain unsatisfied with the selection and price. Out of luck? Not just yet. Check out www.itasoftware .com, a website used by travel agents, travel websites, and the airlines themselves. While you can't book your tickets through this site, it does offer lots of other benefits. You're allowed to choose where you fly from and where you're flying to just like the other sites, but you can also search airports up to 300 miles away from your destinations. In addition, you can see available flights on the days before or after your target dates. It's an awesome tool, too, if you're flying to three or more destinations. Here's an example: New York to Miami to Bangkok, Thailand, and back to New York. Within a minute, we found more than a dozen airline combos, ranging from $1,982 to $8,722.

Once you find the flights you need, booking is a snap. You simply click the "details" icon, which then gives you the flight numbers, booking codes, and fare codes for each flight on your itinerary. At this point, you simply call a travel agent—or call the airlines directly—with the information.

Find Disney savings online. The easiest way to save money on your trip to Disney World is to trim the price of those full-price park passes. Before you plan your trip, it's worth visiting a few Disney-centric discount websites, like www.themouseforless.com and www.mousesavers.com. These and other sites list discount coupons and codes for the Disney theme parks, hotels, cruises, and anything else Mickey-centric. They're at your fingertips with a few clicks of the, uh, mouse.

Sit where you want. Don't let those sneaky airlines put you in the middle seat of a three-seat row. You want to know where the *good* more-legroom, exit-row seats are? SeatGuru.com lists virtually all planes and their seating charts. What's more, with input from fellow travelers, the site tells you where *not* to sit—in other words, which ones have little legroom and are close to the bathroom. The site is an invaluable tool for anyone looking to fly. ◁

Bid—and Win!—with Priceline.com

If your departure city is within the U.S., Priceline.com is a great way to save some dough. Some folks may be intimidated by the "name your own price" gimmick. Here's how you can get the best deal from the site:

☐ As soon as you know what your travel plans are, go straight to www.biddingfortravel.com. This site has a very active online forum at which frequent travelers post their winning bids, and the hotels and neighborhoods with which they've had success. This is a mandatory visit before you bid on anything!

☐ When booking airline tickets, remember that Priceline can place you on any flight (3 a.m. *does* count!) during the 24-hour period of your departure date. For this reason alone, it's best to skip Priceline when booking short trips; you can easily lose two days in travel time.

☐ Booking hotels on Priceline is probably the site's most popular feature. To do so, you bid for a hotel and pick the section of the city and the star level you want. One caveat: If you don't get a hotel at the price you bid on, you can't bid again using the same parameters for 72 hours—you can only bid if you change your search criteria (neighborhood, star level, or price).

☐ A good rule of thumb for hotels: Check other online travel agents, find out how much that kind of hotel costs, subtract 20 percent, and use that figure as your bid on Priceline. You're virtually guaranteed a room.

☐ Car rentals are also a fantastic deal on Priceline. It's a rare day when a $20 bid won't get you an economy rental anywhere.

Airline Confidential
10 Special Ways to Score First-Class Savings, Seats, and More

Redeem your miles wa-a-a-y in advance. "Frequent-flier miles" is a misnomer. When the airlines make them almost impossible to use, they're more like infrequent-flier miles. Well, here's something the airlines won't be advertising anytime soon: They release their booking schedules a whopping 330 days in advance, according to Anne Banas, the editor in chief of www.smartertravel.com. So what does this mean? If you want to use your frequent-flier miles during a peak travel time—say, Christmas—you should start dialing up those airlines on Valentine's Day.

Mix and match airports. It's sometimes cheaper to take a return flight to a different airport than the one you flew out of. Try this little trick: Say, for example, you want to fly from Newark, New Jersey, to Los Angeles. Just for kicks, search for a return flight to a different airport in the region, such as JFK in New York. You'd be surprised to find that it's cheaper to fly back to a different airport than the one you took off from. (Of course, this plan doesn't work if you've parked your car at Newark.)

Get a first-class ticket on the cheap. Airlines don't exactly promote this fact, but it's possible to book a business-class or first-class ticket for the same price as a regular (not discount) coach seat. They're called Q-up, Y-up, or Z-up fares, and they all amount to first-class upgrades of coach fares, according to Laura Powell, a longtime travel journalist and expert. The fares were created by airlines to help business travelers, many of whom work for companies that don't allow them to buy first-class tickets. The website www.farecompare.com helps you search for these fare deals.

Change your ticket penalty-free. Airline employees would probably get in trouble if they ever admitted it, but know this: The fees you're charged when you have to change your airline ticket are negotiable. It happens to everyone— you have your travel arrangements all set, but something comes up, and you either have to add or subtract dates to your trip. So you call the airline, and you're hit with penalty fees, often well over $100 per ticket. Well, don't take it lying down, as the fees can be sliced, diced, and, if you're lucky, waived altogether.

Here's how you do it: When changing the ticket, simply ask the agent if it's possible the fees can be waived. The agent's first response will usually be "No." Ask to speak to the supervisor, and once you do, make your story a good one: Tell them your kid's got a dance recital that you just can't miss. Ask, be nice, and you might just get those tacked-on fees waived. It doesn't cost them anything to do this for you. But what's the airlines' motivation for doing this for you? In some cases, they make even more money if you're changing your ticket from a crowded flight to a less-crowded flight—they can sell that popular seat to someone else at a premium.

Don't settle for the first "bump" offer. You're on an oversold flight, and the gate agents are starting to tempt passengers with $100 in flight coupons if you'll agree to be "bumped" from your seat and take a later flight. Never accept the agents' first offer. What they're not telling you is that they have the discretion to give you even more money. Waiting patiently will be rewarded well during peak travel times, such as spring break or the Christmas holidays: Other travelers will be less likely to want to get bumped when Grandma (or a warm beach) is waiting for them. Make sure you get what's coming to you.

Bump yourself preemptively. If you want to reap the rewards of being bumped from your flight but the gate agents haven't made the offer yet, here's a way to make sure you get to the front

of the line. If you sense the flight is overbooked, go to the agent and offer to be bumped before any announcement is made. How can you tell if a flight is overbooked? One frequent traveler recommends that you observe the gate agents' body language. If they look harried, if there are weather problems at your destination or at the airport from which you're departing, or if there seem to be a lot of people milling about, it's a good time to start the bumping process.

Ask for a free lunch. Who says you can't get a free meal nowadays? Airlines don't advertise this, but if you've been bumped from a flight, you can usually get a meal out of the carrier. As you're being bumped, ask the gate agent if she'll give you some food vouchers so that you can eat while you wait. Most of the time, the gate agents will give you and your party up to $25 in vouchers. These vouchers will be honored at any restaurant n the airport. Not a bad deal for a few hours' wait.

Upgrade your flight experience. It's every traveler's dream: You buy a discounted coach ticket, ask at the gate if you can be upgraded, and before you know it, you're in a big, comfy seat with a flute of champagne in your hand. Stop dreaming—it's not going to happen that way. But if you're willing to spend a little extra money, it's worth asking the agent to "split the difference" on the price of the first-class ticket. If first class isn't booked, which usually happens on less-traveled routes on off-peak travel days, the agent has some discretion when it comes to moving people into first class. Some airlines also let you use your frequent-flier miles to "purchase" an upgrade.

Get your problem solved *after* takeoff. Airlines want you to have a pleasant flight—not because they care about you, but because they don't want you ruining the flight for everyone else. They don't want any part of bad word of mouth. So how does this help you? Once you're on the plane, and once the plane is in the air, it becomes a thousand percent easier to get what you want. Bad seat? Noisy neighbor? The person known as the chief purser can handle all these annoyances. The pilot may be the one flying the plane, but the chief purser is the person running all the other aspects of the flight. Get the

---

WHAT **AIRLINES** DON'T WANT YOU TO KNOW ABOUT Frequent-Flier Miles

Have you ever tried to cash in your frequent-flier miles? It's nearly impossible sometimes. Here are some secrets that your mileage program may not tell you:

☐ Not all flights allow you to use miles for reward travel. Don't even bother trying to redeem miles during high season to top destinations. Some airlines are now being more up-front about these blackout dates, and are listing them on their websites.

☐ It's easier to use your miles for upgrades on tickets you've already purchased than on free tickets.

☐ If you have frequent-flier miles on an airline that is either in bankruptcy or headed that way, use those miles quickly. Even if the carrier goes out of business before your flight, it may still honor the tickets you "bought" with your miles.

☐ Call the airline directly if there's a specific flight for which you want to redeem miles—even if the airline has already said you can't use your miles on that flight. If the day of the flight draws nearer and the plane isn't near capacity, the airline may let you cash your miles in.

---

chief purser's attention—it's his or her job to make sure you're happy.

Let's say you had a horrible experience at the gate. Let the chief purser know. He may offer you a free drink, or food from the first-class menu. He might even offer you an upgrade into first class. "It's important to speak with reason and not look like an air rage customer," one former chief purser said. The longer the flight, the better chance you have of getting moved into first class or business class. (Having an angry customer on board for a two-hour flight is annoying, but having an angry customer for a 14-hour overseas flight is a nightmare for the chief purser.) Ask nicely, explain your situation, and don't be surprised if you end up with more legroom and a filet mignon.

Spill something and get a better seat. Have you ever been stuck with a bad airline seat? Maybe it's next to the bathroom, or next to a screaming baby, or next to a particularly chatty seatmate. How can you escape? "Accidentally" spill something onto your seat. As long as there's another open seat somewhere on the plane, you will be moved. If you don't want to do this, complain about something—anything—that is wrong with your seat. Maybe the headphone jack is loose, or the tray table is shaky. Complain nicely and the flight staff will do their best to accommodate you. ◀

Cruise Control
4 Steps to an Inexpensive, Hassle-Free Sail on a Cruise Liner

Stick to one cruise line. All cruise lines have loyalty programs, and the more you vacation with one company, the better the perks will get—they could be anything from $100 cruise vouchers to private cocktail parties or free bottles of wine. In addition, once you prove that you're a loyal customer, many of the big lines will allow you to skip from brand to brand within the same company and still retain your standing in their frequent-cruiser program. For instance, Royal Caribbean and Celebrity are part of the same corporate structure; once you're a return customer at one, ask if you can use your loyalty points on the other line. Chances are, you can.

Get a group together. Want a free cruise? It's easy. On virtually all major cruise ships, if you can get eight other cabins booked, the ninth one is free. And that one, of course, would be yours. Keep in mind that you don't necessarily need to know the other people in your

Learn the Advantages of Touring by Train

EXPERT INSTANT ADVICE

While traveling by train in North America is not the most popular choice, it's the way to go when traveling abroad, especially in Europe. If you really want to become an expert at this type of travel, you must go to www.seat61.com. It's the most comprehensive site out there when it comes to trains the world over. Don't board without first checking it out.

Wrinkle Spray

Hotels are more than willing to charge guests an arm and a leg for the dry-cleaning service to revive suitcase-squashed clothing. A relatively new product called wrinkle-release spray is an inexpensive solution to hotel laundering. You just hang up your clothing, spray it, smooth out the wrinkles with your hands, and let it air-dry. Several brands are available, including Wrinkle Free, Austin House, and Downy. Look for them in the laundry products section. Or you can try making your own by mixing 1 tablespoon of fabric softener and 1/4 cup of unscented rubbing alcohol with 1 cup of distilled water. Put it in a travel spray bottle and gently mist the garment about a hand's length away.

group. Hang an ad in your church, at the local gym, or anywhere people congregate. Maybe you'll get lucky and get a group together. At worst, maybe you'll make a friend or two.

Haggle with your travel agent. Most people book their cruises either through websites or travel agents. Here's a significant fact that may change the way you book your next cruise: The cruise lines are getting more and more inflexible with their pricing. In the past, cruise lines would quote their prices to travel agents, and the agents would be able to work within a set of parameters. For example, a cruise line would tell a travel agent that a particular cruise should cost between $2,000 and $2,500. Travel agents would be able to negotiate prices with their clients. Now, cruise lines tell agents exactly how much a cruise costs.

Any rebate your travel agent is offering you is coming straight out of her commission. "Cruises don't rebate on their product anymore," says Sheila Gawel, the owner of GalaxSea Cruises and Travel in Toms River, New Jersey. "They believe they have a good product, and they choose a price and stick with it."

What does this mean for the cruise consumer? Well, no matter where you go to book your cruise, the price of the cruise will remain constant—it's the commission fees that will change. So while you can't easily negotiate prices with the cruise lines or websites, you can certainly negotiate prices with your travel agent. Commissions on cruises are normally 10 to 20 percent of the price of the cruise; when you speak to your agent, tell him you want a deal, or you'll go home and book the cruise on your computer.

If there's a problem, just tell someone. Cruise ships have the best customer service you'll find anywhere in the travel industry, according to one veteran of the business. The reasoning is simple: There is plenty of competition for your cruise dollar, and bad word of mouth can sink a ship. So if you ever find anything not to your liking while on board, be sure to speak up. You will be taken care of. Don't like the people at your table? Speak up. Is your cabin too close to the disco? Dance on over to someone in charge. Any problems you encounter are worth discussing with cruise personnel. ◂

Business Travel

4 Tricks for Taking Drudgery and Mishaps Out of Work-Related Trips

Get a practical lightweight carrier. Yes, a leather briefcase looks dapper and professional. However, it's not the most practical piece of luggage when you have to walk several city blocks or a mile of airport corridors. The conventional briefcase is heavy, it's not designed to accommodate the items a modern businessperson needs to carry, and the weight imbalance it creates on your body will wreck your shoulders over time. Instead, buy a bag that is designed to hold your laptop (including an envelope of padding), has pockets for your cell phone and chargers, and can accommodate a change of clothes and a file folder or two. Make sure it's lightweight and—most important—has two backpack-style shoulder straps as well as a handle.

Carry on your laptop. On the upcoming flight, you think you won't need your laptop computer. So why not just wrap some cushy clothing around it and stick it into your checked luggage? That's a bad move, say seasoned business travelers. You not only increase the chances that it might go astray for a few days, but baggage-handling systems have perfected laptop-smashing to a fine art. It may add weight and bulk to your carry-on, but that inconvenience is nothing compared to the hassle of replacing your computer.

Change for a long flight. Aren't you tired of getting off an airplane after several hours and realizing that your suit and dress shirt or blouse look like you've slept in them—because you *did* sleep in them? The solution is to pack a pair of long, lightweight workout pants and a T-shirt in your carry-on luggage. When you get on the plane, change into these informal clothes and put your dress clothes on a hanger. Near the end of the flight, change back again—your clothes will look crisp and clean.

Tame those receipts. Visit an office supply store and buy a small organizer "wallet" about the size of a legal envelope—one with several dividers inside. Make this a staple in your luggage for organizing business receipts. During the day, just stuff all receipts for business-related expenses into the same place—a jacket pocket, for instance. Every night at your hotel, put the day's receipts into the compartments within the organizer, sorted by the categories required by your employer. At the end of your trip, filling out the expense sheet will be a breeze. ◁

SECRET WEAPON

Ethernet Cable

Just about any hotel today will tell you it offers wireless Internet access, and many say they also have Ethernet cables in every room if you prefer a direct hookup. The sad truth is that the quality and reliability of wireless connections vary widely from one hotel to another, and Ethernet cables disappear from hotel rooms as quickly as those little shampoo bottles. In self-defense, drop by a computer or electronics store and buy your own Ethernet cable. Never again will you get caught in your pajamas at night, unable to access your e-mail.

Resorts and Hotels
4 Savvy Ways to Make Your Visit Less Costly and More Enjoyable

Watch those "resort fees." You shopped around for your vacation hotel—maybe even used a bidding website such as Priceline.com. But when you get to the registration counter, you find out that you will be charged an extra $10 to $15 per day as a "resort fee," supposedly to cover such amenities as the swimming pool and fitness club. This is nothing but a ruse to make a hotel's rates appear lower at the time you are scouting for a room, say industry insiders. The hotel knows that by the time you arrive, fatigued from travel and dragging your luggage and kids along, there's no way you're going to refuse your hotel room because of an add-on fee. So at the time of booking, scan the fine print of your agreement and ask the hotel about any fees that are not included in the quote. If you're surprised by such fees at the registration counter, call your credit card company after checking in and ask it to get the fee waived.

Skip resort-area crowds. If you have decided to vacation in a highly touted resort area, here's a rule of thumb from travel insiders: Schedule your vacation for less popular times of the year. For instance, in central Florida—theme park center of the universe—skip the conventional summer season, as well as the holidays and spring break. Mark your calendar for sometime between the end of August and the middle of December, or from January to the middle of February. You will find the traffic, crowds, and line waits markedly reduced—and you'll save a bundle with the off-season rates as well.

Don't get soaked ordering drinks. You might not want to sound like a penny-pinching weenie every time you place an order during your travels, but never assume that prices will be within some range that you have fixed in your mind. At a resort-town restaurant your repeat business might not be important to the management. One tourist reports that a waiter offered the "helpful" suggestion that his group buy margaritas by the pitcher. Later they were flabbergasted to be billed $35 per pitcher—and they had consumed two! Even if the waiter suggests water, make it clear that you're looking for a glass of tap water (free) as opposed to a bottle of water.

Get your government briefing. Your resort may have that safe-and-secure look that you are accustomed to back home, but that could be an illusion. Before you jump on an airliner to that idyllic foreign vacation spot, if you're American, check the U.S. State Department's travel website, www.travel.state.gov. Click on the "Consular Information Sheet" for your destination, print it out, and take it with you. If you are Canadian, go to the Department of Foreign Affairs, Consular Affairs, Information and Assistance for Canadians Abroad (www.voyage.gc.ca). Both sites provide a wealth of information about your destination. Pay particular attention to the security, safety, and crime passages, and heed the warnings you find there—carrying a minimum of cash, for instance, not taking rides with strangers, locking all hotel doors, and using the hotel safe for valuables and documents. ◂

Money on the Road
3 Strategies for Getting the Best Transaction Deals When You Go Abroad

Play your bank cards right. If you have been faithfully ordering traveler's checks every time you hit the road, give up the habit. These days, ATMs are far easier to use. But having a bank card already in your wallet does not mean you are ready to fly overseas. A tiny bit of homework will make the handling of money during your trip go much more smoothly:

- The most economical way to manage money in a foreign country will probably be withdrawing currency from local ATMs as needed with a bank card. But be sure to ask your bank in advance what fees are charged for international transactions. There could be a flat fee, as much as a few dollars per transaction, and it may also charge a percentage point or two for converting the currency. To lower the impact of a significant flat fee, make larger, less frequent withdrawals during your trip.

- Ask your bank of it has a no-fee arrangement for ATM withdrawals from certain banks at your destination. If so, gravitate toward those automatic tellers during your travels.

- Keypads on North American ATMs have letters as well as numbers, which some people use to help them remember their PIN. The ATMs in many other countries have numbers only, so be sure you know your PIN in numeral form before leaving.

- Tell your bank roughly when and where you will be traveling. (Your credit card company, too, for that matter.) You don't want a security-conscious banker freezing your account because a computer tags some unusual transactions.

- Ask your bank if there's a limit on the number of ATM withdrawals you can make during any one day. You don't want to get stuck with an empty wallet because you have "been to the well" too many times.

- Take a backup bank card with you, and keep it in a separate place. You won't get stranded if your original card gets demagnetized. Of course, if you are a couple and each has a bank card, you have an automatic backup.

Trim those transaction fees. Some popular credit card companies tack on as much as three percent in foreign transaction fees. Before you depart on an overseas trip, shop around for a card that offers low fees or even no fees on purchases you make in foreign countries. Make sure it's a card that's commonly accepted in the country you intend to visit.

Don't pay in dollars. Oh, those friendly overseas merchants! Many stores in destinations that are popular with North Americans obligingly post two different prices on products—a price in the local currency and a price in U.S. dollars. Here's the catch: The price posted in U.S. dollars is typically a few percentage points more expensive for you than the going exchange rate. So decline to have your merchandise rung up in dollars. Either pay cash in the local currency, or charge it on your credit card—which, if you followed our advice above, will automatically do the conversion at a much more friendly rate. ◂

Early Schooling

5 Strategies for Helping Your Child Develop the Skills to Succeed in School and After

Start good habits early. We hear all the time from parents of high schoolers that they still have to get on their teenagers to do their homework. Sheesh. What are these parents going to do—go to college with their kids? First grade is the time to start setting the habits that will stay with your child through graduate school. From the moment said child walks in the door after school, have a routine in place that rarely, if ever, varies. A cuddle, a conversation about school, a small snack, and then homework. Only after homework is complete can video games, soccer practice, and other activities occur.

Create the right work space. You wouldn't do your work at the kitchen table, so why should your kids? Set them up with a dedicated space to do their homework and studying, says former New Jersey teacher of the year Tom Kraeutler, who now hosts the nationally syndicated radio show *The Money Pit*. You don't have to spend big bucks at those teacher specialty stores, he says. You can pick up a desk and chairs secondhand, and the rest of the accoutrements at big-box discount stores and home improvement stores. Your shopping list should include track lighting with halogen bulbs or overhead can lights to complement the ambient lighting found in most homes, a storage center, and a dry erase board and bulletin board to enhance visual learning. Choose a dedicated spot that is a different space from where your kids play video games or watch TV, so they learn to associate that space with learning, not entertainment. Also make sure there's adequate airflow and proper temperature to keep the space comfortable.

Keep a file of accomplishments. Beginning in middle school, make a file and label it with your child's name, suggests Annette Riffle, general manager of Kaplan Premier Private Tutoring programs. Start saving all your child's good work (projects, essays, artwork) in this portfolio, and also use it to keep track of all extracurricular activities, awards, volunteer activities, and accomplishments. Also maintain a list of teachers and other adults in your child's life you can call on for recommendations.

Help your kid conquer tests. As a parent of a school-age child, you'd like nothing more than to go into that classroom on Fridays and take your fourth-grader's spelling test for her. Or your eighth-grader's algebra quiz. Get over it! Your job is to raise independent children capable of standing on their own—and taking tests on their own. That doesn't mean, however, that you can't help with tests:

- Make a test calendar. Every Monday, list all of the tests for the following week. Then with your child's help, develop a study schedule—including all reading assignments—so he's not freaking out the night before.

- Speaking of freaking out—don't do it in front of your kid. The cooler you stay about impending tests, the cooler she'll stay. Focus on the fact that it isn't the grade that's important, it's knowing she did her very best.

- Send your child to bed an hour early the night before the test. Sleep is one of the best tools available to

Evaluating a School— Beyond Test Scores

EXPERT INSTANT ADVICE

You've just been transferred halfway across the country, and before you can even think of looking for a house, you have to find the best school district. Forget about test scores, says Eileen Gale Kugler, author of *Debunking the Middle-Class Myth: Why Diverse Schools Are Good for All Kids.* Instead, focus on:

- **The school's overall tone.** For instance, do the educational leaders publicly and privately champion the value of diversity? Do students work on a wide range of topics visible throughout the school? Do students coexist in tension or have they become one community celebrating their diversity?

- **The staff's expectations of students.** What do the principal and teachers expect from the kids? Does the curriculum provide challenge for all students? Are there targeted initiatives aimed at reducing barriers to achievement and decreasing the achievement gap? Are students of color well represented in enrichment activities and rigorous classes?

- **The teachers' active participation.** Do teachers collaborate across grades and across the curriculum? Are they given the opportunity to take part in relevant professional development opportunities? Are they part of collaborative decision-making bodies at the school level and district-wide?

- **The school's resources.** Are there enough books and school supplies? Do teachers have to pay for their own supplies? Are parents and community members motivated to donate time and materials, and are these used in a coherent way that meets the goals of the school?

- **The school's relation to the community.** Is the school a focal point of the neighborhood? Do parents and community members feel welcomed as collaborative partners in the school's success? Does the school use innovative outreach strategies to partner with parents of diverse backgrounds? Does the school have vibrant partnerships with community and business organizations?

consolidate learning and hard-wire it into memory.

- Fix a good breakfast the morning of the test. That doesn't mean a sugary cereal that will leave your child groggy and light-headed just as the teacher hands out the work sheets. Fix something like whole-grain toast with cheese and a piece of fruit. The fiber in the fruit and bread, along with the protein and fat in the cheese, slows stomach emptying and helps maintain steady blood sugar levels.

- When your child brings the test home, go over the test with him so you can both see what he did right and wrong. Then focus on those areas when it's time for the next test.

Be alert to subtle warning signs.
Sometimes you really can't be sure how well your kid is doing at school, especially at a new school or the beginning of a new year before you have had any parent-teacher meetings or received a report card. And you know if you ask your child how things are going, you'll get the standard reply: "All right." But there can be subtle signs that trouble is brewing, and the earlier you are clued in on the potential trouble, the sooner you can try to do something about it. Keep an ear out for how your child describes teachers and courses. A statement that he "hates" a certain teacher or that the teacher is going too fast or gives homework that's too hard may indicate your child is having trouble with the subject and may need a little extra help from you. But be leery of contacting the teacher directly without your child's okay; he may resent your interference, especially if he is in middle school or above. And your whole effort could backfire, because he'll hate the teacher and the subject even more. ◀

Getting Into College
9 Ways to Get an Inside Track on the College Admissions Process

Start gathering recommendations in middle school. Every time your child connects with a mentor or teacher, ask for a letter of recommendation at the end of the school year. That eighth-grade drama coach will write a much more passionate letter just after the play closes than four years later, when your kid is applying to drama school. Your portfolio of recommendations will come in handy for both the admissions and the scholarship processes.

Start looking early. Your sophomore year of high school isn't too soon to begin exploring colleges, says Deborah Spinney, executive director for student development at the University of Indianapolis in Indiana. So get out from behind the video game controls and start attending college fairs, requesting literature from places of interest, and doing some online investigating. Don't feel pressure to make decisions, she says. Just gather as much information as possible to begin getting a sense of your preferences.

Create a timetable with deadlines. Many high school seniors move slower than the federal government when it comes to completing the plethora of forms involved in college applications. Instead, Kaplan Test Prep and Admissions consultant Joan M. Pagano recommends creating a timeline in your child's junior year that includes deadlines for everything from applying to take the SAT (twice) or other admissions tests to submitting a list of supplies needed for freshman year. Link rewards (or punishments) to each deadline. For instance, if your kid meets every deadline through December of senior year, he gets a laptop computer for college. If the "assignment" is due Friday and the kid is late, he loses the use of the car for the weekend. Not only will the tasks get done, but you'll be teaching your child the valuable time management and responsibility skills he needs in college.

Do a few extracurricular activities well. If you're a high school student interested in lining up a good résumé for your college applications, limit your extracurricular activities. That's right—limit them. The majority of college admissions officials say a long list of extracurricular activities is of little or moderate interest to them. They would rather see you specialize in two or three outside activities, do them well, and exhibit leadership and commitment. So focus yourself and go deep. You'll also wind up with more energy for your studies.

Work toward your future. If you already know what you want to do after college, get a head start in high school. For instance, planning to become an architect? Make sure the college admissions staff knows you spent your summer working construction, learning how to build a house from inside out.

Do community volunteer work. Top of your class, president of the student council association, and founder of the French club isn't enough. Today's admissions officers want to see a good measure of community service on your résumé. So volunteer at a soup kitchen, become an aide at a nursing home, offer to become a Big Brother or Big Sister. Not only does it demonstrate that you're an active and responsible citizen, but volunteering exposes you to different peoples, cultures, and organizations in your community.

Don't get sticker shock over high fees. Sure, college in most parts of the U.S. is going to cost some bucks. But those enormous price tags that schools like to wave around on their websites and in brochures—$30,000 a year, $40,000 a year, etc. etc.—are about as realistic as the pricing in a used-car lot. "Students almost never pay that sticker price," says Spinney. Financial aid and other arrangements will make whatever college you choose to attend much more affordable than you think.

Go beyond the campus tour. Visiting colleges is fun, but if all you see of the campus is what the goody-goody in the suit and tie wants to show you, then you're not getting a real sense of what life is like there. Arrange to sit in on a couple of classes in your area of interest, schedule an interview with a professor, go have lunch in the student cafeteria and get kids to tell you what life's really like there. Most admissions offices will even arrange for you to spend a night in the dorms.

Factor in a possible change in interests. You might be 100 percent positive that you're going to be a pre-med major in college, but people change, and nowhere will you change more than during the first year or two at college. So don't choose a college based on your probable major, says Spinney. Instead, make sure the school has strong programs in three or four areas that appeal to you. ◀

LEARNING THE ART OF *SAT* Preparation

Given that the class of 2006 posted the sharpest drop in SAT scores in 31 years, it's clear that there's trouble in test-taking paradise. Joe Jewell—a Rhodes scholar who scored a perfect 1600 on his SATs, was a contributing editor for the book *Up Your Score: The Underground Guide to the SAT*, and is cofounder of prepme.com—offers this advice for SAT takers.

Be comfortable with your calculator

SAT day is not the day to first try out that fancy graphing calculator. Plus, there's nothing on the test that requires anything more than a simple four-function calculator, so stick with the one you use every day in school.

Keep a vocabulary journal

Create a running list of words during your sophomore and junior year. Put three new words on it a day and memorize those words. That's 1,000 new words in a year! Make sure you reinforce the old vocabulary with a monthly review, and try using these new words in conversations with your parents and teachers and in school essays. The more you use the words, the more likely you are to remember them on test day.

Don't practice in the ideal test-taking environment

How will you react on test day if the kid behind you keeps kicking your chair? If the room is too hot? If you didn't get enough sleep the night before? Simulate distractions when you're taking practice tests so you can focus no matter what's happening around you. Try taking practice SATs in a coffee shop or anywhere else with ambient noise. Do this enough and nothing will distract you come test day.

Guess for success

Most questions have one or two answers that are obviously wrong. Eliminate those and then guess from the remaining choices. Don't leave any questions blank, particularly if you can rule out even one answer.

Don't be creative on the essay

Graders score hundreds of essays and scan your essay looking for the same elements: a basic four- or five-paragraph essay with a thesis, topic sentences, specific details and evidence, and a conclusion that restates your thesis. Make sure everything in your essay ties back to the thesis and supports it with evidence.

Paying for College

11 Tricks for Getting Financial Aid When You Head Off to the Halls of Ivy

Grab up local scholarship dollars. When you hear about a national-level $40,000 scholarship, sure, your eyes are going to light up. But you'll shock all the other students and parents when you stack up the mountain of cash from this secret—gleaned from the most successful scholarship hunters: Students can quickly accumulate a six-figure educational nest egg by approaching all of the clubs, community organizations, and businesses right in their vicinity. It's much easier to snatch up $1,500 here and $2,000 there from nearby organizations where there's less competition and a local student is more likely to be a standout.

Search beyond the Web. Every prospective college student on the planet knows to scour the Internet for scholarship dollars. Which means that there will be enormous competition for any scholarships you find there. By all means go after that money. However, while the masses are fighting it out, you'll be scooping up tuition money more quickly if you mine sources that aren't so well publicized. Ask for the financial reference books at your local public library. These are big, fat books full of scholarship opportunities offered by groups that couldn't care less about publicizing themselves on the Internet.

Move fast to apply early. You know the old saying—"The early bird … " Well, it's especially true when it comes to financial aid, says college planning specialist Alisa LeSueur. For instance, you can submit the Free Application for Federal Student Aid (FAFSA) required

for government and private funding as early as January 1 of your child's senior year in high school.

Be wary of school-aid consultants. Paying a financial aid consultant may be a waste of money better spent on college expenses, says Francine Jackson, director of financial aid at Harrisburg University of Science and Technology in Pennsylvania. "There are a lot of scams out there that prey upon families seeking financial support to pay for college," she says. Instead, she recommends that students build relationships with the financial aid professionals at the university to which they've been accepted to ensure

EXPERT INSTANT ADVICE

Here's advice for landing free money for your child's college education, provided by Alisa LeSueur, a certified college planning specialist based in San Antonio, Texas.

- College scholarships are available for children as young as six! Meaning, it's never too soon to start.

- Use the Internet for free resources. A good one: weeklyscholarshipalert.org. But limit the personal information you provide. Some sites sell this information for mailing lists.

- Read the small print. Parents often miss eligibility information on scholarship applications, meaning they miss out on the money.

- Meet the deadline! 'Nuff said.

- If there's an essay or art project required, ask to see what past winners submitted. This tells you what the judges are looking for.

- Look in the local paper for scholarship announcements. Then get the application so you can apply for your kid next year.

- Don't give up! There are thousands of scholarships, and you can't win them all.

they're receiving the funding they're entitled to. Be especially cautious about agencies and consultants that guarantee any specific level of scholarships and those that charge fees. A more legitimate arrangement is a consultant whose fee is a percentage of the aid he helps your child obtain.

Don't overreport your financial status. You know how lawyers tell their clients to just answer yes or no when they're on the witness stand? Well, that's what we're telling you when it comes to completing financial aid forms. If they

don't ask about your mother's antique jewelry, don't tell them! Just identify and report the value of the assets you're required to.

Submit an addendum. While you shouldn't reveal assets you don't have to, you *should* reveal hardships *not* requested on financial aid forms, says LeSueur. For instance, if you just got hit with $100,000 in medical expenses for your wife's breast cancer treatment, say so. Ditto if you're funding four college educations at the same time—including one medical school stint. Just make sure you have the documentation to back it up.

Refile every year. You may think your situation hasn't changed, but even a small increase in debt or reduction in assets can make a big difference. So resubmit your financial aid forms every year. And check the date on the financial aid form to make sure you're using the right one; they change every year.

Keep claiming your kid on your taxes. If you stopped claiming your child as a dependent on your income tax form in the hope you'll get more financial aid, you've just left hundreds of dollars sitting on the table. "Many parents are under the incorrect impression that their income and assets will not be considered in the financial aid calculations if they stop claiming their student on their tax return," says LeSueur, but that's simply not true. The only way children are considered independent in terms of financial aid eligibility is if they're married, have a dependent child of their own, are 24 or older, are in or have been in the armed services, are orphans or wards of the court, or are graduate students.

Early decision can mean less aid.
If you need help paying for college, stay away from the "early decision" admissions process. This is the system in which a university will admit a student months before the rest of the crowd is considered. Yes, this gives the student a better shot at the university he or she most wants to attend. However, you're also making that admissions officer's eyes sparkle: By committing to that one college, you're tipping your hand. Early admission students typically get lower amounts of financial assistance because there's no need for the college to woo them.

Never go "off-season" in your sport. If you're a student hoping to get an athletic scholarship, don't wait until your sport's season to play. Get involved throughout the year—in sporting camps and intramural leagues. Whether you coach younger athletes or participate in a traveling league, the year-round training will show your dedication to the sport and pay off with improved skills too.

Land an inside job at college.
If you're working your way through college, you might as well have a job that dumps bucketloads of cash in your lap rather than a trifling hourly wage. Colleges that offer their students work-study programs get low-cost student labor to help with office work or running the front desk at dorms. What the insiders aren't telling you is this: If you have any choice in the matter, snap up that job in the financial aid office. You'll get a great overview of how the entire tuition-funding system works and you'll get early notice of any scholarship opportunities. You'll have a definite edge over anyone else. ◁

$

3 QUESTIONS TO ASK YOUR
financial aid
Officer

Sure, it was nice of your financial aid office to recommend a student loan company, but what's in it for them? To make sure you're getting the best deal, ask the financial aid officer the following questions, says Raza Khan, president and CEO of the student loan company MyRichUncle (myrichuncle.com).

1 Which loan company offers the lowest rate?

When the financial aid official recommends a certain lender, it doesn't necessarily mean that that lender is offering the lowest rate.

2 Are you making any money from this loan?

Just as Realtors get a cut when they refer you to a mortgage company, so, too, do some financial aid offices when they refer you to a specific lender. It can come several ways:

☐ Revenue sharing. The office gets a percentage of any profits made from the loan.

☐ School-as-lender. The school gets a percentage of the profit made when federal Stafford or PLUS loans are sold to lenders.

☐ Override pools. The financial aid office gets a portion of the profit from your loan to use to pay for other students' tuition. Why should you be paying for other students? Get a lower rate instead.

☐ Old-fashioned kickbacks. These are just what they sound like: cash or gifts given to school officials for referring the lender to you. Khan says she saw some financial aid administrators receiving digital music players, DVD players, gift certificates, and designer briefcases at the 2006 National Association of Student Financial Aid Administrators conference. Just as fancy dinners and Caribbean cruises were often used by the pharmaceutical industry to influence doctors to prescribe certain drugs, these gifts can influence which lenders make it onto a college's preferred lender list.

3 How did you choose this list of lenders?

Why *these* lenders and not others? And are you prohibited from going outside this list to find your own lender? If the financial aid office won't give you copies of any "agreements" between the school and lenders, then something fishy is going on.

Succeeding on Campus
6 Easy Ways to Get Ahead at College Both Academically and Socially

Go with debit, not credit. More than half of all college students have at least one credit card billed to them, according to the American Council on Education, and about 40 percent carry a balance from month to month. Since you're likely graduating with student loans to repay, why would you also want to be saddled with credit card debt at 18 percent or higher interest? Here's an easy way to avoid it. You need to establish credit in your own name, so go ahead and get a card. Then use it once for a purchase, pay off the bill immediately, and cut up the credit card. At the same time, get a debit card that looks like (but doesn't act like) a credit card. In other words, you can't spend more than you have in your checking account. Just make sure you track your debit expenses, or you'll find yourself paying some hefty fines in overcharges to the bank.

Check out student housing in person. Before you request the residence hall with 12 rooms over the suite-like dorms, take a tour. Talk to students currently living there about the pros and cons of the living arrangement and the type of students who tend to choose that particular living arrangement. (Jocks? Brains? Frat boys?) Will you absolutely die of embarrassment if you don't have a private bathroom? Do you want to be stuck in the dorm for meals too? Is a single-gender dorm important to you? Do you want the new dorm with the air conditioning or the old dorm with the fireplace? The more carefully you think through these issues the happier you'll be, says Harlan Cohen, author of *The Naked Roommate: And 107 Other Issues You Might Run Into in College.*

Talk to your roommate *before* September. Most middle-class kids today have never shared a room—until they hit college. So the idea of living with someone else's mess, smells, and personality in a room the size of your closet back home can be, well, quite disconcerting. Never fear! Here's advice for future roommates from Matthew Paul Turner, author of *Everything You Need to Know Before College:*

- Try to meet in person if possible. If that's not possible before school starts, set up a phone call, *not* an instant messaging conversation. Talking is important here, because you're going to be discussing some important issues.

- Have a conversation about cleanliness. If you dust every afternoon and your roomie only changes his underwear every week, there will be problems. Find out now so you can switch before school starts.

- Only share the big stuff. Initially, you might think you should go halfsies on everything in the room—from comforters to pillows and bookshelves. Don't bother. You may never see this person after the first year—or even the first month. Instead, just split the cost of the big items, such as the TV, the refrigerator, and the microwave, and keep the receipts. If you split up, it's easy enough for one of you to buy the other out.

- Decide up-front about sleepovers. If you're fundamentally opposed to premarital sex and your potential roommate has a very involved boyfriend who will be visiting every weekend—and staying in your room—now is the time to either set parameters or switch roommates.

Get to school early on check-in day. If you want the best closet, the best bed, the desk near the window, and the dresser near your side of the room, get there first, recommends college-life author Harlan Cohen. Your best bet? Stay in a hotel near campus the night before, so you're first in line when check-in starts.

Try the A student's playbook. Those competitive students running around with perfect 4.0 grade point averages have a handful of test-taking secrets that they would just as soon keep to themselves. You already know to do the reading and the homework, review the class materials regularly, and to get plenty of sleep the night before the exam. But here are some techniques that separate the A students from the other kind:

- If you're going to skip the occasional class, that's your business. But always attend the class that's just before a test as well as review sessions (if they're at another time). This is when you'll get the best hints about the content of the test. Always ask the instructor to get as specific as possible about the material that will be covered.

- Always find out whether answering incorrectly is any worse than not answering at all. If they're the same, you might as well guess when you have to.

- Eat a light meal or snack before the test so you'll have energy and be able to keep your eyes open. Avoid heavy food.

- Take a watch to help you pace yourself. As soon as you receive your test, scan through it quickly and plot out how much time you will devote to each section.

- Give first priority to the easy questions and those that will earn you the most points.

- Don't let any question bog you down. Skip it for the moment and see if anything else in the test provides helpful information.

- After the test, listen carefully as the instructor reviews the answers. This will give you valuable insight about what the instructor will want on the next test.

SECRET WEAPON

Open Door

Okay, so you're getting along great with your roommate. What about the rest of the dorm? If you want to make friends you'll have for life, leave your dorm door open, says author Harlan Cohen. Other students will be more willing to stop by if there's no barrier that suggests "Don't bother me."

Parents, learn to let go. There's a new phrase circulating among college administrators: "helicopter parents," those who swoop in whenever their kid needs a helping hand. Well, it's time to turn off the engines, Mom and Dad. Instead, follow this advice from Rodger Summers, vice president for student affairs at Binghamton University in Binghamton, New York:

- Don't call the president of the college or university!

- Acknowledge your own feelings about your child leaving and address them, either on your own or with a trained therapist.

- Be familiar with the university resources available and where your child can get help, as well as where you can find answers.

- Keep all contact information and resource material in your night table drawer or in a central location.

- Support and demand degrees of independence from your student. Remember: At age 18, your student is an adult.

- Develop expectations for communication and talk about them before your child leaves home.

- Have a life of your own and recognize that others depend on you besides your college freshman.

- Be supportive but not "hyper" when it comes to your child's college life.

- Celebrate your accomplishments and let go! ◁

5 Most Common Freshman Mistakes

You've heard of that weight-gain hazard called the Freshman 15? This is the Freshman 5—the five most common mistakes freshmen make, courtesy of Deborah Spinney, executive director for student development at the University of Indianapolis in Indiana.

☐ **Assuming college is an extension of high school.** Many students aren't prepared for the quantity and complexity of college work and rely on their high school study habits to get by. A good rule of thumb: Spend the same amount of time studying for a course each day as you spend in that class. If you need help with study skills, seek help from your university's academic support office right away. Don't wait until you're mired in midterms.

☐ **Trying to save money by not buying books.** Do you have any idea how much reading is required in college? If you think you're going to check out the book from the library and save a few bucks, think again. You'll quickly fall behind on your reading assignments and your grades will suffer. Instead, search out bargains online and from students who already took the class.

☐ **Being overly ambitious.** A heavy course load in high school may have been manageable, but it could overwhelm you in college. Set yourself up for success by taking no more than 12 to 14 hours of classes your first semester so you have time to acclimate.

☐ **Ignoring e-mails.** Yeah, yeah, you think e-mail is for ancient people like teachers and parents. Well, here's a news flash: Professors and school administrators use it too. They're not going to instant message or text message you about assignments, grades, tuition deadlines, and the weekend parking ban. So check your e-mail regularly!

☐ **Over- or under-socializing.** If your calendar holds more party dates than class dates, you're overdoing it. Conversely, if your idea of a hot Saturday night is when the air conditioning breaks in the library, you're underdoing your social life. You can't have the ultimate college experience if you never get out of your room. So find activities you enjoy beyond schoolwork—just keep it all in perspective.

Acknowledgments

The author wishes to gratefully acknowledge the help and information supplied by the following sources:

Jim Abbott, handyman franchise owner, Aurora, Ontario

Katie Albright, Sierra Club environmentalist, Ottawa, Ontario

Jennifer Appel, landscape designer-landscape architect, Houston, Texas

Brian Babcock, attorney, Thunder Bay, Ontario

Linda Bacon, Ph.D., nutrition expert, Davis, California

K. George Beck, professor of weed science, Colorado State University, Fort Collins, Colorado

Cheryl Bell, M.S., R.D., L.D.N., healthy living advisor, Chicago, Illinois

Stephen J. Berne, chair restorer and wicker expert, Vancouver, British Columbia

Robin Bond, workplace etiquette expert and employment attorney, Wayne, Pennsylvania

Walt Borchers, vice president, MovieTickets.com, Santa Monica, California

Lee Borden, divorce lawyer and mediator, Birmingham, Alabama

Kathy Brownfield, bathroom fixture industry expert, Richmond, Virginia

Susan Burke, R.D., nutrition expert, Fort Lauderdale, Florida

Bill Burton, casino gambling authority and author, New Britain, Connecticut

Gene Bush, owner, Munchkin Nursery, Depauw, Indiana

Rita Carey, gardener-gardening advisor, Kapat Garden Center, Squamish, British Columbia

Michelle Cederberg, fitness trainer, Calgary, Alberta

Harlan Cohen, college expert and author, Hackensack, New Jersey

Dan Collins, public relations professional, Baltimore, Maryland

Charles Cox, freelance handyman, Beaver Falls, Pennsylvania

William Davis, M.D., medical director, Milwaukee Heart Scan

Stacy DeBroff, mothering expert, Chestnut Hill, Massachusetts

Nancy and Glenn Deines, gardeners for over 50 years, Platteville, Colorado

Jason Denton, author of *Simple Italian Sandwiches* and owner of a panini restaurant, New York City

Laure Dixon, innovative amateur cook and certified wine connoisseur, Nashua, New Hampshire

Kenneth Dotson, chief marketing officer, TicketsNow, Crystal Lake, Illinois

Alison Doyle, former human resources director, Saratoga Springs, New York

Howard Dvorkin, president and founder, Consolidated Credit Counseling Services, Fort Lauderdale, Florida

Steve and Annette Economides, a.k.a. "America's cheapest family," Phoenix, Arizona

Linda Eremita, TreePeople Forestry Educator, Beverly Hills, California

David Felton, executive chef at Pluckemin Inn, Bedminster, New Jersey

Jodi Fitzpatrick, kitchen and bath designer, Fresno, California

Linda Foley, executive director of Identity Theft Resource Center, Washington, D.C.

Louise Fox, etiquette coach, the Etiquette Ladies, Manitoba

Eugene Fram, marketing professor, Rochester, New York

Michael Fugate, furniture sales veteran, Auxvasse, Missouri

Sheila Gawel, owner, GalaxSea Cruises, Toms River, New Jersey

Kevin Gianni, fitness expert, New Haven, Connecticut

James Gibbs, hardware store manager, Richmond, Virginia

Phil Goodin, head of Cherry Creek High School (Colorado) Plant Lover's Club, Englewood, Colorado

Mary Hardy, M.D., director of integrative medicine, Ted Mann Family Resource Center at the University of California, Los Angeles

Edward Hasbrouck, travel writer, San Francisco, California

Mikki Hopcroft, furniture salesperson, Richmond, Virginia

Jan Horsfall, owner of Gelazzi, Denver, Colorado

Douglas Husbands, certified clinical nutritionist, San Carlos, California

Francine Jackson, financial aid director, Harrisburg, Pennsylvania

Daniel Jalkut, software developer, Somerville, Massachusetts

Jennifer James, nurse and long-time gardener, Lafayette, Colorado.

Ingrid Johnson, professor of textiles, Fashion Institute of Technology, New York City

Val Jones, owner, Orchard Park Travel, Kelowna, British Columbia

Charles Joseph, labor lawyer, New York City

Susan Joyce, computer security expert, Marlborough, Massachusetts

Marina Kamen, fitness expert, New York City

Larina Kase, Psy.D., M.B.A., psychologist and author, Philadelphia, Pennsylvania

Kraig Kast, financial expert, Redwood Shores, California

Francine DiFilippo Kent, president, Celebrate a Hero!, Sarasota, Florida

Stanley Kershman, author and debt expert, Ottawa, Ontario

Raza Khan, student loan expert, New York City

Shelley Kincaid, yard-sale maven, Denver, Colorado

Peggy Koontz, remodeling professional, Fresno, California

Brian Korte, computer consultant, Richmond, Virginia

Tom Kraeutler, education supply expert, Lincolnshire, Illinois

Eileen Gale Kugler, education expert, Springfield, Virginia

Dale Kurow, career and executive coach, New York City

Michael Laimo, longtime staffer for Mercury Beach-Maid, a New York City sportswear wholesaler, and also a horror novelist

Katherine Lawrence, professional declutterer, Richmond, Virginia

Alisa LeSueur, certified college planning specialist, San Antonio, Texas

Hugh Lobban, drapery cleaning expert, Lorton, Virginia

Enga Lokey, gardener and part-time landscaping professional, Natimuk, Australia (also part-time resident of Salida, Colorado)

Tom Long, stay-at-home dad, Elkins Park, Pennsylvania

Wanda Martens, appliance repair expert, Mound, Minnesota

Kristina Matisic, bargain hunter, Vancouver, British Columbia

Greg McArthur, Ph.D. in plant ecology, biology professor, part-time garden center employee, Denver, Colorado

Susan McCausland, landscape installation and garden maintenance expert, Beyond Gardens Inc., Boulder, Colorado

Deb McCoy, president, American Academy of Wedding Professionals, Palm Beach, Florida

Jonni McCoy, frugality expert, Colorado Springs, Colorado

Chris McGoey, security consultant, Los Angeles, California

Paul McKinzey, appliance expert, Richmond, Virginia

Ross Melnick, cofounder, Cinema Treasures, West Hollywood, California

Isadore B. Mirsky, C.P.A., Wayne, New Jersey

Donna Montaldo, bargain expert, New Orleans, Louisiana

Susan Louisa Montauk, M.D., professor of clinical family medicine, Cincinnati, Ohio

Birgit Mueller, Emmy Award-winning costume designer for television, based in Los Angeles, California

Brian Muntz, veteran computer consultant, Ajax, Ontario

Sharon Naylor, author, *1,000 Best Kept Secrets for Your Perfect Wedding*, Madison, New Jersey

Stephanie Nelson, frugality expert, Atlanta, Georgia

Marion Nestle, professor of nutrition, New York City

Brent Newbold, CFO, Holy Cow cleaning products company, based in Rocklin, California.

Susan Newman, Ph.D., social psychologist and author, Rutgers, New Jersey

Liz Ngonzi, president of Amazing Taste, an event-planning firm in South Orange, New Jersey

Jeff Novick, director of nutrition, the Pritikin Longevity Center and Spa, Aventura, Florida

Anne Obarski, customer-service expert, St. Charles, Missouri

Robert O'Shea, real estate attorney, Petaluma, California

Joan M. Pagano, Kaplan Test Prep and Admissions consultant, New York City

Michael Palermo, estate planning lawyer, certified financial planner, Lexington, Kentucky

Ryan Peif, landscape design and installation professional, Greeley, Colorado

Gary Peterson, auction expert, Hudson, Quebec

Bruce Powell, Pappy's Motorhome Rentals, Salt Lake City, Utah

Wanda Prychitko, executive secretary, Citizens for Crime Awareness, Winnipeg, Manitoba

Wendy Reed, EPA energy expert, Washington, D.C.

Rick E. Ricer, M.D., family medicine specialist, Cincinnati, Ohio

Annette Riffle, tutor, New York City

Susan RoAne, career counselor and networking authority, Greenbrae, California

Clark Robins, architect and home remodeler, Richmond, Virginia

Nancy Rosebrock, furniture conservator, Asheville, North Carolina

Ron Rupert, chef at Seasons 52, Orlando, Florida

Harvey M. Sachs, Ph.D., energy efficiency expert, Washington, D.C.

Prentice St. Clair, Detail in Progress auto detailers, San Diego, California

Noah Scalin, founder of a community-supported agriculture organization, Richmond, Virginia

Karen Schaffer, career coach, Halifax, Nova Scotia

Lou Schlachter, Ph.D., R.N., teacher of herbal and folk medicine, the College of William & Mary, Williamsburg, Virginia

Liz Scofield, etiquette teacher and director, Zoellner Arts Center, Lehigh University, Bethlehem, Pennsylvania

Brette McWhorter Sember, parenting expert, Clarence, New York

Sheri Sheets, heating and plumbing contractor, Stuarts Draft, Virginia

Karen Sherman, Ph.D., psychologist, Long Island, New York

Kevin Reid Shirley, real estate stager, Washington, D.C.

Frank Silva, manager, Schwartz's Hebrew Delicatessen, Montreal, Quebec

Viviana Simon, Ph.D., director of scientific programs, Society for Women's Health Research, Washington, D.C.

Beth Smerek, assistant manager and bedding plant specialist, Sturtz & Copeland, Boulder, Colorado

Connie Smith, manager, Sturtz & Copeland garden center, Boulder, Colorado

Syble Solomon, financial expert, Rockville, Maryland

Susan Sommers, author and fashion coach, based in New York City

Deborah Spinney, student development executive, Indianapolis, Indiana

Jyl Steinback, senior editor, *Looking Good NOW!* magazine, Scottsdale, Arizona

Bobette Stott, clothing designer, Los Angeles, California

Jeffrey Strain, frugality expert, Cupertino, California

Rodger Summers, vice president for student affairs, Binghamton University, New York

Tina B. Tessina, Ph.D., psychologist and author, Long Beach, California

Mathew Paul Turner, college expert and author, Nashville, Tennessee

Denise Vivaldo, author, *Do It for Less! Parties*, Los Angeles, California

Anna Wallner, bargain hunter, Vancouver, British Columbia

Louise J. Wannier, CEO, Internet clothing retailer myShape, Inc.

Brian Wansink, director, Food and Brand Lab, Cornell University, Ithaca, New York

Lindsay Wombold, health educator, Indianapolis, Indiana

Alan Zell, a.k.a. "The ambassador of selling," Portland, Oregon

Mark Zwick, owner, Phillytrips.com, Philadelphia, Pennsylvania

duct tape, drawbacks of, 118

DVDs, 325

E

ear care, 30–31

earplugs, 30

ear wax, 31

earwigs, 160

EAs (enrolled agents), 245

EBCT (electron beam computed tomograph) test, 19

economic news, 210

eczema, 12

edamame (soybeans), 47

edible wild plants, 81–82

Edmunds.com, 204

education, 349–59

eggs, 86–87

elderberry, elderflower, 45

electrical cords, pets and, 301

electric drills, 122

electricians, hiring, 119

electric toothbrushes, 28

electron beam computed tomograph (EBCT) test, 19

electronic equipment, buying, 180–82

e-mail:
  business, 256
  at college, 359
  identify theft and, 275
  job-hunting and, 249
  telephone vs., 256, 271

employee discounts, 213

employment:
  computer proficiency and, 255–56
  getting ahead in, 254–57
  job-hunting for, 248–52
  mentors and, 254
  promotions and, 255
  quitting, 263–64
  self-promotion and, 257
  termination of, 262–65
  see also workplace

endive, 59

end-user license agreements (EULAs), 190

energy bars, 62

energy conservation, 127–33
  myths about, 133

Energy Star ratings, 128, 130, 131, 132

enrolled agents (EAs), 245

entertaining, 306–7, 310–13

escrow services, online, 227

essential oils, 112

Ethernet cables, 345

etiquette:
  dating and, 304
  at table, 313

evening primrose oil, 45

event-planning, software for, 315

exchange rates, 347

exercise:
  hearing loss and, 30
  heart disease and, 72
  isometric, 74–75
  motivation for, 66–67
  outdoor, 75
  sleeplessness and, 21
  techniques for, 68–69, 74–75
  walking as, 72–73
  women and, 71–72

exercise videos, 71–72

exes, dating friends,' 305

expense reports, 345

extracurricular activities, 351

eye care, 29–30

F

fabric, decorating with, 105

fabric softener, 174

family life, 293–303
  see also child custody; divorce

family outings, 335

Fandango.com, 323

fans:
  bathroom, 121
  ceiling, 133

farmers' markets, 217

farms, pick-your-own, 81

fast-food restaurants, 64

fat, dietary:
  monounsaturated, 17
  restaurant menus and, 316–17

faucets, buying, 122–23

Federal Trade Commission, identity theft and, 275

fees:
  bank, 235
  credit card, 234, 235

fencing, 69

fennel, 58

fertilizer, lawn, 151, 157

festivals, 335

fiber, 60

Field Guide to Edible Wild Plants, A (Peterson), 82

fights, between siblings, 295

filers, stackable, 106

recreational vehicles (RVs), 208

recruiters, human resources, 250–51

references, after job termination, 262–63

refrigerators:
  energy usage and, 128, 130
  maintenance of, 183, 185

registers, incorrect prices at, 216, 236

relationships, romantic, 292–93, 304–5

relatives:
  dealing with, 298–99
  divorce and, 281–82

religious organizations:
  children and, 296
  weight loss and, 56

repairmen:
  hiring, 119–20
  as source of advice on appliance purchases, 181

repairs, do-it-yourself, 120–22

reseeding lawns, 151

resorts, 346

respect, in love and marriage, 293

respiratory illnesses, 15–16

restaurants, 100–101, 316–20
  children in, 295
  fast-food, 64
  recommendations for, 317
  weight loss and, 64, 316–17

restless legs syndrome, 20

résumés, 249, 250

retailers:
  big-box, 188–89
  clothing, 170

dealing with, 220–23
gift cards and, 214
return policies of, 220
warehouse, 221

retaliation, workplace harassment and, 261

retirement planning, 231, 232

return policies, 220

reunions, class, 314–15

revocable living trusts, 245–46

rheumatoid arthritis, 45

riders, for life insurance policies, 243

RN number, 169

roaches, 114

road safety, 199–200

rodents, RVs and, 208

romance, 292–93, 304–5

root cellar, portable, 93

rosebushes, 145

roulette, 331–32

routers, computer, 186, 191

rust, tools and, 119

rust-proofing, for cars, 203

RVs (recreational vehicles), 208

S

sacrifices, choices vs., 297

safety, 267–77
  cars and, 199–200, 276–77

salad dressings, homemade, 85

salads, 52, 64
  bagged, 217
  fat and, 51

sale bins, 223

sales, patterns of, 236

salt, 55

sander, belt, 119

sanitizers, hand, 100

satin-weave cotton, 173

SATs, preparing for, 352, 355

sauce, tomato, 50, 84–85

saucer sled, for garden trimmings, 164, 166

saying no, 27

scams, investment, 239

Schedule C, 244

scholarships, 353, 354
  athletic, 355

schools, choosing, 349

Schwartz's Montreal Hebrew Delicatessen, 88–89

S corporations, 244–45

scratching posts, 301

screen doors, repairing, 120

screwdrivers, 117, 118

sealers, for new cars, 202

season tickets, 327

SeatGuru.com, 339

security:
  computers and, 187, 190–91, 273
  home, 266–68
  personal, 269–70
  telephone, 270–71

selenium, 61

self-hypnosis, weight loss and, 55–56

seniors, free legal advice for, 278

serving size, on food labels, 78

sex, children and, 295

sex-enhancement supplements, 43

shades, window, decorating, 105–6

TAKE ADVANTAGE OF ALL YOUR BENEFITS

Discounts, Deals&Steal$

For Those over 50 Who Don't Want to Pay to Play

Reader's
Digest

The Early Bird Mantra

I will strive to unearth every discount I deserve,
in every part of my life.

I will proudly ask for senior discounts, in the knowledge
that those who offer them want and need my patronage
today and in the future.

I will be a savvy consumer not only because having
extra money is useful, but also because I believe in the
values of simple, frugal, clever living.

I will enjoy the spectacular rewards of being over 50
and share my Early Bird wisdom with others.

I will understand that part of being an Early Bird is
being lighthearted and joyful about everyday life, and that
the pursuit of savings is a game I will always win!

Contents

Wake Up, Early Bird! It's a Whole New Day!

Imagine this: You arise one sparkling and lovely morning. The skies are blue, the birds are chirping happily, the sun is shining. You proceed with your day as you always do: have a nice breakfast, maybe do a little bit of exercise, and take your pooch for a walk. You accomplish that long list of busy errands—paying a few bills, taking the car to be serviced, making arrangements to visit the grandkids, calling the oil company to have your furnace cleaned, visiting the doctor for a checkup. Perhaps you have a cafe lunch with one of your friends before hitting up the library for the newest bestseller you've been waiting for. You come home, have a nice dinner, watch some television, send a few chatty e-mails, and hit the sack.

What's different about this particular day?

Dear reader, *this* day is an Early Bird Day!

As an invigorated member of the Early Birds, you will take advantage of absolutely everything that the world now offers you, in every part of your life. You will reap the extensive rewards that you deserve, now that you are on the right side of 50, whether you're filling up your car with gasoline, buying airline or train tickets, or doing grocery shopping of any proportion. Discounts will appear as if by magic when you go to the movies or go golfing. You will absolutely expect "senior" discounts (little do they know how youthful you are!) to be handed to you as often as possible; be they small or great. They will make a terrific, joyful, thrifty impact on virtually every aspect of your life, and turn the clever art of savvy savings into a game that you win each day, every day. What could be more rewarding?

The Sunny Side of 50

Gone are the days, Early Bird, when you might have felt just a little bit funny asking for senior discounts, or even assuming they existed at all in some places. Never again! And here's why: Businesses want you. *Desperately.* They're not offering "senior" discounts out of respect, pity, or moral obligation. Quite the opposite. We Americans are living longer than ever before; we are living more actively than ever before; and we Early Birders have much more available cash on average than people under 50. Retailers know all this! So if they can win your patronage by offering you special deals, they're banking on you being a regular customer for many years to come. It's the proverbial "win-win" equation that makes our economy so great!

So in the coming pages, our top flight team of Early Bird experts will show you how to live better than ever by knowing exactly what to ask for, how to get it, and making your wisdom, your experience, and your smarts pay off BIG! If you're on the sunny side of 50, the world is your oyster! Here are just a few of the ways in which you can save:

Ka-Ching! Staying at a hotel or a motel? There are hundreds of valuable discounts just yours for the asking.

Ka-Ching! Get your morning coffee for much less—even free—at this national fast food chain.

Ka-Ching! Fill your fridge, your pantry, and your freezer for a song.

Ka-Ching! Take classes at this world-class university for free.

Ka-Ching! Turn your favorite hobby into a cool cash cow.

Ka-Ching! Get totally free checking at your local bank.

Ka-Ching! Get deeply discounted cell phone service.

And so much more—all just for being you!

Discounts, Deals, and Steals is filled with more than 1,900 invaluable tips, techniques, and secrets to great living for far less than you spend now, freeing up time and cash for the things you really want in your life. You'll learn how to get expert medical advice for less; how to look and feel your best for virtually nothing; how to keep in touch with family and friends the world over; how to get the best deals on the right insurance for you, and much, much more. The icing on the Early Bird cake? An A-Z section chock-full of quick, clever, savings ideas for making life not only great, but joyful, fun, *and* thrifty.

So sharpen your pencils and get ready to reap all the benefits that are yours for the taking. The time is now!

Elissa Altman

EXECUTIVE EDITOR,
READER'S DIGEST HOME BOOKS

Finding Gold in Your Golden Years

1

> *Get Discounts, Strike Bargains, and Give Scammers the Boot*

Top Strategies for Getting the Best Bargains

There's no single way to get the best bargain all the time. You have to be ready to go with the flow, to know what to ask for, and then be prepared to ask again, or differently, if you're not getting what you want. Keep your eyes on the prize, stay focused on what you're looking for, and be ready to change tactics, change questions, or even call back later and change whom you're talking to!

Ask for a discount whether it's marked or not. The price on the tag is rarely the price. We've all been deeply conditioned to believe that the number on the tag is the number we have to pay, with tax added on top. But how did that number get on the tag? It's the amount the retailer paid to make or acquire the item wholesale plus a prorated amount that he has to spend to pay his staff and keep the lights on and advertise to get you to come to his store, plus however much more he thinks you, Mr. and Mrs. Public, are willing to pay on top of that (that is, the profit).

Be a savvy senior shopper. Unless you're dealing with a big commercial operation like Wal-Mart or Costco, most retailers and service providers are a lot more interested in moving goods out the door and closing the deal for the service than in making you pay a set price. We are prepared to negotiate when it comes to buying a house or a new car, where we wouldn't dream of paying the asking price, but when it comes to retail shopping, we think that the price on the tag is the final price, and we wouldn't consider negotiating over the price of a coat or skirt. Think again. Depending on where you are and who you're dealing with, you can probably get an additional 10 percent off just for the asking. And if you don't ask, you'll never know.

Tap into your Inner Bargainer. If you've never asked for a discount in your life, that first request can be hard. But guess what? People who do commercial transactions get asked all the time. They're not going to think twice about you and your request. It's all in a day's work to them. You may feel like it's a bigger deal, until you ask for the first time, get your discount, and realize it's nothing but money back in your pocket. So open your mouth and take a stand: "Can you do any better on that rate?" "Is there a lower-priced option?" "Would you be willing to cut your commission?"

Be nice about it. Even though the person you're asking doesn't mind at all if you ask, you've got a better chance at success—and a better chance for a deeper discount—if you ask politely. Even though nobody *minds* giving you a discount, they don't *have* to give you one, either, so if you make the transaction pleasant, you might find the person taking your credit card will do a better deal for you if they've enjoyed dealing with you.

Don't forget about cold, hard cash. Cash is almost always good for a percentage off, and many people find it easier to ask for a discount when using it. There are no residual credit card fees for the merchant, and they can do what they like with cash in hand. If you're new to bargaining, you may find a good place to start is with this classic line: "Can I have a better price if I pay cash?"

Early Bird Secret

Take 10 Off the Top!

Ten percent is the standard amount that any employee will have the ability to take off of a bill without getting additional authorization, so don't expect to go too much higher on a normal transaction. If you're somewhere that the employee is just minding the store and running the cash register, such as a chain restaurant or a mini-mart, for example, then those employees have probably never even been asked for a discount and will think they do not have the authority to give you one. But if you're somewhere where you're dealing with the owner or manager—a small clothing store, a café, or a garage, say—you can likely have 10 percent off just for asking, whether or not you're a senior!

Don't bargain for stuff you don't need. When you start asking for discounts and find that you're racking up savings right and left, you may also find that the practice is addictive. "I got 5 percent off here, 10 percent off there, and a whopping 25 percent off over there!" It's like discovering a secret that was hiding in plain sight but one that hardly anyone else can see. However, you have to curb your impulse if it's simply making you shop more to exercise your newfound negotiating powers. There are no savings in that. Like a comic-book superhero, be sure to use your powers for good—which means scoring discounts only on the stuff you truly want and need.

Always take your due. In addition to asking for special discounts, never overlook anything that was already yours to begin with. There are dozens more subgroups of Americans in addition to senior citizens who are entitled to special consideration. Money off for being a veteran? I was, indeed, in the armed services. Special discounts for firefighters, clergy, police, schoolteachers, nonprofit workers, or municipal employees? Here's my ID.

Free entry for those with disabilities? Yes, thank you. If you're a member, either active or retired, of a special group that America seeks to reward or honor through special offers or discounts, proudly claim the rights that are your due and that are offered with open hearts and hands. You can find out about special offers through professional organizations and special-interest groups that support your profession or status.

Did You Know?

It Pays to Be Carded! You might think you'll be offended if someone offers you a senior discount when you totally don't look like a senior. But you'll likely be far more frustrated and annoyed if you go to the trouble of asking for a senior discount and can't get it because the person doesn't believe you! Be sure to travel with the ID required to take full advantage of any discounts you can get. Whether it's your driving license, your AARP membership card, your AAA card, or any other senior program that you've signed up for, don't get caught out without your little piece of paper that may be your key to senior savings.

Stay one step ahead. Even when the economy feels stable, things change all the time, and in a period of rising inflation or economic downturn, they change even faster. You can stay informed about the big stuff—tax breaks, write-offs, federal benefits—by reading the papers, listening to the news, talking to tax professionals, or inquiring about federal programs directly through the government. Nobody can stay on top of everything all the time, but you owe it to yourself to figure out what you care about and pursue it. Does your tax bill feel out of whack? Read about getting free assistance through the AARP on page 246. Are you tired of paying full-price for ball game tickets, but you love Major League Baseball? Find out how to search for Senior Discount Days hosted by your favorite team on page 138. Are you distressed by your skyrocketing energy bills and want to know what all the fuss is about with new energy-saving lightbulbs? Check out terrific sources of info on federally mandated power saving tips on page 74. The help you need and savings you probably never considered are just waiting for you.

Use your noggin. A little common sense can go a long way toward cutting your spending and saving you money, with or without a special senior discount. Clipping coupons, for example, is a big waste of time and money if you're saving 50 cents on a major national brand when you could have bought the store brand for $2.50 less in the first place. And ordering the three-course lunch special that comes with a free drink is a waste if all you really wanted for lunch that day was a sandwich and a glass of water. Learn to see through the hype to find what the special offer really is and what's in it for you. Don't be swayed by promises of saving a certain amount on an item when you didn't necessarily want that item anyway.

Take a chance. Be willing to take a chance on a big payoff when it makes sense. For example, why pay for all the coverage offered on a rental car if one of your credit cards offers that extra coverage automatically, as so many cards do? If you've had a lifetime of safe driving and you don't do much driving besides the grocery store and church on Sunday, you're probably a safe bet to take a higher deductible on your car insurance. Similarly, if your basement has never flooded and you don't have any ominous trees leaning over your eaves, you're a good candidate to take a higher deductible on your homeowner's insurance, with the payoff of big annual savings in exchange for assuming more of the risk.

Get creative. Don't just take what's offered, and don't just ask for a discount and wait to see what you get. Come up with an idea that helps the service provider help you. Your doctor, for example, may be able to open her sample cabinet and supply you with two weeks' worth of the high-priced antibiotic she's just prescribed—if you ask. Finding the price of beef too high for comfort? See if an area farmer can provide you with a butchered cow to share with a handful of friends who have big freezers. You'll get good local meat for a fraction of the supermarket price. Is the price of gas too high for you to make your monthly trip to the doctor without worry? Ask the receptionist at the doctor's office to help you put together a carpool with patients who live near you, so that two or three of you could make appointments for the same morning and all drive together. It saves money for everyone, it's sociable, and, if you need any more convincing, it decreases your carbon footprint and is good for the planet!

Get thee to the Internet! If you haven't done so already, it's time to face up to the fact: we're living in an Internet world, and if you're not online, you're simply not getting the best deals possible. Many airlines, for example, offer Internet-only fares that are significantly cheaper than anything you can get by booking through a human being on their toll-free reservations lines. In fact, generally, most airlines will tell you that they can't offer you that price over the phone, even if you call and say you saw or heard about it at their Web site.

Let people help you. Always take advantage of an offer of help or a freebie. If your doctor says, "Don't fill that prescription—I have a handful of samples for you," or if your neighbor says, "I'm driving to the grocery store—want to come along, or is there anything I can pick up for you?" then all you have to do is say, "Yes, thank you." If the checkout girl at the grocery store says, "Hey, did you know that we have a senior discount?" she's not trying to offend you (or say that it's time you touched up your grays). Take all offers in the spirit in which they're made, and don't assume anything other than kindness or good nature.

Use both old and new classifieds. You can read the classified ads in newspapers, both in hard copy and online, so there's nothing to limit your search for the best possible price, whether you're in the market for airline tickets or a new car. And if you're not part of the phenomenon that is Craigslist, you should be. Once a tiny site of free ad listings based in California, it's now the go-to site worldwide for classified listings with sites for every major city in the United States and around the world. Looking for an apartment to rent when you go to a wedding in Seattle? Want to find a babysitter for your grandkids at the same time? Need a roofer to fix that leaky spot in the eaves? You can find everything at the listing for your city at www.craigslist.org.

Comparison shop. Even if it seems like the deal of the century, it's always worth doing a little comparison shopping before you buy. It's up to you to use the Internet or the phone, but check to find out what price the competition is offering before you buy anything big, whether it's a lawn mower or a life insurance policy.

Keep your eyes peeled for deals. Special offers are all around, as retailers and service providers seek to draw in new customers. Whether it's a discount aimed at seniors or not, there's no reason you shouldn't take full advantage! Ben & Jerry's ice cream shops, for example, hold a free cone day every year, when you can enjoy a luscious scoop on the house. Starbucks recently took out ads in local papers that included a card that entitled the bearer to a free iced coffee every Wednesday for six weeks. Read the papers, listen to the news, and enjoy everything that's offered!

Let Uncle Sam extend a helping hand. Your tax money goes toward countless free services that are available to all citizens simply for the asking, from tax help to tips on cutting your energy costs. There are countless services available to specific groups, from seniors to veterans to the disabled, and you've already paid for your share through your annual income

Ka-Ching!

Easy Ways to Get Started on the Internet

Don't have a computer? Worried about getting started? Here are some ways to go online for less.

Ask for a hand-me-down. Your son or daughter or one of your grandchildren has probably recently upgraded one of their computers, and you should be first in line to get the old computer. As prices have come down on new computers and laptops and as the technology changes so quickly, people have begun to upgrade more frequently. That castoff might be the perfect thing for you to surf the Internet and send e-mail.

Get an inexpensive laptop. Nowadays, you can buy a new laptop for several hundred dollars, complete with software installed, which will likely include a step-by-step online tutorial on how to use it. There's no excuse!

Use the library. Nearly all public libraries in the United States now have public computers. At busy branches, you may have to register for a time slot, but you can spend your hour online surfing for good deals for that upcoming trip to Mexico or finding the lowest price prescription drugs.

Get connected with a high-speed package. If you've got cable TV, you're just clicks away from having a high-speed Internet connection. "Dial-up," the kind of connection that goes through your phone line, is so slow to download information that many Web sites won't even work through dial-up anymore. Ask your cable provider if it has any special offers to bundle high-speed

service along with your regular cable service—and then ask if it has a senior discount as well!

Take a tutorial. Get moving fast with one of the excellent free Web sites that focus on teaching seniors how to use computers and the Internet as quickly and easily as possible, without assuming that you already understand some aspects, the way your teenage grandson might! Here's a list of terrific sites, many written by seniors for seniors:

www.seniorsguide
tocomputers.com

www.computers
forretirees.com

www.seniornet.org (Click on "E-Learning" and "Online Courses.")

tax. Be sure to get your benefits, too. A good place to start is at the main Web portal for the U.S. government, www.usa.gov, which links you to every single Web page administered by the federal government.

Early Bird Secret

Get Online for Less

Your cable company's high-speed access is fast and simple to set up, but even with a special introductory offer, you'll still pay anywhere from $20 to $30 a month, possibly more with taxes and fees. Instead, consider a free or discount high-speed provider. Few of these services are completely free, but some still offer free connection for a limited number of hours, typically 10 hours a month. That may be great for you to get started, but once you figure out how to use the Web to your advantage, you may want to upgrade. These services are still very inexpensive by comparison, generally no more than $20 a month, for unlimited Internet access as well as full technical support. Check out these reliable providers and get online the cheap way!

www.juno.com   www.mfire.com   www.arcZip.com

Go local. Although there are tons of national discounts just waiting to help you save money as a senior, from national clothing stores, restaurants, and more, the real savings might be hiding in your region. Local and state-wide senior discounts can be a real seam of gold to mine, from towns that focus on making themselves amenable to seniors to states, such as Ohio, that pay more than lip-service to the idea of aid and respect for their senior citizens. While it's comforting and easy to know, for example, that Perkins will always have the same (or similar) Senior Menu from restaurant to restaurant, wherever you go, you can find better and deeper discounts if you push outside the box a bit and ask about senior benefits at your local mom-and-pop stores and restaurants. They may even cook up a senior discount on the spot just for you!

Skirting Scams and Dubious Deals

While you're out there looking for your senior discounts, other, much more insidious operators, are out there looking for you—to separate you from as much of your money as possible. One study says that the average amount a senior loses in a telemarketing scam is as much as $7,000! You'd have to save a lot of money at the grocery store to make up for that kind of loss out of your nest egg. It's crucial throughout life to avoid scams and scurrilous offers, to dodge fakes and protect yourself from tricksters and con artists, but it's a particular problem that plagues seniors. Anyone can get taken in—and a lot of people do. But the fact is that a lot of scam artists tend to target seniors for a variety of reasons, not least being that we're more likely to politely hear them out. You need to keep your head on your shoulders and pay attention when you're the person writing the check or handing over the credit card or bank account info.

Protect yourself with a little bit of care and a modicum of suspicion. Check out these tips for avoiding cons and scams, and take them to heart when navigating the sometimes deep waters of commercial transactions.

10 Secrets to Shielding Yourself (and Your Money) from Con Artists

Although it may seem there are pitfalls around every corner, in fact you can protect yourself pretty easily by taking some standard precautions and sticking to them.

1. Ignore junk mail. Just throw it in the trash. The likelihood is practically nil that there is some kind of offer in unsolicited mail that will benefit you instead of the mailer.

2. Buy a shredder. Shred and tear up all documents containing personal or banking information before you dispose of them. It's not very likely that someone will go through your trash—but if they do, why hand them your identity?

3. Create a trustee or assign a power of attorney. Although this person can be a trusted family friend or family member, you can also have it be a financial adviser or attorney—in other words, a disinterested party. The benefit is that, as you get older, you won't find yourself writing a check for $50,000 from your life savings to some scurrilous operator when you need that money for your medical bills! Your trustee will be able to step in and help prevent it. You may feel that you're giving up a certain measure of control, but in fact it's about protecting yourself and your assets to the best of your abilities.

4. Don't have checks mailed to your home. If you get regular payments, be it Social Security, dividends, royalties, or whatever, have them deposited directly into your bank account whenever possible.

5. Get a Medicare-approved list of drug discounters. You should not buy a drug discount card from a telemarketer, and when you buy the card, you should not need to provide your personal financial information—Medicare already has access to it! If you're asked for personal financials, run the other way, or call Medicare to check on the company's record, at 1-800-MEDICARE (800-633-4227).

6. For home repairs, get referrals. If you need work done on your house, ask friends for referrals to a reputable contractor. Do not hire the guy who knocks on your front door and asks whether you need a new roof or a new driveway surface. If you *do* need these things, you should go looking for the worker, not the other way around. You can ask someone who knocks on your door for a business card and tell that person you want to think about it first. If you do want to use that person's services, contact your local Better Business Bureau first. And never pay more than half of the fee up front—if you do lose money, you won't lose the entire amount.

7. The government does *not* call to drum up business. If someone calls you offering a government grant for repairs on your house, for example, and then asks for a processing fee to give you the grant money, do *not* give them your bank account number. This is a particularly tricky scam because it all sounds very official and correct, right up to the moment you give the caller your personal info. There are indeed government grants for home repair for seniors, but you need to go looking for them by calling your local housing authority and asking for further information. The U.S. government has a lot of programs out there to help you, but they do not have the resources to call and offer you the help—and if they do, it will never come with a fee. You can contact www.grants.gov, the federal clearinghouse for government grants, or call them at 1-800-518-4726 to check the authenticity of the offer.

Did You Know?

Reporting Fraud and Scams There are a number of authorities who want to hear if you've been scammed or approached by a con artist. If someone has come to your home and physically threatened or frightened you, always start by calling the local police or dialing 911. For less urgent matters where your life or health is not endangered, try these:

Federal Trade Commission, www.ftc.gov

National Consumers League's Fraud Center, www.fraud.org

U.S. Department of Justice, www.usdoj.gov/criminal/fraud

8. Have scam, will travel. Be wary of travel clubs that promise you special rates and discounts in exchange for steep annual fees. Why pay an organization thousands of dollars a year to get room rates that you can probably find for less on the Internet? When you agree to accept something, such as a night at a resort, in exchange for listening to a sales pitch, the person doing the pitching is going to be *extremely* persuasive, and will press on your feeling of obligation, thanks to whatever you got: free dinner, hotel, or show tickets, for example. Accepting anything in exchange for listening to a sales pitch does *not* obligate you to buy whatever service is offered. Refuse to sign a contract then and there.

9. Be sure your bills are real. Suppose you receive a notice that your subscription to *Gourmet* is nearly up. You reach for your checkbook, but then think, "Wait, didn't I just pay that?" Check the return address on the bill, which is probably something like, "National Magazine Renewal Service." These scammers make money by collecting from a huge range of victims, who don't balk at writing small amounts for magazines that will never arrive. Many of us are so careless in our bookkeeping that we never even notice and might pay our actual *Gourmet* bill again when the real thing arrives nine or 10 months later. If you want to renew a magazine, check your subscription label or call customer service and find out when it's actually due—and then write your check *only* to the magazine, not to anyone else.

10. Stop and think before you act. The world might seem to be moving quickly, but there's *always* time to stop and think. Ask that the request be put in writing or tell the caller you can't write a check or give out info without the okay of your trustee (even if you don't have one!)—that will generally be enough to end a solicitation. If you do want to pursue the offer, check with the Better Business Bureau or the National Consumer League's Fraud Center. And you can always check the Web at www.snopes.com, a wonderful site that debunks myths, scams, and urban legends right and left, with frequent updates and authoritative research.

Keep Your Privacy Private

The Privacy Rights Clearinghouse is a nonprofit organization that provides a huge range of information on protecting your privacy, from avoiding identity theft to dealing with cell phone abuse. Here's the place to find out exactly what rights you have to privacy when it comes to your medical records or background checks in the workplace. You can also find out how junk mailers get your name and address and how to get off their lists—including how to stop getting junk mail in the name of a deceased loved one. Visit its Web site at www.privacyrights.org.

Simple Ways to Dump Those Pesky Telemarketers

It is estimated that more than half of the victims of telemarketing fraud are over 50. The sad truth is that dishonest telemarketers target seniors for a variety of reasons, not least being that basic courtesy for many seniors makes it hard for them to hang up and impossible for them to accept that the helpful-sounding person at the other end of the line might wish them harm. As your own parents may have said long ago, "There's no free lunch." There are great discounts and bargains, but hardly anything that's just being handed to you for free, especially when it sounds too good to be true. But there are a number of ways to tell whether the call is a scam and the caller is a con artist, and, more important, ways to avoid these calls altogether.

Free things don't cost money. If a caller tells you that you've won a free gift and that all you have to do is pay taxes or shipping or a "claim fee," it's a scam. Never send money to claim a prize or pay a tax or any other reason. Most telemarketing fraud is in the field of prize winning and investments, with "contests" and "sweepstakes" making up a major part of it. Remember that it is illegal in the United States to charge people a fee to enter a contest or claim a prize.

If you have to make a decision *now*, say "No." When a caller rushes you and says that you have to accept the offer right away or it will be rescinded, that's your cue to let it go. There simply are no deals that have to be done in that time frame. If they called you, not the other way around, what's the rush? The only person who's in a hurry is the caller. Even legitimate merchants like to sew up deals quickly, but it's fraudulent telemarketers who insist upon it.

Tell the caller to put it in the mail. A list of terms and conditions reeled off at speed is no way to close a contract. Whatever the rush, whatever the terms, tell them to send the offer to you in the mail if you have any actual interest in it—but keep in mind all the other warnings here when it comes! Nice-looking letterhead is easy to fake, so that's no indication of legitimacy.

Let Your Fingers Do the Walking

There's one foolproof way to know whether the person on the other end of the line is making you a legitimate offer for a service or product that you actually want and need. *Did you look them up in the phone book and dial the call?* If not, all other calls can fall by the wayside. If you really needed or wanted the product or service, you would have gone looking for it yourself and made the call to a reliable purveyor. Anybody calling you is just trying to sell you something that you probably don't need, even if the call is "real."

Don't share. Ever. Never give out personal information to someone who calls you, including your Social Security number or your credit card or bank account numbers.

Have a standard refusal, say it, and hang up. Use whatever phrase you like, but repeat it to all callers, and include the request that they not call again—otherwise you get people saying things like, "I'll call again later." Here's a very useful phrase that's polite and effective: "I'm sorry, this house does not accept solicitation phone calls. Please take my name off your list and do not call this number again." The last sentence is the most important part, and you can say simply that, "Please take my name off your list and do not call back." Practice saying it, keep it on a piece of paper on the wall by the phone to read it aloud if necessary, and then *hang up.*

They're not just making a living. Don't assume that the caller is just someone working a tough job and trying to make a living by selling something on the phone—even if that's what the person tells you! Anyone who cajoles, threatens, pleads, or offers to work out a special price or deal "just for you" (and tries to get your bank account or credit card number) is not just making a living. Is this how you earned your money, or how your parents earned a living before you? Probably not. Protect yourself and your money and hang up.

Put yourself on the Do Not Call Registry. You won't even need most of these defensive measures if you put all your phone numbers, including your cell, on the National Do Not Call Registry. Call 1-888-382-1222 from your home phone to register it automatically, or register your home and cell phone numbers at www.donotcall.gov. After about a month, you should notice a significant reduction in the number of calls you receive, although you may still receive calls from legitimate charities, political organizations, telephone surveyors, and companies with which you have an existing relationship. The rules still apply, though! If you want to donate, ask for the request in writing, or offer your stock rejection phrase.

Delicious Food Savings for Seniors

Big Savings on Dining Out, Cooking In, and Eating Great!

Super Savings at Supermarkets

To be clear, you don't have to be over 50 to want (or get) a great deal on basic necessities—but the fact is that some of the best deals at supermarkets are *only* available to seniors. Many national and regional supermarket chains offer discounts on certain days of the week, and all you have to do is be sure to shop that day rather than another. Since you have the freedom to shop when you like, be the first in line to rack up the savings!

Note: The sample list below was accurate at time of printing, but age requirements, percentage of discount, and other restrictions can vary from store to store, even within the same chain of supermarkets, so be sure to get the specifics from the store where you shop.

A&P Supermarket If you have an A&P Club Card and you're 60 or above, upgrade to a Live Better Wellness Club Card and get a 15 percent discount on fruits and vegetables, a 25 percent discount on healthcare products, plus a 10 percent Senior Citizen Prescription and Family Pet Prescription discount. Details at www.apsupermarket.com.

Bi-Lo Once you register for a Bi-Lo Bonus Card, if you're 60 or older, every Wednesday you can get the Senior Bonus program, which means an additional 5 percent savings. Visit www.bi-lo.com.

Earth Fare This chain of grocery stores in North Carolina, South Carolina, Georgia, and Tennessee offers 5 percent off to seniors 60 and older everday. To find locations, visit www.earthfare.com.

Foodland Some Foodland stores offer a senior discount of 5 percent one day a week. The day of the discount, discount amount, and age requirement varies for each store. Call your local branch for specifics. Find locations and phone numbers at www.foodlandstores.com.

Fry's If you register for Fry's VIP savings card (registration is free) and you're 55 or older, you can save 10 percent on your food bill (less VIP savings, taxes, and coupons) the first Wednesday of every month. Register by visiting www.frysfood.com.

Kroger The first Wednesday of each month, seniors 60 and older receive a 10 percent discount off total purchases, but you have to go to Customer Service to get it rather than having the discount rung up when you pay. You must have a KrogerPlus shopping card and ID. Get details at www.kroger.com.

Ralphs You can get a Ralph's rewards card that lets you save 20 percent on some store brands. You can also save an extra $1 after accumulating $10 in spending on Ralphs private label products. Get details at www.ralphs.com.

Shop 'n Save The day of the week varies according to location, but most offer a 10 percent discount to seniors once a week. Visit www.shopnsave.com.

ShopRite If you're 55 or older, you can get a discount off your purchases at your local ShopRite. The amount of the discount and day of the week it applies varies with each individual store, so be sure to check in advance. You can find your nearest ShopRite by visiting www.shoprite.com.

Wegmans Wegmans wins when it comes to the biggest effort to accommodate seniors among grocery chains: They send Medical Motors buses with wheelchair access to 70 senior-subsidized housing complexes, and they take the residents for free to a Wegmans store to shop. Note: This offer is only open to seniors who live in government-subsidized housing. Find out more at www.wegmans.com.

25 Grocery Items Never to Buy Again

Let's face it: We'll probably never stop shopping in a grocery store for many reasons, nor should we. We just have to be smarter and savvier about it, and vow to never, ever buy certain prepackaged items again because, simply, we don't have to. Why spend when we don't have to? So shelve those mixes and say good-bye to canned broth, once and for all!

1. Gravy Mixes

Got flour? Some butter? Canned or homemade broth? We thought so. If you have these three pantry ingredients, you've got the makings for gravy that will take you from Thanksgiving to July Fourth and every day in between. Here's an easy version that you can modify to your heart's content (try a handful of mushrooms or a splash of wine).

The Gravy Train Gravy

Makes about 2 cups

4 tablespoons unsalted butter
1/4 cup all-purpose flour
2 cups turkey, chicken, or beef broth (low-sodium if using packaged)
1/4 teaspoon salt (or to taste)

1 In a medium saucepan, melt the butter over medium heat and add the flour, whisking until a smooth paste is formed.

2 Continue cooking until the mixture browns to a light toasty color, about 3–5 minutes. Reduce the heat to low and slowly add broth, whisking constantly. Once the liquid is incorporated (about 2 minutes), turn the heat back to medium, and bring to a slow boil until thickened.

3 Taste and adjust for seasoning if necessary. Refrigerate leftovers for 3–4 days or freeze gravy within 24 hours of making it for up to one month.

Modifications: Replace 1/4 of the liquid with dry white wine; add sautéed mushrooms; add oregano, basil, rosemary or sage; adding a tablespoon of sherry at the end gives a sweet, sophisticated punch; likewise, a bit of cream—just a tablespoon—adds decadence and makes this truly "special sauce."

2. Canned, Bottled, or Boxed Soup Stocks

Sure, the canned or boxed stuff is easy, and who doesn't like easy? But if you've bought a chicken for $6, you can make a virtual vat of homemade stock from the leftover carcass (and those veggies and herbs that might be lurking in your crisper) and save yourself a lot of dough in the long run. Once made (usually from stuff that you'd just throw away), stocks freeze well, so make them when you have the ingredients and the time, and you'll never run out. Here's our favorite chicken stock recipe (which can also be made with a turkey carcass, but then it would be turkey stock):

Move-Over-Martha Chicken Stock

Makes about 5 quarts

Carcass, bones, and any attached meat from one 4-pound chicken
1 onion, peeled and quartered
1 large carrot, peeled and cut into 2-inch chunks
1 celery stalk, cut into 1-inch chunks
1 bay leaf
1 parsley sprig
1 thyme sprig

8 whole black peppercorns

1/2 teaspoon salt

1   In a large soup pot over medium-high heat, combine chicken carcass, onion, carrot, and celery. Add 7 cups of cool water, and bring to a boil. Skim off foam and discard.

2   Add bay leaf, parsley, thyme, peppercorns, and salt. Reduce heat, cover, and simmer for 2 hours.

3   Strain stock through a fine mesh sieve into a heatproof bowl. Let cool completely, then refrigerate until cold, and remove fat from surface. Use within 3 days or freeze and use within 3 months.

Freeze this stock in 1-cup containers or ice cube trays for a quick hit of flavor in everything from soups to stews.

3. Packaged Bread Crumbs and Stuffing Mixes

How many "heels" of old bread do you toss out or give to the birds? If you saved them and grated them in a food processor or blender, you would never run out of fresh bread crumbs; if you cubed, tossed them with dried herbs, and toasted them, you'd never run out of stuffing. Freeze crumbs, cubes, and slices in storage bags for up to 6 months.

Early Bird Secret

Stale Bread Reborn

Like croutons on your salad? If you like bread, you'll never have to buy them again. Bread of any kind can be sliced and toasted for croutons or as a surface for any kind of dip or topping.

4. Commercial Tomato-Based Pasta Sauces

Forget about premade pasta sauces, even if they are supposedly made by Butch Cassidy. They can be very expensive because you're paying extra for the bottle. Make your own sauces from inexpensive canned crushed tomatoes or, in late summer, fresh tomatoes, when they're plentiful and CHEAP!

Even better: *you* control the amount of salt, pepper, herbs, and other seasonings that go inside. Here's a quick, simple, and frugal version:

Totally Terrific Tomato Sauce

Makes about 2–3 quarts

2 tablespoons extra-virgin olive oil
2 cloves garlic, peeled and minced
1 medium onion, peeled and diced
2 celery stalks, diced
2 carrots, peeled and diced
2 cans (28 ounces each) crushed tomatoes
Salt and pepper, to taste
Optional: red pepper flakes, dried basil, dried oregano

1 Heat the olive oil in a large soup pot set over medium-high heat. Add the garlic, onion, celery, and carrots, and cook until soft, about 8 minutes, stirring frequently to keep them from sticking to the pan.

2 Add the tomatoes and stir to blend well. Bring to a boil, and immediately lower heat to slow simmer. Cover and continue to cook for 30 minutes, stirring frequently, seasoning to taste with salt and pepper. Add red pepper flakes, basil, and/or oregano as desired. Use within 5 days, or freeze in individual 1-cup containers.

5. Meat and Pasta Helpers

These convenient boxes filled with dried pasta and some flavorings are basically a very expensive way to buy macaroni, whether it's a blend to add to hamburger or tuna, or good old boxed mac and cheese. Bottom line: You're paying between $1.79 and $2.79 for a few ounces of pasta and fake cheese or freeze-dried herbs and spices. On the other hand, 16 ounces of pasta costs about 99 cents. You can mix up your own ground beef, herbs, pasta, and tomato sauce just as easily—and it will taste better, too!

6. Bottled Salad Dressing

The cheap stuff tastes like motor oil so that's no bargain. And the expensive stuff—at $5 and up—can be matched by your own (very frugal) culinary magic at home. Here's how:

Fabulous and Frugal Italian Dressing

Makes about 1/2 a cup

1/2 teaspoon Dijon mustard
2 tablespoons vinegar (red or white wine)
1/3 cup olive oil
Pinch of sugar, to taste
Optional: snipped chives, fresh or dried parsley, fresh or dried tarragon

1 Place the mustard in a medium-size bowl and add the vinegar. Whisk well.

2 Drizzle in the olive oil in a steady stream, whisking to incorporate.

3 Add sugar, to taste, and optional herbs. Pour into a glass jar, seal, and refrigerate for up to 4 days. Shake well to reincorporate ingredients.

Fabulous and Frugal Ranch Dressing

Makes about 1 1/2 cups

1/2 cup mayonnaise
1/2 cup sour cream
2 tablespoons lemon juice
2 tablespoons each chopped fresh parsley and scallion
1 clove garlic, minced
1/2 teaspoon black pepper

Combine all ingredients in a small bowl. Pour into a small glass jar and store for up to 4 days. Shake well before serving.

7. Boxed Rice Entrée or Side Dish Mixes

These consist of two inexpensive ingredients—rice and salt—yet they're priced way beyond either ingredient sold individually. Sure, there are a few flavorings included, but they're probably ones you have in your pantry already.

Buy a bag of rice, measure out what you need, add your own herbs and other seasonings, and cook the rice according to package directions.

The Manager's Special

In addition to the sales advertised in the weekly flyer, supermarkets very often have unadvertised "Manager's Specials"—sales that often occur when the supermarket has an overstock of perishable items such as produce, dairy, bakery, meat, poultry, or seafood. Savings can range from 50 percent to 80 percent off, depending on the item. Inquire at your store's service desk to see if there are any "Manager's Specials" that day or week. These items will be clearly marked on the shelves and, in the case of meat, poultry, and fresh seafood, tagged on the item itself. You may get lucky and find half a turkey breast for $2 (for the entire thing, not "per pound"), and a 3-pound pork roast for $3.

8. Premade Frozen Noodle Side Dishes

No matter how you carefully you prepare these "according to package directions," the noodles and veggies will still come out mushy, because pasta wasn't meant to be cooked in its sauce, and precooked veggies just get softer with every reheating. Again, you have all the items in your pantry to make a perfectly delicious side dish of, say, Pasta Alfredo (okay, you may have to buy fresh Parmesan cheese), or chicken with pasta in cream sauce.

9. Granola Bars

These expensive, calorie-and-sugar laden bars are stacked at the checkout counter because they depend on impulse buyers who grab them thinking they are more wholesome than a candy bar. (They're not.) If you need a quick boost, enjoy a piece of fruit, a hard-boiled egg, a cup of yogurt, or a small handful of nuts.

10. Flavored Water

Why pay a premium price for tap water or spring water with a shot of lemon or orange juice—and food coloring—when you can concoct your own flavors at home? Simply add a tablespoon of cranberry, orange, lemon, or lime juice to seven ounces of cold water, and you've got yourself a refreshing, low-cal thirst-quencher.

11. *Powdered Iced Tea Mixes or Prepared Flavored Iced Tea*

Do the math: If you buy a bottle of packaged iced tea twice a day, every day, at $2 a bottle, you've spent $28 a week (or $112 a month, or $1,344 a year!) on what you can make at home for just pennies. Here's how:

Summertime Anytime Iced Tea

Makes 32 ounces, or 8 to 10 large glasses of tea

About 32 ounces of *fresh cold* **water**

8 bags of black tea or 10 bags of herbal, green, or white tea, or a combination of 10 black and herbals bags

Ice cubes

Optional: Granulated sugar or other sweetener such as fruit juice, and lemon, orange, or lime slices

1 Place tea bags in a *heatproof* glass or ceramic pitcher large enough to hold 32 ounces of water. Bring water to a rapid boil, and pour over the bags in the pitcher. Allow the tea to steep for about 20 minutes, then remove bags with a slotted spoon.

2 Cover and chill for at least an hour and a half or overnight. To serve, pour in an ice-filled glass. Stir in a teaspoon of sugar (or to taste) if you like your tea sweet. Add citrus slices for another layer of flavor. (Note: If you include fruit juice, you will likely not have to use additional sugar or other sweetener.)

12. *"Gourmet" Frozen Vegetables in Sauce*

Sure, you can buy an eight-ounce package of peas in "herbed butter sauce." But why do so when you can make your own? Just cook fresh or frozen peas, add a pat of butter and a sprinkle of herbs you already have on hand.

13. Spice Mixes

Spice mixes like grill seasoning and rib rubs might seem like a good buy because they contain a lot of spices that you would otherwise have to buy individually. Right? Wrong! Look in your pantry, and you'll likely find the same ingredients, so why not make your own like we do? Stored in an airtight container in a cool part of the kitchen, these babies will keep for up to 2 months.

Mama Mia Italian Spice Rub

Makes about 1/2 cup

2 tablespoons dried basil
1 tablespoon dried oregano
1 tablespoon fennel seeds
1 tablespoon garlic powder
1/2 tablespoon salt

Mix all ingredients together in a small bowl, and spoon into an airtight container or jar. Label, and store in a cool, dark cupboard for up to 6 months.

Ooh-La-La French Spice Rub

Makes about 1/2 cup

2 tablespoons dried parsley
1 tablespoon dried lavender
1 tablespoon fennel seeds
1 tablespoon thyme
1/2 tablespoon salt

Mix all ingredients together in a small bowl, and spoon into an airtight container or jar. Label, and store in a cool, dark cupboard for up to 6 months.

5 Things

Not to Buy in a Supermarket

We love grocery stores. Their stock and trade is food—fresh, frozen, canned or prepared—and kitchen staples like paper towels and laundry detergent. But there are a whole host of other items that cost a premium in grocery stores because of the "convenience" factor. You can get them cheaper at a discount department or hardware store, dollar store, or drug store so leave the following items off your shopping list:

1. COOKWARE AND KITCHEN UTENSILS

It may be convenient to pick up a frying pan while you're buying your bacon, but you'll be paying much more than you ought to for it.

2. COSMETICS, TOILETRIES, AND PERSONAL CARE ITEMS

Keep rolling! It might save time to buy your lip-gloss, moisturizer, toothpaste, razor blades, and deodorant at the same time and place you're getting your food, but you'll be paying a premium price.

3. SMALL APPLIANCES

Why buy a toaster for $40 when you can buy the same toaster for $20 dollars at a discount house? The same theory applies to coffee makers, electric teakettles, and hot plates.

4. PARTY SUPPLIES

Okay, you can get your balloons, funny hats, place cards, candles, and name tags in the grocery store. But you could pay a whole lot less getting them in bulk at a party supply store.

5. BATTERIES, LIGHTBULBS, EXTENSION CORDS

Again, these are pricey specialty items at the grocery store, but cheap impulse buys at a discount hardware, department, or dollar store!

All-American Barbecue Dry Rub

Makes about 1/2 cup

1 tablespoon coarse salt
2 tablespoons dark brown sugar
1 tablespoon paprika
1/2 teaspoon cayenne pepper
1/2 tablespoon garlic powder

Mix all ingredients together in a small bowl, and spoon into an airtight container or jar. Label, and store in a cool, dark cupboard for up to 6 months.

14. Premium Frozen Fruit Bars

At more than $2 per bar, frozen "all fruit" or "fruit and juice" bars may not be rich in calories, but they are certainly rich in price. Make your own at home—and get the flavors you want. The only equipment you need is a blender, clean yogurt cups, and pop sticks or wooden skewers.

Save-ery Fruit Pops

Makes 4 pops

2 cups cut-up fruit (strawberries, pitted peaches, nectarines, melon, pitted cherries, pitted plums, pitted apricots)
1 tablespoon sugar or the equivalent amount of your favorite replacement sweetener (optional, depending on sweetness of fruit)
1 teaspoon fresh lemon or lime juice
Water

1 Place the fruit, sweetener if using, and lemon or lime juice in a blender. Cover and blend until smooth. Add 1–2 tablespoons water, if necessary, to create a thick "slush."

2 Pour evenly into 4 yogurt cups or a Popsicle mold. Insert sticks. Freeze until solid.

15. Cocktail Mixes

Premade bottled cocktail mixes (Just add gin! Just add vodka! Just add rum!) are another waste of money because you end up paying for a lot of *water* (!), sugar, and artificial ingredients. It's just as easy and cheaper to make your own drinks "from scratch" with your own fresh fruit juice, sugar, and water.

16. Buttermilk

It's tangy, it's low-fat, and a little bit of it will give zip to all sorts of baked dishes. Why buy an extra grocery item when you can make it yourself? It's simple!

Better than Bought Buttermilk

Makes about 1 cup

1 tablespoon white vinegar or lemon juice
1 cup milk (preferably whole)

Combine vinegar with milk and let stand for 5 minutes before using it (which you should do immediately).

17. Brown Sugar

The more people we asked, the more our suspicions were confirmed: How many of you have an ancient box of brown sugar from a long-ago presidential administration (Kennedy? Carter?) kicking around your pantry, and it's rock hard. Don't chisel away at it; make your own instead with two basic pantry ingredients, and never buy it again. Ever. (Meanwhile, you can still use that rock-hard block if you microwave it in the bag for 1–2 minutes on high, squeezing and checking it frequently until it's soft enough to use.)

Even Better Brown Sugar

Makes about 1 cup

1 cup white granulated sugar
2 tablespoons molasses

Using a fork, combine the sugar and molasses until blended completely. For dark brown sugar, use blackstrap molasses; for light brown sugar, use lighter molasses. Store in an airtight resealable bag in a cool, dark location.

18. Canned Cake Frosting

Ick. The cheap brands taste like petrochemicals, and the premium products are super-expensive. Frostings from scratch are simple and easy to make. Here's our favorite simple one:

Old-Fashioned Chocolate Frosting

Makes about 2 cups (enough to frost a 1-layer cake or a dozen cupcakes)

2 cups confectioners' sugar
1/2 cup unsweetened cocoa
1 stick unsalted butter, softened to room temperature
7-8 tablespoons whole milk
1 teaspoon vanilla extract
1 tablespoon brewed coffee (instant is fine)

Combine all ingredients in a medium bowl, and beat with an electric mixer or by hand until combined and spreadable. Use immediately or store in an airtight container in the refrigerator for up to 3 days.

2 Slippage

> "Hey, wasn't that cottage cheese?"
> "Wasn't this once a green pepper?"
> "We ate chili two nights running,
>   so let's just throw the rest away."

Sound familiar?

It's so common to throw out food that we rarely stop to consider that it's like standing on the front porch feeding dollar bills into the wind. "Slippage" is an economic term for the difference between the estimated costs of a transaction and what you actually pay. When it comes to food, "slippage" is when you buy bananas, eat three, and throw away two. Stop now and save big.

FIGURE OUT WHAT YOU USE FREQUENTLY AND BUY IT—AND ONLY IT—IN BULK.

Everyone knows their staples: cereal, coffee, toilet paper—anything your family always has on hand or might make a special trip to buy. These are the only things you should ever buy in bulk at wholesale stores or discount clubs.

MAKE A MEAL PLAN AND A GROCERY LIST—AND STICK TO THEM.

Your list can be definite while your meal plan is hazy. Say you know you're going out Friday and have something already for Monday but still need to cook Tuesday, Wednesday, and Thursday. Choosing the actual meat or vegetable or pasta can depend on what might be on special at the store, but you're still sticking to your list in terms of basic items to acquire.

19. Flavored Yogurt

Instead of spending money on pricey flavored yogurt, flavor your own plain yogurt with already-in-your-kitchen pantry items: fruit spread or jam, honey, maple syrup, a drop or two of vanilla extract, mashed bananas, walnuts… the possibilities are endless!

Did You Know?

You can save big by blending your own inexpensive, customized specialty sauces and dips, and you'll never look back. Here's how to get started:

1. Trick out a cup of plain yogurt with lemon juice, salt, pepper, and curry powder for an elegant dip for raw veggies.

2. Make honey mustard by mixing half honey, half mustard (either Dijon or spicy brown), and a dash of cider vinegar.

3. Homemade onion dip is fresh, easy, and preservative-free if you mix half sour cream, half mayo with some caramelized onions, chopped fresh parsley, Worcestershire, ground black pepper, and a dash of hot sauce.

20. Trail Mix

Our experts did a national price check and found that, on average, those little bags of candy-coated chocolate nuts and raisins cost about $10 a pound! Make your own for much, much less with a one-pound can of dry-roasted peanuts, a cup of raisins, a handful of almonds, another of candy-coated chocolate, and perhaps some other kind of dried fruit. Keep it in a plastic or glass container with a tight lid for up to three weeks.

21. Granola

Gourmet granola breakfast, especially organic brands, can also run in the $7 to $10 per pound range. If you love granola for breakfast (or as a snack to munch on during the day) make your own with good old-fashioned rolled oats.

Simply Grand Granola

Makes about 6 cups

1/2 cup vegetable, sunflower, or canola oil

1/3 cup honey or maple syrup

1/4 teaspoon salt

3/4 teaspoon cinnamon

1/3 cup skim milk

3/4 cup brown sugar

5 cups whole oats

Nonstick cooking spray

1/2 cup each of any of the following:

Unsalted slivered almonds

Unsalted chopped walnuts

Unsalted chopped cashews

Raisins

Shredded unsweetened coconut

Dried cranberries

Dried apricots, chopped

1 Preheat over to 375°F. Combine the first 6 ingredients in a large saucepan over medium heat until the sugar melts and the mixture is well blended. Remove from heat and add oats, and continue to mix well with a wooden spoon.

2 Spray 2 cookie sheets with nonstick cooking spray, and spread the granola mixture evenly on the sheets. Bake for about 15–20 minutes, checking every few minutes and stirring a few times for even browning and to prevent burning. Remove from the oven, and cool on sheets.

3 When the mixture has cooled completely, transfer it to a large bowl and add the nuts and dried fruits. Store in an airtight container for 3–4 weeks.

22. Canned Soup

Sure, they are convenient, but they are also expensive, not all that tasty, and often contain unhealthy amounts of salt. Make your own healthier, tastier soup in minutes with your homemade stock Add in some fresh veggies, beans, leftover chicken or beef, and freeze what you can't eat right away in portion-sized containers.

Early Bird Secret

We Can Get It for You Tomorrow

Supermarkets sell baked goods and produce that are just approaching or have slightly passed their sell-by dates at 50 percent off (or more) of the regular price. Don't buy baked goods that are rock-hard (unless you want stale bread to make stuffing, for instance) or fruit or vegetables that are badly blemished, and never buy badly dented cans or packages that have been opened—they could harbor bacteria. But with a little care, you can find some excellent buys, such a ripe cantaloupe for a third of the price of its younger cousin in the regular produce department.

23. Salad Kits

Washed and bagged greens can be a time-saver, but they're three and four times more expensive than a head of lettuce. Even more expensive, however, are "salad kits," where you get some greens, a small bag of dressing, and a small bag of croutons. Skip these—you already have the ingredients for croutons (toasted or fried bread) and salad dressing (mayonnaise, vinegar, oil, and mustard, plus whatever herbs you like) at home.

24. Preformed Meat Patties

Frozen burgers—beef or otherwise—are more expensive than buying the ground meat in bulk and making patties yourself. (We timed it—it takes less than 10 seconds to form a flat circle and throw it on the grill!) Also, there's some evidence that preformed meat patties might contain more *E. coli* than regular ground meat. In fact, all the recent beef recalls have involved pre-made frozen beef patties. Fresh is definitely better!

25. Cooking Spray

Don't pay big bucks for compressed air. A small oil-misting bottle will pay for itself when you fill it with your own olive oil or canola oil (the two healthiest).

Off-the-Beaten-Path Food Savings

In addition to getting discounts at your favorite grocery store, there are plenty of other ways for us seniors to get the jump on savings. Shopping for everything in the same place, like your local supermarket, may be convenient but it will never save you the biggest bundle. To do that, you need to shop around a bit more to be sure you're hitting the right places for the right items. So where are your best bets? Here's a rundown of your basic grocery shopping options and of which places tend to have better prices on what.

Visit Your Local Farmers' Market in Season

Stock up on whatever is in season, which will usually make it easier on the wallet. A fringe benefit is that produce might be grown locally, and if it is, it'll likely be cheaper. A dozen eggs fresh from a free-range hen will usually cost the same or less than that mass-farmed refrigerated dozen at the grocery store, and they'll always taste much better. The farmers who sell their goods are not big, commercial, high-volume producers, and the prices they set for their produce may *seem* higher than they are at the supermarket. Guess again.

The farmer is your friend. Make friends with the owners, and let them share their passion for what they do (they may even give you a free sample or at least a taste). Once they recognize you and your tastes, they may save their very best tomatoes or apples for you. Once again, the best of the best is almost always a bargain, since you'll be more likely to eat all of it rather than throw some of it out at the end of the week.

Did You Know?

Farmers' markets are among the best places to pick up free recipes straight from the food source. Farmers are often fabulous cooks and are very willing to share advice on how to prepare the vegetables and herbs that they grow. Don't be shy. Take a pad and a pencil, and promise that you'll always give them credit when your family swoons and says, "Where did you get this recipe?"

It's okay to negotiate the price. Farmers are entrepreneurs and are more than willing to do a bit of haggling, especially if you are willing to buy in bulk those items that can be stored or frozen, like winter squash, apples, potatoes, and green beans.

Time it right for savings. If you want to eat fresh food cheap, hit the market an hour to a half hour before closing and scoop up fruits and veggies, even baked goods and flowers, at a discount, sometimes as much as 50 percent to 75 percent off. Growers always want to unload as much as they can at the end of day, rather than haul it home. Just be sure your afternoon foraging begins with an open mind and palate and empty shopping bags (they often run out of bags at the end of the day). Some sellers are even willing to give away items. If you've never tried Chinese cabbage or fresh fava beans, this may be your chance. If you don't fall in love with the flavor, there's always the compost bin.

Enjoy a berry nice price. Love blueberries and cherries but cringe at the checkout when you buy them in the dead of winter? Shop for them in season, and if you know you love them, buy as many as you can. Place them on a large, lipped baking sheet, pop them into the freezer, and four hours later, you'll have individually frozen, fresh-as-a-daisy berries. Store them in heavy-duty freezer bags for up to six months, and you'll never have to shell out hard-earned dough again to make a succulent, fresh blueberry pie or cherry tart in the middle of January.

Other Food-Buying Choices

Find an ethnic market. One man's butt is another man's tenderloin—*pork butt*, that is! One of our researchers discovered an entire pork butt (which is really shoulder) for 99 cents a pound in her local ethnic market and the same cut—from the same producer—at $4.99 per pound in the case at a neighboring gourmet shop. Ethnic markets will cater directly to clientele who have to stretch their dollars as far as they can go. If you live near an Italian, Spanish, Asian, or African market, take advantage of everything you'll find there. And if something looks unfamiliar to you, ask the people around you for help. You'll be thrilled you did!

Don't forget the dollar store! Paper products, cleaning supplies, and even plenty of canned or dry foods can be bought at the dollar store for…you guessed it: a dollar! Many of these stores sell "odd lots" of brand-name products, generally from overstock. There's no stigma in paying a tiny fraction of the original price for perfectly good products.

Ka-Ching!

The Ethnic Market Versus the Supermarket

We shopped for the same 15 items, below, in a small, East Coast ethnic market and a major chain supermarket in the same neighborhood. Here's what we discovered:

	Ethnic Market	Supermarket
Soy sauce (1 quart):	$2.99	$4.99
Pork butt (6 pounds):	$5.99	$10.98
Corn tortillas (pack of 24):	$1.59	$3.99
Organic eggs (1 dozen):	$2.19	$3.99
Sheep's milk cheese (1 pound):	$3.99	$15.99
Canned garbanzo beans (16 ounces):	$.89	$2.99
Chili sauce (1 quart):	$2.99	$4.99
Broccoli (2 heads):	$2.99	$4.50
Imported Italian pasta (1 pound):	$2.19	$4.99
Imported basmati rice (10 pounds):	$8.99	$19.99
Organic milk (1/2 gallon):	$1.19	$3.29
Imported coffee (1 pound):	$3.69	$9.00
Imported tea (150 bags):	$6.50	$12.00
Chicken sausage (1 pound):	$5.75	$8.00
Canned tomatoes (28 ounces):	$1.99	$4.99
TOTALS	**$53.92**	**$114.68**

Split the goods, share the discounts. A dozen rolls of toilet paper won't go stale sitting in your closet, but unless it's wrapped well and your freezer is huge, 12 pounds of beef just may! What to do? Split a discount club membership fee between a few friends, and then divvy up the goods at the end of your shopping trip. You'll reap the benefits of the lower price, without needlessly throwing out food that's gone bad before you've had a chance to use it.

If you're an avid cook, buy spices in bulk. The markup on spices from major brand names in the grocery-store spice aisle is hair-raising. If you can find a store that sells spices and dried herbs from large bins, you may be pleasantly surprised to discover that the little jar of spices you paid $5 for at the supermarket is 89 cents for about three-quarters of a cupful, weighed out in a little paper bag—when bought in bulk.

Meaty Discounts

If you love meats of all kinds but think they'll cost you a fortune, you're in the right place. With a little ingenuity, you can regularly fill your freezer with the tastiest cuts, and dine like royalty. What's the secret? Read on!

Good-bye, prime time. While it's true that prime meat—the highest quality, dry-aged stuff that the top restaurants peddle for mortgage-payment amounts—is the cream of the crop, it's the less-expensive, more frugal cuts that offer both flavor *and* value. Look for hanger steaks, skillet steaks, London broils, chuck steaks, and bottom rounds, and keep your wallet full!

Do the braise craze. If you've got a few hours to kill on a rainy afternoon, you've got time to make a flavor-packed stew that will yield leftovers for days and weeks (if you freeze them). Brown a chuck roast on all sides in a heavy oven-proof casserole (cast iron is best), throw in a handful of chopped onions, carrots, and celery, pour in a cup or two of inexpensive red wine and a cup of beef broth, cover it, and place it in the oven at 300°F. Voila! Three hours later, and dinner is served.

Give it an airing for more flavor. For maximum taste at minimal cost, unwrap your beef when you get it home, put it on a plate, sprinkle it with a tiny bit of salt, and let it stand, unwrapped, in your refrigerator for up to four hours before you cook it. (Let it come to room temperature before preparing your recipe.) Air-curing is the natural way to age meat and to give it an incomparable flavor boost for practically nothing. Note: Only do this if you're going to be preparing the meat the day you bring it home.

Grind your own and save

big! Sure, we know it's easy, but those immense packages of ground beef are nothing more than an overpriced convenience. What to do? Grind your own! Buy what's on sale (if it's on the bone, slice the bone away and discard it), cube it, and pulse it in your food processor. Store in heavy-duty, resealable bags, and use as you would ground beef—for much less.

Buy in bulk and freeze. Meat, when wrapped well, can keep for up to six months. Remove your purchase from its grocery store wrapping, double-wrap it in your own plastic wrap, and place it in a dated, labeled, heavy-duty freezer bag.

Go hog wild! If you're a fan of pork, you're in luck. Some yummy parts of pig can be had in bulk for surprisingly little money. "Country-style" pork ribs—meatier, more flavorful than their baby back cousins, and far more frugal—are generally sold in large "family size" packages. If it's just two of you, break up the big package into smaller ones and freeze; if you're having a crowd, haul out the slow cooker, layer them on top of sliced onions, add a few garlic cloves and your favorite barbecue sauce, cook it on high for a few hours, and call it summer!

Be a ham. Again and again. Don't bypass that big ham on sale at the grocery store, even if there are only two or three of you at the table each night. It's simple to prepare, and leftovers can be cubed and tossed into pea soup, noodle dishes, burritos, and more. Even the bone can be added to cooking soup for incomparable flavor. Anything left over? Freeze it for up to four months.

Buy the whole bird. Grocery stores count on us to skip the whole bird in favor of cut-up parts, like breasts, thighs, and legs. What do they give us in return? Unnecessary expense. If you learn to cut a chicken into parts, you can save up to $2.99 *a pound* on your next chicken-shopping excursion. (Our researchers found whole chickens on sale on the West Coast for as little as 69 cents per pound!) Here's how to do it, simply and easily:

1. Using a clean, strong pair of poultry shears or kitchen scissors, snip up the backbone and flatten the bird.

2. Turn the bird over, and snip right up the breast bone.

3. Snip one half in half again.

4. Snip the other half in half again.

Removing legs and wings is up to you (keep snipping); if you want boneless breasts, simply pull the bone away from the meat. And feel free to pull off the skin while you're at it. What do you have? Expensive chicken parts, for the frugal price of a whole bird.

Caviar Tastes on an Early Bird's Budget

Living the life of a discerning over 50 gourmet is by no means at odds with big savings. Food is something we have to eat every day, and buying good food doesn't have to be expensive. You, too, can be a gourmet while still taking advantage of big discounts!

Be a cheese wiz! Real Italian Parmigiano-Reggiano (not the stuff in the green cardboard can) is a classic addition to everything from pastas to salads and soups, but it can cost a big bundle. Forgo the fake stuff in the green can, and opt for a clever, more frugal substitute for the real thing: Look for easy-to-find Asiago or Grana Padano—very similar cheeses that cost a fraction of Parmigiano-Reggiano and still deliver a punch of flavor.

Early Bird Secret

Keep olive oil cool.

Olive oil should be stored in a cool, dry place, such as a pantry or on a bottom shelf of a lower cabinet. Kept this way, it will stay fresh for a year or more. Never refrigerate it, and never expose it to heat, or it will turn rancid.

You say expensive imported tomato, I say *not!* Fancy Italian canned tomatoes, called San Marzanos, are delicious, sweet, available all year round, and incredibly expensive. Our secret way around the price? Buy other canned tomatoes on sale, and drizzle them with rice vinegar. The result will be so sweet and succulent you'll wonder why you haven't done this before!

Shelve imported pastas where they belong (on the shelf). Fancy imported pastas are rarely worth their price, and sometimes little more than costly packaging wrapped around an inexpensive product. What to do when faced with a choice? Buy the less expensive brand and

Ka-Ching!

Holy cow!

We don't mean to be disrespectful to Elsie, but that iconic cow is responsible for cuts of beef that can run the gamut from very, very expensive to downright cheap. The best-tasting cut is not always the most expensive; the key is knowing what you're buying, what you can save, and how you can use it to make the most succulent, money-savvy meals around.

Ground Beef — $

Chuck — $

Rib — $ $ $

Short Loin — $ $ $

Sirloin — $ $

Rump Roast — $

Round — $ $

Brisket — $ $

Skirt Steak — $ $

Flank — $ $

Shank — $

$ inexpensive

$ $ moderate

$ $ $ expensive

TIP Although ground beef traditionally comes from the neck of the animal, every cut can be bought whole, cubed at home, and ground by pulsing it gently in a food processor. If a particular cut, like chuck or round, is on sale, it may be less expensive to grind it yourself than to purchase it preground.

cook it one or two minutes less than the box suggests; toss it with already hot sauce of your choice, and serve it al dente—to the tooth, in Italian—for a qualitative, delicious boost at a lower cost.

Dressed to the 99s. Sure, you can find everyday items at your local 99-cent store. But if you look a bit more closely, you'll find loads of tempting gourmet goodies: we found fancy, imported chocolates; wild smoked salmon; smoky Spanish almonds; and sweet roasted peppers. Who knew? (Now, you!)

Grow your own herbs; don't buy them. Why spend $2 to $3 for a tiny packet of fresh herbs in a grocery store, when the same amount of money would have bought you a potted plant of the same herb that could live in your windowsill? Rosemary is an amazingly hardy plant, as are thyme and mint, and the only problem with growing chives is to make them *stop*. Cutting chives merely encourages them to grow faster, so if you toss a handful of snipped chives in your scrambled eggs every few days, you'll never lack for them.

Did You Know?

The Whole Truth about Basil. You can freeze fresh basil leaves whole when they're plentiful in summer or, of course, turn them into pesto that will flavor soups and pastas for months afterward. The secret to keeping pesto is to always pour at least half an inch of olive oil over the surface of the jar to block all oxygen from it. Oxygen browns pesto quickly, but a sealing coat of olive oil (which you can spoon right through when you use the pesto) will keep it fresh and fragrant for weeks in your refrigerator. Better yet? Freeze a batch and enjoy a taste of summer during the winter.

Stock up when the price is right. Buying a gallon of extra-virgin olive oil and decanting it into a smaller bottle as needed adds up to big savings. A gallon will run about $25, depending on the brand and country of origin, but even the most inexpensive oils usually run about $8 a quart—or $64 a gallon!

Want lox around the clock? No problem. You can treat your brunch guests to bagels and smoked salmon without spending a fortune. Just find ways to spread it further: mince up a small package (3 to 4 ounces) of high-quality smoked salmon, and blend it gently with one 8-ounce package of softened cream cheese. Refrigerate it overnight in an airtight container, and it'll be perfect by the time your guests arrive.

Get online instead of standing in line. Looking for the best price on a spiral-cut honey ham? Want that special cheese that your mother used to buy? Get thee to the Internet! Online specialty purveyors can offer a much wider range of goods and often at better prices than brick-and-mortar retailers, even with shipping costs added in. Shop around and compare online prices to get the specialty food you want at the lowest cost.

Be a gourmet saler. Even fancy, high-end gourmet shops will generally price expensive products lower than regular grocery stores, especially during sale times. For example, a busy gourmet market will often have lower prices on better-quality coffee than your supermarket, as well as big sales on items like cheeses and sausages, condiments and jams. The super-sharp Cheddar for which you're paying $6.99 a pound at the supermarket may well be selling for $2.99 a pound at a fancy cheese shop, where it may have come from a small cheese maker and not from a major food conglomerate.

Dining-Out Secrets from the Bird That Knows

For many of us, eating out is fun, and it's also entertainment. We don't go to restaurants simply to get food. We go to enjoy new taste sensations and find interesting flavors, to expand our horizons, and enjoy conversations in a relaxed setting. And if we're heading out to an old favorite, we usually do it because it makes us feel good. And that's a wonderful thing!

But too much dining out is a budget-buster—unless you're getting your full due of discounts. Tuck in a napkin and see.

The Early Bird gets the...discounted meal. Yep, the term came from restaurants, and we'd be remiss not to remind you. Have an early lunch so you can enjoy an early dinner at your favorite restaurant during those hours that seem to be specially set aside to please seniors! Restaurants began Early Bird Specials to fill their dining rooms during the quiet early evening hours when they still had the lights on and the stove hot, but the staff was standing around. They're thrilled to have you there and thrilled to offer you a lower price, so take full advantage of it. Best of all, you'll be home and rested and digested while the later diners are just staggering out to their cars with stuffed stomachs!

Split an entrée. Restaurant portions are so big these days that even if you could eat the whole thing, you probably shouldn't. If you're ordering appetizers and drinks, most restaurants are fine with two diners splitting a main course—some of them will even plate it for you separately in the kitchen and add an extra portion of vegetables!

Early Bird Secret

Get a doggy bag. You paid for it, it's yours, and throwing it away is wasteful and not good for the planet or your wallet. It's hard to find a restaurant that's not delighted to pack up your extras for you. Some fancy restaurants will bring you a chit rather than your food in a bag: You exchange the chit at the coat check for your packaged meal, which is waiting in a small fridge on your way out.

Make a meal out of appetizers. Two appetizers, one after the other, likely offer a more normal portion size and can often be more interesting to eat than a big main dish. For two people, you might order four small appetizers and share everything, and still wind up paying less than ordering entrées.

"Do" lunch. Eat exactly the same food that's on the dinner menu, at nearly half the price—lunch can be even cheaper than the Early Bird Special at dinner! The practice may have begun to lure diners into quiet lunchtime restaurants, but now it's a given, and even busy places are still significantly cheaper than they are at dinner. Some high-end restaurants also offer a three-course lunchtime special that's less than the price of a single entrée ordered off the dinner menu.

Go ethnic. Mexican, Cuban, Middle Eastern, Greek, anything Asian—whether it's Chinese, Thai, Vietnamese, or Indian—can be a bargain. Better yet, you'll probably get food cooked with care and love by people who want you to love their native cuisines, so don't be shy about trying out all your local ethnic restaurants. And don't forget they'll be even cheaper at lunch!

Feed kids free. Whether it's kids-eat-free or buffet night or just the Early Bird Special, be sure to compare prices with the senior discount—the special that week may end up being a better deal! That's especially true when it comes to the grandchildren. Feeding two or three (or more) grandchildren for free, even if you're paying full price for your own meal, will probably end up saving you a lot more than bringing them all for the Early Bird.

Go out for breakfast. The first meal of the day is usually cheaper than any other in a restaurant, whether you're having eggs, bacon, potatoes, and toast for $3 or $4 in a diner or croissants and coffee in a high-end hotel restaurant. It can start your day off right whether it's a Sunday brunch or a weekday vacation. Better still: find a place that serves breakfast all day, and have it for dinner.

Order a whole bottle of wine instead of by the glass. Wine by the glass can add up very quickly, so if there's any chance you or your companion will want a second glass, you're better off ordering a whole bottle. Even if you have wine left over at the end of the meal, you may be able to have the bottle recorked so that you can take it with you. (Laws vary state to state about whether you're able to take leftover alcohol with you, but your waiter will know.)

Fast Food Treats and Tricks

Many fast-food restaurants have unadvertised discounts and special offers for seniors. The reason that they're not widely advertised or visible is mostly because the discount or offer varies from store to store in these franchised restaurants, rather than being a corporate policy across the board. Thus, be sure you check with your local store—one Burger King in town might give you a free cup of coffee while another may not. If it's available, however, the staff is happy to dole out your discount when asked, so don't be shy.

Arby's Company-owned Arby's (more than 1,100 nationwide) offer seniors a value size soft drink or a small coffee for 50 cents. Discounts at franchise-owned restaurants may vary so ask before you order.

Baskin Robbins Got a craving for ice cream or need a special ice-cream cake for your grandchild's birthday party? If you're 55 or older, you can get it at a 10 percent discount.

Early Bird Secret

The Truth about Bottled Water

The moment you sit down, many waiters will ask "Bottle or tap water?" *Never* feel intimidated into ordering bottled water! Tap water is fresh and free, and if you need any better reason, it's also a much "greener" choice because it didn't require a truck to transport it from some spring across the country. Beyond that, bottled water can add untold dollars to your bottom line. One of our experts compared bottled water prices in some of our nation's restaurants, and here is what they found, by city.

Average Restaurant Price of Bottled Water by City

New York $12

Los Angeles $15

San Francisco $15

Dallas $9

Seattle $5

Miami $5

New Orleans $6

Portland (Maine) $4

Fargo ($0. You'll never find it.)

Burger King Most outlets offer a senior discount on beverages. Some stores also extend a free cup of coffee to senior patrons in the morning until 10 a.m.

Dunkin Donuts American seniors run on Dunkin Donut's standard discount of 10 percent for those who are 55 and older.

Fresh Choice Patrons 60 and above get 15 percent off the price of their entire meal every day at Fresh Choice.

Jack in the Box Senior citizens 55 or older receive 50 cents off on any size soft drink beverage of their choice, combo meals excluded.

KFC The buffet at KFC has special prices for customers 55 and above, and some locations offer a 10 percent discount on the cost of your meal, but the senior benefit varies from store to store.

McDonald's As with other franchises, the owner of each store has the right to set any senior discounts or promotions, and the outcome varies widely between stores. Be sure to ask at your local McDonald's and at any other one you visit when away from home.

Pizza Hut Discounts for seniors vary from store to store but in nearly all branches, the senior prices are for dine-in patrons only, not for take-out.

Souper Salad Sign up for the Souper Fresh Club at soupersalad.com to get printable discounts on food as well as a special discount on your birthday.

Taco Bell Many Taco Bell locations offer discounts for seniors, but the details vary by restaurant. Check with your local Taco Bell to see if they participate in a senior discount program.

Tim Horton's This popular Canadian doughnut chain has infiltrated ever deeper into the American market, and they offer seniors a small coffee for 98 cents.

Wendy's Most Wendy's restaurants offer a discount to seniors, such as a percentage off the customer's order or a free small beverage. Discounts vary with individual restaurants, so customers should inquire about the details when they place their order.

Better Dining Restaurants

A wide range of restaurants beyond fast food offer senior discounts, and some of them are corporate-wide, such as the Applebee's Golden Apple program. Others vary from location to location, so be sure to ask when you're trying a new restaurant to make sure you haven't missed any special deals. Some restaurants will offer you a discount based on your membership in AARP if they have no other program—it never hurts to ask!

Applebee's Sign up for and receive your Golden Apple Card at participating locations if you're 60 and older. You'll get 15 percent off the total of your check at any Applebee's all over the United States.

Bob's Big Boy
Patrons 55 and older can sign up for a Senior Discount Card, for a 10 percent discount at participating locations.

Boston Market Chicken-loving patrons who are 60 and above (okay, you don't *have* to love chicken but why else would you be here?) can get a 10 percent discount on their entire order.

Carrows Be sure to order from the special senior menu to get the best prices for Carrows' diners who are 55 and older.

Early Bird Secret

Birthday Discounts

In addition to the senior discount, check around to see if a restaurant you like has any other specials you can profit from as well—and there are few discounts and specials at any restaurant so generous as those they offer for your birthday. Many national chains allow you to register your birthday with them on their Web site or directly at the restaurant, and then they'll send you a coupon or invitation before your birthday to get a variety of freebies and specials that range from a free coffee drink at Caribou Coffee to a free dessert at the Cheesecake Factory to a $30 dinner certificate at Benihana Japanese Steakhouse.

Find out what birthday goodies your own favorite restaurant has to offer, and then sign up your whole family—everyone you love can have birthday treats all year long!

Chili's A senior discount of 10 percent for diners who are 55 and older is available at some Chili's locations, so be sure to ask (and some locations may ask to see your AARP card).

Coco's Bakery Restaurant This western chain has a senior menu called Club 55 for patrons who are—you guessed it—55 and above.

Cracker Barrel Most Cracker Barrel locations have a senior section on the menu offering somewhat smaller portions at a lower price.

Denny's Denny's takes the tastes of their senior patrons very seriously since the company estimates that seniors make up approximately one-third of its customers. It has a senior menu for those who are 55 and above with lower prices for slightly smaller portions.

Elephant Bar Restaurant If you're 60 or older, sign up for the Senior Explorer Card, good for 20 percent off the cost of food at these restaurants.

Friendly's These East Coast establishments with a focus on ice cream have a special senior menu for diners who are 60 and older, which, besides offering lower prices and smaller portions, allows the diner to have a free coffee with breakfast or a small sundae with lunch or dinner.

Golden Corral It varies widely according to location, but most Golden Corral restaurants offer special prices for diners who are 60 and above.

International House of Pancakes IHOP has a senior menu for diners who are 55 and older, but if you want to order off the regular menu, they'll still extend to you a 10 percent discount on your meal.

Old Country/Old Town Buffet/Country Buffet This popular chain of buffets offers a Senior Club Card to patrons 60 and older for $1. The card is good for a year and gives you approximately 10 percent off the cost of your meal when you present it to the cashier at the end of each meal. Using it also enters you in the weekly drawing for a free meal.

Picadilly This Louisiana-based chain of cafeterias, now more than half a century old and popular across the South, offers 10 percent off the cost of the meal for seniors 60 and older from 2 to 5 p.m. every day except Sunday with your Prime Time for Seniors Card. Ask your store manager for one today.

Ponderosa Steakhouse Most locations have special senior menu items at reduced prices for smaller portions. Menu items vary by steakhouse.

Did You Know?

Get a Promotion! Ponderosa Steakhouse occasionally offers some terrific promotions and special offers that you can only get online. Go to www.ponderosasteakhouses.com and sign up for its eClub newsletter to receive news and notices of special promotions. You'll get a special offer on your birthday and other offers throughout the year. While nobody wants to sign up for a lot of junk mail in their e-mail inbox, it's worth it if it's going to bring you savings!

Shoney's If you're 55 and older, be sure to ask your server about their senior discounts.

Silver Diner Diners 55 and older can get 10 percent off the cost of their meals at some locations, while other locations have Early Bird Specials from 4 to 6 p.m. Check with your local restaurant for specifics.

Sizzler If you're 60 and above, you can order from the senior menu, and some locations also have special offers for AARP members when you present your membership card.

Strings Italian Cafe Discounts vary from location to location, but most offer 10 percent to 15 percent off the price of the meal (or sometimes just the entrée) for patrons 62 and above. Sign up for special discounts on your birthday.

Great Life Entertaining

Does having a big crowd of people over and feeding them a lot of delicious food and drinks seem the opposite of saving money? Well, it can be, but guess what? It doesn't have to be. Read on, and you'll see how to save big on food *and* party big with your friends and family.

Cocktails, anyone? Invite people to come from 5 to 7 p.m., which suggests that dinner is not on the menu, even if you end up serving plenty of food, and even if they stay well past 7 (someone *always* does). Serve lots of smaller things—veggies and dips, chips and salsa, hummus and carrots, quiche cut into bite-size pieces—that are inexpensive, tasty, and filling.

Have a sangria bash. You don't have to have a full bar (or anything like one!) just because you're having a party. Sangria is inexpensive, delicious, easy-to-make, and a little goes a long way. Add red wine, carbonated water, sweetener such as honey or orange juice, and a small amount of spirits, such as brandy or triple sec, to a pitcher full of chopped or sliced oranges, apples, or other fruit, and refrigerate for two hours before your guests arrive. Add ice, stir, and your guests will be delighted. For a variation, use white wine, and you have *sangria blanca*.

Have a buffet. Casual buffets lend themselves to clever spending because you can make a large amount of hearty and inexpensive foods, whether it's a giant pot of three-bean chili, a big vat of chicken and dumplings, or a mammoth portion of spaghetti and meatballs.

Don't skimp on starch. There's a reason so many world cuisines center around rice and pasta: they're filling, they're inexpensive, and they can be absolutely delicious. You can serve a smaller amount of an inexpensive meat-based topping, such as beef stew, and an absolutely enormous mountain of buttered egg noodles, and you'll be met with cries of delight rather than whines of hunger.

Early Bird Secret

Serve Caviar Pie

Want to serve something really special but don't want to spend a fortune on it? Make your special ingredient go further. Caviar pie is a great example (domestic caviar can be had for as little as $6 or $7 a jar): Spread a layer of homemade egg salad on a decorative serving dish and smooth over it a layer of softened cream cheese that you've combined with a finely minced red onion. On top, smooth over a small jar of inexpensive caviar, such as "red lumpfish roe." Serve it with crackers—or toast, to make it a little fancier. You just saved yourself $200 on a tin of Beluga!

Go vegetarian. Skip the meat altogether and make a large pot of three-bean chili, a spicy stir-fry with lots of red peppers and broccoli over rice, or a towering bowl of pasta that you can serve with tomato sauce and heaps of cheese. Make a giant pan of cheesy cornbread with chopped jalapenos in it and serve it up with beans. Nobody will even notice there's no meat on the table. (Trust us!)

Start with soup. Most folks love a bowl of homemade soup, which is wonderful because soup is super-inexpensive and supremely delicious—plus, it fills people up before they get to the roast beef! Make a savory leek-and-potato or creamy butternut squash soup. Float some croutons on top of each bowl or—even easier—some bruschetta (toasted slices of hearty country bread brushed with olive oil on both sides and rubbed with a raw garlic clove).

Slow-cook a bigger, cheaper cut. Whether you fancy chicken thighs or boneless country ribs, take advantage and haul out your slow cooker. Sure, you'll have to plan ahead to do this, but the result is a much more deeply flavored dish that you've prepared ahead, which brings down the stress levels on the day of your party, and you'll save lots of money. Your low-priced and plain protein—slow-cooked or in a nice sauce—suddenly becomes dinner-party fancy.

Don't forget the fruit. Fresh fruit in season can turn into inexpensive, show-stopping purées for dessert: try raspberries, blueberries, or peaches (peeled and pitted) in a blender with sugar and lemon juice to taste, and pulse until the sauce is completely smooth (raspberry puree may need to be pushed through a mesh strainer to take out the pesky seeds). The colors of a simple fruit puree are stunning and absolutely delicious when poured over store-bought ice cream. Your guests will swoon!

Take advantage of sales. A batch of "fancy" homemade beef stew can be made ahead and frozen for three months, so if you see something on sale, buy it, make the dish, and freeze it. Why? It may not be on sale when you want to have that big bash, and it'll give you one less thing to worry about come party night.

Decorate seasonally. Don't feel that you need to spend money on flowers or centerpieces when you're having a party. Try using whatever produce looks beautiful just now. If it's spring, place a glass bowl of bright lemons in the center of the table, with a couple of smaller bowls of perfect strawberries to either side. If it's autumn, put a few pomegranates in the center of the table. In the winter, arrange some holly branches and berries. In summer, pick wildflowers or heap up some lovely summer tomatoes. The star of the show should always be the food, so decorations shouldn't be the slightest drain on your party budget.

Turn down the lights and save! When you have votive candles flickering around the room and tapers on the table, surfaces seem to gleam and people's faces glow, making everyone look—and feel—younger, prettier, and happier. If a few cheap votive candles can accomplish that, they're worth every penny. Candles are the easiest, best decorations you can buy, they have the added benefit of hiding dust, and they'll keep your electricity costs down.

Ka-Ching!

The 55-Cent-Per-Person, Slow-Cooked Taco Party

Makes 20 Servings

One of the most delicious ways to entertain a crowd of hungry friends is to slow cook a pork shoulder, pull it off the bone, and have guests assemble their own tacos from the absolutely delicious meat. A recent excursion to our local branch of a national supermarket chain revealed this most frugal, fabulous cut for $1.99 per pound; the biggest one in the case cost a little over $11.00 and served 20 people, making each serving approximately 55 cents. Now *that's* a bargain!

8-pound pork shoulder, on the bone, skin and fat removed
Salt and pepper, to taste
2 tablespoons dried oregano
1 large white onion, peeled and sliced
1/2 cup orange juice

1. Rub pork shoulder all over with salt, pepper, and oregano, and set aside.

2. Place sliced onions in the bottom of a large slow cooker, and place the pork shoulder on top of the onions.

3. Drizzle with orange juice, turn the slow cooker to low, and cook for 6 hours, until the meat is falling off the bone.

4. Let cool and pull meat off bone with a fork. Serve with soft tortillas or hard tacos, and pass around bowls of salsa, shredded lettuce, and grated cheese.

441

Paper, Plastic, or Ceramic?

Get ready for a *big* surprise: one of our experts was convinced that buying good-quality paper plates and plastic cups for a bash she was having would be *more* expensive than buying the real thing. We didn't believe her, until she went out and did it. The result? We'll never buy paper plates and plastic cups again (they're expensive *and* not good for the environment—a double whammy), and well, neither should you. Here's what we discovered:

Quality Paper and Plastic	99 Cent Store Porcelain and Glass
25 paper dinner plates ($8)	25 porcelain dinner plates (50 cents per plate)
25 paper dessert plates ($6.50)	25 porcelain dessert plates (25 cents per plate)
25 paper soup bowls ($9.95)	25 porcelain soup bowls (25 cents per bowl)
25 plastic soda cups ($6)	50 heatproof glasses (25 cents per glass)
25 plastic hot cups ($6.75)	
Total: **$37.20**	Total: **$37.50**

Make it a potluck. If you're having a big crowd, don't be shy about calling for potluck. It's sociable and cheery, and people love to participate and even show off a little with a special dish. Keep things manageable by providing a main course or two yourself (meatloaf and fried chicken, perhaps), and ask others to bring salads, sides, desserts, and drinks. By having a general idea of who's bringing what, you won't end up with 15 pies and very little else on the table.

Splurge on dessert. You might serve a budget-conscious meal of soup and meatloaf, for example, but then pull out the stops with a flourless chocolate cake made with top-quality chocolate and topped with super-premium vanilla ice cream and fresh raspberries, perhaps. Or brew a pot of fragrant coffee and serve it with wrapped chocolates, homemade caramels, or bakery biscotti. One special item or course is the showpiece and everything else can be more ordinary. Not only will nobody mind, but they'll be very grateful for the good time!

Restaurant-Style Dining at Home

You don't have to eat out to enjoy the experience of fine dining. Make it a special night in, and dramatically cut costs on your restaurant-going by arranging a restaurant-type evening for your family in the comfort of your own home. The plan here is to do something very different from your usual routine so that your family gets the entertainment value of a night out at a fraction of the cost.

Light some candles. Put a lovely tablecloth on the table and some fresh flowers. Don't be afraid to treat yourself well. Get out your nice crystal or your wedding china—it's yours, and who better to enjoy it than you? Put on some background music. And turn off the TV!

Did You Know?

The Real Value of Restaurant Wine. Shocking, but true: most restaurants mark up the wines they sell by the bottle at least 100 percent from the price in a wine shop. In other words, if your favorite wine costs $12.99 in a local wine shop, a restaurant will likely put it on its wine list for $25 or $30 or higher. The way around this? Ask if you can bring a favorite bottle from home. The restaurant will likely charge you a corkage fee if it doesn't have a BYOB policy. Better still? Make dinner at home, and keep the wine bill low.

Start with some nibbles. Signal that this meal is going to be something special with the sorts of appetizing little snacks you get when you sit down at a nice restaurant. Put a dish of flat bread or crackers on the table or warm some rolls or slice some hearty bread from the bakery. Put a pat of butter in a small dish, drizzle it with olive oil, and sprinkle with chopped fresh herbs such as chives or rosemary. Add a dish of nuts or olives, and a cocktail—alcoholic or not—and you're ready to enjoy your evening.

Order in. If concocting an interesting dish is your idea of torture rather than a fun afternoon, order in something you've been wanting to try but never have. Picking up one main dish to go will be cheaper than dining out, and you'll save the cost of starter, sides, marked-up beverages, tax, and tip at a restaurant.

Invite everyone to cook. Whether it's family or a small group of friends, organize a group activity in the kitchen that makes dinnertime fun. Set up an assembly line to let everyone fill and crimp dumplings, decorate their own mini-pizzas, or stuff and fry egg rolls. Alternately, let them assemble their own desserts. Put out the fixings for hot fudge sundaes after dinner.

Discount Cooking Gear

Need to replace some kitchen equipment? You won't get a senior discount at Williams-Sonoma! But you can create your own: Open the phone book and find a restaurant supply store. These places are piled high with plain-looking equipment that is actually more professional than the fancy stuff sold in retail kitchenware stores, and *much* less expensive. Do you really need a $75 electric knife sharpener? A rubber garlic-skin remover? No, we didn't think so. (That's why you'll never find one here!)

Free cookware? You bet. One of the cleverest and most frugal ways to stock up on cookware is to hit your local flea market—at the tail end of the day! Most of the sellers are interested in packing up and generally don't want to repack what they didn't sell. One professional cook we spoke to was handed a heavy-duty flame diffuser because the seller didn't want to have to cart it home; another was asked to relieve the seller of a set of nesting cast-iron frying pans for the same reason. Sometimes, it pays to be late.

Make cookware go the distance. Who says you need a special meat pounder? Or an olive pitter? Save $10 instantly (or $20 or $30) by inventing new ways to use the same objects. For example, if you have an empty wine bottle, you don't need a rolling pin (just flour the sides of the bottle). If you have a heavyweight skillet, you don't need a meat pounder. If you have a good knife, you don't need an olive (or cherry) pitter. (Just smash the olive with the flat side of a heavy knife, and the pit will make a hasty exit.)

Shelve the mixing bowls. Need to marinate something? Pour the contents into a resealable plastic bag, toss in the meat, fish, chicken, pork, or vegetables, zip it up, and stow it in the fridge for its marinating time. Need to mix something? Use an empty plastic container. Need to mix something big? Do it in your biggest soup pot.

The Good-Deal Wine Cellar

New research shows that resveratrol, an organic compound in red wine, may help extend your life! If that's not a good reason to enjoy an occasional glass, nothing is. Best of all, there are plenty of bargains and good deals on wine to be found. It helps to know that "expensive" doesn't always equal "good" in the wine world—the challenge is to seek out inexpensive bottles that suit your tastes. Here's how to do that:

Buy by the case. Many wine stores will offer you a 10 percent case discount if you pay with a credit card, or, even better, a 15 percent discount if you pay with cash or a debit card. Some stores offer smaller discounts on half cases.

Ka-Ching!

Buy Where Restaurants Buy

We took a trip to three restaurant supply houses—one in New York City, another in rural northeastern Pennsylvania, and the last in Texas—and came away with a kitchen full of equipment that would make any four-star chef proud. The same selection, priced at a well-known kitchen shop chain, rang in at nearly $2,000, almost 10 times the supply house cost.

The Basics	Supply Store	Gourmet Store
Wire whisk (10-inch)	$5.00	$10.95
Stainless-steel spatula	$2.00	$22.00
Rubber spatula	$1.50	$22.50
Chef's knife (8-inch, plastic-handle, stainless alloy)	$20.00	$399.00
Instant-read thermometer	$6.00	$20.00
Oven thermometer	$3.00	$18.00
Slotted spoon	$1.25	$22.00
3 wooden spoons	$3.00	$29.95
3 graduated-size, stainless-steel bowls	$9.00	$129.95
Metal tongs (9 1/2-inch)	$2.50	$9.50
Sheet pan (18-by-12-inch)	$8.00	$17.00
Plastic cutting board	$7.00	$20.00
Paring knife	$5.00	$13.95
Manual can opener	$2.00	$10.00
Vegetable peeler	$3.00	$14.00
Box grater	$5.00	$34.95
Stainless-steel colander (8 quart)	$8.00	$59.95
Set of cast-aluminum saucepans	$50.00	$450.00
Nonstick frying pan (10-inch)	$15.00	$160.00
Stock pot (10-quart)	$25.00	$340.00
Universal lid	$6.00	$39.00
TOTALS	**$187.50**	**$1,842.70**

Try a different producer. Go looking for smaller or newer producers from lesser-known regions.

Try a different grape. Seek out a less expensive crisp and acidic dry Riesling instead of yet another chardonnay. Ask for a less pricey Argentinian malbec instead of merlot. Go for a Spanish Rioja instead of an expensive pinot noir.

Don't be afraid to ask. People who work in wine stores often do so because they love wine and like to talk about it. When someone says, "May I help you?" tell them you want a terrific, highly drinkable bottle of everyday red for $10, and see what they recommend.

Early Bird Secret

A World of Wine

Who is producing high-value, low-cost wines? Spain remains a good place to look, but don't forget Chile, Argentina, Australia, and even Hungary for lots of good-quality wines at competitive prices. South Africa used to export some bad wines, but the consistency of quality has improved dramatically in recent years while the prices have remained comparatively low.

Go for quantity. The one-and-a-half liter bottles usually cost less than two typical 750-militer bottles, and if you're entertaining, this is the ideal way to go.

Buy the box! The plastic bag-in-a-box style is, oddly enough, an ideal way to store wine. Because the bag is airtight and collapses as you draw off the wine through the box's spigot, air never touches the wine. You can store an opened box for weeks or months without the quality of the wine changing.

Try your luck with Two-Buck Chuck. Trader Joe's famous discount wine sells for less than $4 a bottle. Charles Shaw wines, as they are more formally known, are worth stocking up on. Some wine critics champion them, others scoff at them, but ordinary wine drinkers feel the extremely low price helps the wine slip down easily.

3

Your Castle and Your Car

> Easy Ways to Cut Home and Car Costs

DIY Discounts

Not everyone needs a big remodel or renovation (thank goodness!). But do you need a lot of plumbing or lawn work done or tips on where to find the best hardware deals? Check out these senior discounts on everyday items, projects, and special services before you spend another penny.

Ace Hardware Ace is the place where seniors age 60 and above can usually receive 10 percent off their purchases. Both age requirement and discount amount vary by location, and some discounts may be restricted to certain days of the week, so call ahead. You can find your local Ace store at its Web site at www.acehardware.com (click on "My Local Ace").

Roto-Rooter This national chain of plumbers offers 10 percent off labor (but not parts) to customers who are 60 and older. The age and discount can vary according to location and may not be available for holidays or emergencies, so be sure to ask when you call. At its national Web site, where you can find a number for your local branch, you can also sign up to receive special promotions and coupons via e-mail, which may end up saving you more money than the senior discount. Visit www.rotorooter.com.

City Slickers Can Save Big

If you're on a fixed income and you're finding that home costs are getting the better of you, have no fear! Check out the Department of Housing and Urban Development (HUD), where you can find a national list of budget-friendly urban senior apartments. If you have access to the Internet, visit the HUD Web site, where you can search by state to see what the income limits are and what residences are available in your immediate area. Requirements vary region to region.

U.S. Department of Housing and Urban Development
451 7th Street S.W., Washington, DC 20410
(202) 708-1112
www.hud.gov/apps/section8/

ServiceMaster This umbrella company for a family of brands includes many home services, such as Terminix Pest Control, TruGreen lawn care, and ServiceMaster carpet cleaning. Senior discounts vary widely depending on what service you require and what local company performs the service for you, but you can sign up at its main ServiceMaster Web site to receive special offers and promotions that will also help save you money, such as $20 off a carpet cleaning or a free termite inspection and then 10 percent off the first treatment. Visit the Web site at www.servicemaster.com or call the toll-free number: 1-888-WE-SERVE.

Did You Know?

The Poison-Free Way to Get Rid of Pests Alcohol—plain old cheap-as-dirt rubbing alcohol—kills ants, not to mention roaches, better and more safely than dangerous poisons. Place the undiluted alcohol in a spray bottle and squirt when you see a roach. Just a few squirts will do. Clean your counters and areas where you see ants and then spray with the alcohol. Don't rinse it. The ants will become dehydrated when they walk through the alcohol and die. Simply buff away any "clouding" from countertops if necessary.

35 Ways to Accident-Proof Your Property

It's a beautiful day, and you are looking forward to visiting with friends out on the deck or maybe serving a special dinner in front of a roaring fire. But instead, you or one of your friends ends up sitting in the emergency room because you fell, got burned, or got cut. Serious household accidents do happen—more than 7 million times a year. Taking simple precautions and making easy changes around the house can help avoid personal harm and related hospital and aftercare bills.

1. Make sure you have secure, easy-to-grip handrails along all stairs.
2. Ensure loose carpeting and tiles are secured to the floor.
3. Use a contrasting paint color to draw attention to short flights of stairs. Or, place nonskid tape on the edge of each tread.
4. Arrange furniture so it provides ample space for walking, especially if there is someone in your home who uses a cane, walker, or wheelchair.
5. Secure light pieces of furniture so they do not move if someone leans on them.
6. Secure electrical and telephone cords to walls to minimize tripping hazards.

7. Use nonskid safety strips or a nonslip bath mat in the tub and shower.

8. Consider installing a grab rail on the edge of the vanity or shower wall. (Do not use a towel bar. It's not a substitute for a genuine grab rail.)

9. Use automatic night-lights that turn on in the dark and stay off when light.

10. Make sure tile and vinyl floors are dry after cleaning or spills before walking on them.

11. Keep outdoor walkways and paths clear of leaves and other debris.

12. In wintertime, be sure to clear walkways of snow and ice, and place kitty litter, rock salt, or gravel on wet, potentially icy surfaces.

13. Fence in pools and water features, and keep surrounding areas clear of toys, leaves, and other items that someone could trip or slip on.

14. Store outdoor extension cords when not in use.

15. Pick up tools when not in use, and never leave a rake, manual rotary mower, or shovel on the ground.

16. Install smoke alarms on every floor—and make sure they work. About one-third of all smoke detectors don't function because the batteries are dead or missing.

Safety First

Fires kill more than 4,000 Americans and injure an additional 25,000 people. The leading cause of fire deaths: careless smoking. Another great reason to butt out of that bad habit! Other causes of accidents at home include taking medicines or swallowing poisons like household cleaners by mistake (in the case of small children, this is a real problem); getting bumped, bruised and burned; drowning; and gun accidents. Here are some safety changes that are oh-so-easy and oh-so-very-worth-it!

17. Lock liquor cabinets, and remove all poisonous household items from accessible locations.

18. Keep medicine out of reach from small hands—and clearly marked for big ones!

19. Install lights in medicine cabinets so mistakes are not made when taking medicine.

20. If you have babies and tiny tots around, or visiting regularly, cover sharp edges with rubber cushioning.

21. Remove glass shower doors or replace them with unbreakable versions.

22. Set the hot water thermostat below 120° Fahrenheit to minimize the chance of burns—especially important if you have small children or elderly people in your home regularly.

23. Use faucets that mix hot and cold water, or paint hot water knobs or faucets red.

24. Install toilet guardrails or provide a portable toilet seat with built-in rails.

25. Store firearms in a locked cabinet, and keep bullets in a separate locked cabinet.

26. Cover outlets with childproof outlet covers to minimize the chance of shock. This may also minimize drafts in your home!

27. Keep very small sharp objects like tiny nails, razors, and pins out of reach of small hands (which are usually attached to curious mouths).

28. Make sure televisions and other large objects are secured safely to strong surfaces or the wall. (One great feature of flat-screen TVs is that they can be secured to a wall and out of reach of people who could bump into them or pull them down on top of them.)

29. Likewise, make sure pictures are secured to walls and out of reach of inquiring hands.

30. Keep knives on a knife rack high on the wall and out of children's reach or in a secure rack in a cabinet with a child lock.

31. When cooking, do not wear loose-fitting clothing or dangling sleeves that could catch fire on a burner.

32. Never leave food unattended while cooking—including food on the outdoor barbecue.

33. Keep space heaters away from curtains, furniture, and any other item that could catch fire, and unplug them when they are not in use and while you are sleeping.

34. Don't use electric appliances with frayed cords. Replace the appliance or the cord.

35. Keep one fire extinguisher in the kitchen and one near bedrooms, and know how to use them.

The Home

How safe are you? Taking this 5-minute, 10-question quiz helps you identify potential trouble spots quickly—and will get you thinking about emergency preparedness ahead of time. Any question that gets a "no" should be addressed immediately.

1. Do you have a NOAA (National Oceanic and Atmospheric Administration) Weather Radio or other battery-operated way (transistor radio or TV) to monitor news and weather in case of an emergency or a blackout?

2. Do you have a family emergency plan in place that includes two possible evacuation routes, a designated meeting place, and an alternative place to stay?

3. Have you created an emergency survival kit, the most basic of which should include a battery-operated radio (see question 1); drinking water; packaged, nonperishable food (like canned beans, tuna, and veggies); can opener; flashlight; flare; whistle; extra batteries; first aid kit; and a conventional land-line phone (cell and cordless phones don't work in blackouts)?

4. Is your house number clearly visible to firefighters, law enforcement, and other emergency workers? Reflective 911 emergency house numbers are available for low cost or free under some circumstances from all municipalities. If you are unable to install your own, your community will even send someone to do it for you.

Safety Quiz

5. Do you know how to turn off utilities including water, power, and gas?

6. Is your driveway accessible to emergency vehicles at all times—meaning that there is adequate clearance on both sides and a large vehicle like a fire truck would be able to make a wide turn into your driveway? Is there enough space to turn around?

7. Do you have a plan for covering windows and doors in the event of a weather disaster or other emergency? Likewise, do you have a way to cover or reinforce your garage door?

8. Are lawn furniture, children's toys, gardening tools, trash cans, and any other large, moveable objects stored away from stairs and exits? Do you have a secure place to store these items in case of high winds?

9. Have you cleaned leaves and debris off of or away from your walkways, roof, gutters, and air-conditioning units?

10. Are stair railings, both inside and out, secure and sturdy?

Dim Electricity Bills

So many of us take electricity for granted: We plug "it" in—whatever it is—and off it goes. Lights, heat, well pumps, washing machines, dryers, computers, televisions, stereos, treadmills, your stove, your fridge…virtually everything in your home runs on an electrical current, and this means big bills at the end of the month. The good news is that there are savvy ways for seniors to save, if you know what to do!

Low-Income Home Energy Assistance Program Low on income and big on energy costs in the heat of the summer? No problem! The U.S. Department of Health and Human Services allocates federal funding to the Low-Income Home Energy Assistance Program (LIHEAP). Its primary focus is immediate assistance with home energy—whether it's a summer heat wave or the dead of winter—to seniors who have very low incomes. The LIHEAP Clearinghouse provides free telephone and e-mail referrals to people who need help applying for energy assistance. Call the National Energy Assistance Referral (NEAR) at 1-866-674-6327 from 8 a.m. to 6 p.m. (Eastern Time) or visit its Web site at www.liheap.org. You may also send an e-mail to NEAR at energyassistance@ncat.org, with your city, county, and state in your e-mail message.

National Fuel Funds Network Hot enough for you? The National Fuel Funds Network helps eligible seniors find assistance with energy costs on a local level. Check out its Web site at www.nationalfuelfunds.org or call 1-866-674-6327.

Energy Star Ratings If you change just one lightbulb in your home to an Energy Star approved bulb, it's as good for the environment as not driving your car for *two weeks*—and the energy savings is not only good for the planet, but it also adds up to dollars in your pocket. You can make significant changes in your carbon footprint and in your power bill by using products approved by Energy Star, a joint program between the U.S. Environmental Protection Agency and the U.S. Department of Energy. Using Energy Star techniques, advice, strategies, and approved appliances and lightbulbs, Americans saved $17 billion on their utility bills in 2009. Make sure you get your share of the savings! Check out the Energy Star Web site at www.energystar.gov for a wealth of hugely practical energy-saving techniques.

13 No-Cost Ways to Reduce Energy Bills

Small, inexpensive changes to the way you use energy around the house can significantly reduce your energy costs—from heat to hot water. Once you make these changes, the only thing you'll notice are lower bills.

1. **The big chill.** Our experts say that you can save up to $63 per year by washing all your clothes in cold water instead of warm or hot.

2. **Fully loaded.** Full loads of laundry and dishes result in maximum efficiency and help you avoid water waste. Air-dry dishes—and clothes, if you can—for even more savings.

3. **Lose the lint.** If you must dry clothes in a dryer, always clean the lint filter after every load to maintain peak drying efficiency (not to mention reducing the risk of fire).

4. **Separate heavy from light.** Dry towels, bedspreads, and other heavy items separately from lighter-weight items to increase drying efficiency.

5. **You're all wet.** Take showers instead of baths and install a low-flow showerhead to save on water and heat.

6. **No drips allowed.** Fix leaky faucets. Even a little drip can add up to a big-time water bill.

7. **Bundle up.** Insulate hot water pipes and water heater with approved insulation materials for efficiency. Your heating bills will be reduced up to 10 percent.

Film and Function

The summer sun streaming through your windows helps cut down on electric light usage, but it can also make your air conditioner work two to three times harder (that's a bill we don't want to see). Install non-light-blocking reflective window film over clear glass to reduce cooling costs by 5 to 15 percent (far more than the cost of the film)! Look for apply-it-yourself, high-tech, "spectrally selective" film that permits daylight to enter your rooms while blocking solar heat gains. Peel the film off around the time you turn the heat back on—in many parts of the country that's mid-October—or as soon as you no longer need the air conditioner.

8. **Turn it off.** Turn off lights, TVs, computers, and other electronics when they are not in use.

9. **Let there be (better) light.** Replace your most-used conventional incandescent bulbs with long-lasting, energy-saving compact fluorescent bulbs. Use the

sun as your main source of light during the day whenever possible—so open up those drapes and pull up the blinds!

10. **Filter savings.** Clean or replace air-conditioning and heating-system filters monthly for maximum efficiency.

11. **Air-dry for freshness and savings.** One of the cleanest, freshest, most frugal ways to dry your clothes is—you guessed it—outside on a line (weather permitting).

12. **Do the glow test.** Wait until after dark to walk around your house (with a flashlight!) to see what is "glowing." The results will amaze you: your power strips, your computers, your DVD player, your cable box, your microwave oven. Although you may not be actively using them, all of these items in your home are perpetually "on" and eating electricity, unless you pull the plugs when they're not in use.

13. **Keep your freezer full.** If your freezer is empty, you can be sure that it's working overtime to keep the space icy cold. Remedy this by filling it with a large stone, a bucket, a milk jug filled with water—anything that will take up space; the freezer won't work as hard and therefore will use less electricity.

Cut Cell Phone Costs

Buying minutes as you need them may seem like a good idea, but you almost always wind up paying more. By the time you've added in the cost of scrambling to use minutes before they expire, and the inconvenience of never quite knowing how many minutes you have or how many you just used up on a long-distance or "roaming" call, those pay-as-you-go phones aren't a good bargain. But don't do without: a cell phone is a necessity today. Check out these plans for great senior savings:

Verizon Nationwide 65 Plus Plans If you're 65 or older (age verification required), you can sign up for one of Verizon's 65 Plus Plans for $29.99 a month. That rate gets you unlimited calls with any other user on the Verizon cellphone network, 200 monthly anytime minutes, and 500 night and weekend minutes. You can also get a free senior-friendly cell phone such as the Samsung Intensity with a large keypad for visibility, dedicated 911 buttons, and special "In Case of Emergency" buttons. There's a $35 activation fee, and additional minutes beyond the plan are billed at 45 cents per minute (so don't go over your minutes!). There are no domestic roaming or long-distance charges within the United States or Puerto Rico. Find out more at www.verizonwireless.com.

Ka-Ching!

Save Energy,
Save the Planet, and
Save on Your Taxes!

Planning to do some renovation work on your home? Need to bring an old electrical or plumbing system up to date? Before you do, check out your opportunities to install federally approved energy-efficient systems in your home, and then sit back and reap the benefits when tax time comes. The recently enacted American Recovery and Reinvestment Act (ARRA) of 2009 contained a number of new or expanded tax benefits on expenditures to reduce energy use.

"These new, expanded credits encourage homeowners to make improvements that will make their homes more energy efficient," said IRS Commissioner Doug Shulman. "People can improve their homes and save money over the long run."

Homeowners now get bigger tax credits for making energy efficiency improvements or installing alternative energy equipment. Highlights of the new benefits include:

1. A uniform credit of 30 percent of the cost of qualifying improvements—such as adding insulation, energy-efficient exterior windows, and energy-efficient heating and air conditioning systems—up to $1,500. The uniform credit replaces the combination of a 10 percent credit for some property and a credit equal to cost for other property.

2. The limit on the amount that can be claimed for improvements placed in service during 2009 and 2010 was raised to $1,500 from the old $500 lifetime limit.

3. The cap on the 30 percent tax credit for alternative energy equipment installed in a home—such as solar water heaters, geothermal heat pumps and small wind turbines—has been eliminated, beginning with the 2009 tax year.

You'll need to file Form 5695 along with your receipts in order to claim these credits.

Details on the wide range of energy items is available in the special Recovery section of irs.gov, see Fact Sheet 2009-10.

AT&T Senior Nation 200 Plan If you're 65 and older, the Senior Nation 200 Plan, for $29.99 a month with 200 anytime minutes and 500 night and weekend minutes and unlimited minutes with anyone else on AT&T's network, may be perfect for you if your loved ones and friends are also AT&T subscribers. Both plans require a two-year activation and a startup fee ($36 for AT&T or $35 for Verizon), and your monthly bill, with taxes and fees, will likely be more like $35 to $40, rather than $29.99, but if you use your cell phone for all your long-distance calls, it might be a major savings. Visit AT&T at www.wireless.att.com.

Save on Those Phone Bills

Ever since 1876, when Alexander Graham Bell spoke those fateful words into his rudimentary telephone—"Mr. Watson, come here, I want to see you"—phone costs have only gone up. But seniors now have a wealth of ways to bring them back down, including the amazingly cheap world of Internet calls. Find ways to get your telecommunication bills back in line with reality with the discounts and tips below.

Internet Phone Service If you already have high-speed Internet service in your home (which we highly recommend to surf the Web for the very best senior deals and information), you can also use that connection for your regular home phone service. For an additional monthly fee, your Internet service provider can send you a small box that you plug into the back of your modem, and then you plug your regular phone into that. The phone will sound exactly the same as using a regular phone service, but now your voice is going out across your high-speed Internet line rather than your old phone line. What's the downside? If your Internet service goes down (which is rare but happens occasionally), your phone goes out, too. (It returns instantly when the Internet comes back up.) Also, using Internet service for your phone means that 911 dispatchers can't find your physical location if you dial 911 and are unable to speak your address. What's the upside? You'll get significantly reduced monthly costs on phone service and unlimited national long distance for one low price, usually around $20 per month.

Skype If you have grandchildren living across the country or even out of the country, here's a totally free, absolutely delightful way to see their faces and talk to them and let them see you. Skype is a free Internet program that you download onto your computer. The person you want to call must download the program, too, for free. Then, you both open Skype, one of you "dials" the other by hitting the green button on the Skype screen, and the other person

Ka-Ching!

Information Please?

Long ago, dialing Information was a free service from the phone company, but, like everything else, prices have crept up. It can cost as much as $3 to find a number! Don't ever pay for phone information again. If you have a cell phone (and if you don't, you should! See pages 76 and 78 for sweet cell phone deals for seniors), there are heaps of *completely free* services to help you out:

1-800-GOOG-411

Just dial this number from any phone, cell or regular, and you can ask for any listing across the United States and then be connected, all for free. You can also interrupt the computer voice to say "Details," and it will read you the listing, or say, "Text," and it will send the information directly to your cell phone.

1-800-FREE-411

This is another free information service, but it requires you to listen to a 20-second ad before giving you the listing you require.

1-800-2-CHACHA

Wonder when the Hoover Dam was built? Curious about the signs of a heart attack? Want to know what the temperature was in New York City on February 7, 2003? Call 800-2-CHACHA from your cell phone and ask. Thirty seconds later, you'll get a text message to let you know they received the question and are working on it. And in a minute or two, you'll get the answer as a text on your cell phone, along with a link to the Web page where the researcher found the info. You pay the fee, if any, that your cell phone provider charges for receiving a text—typically 10 cents—but otherwise it's a free service.

1-866-JOTT-123

First you have to sign up at www.jott.com, then Jott becomes your personal message service. Call it and say something like, "Remember to take the casserole out of the freezer," speak the date and time to send the message, and when you get home at 6 p.m., the text will appear on your cell phone, beeping you that a message has arrived. You could also have it call your relatives or friends—anyone whose information you've registered—and send any message at any time you like, at any time or day in the future. For free.

"answers" by hitting their green button. Lo and behold, you can hear their voice and see their face on your screen, and you can talk as long as you want for absolutely free. This service assumes you have a computer equipped with a camera and a microphone, as nearly any computer does these days, and also requires high-speed Internet access. Visit www.skype.com.

The Skinny on Car Insurance

You're a great driver, right? Of course! But just when you feel it's time you were due a nice discount on your premiums because you're getter older, the insurance companies start questioning your abilities because you're getting older! Nonetheless, there are insurance companies that understand that seniors with safe driving records deserve a discount.

Early Bird Secret

Extra Insurance Discounts

Whether or not the insurance agent mentions it to you, many insurers offer additional auto discounts if:

• you're retired from the military;

• you're retired from a government job;

• you complete a defensive-driving course;

• you're insuring multiple cars; or

• you have a completely clean driving record for 5–10 years or more.

If you fit the bill for any of these categories, be sure to ask about discounts, no matter which insurance agent you're talking to. And if you get the brush-off, there are plenty of other insurers in the sea! Ask around before settling on a policy that doesn't take any of these categories into account.

The Hartford In partnership with the AARP, The Hartford offers an AARP Auto Insurance Program that it says has potential savings of up to $402 in the first year alone. It also has a Six-Point Claim Guarantee that the company promises will make for fast, no-hassle claim payments. You can use the phone or make your claim online round the clock, with 24-hour claim service and an Online Customer Center to manage your policy. The AARP insurance plan offers Lifetime Renewability, which is important as you age because it ensures that, as long as you are able to meet some specific requirements, your policy will never be canceled. Since you are eligible to join the AARP beginning at age 50, this could be a good move. Visit www.thehartford.com (click on "Auto" under the heading "AARP-endorsed products").

Prime Time for Seniors at Geico If you're 50 or older and are not trying to insure any drivers under the age of 25 on the same policy, you can get a Prime Time contract for auto insurance with Geico. The policy offers guaranteed renewal, and it is only available to drivers who have had no accidents or violations in the previous three years. The vehicle being insured must be for personal use only and may not be used for any business purposes. Find out more at www.geico.com.

Make Your Wheels Roll Longer

There are some people who think of their cars as extensions of their personalities—and Early Bird, you are no exception. We all live in a car culture. A lot of us consider our drive time "our" private moment, and we really savor the freedom of being on the open road (whether it's a drive to the drugstore or a road trip down the Dixie Highway or Route 66), listening to our favorites tunes on the radio, or even doing a little singing ourselves. New car prices rise every year, so the key is to keep your vehicle roadworthy for as long as possible, and you want to take care of it at Early Bird rates! By making the effort to care for your car—lengthening its life and its mileage and maintaining the engine in optimal condition—you can save yourself some real money.

A fine finish. Drive your car through a car wash regularly to get rid of things like salt, mud, grit, grime, bug and bird splatters, and road gravel and tar. "Road dirt" causes permanent pitting and scarring, leaving open the possibility for rust and deterioration. And don't necessarily go for the bottom rate at the car wash. Some places put a polytetrafluoroethylene-based

(PTFE) product on as a final protective layer—the very same material used on Teflon frying pans. If you prefer to do this yourself, it's available under various brand names at automotive stores and in the automotive department of discount stores.

Keep it under wraps. When you are not driving, keep your car in a garage, underneath a carport, or in some sort of covered parking. If you must park in an open driveway, use a car cover—sort of like a water-repellant slipcover for your car. Left under the baking sun, a car's paint finish will oxidize—dark colors and red in particular are most susceptible to this kind of damage.

Stay in tune. Just like you need an annual physical, your car benefits from tune-ups. A well-tuned car runs better, consumes as much as 33 percent less fuel, and extends the life of all other car parts. By adhering to the manufacturer's recommended maintenance schedule, you can save up to $300 a year *over* the cost of a tune-up.

A Clean Discount

Go to an independently owned car wash rather than a national chain, and you're much more likely to get a discount just for the asking. In fact, if you call ahead and ask to speak to the owner or manager, you can probably get your own 10 percent senior discount simply for taking the trouble to request it. And if you become a regular customer, neither you nor the owner will ever have cause to complain about it!

Change is good. Most expert mechanics say regular oil changes—every 3,000 miles, no matter what kind of oil you use—keep your car's engine running smoothly. Heat, friction, and oil oxidizing over time result in sludge, otherwise known as "engine killer."

All tired out. Good, well-cared-for tires keep you safer and increase your gas mileage. Steel-belted radial tires with tread patterns chosen for the worst kind of conditions you regularly face (such as snowy, rainy, muddy, hot, or cold) are best. Make sure tires have the correct air pressure. Underinflated tires burn 5 to 10 percent more fuel. Overinflation causes wear to front-end parts. Get a wheel alignment, tire balance, and rotation once a year; unbalanced tires wear out suspension.

Go for heavy metal. Platinum plugs give you peak performance, and they do not need to be changed for 60,000 to 100,000 miles—three times longer than the life of standard plugs. They cost a bit more initially, but you save down the line on replacement parts and labor.

Fresh air fund. Have your air filter checked every month or two; a dirty one uses more gas and can shorten the life of your engine.

Put on the brakes. Your mechanic can check brake pads when you bring your car in for inspection. Otherwise, they need to be changed if you hear the squeal of the wear bar. An inspection process should include a check of your car's drums, rotors, and other brake parts to ensure they are in good working order.

Senior Discounts on Car Maintenance

While insurers might be a trickier bunch from whom to get a good senior discount, many national chains that provide car-maintenance service are delighted to make the extra effort for seniors. Even if your local shop is not part of a national chain, there's a good chance that you can get 10 percent off the cost of the parts or the labor or both, merely by asking. And let's face it: As you get older, even if you once knew how to change your oil, the thought of crawling under the car and doing it yourself gets less appealing every year! So take advantage of senior discounts, as well as special offers, promotions, and coupons at the following:

Make mine Meineke. Meineke Car Care Centers can put a new muffler on your car in about an hour or less, and if you're 60 or older, many locations will also offer you a 20 percent discount on the service. These car shops can handle oil changes, brakes, exhaust, and many other service issues. As with many national chains, the age requirement and the discount varies, so be sure to check when you bring your car in. At its Web site, www.meineke.com, you can type in your zip code and print out a variety of coupons that are accepted at Meineke locations near you, such as 50 pecent off brake pads and shoes, or $10 off belts and hoses, or a free battery check.

Trust the Midas senior discount. Midas offers 10 percent off parts and services to seniors who are 60 and above, although the discount and age requirement can vary from location to location. Be sure to check when you take your car in, and be sure to visit its Web site to print out coupons, such as an oil change package for $19.99, which includes a tire inspection plus a courtesy check of brakes, filters, fluids, belts and hoses. You can also search for your car's make and model at its site, www.midas.com, and find the manufacturer's recommended maintenance schedule.

Take it off at JiffyLube. There are more than 2,200 locations of JiffyLube across the United States, and most of them will offer at least 10 percent off the cost of your oil change or tune-up for seniors age 60 and above. The age requirement and discount rate vary according to location, so be sure to ask, ideally *before* you get the service and not after. JiffyLube has a useful locator function at its Web site, www.jiffylube.com, and you can also sign up for special offers that may save you more than the discount, as well as find coupons and promotions, such as $5 off the price of an oil and filter change.

Gasoline Savings

In this time of continually rising gas prices, going to the pump can be expensive and alarming. Taking a trip to the store just for a quart of milk seems ridiculous when the cost for the gallon or two of gas it requires is many times the price of the milk. There are, however, a few things you can do to keep your gas costs as low as possible.

Pay the least amount possible. There are some terrific Web sites where rabid Web watchdogs obsessively track the price of gas at stations all over the United States. If you really want to know where the lowest gas prices are in your area, check one of them out and do a search for your street address, town, or zip code. You'll instantly get a listing, station by station, of the latest prices. Of course, make a decision about whether it makes sense to drive five miles out of your way to save 2 cents a gallon. Check out www.gasbuddy.com; www.gaspricewatch.com; or gasprices.mapquest.com.

Compare your car's mileage to other models. The U.S. Department of Energy has a list of all the current car models and the mileage they get, with information on common makes and models dating from 1985 to the present. This very helpful site, www.fueleconomy.gov, also includes a gas mileage calculator to help you figure out your own mileage; a Q&A section on current gas prices and the outlook for upcoming rates; information on alternate-fuel and super-efficient vehicles; and a very interesting, entertaining section on the future of automobiles. A sample: The 2006 winner of an annual competition for a fuel-efficient vehicle (the driver must be enclosed, there must be at least three wheels, and the vehicle must be powered by a small four-stroke engine) was the University of British Columbia, whose entry got a record 3,145 miles per gallon!

Get a tax credit for energy efficiency. If you buy an energy-efficient vehicle, you may be eligible for special state and federal tax credits on the car. Check out the Web site of the U.S. Department of Energy Efficiency and Renewable Energy at http://www.eere.energy.gov/afdc/incentives_laws.html. It has an interactive state-by-state map to let you search rules and regulations regarding tax incentives for fuel efficiency.

Early Bird Secret

Go Where the Trucks Go

One of the very few gas stations that offers an actual gas discount is Flying J, a national chain of truck stops, which you probably see regularly off the highway. Make a point to pull in—and sign up for one of its loyalty incentive programs. Once you've got a membership card in its RV RealValue Club or its Flying J Rewards Club, you won't want to buy gas anywhere else. Both clubs offer a membership card that tracks your purchases at Flying J. Spending anywhere from $10 to $400 a month on goods and services—such as restaurant and J Care service center purchases—can earn you anywhere from a penny to 30 cents off a gallon (generally there is a per-month limit on how much gas you can buy at the discounted rate).

If you've ever bypassed a truck stop looking for a "regular" gas station, think again! Find out more at www.flyingj.com.

The Fine Art of Hypermiling: Going Farther on Less Gas

If you can't get your hands on a hybrid, fear not. Here are simple steps you can take to go much farther in a regular car. In fact, simply maintaining your car can improve mileage by 19 percent. In its most extreme form, gas savings is called "hypermiling" or the art of wringing every last ounce of fuel efficiency out of any car. Many of the techniques embraced by hard-core hypermilers (who tend to be 20-something zealots who are obsessed with wringing every last ounce of performance from their cars) don't meet the average person's commonsense requirements in terms of comfort and safety (they coast down long hills with the engine off, for example). But many others are commonsense approaches to making your gas purchases good to the last drop. Here are a few to get you going.

Go forward. Always park so that you can pull forward rather than waste gas backing up. This can improve your mileage 25 percent (some experts say this might be an underestimate)!

Go the speed limit. The U.S. Department of Energy says that by following the speed limit and swearing off aggressive driving (rapid acceleration and deceleration), drivers can improve mileage by anywhere from 12 to 55 percent. Edmunds.com tested the idea and got similar results. They also found that using cruise control improved mileage by an additional 7 percent.

Stop idling. This leads to mileage improvements of up to 19 percent. If you're going to be at a standstill for 10 seconds or more, say at the drive-through lane at a fast-food joint or an outdoor deposit at a bank, it's better to cut the engine and do your business inside.

Warm up with a long drive. Modern cars don't become fully efficient until the engine is warmed up, so if you plan on running a series of errands, drive to the farthest location first and then work your way back—a series of short stop-and-start trips will never allow your car to reach maximum efficiency.

No junk in your trunk! For every 30 pounds of extra weight your car carries, miles per gallon decreases by anywhere from one-tenth to one-hundredth of a percent. That may not seem like much, but mile per mile it adds up. So de-clutter your car!

Avoid hard stops and starts. Rapid acceleration and hard braking, completely avoidable actions, just throw gas away. Instead of braking hard at a red light, coast from a distance. Come to stops slowly and gradually (if there is no one behind you, coast to the red light if you can).

4

Looking Good, Feeling Great

Cheaper Medicine, Cosmetics, Haircuts, Glasses, and More!

467

Get Thee to a Gym!

If you've never been to a gym in your life, get ready for some fun! Many national chains have special classes for seniors and physical trainers available to take you through an exercise routine or even a round of gentle weight lifting that's tailored to your needs. The result? You'll feel younger, fitter, more energetic—ready to go out there and enjoy all the other discounts that are available to you! Check out these examples, and don't forget to check with your local gym, fitness center, or recreation center, if a branch of one of these isn't nearby.

Curves This worldwide chain of fitness centers caters specifically to women, with special classes and exercise equipment that takes women's comfort into account, plus you never have to wonder if the man on the treadmill is gazing at your bared midriff when you stretch! AARP members can join Curves for an enrollment fee of $49, which is a savings of $100 from the usual fee. What's more, Medicare may cover the cost of your membership—check with your health-care provider. Type your zip code into the Curves Web site (www.curves.com) to find a branch near you, or call 1-800-848-1096.

Gold's Gym Senior discounts vary according to location since all the gyms are independently owned and operated, but a Gold's Gym representative in a Florida location said, proudly, of his center's discount: "It's pretty big!" Check with your nearest Gold's Gym and see how big your senior discount is. The Web site—www.goldsgym.com—can help you locate the nearest facility. AARP members can join Gold's gym for a $49 enrollment fee and save up to 20 percent off membership costs.

YMCA Many (many!) YMCA locations offer programs specifically geared to seniors, such as yoga or tai chi, and some also offer community-based activities such as lectures, social gatherings, and senior outings. Check with your local Y and find out what's on offer.

The YMCA is also a participating member in the SilverSneakers program, so you're in luck if there's a Y nearby! Check the Web site at www.ymca.net to find a Y near you, or call 1-800-872-9622.

Eyesight

Do those darn glasses not work as well as they used to? You have nobody to blame but yourself if you're not getting regular eye exams—vision can change, and you need your prescription to keep up. The days of bifocals that didn't let you see well either close up *or* far away are over. Modern optometry is keenly attuned to your changing vision needs, whether it's merely a pair of reading glasses or a high-tech pair of trifocals. Best of all, you can get your new glasses at a discount.

LensCrafters LensCrafters offers discounts to AAA and AARP members from 10 percent on contact lenses to 50 percent off specials on regular lenses. Check the Web site www.lenscrafters.com for their current discounts.

Pearle Vision It always pays to be a AAA member, and not only for your car: present your card and get a discounted eye exam, 30 percent off eyeglasses (frames, lenses, lens options), 30 percent off eyeglass accessories, and 10 percent off contact lenses. You can also get 30 percent off eye exams and 15 percent off partials. Present your AARP card and you can get a discounted exam, 30 percent off complete eyewear, 20 percent off non-disposable contact lenses, 10 percent off disposable contact lenses, and 20 percent off accessories. Visit www.pearlevision.com for the most recent deals and discounts.

The MD Foundation This little-known organization offers information on macular degeneration and the most recent scientific research into its causes and cures. You can read its regular newsletter, "The Magnifier," at its Web site, www.eyesight.org, where you can also listen to an audio version of the newsletter. You can also phone and ask for a free subscription at 888-633-3937.

Get a Salon Look for Less

As much as we might all wish for it, there is one basic truth about hair care: the wash-and-go cut, simple-and-easy hairdo is essentially a myth. Nobody rolls out of bed with perfect hair. Hollywood celebrities look the way they do because an entire hair and makeup team spent hours working before the celebrity ever set foot out the door. Most of us can manage without a team of stylists, but having someone else trim and style our hair now and then makes a big difference. We all know that to keep your hair looking good, you have to spend a little *time* on it. The good news is that you don't have to spend a lot of *money*.

Turn gray into gold! As hair grays, it becomes somewhat coarser than when it had its natural pigment, partly due to the natural loss of oils. Turn down the heat, if possible, on appliances such as curling irons, and use the low setting on blow-dryers because gray hair is more likely to be damaged, and damage on gray hair can take the form of a yellowish cast. Yellowing can also come from exposure to sun, smoking, hard water, and even from medication. Lavender- and blue-toned shampoos are an inexpensive way to counteract yellowing, but use them alternately with your regular shampoo to prevent the hair taking on that bluish tone.

Wash, rinse, repeat—not! Washing your hair twice in one session is an old marketing trick designed to make you use your shampoo up twice as fast. Double-shampooing strips all the natural oils out of your hair as effectively as paint thinner. Hair should never be "squeaky clean" because that's the same as "super-dry." Even people with naturally oily hair merely rev up their oil production by stripping all the natural oil from their scalps. One of our top experts, a partner and senior stylist at an upscale New York salon, recommends using shampoo on your hair not twice in one wash, but only every second wash. "Put in a little conditioner on your hair the days you're not shampooing," he says, "And be sure to rinse it out very well in warm water, so it doesn't start to build up on the strands. The days that you do shampoo, use about half the amount." The benefit to this system? Healthier hair with more body and shampoo costs that are cut in half.

Did You Know?

Don't use any clarifying shampoo, either store-bought or homemade, if you have just colored your hair, because it can remove some of the color and leave your newly coiffed head looking a lot less lustrous and evenly toned. But it's a great idea to use a clarifying shampoo just *before* you color your hair. Removing all traces of buildup allows the hair to take the color much better, and thus the color will last longer.

Baking soda for healthy hair! Your hair will look shinier and bouncier if you remove all traces of styling products and conditioner every six weeks or so. But do you need to buy a special clarifying shampoo? Not if you already have a box of baking soda in your cabinet. Mix a tablespoon of baking soda with two tablespoons of white vinegar and work it into your hair. Rub it in well all along the hair strands and then rinse thoroughly.

Stay away from too much of a good thing. Shampoo, conditioner, gel, mousse, hairspray—whatever you're putting on your hair, you're probably using too much of it. Try using half of the usual amount of everything you put on your hair, from shampoo and conditioner to gels and hairspray. You'll prevent (or slow) product buildup, allowing the products to be more effective, and you'll make a bottle or tube last twice as long—cutting the price effectively in half.

Ka-Ching!
Lace On Those Tennies!

The SilverSneakers Fitness Program is just what the doctor ordered if you're an in-the-know Early Bird. This terrific program offers:

CUSTOMIZED SENIOR WORKOUT AND HEALTH CLASSES

HEALTH EDUCATION SEMINARS

SPECIALLY TRAINED SENIOR ADVISER

The best part? It's *free* if you're a member of a participating Medicare health plan.

SilverSneakers provides a membership in a fitness center near your home. If no participating gyms or fitness centers are nearby, the SilverSneakers Steps program will provide you with a Personal Exercise Tracker, a recommended fitness program to get you started, newsletters, tracking logs, and a toll-free number where you can call for advice.

If your health plan covers the cost of SilverSneakers (and many do—just call the toll-free number on your health plan membership ID and ask), then all you have to do is take that ID to a participating fitness center and sign up. It's that easy to find a community of either like-minded exercise buffs or tentative beginners just like you! Find out more at www.silversneakers.com.

Sleep like a princess for Rapunzel-like locks. Your hairstyle rumples less if you sleep on a satin pillowcase. Cotton pillow covers (yes, even those 400 thread-count sheets) roughen the cuticle more, but satin allows the hair to slip smoothly over the surface as you roll and turn in your sleep. Satin allows you to preserve your do overnight. If you've spent a lot of time getting styled the day before, a night on the satin will help leave it magically preserved in the morning and ready to face another day.

Baby those tresses. Don't pay premium prices for high-end shampoos that are specially formulated for colored or permed hair. An inexpensive bottle of baby shampoo will treat your hair just as gently and will also allow the color or perm to last much longer.

Give it a natural shine. To bring out your highlights without a lot of expense, use an astringent rinse last thing while washing your hair. For lighter-colored hair, combine 1/4 cup of lemon juice with 1 cup of warm water and pour it over your hair. To bring out the highlights in darker hair, mix 1/4 cup of white vinegar with 1 cup of warm water.

Skin and Makeup Savings

Did you know that you can buy a skin cream that costs $600 an ounce (we're not kidding) and contains a chemical that's supposed to regenerate dead skin faster than normal, and it's only available at a few exclusive boutiques? Did you further know that this super-pricey skin lotion comes backed by "clinical trials" that assure you this product will change the way your skin looks in mere days? Further still, were you aware that these same trials are always paid for by the manufacturer of said cream? The truth? We never get to hear how a bottle of drugstore moisturizer measured up by comparison.

Fortunately, you can do far more practical and downright inexpensive things for your skin that will make it look just as good—and, probably, better—than that of the woman who's praying that her $600 worth of face cream makes her look like a 20-year-old. Here are some straightforward and inexpensive skin-care ideas that save time and money!

Borrow your grandmother's skin-care tool kit. What's the trick to great skin? Listen to your grandmother and pare down your supplies. According to a top dermatologist in New York, you can count on three fingers all you need for great skin health. What's in the arsenal? A moisturizing soap, moisturizer, and sunscreen. End of story. Anything else might make you *think* you're helping your skin, but the truth is you're just wasting time

Ka-Ching!

"Do" Discounts

Major national chains offer varying discounts for seniors, so be sure to check at your location. If all you want is the occasional trim, or a wash and blow-dry, check to see if you have a local barber training school or hairstyling school (most towns have some such institution—your hairdresser may be able to tell you where!). These places are glad to get willing models, and as long as you only want something simple—a color rinse, a trim, a blow-dry—they're usually worth the small fee you'll pay. Or you can get slightly more seasoned professionals to do your do for a nice senior discount at the following chains:

SUPERCUTS

Haircuts are $2 off the regular adult price for patrons 60 and older at this national franchise with over 2,000 locations. Discount and age requirements may vary by location so please call before you go. To find a salon near you, visit www.supercuts.com.

GREAT CLIPS

If you're 65 and older, you can get a haircut at a discount off the regular price (which differs with individual salons). Visit www.greatclips.com and click on Salon Locator for the GreatClips near you.

THIRD DIMENSION

Located in Washington and Oregon, these salons offer their clients 60 years and older, 10 percent off the regular price of any service that is performed Monday through Thursday, between the hours of 9:00 a.m. to 3:00 p.m. For salon locations, visit http://www.3dsalons.com.

and money on special eye or neck creams—moisturizer is moisturizer, so find one you like and stick with it.

Stay out of the sun. There's no such thing as a healthy tan. Tanned skin is effectively damaged skin, and nothing ages you faster or worse or puts you more at risk for skin cancer than cumulative exposure. As you age and your skin becomes thinner and more delicate, it's even more important that you use sunscreen on your face and neck (and ideally on your chest and the backs of your hands) *every day*, whether it's blazing hot summer or the middle of winter. Sun damage occurs year round, especially during hazy, cloudy days.

Get enough sleep. When you get a poor night's sleep, it shows on your face in the morning as surely as if it was written across your forehead in marker. Getting enough rest is one of the number-one beauty treatments, more important than any soap or moisturizer or makeup. Go to bed a little earlier and try not to worry—you're saving money *and* looking good!

Slice a cuke to lose those dark circles. While you're working on getting more beauty sleep, do what you can to lessen the effect of those telltale dark circles under your eyes. A slice of cold cucumber on each eye will reduce puffiness, as will a cold wet tea bag on each eye, but the best trick of all is cold, freshly grated potato. Wrap the damp shreds in one layer of cheesecloth (or one layer of a dampened, squeezed-out paper towel, if you're fresh out of cheesecloth). Recline and lay a potato packet over each eye, and rest for 15 to 20 minutes. When you discard the packets and rinse your face in cool water, eye puffiness will be noticeably reduced—as will fine lines around the corners!

Drink enough water. Skin hydrates from the inside out, so it doesn't matter what you're slathering on the surface if you're not drinking enough water. Researchers have backtracked a bit from the old recommendation of eight 8-ounce glasses a day, independent of any other beverages. Now we are told that the coffee or juice or soda you drink does count toward your daily water requirement, but nobody has backtracked from the fact that simple, unadulterated, really inexpensive water is still the healthiest drink there is.

Ka-Ching!

See a Celebrity Stylist for Pennies

Some of the top styling salons—the ones you see in celebrity magazines—charge up to $600 for a cut. Although their prices are insane, these people truly give you a terrific haircut and style that actually looks like you're a celebrity, so it can be well worth seeing one of them.

What?! The secret is to go to one of their modeling sessions. "Hair models" are the people whom salons use when training their staffs. Many upscale salons have very advanced hair-model programs, offering cuts, color, and styling—all for free. Some require you to come to an assessment session so they can see if you have hair they want to work on. Super-curly or super-short-haired clients, for example, probably will not qualify; some salons also won't color your hair if you have used certain coloring products within the last year.

Once you pass the test, you're usually in the door for regular cuts, color, and stylings as long as you meet all their criteria. Call the fanciest salon in your area and ask if they have a hair-model program, or do an Internet search for "hair model" and the name of your city. You'll feel like Dorothy sitting in the beauty salon in Oz!

The rules tend to be strict for getting these fancy and fabulous haircuts for free, even though nothing will be done without your consultation and approval. If you prefer the more traditional route of deciding exactly when you get an appointment and exactly what's going to happen while you're there, stay away. If you have some flexibility in terms of time, and you're willing to discuss various styles, however, you'll look like a million bucks for *free!*

Early Bird Secret

Say Hello to Sally

Sally Beauty Supply, the largest beauty supply store in the nation, also has stores around the world: in Ireland, Mexico, and Japan. They also have a very generous senior-discount policy, offering seniors 55 and older a discount of between 5 percent and 25 percent on non-sale items every day. The discount varies according to which product you're buying, and participation may vary according to location, but whether you need cocoa butter for your chapped hands or new hot rollers, the price may be just right at Sally! Visit www.sallybeauty.com for more information.

Exfoliate and glow! Especially in cold weather, skin can start to look rough, tired, and dull. The key to getting back your glow is to exfoliate, or rub off the dead skin cells clogging the surface of your skin, and you can do this once a month (but don't do it if your skin is already irritated or broken out). In a small dish, mix 1/4 cup raw rolled oats (either quick-cooking or traditional oatmeal is fine) with 2 tablespoons olive oil and 1 tablespoon of cornmeal. Add a few teaspoons of warm water until the mixture forms a paste. Wet your face with warm water and gently rub this mixture onto your skin with gentle circular motions. Stay away from the delicate skin around your eyes, but don't forget to massage the skin under and around your nose. Rinse well with warm water and pat dry very gently.

Have a facial. It's true: You don't need a lot of products for basic upkeep, but a once-in-a-while facial can leave your skin feeling soft and refreshed, and it's a great stress reliever. It promotes blood flow to the surface, and the whole process makes you feel and look more relaxed. And it doesn't need to cost more than a few pennies. An excellent facial for any skin type can be made from items that are already in your kitchen. Smooth one on, put your feet up, tip your head back, and let the stress flow out of you for 15 or 20 minutes. Whatever facial you use, be sure to moisturize your face generously after you're done.

Normal skin: Plain yogurt smooths and soothes almost any kind of skin, and it's the simplest mask there is. A full-fat yogurt feels creamiest, but even low-fat varieties give good results. (Nonfat yogurt is okay, but it won't feel as nice when you smooth it on.) Smooth a few tablespoons of yogurt directly on your face, or combine it with a teaspoon of honey, which moisturizes, and 1 or 2 drops of tea tree oil, a natural astringent. Allow to dry for 15 minutes, then rinse with warm water.

Oily skin: Clay masks are classic to help dry out oily skin, and you may be able to find facial clay at a health-food store. If so, combine 2 tablespoons clay with 1 teaspoon of honey and enough water to make a smooth paste. Smear all over your face, avoiding the eye area. If you can't find clay, smear unflavored milk of magnesia over your face (avoiding the eye area, as always). Whichever you choose, allow it to dry for 20 minutes before rinsing with warm water.

Dry skin: Mash half a ripe banana with half a ripe avocado using a fork, and blend in a tablespoon of warm olive oil (you can warm a bit in a cup in the microwave). Smooth it generously all over your face, avoiding the eye area. Leave on for 15 to 20 minutes, and then rinse well with warm water.

Skin with large pores: Put an egg white into a cup and beat it with a fork until it starts to get foamy. Smooth this over your clean skin and allow to dry. Rinse off with lots of warm water, buffing gently with a soft washcloth if necessary, and then moisturize.

Homemade Beauty and Health Products

The best discount of all might be the cost of making some of your beauty products at home. Most dermatologists agree that putting too many chemicals on your skin isn't good for it—especially as you get older and your skin is more delicate. Therefore, the best beauty products can be the simplest, without harsh alcohols and soap. In upscale beauty departments, the most natural products with the fewest chemicals are nowadays the ones that command the highest price! How have we come to this inverted way of doing business? Fortunately, homemade beauty products are easy to make, extremely effective, and can replace nearly every manufactured item in your bathroom cabinet. You'll look and feel better and keep your skin soft and smooth, your hair gleaming, and your cheeks and lips shining with health.

The "Spot Test" Rule

Before you put any homemade beauty product all over your face (or before you put any manufactured one that you've never tried before), do a spot test. Put a dab of it on the inside of your forearm. Leave for 10 minutes, then rinse off. If the skin is in any way discolored, reddened, or itchy, don't put that product on your face! You won't be surprised to find, however, that homemade facials such as yogurt and eggs tend to be much gentler on the skin than manufactured products, which often contain irritating levels of alpha hydroxy acids.

Bath products

"Soaking in bath salts" has a Victorian sound to it, but people have known for generations that a warm tub of water full of mineral salts helps relax the body and eases muscle aches, reduces inflammation, and can even soothe the skin. (We're not talking about table salt here.) Epsom salt, available in any drugstore, is in fact magnesium sulfate and contains no sodium chloride at all, but it can be used in place of "bath salt" in any bath soak recipe. Regular sea salt is usually damper and grayer than table salt and is full of minerals such as magnesium and calcium; it, too, can be used in the bath with good results. The amounts below are for one bath. You can either mix the ingredients in advance and package them for later use, or put the ingredients directly into the tub under hot running water.

Lavender Bath Soak

This bath is a classic soother of both mind and body.

> 1/2 cup bath salts
>
> 1 tablespoon baking soda
>
> 5 drops lavender essential oil

Rosemary Bath Soak

This bright, herbally scented bath is invigorating and wonderful if you need a lift.

> 1/2 cup bath salts
>
> 5 drops rosemary oil
>
> 5 drops tea tree oil

Rose Milk Bath

Ideal for irritated skin, the milk and baking soda in this bath make your skin feel soft and smooth.

> 1/2 cup powdered milk
>
> 1/4 cup baking soda
>
> 15 drops blended rose oil

Oatmeal Bath

This is an extremely soothing bath for itchy, dry, or sunburned skin and perfect if you or a loved one has gotten into poison ivy.

1/2 cup oatmeal, ground to a fine powder in a coffee or spice grinder

1/4 cup powdered milk

1/4 cup baking soda

5 drops of your favorite essential oil

Bay Leaf Bath

This is a time-honored home preparation thought to ease strained muscles.

10 large bay leaves

1 pint of boiling water

Steep bay leaves in a boiling water for 10 minutes. Remove the bay leaves and pour the liquid directly into a hot bath.

Early Bird Secret

The Correct Epsom Salt

When you're looking for Epsom salt at the drugstore, don't buy the small box or bottle that contains about half a cup for $2 to $3. The small containers are for people who want to take their Epsom salt internally, a teaspoonful dissolved in water as a laxative. Look in the housewares section or ask in the pharmacy for the large containers—bags or boxes that hold a pound or more and that sell for $1 to $2. You need a lot more salt if you want to soak in it or use it as fertilizer in your garden.

Hand and body lotions, balms, and oils

Homemade hand lotion is more like the old-fashioned, thinner type of lotion our grandmothers used. It won't be as thick as a manufactured hand lotion, but it will generally be absorbed by the skin faster and feel much less greasy. A hand cream will be thicker and is better for dry skin or nighttime use. Whatever you choose, the active ingredients are usually the same: glycerin and/or petroleum jelly and maybe some beeswax or cocoa butter. All of these are available in their base form in nearly any drugstore, and you can combine them with various fragrances and other ingredients to make a truly personal body and hand moisturizer. For each recipe below, mix the ingredients in a small jar or tub and shake before each use. Store in the refrigerator and use each batch within five days.

Lavender Hand Lotion
- 1/4 cup glycerin
- 1/4 cup rose water
- 4–5 drops lavender essential oil

Lime Body Lotion
- 2 tablespoons glycerin
- 1 tablespoon fresh lime juice, strained

Lemon Body Lotion
- 2 tablespoons glycerin
- 1 tablespoon fresh lemon juice, strained

Orange Body Lotion
- 2 tablespoons glycerin
- 1 tablespoon fresh orange juice, strained
- 3 drops orange oil

Instant Hand Softener

2 tablespoons baby oil

3 tablespoons sugar

Rub and massage all over your hands, then rinse gently in warm water and pat dry.

Super-Soothing Hand Cream

1/2 cup oatmeal, ground fine in a coffee or spice grinder

1 tablespoon yogurt

2 tablespoons sweet almond oil

1 tablespoon rose water

1 teaspoon honey

Stir together and store in the refrigerator. Rub generously on itchy, dry hands and allow to soak in, then rinse with warm water.

Strawberry Foot Balm

1/2 cup fresh strawberries

3 tablespoons sugar

2 tablespoons olive oil

Mash strawberries (discard the stems first) with sugar and olive oil. Rub all over your bare feet and relax for 10 minutes. Rinse well with warm water and follow with Peppermint Foot Oil.

Peppermint Foot Oil

2 tablespoons sweet almond oil

1 tablespoon olive oil

12 drops peppermint essential oil

Lip balms and glosses

Making lip treatments at home is extremely appealing when you consider that this is the one cosmetic you actually tend to "eat," whether you mean to or not. The stickiest gloss eventually disappears off your lips, and it probably didn't get wiped off—you gradually ingested it. Taking that into consideration, wouldn't you rather know exactly what went in before you slather it on? With these simple versions, you can feel sure that your lip balms are simple and pure. Lip balms may require melting to get all the ingredients to combine, so use care if using the microwave.

Peppermint Lip Balm

1 tablespoon cocoa butter

1 tablespoon beeswax

2 tablespoons sweet almond oil

5 drops peppermint oil

Melt the cocoa butter and beeswax in a small container in the microwave for 10 seconds, then stir in the oils. Pour into a small container and allow to cool.

Honey Lip Balm

1 tablespoon petroleum jelly

1/2 teaspoon honey

Melt in the microwave for 10 seconds, then stir to combine. Pour into a small container and allow to cool.

Homemade Lip Gloss

6 teaspoons sweet almond oil

2 teaspoons beeswax

1/2 teaspoon honey

7 drops peppermint oil

Melt the oil and beeswax together in the microwave for 10 seconds, then stir in the honey and peppermint oil. Pour into a small container and allow to cool.

Basic Toothpaste

The simplest mouth cleaner possible is to combine three parts baking soda with one part salt. Shake about a teaspoon of this mixture into your palm and dab your wet toothbrush bristles in it, and brush as usual. Your teeth will feel as smooth and freshly polished as if you had just left your dentist's office.

Mint Toothpaste

If the salty taste of basic toothpaste isn't to your liking, make a slightly fancier, minty, and equally effective cleaner.

2 tablespoons baking soda
1/2 teaspoon salt
1 tablespoon glycerin
10 drops oil of peppermint

Combine all ingredients. Add a few drops of water, if you like, to achieve the correct paste consistency, and store in a tightly covered container.

Natural Teeth Whitener

1 teaspoon baking soda
1/2 teaspoon table salt
hydrogen peroxide

In a small container (or in your clean palm) combine baking soda, table salt, and a little hydrogen peroxide, just enough to make a paste. Dip your brush in this mixture and brush as usual, paying special attention to the front teeth.

Basic Mouthwash

Nearly all commercial mouthwashes contain alcohol as a major ingredient. If you use one daily, you may find that eventually your mouth starts to dry out more and more, becoming uncomfortable and, paradoxically, increasing the likelihood of the very bad breath that mouthwash is supposed to combat. Homemade mouthwashes are a much gentler rinsing agent and can be infused with a bit of herbal or spicy flavor. Make them in small quantities and use each batch within a week. Gargle with 1/4 to 1/2 cup a day, as you like. For added refreshment, store your homemade mouthwash in the refrigerator.

Basic Mint Mouthwash

- **2 cups water**
- **2 teaspoons baking soda**
- **2 drops oil of peppermint**

Combine in a small bottle, cover, and shake.

Basic Cinnamon Mouthwash

- **2 cups water**
- **2 teaspoons baking soda**
- **2 drops oil of cinnamon**

Combine in a small bottle, cover, and shake.

Fresh Mint Mouthwash

- **3 cups water**
- **1 handful fresh mint leaves**
- **1 teaspoon fresh rosemary leaves**
- **1 teaspoon anise or fennel seeds (optional)**

Boil the water and drop in the leaves and seeds. Steep for 10 minutes, then strain, bottle, and store in the refrigerator.

Saltwater Dental Wash

This is particularly good at removing stray food particles and helping ward off gum disease.

- **1/2 cup warm water**
- **1 teaspoon salt**

Combine warm water with salt, swish and gargle. Mix each batch fresh as needed.

Department Stores That Discount

Department stores are a reliable source of senior discounts because so much of their goods are discretionary as opposed to necessity. It's worth the while of these retail outlets to court the patronage of a group of customers who wield, by some estimates, nearly 80 percent of leisure spending. So you'll often find a slightly higher percentage off—15 percent or 20 percent, say—than you might at a grocery store. Look out for good sales at your favorite department store, and then breeze in and get your additional discount on top. You'll be glad you asked! Here is just a selection of discounts you get.

Early Bird Secret

Secondhand Discounts

You might think that secondhand clothes at Goodwill and the Salvation Army are inexpensive enough, but don't forget to ask for your senior discount when shopping there as well!

Goodwill offers a 10 percent to 20 percent discount to customers 55 and above, depending on which location you're shopping.

The Salvation Army offers seniors 55 and older discounts that range from 15 percent to 50 percent off, depending on the location. Some stores offer these discounts to seniors every day, while others only offer them on Wednesdays. Check with your nearest store and don't forget to ask!

Banana Republic Nearly all Banana Republic stores offer a 10 percent senior discount every day, but check with the cashier before your purchase is rung up. Find a store near you at www.bananarepublic.com.

Bealls If you're 50 years or older, you'll save 15 percent on all your purchases on the first Tuesday of every month, 20 percent if you use a Bealls Credit Card. You need to sign up with a sales associate. For details of Club 50 Plus, visit bealstx.com and click on Customer Rewards.

Belk This chain of upscale department stores across the South and the Midwest has a Seniors Day the first Tuesday of every month. If you're 55 or older, take an extra 20 percent off all sale purchases storewide and 15 percent off Home and Shoes with your Belk Rewards Card.

Bon-Ton Check with your closest Bon-Ton store to find out which day of the month is Senior Day (it's often a Wednesday). If you're 55 and older and using a Bon-Ton credit card, the discount is 20 percent. It's 15 percent off if you use any other type of payment. All purchases from the home department (sheets, towels, curtains, etc.) are 10 percent, no matter what payment type you use. Visit its Web site at www.bonton.com.

Dress Barn Customers 62 and older can take an additional 10 percent off their entire purchase every Tuesday, although the day and the percentage may vary at some locations. Check out details at www.dressbarn.com.

Goody's Customers who are 50 and older can save 15 percent off their purchases on the first Tuesday of every month, 20 percent off if you use a Goody's Credit Card. You need to sign up with a sales associate. To find out more, go to www.goodysonline.com and click on Club 50 Plus "Customer Rewards."

Kohl's While Kohl's does not offer a standard senior discount, every December they advertise several senior days when seniors can take an extra discount off their purchases. The percentage and the days vary from store to store, so be sure to ask, especially when you're doing your holiday shopping! They offer senior days occasionally throughout the rest of the year, but you'll have to check with your individual store. Kohl's Cash may be an even better deal than a senior discount: for every $50 you spend, you get $10 in Kohl's cash, effectively giving you back 20 percent of the purchase price to spend on your next visit. (The senior discount and the Kohl's Cash are not mutually exclusive, but you'll receive the "cash" reward based on the discounted final amount, not the base price.) Find out more at www.kohls.com.

Lord & Taylor If you're 62 and older, Lord & Taylor may give you a 15 percent discount on Wednesdays, but this may vary from store to store, so visit customer service to confirm, and then shop happily!

Meijer One day a month (the day varies according to the store but generally on a Monday or Tuesday), Meijer has a Senior Discount Day offering customers 55 and up 15 percent off all general merchandise purchases. Get details at www.meijer.com.

Peebles If you're 50 or older, you can apply with any sales associate at Peebles (find a store near you at www.peebles.com) for a Club 50 Plus card, which allows the holder to save 15 percent on all purchases on the first Tuesday of every month, 20 percent if you use a Peebles Credit Card. Proof of age is required.

Ross Ross Stores have a Tuesday ClubDiscount Day for customers 55 and older. By becoming a member of the program, customers are entitled to 10 percent off their purchases on Tuesday. Sign up at the customer service desk during store hours and show ID with your age or date of birth and the store will issue you a card. Visit their Web site at www.rossstores.com.

Welcome to Senior Discount Village!

La Grange Park, a town in Illinois that bills itself as "The Village of Roses," is also the Village of Senior Discounts. In 2001, they formed a commission on Aging Well that has not only led to a series of initiatives to make the town senior friendly, such as free 911 cell phones for seniors and a Walk for Health program, but they have also coordinated local businesses in offering senior discounts.

If you're 65 and older, you can enjoy a minimum of 10 percent off a wide range of goods and services in the town each Wednesday. There are nearly 30 businesses participating, and each one displays an "Aging Well" discount sign. That's a town that knows how to live well. Find out more at www.lagrangepark.org.

Outlet Shopping

"Outlets" used to mean a decrepit wholesale store attached to a factory, such as bread outlets offering overstock and day-old goods. Nowadays an outlet is more likely to be an upscale complex of high-end stores, and the prices don't always seem *that* much lower than what you'd pay at the same store in the mall. But outlets are also eager to build their status as "destination" shopping—and if they want you to make a day trip out of it, then an added discount can only help.

Chelsea Premium Outlets

This parent company of outlet complexes has stores across the United States, and the names vary: Woodbury Common Premium Outlets is near New York City, for example, and Napa Premium Outlets is in California. You can locate the one nearest to you through the map on its Web site, www.premiumoutlets.com. You can get an additional 10 percent discount off your purchases at participating outlet stores (ranging from Old Navy to A/X Armani Exchange) every Tuesday with their 50 Plus Shopper Perks Program. Show a photo ID when paying and you *automatically* receive your discount. You can also join its VIP Shopper Club at its Web site and receive exclusive online coupons and e-mail updates for sales and special events.

HSN Outlets This chain of outlet stores offers Senior Discount day every Tuesday in all the outlet stores of the complex. If you're 50 or older, you get an additional 10 percent off your total purchases—with a maximum savings of $50. (That means, once you spend $500, you should put your credit card away until the next Tuesday!)

Prime Outlets Prime Outlets are mostly east of the Mississippi. You can pick up a Senior Savings Guide near the food court in each outlet complex and figure out what your savings potential is at every store. Find out more at www.primeoutlets.com.

Don't Re-buy Your Clothes: Clean Them!

Found the linen suit of your dreams that will need professional pressing every time you wear it? How about a gorgeous silk blouse marked "Dry-Clean Only"? We feel your pain, because a lot of dry-cleaning is not only bad for your pocketbook, but it can actually damage your clothing, and do a lot worse to the environment. More and more cleaners are attempting to switch to "healthier" chemicals, but the fact remains that most dry cleaning is still accomplished by powerful solvents that are potentially toxic. Here's how to cut down on your dry-cleaning bill and those solvents' impact on the environment, and maybe make your clothes last a little longer in the meantime.

Spot clean. If you get a spot on a "dry-clean only" item, remove it yourself, instantly, with a portable spot cleaner. Before you ever wear the item, test a spot on an inside seam with a bit of the cleaner, and make sure it does not leave a visible mark on the fabric. Then carry your spot cleaner with you and use it, fast, as soon as you dribble a drop of coffee or spill a little ketchup.

Air it out. Refresh a dry-cleanable garment each time you wear it rather than rolling it in a ball to take to the cleaners. Put it on a hanger and allow air to circulate around it rather than tucking it in an overpacked closet or throwing it in a pile. Hang it in the bathroom while you shower, and let it steam a bit to relax wrinkles and allow odors to dissipate.

Press it. You *can* iron a "dry-clean only" outfit without harm if you keep the heat low and don't iron too much. Avoid any obvious stains and try not to iron over areas where stains may emerge, such as under the arms or over the chest and belly.

Make your own home dry-cleaning kit. There's no need to spend a lot of money on those kits, which will provide you with a solvent and a "freshener," also known as a "dryer sheet." Put the garment in the dryer with a regular dryer sheet for 10 to 15 minutes, on medium heat, and you'll find that it's nearly the same as taking it to the cleaner: freshened, sweeter smelling, and with most of the wrinkles released. (Don't overdry, and be sure to remove the garment and hang it up promptly, or you'll set the wrinkles back in.)

Hand wash. Why should a silk cardigan be dry-cleaned when silk is supposed to be one of the toughest natural materials on earth? Knitwear, linen, and silks are especially likely to be hand-washable. (Men's suits, not so much—it's not that it will ruin the fabric in most cases but it *will* ruin the shape.) Use cold water and a delicate detergent. Lay knitwear flat to dry, or reshape the garment on a hanger to dry; be sure to use a wide hanger that reaches to the shoulder seams, so that the item doesn't end up with little marks at the shoulders where the hanger caught it.

The Top 12 Heart-Happy Foods

When you put wholesome, unrefined, unprocessed foods into your body, you are helping to promote glowing health and reducing all sorts of health risks like obesity, diabetes, high blood pressure, and stroke. That in turn can reduce doctor visits, improve your good mood, and lower stress. Best of all, ounce for ounce, pound for pound, real "whole" food costs a lot less than packaged junk. You get a much bigger bang for your buck, and it tastes better, too. Eat a balanced diet full of a variety of fresh foods, like these 12 superstars, and you'll have plenty of reasons to smile.

1. Almonds Vitamin B2 (riboflavin), vitamin E, magnesium, and zinc all help to make a handful (about 1/4 cup a day) of crunchy almonds good for your heart and your mood. B vitamins and magnesium help produce serotonin, which helps regulate mood. Zinc has also been shown to fight some negative effects of stress, while vitamin E is an antioxidant that

5 Smart

Where to shop? Super-sales at major department stores can yield discounts much deeper than what the store offers you as a senior, especially if it's end of season. You can also get creative about the places you buy things and think outside the big-name box—there are serious savings in shopping a bit off the beaten track, in the best possible way, such as vintage stores or designer overstock.

1. CHAIN BARGAIN STORES

Places such as Ross and T.J. Maxx not only offer senior discounts but can also offer treasures if you're willing to plunge in up to your elbows and pick over the bargain racks. The racks at the front of the store have become less of bargains over the years, offering full-price merchandise from lesser labels. Move straight on back to the "Clearance" sections and start to sort. This is where you can often find real designer goods at major discounts. Subtract your senior discount from the rock-bottom price, and you've got a real deal!

2. OUTLETS

Outlets used to be the first outpost of the bargain hunter, but as this business has become firmly entrenched, outlets sometimes sell their own brands, such as the Gap Outlet label, offering clothes that never make it into actual Gap stores. Full price at outlets is suspiciously like full price at the regular store! Happily, the senior discount at a large outlet center is usually for all the stores in the entire outlet, and it's usually a higher discount than the stores might offer individually.

3. OVERSTOCK WEB SITES

Here's where you can get real bargains on designer labels. Type into a search engine (such as Google) the

Places to Shop

name of the item or designer that you want and the word "overstock." You'll find a range of sites selling brand-new stuff, usually with tags still on, at complete bargain-basement prices.

4. VINTAGE, CONSIGNMENT, AND THRIFT STORES

Like any store, these eclectic selections can be hit or miss. They're not the types of places to find something highly specific, along the lines of, "I need a blue raincoat right now," but they are the place to find a true bargain on some very distinctive pieces: a Gucci handbag, hardly used, for $15; a pair of Chanel shoes never worn, for $5; perhaps a velvety suede coat, tags on, for $20. Basics can be found for literally cents on the dollar, such as a skirt for 50 cents or a stretchy top for a quarter. These types of stores offer the thrill of the serious bargain and the hunt for the unexpected (and unexpectedly inexpensive) in exchange for giving up control—you never know what you might get on a given day, but it will likely be fabulous and cheap!

5. TAG SALES, YARD SALES, GARAGE SALES

Sometimes a risky place to buy clothes because people are inclined to overprice something that means a lot to them. They know they paid $200 for that winter coat two years ago, so they put it in their front yard for $45, when to you it's only worth $5 or $10. Bargain gently in these situations, and you might end up with a really good deal. Ask, "Do you have a senior discount?" and you'll probably make the owner smile and give you one!

destroys the free radicals related to stress and heart disease. They're the perfect snack—so much better than a bag of chips. Or, add some slivered beauties to your morning oatmeal.

> *Early Bird Buy:* Buy roasted and unsalted almonds from a bulk bin, and get just what you need at a lower per-pound price than packaged nuts.

2. Asparagus

Asparagus contains heart-healthy anti-inflammatory nutrients like folate and vitamins C and D. It is also low in calories and quick cooking. Sauté it with sugar snap peas and toss with whole wheat pasta, olive oil, lemon juice, and a bit of freshly grated Parmesan cheese and pepper for a meatless meal fit for a (very healthy) king or queen.

> *Early Bird Buy:* Buy it fresh during spring and early summer, when local crops are harvested. Canned asparagus lose something in translation, so they are best left on the shelf, but frozen make a passable substitute for the fresh stuff.

3. Beans

These versatile legumes contain more protein than any other plant food—just one cup provides a quarter of what we need each day. They also provide heart-healthy and stress-busting B vitamins, iron, and all-important calcium. Plus, they are considered "nature's scrub brush" because one serving's 15 grams of fiber goes through the intestines and sops cholesterol and takes it away (you know where). Use beans in soups and stews or create a vegetarian chili with kidney beans, tomatoes, carrots, celery, and a little bit of hot pepper. Puree a rinsed and drained can of white beans with two tablespoons of olive oil, a small clove of garlic, and salt and pepper for a Mediterranean-style veggie dip.

> *Early Bird Buy:* Stock up on canned beans when they are on sale; dried beans are always less expensive than canned but take longer to soak and cook.

4. Blueberries

Almost all fruit is good for you—cherries, strawberries, mangos, peaches—yum! But these blue-hued beauties work overtime to provide you with antioxidants and vitamin C, both potent stress busters. They're low in calories and sugar, so you can snack on them to your heart's content without an ounce of guilt (or fat). Blueberries are also a good source of fiber, which can help relieve the cramps and constipation that can occur when you're stressed out. Pile 'em on cereal, eat them fresh from the basket, or blend them with some plain yogurt, a banana, and some ice for a fabulous smoothie.

> *Early Bird Buy:* Summertime is berry time; otherwise frozen berries are a better bargain in winter (and may be fresher than imported berries that have traveled many miles to get to your store).

Ka-Ching!

Farmers' Market Senior Discounts

If you tend to drive right on by all the jewel-toned produce on roadside stands or avoid visiting green markets and farmers' markets because you're afraid the prices will be all over the map (whereas you know for sure what an apple will cost you at the grocery store), then a program called **Senior Farmers' Market Nutrition Program** (SFMNP) is perfect for you. The SFMNP is a program that provides qualifying senior citizens with coupons for certain foods at farmers' markets, roadside stands, and community-supported agriculture programs. It ensures that low-income seniors have access to healthy and delicious produce direct from the grower.

Congress authorized $20.6 million for the SFMNP through 2012. Here are examples of how some states administer the program:

Florida offers 10 coupons worth $4 each (redeemable from April 1 through July 31) to low-income seniors 60 and older living in Alachua, Bay, Jackson, Leon, Sumter, Suwannee and Union counties.

Washington State provides low-income seniors 60 and older with $40 in assistance. The maximum gross monthly income for eligibility for an individual is $1,669. The program runs from June through October.

Alabama offers low-income seniors of 60 and above a book of $4 vouchers to use between April 5 and November 15. For a single-person household, the annual income must be $18,200 or lower. For couples, the annual income must be $24,500 or lower.

Who qualifies? Low-income seniors are generally defined as individuals who are at least 60 years old and who have household incomes of not more than 185% of the federal poverty income guidelines—which are posted anew every year. If you already qualify for food stamps or other food assistance, you may already qualify for this program. You can get more information and help defining your status at the USDA Web site, www.fns.usda.gov/wic. Click on "SFMNP State Agencies" for a full contact list, state by state.

5. Broccoli Broccoli is packed with B vitamins and folic acid, which has been shown to help relieve stress, anxiety, panic, and even depression. Steam broccoli in the microwave (rinse and chop it, place it in a glass or other nonreactive bowl, and cover it with a damp paper towel, not plastic wrap) for a few minutes for optimal nutrition. Add a squeeze of lemon juice, a drizzle of extra-virgin olive oil, and, if you dare, a sprinkle of red pepper flakes for punch, and you've got yourself a sublime yet simple side dish.

> *Early Bird Buy:* Fresh stalks are available all year round, and you can stock up on broccoli when it is on sale. Just blanch in boiled, salted water for 3 to 4 minutes, then freeze for up to two months.

6. Chocolate Dark chocolate (at least 75 percent cocoa; 85 percent is best) is not only a stress reducer—who doesn't love a piece of chocolate?—but it is heart-healthy, too! One study, conducted by researchers at the University of Scranton in Pennsylvania, showed that eating 6 ounces of dark chocolate a day lowered bad cholesterol. And that's not all. Another researcher found that cocoa contains phenols—antiseptic, anti-inflammatory compounds that reduce your risk of heart disease by keeping fat-like substances from oxidizing in the blood and clogging your arteries. Do you really need a serving suggestion for chocolate?

> *Early Bird Buy:* After-holiday sales are one way to find good buys on this good-for-you confection.

10,000 Steps a Day Keep the Doctor Away

Research has shown that taking 10,000 steps every day helps you lose weight, lower your blood pressure, fight off depression, and stay fit and active. And no wonder: 10,000 steps is the equivalent of five miles! There's no need to reach that upper limit. Many of us could simply double the amount of steps we take and achieve big results without ever coming near the 10,000 step level.

But how in the world can you tell how many steps you're taking? Buy a pedometer, an inexpensive device that attaches to your shoe or waistband, so that the vibration registers each step throughout your day. If you're only taking a thousand steps, you need to get out more!

7. Leafy greens Spinach, kale, dandelion greens, turnip tops, and Swiss chard—they're all amazing foods that provide iron plus lots of vitamin C, both good for strong bones, teeth, and hair, and vitamin A and magnesium, both of which are excellent at helping you maintain calm. Sauté one or more type of greens with lemon or orange juice and garlic, or purée with a little low-sodium chicken or veggie broth and white beans for a satisfying soup.

> *Early Bird Buy:* Fresh, loose greens are generally less expensive than washed and bagged. Frozen spinach is a fabulous bargain. Stock up when it's on sale and store in the freezer for up to three months.

8. Lean beef

Surprised this is on the list after hearing admonitions from experts about avoiding the red stuff? Don't be. Beef is a substantial stress buster. It's loaded with zinc, iron, and B vitamins (not to mention protein), all known for keeping us calm and happy. It is also satiating, meaning you feel fuller longer (hunger pangs can cause irritability and anxiety). Avoid fatty cuts, and stick to lean cuts like flank and skirt steak, and 95 percent lean ground beef. Or, look for cuts marked "round" or "loin," such as top sirloin, bottom round (great for pot roast), and tenderloin—they are the kindest cuts in terms of fat content. And limit your intake to 4 to 6 ounces when you do enjoy it.

> *Early Bird Buy:* Meat can be pricey, but luckily the leanest cuts are also the least expensive. Supermarkets have weekly specials on cuts like London broil (perfect for quick grilling or slow pot roasting) and bottom round. If you have room in the freezer, unwrap the meat and rewrap it in freezer paper or wax paper, then place it in a freezer bag to reduce the chance of freezer burn.

9. Salmon and other fish

Most kinds of fish are loaded with B vitamins, particularly the renowned stress fighters B6 and B12. In fact, B12 is one of the most important vitamins in terms of serotonin production; a vitamin B12 deficiency can even lead to depression. Omega-3 fatty acids are prevalent in salmon (Alaskan wild is the best; farm-raised is the least desirable) and tuna—even the canned stuff. Grill or pan-roast fish, and serve on a bed of leafy greens with a side of lentils and carrots for a true power meal. Or, toss rinsed and drained water-packed white albacore tuna with a tablespoon of extra-virgin olive oil and a teaspoon of drained capers and serve on a bed of salad greens. You'll be doing swimmingly after meals like those!

> *Early Bird Buy:* Canned salmon and wild Alaskan tuna are great buys, especially when they go on sale. They last almost indefinitely in your pantry.

10. Sweet potatoes

Talk about a nutritional powerhouse! The more color a veggie has the better it is for you, according to nutritionists—and sweet potatoes might be the brightest of all. Potent antioxidants found in sweet potatoes help to shield our hearts. Plus, their sweet taste makes them delicious enough to eat for dessert. But if you don't want to go that far, try chunking them up into 1-inch squares, roasting them at a high heat (400 degrees) for

10 Ways to Have a **Healthy**

We all know eating right and getting regular exercise is good for you and helps you live longer (regular exercise alone can extend your life by 1 1/2 years according to some experts), but did you know that it can also save money by reducing medical and medication bills, reducing your risk of heart disease, and lessening the risk of catching cold? Here are 10 ways to start getting active that are so cheap—free, in fact—that they're like money in your pocket:

1. ADOPT A DOG.

And then take him or her for daily walks. In the long run, it's less expensive than joining a gym and a lot more fun. It also helps broaden your social circle (very healthy!) by putting you in contact with other animal lovers.

2. FIND A WALKING PARTNER.

Same theory, only this time we're talking human, not canine. Sharing activities with a friend makes it more likely you will stick to an exercise regime.

3. WALK THE MALL.

Your mall provides a traffic-free, climate-controlled area to take a healthy stroll—for free. Some malls encourage walkers by opening early to accommodate them. Inclement weather will never stop you from stretching your legs again!

4. GO OUT OF YOUR WAY.

Take the stairs instead of the elevator if you can, park farther from the store entrance, use the self-serve line to check out and pack your own groceries—whatever you can do during the day to add movement to your routine will get you going, build strength, and burn calories. And it's free.

Lifestyle

5. GO DANCING!

If there is no place in your town (like a swing-dance society or square-dance club) that offers free dancing venues, then turn up the radio and dance at home.

6. WATCH TV.

FitTV is just one cable station that offers free exercise programs all day. Some public television stations include early morning yoga, tai chi, and stretching programs you can follow along with.

7. BABYSIT THE GRANDCHILDREN.

When was the last time you ran after a toddler? Uh-huh. That burns a lot of calories, not to mention the free resistance training you get every time you pick up the little princess (or prince) and put her (or him) down in another room.

8. VOLUNTEER.

Many communities offer property tax reductions to people—usually those 60 and older—who work for the community a certain number of hours. Find out if there is something active you can do, like planting bulbs in the town square or substitute teaching.

9. WORK.

Get a part-time job. Again, think of it as getting paid to exercise. Even working a few hours in a department store, florist shop, or grocery store can give you the activity you crave, some extra cash, and an employee discount to tack on top of your senior discount!

10. FOOL AROUND.

Canoodling with your partner is a free, fun way to add some calorie-burning movement to your daily routine—and it will certainly cheer you up and brighten your day!

about 30 minutes, and then tossing them with some chopped dried plums (better known as prunes) for a tempting and unique side dish next to roasted chicken or turkey—or as a vegetarian meal on its own.

> *Early Bird Buy:* Sweet potatoes are available all year round. Cut down on waste by storing sweet potatoes in the fridge away from onions; unlike white potatoes, sweet versions deteriorate quickly when they are not kept chilled.

11. Walnuts Another powerful nut! Walnuts contain alpha-linolenic acid, or ALA, an omega-3 fatty acid that is similar to the one found in salmon and herring. A handful of walnuts a day as a snack is an easy way to get this important nutrient. Or, scatter a few on top of a salad for a satisfying crunch. Or, add some to your oatmeal along with raisins or dried cranberries for a power breakfast.

> *Early Bird Buy:* Like almonds and other nuts, walnuts are cheapest when bought from bulk barrels. Keep them in the freezer for the longest shelf life.

Freeze Nuts for Freshness

Store nuts in the freezer to keep them from going rancid. They last several months this way, and you won't end up throwing them away.

12. Whole grains Cracked wheat, barley, faro, millet, and quinoa are just a few of the 19 whole grains you can cook with and enjoy in all sorts of dishes. Whole grains digest slowly, keeping you feeling fuller, longer. Plus they boost serotonin levels and make you feel happy—and they brighten your mood because they're so delicious! A half-cup serving size of any whole grain alongside a serving of veggies and lean protein should have you strolling on the sunny side of the street in no time. Follow packaging directions for preparation, but realize that most whole grains don't require any special technique. However, toasting them in a dry pot for a few minutes before adding water adds depth of flavor.

> *Early Bird Buy:* Purchase in bulk at health food stores and freeze for freshness.

Saving at the Drugstore

You're getting exercise, and you're eating healthy and staying fit (not to mention the fact that your clothes are stupendous bargains!), but still, everyone needs prescriptions filled from time to time. Not everyone, however, can get the discount on prescriptions that you can get. And in today's climate of increasingly high-priced medication, that senior discount is something to be especially thankful for. Here's a roundup of your best bets when it comes to knocking a few dollars off your prescription prices:

A&P Supermarket If you sign up for an A&P Club Card, customers 60 and over can get a 10 percent Senior Citizen Prescription Discount. Get details at www.apsupermarket.com.

CVS/Longs Drugs At CVS or Longs Drugs, (which is now a part of CVS), you can sign up for a CVS/pharmacy Health Savings Pass for $10 per year per person. With the pass, you can get a prescription with a 90-day supply of over 400 generics for $9.99 and 10% savings on MinuteClinic services at over 6,300 CVS/pharmacy locations nationwide. You can fill prescriptions online for home mail delivery or pick-up in-store. Stop by your local store to sign up or visit www.cvs.com.

Hannaford This grocery store chain does not treat its pharmacy like an afterthought. There are significant drugstore sections in Hannaford branches, with pharmacists available for consultation. They offer an R_X Healthy Saver Program, which is not only for seniors and is well worth joining. Anyone can apply, either with or without insurance, and you'll receive a Healthy Saver card to present when paying for drugs. If your drug is one of 400 in the program, you'll receive your prescription for $4. You can also receive a 90-day supply for $9.99. Visit Hannaford's Web site at www.hannaford.com (click on "Be a Hannaford R_X Healthy Saver").

Kmart If you're 50 and over and uninsured, you can sign up for Kmart's GoldK Program, which is free. You get a GoldK card, which lets you save 5 percent on diabetes prescription items (not all items apply), up to 10 percent on brand-name drugs, and up to 20 percent on generics. If you have an 80/20 prescription deductible plan, where you pay first and submit receipts later for reimbursement, you can still use the GoldK card. Visit the Web site at www.kmart.com (click on "Pharmacy", then on "GoldK Program").

Kroger Although it's not just for seniors, Kroger offers a generic drug discount program that lets you buy a 30-day supply of a list of generic drugs for $4, or $10 for a 90-day supply. Find details at www.kroger.com.

Osco Pharmacy at Shaw's Supermarket Depending on the location, the Osco pharmacy of Shaw's Supermarket offers approximately 10 percent off your prescription, depending on the drugs. The discount will likely be higher for generics. The age requirement can vary so check at your location. Visit its Web site at www.shaws.com.

Rite Aid Eckerd and Brooks have been absorbed into the Rite Aid family, which offers a Living More program for customers 60 and older. When you apply for a Living More card, which is free, you get 10 percent off prescriptions for which you pay cash. Your card also gets you 20 percent off your purchases the first Tuesday of each month, with 10 percent off on the other Tuesdays of the month, and 10 percent off Rite Aid brand products every day, with other occasional special offers and discounts for Living More members. Find details at www.riteaid.com (click on "Pharmacy," then "Living More").

Stop & Shop If you use your Stop & Shop card, you pay only $9.99 for up to a 90-day supply of a list of generic drugs. Find out more at www.stopandshop.com.

Target Target's in-store pharmacies now offer more than 400 generic drugs for $4 per 30-day supply or $10 for a 90-day supply. The pharmacist will give you a print-out of the list of drugs, or you can search for your drug's availability at its Web site (www.target.com and click on "Pharmacy") or stop by your local branch.

Walgreens If you do not have prescription drug coverage or your insurance does not cover all your prescription drug needs, you can sign up for a Walgreens Prescription Savings Club. There is a fee of $20 a year for individuals or $35 a year for families, and then members can receive a three-month supply from a list of about 400 common medications for $12.99. Find out more online at www.walgreens.com, and visit your local store to sign up.

Early Bird Secrets

Good Health Info

AARP and Walgreens have a partnership to provide health-care information specifically for seniors. For free, you can download brochures on topics such as how to manage your medication, generic vs. brand-name drugs, traveling with medication, caregiving resources, and much more. You can also order through the Web site printed copies to be sent to you for free: www.walgreens.com/aarp/resources.jsp.

Ka-Ching!

Taking Health Costs Off Your Tax Bill

Even when you have insurance, it can be surprising what you have to pay out of pocket—a co-pay here, a test bill there, an unexpected supplementary cost on a prescription, and suddenly it all adds up. Keeping detailed records of the money that you spend on health care may seem like a bit of a hassle day by day, but you'll be glad you did when tax time comes! Unreimbursed medical expenses that add up to more than 7.5 percent of your total income are fully deductible from your year-end taxes.

Here's a list of the kinds of medical expenses that the IRS will let you deduct from your year-end taxes. Again, keep all your receipts carefully for every medical expense, and remember that you can't deduct over-the-counter medicine and most cosmetic surgery. Check with your tax preparer or go to www.irs.gov to confirm this year's deductible expenses. During tax season, you can get live help from the IRS on the phone at 1-800-829-1040.

- Visits to dentists, doctors, chiropractors, acupuncturists, therapists, and other medical practitioners
- Laser eye surgery
- Hearing aids
- Prescription drugs
- Lab fees
- Prescription eyeglasses and contact lenses
- Crutches, walkers, wheelchairs, and other mobility devices
- Dentures
- Guide dogs
- Health-care premiums and long-term care policies
- Some health-related transportation, such as trips to doctors' offices

Wal-Mart Wal-Mart offers the same deal: $4 for a 30-day supply, $10 for a 90-day supply on a similar list of generics. They also have good prices on items such as mobility aids, diabetic supplies, blood pressure monitors, and more. Learn more at www.walmart.com (click on "Pharmacy").

Getting Free Medical Advice

Medical costs are rising by the day, but there are still plenty of good deals out there—if you know where to look. It's always better to prevent a medical condition than to treat one, so take the opportunity to accept the free screenings and advice offered on many fronts to keep yourself as healthy and well as possible. Many drugstores and in-supermarket pharmacies offer screening services for free or for a small fee. While screenings are usually offered by health professionals, generally they are not run by doctors, so don't hesitate to follow up with your regular physician if a screening uncovers any abnormalities or concerns.

Osco Pharmacy at Shaw's The pharmacies at Shaw's Supermarkets offer regular free and low-cost screenings, ranging from diabetes, blood pressure, and bone density, to flu and pneumonia vaccinations. Visit the web site www.shaws.com (click on "Pharmacy," then "Health Screenings" to find a schedule).

Publix Publix grocery stores have low-cost health-care checkups such as an osteoporosis screening for $15, free blood pressure screenings, and cholesterol screenings ($20 for total lipid; $15 for non-fasting screening). Get details at www.publix.com.

Target Target Clinics are available in Minnesota and Maryland and provide treatment for patients ages 18 months and older for many common illnesses and injuries with most services costing in the $59 to $69 dollar range. To find locations, go to www.target.com and click on Pharmacy and Target Clinic.

Wal-Mart Health and Wellness Centers It's hard to drive far in the United States without passing a Wal-Mart somewhere in your vicinity—and that's a good thing when it comes to low-cost clinics. Wal-Mart now offers 68 low-cost clinics across eighteen states, where a typical visit costs about $65. (The Web site, www.walmart.com, has a clinic locator to see if there's one near you. Click on "Pharmacy," then "Health and Wellness Center.") They generally assist with minor health issues, not emergency care, but they're a good place to go if you need help with earaches, flu, respiratory infections, and other basic concerns.

Enjoying Your
Free Time

5

Indulging in Life's Little Luxuries
without Spending a Lot of Money

Deep Discounts on Hobbies and Crafts

Whether you've been pursuing a hobby all your life, or just wished you could find a few minutes each week to begin one, now is the time to turn your attention to the activities you love. And there are added benefits to having a hobby: it fosters creativity and community, it helps you relax, and it keeps your mind keen and actively engaged. What you began as a leisurely pastime can sometimes take on a life of its own. If your hobby actually produces something—whether it's paintings, summer tomatoes, or needlepoint pillows—you might find that the demand for what you produce outstrips the supply. Whatever you create, there's always the opportunity to enjoy the outcome yourself, to give the item as a gift, or possibly even sell it at a craft fair or church bazaar.

Strum and Toot Without Spending a Dime

It happens to all of us—life gets in the way of something that we used to do (or want to learn), like playing an instrument, and it falls by the wayside. It's only when we sit down to it that we realize how much we loved doing it after all! You may not be a Liberace or Chet Atkins, but if your hobby involves a musical talent, then put it to good use, and reap the benefits.

Play it again, Sam. If you love to play the piano, go ahead and make it part of your life again! Church choirs, grade school shows, dance schools, senior centers—they're all wonderful places to offer your skills and talents tinkling the keys. If you volunteer, your offer will almost always be accepted (assuming you're not a beginner).

That old six-string. Always wanted to learn to play the guitar but never found the time—or money!—for lessons? Forget the extra cash. All you need is an Internet connection and a guitar. There are dozens of sites on the Web that offer step-by-step videos and lessons to teach you to play *all for free*. Check out sites such as www.justinguitar.com or www.guitarmasterclass.net to get an idea of what's out there. And then get ready to strum along!

Gimme (sheet) music. Dust off your instrument, whatever it is, and treat yourself to some new music. Don't worry if you can't get to the music store to buy a paper copy. The Internet can give you music to just about any song you can remember and everything else as well. Sites such as www.freesheetmusic.net or www.findfreesheetmusic.com have countless scores and arrangements available to download for free. If you're looking for a lovely arrangement of "Danny Boy"—be it for the accordion, the violin, or the bagpipes—you can find it for free on the Internet.

Practical Crafts...Practically Free

There are few things as satisfying as making something useful by hand, whether it's a handmade book, a quilt, or an heirloom piece of furniture. Supplies can be specialized and tools can be expensive to purchase, so consider ways to try out a craft, such as taking a class or learning from a friend, before you splash out on something that you may not want to continue. When you do find your calling, whether it's smocking handmade children's clothes, nature photography, or throwing pots, don't hesitate to get yourself the necessary professional implements you'll need. Your loved ones will treasure your efforts, and you'll have the deep satisfaction of a project well done.

Say cheese! Taking digital photos frees you up to shoot like a professional, and you get instant results. First, you're not wasting film by snapping photos over and over to get just the perfect shot. Then, you can download them to your computer and print only the ideal picture. Printing at home can get expensive since you have to buy photo paper and those expensive color ink cartridges that run out so quickly. Instead, compare prices and see if it's a better deal, depending on your printing habits, to print from a photo site such as www.snapfish.com or www.shutterfly.com. You upload the photos to the site from your computer, and they make prints and mail them to you.

Be sew-cial and join a bee. Love to partake in this treasured, practical hobby of American women everywhere? There's no more social way to sew or quilt than to join a bee, and while you can piece together quilts at home by yourself whenever you have the time, there's real pleasure in joining a quilting class or club and putting the whole shebang together with your peers. Ask about local clubs at your favorite fabric shop, or log on to your favorite search engine, type in "quilt club" and the name of your town, and you may be surprised to find how many quilters are stitching away near you.

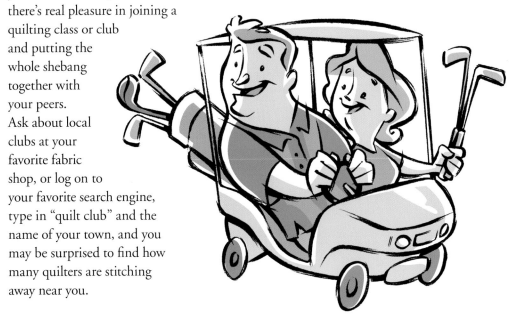

Got feet of clay? Throwing pots is addictive. It may not sound exciting at first, but wait until you put your hands on a damp mound of clay spinning on a wheel. It spins and hums and shapes into a pot beneath your palms like a living thing, and the results can be magnificent, even for beginners. Because pottery requires specialized tools—such as a wheel and a kiln—that aren't easily available to home users but are more readily found in classes or clubs, pottery can be a surprisingly social hobby as well as an immensely satisfying way to work with your hands. Visit your local community college or pottery shop and just ask, "Where can I learn this art?" and they'll be happy to guide you.

Make an heirloom. Woodworking creates instant family heirlooms, whether it's an inlaid tabletop or a plain wooden spoon. Develop your woodworking skills with classes at community colleges, or ask at your local lumberyard if there are any woodworkers' groups you can join. Woodworkers are a passionate bunch, eager to share knowledge, and the only thing they like more than creating beautiful items with wood is talking about the process and showing off their handiwork. There are also a lot of community Web sites where you can get advice and learn advanced techniques, such as www.woodweb.com.

Did You Know?

The Statue of Liberty–Ellis Island Foundation, in partnership with the National Park Service, not only preserved and restored the Statue of Liberty and Ellis Island, the main entry port for millions of immigrants to the United States, but also created the American Family Immigration History Center. This is a terrific place to visit if you're in New York and go to Ellis Island, but you don't have to make a trip to get the records of your forebears who may have passed through Ellis Island when they first came to America. On the Web, at www.ellisisland.org, you can search millions of passenger records for free to find your own ancestors who made the brave journey from their home countries. If you're looking to find out how you came to be who you are today, Ellis Island may be the place to begin. And make sure to ask for that senior discount when you visit!

Sew fabulous! If you've got a way with a needle, you can turn your hand to many crafts, besides quilting, embroidery, and needlepoint. You can also make stunning baby clothes, napkins, and pillowcases, and decorative tablecloths, towels, and runners that will be treasured by you and your family for years. Ask at your local fabric shop or community center about

Ka-Ching!

Saving at the Craft Store

Retailers of crafts and hobby supplies are less inclined to offer discounts to seniors because seniors make up a big part of their customer base in the first place. Jo-Ann Fabric and Craft Stores, for example, one of the largest chains of fabric and craft material in the United States, no longer offers a senior discount. (They do, however, offer special preferred customer coupons for patrons of any age, so be sure to ask at your nearest Jo-Ann's.) You're more likely to find a senior discount at your little local mom-and-pop fabric store, where the service tends to be more personal and the management is more concerned with the needs and opinions of the customers. If you're an avid crafter and a discount is not readily apparent, try this:

1. Patronize a smaller craft or hobby shop instead of a major national chain. If the owner or manager is the person ringing you up, that person also has the power to give you your own personal senior discount on the spot.

2. Ask for a senior discount—or ask why there isn't one! Some fabric and quilting shops, for example, may offer 10 percent off for seniors on Tuesday mornings or another day, but they may not post a sign to that effect. When the cashier is ringing up your fat quarters and roll of batting, say, "Do you have any senior discounts?" You might pay full price for that particular transaction, but you can come back on Tuesday if you need more supplies.

3. Buy it online. If you need a regular source of materials, whether you make stained glass or homemade paper, or build wooden ships or birdhouses, you can compare prices and probably find it cheaper online—including shipping.

If you *don't* happen to live near Red Bank, New Jersey, the site of Hobbymasters, which bills itself as the oldest and largest hobby store in the United States, you can still access it for orders online and receive its senior discount of 20 percent—far more generous than most craft stores! Visit www.hobbymasters.com or call 1-877-MR-HOBBY.

classes and sewing groups, and join up with experts to refine your art to its highest level. The Internet is also a rich resource for the needle arts, from free patterns and designs to contacts with other needle workers in your area.

Plant your family tree. Just because your children or grandchildren haven't asked doesn't mean that they don't want to know about their family history. We all like to know where we came from, and it becomes all the more fascinating when you begin to uncover fun facts and details about your forebears. If you know a few basic facts about where your family came from, there are a number of places you can start searching for free, including www.genealogy.org and www.familysearch.org. You can also find downloadable trees to print out and share with your family members.

Low-Fuss, Low-Cost Gardening

Growing a garden these days has become more than the simple pleasure of working the soil. A vegetable or herb garden can make a significant difference to your food bill, and a package of perennial seeds will provide years of annual color! Early Bird gardeners in the know are attuned to tons of ways to do what they love without spending a fortune in seeds or plants, bending over in the hot sun, or canning for hours in the kitchen.

Plant in containers, eat what's fresh while it's fresh, and give away the rest—to your family, your neighbors, your church, or a local soup kitchen. A bag of seasonal homegrown veggies is a gift worth its weight in gold to a non-gardener. You can also plant other gardens that don't require you to find recipients.

Throw it in, watch it grow. Forget about pricey annuals, and, instead, plant what will give you years of pleasure. Two of our senior gardening experts agree that the bright blues and purples of Nepeta (otherwise known as catmint) and varying yellow hues of coreopsis make a garden pop in the most persnickety of soil conditions. The best news is that all you have to do is sprinkle the seeds along the ground before a light rain, and you'll have color for years, without fuss.

The Early Bird, no-maintenance lawn. Wait! Don't kill that moss that's creeping across your lawn. Dig up the grass nearby and let the moss grow instead. Moss gardening is a steadily growing trend, because it's lush, velvety, and beautiful to walk on and look at, and it requires absolutely no mowing. All it needs is shade, a bit of moisture, and, ideally, poor quality, acidic soil. The EPA estimates that the average suburban grassy lawn requires 10,000 gallons of water annually, while a moss lawn requires about 1 percent of that. Check out www.mossacres.com or call 1-866-GET-MOSS for tips on moss gardening and to buy a moss starter kit.

Herbs for a song, with parsley, sage, rosemary, and thyme. An herb garden doesn't require quite the same commitment level as a vegetable garden. You don't need to work the soil as deeply or tend the herbs as much. But the results are delightful, colorful, and fragrant. Many herbs, such as chives and cilantro, bloom with bright flowers as the growing season progresses. And what could be nicer than walking through your herb plants in the evening, trailing your hands across the leaves to release the fragrance of a rosemary bush, a bed of peppermint, a tangle of delicate thyme, or a bunch of basil? And whether you make pounds of pesto or dry some sage to enrich your Thanksgiving stuffing, an herb garden can enrich your life all year.

The No-Bend, Ouch-Free, Early Bird Garden

6 WAYS TO CULTIVATE WHAT YOU LOVE FROM AN UPRIGHT POSITION

Even if you love gardening, it's strenuous work. Our experts came up with the following six ways to grow great grub, herbs, and flowers without ever bending over.

1. Install window boxes on your front and back deck railings or sills, and plant everything from cherry tomatoes to baby carrots, radishes, herbs, and flowers (anything lightweight).

2. Invert a large planter and put another planter on top of it, at waist height, for visual design interest and elevation.

3. If you must sit, borrow a child's tricycle to wheel from one growing area to the next.

4. Sharpen and use your long-handed tools, like scuttle-hoes, rakes, and border shovels.

5. Extend the handles of your shorter tools by duct-taping them to full-length broom handles.

6. Cultivate easy-to-grow perennials immediately after a rain, when the ground is still workable. Rake up the soil to loosen it, sprinkle in perennial seeds, rake back the soil, and walk away.

Cultivate a cutting garden. If you've only ever bought flowers from a store, you may be surprised at how easy it can be to grow a "cutting garden" of flowers. Hardy brown-eyed Susans or Michaelmas daisies, bright zinnias or snapdragons can grow in a season and be ready to fill vases, bouquets, and photographs by midsummer. Heavy-headed peonies or heirloom roses may take a year or more to establish before they start to bloom, but once they get started, they'll bring you joy for seasons to come.

The (new) Victory Garden. When food prices are as high as an elephant's eye, it's time to grow some food! A vegetable garden isn't expensive to begin, but it does require a fair amount of effort. Get the grandkids to come help you turn the soil and break up the clumps, or, even better, see if you can find a helpful neighbor with a tiller. Once you've dug your plot, it's easy and inexpensive to grow many, many veggies from seed, from beans and squash to pumpkins and lettuce. Other plants, such as tomatoes, are often best grown from bedding plants. If you've never planted a garden before, give it a try—nothing tastes as sweet as a pea you grew yourself!

Find your inner Johnny Appleseed. There are plenty of fruit trees and plants that will produce in a year or two—and blueberries are high on that list. Blueberries are now grown commercially in 38 states, so you've got a good chance of living in a climate that will support these luscious little jewels. Invest in a couple of blueberry bushes at a local nursery, and you may find yourself making blueberry pancakes and muffins with your own supply before summer is out. You can also find apple, pear, and peach trees of medium size that will produce by the following season—just be sure to plant more than one for cross-pollination, and be sure to keep a close eye out for pests.

Early Bird Secret

Serious Sales on Fruit Plants and Trees

If you're serious about putting in a fruit garden, wait until the end of the season and buy all the plants you like at the local nursery, where they'll be going cheap. Ask for advice from the experts at the nursery on whether the plants can winter over in your climate zone when they're going in the ground so late in the growing season. Most plants can survive but may need special mulching or covering. And the upshot is that you'll have gotten a terrific deal on your garden, sometimes as much as 75 percent off!

Senior Perks at State and National Parks

America's great national parks are so senior-friendly that you might think the government has just been *waiting* for you to retire in order to welcome you with open arms into the park system! From free passes to special packages and discounts, the park services of the nation and of each state offer an enormous wealth of advice and assistance to Americans over 50. Get outdoors and enjoy your national parks—at greatly reduced rates, with lots of special benefits thrown in.

State parks have varying senior discounts from park to park and state to state, but below are some of the best deals around for getting into parks and enjoying amenities at the best possible rates!

Alabama State residents are eligible for discounts on a park-by-park basis. For more information, visit http://www.alapark.com.

Blue Springs State Park
2595 Hwy. 10
Clio, AL 36017
334-397-4875
$1 admission fee for those age 62 and older (normally $3 for adults)

Chewacla State Park
124 Shell Toomer Pkwy.
Auburn, AL 36830
334-887-5621
Seniors 62 years of age and older: $1 (normally $2 to $3 for adults)

Frank Jackson State Park
100 Jerry Adams Dr.
Opp, AL 36467
334-493-6988
Senior Citizens age 62 and older get in for 50 cents ($1 regular admission)

Lake Lurleen
13226 Lake Lurleen Rd.
Coker, AL 35452
205-339-1558
Seniors 62 years of age and older can enter for $1 ($3 regular admission)

Meaher
5200 Battleship Pkwy. E.
Spanish Fort, AL 36577
251-626-5529
Senior citizens age 62 and older get in for 50 cents ($1 regular admission)

Monte Sano
5105 Nolen Ave.
Huntsville, AL 35801
256-534-3757
Seniors 62 years of age and older: $1 (normally $2 to $3 for adults)

California's Early Bird Park Bargain

California offers to those 62 years of age or older a $1 discount for vehicle parking and a $2 discount for family camping in state-operated parks, year round. Its even better deal, however, is the Golden Bear Pass. It's available to anyone receiving Aid to the Aged, Blind, or Disabled, or to any person 62 years of age or older with income limitations, so an application with income verification is required. It provides free entrance to all parks.

There's also a Limited Golden Bear Pass for those 62 years of age or older, which costs $10 and provides free parking between Labor Day and Memorial Day. Contact:

California Department of Parks and Recreation
1416 Ninth St.
Sacramento, CA 95814
800-777-0369, 916-653-6995
www.parks.ca.gov

Colorado Aspen Leaf Pass. This $30 pass, for all Colorado residents 64 years or older, provides unlimited access to all Colorado State Parks for one year. It has the added bonus of 50 percent off camping, Sunday through Thursday, excluding holidays. Visit: www.parks.state.co.us.

Connecticut The Charter Oak Pass is free to any Connecticut resident age 65 and older. Free admittance is also provided for the Charter Oak pass holder when visiting Gillette Castle, Dinosaur or Fort Trumbull State Parks, or fishing at the Quinebaug Valley Hatchery, as well as free parking at these places. It can be obtained through the mail or in person. Visit: www.ct.gov.

Delaware Delaware residents 62 and older get free entrance to most parks with a $12 pass which can be ordered online at egov.dnrec.delaware.gov.

Florida Florida residents who are over 65 pay only half the camping fees at state parks. Silver Springs Park is not a state park, but it offers an annual Silver Pass to adults 55 and over for $44.99, with free admission and parking and VIP entry for concerts. The daily admission is $29.99.

Georgia Seniors 62 and older get half off the usual fee of $50 for the annual ParkPass or they can join the Friends of Georgia State Parks & Historic Sites, and get both the annual Park Pass and the Historic Site Pass for $30, a $15 savings. Visit: www.gastateparks.org.

Hawaii Seniors pay no fees for the state parks in Kauai, Oaho (except Diamond Head Monument), Maui, Molokai, or Hawaii.

Idaho Those 62 or older will receive 50 percent off camping fees within the following Idaho State Parks:

Dworshak, Heyburn, Winchester, Lake Cascade, Three Island Crossing, Bruneau Dunes, Bear Lake, Lake Walcott, Massacre Rocks. Discount is valid midweek on stays Monday through Thursday (excluding holidays).

Illinois Adults 62 or older who are state residents receive camping fee discounts, the amount depending on the site. Generally, Monday through Thursday campers receive 50 percent off the fee.

Indiana Just $18 gets you a Golden Hoosier Passport, when you're an Indiana resident at least 65 years of age. It admits the driver and passengers of noncommercial vehicles to state parks which charge a gate fee. Visit: www.in.gov.

Kansas Kansas resident seniors 65 and older pay half of the regular price, which can vary from park to park. Visit: www.kdwp.state.ks.us.

Kentucky Residents age 62 and older receive a 10 percent discount on camping and lodging fees with valid ID.

Louisiana Admission to state parks, historic sites, and preservation areas is free for all seniors age 62 and older, with these exceptions:

Hodges Gardens State Park
$4 for seniors (62 and older)
Rosedown Plantation SHS Fees
$8 per senior citizen (ages 62 and over)

Maine All citizens 65 and over receive free admission to parks for day use with proof of age. Visit: www.maine.gov.

Did You Know?

Maryland's Golden Age If you're 62 or older and a resident of Maryland, you can apply for a Golden Age Pass that's good for your lifetime. It allows free entry to all state parks as well as half off the fees for camping from Sunday through Thursday. The pass is available via application online or at any of the park offices, and proof of age is necessary. Once you've got it, you're ready to hit the trail! Visit: www.dnr.state.md.us.

Massachusetts The Massachusetts Senior Pass, which is for state residents 62 and older, allows free parking at state parks for the vehicle occupied by the pass holder. Visit: www.mass.gov.

Michigan Those 65 and older can get a permit for $6 that admits you free into all state parks, and a hunting or fishing license for $6 a year. Visit: www.michigan.gov.

Montana Residents age 62 and older receive free fishing and conservation licenses and pay reduced fees for hunting licences and camping. Visit: www.fwp.mt.gov.

Nevada Residents of Nevada for at least five years who are 65 and older pay $15 a year for a permit that provides entrance to all parks and use of camping and boat launch facilities. Visit: www.parks.nv.gov.

New Jersey Residents who are 62 or older can get free passes from Parks and Forestry Division, allowing free admission and parking at all state parks and historic sites. Visit: www.state.nj.us.

New York New York residents over 62 are allowed into all state parks for free except on holiday weekends. Visit: www.nysparks.com.

The Golden Buckeye

Any Ohio residents with a driver's license or state ID automatically get their Golden Buckeye card mailed to them for their 60th birthday—and it's quite a gift. Accepted by more than 20,000 businesses in the state, it offers seniors in Ohio discounts on everything from food and prescriptions to entertainment and clothing. Among other things, Golden Buckeyes receive 50 percent off camping fees at all state parks from Sunday to Thursday, 10 percent off the rest of the week, and 10 percent off all cottage and lodge rates. Visit: www.goldenbuckeye.com.

Pennsylvania Adults 62 and older get $4.50 off the base campsite rate with valid ID. Visit: www.dcnr.state.pa.us.

Rhode Island If you're 65 or older and a resident, you're entitled to half off beach and golf fees. Visit: www.riparks.com.

South Carolina Those 65 and above receive 35 percent off entrance and amenity fees (for fishing, camping, golf, etc.), and residents of that age may buy a Palmetto Passport for $25, half the standard price, which is good for free admission for one year. Visit: www.southcarolinaparks.com.

Tennessee Resident seniors 62 and older receive varying discounts according to the park. Visit: www.state.tn.us.

Texas Residents 65 and older who meet certain eligibility requirements can receive a free Texas Parklands Passport which admits them to state parks for 50 percent off the usual price. Visit: www.tpwd.state.tx.us

Utah A $35 Utah Senior Adventure Pass is available online or by mail, allowing free day-use entrance to all state parks (a savings of $40 off the regular pass price) and $2 off camping fees. Visit: www.stateparks.utah.gov.

Vermont Residents 62 and older can buy a Green Mountain Passport from their town clerk for $2 that allows the holder free entrance into any state park. It is valid for the holder's lifetime. Visit: www.vtstateparks.com.

Early Bird Secret

Senior Pass to National Parks

If you're not yet 62, the America the Beautiful – National Parks and Federal Recreational Lands Pass is available for $80 and admits up to four adults and one noncommercial vehicle to any national park for one year. But if you're 62 and older, you can get the same pass for $10, and it's good for your lifetime! The Senior Pass admits three adults besides the pass holder, and children under 16 are free. The pass also provides 50 percent off many amenities requiring additional fees, such as camping, swimming, boating, and special interpretive exhibitions and tours (the 50 percent discount is not available at all parks). The pass must be purchased in person at a park, and you must show proof of age (your driver's license is just fine).

Virginia The Lifetime Naturally Yours Passport is available to residents age 62 and older for $110, allowing admission and parking for free at all state parks, but there are varying packages, such as the one for boaters, including launching fees, which includes lifetime launching fees and costs $314. Seniors may also buy annual passports for less, such as the one-year Passport Plus for $33. Visit: www.dcr.virginia.gov.

Washington Qualifying residents 62 and above can get a Senior Citizen Limited Income Pass for free, which offers half off camping and moorage fees. Visit: www.parks.wa.gov.

West Virginia Admission to all state parks is free to all users, but residents over 60 receive a Golden Mountaineer discount card, that entitles the holder to discounts at retail businesses all over the state, including camping fees at parks. Visit: www.wvstateparks.com.

Wisconsin Residents over 65 pay half-price for licenses and annual admission permits. Visit: www.dnr.state.wi.us.

Wildly Low Admissions to Zoos and Aquariums

And yes, it really is true! Zoos (and aquariums) are no longer the musty places they once were. In fact, they offer incredible learning and educational programs and opportunities to volunteer. The best part? They're not just for kids anymore. Check out the Early Bird savings at these worlds of wonder, and you'll become a regular.

Atlanta Zoo Adults 55 and older can get $10 off an annual membership card that allows express entry into the zoo for the cardholder and one other named beneficiary, with 10 percent off admission for all other friends and family. Visit: www.zooatlanta.org.

Brandywine Zoo (Wilmington, Delaware) Senior citizens pay half price, or $2, from October 1 to May 31, and pay $4 instead of $5 from June 1 to September 30. Visit: www.brandywinezoo.org.

Dallas Zoo Seniors age 65 and older are admitted for $9 instead of the regular admission price of $12. Visit: www.dallas-zoo.org.

Indianapolis Zoo Seniors 62 and older are admitted for $9.50, instead of the regular admission of $14.50. Visit: www.indyzoo.com

Monterey Bay Aquarium Seniors 65 and above get $2 off the standard admission of $27.95, and get free admission for two seniors with a senior membership for $50, all tax deductible, compared to the standard membership for $75. Visit: www.montereybayaquarium.org.

National Aquarium (Baltimore, Maryland) If you're over 60, you get $1 off the standard admission of $28.95. Visit: www.aqua.org.

Oakland Zoo The regular adult admission is $11, but seniors 55 and above get in for $7.50. Visit: www.oaklandzoo.org.

San Diego Zoo For $50, a Single Senior Membership entitles the holder to one year of unlimited admission to the Zoo, the Wild Animal Park and Skyfari Aerial tram, a $29 discount over the Individual memberships. Residency requirements apply. Visit: www.sandiegozoo.org.

Early Bird Secret

Become a FONZ!

Being a Friend of the National Zoo (FONZ) can have significant benefits whether or not you live near the nation's capital. Although the National Zoo is always free to everyone, the Senior Membership, for $40 annually (instead of $45 for an Individual Membership), also gives you free or discounted admission to 100 zoos around the United States. It also provides the following benefits, plus the knowledge that you're supporting the zoo in its mission of being a leader in conservation, research, and education:

• Free parking while visiting the zoo

• Up to twenty percent off at in National Zoo stores

• *Zoogoer* magazine and Wildlife Adventures newsletter

• Annual member event

• Discounts on tickets to popular zoo events

• Invitations to previews of new exhibits

Find out more at www.nationalzoo.si.edu, or call 202-633-3038.

Shedd Aquarium (Chicago, Illinois) Seniors 65 and up get in for $21.95, reduced from the usual $24.95 for the day admission Shedd Pass. Visit: www.sheddaquarium.org.

South Carolina Aquarium (Charleston Harbor) Seniors 62 and older get $1 off the adult $16.95 admission. A better deal, if you live in the vicinity, is the Grandparent membership level, which is $80 for two senior adults plus all grandchildren free, compared to the Family

membership of $90 for two adults with all children free.
Visit: www.scaquarium.org.

Scoring Savings on Spectator Sports

If you love to watch or play sports, you're a lucky Early Bird. While the cost of tickets and equipment continues to rise, there are great deals out there just for you. So step up to the plate, and swing for home!

Pro Ball for Less Dough

Ka-ching, indeed! Professional league sports have become unbelievably pricey. (They have to be to pay all those incredible salaries.) The fact is that going to watch a baseball game on a Saturday afternoon or a seeing a basketball team in all its tall glory used to be an entertainment within reach for regular joes, but these days you might have to take out a second mortgage to get courtside seats or sit somewhere other than the farthest part of the outfield—and that's before you've paid for parking, bought a T-shirt or pennant, or even had your first $6 soda and $8 hot dog! Still, there's nothing like the thrill of a live game. So what's a sports fan to do? As they say in the big leagues…punt!

Seniors Have a Ball at Big-League Games

The National Football League, National Hockey League, and National Basketball Association do *not* offer specific senior discounts, but some teams hold special senior days at specific games. The schedule changes each season, so you'll need to check specifically with your team. You can find your way to every team's season schedule and their ticket prices through each league's main Web portal:

www.nfl.com

www.nhl.com

www.nba.com

Take me out. Baseball is your best shot for a discounted game, if you insist on the major leagues. Senior discounts are not available to every game or every team in Major League Baseball, so it's important to check with your team. Many teams offer special senior citizen appreciation days, when the tickets are discounted, and there are special events, such as a "Senior Stroll the Bases Night." What's pretty constant is this: Baseball fans 60 and older can usually get half off of non-premium seat prices on certain days during the regular playing season. The days vary according to each team's schedule, but you can check your team's schedule at www.mlb.com.

Games That Are Less Pricey, but Just as Exciting

If the major leagues can't be bothered to offer you a special discount, you can leave the major players to their multimillion-dollar contracts and look around for other exciting and less expensive options to indulge your love of the game—any game. Local sports teams offer the best bet for the thrill of a roaring crowd without the chill of the roaring ticket prices.

Friday night lights. There's nothing like the drama of a hotly contested game between two local high school rivals, and many communities turn out in force to support their teams, whether they're related to the players or not. Sit in the bleachers like everyone else and wave a pennant for your favorite youngsters.

Conference me in. Check out your local college's prices on basketball and football games. If your team is in the top of the NCAA or a major conference, it might cost nearly as much as a professional team. But if your guys are mid-list, season tickets will bring all the excitement of live games—cheerleaders and marching band included!—for a fraction of the cost of the big leagues.

Watch the women. Women's sports have become very popular, but the ticket prices still aren't as high as those of the top men's teams. Even if you're bemoaning the injustice of it, buy a ticket to the big game—you can show your support *and* get a bargain on some serious sports.

Watch something new. Colleges and universities offer a wealth of sports to watch. Check out your local college's offerings and try something new—soccer, lacrosse, rugby, tennis, ice hockey, field hockey, or even snow boarding, if you live in northern climes. Check out a sport live that you've only ever seen while flipping through the TV channels on a Saturday afternoon. You may find you're a real rugby fan!

Take me out to the (minor league) ball game. Farm teams offer all the fun of an old-fashioned baseball game at a pittance. You'll have enough money left for hotdogs *and* popcorn *and* peanuts if you're sitting in the bleachers of your local baseball team—and you might see a star in the making, just waiting to be called up to the big leagues.

Special Offers for Sports Participants

Now we're talking! If you want to go sit and watch a major team, there aren't a lot of discounts. But if you want to get off your duff and actually *play*, there's a whole world of bargains and special offers to entice and welcome you into participating.

Old Folks on Spokes? That's how this Senior Cycling company bills itself, even though nothing could be further from the truth! It caters to cyclists 50 and above, and its tours are arranged according to difficulty level, from beginner to intermediate to advanced, so there's something to suit every rider, along with good food and a support van. Recent tours included Bike the Florida Keys, Bike the Great Allegheny Passage, and Bike the Erie Canal! Find out more at www.seniorcycling.com, or call 540-668-6307.

Elderhostel bike tours. This remarkable organization that also has educational, hiking, and travel programs counts among its many great activities the opportunity to tour with similarly minded senior cyclists all around the United States and Europe. Depending on the tour you choose, you'll pedal about 30 miles a day. Bikes are provided, along with all food and accommodations, and a support van to carry the luggage and you, if you can't go another mile. Visit www.elderhostel.org or call 1-800-454-5768.

Women on wheels. The average age of Woman Tour cyclists is 54 on shorter tours and 59 on longer cross-country tours. According to this organization, its oldest cyclist so far was 79. So you'll be in good company as a senior in this group specifically devoted to organizing bike trips for women. You can get a 5 percent discount if you're one of the first six to sign up for a tour, or a 10 percent discount on the second tour if you take two tours within 180 days. Bring a friend on her first trip with the group and you get 5 percent off your trip. Find details at www.womantours.com or call 1-800-247-1444.

Tennis, anyone? Joining the United States Tennis Association (USTA) for $40 a year allows you to participate in the many senior tournaments it organizes throughout the year and all around the country (often for an additional fee). Tournaments are broken up by age, and the Senior Division

Ka-Ching!

Batter Up, Peewee!

One of the best, cheapest, most thrilling, delightful, and true-blue American ways of enjoying the best in sports is going straight to where it starts—the peewee leagues. Yes, Little League is right up there with the big league for excitement. Not only do you get to watch and cheer for kids who are proud as punch to be out there on a Saturday afternoon with the promise of sliding into home, but you get to watch future champs in the making, for free. Gather up a few friends and neighbors, bring some lawn chairs and a tube or two of sunscreen, pack a cooler with some homemade sandwiches, and make a day of it. It'll cost pennies. Our experts made a list of the top 10 items to bring to a Little League game to keep the costs down and the pleasure up:

2. ICE COLD SODAS OR BOTTLED WATER*

3. BROAD-BRIMMED HAT

4. COLD FRIED CHICKEN WRAPPED IN WAX PAPER*

5. COMFY FOLDING CHAIR

6. THERMOS OF ICED TEA*

1. SUNSCREEN

7. BIG BAG OF CHIPS

10. CHOCOLATE CHIP COOKIES

8. PAPER FAN

9. HOMEMADE COLESLAW*

*These are traditional. Pack them on ice in a cooler, and make sure they stay cold until consumed.

includes women's tournaments for players 85 and above, while the men's group has tournaments for those older than 90. Tennis is truly a lifelong sport! You also get discounts on tennis supplies, tennis camps, and tennis resorts. Visit www.usta.com or call membership services at 1-800-990-USTA (8782).

Squash: more than just a vegetable. Aficionados promise that, despite its fast pace and highly competitive nature, squash—traditionally known as squash racquets—is the game of a lifetime. This means that once you're hooked (one of our experts is a die-hard fan), you'll play for life. The United States Squash Racquets Association (USSRA) holds many age-appropriate competitions all over the country, on both public and private courts. Most universities have at least a few public courts on the premises, and a simple call to the team coach is a great way to get in the door. For more information, visit www.ussquash.com.

Early Bird Secret

There's Gold in Senior Golf

The National Senior Golf Association is the original and oldest provider of amateur golf events in the United States, and it exists to make the game as pleasant, enjoyable, and accessible as possible to seniors.

The organization defines senior as 50 and up, but it welcomes any age members, although only those over 50 can win awards at its tournaments. Membership costs $35 a year, and a new membership brings with it a $50 gift certificate for use at a Senior Golf event.

Membership provides access to its senior tournaments at golf courses around the United States and the world and assistance in booking reduced-rate travel, as well as discounts on computerized golf club fitting or a discounted rate on shipping your clubs ahead of you to any course around the world. Visit www.nsgatour.com or call 1- 800-282-6772.

It's not just for Arnold Palmer. With membership billed at just over $4 a month for singles or $7 a month for a couple, the benefits of owning the Golf Card includes free green fees with the rental of a power golf cart for two rounds of golf a year at 600 participating golf courses. You also get up to 50 percent off the combined cart and green fee for two rounds per year at an additional 2,400 courses, as well as savings at Stay and Play resorts, chances to test products, discounts on car rentals, and free copies of *Golf Traveler* magazine. Find out details at www.golfcard.com or call 1-800-321-8269.

Walking the world over. Walking the World is a group for walkers 50 and older who take trips from 10 to 14 days through different regions. Upcoming walks include Costa Rica, Utah, and the wild outback of New Zealand. For details, visit www.walkingtheworld.com or call 970-498-0500.

Lace on those trekking shoes. If you want adventure on your walk, look no further. ElderTreks specializes in the far-flung for those over 50, whether it's hiking the Silk Road through Pakistan, exploring Mongolia on camelback, or hiking to the stunning ruins of Angkor Wat. Visit www.eldertreks.com or call 1-800-741-7956.

Hiking with America's mountaineers. The Appalachian Mountain Club, America's most famous hiking organization, runs a number of programs specifically for those 50 and above. Recent offerings include moderate hikes of three to six miles to examine the June flowers in bloom along the Appalachians, as well as five-day trips to Adventure Camps, which include hikes to special huts deep within the mountain range. Find details at www.outdoors.org or call 617-523-0655.

Move Over, Mark Spitz

The National Senior Games Association is the umbrella group overseeing all the individual states that host Senior Olympics, for competitors 50 and above, and it hosts the National Senior Games, which take place every year ending in an odd number (2011, 2013, etc.) in the fields of archery, badminton, basketball, bowling, cycling, golf, horseshoes, race walk, racquetball, road race, shuffleboard, softball, swimming, table tennis, tennis, track and field, triathlon, and volleyball. You must qualify at the state or local level competition, held in even years (2010, 2012, etc.) to take part in the national competition. For more information on Senior Games held in your state, check out the Web site at www.nsga.com.

Ski (and more) with The Over the Hill Gang. Founded as a ski club, this group for adventurous and hardy seniors over 50 has expanded into learning golf in Arizona, biking in Europe, treking coast-to-coast in Costa Rica and sailing in Turkey. And its skiing options include St. Moritz, British Columbia and Spain. The Over the Hill Gang International does not run vacations for folks who mostly want to put their feet up! But if you crave the powder or the call of the wild, these are your guys. Membership is $60 a year, and that gives you discounts on lift tickets at 100 ski areas in the United States and Canada. Visit www.othgi.com or call 719-389-0022.

Going Back to School Without Going Broke

Learning keeps your brain active and keeps you young! Colleges and universities welcome seniors back into their hallowed halls because mature students bring a lot to the party when it comes to learning and classroom discussion. Nearly every college and university has a continuing education program that allows seniors to attend classes for credit or to audit them for no credit. State schools are a wonderful place to start if you're looking for low-priced classes; some states have particularly good programs that offer seniors free tuition. Even if you don't see your state in the list below, it's worthwhile to contact your closest state-funded university or college and ask about its requirements for senior students. The university may offer you a deal even if it's not mandated by the state legislature, as it is in most of the cases below.

Alabama The Alabama Commission on Higher Education has a free tuition program for any resident 60 or older who meets the requirements to attend any two-year post-secondary educational institution.

NO KIDDING?

Audits Can Be Fun!

To audit a class means literally to "listen" to it, rather than taking the class for credit. Auditing doesn't mean that you only have to sit and listen, however. You can take part in the class just like any other student. The difference is that you're there merely to enjoy and educate yourself, and auditors don't have to do the homework, write the papers, or take the tests (although some professors may allow you to do so if you wish).

Alaska Any resident eligible to receive full Social Security retirement benefits has been able to attend state-funded colleges for free, but the recent leap in oil prices and the financial instability of the Alaska state college system has led officials to temporarily halve the waiver.

Arkansas Residents of Arkansas 60 and older may attend Arkansas State University for credit and for free. All tuition is waived.

Colorado Residents 60 and older may enroll tuition-free at UC-Denver on a no-credit audit basis.

Connecticut Citizens 62 and older may attend any public university or college in Connecticut for free.

Delaware Residents of Delaware 60 and above may attend the University of Delaware for credit tuition-free.

Hawaii The University of Hawaii-Mānoa has a Senior Citizen Visitor Program that allows senior citizens to audit classes for free, but those wishing to attend for credit must pay full tuition.

Indiana Purdue University waives tuition for Indiana residents 60 and older taking undergraduate courses.

Kansas Wichita State allows residents 60 and above to audit courses without tuition.

Kentucky The University of Louisville waives tuition for residents of the state who are 65 and older.

Maine Residents 65 and older for whom tuition would be a financial hardship may apply to have their tuition waived at any University of Maine campus.

Did You Know?

Even if you can't go back to school for free, you *can* go back to school near you with the Osher Lifelong Learning Institute (OLLI, formerly Learning in Retirement), designed specifically for seniors. The Bernard Osher Foundation was founded in 1977 to support higher education, and the foundation now supports senior learning programs on 115 campuses across the United States, at universities such as Harvard, Penn State, and the University of Southern Maine, which hosts the OLLI program's National Resource Center. Contact the center or surf its comprehensive Web site (www.osher.net) to find an OLLI program at a college or university near you. You may also call 207-780-4128 or write:

OLLI National Resource Center
University of Southern Maine
PO Box 9300
Portland, ME 04104-9300

Ka-Ching!

There are heaps of free and inexpensive courses available on the Internet. If you want to go back to school in the privacy of your own home, give it a whirl!

FREE ED!

A site wholly devoted to education for education's sake, this site provides courses in a huge range of topics, all entirely free. The upside is that you can range as far and wide as you like, never even completing a course if you find you prefer a different one. You don't have to register, you don't have to do homework, and you don't get a grade. The downside is that you won't have a live teacher or fellow students with whom to discuss anything. But if you want to travel widely in the realm of self-education, this site is waiting with open arms. Get going at www.free-ed.net.

SENIOR SUMMER SCHOOL PART I

Travel programs with a strong educational bent are the focus of Senior Summer School, which takes place on campuses and at universities across the United States, allowing seniors to immerse themselves in the local culture with tours and events in different cities. Enjoy Burlington, Vermont, from the base of St. Michael's College, or get to know America's heartland at University of Wisconsin-Madison. Find out more at www.seniorsummerschool.com or call 1-800-847-2466.

Online Higher Learning

SENIOR SUMMER SCHOOL PART II

The online part of the Senior Summer School program is made up of courses from a number of schools, generally in a six-week online class and offering a wide range of topics, from art history and accounting to math, marketing, and Web design. The online courses are complete with class (online) discussions, quizzes, and final exams—and all for $99 a class. Sign up at www.ed2go.com/ssschool.

OPEN CULTURE

At www.oculture.com, you'll find a site that is essentially one-stop shopping for continuing education, from podcasts of lectures and courses at great universities around the world to thought-provoking essays and videos. Nearly all the content is free, but it also points you to sites such as www.extension.harvard.edu where you can register for online courses at Harvard for a fraction of the usual cost.

MIT

The Internet offers some amazing things, but it's really remarkable that it will let you take classes at the Massachusetts Institute of Technology for *free*—in any subject that interests you. Go to http://ocw.mit.edu, find a subject, and you can either read the course or download some mp3 files of lectures and listen to them just like any student sitting in the lecture hall. Many of the courses also include class notes to help you catch up, along with lists of the course reading.

Massachusetts State residents who are 60 and older may register tuition-free for credit courses any of the state-funded colleges or universities.

Missouri Residents 65 and older are exempt from tuition at Missouri state schools.

Montana State residents 65 and above may have their tuition waived at any publicly funded Montana college.

Nevada Students 62 and older who are state residents may register for courses at the University of Nevada-Reno without paying per-credit registration fees.

New Hampshire Residents 65 or older who are not enrolled in a degree program may take two for-credit courses per academic year tuition-free.

New Jersey Rutgers allows residents 62 and older to audit courses without paying tuition on its Camden, Newark, and New Brunswick campuses in the spring and fall only.

Did you know?

Wisdom Wins the Race! Recent studies have shown that our brains take in information differently from those of younger people. One study found that young people in a test group could all plow quickly through a text, ignoring the words or concepts that they didn't understand, and could parrot back the major ideas with speed. Thus young people appear, superficially, to be getting the ideas faster and more easily. The older people in the study group, faced with the same material, worked far more slowly, stopping to take in, understand, and fully integrate any unfamiliar concepts and words. Researchers concluded that this phenomenon might actually be the visible sign of...wisdom. Only age can bring that level of concentration and understanding, so never think that a return trip—or a first-time visit—to school won't be worth your while!

New Mexico Each public, post-secondary, degree-granting institution in New Mexico may only charge senior citizens $5 per credit hour, on request by the student.

North Carolina The Senior Student Tuition Waiver allows North Carolina residents 65 and older to attend classes for credit (or take online courses for credit) at all North Carolina public universities and state community colleges for free.

Ohio Residents 60 and above can take classes for free at Ohio State University.

South Carolina Senior citizens 60 and above may enroll at the University of South Carolina-Beaufort for free, provided they wait to register until the third day of class. (Registering prior to that will incur the usual tuition.)

Texas Any Texas resident 65 or older may audit classes at any publicly funded university or college for free. Residents 55 to 64 may attend classes at a reduced tuition.

Utah State residents 62 or older can audit any University of Utah class numbered 1000 or above for $25 per semester.

Virginia Any resident age 60 or older may audit any class in any publicly funded Virginia college or university for free. You are only guaranteed free classes for credit if you made less than $15,000 the previous year.

Volunteering for a Cause

Volunteering during your retirement may turn out to be the most rewarding work that you have ever done. Senior volunteers are always in great demand because they bring a lifetime of wisdom and experience to every project they undertake, and that's an immense benefit for everyone involved. Because of this, there are dozens of organizations coordinating senior volunteering on a national level, as well as state and local organizations, that can help pair you with the volunteer work that best suits your needs in terms of interest, time, and expertise.

Although many seniors have the time and energy to volunteer, a lot of them don't do it simply because *nobody asks them*! If you don't know that you're wanted, it can be intimidating to go look for a volunteer position. Most volunteers age 55 and older find their volunteer positions through their church or religious institution because they attend on a weekly basis and the opportunities arise. Many, many nonprofit and charitable organizations are eager for your assistance but don't know how to reach you, so you can be sure that you'll be received with open arms.

Ka-Ching!

Take a Vacation with the National Trust

The *British* National Trust, that is, an organization overseeing the cultural heritage of the United Kingdom. It offers "Working Holidays," many specifically limited to volunteers ages 40 and older, which allow you to live and work for a few days or a week on the grounds of one of its national historic houses or estates. It's like getting a dream vacation for nearly nothing: You pay a minor fee, about $150 a week, for food and accommodation, which might be austere hostel-style dormitories, but, then again, might be an extremely comfortable gardener's cottage on a grand estate. Each working vacation group usually includes about a dozen volunteers, and in the evenings, the volunteers prepare dinner together.

You can choose your working holiday at the National Trust's Web site by selecting the region of the United Kingdom you wish to visit and the approximate dates you're available, and the site will offer you a selection of possible holidays. Some recent offerings included:

Repairing dry stone walls and upgrading Lakeshore paths for wheelchair access in the countryside around Wasdale.

Managing woodlands and wildlife habitats on the banks of the Menai Straits as you earn your John Muir award.

Learning tree identification while you help wardens run the countryside education program for local primary schools.

Each Working Holiday tends to fill up quickly, so you may have to plan far ahead. But for the price of a plane ticket and a little hard work, you can have an extremely inexpensive holiday and a truly unique experience. To find out more, go to www.nationaltrust.org.uk (click on "Get Involved with the National Trust").

The American branch of the National Trust is called The Royal Oak Foundation, at www.royal-oak.org, and you can join from the United States. Membership gives you free admission to all the properties of the National Trust, which you can visit when you're done with your Working Holiday!

National and International Volunteer Organizations

Many venerable institutions such as the Peace Corps and Senior Corps exist to help match knowledge with service, but there are also plenty of places that exist for the sole purpose of pairing you up with the right opportunity. If you don't find what you want at one place, check another. Positions, openings, and opportunities change frequently, so search around to find the one that suits you.

Peace, baby! Interesting enough, you can still, all these years after Camelot, answer President Kennedy's call to service and join the Peace Corps, which defines "Older Americans" as anyone age 50 and beyond (there is no upper age limit for Peace Corps volunteers). Couples must apply separately and each qualify as a volunteer, but once that happens, there are joint postings for couples at Peace Corps sites around the world. Forget traveling in an RV—if you want *real* adventure, learn to speak Swahili under the Peace Corps' auspices and go teach schoolchildren at a remote outpost in Kenya!

Even if you feel a bit less adventurous than that, there are countless opportunities all around you for volunteering.

Peace Corps
Paul D. Coverdell Peace Corps Headquarters
1111 20th St., NW
Washington, DC 20526
1-800-424-8580
www.peacecorps.gov

Corpsman, Corpsman! The Senior Corps is an independent federal agency dating back to 1965, when the Foster Grandparent program was founded to help seniors with limited incomes give something back to their communities. It was so quickly successful that it expanded into the three main parts of the organization that are still active today:

- Foster Grandparents, which hooks up volunteers age 60-plus with children who need the stabilizing influence of older adults;
- Senior Companions, which lets volunteers age 60-plus assist older adults with daily activities; and
- RSVP, a volunteering clearinghouse with a wealth of opportunities for community and local work available to Americans age 55 and over.

Senior Corps
1201 New York Ave., NW
Washington, DC 20525
1-800-424-8867
www.seniorcorps.org

He ain't heavy; he's my (little) brother! For as little as four hours a month (or as much more time as you have), the Big Brothers Big Sister program can make a huge difference in the life of a child who may have a home environment that's less than ideal. This program involves pairing you with a child in your area and allowing you to get to know that child and spend some quality time with him or her. Whether you go to a baseball game or have a picnic in the park, the benefits are incalculable.

Big Brothers Big Sisters National Office
230 N. 13th St.
Philadelphia, PA 19107
215-567-7000
www.bbbs.org

Did You Know?

Senior Environmental Employment Program A program of the Environmental Protection Agency (EPA), the Senior Environmental Employment (SEE) Program is a unique setup that pairs retired Americans with EPA labs and regional EPA offices around the country. Once there, generally on a short-term stipend or contract, they bring their specialized skills to bear on environmental issues. The SEE Program is for retirees age 55 and above, and mostly requires professional qualifications for participation (engineers, scientists, accountants, grant writers, technicians), but if you have a profound interest in working on environmental issues, some of the work is clerical and requires only your passionate interest rather than your lifetime of professional experience. Contact the SEE Program or check out its Web site to see if it's right for you.

SEE Program
U.S. Environmental Protection Agency
1200 Pennsylvania Ave., NW, MC: 3605A
Washington, DC 20460
202-564-0420
www.epa.gov/epahrist/see/brochure/backgr.htm

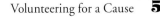

If you build it…Don't think that volunteering for Habitat for Humanity will require you to cart around wheelbarrows full of bricks. There are many volunteering jobs with Habitat that don't require physical labor—but if you would like to build, or just wield a paintbrush, Habitat is happy to teach you how. Check out its program called Women Build, which teaches women the skills they need to go out safely on a job site. Call 1-800-422-4828 (1-800-HABITAT) or visit the Web site at www.habitat.org.

Smokey says…join the National Park Service. If you're fortunate enough to live near a national park—and many of us do, even in urban areas—you can volunteer to do practically anything. The parks are frequently in need of help in a huge variety of ways, from excavation and construction to making an inventory of plant life. The National Park Service has a wonderful Web site that lets you find your closest park and all the upcoming events requiring volunteers, with the specific contact information for each event. Visit www.nps.gov (click on "Get Involved").

Early Bird Secret

Start Close to Home

When you're considering what kind of volunteer work you want to do and where, it can help to think local before you think national (or international!). While major programs that involve travel with the Peace Corps or Habitat for Humanity can be exciting, it can be just as rewarding—and a lot less tiring—to do lower-key but equally vital volunteer work in your own community or neighborhood. Consider places such as these in your own town:

• Schools, colleges, youth groups, sports teams, preschools, day-care centers, after-school programs

• Retirement and assisted-living communities, Meals on Wheels, church- or community-sponsored soup kitchens, Neighborhood Watch organizations

• Prisons, halfway houses, drug rehab centers, shelters for the homeless or battered women and children

• Community theaters, bands, choirs, orchestras, dance troupes, art museums, civic clubs

• Local parks, monuments, battlefields, historical homes and markers

Assistance with Volunteer Opportunities and Placements

If you're not sure where you want to volunteer or what exactly you want to do, you'll find a huge range of ideas and opportunities from these organizations.

Experience Corps Experience Corps is specifically designed to utilize the talents and accumulated knowledge of Americans over the age of 55. It currently has branches in 19 major cities across the country. Check out its Web site at www.experiencecorps.org to see if there's an Experience Corps opportunity near you.

Network for Good If you don't have a lot of time for volunteer work but still want to be involved in assisting charities and the needy, Network for Good can help you, with a few simple clicks, direct your money to places where it will be put to work for you. The network vets the organizations and charities that they help benefit to be sure that your funding is getting into the right hands, and they also provide a network of places where you can actively volunteer, not to mention a useful list of questions to ask yourself when considering volunteer work.

Network for Good
7920 Norfolk Ave., Ste. 520
Bethesda, MD 20814
1-888-284-7978
www.networkforgood.org

Volunteer Match This is another clearinghouse to put people together with the best volunteering positions for their skills and talents. At its Web site, you can type in your location and a keyword of what interests you, such as "health care" or "children in need," and it will search opportunities for you from its database of more than 60,000 non-profit organizations.

VolunteerMatch
717 California St., Second Floor
San Francisco, CA 94108
415-241-6868
www.volunteermatch.org

1-800-Volunteer.org This is a national database organized by the Points of Light Foundation that allows users to search, in English or Spanish, for volunteer opportunities all over the United States. The site works in partnership with more than 75,000 organizations across the country. To use the site, you must first register for a free account, and then access to all information is free. Visit www.1-800-volunteer.org or call 1-800-VOLUNTEER (865-8683).

Keeping Cultured

> *Amazing Ways to Go Out on the Town—on a Shoestring*

Big Savings at the Big Screen

The price of movie tickets has been climbing steadily since the first silent movie thrilled the public more than 100 years ago, and don't we feel it! In New York and Los Angeles, movie tickets are headed for $12—and that's evenings *and* matinee. If you live anywhere in between, you've got a much better shot at saving a little money for some scrumptious popcorn. In addition to a rundown of the standard senior discounts at the major cinema chains, here are some cinema-tastic tactics that will fulfill your craving for the silver screen. Are you ready for *your* close-up? We thought so!

Always on a Tuesday (never on a Sunday). It might be because it follows one of the busiest days of the work week (when most folks just want to head home), but Tuesday nights are notoriously slow movie nights––so slow, in fact, that many theater chains slash their ticket prices by 20 to 50 percent. Call your local theater to make sure it's on board, and if not, ask why. Inquiring minds generally get favorable responses.

(Never say never.) Sometimes on a Sunday. Three cheers all around for that great American institution, the Sunday matinee. Tickets are usually 30 to 40 percent lower than at other times, and if you get a senior discount, you may be entitled to even more off the discount.

Be artsy. Independent theaters—the ones that show foreign and short-run films—generally price their tickets 10 to 15 percent lower than chain theaters. Why? Independent theaters are usually smaller, as are their audiences, so it's important to them to draw more viewers.

Early Bird Secret

Free Movie Passes Online

A number of Web sites offer access to free movie screenings. Some of the showings are promotions by the studios hoping to stir up advance buzz; others are actual passes you can print out and take to the cinema with you; and some are discounted tickets (although the discount rarely reaches higher than the 35 percent you may already get on a senior ticket). Some sites also allow you to purchase packs of tickets at a reduced fee, which is generally lower than the senior price. Visit these sites to find bargains: www.iscreenings.com, www.freemoviescreening.net, and www.wildaboutmovies.com.

Use your rank. Are you active-duty military personnel? If so, you can gain entry to all National Amusements theaters for $7 (general admission) or $5 (during matinees).

Be a star! Many theater chains, like National Amusements (in Connecticut, California, Iowa, Kentucky, Massachusetts, Michigan, New Jersey, New York, Ohio, Pennsylvania, Rhode Island, Virginia, and as a far away as Wales, Russia, and Argentina) offer special rewards programs that result in free tickets, free snacks, and more. The StarPass Membership (http://www.nationalamusements.com/programs/star_pass.asp) is free. Each time you make a purchase at a participating theater, you will earn 10 credits on the dollar, redeemable for tickets and much more.

Enjoy the classics. If you love the best of the silver screen (from the 1930s to the 1980s), you may be in luck. Many theaters show classics during off hours (usually in the early afternoon), at a deep, deep discount. One of our experts in New York discovered a Long Island-based program called Silver Screen Classics, for which the price of admission is $2 per ticket.

Lights, camera.... Some of us who would never ask for a senior discount anywhere else are thrilled to get one at the movies. Maybe that's because the movies tend to post the discount price clearly, up high, behind the cash register—why can't everyone else do that? In any case, there's nothing better than sitting in the cinema, enjoying your popcorn, with the knowledge that *your* ticket came at a discount, often as much as 35 percent off. Actual discounts vary all over the country, as do base ticket prices, and the age restriction may vary as well, but this is the general rundown of senior discounts at a sampling of the major movie chains.

- AMC Loews: Senior discount for ages 60 and older (62 at some locations).
- Carmike: Seniors age 55 and above get a discount.
- Clearview: Ages 62 and above get a senior discount.
- Imax: Discount for ages 65 and above.
- Regal: Seniors age 60 and above get a discount.

Theater Discounts On, Off, and *Way* Off Broadway!

Think that you can't afford the luxury of live theatrical performances? Guess again! We discovered that actors don't like empty seats, but more important, neither do producers and theater owners. The result? There are heaps of special discounts to help fill the house when it comes to showtime. You won't find actual senior discounts to a Broadway or West End of London show, but there are plenty of other ways around paying full price. (And that's a good thing, because box-office ticket prices for top Broadway shows can run as high as $200.)

Make friends with Craig. Craig's List, that is! Go online to www.craigslist.org and search in New York, Boston, Chicago, and Los Angeles for half-price tickets. Make sure you proceed with caution, and verify the tickets are legit. Most are fine, as people whose schedules have changed offer them as a way of trying to make up their losses.

Taking stock. If a trip to a big city isn't in your future, don't forget about regional theater and summer stock. Many plays headed for Broadway travel to one of the country's 1,800 regional theaters for tryouts. Ticket prices are much less than they will be once they hit the big time. According to *Time Magazine*, the five best regional theaters in the country are: Goodman Theatre, Chicago, Illinois; Oregon Shakespeare Festival, Ashland, Oregon; American Repertory Theatre, Cambridge, Massachusetts; Guthrie Theater, Minneapolis, Minnesota; and South Coast Repertory, Costa Mesa, California.

TKTS, get your TKTS. Why do people line up in all weather at the Times Square branch of TKTS in New York City? Because it's the place to get same-day tickets to nearly everything on Broadway for 50 percent off. The Times Square location of the Theater Development Fund's ticket booth opens at 3 p.m., and the long, twisting rope of a line starts to form hours before that. You can generally get anywhere from 20 to 50 percent off nearly everything on the Great White Way, and on lots of other shows around the city. TKTS is cash only, and there's a small handling fee of about $4.00 per ticket, but it's worth it for the major savings. Visit www.tdf.org/tkts for more information.

The Early Bird Who Heads South Gets First Crack at Bargain Tickets

If you're visiting Manhattan, skip the lines in Times Square for the TKTS booth and hop on a subway to the South Street Seaport TKTS booth. This one opens at 11 a.m., and the lines tend to be much shorter and faster-moving—it's where the locals go to buy tickets. If you're in Brooklyn, you can also take advantage of the recently opened Brooklyn branch. The outlying branches are selling the same tickets at the same discounts, but without the staggeringly long lines. You can get to South Street Seaport, buy your tickets, have lunch, even, and be back uptown before the Times Square branch even opens!

Visiting London? The best way to score half-price tickets is to check out the British version of New York's TKTS. In London it's known as tkts, and the kiosk is in Leicester Square. You must turn up in person and have an open mind—there's no telling what plays or musicals will be available. Popular shows that are sold out in advance are likely unavailable.

Get online, wherever you live. Wherever you live in this country, virtually every metropolitan area and university town offers great theater for less. While you may not be able to find a TKTS booth for half-price tickets, you can find similar bargains by logging onto the Internet and going straight to TheaterMania.com. This site lets you buy tickets in advance at up to 40 percent off for plays in New York, Boston, Chicago, Dallas/Ft. Worth, Washington, D.C., Las Vegas, Los Angeles, Philadelphia, San Francisco, and more. Registration is required but free, and there are special sections and discounts on shows specifically for children, if you're trying to introduce young grandkids to a love of the theater. Visit www.theatermania.com for more information.

To be or not to be...free! More than 400 years after the great Bard sharpened his quill, Shakespeare would be delighted to know that we can all enjoy his plays for free. Many metropolitan areas have theaters that offer free Shakespeare in the summer, not least in Central Park, where New Yorkers in the know wait in line to get free tickets to world-class productions at the Delacorte Theater, some of which later even transfer to Broadway. Many smaller communities offer free Shakespeare, usually in the summer. If you don't live near one of these places, check your own arts pages to see if there are any upcoming performances.

Boston, Massachusetts: www.citicenter.org
Cleveland, Ohio: www.cleveshakes.org
Louisville, Kentucky: www.kyshakes.org
New York, New York: www.publictheater.org
San Francisco, California: www.sfshakes.org

Take it play by play, and fill a seat. Apply for membership to the private organization Play by Play, which helps to fill seats that might otherwise go empty, and you can see top Broadway shows for $4.00 a ticket! There's an online membership fee of $99 a year, as well as an $8 processing fee, and you must apply by phone. Once you've been accepted as a member you can find out what shows are available online, choose one, and reserve two tickets for it—for $4.00 each. For your annual fee and the per-ticket fee, you can see as many shows as you can possibly sit through. The rules are clearly defined, if strict, but the benefits are nothing short of fantastic. If you live anywhere near New York City, it's the sweetest ticket deal imaginable. Visit www.play-by-play.com or call 212-868-7052 (phone membership is $125, plus $8 processing fee).

Usher in great savings. If you love theater, volunteer to be an usher and odds are you'll get to see every play you work for free. Even if you truly love the lights of Broadway and you live in New York City, you can be an usher and see all the shows you like, while helping patrons get seated and get their Playbills. The task is not onerous, and usually these positions are filled by theater-loving seniors. This is not an option for visitors since there's a certain commitment level expected of volunteers. If you're interested, inquire at the theater where your favorite show is playing, and ask for details on how to volunteer.

Attend a festival. A great way to see upcoming world-class plays while they're still at bargain-basement prices is the Summer Play Festival at the Public Theater in New York City. The Public's festival, which runs throughout July, offers cutting edge new drama for the rock-bottom price of $10 per play. Check out this year's offerings at its Web site. If you miss the thrill of live theater in your hometown, $10 a show might just lure you to NYC! Note: The SPF is on hiatus in 2010 but plans to return to the Public Theater in 2011. Visit www.spfnyc.com for more information.

Go back to school. If you live in or near a university town, you're in luck. Some of the best, most enthusiastic young actors and actresses take part in university theater, often with the help of one special star who shows up to draw the crowd. University theater companies also usually offer a senior discount as well, so make sure to flash that driver's license!

Stage your own play. Want to be on the other side of the stage? ArtAge's Senior Theatre Resource Center helps seniors fulfill their theatrical aspirations with a big selection of plays; all the tips and advice you could ever need to stage a play, including help with production design, publicity, and marketing; and even professional consulting on how to write a grant proposal if, for example, you are looking for funding from your arts council to aid with a local production. Some productions take place in retirement homes and communities, others through religious groups or social organizations, and some troupes have taken on a life of their own with advertising that brings together seniors who didn't even know one another prior to putting on a show together. Look for details on how to get a theatrical production started with your own friends—or find out where seniors are performing near you and go support a Senior Theatre production! For more information, visit www.seniortheatre.com.

Be an extra. Not in the show—in the audience! For an $85 annual fee and a $30 reserve fund to start (for a total setup fee of $115), you can help "paper" a house—fill the seats—of events all over New York City, from top Broadway shows (less likely) to concerts and experimental theater (often lots of seats available!), anything that needs an audience. Once you've applied, you receive a password for online access to find the list of shows on offer, and each ticket costs $3.50. You can get one or two tickets, based on availability. For an additional donation of $50 when you sign up, you can get up to four tickets per show, when available, for a year. For more information, go to www.audienceextras.com or call 1-212-686-1966.

Money-Saving Museum Deals

Love art, history, horticulture, animals, rock 'n' roll, Harley-Davidsons, robots, bananas, or even hats? You're in luck! Museums of *all* sorts, galleries, and botanical gardens offer deeply discounted admission for seniors (and sometimes free admission on certain days during the week—usually weekdays or weekday evenings). If there's something that interests you, there's probably a museum dedicated to it, so let your fingers do the walking.

Get (free) culture at the Met... New York's Metropolitan Museum of Art, that is. Like many cultural institutions, its entry fee is not a requirement; it's a "recommended" admission fee. So if you're in the Big Apple and feel like spending a few glorious hours at one of the nation's most magnificent museums—home to everything from a colossal Egyptian sphinx to a priceless Stradivarius violin to the portrait of George Washington that eventually wound up on our dollar bill—then march up to the counter and lay down any amount you like, from two cents to the suggested admission of $20, and you'll be admitted with a smile and no questions asked.

Are you named Isabella? If so, you're in for a pleasant Beantown surprise: the Isabella Stewart Gardner Museum, located a few blocks from Boston's Fenway Park, offers you free entrance for life if you share the name of the mansion museum's original owner and resident. If you're not named Isabella but you are a senior, you can get in for the senior discount rate of $10 instead of the regular admission fee of $12.

Go corporate. Many corporations—from Chase Bank to *Forbes* magazine—have stunning art collections that the public can visit for free at the corporate headquarters. If you live near the national headquarters of pretty much *any* major company, call its main information number and ask if it has a gallery that's accessible to the public. You'll likely see some delightful sculpture (and some very large paintings)!

Ka-ching!
Free Cultural Events in Your Own Backyard

You don't need to travel to major cities to find museums and theaters. Check your local newspaper listings for events such as these—nearly always free and delighted to see you.

BOOKSTORES:

Authors travel the country pouring their hearts out in bookstores, whether reading from their newly published tomes, talking about them, or signing them. Most bookstores that host regular events have newsletters and Web sites, but you can get a better scoop if you get to know your local bookstore employees. Find out what visiting scribe they're excited about and show up in time to get a ringside seat. And if you're the only one who comes? You'll get a private show, and the author and employees will be eternally grateful that you bothered!

GRAND OPENINGS:

Art galleries, exhibitions at your local museum or civic center, new shops and stores—whenever something new is opening, there's usually a public party to lure you in. Scan the newspapers, look for banners, ask your friends to come along. Opening celebrations often include free food, free drinks, and sometimes live performances. Who can resist? And the price is right.

POETRY READINGS, OPEN-MIKE NIGHTS:

For the price of your latte at a comfy coffee shop or perhaps a gin-and-tonic at a slightly wobbly table, you can get a ground-floor view of what today's upcoming talents are up to. The really bad performers are entertaining in their own way, and on any given night, there are always a few gems.

LIVE MUSIC PERFORMANCES:

Depending on where you live, there's probably nearly free live music and concerts happening all the time. From practicing choirs to jazz guitar to indie singers and string trios, musicians, like any artists, like to share their stuff, and generally the price of admission is not high.

LOCAL THEATER:

At a high school near you, dozens of teenagers are preparing to act their hearts out in *No, No, Nanette; Godspell;* or *Hamlet;* and they'd love it if someone was in the audience besides their parents. There are also community theaters and one-off performances of small, traveling troupes. Get one of these usually inexpensive tickets and give it a whirl. If it's opening night, community theaters may serve free cheese and wine!

STREET SINGERS, PARK PERFORMERS:

This is how to catch music on the run, without sitting down for it. If you live in an urban area, chances are someone is singing or playing an instrument in a pedestrian passageway or in your local park. And sometimes they're enormously talented. Take the time to stop and listen. When virtuoso violinist Joshua Bell played his Stradivarius at an entrance to the Washington Metro (as a little experiment for the *Washington Post*), only seven people of more than a thousand who went by paused to listen.

Borrowed admission. Most public libraries offer *free* passes to selected museums and other area attractions. These are kept at the library's circulation desk and are available to card-holding library patrons. Below you'll find a mere sampling of the offerings available at the libraries where we inquired—ask at your local library and see what's on offer:

- The Boston Public Library furnishes numerous free and discounted passes at its main and branch locations.
- The Chicago Public Library issues Kraft Great Kids Museum Passports for up to four family members.
- The Mill Valley (California) Public Library offers free museum passes.
- The Huntingdon County (Pennsylvania) Public Library offers museum passes to its patrons.
- In Michigan, public libraries offer patrons a free Museum Adventure Pass to over 25 museums, and nature, art, and histroric sites.
- The Minneapolis Public Library offers patrons passes to museums, zoos, and other attractions.
- The Ottawa (Canada) Public Library furnishes passes to more than 30 Canadian museums and historic sites.

The Modern for free. The Museum of Modern Art (MoMA) in NYC does *not* offer a suggested admission: $20 is the price, take it or leave it, unless you're a senior 65 and older, with ID, in which case you only pay $16. Or you can take advantage of Free Friday Nights, sponsored by Target, which allow visitors into the museum for free between 4 and 8 p.m. These "tickets" cannot be obtained in advance, so you have to line up with everyone else and wait your turn for admission. If you want quiet, go for a morning admission at the senior discount price, because even these spacious galleries are jam-packed on a Friday night, but it's a cheerful hubbub and will convince you more than anything that art still matters!

Go to Washington, DC. The Smithsonian Institution consists of 19 museums, including the delightful National Air and Space Museum, the National Portrait Gallery, the National Museum of American History, the National Museum of African Art, the Hirshhorn Museum and Sculpture Garden, and many more. Admission to all of the museums that are located in Washington, DC (which is everything but the Cooper-Hewitt in New York) is free.

Our Nation's Most Offbeat (and Inexpensive) Museums

For mere pennies on the dollar, you can gain entry into any of the following museums, which run the gamut from the sublime to the, well, just plain kooky.

American Clock & Watch Museum, Bristol, Connecticut

Burlingame Museum of Pez Memorabilia, Burlingame, California

Circus World Museum, Baraboo, Wisconsin

Cuba Cheese Museum, Cuba, New York

Frederick's of Hollywood Lingerie Museum, Los Angeles, California

The Hat Museum, Portland, Oregon

Haverstraw Brick Museum, Haverstraw, New York

Kansas Barbed Wire Museum, LaCrosse, Kansas

Liberace Museum and Foundation, Las Vegas, Nevada

Lizzie Borden Museum, Fall River, Massachusetts

Marvin's Marvelous Mechanical Museum, Farmington Hills, Michigan

Museum of Bad Art, Dedham, Massachusetts

Mütter Museum, Philadelphia, Pennsylvania

New York Museum of Water, New York, New York

Sing Sing Prison Museum, Ossining, New York

World Kite Museum, Long Beach, Washington

Check out great design at the Cooper-Hewitt. For the New York City branch of the Smithsonian, filled with wonderful examples of design past and present, the regular admission is $15, but seniors are $10—unless you're already a member of the Smithsonian Institution, in which case admission is free.

Get a City Pass. A City Pass allows substantial discounts on many museums and other attractions and also allows you to skip the long lines in many places and march right in through special entrances. Whether you're visiting Atlanta, Boston, Chicago, Hollywood, Houston, New York, Philadelphia, San Francisco, Seattle, Southern California, or Toronto, a City Pass can be a wise investment in terms of money and time. You don't even need to prepurchase: a City Pass can be bought at the main ticket window of any of the attractions included. Visit www.citypass.com or call 1-888-330-5008.

When in the Apple, stop in at the Whitney.

Regular admission to this stunning collection of American art is regularly $18, but seniors 62 and older with ID can get in for $12.

Go to the Guggenheim.

If you only know what the famous spiraled shell-like exterior looks like, treat yourself to an interior view as well with a senior discount price of $15, down from the regular admission of $18. On Saturdays from 5:45 until the 7:45 p.m. closing, you can visit the Guggenheim in Manhattan on a donation basis, paying what you wish for admission—the tickets are not "free," since you must pay something, but the amount is up to you. The final tickets that night are issued at 7:15 p.m.

Get to the Getty. Admission is free to this Los Angeles collection of Western art dating back to the Middle Ages, but you must have a timed ticket to visit the Getty Villa in Malibu, with its unparalleled collection of ancient Greek, Roman, and Etruscan art. (Note that parking is $15, but free after 5 p.m.) Save yourself the hassle by checking for availability online at www.gettymuseum.us, where you can order your free ticket and print it yourself. You can also call 310-440-7300 to book your visit.

Climb those famous steps like Rocky.

The Philadelphia Museum of Art is $16 regular admission but seniors 65 and older with ID can get in for $14. The first Sunday of every month is pay what you wish. For more information about membership and current exhibits visit www.philamuseum.org.

Visit the Windy City's Art Institute of Chicago.

Entry to the Art Institute is $12 for seniors 65 and older with ID, a savings of $6 off the regular admission. You can also enter free from 5 to 8 p.m. on Thursdays, sponsored by Target.

Way out west at the Los Angeles County Museum of Art. Seniors 62 and older with ID get in for $8 instead of $12 to visit the world-class collection of LACMA.

Did You Know?

Many Museums Only Suggest an Entry Fee Most museums in the United States have a "suggested" admission fee for entry? This means that if you can't pay the suggested senior rate (which is likely already discounted), or you'd simply rather pay less, you can do so. Museums nearly always have discounted admissions, from free admission for children to special student prices and senior discounts, because they're eager for you to attend. To find out more information on rates, including info on museums close to you or on museums you plan to visit while traveling, check out the Web site Museums of the World at www.museum.com, which gives you admission hours and prices on literally thousands of museums and galleries throughout the world.

Concerts, Opera, and Live Music Festivals on the Cheap

Do you crave the transporting sounds of classical music, yearn for the sweet-hot swinging vibes of jazz, or pine for a moving and memorable aria? Don't stay home because live music prices seem out of reach! Early Birds have awesome options when it comes to getting their fix of live music. While it's true that drink minimums and cover charges can add up at big-city nightspots, and concert tickets can range anywhere from $25 to more than $100, you can still hear world-class musicians perform for very little and sometimes even nothing! Many churches, universities, and colleges offer free or very low-cost concerts that are open to the public. Government art grants or private foundations generally subsidize these concerts—lucky for you! A random search on the Internet turned up loads of fascinating performances. For example, the Old Church in Portland, Oregon, (www.oldchurch.org) offers free "Sack Lunch" concerts on Wednesday afternoons and low-priced jazz and classical concerts for less than $15 a ticket, with a senior discount for music lovers 65 and older.

How do you get to Carnegie Hall? With a discounted ticket! (And, of course, it never hurts to practice.) While concert prices vary greatly depending on the venue within Carnegie Hall and who's playing what, there are senior discounts for certain shows. Senior discounts are available at the box office and only sold up to one hour before showtime. To find out when senior discounts will be available, visit Carnegie Hall's Web site and sign up for its biweekly e-mail newsletter, "At a Glance." You can also call the box office on the day of the event to see if discounted tickets will be available. Visit www.carnegiehall.org or call 212-247-7800.

Stay in tune with the Boston Philharmonic. Seniors can get discounted tickets to most shows as well as "rush" tickets on the day of the show, only at the box office. Rush tickets are also available to students, so you'll need ID, and you may need to stand in line! Get details at www.bostonphil.org or call 617-236-0999.

When in Beantown, shop at BosTix. Hear the Count Basie Orchestra or listen to classical music under the stars; catch an Elvis tribute band or hear a moving performance of *Carmen*—all for half-price when you shop at BosTix. Run by the nonprofit organization ArtsBoston, BosTix is one-stop shopping for any cultural event happening in Boston, from bands and orchestras, operas and musicals, to dance and theater, too. They operate two ticket booths, one in Faneuil Hall, the other in Copley Square, which open at 10 a.m. daily (11 a.m. on Sundays) and sell discounted day-of-show tickets. All tickets are cash only, but the savings are 50 percent off. You can also buy half-price tickets in advance at its Web site: www.bostix.org.

Early Bird Secret

RUSH Over to Carnegie Hall

The cheapest way to hear world-class music at Carnegie Hall is to come to the box office clutching a crispy new $10 bill on the day of the concert you want to hear. That's when a limited number of Public RUSH Tickets are available for concerts in the Stern Auditorium and Perelman Stage. It's best to get there (at 57th Street and Seventh Avenue) when the box office opens (at 11 a.m. Monday through Saturday and at noon on Sunday) because limited means when they're gone, they're gone. Visit www.carnegiehall.org for upcoming events.

From jazz to opera at Lincoln Center for less. The Lincoln Center in New York City is actually a complex of 12 resident organizations: Lincoln Center for the Performing Arts; the Chamber Music Society of Lincoln Center; the Film Society of Lincoln Center; Jazz at Lincoln Center; the Juilliard

School; Lincoln Center Theater; the Metropolitan Opera; New York City Ballet; New York City Opera; New York Philharmonic; the New York Public Library for the Performing Arts; and the School of American Ballet. Each organization has its own policy on senior discounts, but they are indeed regularly available for many performances and presentations. The best way to find out for sure is to contact the box office about what you want to see and reserve your discounted ticket directly through them. Visit www.lincolncenter.org for more information.

Opera Carolina. The vibrant opera community of Charlotte, North Carolina, which tends to offer classics such as *The Marriage of Figaro* and *The Barber of Seville* during its regular season, offers seniors a standard discount of 10 percent off the base ticket price, and proof of ID may be required. An even better deal, if you qualify, is the military discount of 15 percent. Find out more at www.operacarolina.org.

Long Leaf Opera Festival. Based in Chapel Hill, North Carolina, Long Leaf is the only opera company in the United States dedicated to presenting fully staged operas that were originally written in English. If you want to understand exactly what's going on onstage without reading subtitles (or "supertitles," as used at New York's Metropolitan Opera and many other opera houses), then Long Leaf is for you. They are also committed to making opera as affordable and comfortable as possible, with audience members encouraged to wear anything they like to performances, other than hats and big hair! Ticket prices are as low as $20 per performance. Get details at www.longleafopera.org.

SPTs at the Kennedy Center. SPTs, or specially priced tickets of 50 percent off, are available at the Kennedy Center in Washington, DC, for seniors 65 and older with valid ID. (They are also available to military personnel, those with disabilities, and those on a fixed income.) The tickets are subject to availability and can be ordered in advance except for any Saturday night events or Friday night *Shear Madness* performances. (When ordering in advance, ID must be shown at pickup.) Go to www.kennedy-center.org or call 1-800-444-1324 for information.

Grand deals for the Grand Ole Opry. There are a number of ways to get several dollars off your ticket to a performance at the Grand Ole Opry, both at the current Opry House and the old Ryman Auditorium, where the Opry was held from 1943 to 1974. The best bet is to book online, either with a tour group, which will give you a few dollars off your ticket and may include round-trip transportation to your hotel as part of the price. Visit www.opry.com/fancoupon.aspx or call 1-800-733-6779.

Branson for less. The Ozarks have always been known for music, and with the huge variety of shows available in Branson, Missouri, you can find far more there nowadays than foot-stomping country. The Branson Tourism Center, while not offering specific senior discounts, has mountains of discounts on everything from food and lodging to last-minute show tickets. The site claims to have sold more than 1,000,000,000 tickets to Branson shows, so they ought to know what they're doing by now! Log on to www.branson.com or call 1-800-785-1550 for more information.

Summer Folk Festivals

THEY'RE NOT LIKE WOODSTOCK ANYMORE!

One of the most underrated ways to enjoy live music inexpensively is to visit a summertime music festival. They're comparatively inexpensive, and you get to listen to fabulous music, usually while surrounded by like-minded people. All over the United States each summer, people congregate for weekends of music and dance, staying in local hotels, RVs, or campgrounds, and enjoying the delights of music in an outdoor setting. Many of these festivals, true to the family atmosphere most of them engender, offer a senior discount. Here is a list of some of the biggies:

- **Augusta Heritage Center Bluegrass Week,** Elkins, West Virginia

- **Beartrap Summer Festival,** Casper, Wyoming

- **Bitterroot Valley Bluegrass Festival,** Hamilton, Montana

- **Cumberland Dance Week,** Nancy, Kentucky

- **Falcon Ridge Folk Festival,** Hillsdale, New York

- **Founders Title Company Folk and Bluegrass Festival,** Salt Lake City, Utah

- **Kerrville Folk Festival,** Kerrville, Texas

For more information about what's going on in your neck of the woods, log on to festivalfinder.com where you can search by your favorite genre or use the Find By feature to locate festivals by date, location or name.

Live (and Free) Television Show Tapings

Live TV tapings can be a real thrill—the lights, the camera, the roar of the crowd all make for a fabulously free experience! Getting tickets to a live show used to be a rarity, but these days there are plenty of shows shot before a live studio audience and plenty of ways to get them. From David Letterman and Rachael Ray to Jon Stewart, Stephen Colbert, and Jimmy Kimmel, talk shows are the first line of tickets. You might have to win the lottery to see Oprah, but someone has to fill those seats, so you might as well throw your name into the hat. And if you don't get tickets to anything else, you can always go by Rockefeller Center if you're visiting New York City, and say "good morning" to the hosts of the *Today Show*, who regularly come outside to greet their guests on the plaza outside Studio 1A at NBC. Here are some leads to getting your free TV tickets. If you manage to get into *Saturday Night Live*, your kids will be thrilled!

TV sitcom tickets. Ever dream of being in a live studio audience? If you live in Los Angeles, here's your chance! Go to TVTickets.com, a direct hookup to a plethora of sitcom tapings of current network shows, nearly all of which are taped in studios in and around Los Angeles. You can search among the listings of currently taping shows; read all about each sitcom, its stars, and cast of characters; and check out the schedule of shoot dates. Then you can submit your request for tickets up to 30 days prior to the tape date you wish to attend. When you click "Submit," your map to the studio and your free ticket will be generated for you to print. Recent shows available included *The New Adventures of Old Christine* with Julia Louis-Dreyfus and *According to Jim* with Jim Belushi.

Watch a pilot taping. Pilots, which are essentially a "sample" of a new show for the networks, often require live audiences for their shoots. You can get tickets to see new shows being shot through Audiences Unlimited, which reminds visitors to the site that, once upon a time, *Seinfeld* and *Friends* were both just pilots before they were massive hit shows! The free tickets from this site are all for studios in and around Los Angeles, so if you're just visiting, they ask that you provide them with a working cell phone number so they can contact you with any changes. Maybe you'll get lucky and be there for the birth of a winner. Go to www.audiencesunlimited.com to learn how.

Saturday Night Live. The days of John Belushi and Chevy Chase may be long gone, but tickets to *Saturday Night Live* are among the most sought-after in TV tapings, and tickets are given out by lottery once a year. In August, you can submit a request via e-mail to snltickets@nbcuni.com. You can only send one e-mail per household, and you cannot select the date you would like to attend. If your request is successful, you receive two tickets for a randomly selected date. Alternately, you can try for a standby ticket at 7 a.m. on the morning of a taping. Tickets are distributed on the 49th Street side of 30 Rockefeller Plaza, and you can choose between the 8 p.m. dress rehearsal or the 11:30 p.m. live taping. Standby ticket holders are required to keep their places in line until the taping, with only minimal breaks allowed. Get more info at NBC's Web site: www.nbc.com/Tickets.

Take a Seat at Your Favorite TV Show Tonight

Want a quick way to get onto the set of a television show? If you're flexible—not to mention available during the daytime, when most of these shows tape—you can get tickets at Free TV Tickets for that same day or during the next week or so for anything taping in Los Angeles. This Web site (www.tvtix.com) is both a clearinghouse for those who want tickets and a seat-filling machine for the show's producers, who never want their stars to be talking to a half-empty house. Even if you're just visiting LA, you can visit the Web site in the morning and be sitting in a studio in Culver City that afternoon. Tickets are free and must be printed directly from your computer. Certain dress codes apply. These are always specified and usually include things like, "No shorts, no hats, no white shirts" (which don't look good when the camera scans the audience). Recently available tickets included: *Let's Make a Deal*, *Dr. Phil*, *Mike & Molly*, and *Pair of Kings*.

Oh, Oprah! Getting tickets for *Oprah* is much like winning the lottery—and if you do manage to get on, you may really feel that way, since who knows what she'll be giving away that day. Oprah's show tapes in Chicago from August to November and January to May, and while the show is on hiatus, no reservations are given out. Visit the Web site for information on how to call for a reservation when the show is taping: www.oprah.com. You'll also find information on how to send an e-mail request for a last-minute ticket.

The Daily Show with Jon Stewart. If you're going to be in New York City for any stretch of time, this is one of the hottest free tickets in town. Send an e-mail request to requesttickets@thedailyshow.com.

Late Show with David Letterman (and other CBS shows).

Forty-five years after the Beatles made their infamous appearance onstage at the Ed Sullivan Theater on Broadway at 53rd Street in New York City, funnyman David Letterman calls the historic space home. Representatives are available in the lobby of the theater to take ticket requests and let you know if any seats are available for that day's or week's tapings of the *Late Show with David Letterman.* Those tickets are awarded randomly, and requests are taken Monday through Thursday, 9:30 a.m. to 12:30 p.m., and Saturday and Sunday, 10 a.m. to 6 p.m. You can also request a standby ticket starting at 11 a.m. on the same day you wish to attend by calling 212-247-6497. To submit a request online, go to the CBS Web site, choose David Letterman from the Shows listing, and click on Tickets—which is how you get information on tickets to other CBS shows such as *The Price Is Right.* Visit the CBS Web site at www.cbs.com for complete instructions.

Theme Parks and Attractions at Bargain-Basement Prices

It might seem unlikely that theme parks would be the place to find seniors, but in fact we make up a big part of the visiting audience. We may not necessarily be there to ride the roller coasters, but many of us visit a lot of major attractions every year both to take our families along (roller coasters are for grandkids) and to be entertained ourselves.

And what a way to be entertained! America is filled with thrilling theme parks, some time-honored, such as Cypress Gardens, and others, such as the planned Wizarding World of Harry Potter, thrillingly new. Many, many attractions offer senior discounts, which are usually clearly posted when you buy tickets. If you're buying on the Web in advance of your visit, you may find even better prices or specials that won't be available at the front gates, so be sure to check before you go.

Early Bird Secret

Mickey's More Fun (and Affordable) in the Off-Season

Walt Disney World and Disneyland are among the few major parks in the country that don't offer any senior discount—and despite the top-notch fun, the Mouse can get pretty expensive. Minimize your costs by taking advantage of special package deals that include lodging and by visiting off-season, such as in October or January. Off-season trips can be far more pleasurable because the parks aren't as crowded, and the lines are much shorter. Be sure to book well in advance to get the best offers, because you'll pay a premium if you're rushing to book at the last minute. For that winter trip, you should start searching the Internet for a good package deal in October. Find some deals at www.mousesavers.com or www.allearsnet.com.

What a sweet deal! Hershey Park, the wonderful chocolate-themed playground in Hershey, Pennsylvania, has a two-tier senior discount that saves you a significant amount. The regular admission ticket for one day is $52.95, but seniors 55 and up can get in for $31.95. And if you're 70 or older, it costs $20.95. The two- and three-day passes are also enticing—$52.50 instead of $70.50 and $77 instead of $99, respectively. What's more, Hershey Park has a special "Sunset Admission" price structure: If you enter the park after 3 p.m. on days when the park closes at 6 p.m., or after 5 p.m. when it's closing at 11 p.m., regular admission is $26.95, discounted to $22.95 for those 55 and above, and all the way down to $15.95 for those over 70. For more information, visit www.hersheypark.com.

A "berry" nice farm. California's Knott's Berry Farm offers deep discounts to seniors 62 and older. A regular adult ticket for one day costs $53.99, but the senior price for one day is only $23.99—less than half the price. Knott's is affiliated with Soak City water parks, with locations in San Diego, Orange County, and Palm Springs, also have senior pricing: $19.99 for those 62 and older instead of the regular admission of $25.99. Annual passes to Knott's with unlimited admission are also favorable to seniors: $59.99 instead of $64.99 for the regular pass. Go to www.knotts.com and let your fingers find you savings!

Visit Shamu and Flipper's digs for less. There are three locations of Sea World—Orlando, San Diego, and San Antonio—and the senior discounts are not consistent across all locations. In San Diego, the park offers "Terrific Tuesdays" for guests 50 and above, with special activities just for seniors, including a complimentary breakfast and special symposiums, for $61 for one day (which is, in fact, the same as the regular admission for a day but with added activities). San Diego also offers those 50 and older a discount on a Silver Passport, good for a year of free Sea World admission, for $89 instead of $99. If you buy your ticket to the Orlando park online, you can get $10 off the standard $69.95 admission. Get details at www.seaworld.com.

A universe of savings for seniors. At Universal Studios in Orlando, there is not a senior discount, but there is special pricing for Florida residents who buy their tickets online. You get a two-day, two-park ticket for $75, a savings of $59.99 over the regular two-day, two-park ticket price. It also saves you time because you print your tickets out at home and go straight to the front gate. And Universal also includes a coupon book with $150 in savings. Go to www.universalorlando.com and watch your savings add up.

The Early Bird's Garden of Eden. There is not a specific senior discount for either Busch Gardens locations in Williamsburg, Virginia, or Tampa Bay, Florida, but AARP members can present their cards for discounts at the parks. A regular tickets at Williamsburg is $61.95 and Tampa is $74.95, but Williamsburg offers special pricing and promotions for Virginia residents as does the Tampa Bay location for Georgia and Florida residents. Visit www.buschgardens.com for more information.

Super Savings on Other Points of Interest

Not everything classifies as a theme park, and there may nary be a Van Gogh in sight or a Chopin étude within earshot, but plenty of other cultural attractions offer a lot of thrills and informative excitement and senior discounts at the same time.

Move over, Henry Kissinger. Talk about excitement! At its gleaming, imposing headquarters on the East River in New York City, the United Nations is a fascinating tour, especially if you've ever seen Alfred Hitchcock's

Ka-Ching!

10 Absolutely Free and Peaceful Things You Can Do to Amuse Yourself

Don't want to go out to some big event? Not looking for a show or a spectacle but merely to enjoy the quiet company of a friend or spend a few hours communing with yourself? These kinds of quiet amusements often lead to the most pleasurable hours that we spend in life, either alone or with others, so, hey, don't forget about the small stuff when you're looking for something to do.

1. Go for a walk. Whether it's a beautiful, sunny day or there's snow falling, dress appropriately for the weather and go outside. Your neighbors may have never before seen you strolling around the block rather than driving around it, but what's especially nice about walking around your own neighborhood is how quickly people get used to the fact and start waving or stopping to chat. They might never come ring your doorbell, but they may be glad to see you as you go by.

2. Read a book. It sounds simple, but some people may recall that in the days before TV, books were a major source of entertainment. And they can be again. Pull out a classic, or borrow the latest number-one best-selling novel from the library. Surf around on Google, which is working on scanning the libraries of the world, and you can read the full text of hundreds of thousands of books (and plenty more to come) all for free.

3. Listen to a book. Audio books can be a terrific way to reacquaint yourself with your favorite classics or to get into a brand-new novel. Sometimes the performance by the reader is truly outstanding and can bring out nuances in the text that you might not even have noticed while reading. If you listen to one while driving or doing housework, you can tell yourself you're using a bit more brain power. Audio books can be checked out at the library and many can be downloaded free on the Internet (try www.freeclassicaudiobooks.com).

4. Join a book club. One of the pleasures of a good book is talking about it with others afterward. Start a book club with like-minded friends or join a group of interesting strangers. If you have no idea where to start, ask at your local library—they can hook you up.

5. Watch a movie. If you've got cable TV, you probably have more movies than you'll ever want to see. But, ideally, you also have Turner Classic Movies (TCM), which is showing something good at this very moment. They have all the golden oldies in black and white; it's a rare film on this channel that's in color. From all-day tributes to Cary Grant and Greta Garbo to Westerns that run all day Saturday to the earliest silent movies on Sunday nights to documentaries about filmmakers from the Golden Age of cinema, they've got it all, and it's all commercial-free. Watching this channel is a film education.

6. Go to a movie. From half-price matinees to second-run cinemas for a buck or two a pop, going to the movies can be really cheap. Just don't be suckered into paying 10 times as much for popcorn and a soda as you paid to get in.

7. Watch TV. Have you given up regular TV because the advertising has become so pervasive on the network channels? Are you tired of watching the umpteenth reality show about nothing? If you have a computer with a high-speed connection, you can stream your favorite network shows directly off their Web sites with no commercial interruptions. And find free classic episodes from the Golden Age of TV on http://video.tvguide.com/episodes.

8. Listen to music. So many of us treat music like a background noise. But real music lovers sit down and give their favorite CDs as much attention as any reader gives a book. Put on your headphones, close your eyes, and really listen to your favorite recording.

9. Learn to speak a new language or play an instrument. Gave up French after high school? Found your son's old guitar in the upstairs closet? You can get language and music training tapes, videos, and DVDs at the library, or, perhaps even better, you can learn on various Web sites: www.youtube.com has video guitar lessons from various masters (as does www.ultimate-guitar.com), and www.livemocha.com is a site where you can study languages completely free and be tutored by native speakers.

10. Build a puzzle or play a game. People might laugh if you tell them you love puzzles, but put one out on a card table and most people set to without hesitation. Puzzles are very absorbing, as are crosswords, Sudoku, and anything else that challenges your brain and keeps it active. Play chess with an old friend, or better still, teach your grandkids to play backgammon, Scrabble, or dominoes, for a little bit of old-fashioned excitement.

classic film, *North by Northwest*, where Cary Grant suddenly finds himself in the UN holding a knife in the back of a newly deceased diplomat. Trust that your visit will be far less eventful, and pay the discounted rate of $11, as opposed to the regular admission price of $16.

Run for the roses—and the savings. Our experts considered putting this listing in the sports chapter, but in fact, Churchill Downs is one of Kentucky's greatest cultural spots of interest. On regular racing days at the home of the Kentucky Derby, general admission at the front gate is $3, but seniors are admitted for $1. Place your bet wisely and maybe you can move your seat to Millionaire's Row instead!

Honk if you love a deal! One part educational, one part recreational, and two parts fascinating fun, the Henry Ford Museum in Dearborn, Michigan, offers a discount to visitors 62 and older. Seniors save $1 off the regular $15 Museum and $22 Greenfield Village tickets. For more information, see www.thehenryford.org.

Safe and Savvy Travel

> *Amazing Seniors-Only Deals on Excursions and Lodgings.*

Getting the Best Deals on Airfares

In the early days of commercial air travel, people used to dress up, dine sumptuously in midair, and arrive rested and refreshed. Nowadays, with skyrocketing fuel costs and increased expenses at every turn, the skies just aren't quite as friendly as they used to be. In an attempt to lower their costs and save money, airlines are cutting corners right and left—no more pillows, no more food, less legroom, checked baggage fees—and, more to the point, senior airfare discounts have become a lot scarcer than they used to be.

Because so much travel is now booked by individuals on the Internet and airlines no longer need to wait to publish fares in a newspaper, for example, speed rules when it comes to the airlines' response to fuel prices and passenger demand. Fares can change, quite literally, from minute to minute on the Internet, and so can the availability and/or existence of senior discounts. Fear not! This can all be turned to your advantage. With a little flexibility, patience, and savvy, there are still plenty of ways that seniors can get those skies feeling a little friendlier again.

Start shopping well in advance of your trip. Good news if you're Internet savvy: It's hard to beat online prices when you're booking a flight. If you're planning a big trip, or even a holiday break to see the grandkids, check out fares a few months in advance to get an idea of the going rates. Many of the largest travel sites, such as www.orbitz.com, have features that will automatically "fare watch" for you and send e-mails when the fare for your route goes up or down significantly.

Get on the phone. Most airlines' Web sites do not publish senior fares, which usually kick in at age 65. Delta Airlines, for example, specifies that senior fares are not available through online bookings, so you'll have to get on the phone. Ask the reservations agent specifically about senior pricing, which, when available, is generally about 10 percent off the base fare. That amount, however, will often be higher than the airline's special offers. Don't hesitate to ask the agent if there is a lower fare than the senior discount, and if so, whether it can be booked for you over the phone.

Visit the zoo. Travelzoo, that is! Spectacular deals are to be found at a Web site called Travelzoo.com. Sign up for the Travelzoo Top 20 newsletter (www.top20.travelzoo.com) and receive a weekly email with the twenty best travel deals for that week. Two recent postings had a 6-night trip to Ireland including air and a rental car for $599, and a suite at the 5-diamond Venetian resort in Las Vegas with breakfast for $159.

Ka-Ching!

Seven Travel-Savvy Ways to Save Time, Money, and Your Back

Gone are the days of loading up two "rollerboys" to take on a weekend excursion for you and your sweetie, or of dressing up as though you were embarking on a transatlantic journey on the *Queen Mary*. Here are our experts' surefire ways to make air travel as smooth as possible for yourself and your wallet.

Invest in a lightweight, microfiber, rolling carry-on: You'll be less inclined to overpack and less likely to go over the airline's allowed weight limit.

Pack one pair of shoes. Make the ones you wear on-board slip-ons, like loafers. The Transportation Security Administration (TSA) and your fellow passengers will thank you when it comes time to remove them.

Decant your shampoo. No need to pack whole bottles into your checked luggage. Buy inexpensive 3-ounce plastic bottles at your drugstore, and decant at home.

Stay away from salty snacks. The TSA now demands that any snacks brought on board be purchased after security check-in. Stick with fruit and cheese, and beware salty chips: you'll get dehydrated faster once aboard and be forced to pay premium prices for bottled water.

Pack one lightweight sweater suitable for day or night. Unless you're visiting the Arctic, there is no reason to travel with your entire winter wardrobe. Choose carefully, and pack lightweight clothes that can be layered.

Stick with one color scheme. Our experts uniformly agree that packing clothes that are black or white is the wisest way to travel. Everything will always match, black can be very dressy (or not), white always looks crisp, and you can brighten up outfits with a simple, lightweight scarf.

Avoid checking luggage. Packed intelligently, a carry-on rolling bag can work for trips as short as a weekend or as long as a month. Another reason to go this route: airlines are all starting to charge for checked luggage.

Did You Know?

During the holiday season, you'll get the best, cheapest seats if you travel on, not before, a holiday. You can reap significant savings if you book your flight for Thanksgiving or Christmas Day. Most people want to be there in advance of a major holiday, but if you're planning to spend time with your family for several days or weeks after the event, why not travel the day of the holiday and reap the benefits? It will give you even more to celebrate.

Look before you leap at a super-sale price. The hot sales are generally the first thing you see on the home page of an airline or travel site, but surf around and compare prices first. Be sure to read the fine print on the super-sale price to make sure it doesn't have restrictions you find too onerous. It can be tempting to jump at the lowest fare you see, but you may discover it has taxes and fees that raise it higher than the next price up from the "sale," or even that it's only a one-way price, cleverly worded to make that fact hard to figure out until you're already typing in your credit card number!

Fly on Tuesday, Wednesday, and Saturday. Airfares tend to be lower midweek and on Saturdays, a fact that is driven largely by the needs of business travelers, who typically pay more on the other days while traveling for work because their companies are paying. Because airlines generally have a slightly lower demand for Tuesday, Wednesday, and Saturday, you can save anywhere from $10 to $100 off the price of the same domestic destination on Monday, Thursday, Friday, and Sunday.

Spending Less on Lodging

Hotels rooms are a commodity that can be even harder to pin down than airfares, because Internet rates can change, if possible, even faster. But a little research in this field can pay off big because hotel rooms are very much a business of supply and demand. A large booking for a convention might make the price on the remaining rooms in a hotel go sky-high, no matter that you saw them the day before at a much lower rate. Conversely, booking on the Wednesday before a slow weekend may see rates plummet through the floor, with the hotel delighted to get you in to fill all that empty space! If you're a senior, however, all those convention-goers can step aside while you claim your special rate, no matter what the demand, since it's hard to find a hotel, motel, bed-and-breakfast, or inn that *doesn't* have a senior discount of some sort. The standard rate, even at the most basic motel, is usually

10 percent off. With plenty of advance notice or a little bit of last-minute wrangling, you may be able to get 15 percent or even 20 percent off. The caveat: These rates are rarely posted, so be prepared to ask.

Check the Internet rates first... Go to your chosen hotel's Web site and check all advertised prices and special promotional deals. Then type in your specifics (dates, arrival times, king, queen, suite, etc.) and see what rates you're offered for the time you want to stay. Search "senior discount" if it's not obvious where to find that rate (and if there's a site-specific search box). Write down the rates but don't book anything on this research visit.

...and then call the hotel directly... If you dial the toll-free national reservation number for a major chain, you'll be duly quoted the rack rate, along with standardized promotional offers and senior discount. But if you want the best possible rate—and why wouldn't you?—call the actual hotel in the city where you want to stay. The hotel's on-site reservations clerk has the most updated information on supply and demand in that hotel and can potentially offer you a much better rate than you'll ever get from the operator at the national switchboard—and may even quote you a better senior discount.

...and *then* make the best deal. If the hotel's own reservations clerk can't beat the rates you researched on the Internet, ask why not—and then see if you can book at the better rate you already found. If it's a published deal, you should be able to book it via phone or Internet, even though you had to check both to find it!

Go against the grain. If you're heading to a unique bed-and-breakfast in a prime countryside location, its weekends are likely booked while its weekdays may be surprisingly quiet. If your goal is a national chain's city-center hotel in a major metropolitan area, business travelers likely stream through all week while the corridors echo on weekends. If you're traveling for leisure and can be flexible, get much lower rates by doing a "reverse commute" on visits, and try to make reservations to stay when everyone else is not.

Bring all your ammo to bear (politely!). Ask for the senior discount, then ask if there's a AAA discount or perhaps a separately negotiated AARP discount for card-carrying members. Don't forget to ask if there are any other discounts for military or government employees, if that applies to you, and then ask if you can double up on any of these discounts! Depending on demand for the dates you want, you may find a reservations operator who can do you a particularly sweet deal.

Staying Off-Season Yields Big Savings

One of our experts visited a major ski area in Colorado, midsummer, midweek. Instead of staying at a motor inn, she called the area's premium resort, which was virtually empty. The result? She was able to book a four-star room for the price of a basic room in a motor lodge. Remember: It always pays to use your noodle.

Plan well in advance. If you're going for the straight senior discount at a major hotel—as opposed to a special promo rate or last-minute deal—be sure to book well in advance. Some hotels impose restrictions such as a 21-day advance notice or a non-refundable credit card deposit.

Always confirm. Once you've asked for and received the senior discount, be sure to confirm again when you check in and *before* the bill is prepared when you check out. "There's many a slip," as they say, and you may find it more difficult to insist on your senior discount if you've already been presented with a final bill that doesn't include it.

Make your own senior discount. A hotel may set aside a limited number of rooms that can be booked at a senior discount price. If you find that you can't get the rate you want for the date you want, ask about the following weekend, or month, or another date that's convenient to you. If not, ask if the hotel can do something else for you instead: Upgrade to a bigger room or suite at the basic-room rate? Free parking? Restaurant or theater vouchers? One or two little perks can add up to more than the 10 percent you might have gotten as a discount.

Join the club. If you travel often, whether for business or pleasure, pick a hotel group and try to stick with it. Many of them have programs such as the Hyatt Gold Passport or Starwood Preferred Guest that, when you reserve a room under your member number, will allow you to earn points or rewards for stays, and that can result in free stays, additional discounts, restaurant vouchers, and other perks down the road. Some will also let you redeem points for airline miles or other bonuses and incentives.

Scoring Deep Senior Discounts at Chain Hotels

Even if a hotel is part of a major international chain, there's a good chance that the hotel is independently owned and operated like a franchise; as a result, the discount you're able to get may vary from place to place. A 10 percent discount—be it a senior discount, a AAA discount, or an AARP discount—is pretty easy to get at just about any hotel chain. The particular benefit to the AARP discount is that the discount starts at 50 for the long list

Ka-Ching!
Major Travel Savings,

COURTESY OF THE AARP

Over 50? Here's something to celebrate: Get an AARP card and you will never have to pay full price again at a hotel. The following AARP partner hotels will offer you a senior discount of at least 10 percent off the standard rate (and often a lot more off the rate at luxury properties—sometimes as much as 50 percent). Always be sure to check for specials that may give you an even better rate.

If you're an AARP member, you should also look into the AARP Passport Program—it's a one-stop shopping site for a wealth of travel options. When you're looking for a travel discount, it's likely that AARP has been there ahead of you and already negotiated a rate for its members—and always with the added benefit that you can start getting the discount at 50, instead of waiting for 60 or 62, as many outlets require. Booking through the Passport Program ensures that you automatically get any AARP-negotiated discount with any travel operator or cruise line or hotel without having to ask. Visit www.travelocity.com/AARP/home for more information.

Hotel	Phone
Baymont Inn & Suites	1-800-364-6072
Beaches Resorts	1-866-498-3218
Best Western	1-800-618-2277
Cambria Suites	1-877-424-6423
Clarion Hotels	1-800-424-6423
Comfort Inn	1-800-424-6423
Comfort Suites	1-800-424-6423
Days Inn	1-800-364-6072
Econo Lodge	1-800-424-6423
Four Points	1-877-778-2277
Hampton Inn & Suites	1-800-426-7866
Howard Johnson	1-800-364-6072
Knights Inn	1-800-364-6072
La Quinta Inns & Suites	1-866-573-6722
Luxury Collection	1-877-778-2277
MainStay Suites	1-800-424-6423
Quality Inn	1-800-424-6423
Ramada	1-800-364-6072
Rodeway Inn	1-800-424-6423
Sandals Resorts	1-866-498-3218
Sheraton	1-877-778-2277
Sleep Inn	1-800-424-6423
St. Regis Hotel	1-877-778-2277
Suburban Extended Stay Hotel	1-800-424-6423
Super 8 Motel	1-800-364-6072
Travelodge	1-800-364-6072
W Hotel	1-877-778-2277
Westin Hotels & Resorts	1-877-778-2277
Wingate by Wyndham	1-800-364-6072
Wyndham Hotels & Resorts	1-800-364-6072

of AARP partner hotels. At other hotels without an AARP agreement, the senior discount generally doesn't kick in until age 60, 62, or even 65. Getting an AARP discount at a hotel means you can get 10 to 15 years' worth of extra discounts!

Here's a rundown of the AARP savings that you can get at many of the major hotel and motel chains across the United States. Our information was correct at press time, but, as always, be sure to ask about the discount and confirm when you book.

You have a Choice. If you are an AARP member 60 or older, Choice Hotels offer a 10% off Senior Rate on advance reservations when you call their 800-424-6423 line. Sign up for their Choice Privileges membership, and save up to 20% on advance, prepaid bookings. Members earn points for free stays, travel on Amtrak, cruises, restaurant gift cards and gas cards and also qualify for Airline Rewards, frequent flyer mileage on domestic and international airlines. Get details and enroll at www.choicehotels.com or call 1-877-424-6423.

Get Marriott for less. If you're 62 or older, you can save 15 percent off a room at any of Marriott's more than 2,000 locations worldwide, including:

Fairfield Inn
Marriott Courtyard
Marriott Vacation Club International
Renaissance
Residence Inn
Springhill Suites
TownePlace Suites

You can book up to two rooms per visit at the special senior rate, but you must present valid proof of age when checking in. Visit www.marriott.com or call 1-888-236-2427.

Discounts at "The World's Hotel Company." The InterContinental Hotels Group offers travelers 62 and older a discount that varies somewhat depending on which of its family of hotels you're booking:

Candlewood Suites
Crowne Plaza Hotels and Resorts
Holiday Inn Express
Holiday Inn Hotels and Resorts
Hotel Indigo
InterContinental Hotels
Staybridge Suites

Be sure to ask for the discount, and join its Priority Rewards club to rack up points each time you stay at an IHG hotel. Visit www.ihg.com or call 1-877-424-2449.

Shine on at Starwood. The luxury properties owned by Starwood Hotels have an agreement with AARP that offers significant discounts. You can get 5 to 15 percent off with your AARP ID. Starwood also has a Preferred Guest Program that lets you accrue points to be exchanged for free stays later—and one of the benefits is that it requires far fewer points to do so than most luxury hotels, and there are no blackout days on using those freebies. The participating Starwood Hotels are:

Aloft Hotels
Ascend Collection
Element Hotels
Four Points by Sheraton
Le Méridien
Luxury Collection
Sheraton
St. Regis
W Hotels
Westin

Visit www.starwoodhotels.com for information. The individual hotel chains also have toll-free numbers.

Embassy Suites. With Embassy Suites, a part of the Hilton Hotels group, you can get a discount with your AARP card. While the Hilton group has discontinued its Senior HHonors program, it may be worthwhile noting that Embassy Suites offers a discount to government and military employees with ID. Visit www.embassysuites.com or call 1-800-EMBASSY.

High on the (Hyatt) hog. Because the Hyatt corporation has an arm that specializes in luxury assisted-living residences for seniors, you might expect that it would offer senior discounts at Hyatt Hotels and, in fact, it does. Seniors can save up to 50 percent off the rack rate, although the actual percentage may vary depending on where you're staying. Some hotels do not participate so call 1-888-591-1234 to find out specific details for the hotel location of interest to you.

Early Bird Secret

Booking the Unknown Can Save Big Bucks

Like to gamble—with your hotel reservation? Go to www.hotwire.com or www.priceline.com, and book your hotel in your destination of choice. You can choose from a range of two-, three-, and four-star hotels in major cities across the United States at bargain basement prices. The deal at these "opaque" sites, as they're called, is that hotels with rooms unsold post them anonymously. The details are usually pretty specific, such as the general neighborhood, the star rating, the price, even the check-in and check-out days for which that price is valid. The catch is that you won't be told *which* hotel you'll be staying in or its address until you've already paid. So if you find you don't like it, it's too late—no refunds, buddy. But if you're flexible and don't mind taking a risk, you can save a whole lot of money and, with a bit of luck, enjoy a stay in a luxury hotel.

Getting "rad" at the Radisson. Even though we've been telling you over and over to check and compare rates, Radisson makes it easy for you in the Specials and Packages page of its site. Visit its Web site, and if you click on one of the changing roster of "Hot Deals" hotels, you have the option of searching for the lowest available rate, the AAA rate, the government rate, and the senior citizen rate. Take a moment to view them all and see what you find. And then don't hesitate to call its reservations line and see if there's anything you may have missed! Go to www.radisson.com (Click on Specials and Packages, then Hot Deals) or call 1-888-395-7046.

Bargains at Bed-and-Breakfasts...and Beyond

Because the vast majority of bed-and-breakfast inns are relatively small and private affairs, there is no consistent senior discount, but there is almost always someone capable of making decisions on the other end of the phone line. You're more likely to get a senior discount at a larger inn. If you ask at a small B&B, such as one with three to four bedrooms where your hostess may also be the owner, cook, dishwasher, and bed maker, you may be imposing more of a burden on her than you would be by asking at a larger establishment. Then again, it never hurts to ask! Meanwhile, there are lots of other exciting alternatives to traditional lodgings.

Join the Evergreen Club. A special and almost ridiculously inexpensive lodging option just for seniors comes from membership in the Evergreen Club. This organization is specifically for those 50 and over and consists of more than 2,000 members who open their homes to serve as B&Bs each for just one guest or couple. With your annual membership—$60 for singles or $75 for a couple—you get a catalog twice each year with the full listings and photos. You choose where you want to go, call the host, and plan your visit. The club asks that you pay your host a small amount, less than $25 per night, toward expenses. It's a way not only to travel without excessive costs but also to make real friends and connections around the country. Visit www.evergreenclub.com or call 1-815-456-3111.

Swap your space! Even before the Internet, savvy travelers around the globe were putting their names on house swap lists. Since the Internet, the trickle has become a deluge. The lists pair people who want to visit each other's cities or countries, and you go stay at their home or apartment while they come stay at yours—all for free. You get the comforts of home, an exciting place to visit, and no hotel bill. You can sign up for fee-based online organizations that give you access to other members and photos of their homes. The benefit to this is that you can go with a swap site that's specific to seniors (so you can be sure that you won't have college students on spring break in your Florida apartment!). If you're new to the world of house swapping, visit these sites for more information:

www.seniorshomeexchange.com
www.homeforswap.com
www.homeforexchange.com
www.craigslist.org (Choose a city and click on Home Swap under the heading Housing.)
www.sabbaticalhomes.com (This is mainly a swap site for academic professionals, but others are welcome to search it as well.)

Welcome Traveller. Similar to the Evergreen Club, but free to join, Welcome Traveller is unusual in that members can distinguish themselves by their interests. If you're a crafter or quilter, a runner, or an educator, for example, you can stay with like-minded hosts who welcome you into their

Ka-Ching!

Vegas Is Not Just for Gambling!

Okay, we have to be clear: The whole point of Las Vegas is to separate you from your money as pleasurably as possible. Don't go expecting to come home richer in much of anything other than experience. This hot city is an amazing destination for folks of all ages. Here's how to keep your cents and sense about you:

In 2009, visitors to Sin City gambled an average of $559 each, and played for an average of 3.9 hours a day. More than half (59 percent) of those who gamble play slot machines.

In 2009, Las Vegas casinos took in $8.8 billion in gross gaming revenue.

In Nevada, there's one operating slot machine for every 13 residents.

Fifteen Las Vegas casinos have been imploded since 1993.

The Las Vegas Strip has 15,000 miles of lighted neon tubing.

In 2009, Wayne Newton — "that's Mr. Las Vegas to you"—celebrated 50 Years on the Strip with a show at the Tropicana Las Vegas.

GET A PACKAGE.

Las Vegas makes its *real* money in the casinos, so they're interested in getting you there, and finding you somewhere to sleep, in a very reasonably priced way. Check out the packages on offer from hotels, airlines, and tour operators. This is one case where the super-low rate might, in fact, be the super-best deal, without a lot of hidden fees and surcharges.

STAY ON THE STRIP.

Don't assume that you have to avoid the biggest, brassiest, brightest places on the Strip to save money. Those hotels are also the ones that are likeliest to have super-low rates to keep the rooms full and thus keep the restaurants and casinos buzzing. Unless you're staying at the super high-end places, such as the Bellagio (where suites can be north of $1,000 a night!), you can probably stay at a three-star hotel in a very nice room for as little as $60 to $70 a night.

DON'T BOOK A SHOW IN ADVANCE.

Show tickets can be had on the day of the show for as much as 50 percent off. Unless you're absolutely determined to see one specific show, wait until you get there and see what kind of special offers await you at your hotel, in the casino, or at the box office. At the very least, you're sure to get $5 to $10 off unsold seats at the last minute.

NEVER RENT A CAR.

Whether you're staying right on the Strip or on a quieter street, all your travel can be done on foot or in a taxi for less than the cost—and hassle—of renting and parking a car. Be aware that the complimentary airport shuttle that came with your hotel booking may take a lot longer and be a bit hotter and more crowded than a taxi, but if you're prepared to expect that, it's certainly your least expensive option for getting to and from the airport.

The Rio and Wynn casinos don't have floors that begin with "4." The number is bad luck in Chinese culture.

TAKE THE BUS.

Traveling up and down the Strip and getting to your hotel and other attractions, hop on the Citizens Area Transit bus that runs up and down the Strip. A one-way trip is $1 for seniors 60 and older with ID. If you're doing a lot of moving around, you'll do better with the 24-Hr. General Market Pass—good for unlimited trips. It's $2 for seniors, instead of the regular price of $5.

homes simply to be hospitable, and to go visit others in their turn. There is also a category for travelers, either couples or singles, who are 50-plus and for women traveling alone. (You can simply register as General Interest traveler, too, if you prefer.) Visit www.welcometraveller.org for more information.

Wrangling Rock-Bottom Prices on Car Rentals

Senior discounts can be a tightrope walk when it comes to car rentals. Too young and you won't get a discount—too old and you won't get a car! Many, many companies provide a good discount and make special accommodations for their senior renters, and the tips here will help you get the best rate you can, wherever you're renting.

Check the AARP rate. As always, AARP has already negotiated discount rates for its card-carrying members with partner companies. For cars, there's a wide range of benefits, not only in terms of discounts off the weekly rate, but also other perks such as free upgrades. Here are some recent offers from partner rental companies at the AARP travel site, and new offers arise all the time.

Alamo: Free upgrade, last-minute weekend rental for $18 per day.
Avis: Rent for five days, pay for four.
Budget: Take $25 off a weekly rental.
Enterprise: Free upgrade, 5 percent off a rental.
Hertz: Get $50 off weekly rental, free day on weekend rental.

When in Rome... If you're going to Europe, reserve your car through Auto Europe. This organization has more than 4,000 car rental locations around the world, and it also rents specialty cars and RVs. Its excellent prices will be quoted in dollars, and you confirm and pay on your credit card at the time of booking, which can be a real benefit if the dollar takes another dramatic slide before your trip (or could end up losing you some money if the dollar suddenly rallies). It also has 24-hour customer support on its toll-free U.S. number, and the Web site lists toll-free numbers from every country in Europe so you can always call for support. Write down the number for the country you're visiting before you go. The base rate at Auto Europe is likely to be less expensive than the senior discount at a larger corporation, so be sure to compare it before you make your decision. Recent special deals included a free Portable GPS with minimum 5 day car rental, free upgrade with early booking, and 15% off a Mercedes-Benz or other luxury car rental. Visit www.autoeurope.com or call 1-888-223-5555 for information.

You May Be Too Old to Rent a Car

If you're planning to rent a car outside the United States, be aware that there are some countries that impose an upper age limit on rentals. In Ireland, for example, you may pay an extra fee if you're over 70, and in Ireland and Israel, you can't rent a car at all if you're over 75. Similarly, in the United Kingdom and Northern Ireland, 69 is the age limit for rental at many agencies, although some will allow rentals for drivers over 70 by adding a hefty fee. Greece, Turkey, Poland, Malta, Romania, and the Czech Republic limit rentals for those over 70, and many Denmark agencies don't rent cars to drivers over 80. If you're close to or over the limits, check and then check again when booking your car—even if the American branch of a large agency tells you it's okay. Its European counterpart may disagree, so check with the source to be sure you're not left without wheels at the end of a long flight.

Go National. To find the best car rental deals National has to offer, visit their Web site and click on Car Rental Specials to Go, where the latest local, regional and international rates plus e-coupon discounts can be found. These include daily, weekly, weekend and one-way rental car specials as well as their Last Minute travel discounts, available for a limited time only so check weekly. Reservations online at www.nationalcar.com or call 877-222-9058.

Enterprise, Dollar, and Thrifty. Enterprise offers weekend rates starting at $9.99 per day for Friday through Monday rentals and special discounts and rental coupons when you sign up for Email Extras. And they pick you up. Dollar and Thrifty give you a 10 percent discount when you pay with the American Express card. Check the Web sites for other specials and offers at www.enterprise,com, www.dollar.com and www.thrifty.com.

Don't rent at the airport. It's more of a hassle, but if you use the rental company that's *not* actually in the airport terminal, you'll nearly always get a lower rate. Look for the fine print when you're booking. It will say something like, "shuttle available from Terminal A" or "at 1234 Route 10," and that generally means you're going to have to go an extra mile to get there, so to speak. Hertz will never be outside the terminal. Enterprise might.

Rent for a week. The weekly rental rate is always better than the daily rate, so always inquire about it, even if you only need the car for a few days. Depending on the renter, it might be less expensive to return the car after four days of a weekly rental than to pay for four individual days—especially if there's a weekly special at the moment.

Big Savings on International Travel

The weak dollar means that there's been enough of a drop-off in European travel from the States that the industry is more eager than ever to lure Americans to the Old Country. Nonetheless, deals need to be very good to offset the dramatically higher costs, now that the euro is worth so much more than the dollar. Some Americans decide just to ignore it—if that café au lait costs $8, that's just the cost of seeing the City of Lights!—but savvy travelers want to squeeze every ounce of good out of their dollar when it doesn't stretch as far as it used to.

Go out of season. Getting to Europe in winter costs a lot less than going there in the height of summer, when you can hardly walk down the streets of perennially popular cities such as Florence or Venice. Book your travel for times when hotels aren't packed and tourist attractions have some breathing room. Go to the Caribbean in June or July rather than January—the temperatures on the islands tend to stay consistently warm, so chances are you won't find it much hotter than the place you left!

Globetrot on the cheap with Elderhostel. Elderhostel is the granddaddy of senior travel organizations, helping seniors travel the globe since 1975. Elderhostel runs more than 8,000 programs across all 50 United States, in 90 countries—and on all seven continents. Sail a Swedish ice-breaker to Antarctica to see whales. Or ride a camel through the burning sands of Egypt. It's hard to conceive of a trip that Elderhostel doesn't already run in some form. Order a catalog or take a spin through its Web site for inspiration, whether you've always meant to visit Mount Rushmore, study art at a New York City museum, go bird-watching on the Georgia coast, or ride a horse through Shawnee National Forest. It's a not-for-profit organization so you can't beat the prices compared to the typical for-profit tour operator. The Web site features a long list of U.S. multi-day trips for under $600. It's also reassuring to go with the pros, who have been doing this so well for so long. Visit www.elderhostel.org or call 1-800-454-5768 for information.

Take a cruise. You're far more immune to the high costs of gas, lodging, and food for Americans on the ground in Europe if *you're not on the ground*! Take a cruise that hits major ports of call around Europe, so that your primary food and lodging expenses are already covered, on the ship, in dollars. This way, you're far more protected from currency fluctuations that could leave you gasping at the exchange rate of your hotel bill.

Early Bird Secret

Lock In the Price before You Go

As the euro, the British pound, and other currencies have strengthened against the dollar, tour operators have become keenly aware that the exchange rate can be a significant deterrent to travelers who might otherwise have been eager to hop a plane across the pond. Thus, a number have offers that lock in the dollar rate you pay for the accommodations and travel in Europe before you go. Of course it's a gamble: If the dollar keeps weakening, you can come out significantly more ahead than if you were paying in euros. But if the dollar suddenly rallies, you could end up paying significantly more. The key? Find out the exact rate at which the tour company proposes locking in your price, and then make a decision based on the best possible information available to you: Does the dollar seem to be trending up or down? How far away is your trip? (Six months away is riskier than two months away, for example.) And, not least, use the Internet to research the local price if you weren't buying a package through an agency. Too much padding on your hotel bill to make up the agency's profit might make it all a wash.

Take the train. If you are a European senior citizen, your train travel would be free. Many countries, such as Ireland, present citizens with a free rail-travel pass when they turn 65. The good news is that even Americans get to take advantage of Europe's generous senior travel discounts, when it comes to rail travel. If you're 60 and over, you can buy a Flexipass for 15 percent less than the standard cost of a first-class pass. First class can be quite luxurious on a British train, with large plushy seats and waiter service, but the second-class pass, for any age, is almost 30 percent cheaper than first class, so you may want to save that extra 15 percent and just go second class, which is perfectly comfortable. That's not necessarily so in France, where first class is *decidedly* nicer, and a first-class pass for seniors costs less than $300 for travel three days out of a one-month period. Additional days can be purchased at the discount price for about $40. For more information, contact www.britrail.com or www.raileurope.com.

Fly local. If you're headed to Europe and plan on flying between countries once you get there, don't book every leg of your trip through an airline based in the United States. Instead, go online and check out the local discount airlines, such as Ryan Air (www.ryanair.com), which flies all over Europe for a fraction of the price of other airlines, including specials where one leg of your

Mais Oui!

Traveling to Spain and don't even know how to ask for a *cerveza* in the local tongue? Many specialized language courses are geared specifically toward older adults, and a bunch even have a study-abroad component. Check out these and you'll be able to *hablar español* and *parle francais* before you know it!

AMERISPAN STUDY ABROAD

This company offers opportunities to learn over 15 languages in more than 45 countries. Visit www.amerispan.com or call 1-800-879-6640.

THE CHAUTAUQUA INSTITUTION

Based on Lake Chautauqua in New York, this institute offers a "55-Plus Residential Week" with programming that presents lectures, discussions or films. The Exploritas Programs offer learning adventures for 55+ adults with domestic and interational travel. For information on their Encore Chorale Camp at Chautauqua for singers, visit EncoreCreativity.org. More information is available on the Institute's Web site at www.ciweb.org or call the Office of Group Sales and Senior Programming at 716-357-6262.

CLOSE UP WASHINGTON

Ever want to know more about how this country *really* works? Attend a week of seminars in the nation's capital and get an insider's perspective on politics. Visit www.closeup.org or call 1-800-256-7387.

ELDERHOSTEL EXPLORITAS ROAD SCHOLAR

This new program from Elderhostel offers domestic and international active experiential learning programs with small groups (no more than 24) of active Explorers. Features include hands-on presentations in the field, behind-the-scenes experiences that would be difficult

Language?

or impossible to arrange on your own, ideally located accommodations and independent time to explore topics of interest to you. Recent offerings included Cultural Heritage and Traditions of Japan, Turkey's Living Treasures and Switzerland by Rail. Closer to home trips included Essence of Hawaii, Ride Colorado's Historic Railroads and Northwest Currents: Seattle to Victoria, BC to San Juan Island. Details at roadscholar.org or call 1-800-454-5768.

EXPERIENCIA CENTRO DE INTERCAMBIO BILINGUE Y CULTURAL AC

Learn to speak Spanish quickly and easily at this school in Cuernavaca, Mexico, that caters to students of all ages. Visit www.mexicoamigos.com or call 866-477-2647.

NATIONAL REGISTRATION CENTER FOR STUDY ABROAD

This organization offers programs specifically for mature adults, with programs in many countries. Find out more at www.nrcsa.com or call 414-278-0631.

SMITHSONIAN RESIDENT ASSOCIATE PROGRAM

Established as a division of the Smithsonian Institution, this continuing education program offers seminars and study tours. Membership is $35 and offers you 25 to 40 percent off on trips and programs. Get details at www.residentassociates.org or call 202-633-3030.

trip might cost, for example, two euro. Be aware that discount airlines tend to fly into lesser known airports, often outside the major city you're flying to, but hop on a bus (at the senior discount) or pick up your rental car (again, don't forget that discount) and enjoy the savings. But how could you possibly know what all the little low-cost carriers are in Europe? Simple. You'll look them up at flycheapo.com, a Web site that gives you all the names and where they fly (although you'll have to go to each airline's own Web site to book your flight). The name may be a little silly, but it's what we're trying to do!

8

Family and Friends

> *A Good-Times Guide to Living It Up with Your Loved Ones*

Good Grandparenting, the Early Bird Way

Congratulations! You now have the quality time to spend and wisdom to share with the little ones. But what kind of grandparent can you be? Well, there are as many kinds of grandparents as there are people. There is no one right way to be a good grandparent. Some grandparents are willing and able to spend ample time with their grandkids, while others may only see them on holidays. Grandchildren, especially when they're young, just want to know that you love them, and there are many, many ways to express that fruitfully, without spending boatloads of cash.

Give them your time. If you have already retired and live close to your grandkids, your time may be the most valuable gift you can give them and your own kids. Most children would rather have their kids in the care of a trusted family member than in the care of a babysitter or day-care center. So all three generations will benefit if you are able to spend time with your grandkids regularly.

Give them treats. Why not? It's a grandparent's prerogative, right? (Right!) If you are not able to see the grandkids as often as you'd like—if you are still working or if you live far away—you might plan a short vacation for them, with you as the destination. When you do see them, just make sure the time is as special as possible. Schedule outings that might be enjoyable or memorable. Just make sure that you are focusing on the little ones when you visit. It can be easy to get caught up in grown-up pursuits or just want to relax but undivided attention from Grandma or Grandpa is treat enough for most kids.

Give money. Okay, we admit, it's pretty transparent. But we're not talking about fives and tens here. If you have the means to do so, consider helping your kids save for their kids' educations. You can set up or contribute to a 529 college savings plan for your grandkids (see page 243). They will certainly appreciate it later.

Help out with child care. Not every parent can afford child care, and if you live close by, they may not have to. Moreover, lucky is the child who has grown up under the watchful eye of a doting grandparent. Just make sure that you take these precautions:

- Childproof your home. Store medications and cleaning products where kids can't reach them. Consider using gates to close off rooms in which there are fragile objects or dangerous stairs.
- Adjust to your limitations. You may not move as quickly as you used to, so if you are taking the children for walks around the neighborhood, the

11 Things

to Do with Your Grandchildren That Cost (Almost) Nothing

1 Plan a **picnic** at your local park or beach.

2 Take them to a **storytelling** session at your library.

3 Teach them how to **putt** into a plastic cup in your backyard.

4 Teach them how to make **pizza** (with store-bought dough, if you prefer), and let them add the toppings.

5 Have a picture drawing **contest** of each other.

6 Make **chalk drawings** in the driveway.

7 **Water plants** with a plastic mister bottle.

8 Go **fishing**.

9 Start a **scrapbook** of magazine clippings, mementos from their visit, or photos of their parents.

10 Visit the local **fire station** (make an appointment first).

11 Play **dress-up**.

museum, or the mall, make sure you can keep track of them, whether this means using a stroller, a walking harness, or training them well not to run off. Be sure that you are able to operate all car seats and gear properly.

- Refresh yourself on first aid. Do you remember how to do the Heimlich maneuver? Do you remember basic first aid? Freshen up before you take responsibility for small children.

- Prepare for their arrival. Make sure that your house is a welcoming place. You have nutritious food and snacks for the kids and a cozy, safe place for napping and relaxing.

Pass on your Early Bird wisdom! Children are most enthralled by the simplest pleasures. Learning to blow the fluff off of a dandelion with Grandma can easily become one of the most memorable moments of a person's childhood. Need some inspiration? Think back to your own grandparents and what they taught you. Usually the lessons related to everyday tasks, but they were precious nonetheless and stuck with you forever. This falls into "The Best Things in Life Are Free" category.

Show them where they came from. Kids absolutely love history, so take the little ones to visit the places of your past and, if possible, those of your parents and grandparents. Show them the school you went to, your childhood home, and so on. Tell them stories of your past—that your own grandfather rode to school on a horse because there were no cars back then; that your grandmother kept chickens in the backyard, and you were in charge of feeding them. Whatever the family stories are, no matter how small, they will help give your grandchildren a sense of their place in the world.

Get them cooking! Kids love to get their hands dirty, and there is no better place to do that than in a bowl of bread or biscuit dough. Or, make it a real learning experience and pass down simple family recipes. You can talk about where your family originated, who invented the recipes, and why they are so beloved. And then you eat the result!

Go for a stroll, for free. Just because the grandkids are small doesn't mean they shouldn't exercise. (Quite the contrary! Remember that exercise can help prevent obesity in children and help you preserve your own health at the same time.) Take them to the park. Walk them around the block. Play catch. Rainy outside? No problem. Get thee to a bowling alley and exercise your senior discount!

Read to them. Go to the library together and rediscover the books of your youth. Share the story of *Mike Mulligan and His Steam Shovel* by Virginia Lee Burton with little boys. Read the girls the *Betsy-Tacy* by Maud Hart Lovelace. Share books on the topics you find meaningful with them. And help them find books on topics that they are excited about. Help them sign up for library cards—it's a thrill to have one of your very own! Most libraries have excellent outreach programs for kids. Visit the American Library Association site at www.ala.org to find links to libraries in your area, news, and reading suggestions.

Top 10 Must-Read Books for Kids and Their Grandparents

Granted, we all have our favorites, but our experts found that these books had major staying power when read to young children. Feel free to add to this list or start your own!

1. **Ramona the Pest** by Beverly Cleary

2. **From the Mixed-Up Files of Mrs. Basil E. Frankweiler** by E. L. Konigsburg

3. **Charlotte's Web** by E. B. White

4. **Stuart Little** by E. B. White

5. **The Adventures of Huckleberry Finn** by Mark Twain

6. **Where the Wild Things Are** by Maurice Sendak

7. **Harold and the Purple Crayon** by Crockett Johnson

8. **The Lorax** by Dr. Seuss

9. **Blueberries for Sal** by Robert McCloskey

10. **Rabbit Hill** by Robert Lawson

What are *your* favorites?

Get growing and plant some herbs or vegetables. Doesn't matter whether you live in the country, in a house, or in an apartment, all you need is a sunny spot or window, some dirt, a few small pots, and a package of seeds. Let the little ones scoop out the dirt with a small child's shovel (or better yet, their hands), and use their pinkies to poke holes for the seeds. If you're planting seedlings, show them how to transplant and pack the new soil around the "baby" plant. When the goods start to grow, let them do the harvesting!

Introduce them to the classics! Most kids just love movies, and this is your chance to get them interested in the classics that have entertained generations. You may think that middle schoolers wouldn't enjoy a Mickey Rooney–Judy Garland movie, but guess again! Here are our experts' favorites:

Musicals: *Singing in the Rain; The Court Jester; The Sound of Music.*
Comedy: Anything featuring the Marx Brothers or the Three Stooges; *It's a Mad, Mad, Mad, Mad World; The Absent-Minded Professor.*
Animals: *Black Beauty; The Yearling; Old Yeller* (have hankies handy for the kids and you).
Classics, old and new, for little kids and grown-up kids: *Mary Poppins; Lady and the Tramp; Cars; Beauty and the Beast; The Little Mermaid; Hans Christian Andersen.*

Listen to good music. Rainy out and nothing to do? Spend the day listening to music! Dust off that old record collection and show them what vinyl really sounds like! Then listen to their favorite songs. Make sure you give and take and don't get hooked on that expensive iPod. By the end of the day—who knows—you might be able to rap!

Visit a museum. Museums are amazing places for children, and you'll probably both get age-related entry fee discounts. Similar to the mall on a rainy day, they have wide open spaces for kids to explore, and you to get some exercise, but museums don't offer as many temptations for you to spend money on frivolous things. You can just wander around, of course, but why not create a treasure hunt for your grandchild? Count the princesses, knights, flowers, dogs, or whatever appeals that you see in the artwork. Talk about the different types of pieces you see—is it a sculpture, a painting, a tapestry? Even if you find museums crushingly boring, remember: There are museums for every kind of person, including ones dedicated to fire trucks, soup tureens, nuts, sports cars, tennis, rock and roll, and even bricks! (No kidding! Visit the Haverstraw Brick Museum in Haverstraw, New York.)

Make something. Break out the paints, the toothpicks, the glue, the construction paper, the crayons. If you have access to a computer, you're in luck. The Internet has a world of advice for fun projects. Just search on Google for "family crafts," and you'll come up with abundant listings, including sites like these:

http://familycrafts.about.com/
http://crafts.kaboose.com/
http://www.amazingmoms.com

Otherwise, a box made of Popsicle sticks is always a big hit, especially when decorated with some seashells!

Get them outside! Where they used to play outside until dark, many children now play in front of televisions and computers. What to do? Grab a birding book, lace on their tiny hiking boots or sneakers, and go for a nature walk, right in your own neighborhood. Look for different kinds of birds and wildlife, and see if the kids can remember the names of trees. It costs nothing to be outside, and the rewards are enormous—for everybody.

Teach them about spirituality. You can share your faith with your grandchildren for no money at all. It's a gift that will give them comfort and a connection to you throughout their lives. Take the kids to services or special events with you. Read them stories that explain your religion. Tell them family stories about your parents' and grandparents' faiths.

Forget Computer Games!

Strange but true: Most kids just love old-fashioned board and card games. If you don't have any, see if any of your neighbors do, or scope out local tag sales where they can be had for very little money. Our experts found that there were favorites among children polled, including:

Candyland

Monopoly

Connect Four

Checkers

Rummy

Old Maid

Dominoes

Older kids even took to card games like pinochle, contact bridge, and backgammon!

You be the student. Ask the grandkids to teach you something from their worlds. Together you can play Wii, make a video for YouTube, learn the lyrics to a hit song, or another activity that you would be unlikely to explore without a child's help and that will make you the coolest grandparent on the block.

Preserving and Sharing Memories

So many of us have our most precious photos and mementos in shoe boxes in the closet. Thankfully, today's technology can rescue even the most dog-eared pictures and enable you to restore them for next to nothing and share them with everyone in your family. Go ahead and haul them out and preserve your past for future generations.

It doesn't matter what you've got: old black and white Polaroids, Kodak Instamatic snapshots, SX-70 "instant" color photos from the 1970s—old photos of people near and dear to your heart are worth their weight in gold and are worth preserving, protecting, and sharing. If you are a real photo fan, think about contacting your friends and family from around the country and have them send you their images, too. You be the designated copier, and once you're done, everyone will have complete sets of images.

Storing Treasured Photographs

How many bags of photos do you have lurking around your house? If you're like us, you have them in every room of the house. This is definitely not the best or most efficient way to store what really are prized possessions. How to keep them safe? Read on.

Find a dry closet. If you're relegated to storing your old photos in a closet, make sure that it's a dry closet. Keeping your photos in the damp basement will hasten curling and disintegration.

Use protective papers and mattes. Make sure protective papers or mattes are acid-free and lignan-free and are intended specifically for photo preservation. Paper should be made from cotton or purified wood pulp. Plastic sleeves should be polyester or polyethylene, not PVC.

Store in albums or boxes. Photos can last for generations if you store them correctly in photo-specific boxes or albums, taking care to make sure that edges don't dent and the photos don't curl.

Sign them to remember. Label photos with a soft pencil on the reverse side in the margin. Never use a pen and never write on the surface of the photo or the rear surface of the photo.

Frame and clean! If you choose to display your photos for all to see, do so in a UV-protective glass frame, which will reduce fading. Clean the glass covering framed photos sparingly and with a soft rag; refrain from spraying glass cleaners directly on the glass itself because it can seep under the edges and damage the photo.

Early Bird Secret

Old Photos Make Great Christmas Gifts!

It's true! If you come across a stash of old photos long forgotten but much beloved, take them to a local photo lab—which may offer you a senior citizen's discount— and have them reproduced. Pop them into inexpensive frames, and surprise friends and family with one of the most heart-warming, thoughtful gifts they'll ever receive. One of our experts framed five long-forgotten family images from the 1930s for her older aunts; the result was sheer delight!

Making Copies of Your Favorite Images

Photos, like many other things in life, alas, fade. The only surefire way to protect old photos to guarantee that they will last for generations is to have them copied, reproduced, or digitally duplicated. You'll be glad you did, and so will your loved ones!

Make color photocopies. The most inexpensive way to reproduce photographs, it's also not ideal because of quality issues. Choose this route for second-tier photos and make sure to copy them onto good-quality, acid-free paper.

Have the photos shot. Ever wonder how museums make posters of famous paintings? They "shoot" them using a film camera, and get a negative produced that then can be reprinted at any size, on any sort of paper. You can have the same thing done for high-value photographs, and the result will be a quality reproduction along with a negative (so you can make more reproductions in the future). Check with your local university's photography department, and you may be able to have a student provide services at a steep discount.

Go digital. This is, by far, the soundest way of making sure your valuable images are both able to be copied, retained in tip-top shape, filed for easy sorting, shareable, and printable at any size. To do this, have your photos scanned—anyone from a teenager with a scanner to a photo shop can do this for you. Then, have the scanned images saved to a CD or a photo Web site, like snapfish.com or flickr.com, and you'll be able to print copies whenever you want them. File away the CDs by event, name, or year.

Reaching Out and Touching Someone—with Technology

One of the best ways to stay in touch with friends and family who live far away is to make audio or video messages with just a recorder or a camcorder. Although they are still referred to as videos, nowadays nearly all moving pictures of your family will be shot with a digital camera, making the results instantaneous. Here are some ideas to make your home videos original and fun.

DIY StoryCorps: *Family Interviews Are Worth Their Weight in Gold (and Won't Cost a Penny)*

Back in 2003, a national project called StoryCorps: The Conversation of a Lifetime, captured the country's attention and spread like wildfire. A recording booth was set up in New York's Grand Central Station, and folks like you and me stepped inside with a loved one, and one interviewed the other. Eventually, the project went national and the results—now into the hundreds of thousands—are archived at the Library of Congress. Why not be your own StoryCorps? Give an interview to one of your kids or grandkids, tape record or videotape it, and it will become a treasured gift to your family.

Move over Bruce Springsteen! Why not make your own music videos? Record a few songs that your grandparents taught you. Sing the kids that special song you danced to at your wedding. Have someone tape you while you bounce a grandchild on your knee and sing "The Itsy Bitsy Spider." If you don't like to sing, read your favorite poem and explain what you like about it.

Give a house or garden tour. Do you have a fabulous green thumb, resulting in spectacular summertime blooms that are the envy of your

7 Ways to Make Digital Photography Pay Off

Thinking about hiring a photographer to document a special event? Think again! Become your family and friends' photographer of record, and save yourself—and them—a bundle by going digital.

The highest cost you'll incur will be the price of the camera ($89 and up). You can download the results onto your computer, e-mail them to friends and family, and let them print whatever they want (or not). No developing costs, no mailing fees, instant results, and you get to delete any shots where you accidentally stuck your thumb in front of the lens.

With a digital camera, you can:

1 Photograph your grandchild's first day at school and have the entire family see the results (wherever they live) almost instantly.

2 Get snap-happy at your family reunion cookout.

3 Photograph your child's wedding.

4 Offer to take neighborhood prom pictures.

5 Be a home food photographer and show off your hubby's culinary creations.

6 Offer to be chief photographer on your next vacation.

7 Photograph your local Little League games.

friends? Do you grow your neighborhood's greatest tomatoes? Grab that digital video camera, take a walk around your garden or house, and give a grand tour. If it's spectacular enough, your local garden club may even put you on its list as a formal tour stop next season!

Transfer tapes to digital video. Do you have a bunch of old Betamax or VHS or even Super 8 family movies in your closet that your family hasn't seen in years? Digitize them by sending them to www.preserve-your-memories.com. For a nominal fee, they will send you a DVD with your selected movies, and they'll last for years.

Telling the Story of Your Life

What better treasure could you leave your family than your memoirs? Think about it: Your whole family will see you, your parents, your siblings, and your grandparents in a way that they never otherwise could. Sound daunting? It isn't! There are many resources to help you along, including a number of excellent books and Web sites that can boost your creativity and jog your memory.

You're not being graded. Rule number one when writing for yourself is: There are no grades! No one will check your grammar or grade you on how quickly you complete your project. All you need is a pen or pencil and some paper, or a computer. Sit down and tell your story.

Remember life's little pleasures. The smallest everyday occurrences are often the most interesting, so don't feel that you have to focus on life's landmark events: the weddings, graduations, and so on. How about when you learned how to drive a car? Or taught junior how to ride a bike or read? How about that spectacular cake your grandmother taught you how to make, that you now bake every holiday? Get creative!

Is it a memoir or a novel? Feel free to write your tale in whatever format suits you. Here are some ideas of quirky ways to pen those stories:

- Lists. You could easily fill a book with various lists: my favorite songs; what I wanted to be when I grew up; my favorite friends; my most memorable moments in the kitchen; most memorable moments with my husband; favorite vacations; and so on.

- Cookbook. Many memoirs and novels interweave the author's recipes. Yours can, too. If food is important to you, pass down your recipes and memories all in one place.

- Book of answers. What are the questions you wish you had asked your own mother or grandmother? Ask them of yourself and offer the answers. The book will be in question-and-answer format.

- Mixed media. Like a scrapbook, add photos and ephemera to your memoir. You can let the objects you paste in determine what you want to say in writing.

Scrapbooking on a Shoestring

What was once a matter of simply pasting photos into an album has become a multimillion dollar industry. It's never been easier to find high-quality scrapbooking materials than now, but why buy them when you can make them for virtually nothing? Scrapbooking lets you creatively catalog your past. And a huge benefit of the hobby's popularity is that it has a social component. You can find scrapbooking groups or take scrapbooking classes, which makes it even more pleasurable and makes it easier to meet new friends if you've moved. It creates an easy, seamless way to talk about your interests and your past.

Early Bird Secret

How to Be a Scrappy, Money-Saving Scrapbooker

Scrapbooking is a great way to pass the time, *and* you end up with a treasure that will delight family and friends. Unfortunately, supplies can really add up, so follow these tips to save money on the bells and whistles.

Put the scrap in scrapbook! Ask your local wallpaper store if there are sample rolls being thrown away, and graciously offer to take them. Visit the last day of your local annual library sale to see if design books are being tossed. Save gorgeous wrapping paper every time you open a gift. You'll harvest beautiful patterns for your albums this way.

Make your own stickers. Look through old magazines for images that can become your own signature stickers. If you see something you like and want more than one, make color copies. You'll save a fortune.

Print out the letters. Instead of buying them, print out alphabetical letters from your computer. Just cut the shape out and glue where you want them.

Second that notion! Forget about buying expensive gewgaws and doodads for your scrapbook. Raid your sewing kit, or visit a notions store, where you can get things like thread, lace edging, and more—for less.

Writing

Here are some questions to help spark your memory as you pen your autobiography.

Family and Friends

Which of your family members do you most resemble?

Who resembles you?

What is your favorite family story or legend?

Do you know anything about the day of your birth?

What is your earliest memory?

What was your childhood room like?

What were your parents like?

What did you like best about the neighborhood where you grew up?

Who were your childhood friends?

What games did you play?

School Days

What do you remember of elementary, middle, and high school?

Did you have favorite teachers?

Who was your best friend in each grade?

Were there special moments that you remember: pranks pulled, outings enjoyed, subjects you loved to study?

Were there outfits you liked to wear to school?

What was your best subject?

Did you play sports or join clubs?

Your Story

School Days

Did you go to the prom?

What did you do during summer vacations?

When did you get your driver's license?

Who taught you to drive?

Did you attend college? Where did you go and what did you study?

What was the most valuable thing you learned there?

What music did you listen to?

Work

When did you first leave home?

What was your first apartment or house like? Did you have roommates?

How did you decorate your house?

What did you wear to your first interview?

What was your first real job like? Describe an average day.

What was your first boss like?

Do you remember your first paycheck?

What were your special indulgences back then?

Of all the jobs you've had, is there one you really loved?

Did you have to travel for business? What were your best trips?

continues

Writing Your Story

Love and Relationships

When did you have your first date?

Your first kiss?

What are your three favorite love songs?

How did you and your true love meet?

What was your wedding like? Your honeymoon?

What were your best vacations?

What happened on the days your children were born?

What were they like as toddlers? As schoolchildren?

What made you most proud?

Finding a group. It's far easier to find a scrapbooking group than you might think. Check with your senior center or even a local gallery owner to see if someone is holding classes. One of our experts in Montana turned up a senior-specific class at the Paris Gibson Square Museum of Art in Great Falls—and better still, the class was free!

Starting a group. Can't find one? Start your own! Let all of your friends and neighbors know that Tuesday afternoon at your place is scrapbook day, and invite everyone over. Ask your friends to bring a shoebox filled with their materials and a scrapbook. You supply the tape, the soda pop, and the snacks!

The sky's the limit! Don't throw away that movie stub! Hang onto that postcard! The best bits of ephemera to save for your scrapbooks are newspaper clippings; report cards; party and wedding invitations; stubs from concerts, movies, and sporting events; stubs from airline or train tickets; cards and letters; favorite menus; play programs; announcement cards; and receipts from trips and vacations abroad (or at home!).

Getting to the Root of Your Family Tree

Genealogy research is booming along with us Boomers, who are all grown up and are now interested in finding out about our forebears. Thankfully, the Internet has made this much easier. It has given us the means to connect to faraway lands and old records almost instantly, and computer software has made mapping your family tree a piece of cake. What are the benefits to tracing the past? Read on to learn more!

Connecting with your family. The easiest place to begin your research is with your family. And it's one of the most pleasurable, too. This process will cause you to strengthen your bonds with your family and give you an excuse to see people. It may also cause you to reconnect with lost family members as well as discover new family that you never knew you had.

You'll get to travel. You may need to travel if you get serious about your research. There is a lot you can do over the phone and on the Internet, but in some cases, nothing can take the place of a personal visit.

You'll get to play Sherlock Holmes. Tracing family history often necessitates a lot of sleuthing. You'll find yourself turning over rocks and dusting off old papers to learn as much as you can about your family. Here are a few places to start:

- Old files. Many old files are not electronic and never will be. If you want to get a look at the real estate deed on your mom's birthplace, you will probably have to visit the local town hall and dig it up yourself. Make sure if you are planning a visit in which you want to access records or do local library research that you have checked the hours of operation of the town hall, library, historical society, and any place else you'd like to go.

- Conduct interviews. If you found out that your grandfather's best friend is still alive, you might want to see him in person. You will be more likely to see photos and other mementos if you can pay a visit yourself.

- Sightseeing. If your mother came from, say, Ireland, and you've never been, why not book a vacation there? You may be able to do some genealogy research while you are there. At the very least, planning a visit will cause you to focus on the place. You might want to read some books about it in advance. And while you are there, you may find family. Even if you don't, you'll have the chance to speak to the locals about what life was like in your mother's day.

You Don't Have to Leave Home to Get Started

Starting research on your family history is as simple as turning on the computer. There are many hundreds of excellent Web sites designed to aid you in your search for your past. Most of the sites are good for doing preliminary research, like determining what your father's hometown will have to offer as you delve into his past. Will there be a town library? A town hall? You might find other useful information on the Internet, like what your father's hometown used to look like or what the various historic buildings looked like. Here are some great places to start.

http://www.archives.com

http://www.cyndislist.com

http://www.accessgenealogy.com

http://www.refdesk.com/factgene.html

http://www.ellisisland.org

You'll grow a beautiful tree. If you're planning on putting the results of your research into tree form, you may wind up with something stunning. Some family trees are gorgeous works of art. They can be drawn on large papers, the lettering done with calligraphy. They can be cross-stitched into muslin alongside designs that represent the people. They can be made into a kind of scrapbook, with photos and clippings interwoven with the family tree. Your family tree can be as beautiful or as simple as you like.

You'll uncover valuable information. Your research may lead to important information about your family. It may put your mind at ease about strange choices in the past that were made or inheritances that were given. In these days of rapidly advancing science it may solve family medical mysteries. A look at the life spans of your forebears might give you crucial information about your history that your kids and grandkids could benefit from.

The 7 Keys to Solving Your Geneological Puzzle

It's an exciting challenge to try to complete the puzzle of where you came from, but figuring out where to begin can be overwhelming. Break the process into its individual parts and it's easier. These are the first places to start your quest:

1. People. What could be easier than just asking a simple question and receiving an answer from someone who remembers? The more information you can glean from your relatives and neighbors, the more smoothly the rest of the process will be.

- First step: Sketch out a rough family tree, and then ask each member of your family to help fill in the blanks. Does anyone remember the street on which grandma lived? Which church did the family attend? What was the name of the guy Aunt Sally married? Did Jean and David have four children or five? Isn't one of their kids living in the next town? Does anyone have his number?

- Next: Ask family for any documents they might have that you can borrow. This could be birth certificates, diaries, newspaper clippings. Be organized as you collect precious materials. Note what you received, when and from whom, and the date on which you returned it. Some things that you receive may appear to have no value, but they might be a crucial link that will lead you someplace else.

- Finally: Take notes as you speak to your loved ones. Little things they say like, "Oh, if only Charlie Farrell were alive—he'd remember!" might be useful. Charlie Farrell might have passed on, but his daughter may remember and like to speak to you. Follow up on everyone and every place mentioned. Find out as much as you can about who Charlie Farrell was and where he lived and if he had any family. Every piece of information you receive should ideally lead you to another piece of information. Don't worry if you feel the path is crooked. It may eventually lead you to where you want to go.

2. Town halls. Town halls keep information on property sales, marriages, births, deaths, taxes—all the big stuff in life. Researching your family will be much easier if you have something to go on—ideally, gleaned from family members or family papers: the street address of your family's house, your mother's birth and death dates, her parents' names. Before you plunge into public records, have as much material at your fingertips as possible.

3. Libraries. The library in your father's hometown probably keeps back issues, likely on microfiche, of the local paper. Find out how far back the records go. You might be able to find mention of your father's Little League team or Christmas pageant. Enlist the librarian in your search. She will probably be delighted by a challenge and have other ideas for you. There may be records besides newspapers that she can point you toward, including material from the local schools, like yearbooks.

Early Bird Secret

Check and Check Again

Our genealogy experts offer two key tips that may prove invaluable in doing family research.

Check your facts. There is a lot of bunk that gets passed down through the years. Just because Aunt Margaret said it's true doesn't make it so. And realize that sometimes mistakes were made in old records. Dates are transcribed with errors or false assumptions made. Don't let a clerical error throw you off. Make sure you dig for the truth.

Tinker with spelling. We've all heard the stories of immigrants whose long names were changed for simplicity at Ellis Island. Some families Americanized their own names to avoid discrimination. The Medvedevs became the Medveds. The Stramskis became the Strams. If your name is Griffin and you pull up a listing for a Griffen, take a look. Could be that a town clerk made a simple error. Don't overlook misspellings and variations, or you might be passing over a pot of gold.

4. Churches and synagogues. Houses of worship usually keep excellent records of their members. If you know where your family worshipped, you should be able to find records of marriages, baptisms, bat mitzvahs, and so on, depending on your faith.

5. Cemeteries. Cemeteries also keep good records and should be able to give you basic information on your family. You can simply read the grave marker, if you know where it is, to receive the fundamentals. Or you can ask for a more detailed record of the burial plot, who is there, their names, and birth and death dates. Many a family secret is discovered this way. Did you know that Aunt Hilda was Elmore's second wife?

6. Historical societies. These institutions act as your town's memory bank. They are filled with eager and helpful volunteers who will be delighted to aid you in your search for information about your past. Use this invaluable resource that many towns offer. Not only do most historical societies keep written records, they often have excellent photos of the town. Think of how meaningful it would be to find a photo of the snowy street where your father used to sled when the trolley couldn't run.

7. Immigrant resources. If your family came to this country within the last few generations, you may be able to get help at a resource center devoted to your country of origin. You can check the Internet, the phone book, and community newspapers to find out what may be available in your area. One of the biggest immigrant resources in the country is the museum at Ellis Island. More than 12 million immigrants to America claim New York's Ellis Island as their gateway to a new life. Ellis Island was open from 1892 to 1954. If you think that a relative of yours might have entered the country this way, check the Web site at www.ellisisland.org. You may be able to see the manifest entry and even a photo of the ship they arrived on. Incredible stuff! Every genealogist can use the free forms that the site offers as well as the advice on tracing your family. It's definitely worth a visit.

Reconnecting with Pals from the Past

Make new friends but keep the old. One is silver and the other gold. Remember that little ditty? It's easy to fall out of touch with old friends. Our middle years are dominated by working and bringing up babies so it's easy to let relationships slide. Your retirement years mark the perfect time to reconnect with old friends. They are likely in the same boat. The kids are grown, the job is winding down. Suddenly there is time for socializing again. Try these methods of getting back in touch with old buddies.

Staying in touch. What is true of genealogy research is true of finding old friends: Asking people is the easiest and most pleasurable first step. Call up the people you are still in touch with and ask if they have been in touch with other friends. Get contact information from them. Even if the old friends they are talking to are not the same as the ones you are looking for, they might be useful because the friends-of-friends might be in contact with the people you want to reach. This friends-of-friends strategy works well of school networks and old neighborhood networks, where there may have been large and overlapping rings of friends.

Remember your alma mater! Get back in touch with any schools you attended—high school, college, or any professional programs. Most colleges have active Web sites with a section dedicated to alumni affairs and many high schools do, too. You can sign up for the site, and you'll have access to the alumni directory and the alumni notes. Reunions usually take place every five years, with the "0" reunions—10, 20, 30, and so on—being considered the big ones. If you decide to go to a reunion, make your plans clear to your classmates. Sign up early when the paperwork comes around because the more people that are signed up, the more likely others will be to follow.

Did You Know?

Your Alumni Gift Matters If you get involved in your old school's affairs, consider giving money. Even if it is a modest sum, your contribution will matter. If you are still working and you work for a large firm, your employer may have a matching gift program where it will give the same amount you do, essentially doubling your contribution. If it doesn't, no matter. Your participation is what counts. When your school goes to solicit money from foundations, it is more likely to get help when the rate of alumni participation is high. So your $25 or $50 or more will go a longer way than you realize. And remember the tax deduction!

Your Fuzzy, Furry, and Feathered Friends

They make your blood pressure and cholesterol drop. They can ease depression and loneliness and increase your security. They force you to get out and get some sunlight and exercise. Three cheers for our pets! Our four-legged family members are the very essence of easy companionship and unconditional love. Many retirees find that they spend more time with their pets than anyone else upon leaving the workplace. In fact, they dote on them. And why shouldn't they? The kids are grown up. The grandkids are away or in school. We should all have someone to spoil.

Your Dog Is Good for Your Health

The link between pets and good health is no joke. If you do not have a pet but are thinking of getting one, consider these benefits. Pets have been proven to:

- Lower cholesterol, triglycerides, blood pressure, and stress;
- Raise energy and exercise levels (especially dogs);
- Restore a sense of usefulness and meaning;
- Offer companionship;
- Connect you to the world (especially dogs—you meet people as you walk them);
- Offer security (especially dogs); and
- Occupy your time with care and play.

Finding the Right Pet for You

If you are in the market for a pet, first talk to pet owners about their experiences. Go to the local dog park if you are thinking about a dog, or if you think you'd like a cat, visit the pet store and chat up the lady buying kitty litter. You need to make sure that you will choose the pet that best suits your lifestyle and personality.

Man's best friend. Dogs are goofy, loving, and responsive to you. They can also be messy, energetic, and time consuming. If you think you'd like a dog, realize that you'll have to walk it three or four times a day (or hire someone to help you). And you'll need to make sure you are home enough to be a good companion. If you are interested in bringing a pooch into your life, ask yourself the following questions:

- Do I want a puppy or an adult dog?
- Will I buy one from a breeder or rescue one from a shelter?
- Have I puppy-proofed my home?
- How much do I know about the breed I'm interested in?

Make sure you have the answers to these questions firmly in place before you do something on impulse. Dogs are a long-term commitment. But they'll repay every ounce of love you give them with double that amount.

What's new, pussycat? Ever hear the expression "It's like herding cats?" There's a reason for it: While they may be elegant and charming, they are also more aloof and resistant to training. They may scratch things—you or the furniture. And they may not cuddle on your schedule, only theirs. But they don't need to go outside. They are small and portable. And they don't mind being home without you. So if you have a demanding schedule for work or play, they might be just the thing for you.

Birds of a feather. Birds are not as cuddly as dogs and cats, but they are certainly affectionate and love their people. They are easier to take care of than dogs because they don't go outside. Some birds live a very long time. Parrots can live 40 to 80 years. Even parakeets are long lived at an average of 18 years. If you plan to get a bird, realize you may be in for a lifelong commitment, and make arrangements for the animal in your will.

Fishing for compliments? Fish, like cats, are elegant. Their graceful turns around the aquarium are positively hypnotic and calming. They don't require too much maintenance, but you do need to clean the aquarium, and you might need help with that. Depending on the size of your aquarium, you may need to hire someone to come to your home to care for the fish when you take a vacation.

Other creatures to love. There are other choices out there—rabbits, gerbils, lizards, snakes, and more. Make sure you fully investigate the pros and cons of an animal before you commit to it. Many of these pets are small and quick and untrainable, which can make them challenging for people who are slowing down or have conditions like arthritis or back pain.

NO KIDDING?

Seniors Get Free Pets!

If you are longing for the companionship of an animal but just can't see spending a hefty fee to adopt one, ask the shelter to waive its fee. Some shelters and rescue groups get grants from corporations and the government to pair seniors with pets. Examples of programs include Purrfect Pals, which matches senior cats with senior folks (http://www.purrfectpals.org/About/SeniorsProgram.asp) and Purina Pets for Seniors (www.purinapetsforseniors.com), which offers pet adoption assistance.

How Much Is That Doggy in the Window?

If you plan to buy a gerbil or a fish or another offbeat animal, a store is fine. But for dogs and cats, it's the worst place you can go. Dogs that end up at pet stores are often born in "puppy mills," terrible farms where canine mothers do nothing but breed, and animals are not carefully bred, which can lead to congenital defects. Puppy mills also churn out animals that are not in tip-top health. You don't need the heartbreak of bringing a dog home and bonding with it, only to have it die a week or a month later. So if not to a store, where to go?

Going to a shelter. Think of the dogs and cats—and sometimes birds and other animals—you find at shelters as "certified preowned." These are animals that for one reason or another have lost their homes and need new ones. You'll find all kinds of breeds and ages and conditions at a shelter, and you should look to the shelter staff to help match you up with the right animal for you. Adoption fees are usually minimal so this is the humane and economical choice. The best place to start browsing is on Petfinder (www.petfinder.com). You'll get a sense of the range of animals looking for homes, and you'll be connected to shelters in your area. Other places to look include The Pooka (www.thepooka.com/rescue.html), the American Society for the Prevention of Cruelty to Animals (www.aspca.org), and humane societies (www.americanhumane.org and www.hsus.org).

Going to a breeder. If you know what breed of dog you'd like and you don't mind paying top dollar for it, then go to a reputable breeder. The American Kennel Club (www.akc.org) can recommend breeders in your area.

Going to breeder rescue organizations. Something of a cross between shelters and breeders, these are organizations that are dedicated to taking care of homeless dogs of a specific breed. So if you'd like, say, a corgi, you can research if there is a corgi rescue group in your area and see if there are any dogs that need homes.

Fetching Ways to Have Fun with Your Pets

Beyond offering love, companionship, and tons of health benefits, pets also offer a wonderful chance to meet new people and pursue new activities. Some of our favorites include the following.

Volunteer opportunities. The connection between good health and animals is so strong that many hospitals and nursing homes invite people and their pets to visit patients. The best way to pursue this is through a service organization like the Delta Society (www.deltasociety.org). The Delta Society registers you and your pet and teams you with people who will benefit from a visit. It operates in all 50 states and 11 countries. The training to be a "Pet Partner" is minimal, and many kinds of animals can participate, from dogs and cats to goats and pigs!

Dog shows. If you have a purebred dog that is "intact"—not spayed or neutered—you can show your animal at dog shows. Most people have seen the Westminster Kennel Club Dog Show, the New York City-based dog show that is broadcast every year on TV. What you may not realize is that there are many smaller, regional shows that happen throughout the year. Check with your breeder about getting started or contact the American Kennel Club (www.akc.org) for more information about showing and other dog events.

Agility training. Agility training is a rapidly rising sport that is getting dog lovers together in the fresh air with their pooches for some fun and exercise. If your dog loves you so much you think he'd jump through hoops for you, take him outside and see if that's true. There is a lot of information on the Web about this at sites like www.agilityability.com.

Did You Know?

Keeping a Pet Can Get Costly Pet care costs can add up, but ask a pet owner if she has any regrets and the answer is bound to be "Absolutely not!" This chart will give you a sense of how much your pet will cost you each year. These numbers do not including start-up costs like buying a crate or having a dog or cat neutered. Nor do they include grooming, which will be a big expense for some dogs, very little for others.

Dog: $400 to $750, depending on its size.

Cat: $500

Rabbit or guinea pig: $700

Parakeet: $100

Fish: $50

In the Dog House, Not the Poor House

It's absolutely true what they say: Take care of your pets, and they'll give you years of love and affection, not to mention pennies in your pocket instead of a veterinarian's. Here's how to keep the expenses down.

Spay or neuter. You will have fewer health problems down the road. Contact the ASPCA to see if you can get a discount on this. Find details at www.aspca.org.

Keep them trim and fit. Just because Ralphie wants a biscuit doesn't mean you have to give it to him. Obesity in pets has very similar effects as it does in humans. It can exacerbate or cause heart disease, joint pain, and diabetes, all of which are expensive to treat. So make sure to feed them high-quality food, and get them outside for some exercise (if you have a pooch).

Find a great pet clinic. Pet superstores like Petco often offer basic health care on site, so make sure to check with your local branch. You can also check with your animal shelter to see if it can recommend affordable services. Your local pet store might even offer a senior pet health day in which just seniors get free basic pet care.

Shop around for pet medications. If your vet's prices are too high, comparison shop to get the best deal. Ask the vet for a prescription, not the actual pills. You may be able to get the drugs for less elsewhere. Try www.kvsupply.com, www.discountpetmedicines.com, www.discountpet-drugs.com, and www.1800petmeds.com.

Ask your vet for a discount. Your vet may be happy to give you a senior discount, so make sure you ask. If he isn't able to, he may refer you to someone who will.

Coping with the Loss of a Beloved Companion

The death of a beloved pet can be just as devastating as the loss of a person. Pets are members of the family, and you may never be closer to yours than when you are a child or a retiree, spending lots of time playing, snuggling, and bonding. Follow these tips to ease the pain.

Allow yourself to grieve. You have the right to feel sad. Your pet was a beloved companion, friend, and family member. Don't hesitate for a moment to let yourself grieve this loss as completely as you would any other.

Get support. If you are feeling despair, consider getting help from a professional. Your church, your hospital, even your vet may be able to point you to inexpensive, often free resources that will help you get through this difficult time.

Honor the memory of your pet. Will you buy a burial plot for the cat or will you bury him in the backyard? Do you want the doctor to handle his remains and just have your memory? Are you considering cremation, which is surprisingly inexpensive? Your vet should be able to help you make a decision.

Hold off on getting a new pet. It can be tempting to try to replace your beloved friend right away. Dealing with a new animal, especially a kitten or a puppy, seems like it would offer delightful and consuming distraction. Give yourself time to grieve for your late pet and only start thinking about a new one when you believe you will not be looking at the animal as a replacement. Experts suggest that you not give your new pet the same name as the old one and that you try to create a visual distinction between the two, as well to remind yourself that this new pet is its own beast.

Early Bird Secret

You Can Provide for Fido after You're Gone

The Humane Society of the United States offers a free kit to help you plan for your pet's care after you are gone. "Providing for Your Pet's Future Without You" contains a six-page fact sheet, wallet alert cards, emergency decals for windows and doors, and caregiver information forms. Send an e-mail to petsinwills@ hsus.org and check the Humane Society's Web site (www.hsus.org) for other information and goodies.

Taking Care of Business

*Figure Out Your Finances
Once and for All*

Collecting the Social Security You're Entitled To

President Franklin Roosevelt initiated Social Security in 1935 as a way of supporting older Americans. The program was to ensure that those who were no longer in the workforce, or who couldn't find a job, would still have a safety net. In an ideal world, retirees use a combination of private savings including IRAs and 401(k)s, pensions, and a part-time (or full-time!) job to provide income in their golden years. Most of us don't do that. It is estimated that 20 percent of married couples and 41 percent of unmarried people rely on Social Security benefits for 90 percent or more of their retirement income.

Know when you're eligible and when to start collecting.

We all think of retirement as starting at 65. But does it? Not anymore. The government has adjusted the age at which you are eligible for full retirement benefits. How to figure out what is coming to you and exactly when? If you were born in or before 1943, you are eligible for full retirement benefits now. If you were born between 1943 and 1954, you are eligible at the age of 66. If you were born between 1955 and 1959 you will be eligible sometime in your 66th year. If you were born in 1960 or later, you will be eligible at 67. When you actually begin to collect benefits is one of the most important decisions of your retirement, and there is no right answer. To determine what timing is right for you consider these points:

- Your life expectancy. Are you in terrific health? Does longevity run in your family? The average American lifespan today is 77.6 years old. If you (and your doctor) believe that you have a good chance of living a long time based on family history and your great health now, you may want to delay receiving benefits for as long as possible to ensure that you will receive higher payouts when you are older and need them more.

- Your other liquid assets and income. Do you have a pension? A 401(k)? If you have other assets from which you can draw, again, it might be best to delay receiving Social Security and treat it like the safety net it was intended to be.

Did You Know?

You Can Be a Really Early Bird! You may be able to start receiving retirement benefits as early as age 62. Your benefits will be reduced because you will be starting earlier than most Early Birds. Your draw will probably be about 75 percent of what you would receive if you waited for full retirement age.

- Your work life. Do you still work? Do you enjoy it? If you find your work—and your paycheck—enjoyable, then why not keep at it? Work keeps you connected to your friends and your community and may give you a sense of purpose. As long as you are still working, there is likely little point to collecting a Social Security payment. You probably want to sit on that Early Bird nest egg a little bit longer.

- Your spouse. If your spouse did not work outside the home, then he or she is entitled to 50 percent of your benefit while you are alive and receiving benefits. This makes the case for receiving your benefits early.

- The economy. Take the recent economic downturn into account when making your decision. You might be better off taking Social Security sooner rather than later if you have other investment assets like a 401(k). The longer you delay tapping into your investment portfolio, the more likelihood the stock market will continue to rally, and you may recover some of your losses.

Always check your statements. Each year, you receive an estimate of your Social Security benefits. Open it, read it closely, and make sure it's correct! If something is wrong, contact the Social Security Administration immediately to have it corrected.

Know that you may be entitled to more than your own benefit. If you and your spouse worked, you are entitled to the greater of 50 percent of your spouse's benefit or your own benefit.

Early Bird Secret

Waiting for Payments Pays Off

Are you able to wait until you turn 70 to receive your Social Security benefits? If so, you will receive an additional monthly benefit, which may be as much as 8 percent for each year beyond your full retirement age that you waited to receive your checks.

Take advantage of direct deposit. Did you know that you can have your check deposited directly into your bank account, be it checking or savings? This way you avoid having checks get lost or delayed in the mail.

Don't forget the ex! If you were married for at least 10 years, you can collect benefits based on your ex-spouse's earnings. Your benefits will stop if you remarry.

See your accountant. If your income is more than roughly $34,000 as a single filer or $44,000 as a married joint filer, you may have to pay tax on 85 percent of your benefit. Each year, these income limits are adjusted for inflation; your accountant can help clarify your Social Security tax liability.

Collect your benefits overseas. You are eligible to receive your benefits even if you move abroad. (There are a few exceptions—Cuba and North Korea among them—but these are unlikely to be your retirement destinations.)

Free Retirement Help Is a Click Away

If you are computer savvy, you'll be pleased to know that there are many free calculators available to help you run the numbers of your retirement. Here are some of the best: http://www.ssa.gov/retire2/index.htm and http://money.cnn.com/retirement and http://bulletin.aarp.org/yourmoney.

Learning the ABCs of Medicare

Medicare is the federal health insurance program for American senior citizens, and generally speaking, it works very well. If you are turning 65 soon, you need to start planning your transition from private insurance to Medicare so that you don't miss any deadlines and can get the preventive care that you need. If you are 65 and already collecting Social Security benefits, you do not need to sign up for Medicare; you will receive your Medicare card automatically in the mail. If you are *not* planning to receive Social Security benefits when you turn 65, then you need to sign up for Medicare three months before your 65th birthday (just call 1-800-772-1213 or visit www.medicare.gov online). You should sign up for Medicare parts A, B, and D.

Familiarizing yourself with the labyrinthine maze that can be the Medicare system is the key to getting all of the benefits you deserve. Recently passed legislation means that there may be some adjustments to the coverage, but we asked our Medicare experts to walk us through the basics to help you find your footing. Armed with this knowledge, you'll be the savviest Early Bird around:

Medicare Part A. This is the part of Medicare coverage that relates to hospital treatment. It covers:

- Inpatient hospital services (up to 90 days per "spell of illness")
- Skilled nursing facility services (up to 100 days per spell of illness after a hospital stay of three or more days)

Ka-Ching!

The Fine Print Is Money in Your Pocket

Medicare scams abound and often involve some very familiar names in the insurance industry. Several of our experts uncovered shady practices, including more than a few companies that promised beneficiaries they'd receive better coverage with private insurance than they would on Medicare Part C. When it came time to cover the beneficiary for procedures as ordinary as a broken hip or cataract surgery, their claims were denied. Keep your money in your pocket, and always read the fine print. If your plan sounds too good to be true, it definitely is. Here are some basic ways to avoid scams:

Never open the door

to insurance salespeople. If they call you on the phone, hang up.

Never, ever give your personal information

to anyone claiming to be a representative of Medicare or a private insurance carrier. This goes for your birth date, your Social Security number, your Medicare number, or your address.

Read the fine print.

If you decide to buy additional coverage, make absolutely sure it is from a company that really works with Medicare. This information is easy to find on the Medicare Web site: www.Medicare.gov.

- Home health care (up to 100 visits per spell of illness after a hospital stay of three or more days)
- Hospice care
- Inpatient psychiatric care (up to 190 days during your lifetime)
- Blood (you pay for the first three pints per year)

Medicare Part B. This part of Medicare coverage relates to ordinary, daily medical care. It covers:

- Physicians' services, including office visits and a one-time physical examination for new beneficiaries.
- Medical equipment (for example, wheelchairs and oxygen) and supplies
- Outpatient hospital services
- Outpatient mental health services
- Lab and diagnostic tests
- Outpatient occupational, physical, and speech therapy
- Home health care not preceded by a hospital stay and visits over the 100-day Part A limit
- Some preventive services (for example, mammograms and diabetes screening)

Medicare Part C. Medicare Part C is also known as the Medicare Advantage plan. It basically bundles Parts A and B and has services provided by a private insurer, which include HMOs.

Medicare Part D. This part of the plan is the prescription drug program.

Sure Ways to Lower Your Insurance Premiums

The best way to be a savvy Early Bird and to save save *save* everywhere from health insurance premiums to prescription costs is…you guessed it: don't get sick! The truth is, maintaining good health goes a long way to preserving your happiness as well as your nest egg. Make sure that you are doing what your doctors agree will keep you younger longer. Bad habits may be challenging to break, but they may also result in better health not only for you, but for your bank account, too! Replace them with great habits, and you'll have more than savings to bank on.

Stop smoking! It's smelly, smoky (of course), and your grandkids probably yell at you when they see you light up. But beyond that, smoking aggravates high blood pressure and diabetes, is a documented cause of heart disease, and can lead to emphysema and lung cancer. If those weren't reasons enough to quit, consider the cost: the price of cigarettes is increasing all the time, from $5-7 per pack—and much more in some places. For someone who smokes a pack a day, that's $1,800 a year. Experts estimate that tobacco use costs the United States about $167 billion a year in direct medical costs and lost productivity. Furthermore, if you are in the market for life insurance or disability insurance, your rates will skyrocket if you are a smoker; in fact, most smokers pay double the amount that nonsmokers pay for their health insurance. The good news? Most insurers consider you a nonsmoker if you haven't had a cigarette in a year. Quit today!

Protect your bones. If you're a woman who has gone through menopause, you have likely started to lose bone mass already, and you will continue to unless you do something to stop it. The first thing to do is to have your bone mass measured by your doctor so you know where you stand. And then get to work!

Work on your balance. Exercises that increase your ability to balance well, like yoga and tai chi, are widely praised. The better your balance, the more you protect yourself against falls. The fringe benefit? Both activities are low-impact, increase flexibility, and are weight-bearing.

Enjoy red wine on occasion. If you do drink wine, make it red, which contains a key component called resveratrol. Studies have shown that a glass with dinner may benefit your heart, blood sugar, and overall health.

Stop and smell the roses. Retirement doesn't guarantee stress-free living: studies have shown that many American retirees are still as overextended and overstressed as they were when they were in the work force. This stress can put unnecessary strain on your general health, specifically, your heart, your immune system, and your metabolism. What to do? Take a slow, mindful walk; look at the trees; go to a museum. In other words, get quiet. Your body and mind will thank you.

Be a pear, not an apple! Doctors believe that your waist-to-hip ratio is a very strong measure of cardiac health. In other words, aim to be a pear, not an apple shape, and try to keep belly weight to a minimum. Check in with your physician, and once they okay it, do some light cardio exercise at least three times a week, and get involved in your community. People who have close ties to their communities and who are active and social with family and friends have been shown to live longer than loners. Life is a party—join in!

6 Pill-Free Ways to Get Your Calcium

You may have to take a supplement prescribed by your doctor, but if you don't (and even if you do), increase your calcium intake by:

1. **Eating leafy greens.** A serving of collard greens contains the same amount of calcium as an 8-ounce glass of milk.

2. **Opening up a can of sardines.** Three ounces of sardines is a delicious way to get more calcium and omega-3 fatty acids into your diet. Mash up a can with half a cup of low-fat cottage cheese, and enjoy on whole grain toast, for added benefit.

3. **Drinking your orange juice.** An 8-ounce glass of orange juice contains 25 percent of the recommended daily calcium intake for folks 51 years and older.

4. **Going a little nutty...**For nuts, that is! Roasted, unsalted almonds are a boon to calcium, so grab a small handful (some experts recommend 12 almonds) once a day.

5. **Saying cheese!** Eaten in moderation (like everything), cheese includes among its health benefits hefty doses of calcium. Look for lower fat varieties, like goat cheese and mozzarella, to enjoy as a snack.

6. **Doing light weight-bearing exercises.** Studies have repeatedly shown that lifting light dumbbells regularly can actually build bone mass—not just stave off bone loss.

Follow doctor's orders. Although pills are more expensive than ever, they are cheaper (and less traumatic) than a major health crisis, so take your medications as directed; you are spending money to save money. Other ways to save? Get regular checkups. Women should have regular mammograms and pelvic and breast exams. Men should have regular prostate exams. Everyone should have a colonoscopy at age 50 (or earlier if suggested by your physician) and once every 10 years afterward if their first screening is normal. See the dentist every six months, and always remember to floss your teeth (a strong connection between gum health and heart health has been established—that little waxy string may save your life!).

Maximizing Retirement and Rainy-Day Savings

Just as your body needs quality care and attention (and hopefully, you already take our expert advice to give it everything it needs to stay healthy), so too does your financial life. Savvy Early Birds know the ins and outs of the system—how to reap the benefits of long-term savings, how to make the most of short-term investments, and how to come out smelling like a rose. Some of the most familiar investment tools for Early Birds are pensions, IRAs, 401(k) plans, and annuities.

Pensions and Annuities: What's the Difference?

Pensions: the Packards of retirement plans. These are big, comfortable financial vehicles that have all but disappeared. For most of our parents and grandparents, pensions were a major part of their retirements. Back then, you worked at the same company for 40 years, got your gold watch and retirement party, and then started collecting your pension, which supported you for the rest of your life. Nowadays, most companies offer contribution plans, like 401(k)s, rather than traditional pension plans.

If you do expect to receive a pension from a reliable employer, you will receive compensation in the form of a percentage of your former salary. Here are the few things you may need to think about:

- Are you going to take the maximum contribution, spread it out over your lifetime, and gallop off into the sunset?

- Do you prefer to take a reduced contribution, but one that will continue to compensate your spouse after you die? If your spouse is much younger than you are, this might be the right bet.

- Are you entitled to Social Security? Some people who receive a pension, like some state employees for example, may not be eligible for Social Security. Make sure you know what you are entitled to as you plan your retirement so you don't come up short.

Understanding annuities. Annuities act as a safety net to guarantee you an income for the rest of your life. They are a conservative tool meant to give you peace of mind and guarantees. You hand an insurance company a wad of cash, and they guarantee you an income on that money, the amount of which depends upon how much you contributed. Annuities can get complicated so if you like to keep things simple, look for fixed annuities from a reliable seller.

Early Bird Secrets

How to Shop for Annuities

You wouldn't buy a carton of milk without looking at the price and making sure you were getting the best deal, right? Same goes for buying an annuity. The most important thing to do when considering one is to comparison shop. There are a huge range of annuities out there, and some of the exact same investment tools can have very different prices. Here's how to do it.

Make a note of all of the features you are looking for, and then compare the plans of several companies.

Make sure you are comparing the exact same terms so that you get an apples-to-apples comparison that is accurate.

Insist upon knowing *all* of the fees or commissions of each plan up front. Companies don't like to disclose these so you may have to push. You don't want hidden or unnecessary costs to pick away at your valuable nest egg.

Is an annuity right for you? If you receive a pension that you can live on from a reliable source—an example would be a teacher who is receiving a pension from the state—then you may not need an annuity, which is afixed income similar to a pension. On the other hand, if you are living on a small Social Security check and a small nest egg that you feel you are dipping into too much or that has eroded in a soft economy, an annuity may be right for you.

How much risk can you stand? Do you want to turn over most of your savings to an annuity? Or do you just want your annuity to be a part of you retirement strategy? The answer will depend on how risk-averse you are: If you want to play it safe and you are sure that the annuity will pay you enough to survive for the rest of your life, then it may be for you. If you don't mind some risk, then maybe only a part of your savings should be converted to an annuity. Another issue to consider: Do you want to leave any money to your children and grandchildren? In most cases, once you buy an annuity, your money is gone, no matter if you die a year later or if you live another 30 years. No money from that annuity will be left for your heirs.

Do you need an annuity? Investment advisers suggest an easy back-of-the-napkin calculation to help you decide if you need an annuity and, if so, how much money you need that annuity to yield. They call it the Income

Gap Calculation. First, tally all your sources of income: pension, Social Security, investments, and anything else. Second, tally all of your expenses: your rent or mortgage, food, travel, entertainment, and most importantly, health care. Third, subtract your expense money from your income money. If there is a negative balance, then that is your income gap—the amount of money that you need to maintain your lifestyle. An annuity might be the perfect thing to fill it in.

When is the right time to buy an annuity? The answer depends on whether you need a long-term income stream or a short-term one. Should you wait until later in your retirement when your savings may have shrunk and your lifestyle may have become quieter (and less expensive) to buy an annuity? Or do you want to use an annuity as a way of delaying dipping into your other investments or starting to collect Social Security? There are annuities for both of these scenarios.

Did You Know?

Understanding the Drawdown Rule The 4 percent drawdown rule is something that may give you peace of mind. It used to be thought that a retiree could comfortably pull 6 percent or so from savings annually and not be at risk for outliving his or her money. But studies have changed the prevailing wisdom. Nowadays, conservative advisers believe that if you stick to 4 percent a year, you will always have enough money to live on (but voices on the horizon are suggesting that other factors, such as the psychology of the individual, must be taken into account). To start, look at your savings, calculate 4 percent, and add it to your fixed income—things like pensions and Social Security. Try again with a number like 6 or 8 percent. Are these number something you can live on—even if you live to 100? Great! If not, it's time to see an investment adviser to make a new plan.

Building Up Your Retirement-Cash Coffers

Know the nuts and bolts of 401(k)s. For most investors, this program will make up the bulk of their retirement savings. Whereas once the company you worked for might have offered you a pension, now most companies offer a savings plan in the form of the 401(k). These plans enable you to put away a portion of your own earnings before taxes are taken out, which reduces the amount of your take-home pay, which in turn reduces your taxes. The earnings are taxed when you start making withdrawals in retirement, but, presumably, you'll be in a lower tax bracket when you retire so you'll save again.

The secret to making the most of your retirement savings. Simply contribute the maximum possible to your plan. If you are not able to contribute the maximum amount, make sure you at least contribute enough to get the full benefits of any matching contributions your company offers. If you are over 50, take advantage of the "catch-up" provision.

Invest sensibly. Invest your money for the long term, and understand the offerings of your plan. Diversify your portfolio, choosing a selection of stocks and bonds. Traditionally, if the stock market drops, the bond market increases. Make sure you keep an eye on how your funds are doing, and reshuffle accordingly, as the market changes.

Leave your money alone. You are able to withdraw from your 401(k) for hardship or to buy your first home. Resist the urge to do so! You must repay the money you borrow, which means that you must stay at the company until you've done so. And you are not maximizing the effects of tax-advantaged compound interest if your money is not in the account.

Play catch-up if you're a late starter. Not all of us start saving when we should; thankfully it is possible to play catch-up by making, literally, "catch-up" contributions. Start putting the maximum into your retirement plan (if you aren't already), and if you are over 50, take advantage of the catch-up contributions, which enable you to add much more. You can add an additional $1,000 a year to an IRA and an additional $5,000 a year to a 401(k).

Postpone your retirement if you can. Every year you don't retire is another year that you are saving for retirement and not breaking open your nest egg. You can look into cutting back your hours, going freelance, becoming a consultant in your field, or finding a new part-time job. For many people, not going straight from full-time work to retirement is the best option as it eases the transition in addition to creating a financial buffer.

Cut your spending! You are already a savvy spender and saver but maybe your belt needs to be tightened even more. Are there areas in which you can do even better? Can you cut back from two vacations a year to one? Do you really need two cars when one would do? Is there still some waste in your food budget? Take a good look at your budget, and whatever you can trim out should be saved for retirement.

Consider relocating. Is it cheaper to live in New Hampshire than New York? You bet! Not only is the cost of living more favorable, but there is no income or sales tax in New Hampshire. Relocating is not for everyone, but the time to start thinking about it is well before retirement. For instance, if you are going to sell your New York-based business and move to New Hampshire, the time to sell is *after* you have established residency in New Hampshire. Then you'll really take advantage of the fact that the granite state does not tax residents on their income.

Get Free Retirement Information

There are terrific resources on the Internet to help you plan your retirement. They range from simple to very complex and can run all kinds of scenarios, from when you can retire to how long it will take you to earn a target amount of money. Here are a few:

http://www.smartmoney.com/personal-finance/retirement
http://individual.troweprice.com/public/Retail/Planning-&-
   Research/Tools-&-Resources/Retirement-Planning
http://www.fool.com/calcs/calculators.htm.

Are You Financially Fit?

You take good care of yourself, knowing that your body won't hold up if you don't treat it right. Guess what? Neither will your money. What to do? Give yourself an annual checkup to make sure that your finances are in the best of health. The ideal time of year to do this is in the fall so that you still have a couple of months left in the year if you've forgotten to do something.

Make sure you contributed to your plans. Did you contribute the maximum that either you can afford or the government allows to your IRA, 401(k), and 529 college savings plan? If not, make sure you do by the proper deadlines.

Check your investments. Do your accounts need to be rebalanced? If some funds are doing very well and others are underperforming, you may find that your allocations are no longer balanced. Make sure that the distributions align with your wishes and your risk tolerance. If you are not sure how to balance your portfolio, consider an age-based (also called life cycle) fund. These funds adjust the risk every year, becoming more conservative the closer you get to retirement.

Watch the taxes. You can reduce your tax exposure by making sure that traditional IRAs, which grow tax-deferred, hold your assets that pay high dividends. Transfer high-growth but low-dividend stocks to your taxable accounts.

Check your beneficiaries. Make sure that if you don't live to enjoy your savings, your loved ones will. Be certain you have named the beneficiary of your choice and that your wishes haven't changed in the wake of a big event like a birth, death, or divorce. Many funds send you a beneficiary review form every few years; if you have never received one, be sure to ask.

Consolidate your funds. Hardly any of us spend our whole lives working at one company anymore, which can mean that by the time we hit retirement, we have accounts scattered around at a number of companies. Decide whether to keep the funds where they are or to roll them over into an IRA. If you choose the former, keep track of your money in its various accounts; if you choose the latter, make sure you do a direct rollover so that you don't take a tax hit.

Did You Know?

Understanding the Sandwich Generation Two out of five families in which the parents are in their 50s include a child who is still a minor. Welcome to the sandwich generation in which seniors struggle with helping their own aging parents, preparing children for life on their own, and planning for retirement. This begs the question: retirement or college savings? If you can't save for both, which is more important?

The answer is retirement. Why? Because you can finance your child's college tuition. You cannot finance retirement. There are loans, student work programs, scholarships, and other tools available to pay for college. No such luck for retirement. So if you are in your 50s, move retirement savings to the front burner and turn up the heat!

Giving to Family, Giving to Charity

You've saved for years, you've pinched every penny, and now it's time to enjoy your golden years. One of the great rewards of hard work and careful spending is being able to help your family. While you may have carefully planned where your money will go after you die by making sure that your will is in order and maybe even setting up trusts for your heirs, you may not have considered giving money away during your lifetime. Living gifts can be one of the true joys of your golden years. It's nice to know that your family will be taken care of after you're gone, but it can't compare to the pleasure you'll receive by seeing with your own eyes how much your money can make a difference to your children, grandchildren, and even charitable organizations. Here are some of the ways in which your dollars can help.

Helping with tuition. Tuitions have skyrocketed over the last decades, and it is not at all uncommon for colleges to charge over $30,000 a year—not including room, board, and supplies! That can be a heavy burden on parents who are trying to fund their own nest eggs while they worry about how to finance their kids' educations. Consider opening 529 college savings accounts for your grandkids. These plans are:

- Run by most states. Make sure that your plan allows students to attend college out of state. Many do. Visit www.savingforcollege.com for more details.

- Tax-advantaged. You may be able to deduct your contributions from your taxes, and the interest on the money you save grows tax-free. Best of all? The contribution limits are high! Most plans have around a $60,000 limit per year and a $200,000 lifetime limit.

- In your control. You decide what funds to invest in. And your grandchildren cannot access the money themselves. There won't be any worries that the money will go toward anything other than legitimate school fees.

- Sometimes helpful in getting discounted tuition. More and more colleges and universities are encouraging families to use 529s by offering tuition discounts to those who do.

- Easy to transfer back. If your grandchild decides not to go to college, you can change your beneficiary, or you may get your money back after you pay tax and a small penalty on the earnings.

Giving gifts of cash. You are free to give as much money as you like to anyone at any time. But be careful! You—the donor—will have to pay a "gift tax" if that amount is more than $12,000 a year. The recipient does not pay tax on gifts. Your lifetime tax-free limit on gifts to one person is a whopping one million dollars. And gifts are deducted from your estate tax exclusion, which is even more: in 2009, the amount was three million five hundred thousand dollars! This means that if you give your child $100,000 during your lifetime, the amount of money that can flow from your estate tax free would be $3,400,000 (these numbers undergo occasional adjustment, so check with your accountant for the most up-to-date information before making a gift).

Taking advantage of the Uniform Gifts to Minors Act.

If you'd like to give to your grandkids but you don't want to contribute to the 529 and you don't want to give them cash, take advantage of this nifty way to give. You can fill out a set of papers with your banker that will enable your child to receive money into an account (the $12,000 a year limit applies), but the child will not be able to access the money until he turns 18 (or whatever age you choose). Here are two caveats to be aware of:

- Don't name yourself as the custodian. You will have to name a custodian who will manage the money until your grandchild comes of age. If you are the custodian, when you die, the account will be included in your estate and subject to taxes and delays.

- Consider how this will affect financial aid for college. The money in your grandchild's account will be considered when it comes to financial aid. It might reduce scholarship possibilities.

Early Bird Secret

Use Your Noodle for Tax Savings

If you've come into some extra money and want to pass it on to your children, you can avoid taxes and maximize your gift. Say you and your spouse have come into $50,000 unexpectedly and would like to pass it on to your son. Will it take you four years to give him the money because of the $12,000-a-year limit? Heck, no! You and your spouse can each give him and his wife $12,000. That's $48,000 in one year with no tax implications. You can enlarge your gifts even more by each giving money to his children!

Gifts that have multiple benefits.

Your family will certainly appreciate gifts of cash or college savings money. They may also appreciate gifts that aim to do greater good in the world. Gifts that enrich charities may also enrich your soul and pass on valuable lessons about your values to your heirs. Consider these ways of giving:

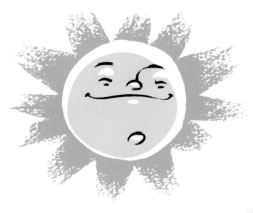

- Sponsor a child. You can sponsor a child through any number of organizations including www.savethechildren.org; www.sos-usa.org; and many others.

- Sponsor an animal. You can sponsor an endangered animal through www.worldwildlife.org. Check your local animal shelter for opportunities to help with abandoned pets.

- Give a gift to a family in need. You can give an African family a goat. Go to www.oxfamamerica.org for ideas. Or give a childless American a toy for Christmas through your local newspaper or other organization.

Charitable remainder trusts. One living gift that will keep on giving in a very real way is a contribution made to a charitable remainder trust. You donate your money to charity and then you receive income from the gift for the rest of your life, much like an annuity. The upshot?

- Tax benefits. You do not pay capital gains tax on the assets you donate, and you get a tax deduction. In addition, your estate taxes are lowered because your gift is no longer a part of your estate.

- You have little control. Your gift is irrevocable. You cannot change your mind years later and get the money back. But you can have some say in how the assets are invested.

- Pleasure. You get the benefit of seeing your money appreciated and used. You may get invited to organizational benefit dinners or have a plaque dedicated in your honor. This is not something you would experience if you left the gift in your estate.

- Risk. There is some risk attached to a charitable trust. You must do your homework to make sure that the institution you give to is solvent so that your gift will not be wasted and so that you will continue to receive your annuity. Some states are highly regulated; others less so. Once you have chosen a charity to contribute to, call your state's insurance department and make sure that the institution is worthy of your attention.

Did You Know?

There Are Three Kinds of Charitable Remainder Trusts

Charitable remainder annuity trusts: These pay a fixed amount each year—very similar to classic annuities backed by insurance companies.

Charitable remainder unitrusts: These pay a fixed percentage of the trust's value every year. The trust's value may fluctuate according to how it is invested and how the stock market is doing.

Charitable pooled income funds: These are set up by the charity and enable many donors to contribute to the same fund. Think mutual fund meets annuity.

Tax Tips That You Can Bank On

There is a world of financial advice out there for seniors, much of which is discounted or free. Even if you end up paying top dollar for tax and planning advice, a good certified financial planner and CPA will earn back what you pay them in no time. Here are some great places to start.

Free advice. Free tax and financial advice is something most people either don't know about or are wary of. The Volunteer Income Tax Assistance program (or VITA) is run by the Internal Revenue Service (IRS). It pairs people of moderate income (usually $40,000 and less) with tax experts who offer free advice and is worth its weight in gold (almost).

Senior-specific free tax advice. The Tax Counseling for the Elderly (TCE) program is similar to VITA. Also run by the IRS, it is staffed by trained volunteers and caters to people 60 years old and above. Tax-Aide is part of the TCE program, which is sponsored by AARP. During peak tax preparation season, before April 15, there are 7,000 locations around the country where seniors can receive free advice.

The IRS itself has a help line that is open 24/7: 1-800-829-1040. Ask about the VITA, TCE, and Tax-Aide programs there. You can get more information on Tax-Aide (and taxes in general) at the AARP site: www.aarp.org.

CPAs and CFPs. Sometimes, the best advice must be paid for, and this is where a good certified public accountant (CPA) or certified financial planner (CFP) comes in. Our experts agree that these two kinds of advisers, at best, can save you a ton, both on your taxes and in your investments. But there are some things to do before you hire one:

- Check the person's credentials. You want to make sure that an accountant is a CPA (certified public accountant) or that your financial planner is in fact a CFP. If you are not sure, ask for the person's license number and check credentials through your state's licensing office.
- Pay by the hour. It might sound expensive to pay by the hour, but it will be a savings in the long run. If you are not using a fee-based planner, you are paying a percentage of your portfolio or commissions.
- Retain control. Never sign over control of your accounts to your financial planner, and if you are pressured to do so, find a new adviser. Remember movies in which the accountant ran away with all the money? You won't have that problem if you don't let anyone else access your assets.

Reel in Big Refunds with These Write-offs

We all know people who have tried to deduct some crazy things from their taxes: doggy day care, consulting fees for the arsonist who accidentally torched a fizzling business concern, cable TV (it's research, right?); the list goes on and on. But there *are* some excellent, off-the-beaten-track tax deductions out there that will help fund your lifestyle—if you take a little time to uncover and pursue them. As always, remember that tax law changes from year to year, so check with your accountant or financial adviser on the current regulations and specifics regarding any write-offs you're hoping to take. However, many deductions continue to exist each year, and only the details might change a bit, such as how much per mile you can deduct for transportation costs to and from medical treatment. Then check out the following unusual and surprising deductions, and ask your financial adviser about others—they can really add up.

Yes or No?

I've just installed a chairlift for my husband. Can I deduct it?

Chairlifts added to a home are tax-deductible; elevators are not. A lift to help you up and down the stairs is considered a legitimate expense to help a handicapped person with mobility, whereas an elevator is considered a capital improvement that increases the value of your home and thus is not deductible.

What about medical costs? Even with health insurance, out-of-pocket medical expenses can amount to a lot in this day and age, but the IRS generally won't let you deduct them from your federal income tax unless they total more than 7.5 percent of your adjusted gross income. However, in addition to insurance premiums, there are a lot of other ways to count medical expenses. Taken all together, they may well push your costs toward that magic threshold. When calculating your costs, don't forget:

- Insurance payments taken from after-tax dollars. If your monthly premiums are not automatically deducted from your pretax income, as they generally are if your insurance plan is through your employer, then you're likely paying for them out of income that has already been taxed—and thus they become a deduction. If you have long-term care insurance, this is usually taken from after-tax money and can be deducted.

- Uninsured medical treatments and accessories. False teeth, extra glasses, hearing aids, contact lenses—if you're wearing or buying these things on the advice or prescription of a medical practitioner, they count toward your total medical deductions.

- Travel to and from medical treatment. This allowance generally runs in the range of 20 cents per mile. If you drive 10 miles each way to the doctor, that's a $2 deduction per visit—and don't forget the trips you take with dependents.

- Medical conferences. Even if you're not a medical practitioner, you could attend a conference concerning a malady suffered by you or your dependents and deduct the costs of travel and admission (though not the cost of food and board, so don't treat it like a vacation!).

- Specialty treatments. Costs of alcohol- and drug-abuse treatment can be deducted, as well as laser vision treatment (check on that first with your medical practitioner or financial adviser if you're planning to take a write-off).

- Medical hardware. If you have to buy crutches or a wheelchair or have to install handrails in your home, these items may be deductible. Structural work on your house to assist in medical conditions, such as widening doorways or adding ramps, can also be a write-off, with a doctor's advice and IRS approval. Also, if your doctor recommends that you add a special filter to your home heating system, for example, to help with your allergies or asthma, you may be able to deduct part of that cost on your income tax.

Yes or No?

My husband does a little handyman work as a hobby, but everything else in our tax life is very straightforward. Can I deduct the costs of his tools on our joint return?

Probably not.

Nearly all these specialized deductions are *only* for people who itemize on their tax returns, not for people who fill out a 1040EZ and take the standard deduction. The exceptions tend to be for educational deductions, which are considered an "above the line" deduction by the IRS and can usually be taken on the EZ form.

Should I itemize?

Only if you're deducting more than these standardized amounts (but always be sure to double-check this year's amounts):

Single or married filing separately: $5,700

Heads of household: $8,350

Married couple, joint return: $11,400

If your total deductions (including mortgage interest, medical expenses, and charitable contributions) are higher than these thresholds, you should itemize. If less, you're better off taking the standard deduction.

Mortgage points. If you took out a mortgage in the tax year, whether for your first or second home, the fees you paid the lender, also known as mortgage points, can come off your taxes *even if you didn't pay them.* In many cases, a motivated seller will cover the points of the mortgage (that is, pay those fees for you) but for federal tax purposes, the buyer taking out the mortgage—not the seller—gets to deduct them.

Traveling for good. If you traveled to do charitable work, your travel costs may be deductible, whether it's the standard mileage rate for driving your car around for the local branch of Meals on Wheels, traveling to a different state to build houses for a charitable organization, or ferrying your Girl Scout troop to an event. You can also deduct fees for parking and tolls paid.

Yes or No?

I've just made a clothing donation to Goodwill. Do I need a receipt to deduct the monetary equivalent of the donation?

Whether you donate cash or an item, if the value is greater than $250, you must get a receipt from the receiving organization, which itself must meet IRS guidelines.

Deduct good works. In addition to your travel, you can deduct any materials or supplies you purchase specifically for a charitable group, such as office supplies for the group's use. You can also write off the costs of a uniform, such as the outfits that some hospital volunteers wear or those of a Boy Scout troop leader; it also means any upkeep on that uniform, whether it's a dry-cleaning bill or paying a tailor to hem it.

Educational costs. Go back to school yourself and earn tax credits toward the cost of your tuition. Up to $4,000 of tuition and fees can be deducted *even if you don't itemize.* Note that the coursework must be for credit, not sport or hobby classes (unless they are required as part of a degree program), and the $4,000 ceiling is for your entire household, so you can't deduct $4,000 for your own continuing education and another for your dependent child who's a full-time student. However, recent adjustments have made this credit accessible to a broader range of taxpayers, so be sure to check if anyone in your family qualifies.

Deduct your savings. If you're a moderate- or low-income household, the IRS allows you to deduct half of the first $2,000 you put away for retirement in your traditional or Roth IRA. Because it's an IRA, you get to deduct the $2,000 from your overall income, and then you get an additional $1,000 credit on your taxes—it's quite an encouragement to save!

Taking a loss. It's cold comfort if you've been the victim of vandalism to your property or outright theft, but these are losses that can often be deducted on your tax return. If the amount of the loss is more than 10 percent of your adjusted gross income, subtract $100 off the total amount of loss and deduct the rest. You can also deduct damage from an automobile accident—unless the accident was due to your negligence as a driver.

Random receipts. Deducted everything you could think of and still have lots of receipts in your desk drawer? There might still be room for some "miscellaneous" deductions, as long as they total more than 2 percent of your adjusted gross income. This category can include subscriptions to professional journals, fees for membership in professional organizations, certain costs for hobbies, and other expenses. The advice of a professional tax preparer can be a real benefit when you get into this hazier side of deductions, but that's okay: That person's fees are deductible as well!

Yes or No?

Are there any charitable donations that are not tax-deductible?

Yes.

1. The value of your time given in volunteer work, or the value of the income you might have forfeited while volunteering.

2. Money given to any group that was formed to lobby for changes in the law.

3. Money given to an individual, no matter how much the person needed the aid.

4. Personal expenses while volunteering, such as the cost of gas, lodging, or meals (although transportation can be deducted at about 14 cents per mile).

5. Money given to civic leagues, homeowner associations, chambers of commerce, and sport or social clubs, unless these clubs specifically meet IRS guidelines for charitable institutions.

6. Fees to appraise the value of property you are donating (although the value of the property may well be deductible).

Public debt. Any money you contribute to the U.S. Treasury to help relieve public debt is directly deductible from your personal tax bill. Public debt is the money that the government "borrows," through selling savings bonds and securities, to keep itself running. You can help lower this debt by sending a check made out to the Bureau of Public Debt along with your tax return, and you can deduct the exact amount as a charitable contribution.

Asset appreciation. If you bought $100 worth of stock in Google when it was just starting out and that stock is now worth $1 million (or whatever Google is worth these days), you could donate that stock to a charity and deduct the full $1 million, not the original price that you paid. This assumes that the charity is set up to receive appreciated property, and also that you're willing to give up your Google stock! The benefit to an appreciated-asset donation is that you pay no capital-gains tax and take as a deduction the full value of the property.

Choosing Insurance That's Right for You

You should have life insurance if you think your dependents will suffer hardship in the event of your demise. If you have enough money saved that your spouse and children will be able to live off of your savings and retirement plans, you probably don't need life insurance anymore. But if your spouse and children rely upon your income, then you need to calculate how much money they would need to survive without it. Consider these points as you make your decision:

Do you have life insurance through your employer?

Many employers offer automatic coverage, so if you are retiring and had been relying on your company's life insurance, you need to make new plans.

If you have a plan, is it current? If you bought life insurance
many years ago when your family was young, the plan, which may have lasted for 20 years or so, might expire soon. It's a good time to review your coverage, see when it ends, and decide whether or not you need to extend it.

Choose between term or whole life insurance. If you decide
that you do need insurance, keep it simple! Look for term life insurance. Most people don't need permanent or whole life, which is more of an investment vehicle and is very complicated.

Long-Term Care Insurance

Americans are living longer than ever, which is great news. But the dark side of longevity is that more of us may need health care that goes above and beyond the basics. At some point, we may need home care, or we may need to be cared for in a long-term care facility. And these are expensive! More and more people are buying long-term care insurance, which is designed to protect your assets, minimize the financial burden on your family, and give you some control over the quality of care you'll receive.

Ka-Ching!

The Secrets to Keeping Life Insurance Costs Down

Before you have a physical to obtain life insurance, there are a few things you can do to try to make your premium lower.

Lose weight	That spare tire will cost you, so try to unload it.
Quit smoking	You are considered a nonsmoker if you haven't smoked for a year.
Eat well for a week	Cut way back on sugar, salt, and fatty foods.
No alcohol	Don't drink any alcohol for at least three days before the exam to make sure your liver enzymes aren't elevated.
No caffeine	Cut out the caffeine the day before and day of the exam. Caffeine elevates blood pressure.
Reduce medication	Don't take any medication that you don't have to—ibuprofen, aspirin, decongestants, and so on. Do continue to take doctor-prescribed meds for serious conditions.
No exercise	Don't do anything strenuous the day before the exam.
Fast	For 10 hours before your exam, consume only water, but only if your health permits.
Sleep	Get a good night's sleep the night before your exam. The more relaxed you are, the better chance you have of doing well.

If you are shopping for long-term care insurance, consider these points carefully:

When should you buy coverage? Do you want to buy coverage now or wait until you are older? The older you are the higher the premiums will be, and there is no guarantee you'll get coverage if you develop a costly condition. On the other hand, the younger you are, the more time you'll spend paying the premiums.

What kind of coverage will you need? You can choose coverage that will only pay for home care or only pay for a nursing home. Or you can do a mixture of care styles.

What is the daily or monthly benefit? This is the amount of money the insurer will pay for each day or month of coverage. If your care costs more than your benefit allows, you need to pay the difference.

What benefit period will you choose? Do you need a fixed benefit period of several years or do you need the care to last the rest of your life?

Is there an elimination period? If the coverage makes you wait for a while, sometimes as long as three months, you'll pay for your care during that time. The longer the elimination period, the lower the premium.

Do you need inflation protection? Most experts we spoke with said yes; with inflation on the rise, it pays to be protected.

Setting Up Sound Wills and Trusts

Everybody should have a will, especially people who have others relying on them: parents with young children and couples who rely on one another's income and assets. If you die without a will, as two out of three Americans do, the government is left to decide what happens to your estate—not a desirable option. Making a will is relatively simple and straightforward.

Hire a lawyer. While do-it-yourself forms have proliferated on the Internet and much software is available for the most straightforward wills, you may find that it's nonetheless preferable to use a lawyer. An attorney drafted will is far less likely to be found invalid, and your heirs will be less likely to be able to overturn it.

Choose an executor. Make sure you choose someone reliable, close to you, and best, someone who does not stand to gain from your demise. If you choose a beneficiary as an executor, you can run into trouble with conflicts of interest. If you ever have a falling out with your executor or he or she dies, make sure you update your will and name a new executor.

Choose a guardian. If you have minor children, you must name the person who is to care for the children. Make sure that you have asked permission of the guardian you choose. The point of a will is to protect your heirs; you don't want any surprises.

Include specific instructions. Most will boilerplates do not include this but it's a nice addition. A letter of instruction outlines who gets which of your possessions. If you do not explain your wishes, then your executor will have to make difficult choices, and your family may find itself bickering over Aunt Mary's knickknacks.

Keep the will someplace accessible. Make sure that your will and other important documents are kept someplace where your family will be able to find them easily. It's nice to have a safety deposit box for important documents, but in the turmoil of a family's loss, your children will be more likely to find your papers if they are in a filing cabinet in the house. An original copy should be kept elsewhere, too, in case of burglary or fire—at your lawyer's office certainly and in a safety deposit box, as well, if you like.

Living Wills

Just as you have a will that dictates what will happen to your property after you die, you should have a living will that dictates what you want to happen to your body should you require medical treatment and not be able to tell doctors what you want. Here are some things to consider when writing your living will:

Have it drawn up by a lawyer and notarized. If you decide to use a form that you find on the Internet or use legal software, make sure that it will be recognized by your state and that you have the final result notarized.

Be specific. Do you want to be kept alive no matter what? Do you want heroic measures taken to save you? Would you approve being kept on a respirator? For how long? Under what circumstances? Are you planning to be an organ donor? There may be many things to think about at the end of your life. The more you can plan in advance, the happier you will be with the management of your care.

Include a health-care proxy. If you are a not able to make your health-care decisions for yourself, who will make them for you?

Give a copy to your physicians and executor. If you are being treated for a condition, make sure all of your doctors have a copy of your wishes. If you end up needing care unexpectedly, make sure that your friends and family know where you keep your important papers so they'll be able to find your living will.

Living Trusts

A living trust, or a "revocable trust" as it is also called, allows your heirs access to your estate without a messy and public trip to probate court. A living trust is also useful in case you become incapacitated. For instance, if you need to check with a trustee to access a large sum of money, you will be less likely to be scammed by a caregiver. Your trustee will review the reason for the withdrawal, and if the money is not going directly to your care—say, instead, into the pocket of an unscrupulous employee—your trustee will realize what's going on and be able to protect you. Here are some key reasons why a living trust might be right for you:

It allows you to pass your assets on in an orderly way. If you die leaving a minor child, for example, a trust enables the child to not inherit a lump sum, but puts the money into the control of a designated trustee until the child is of a reasonable age to handle the money.

It protects you in case you become incapacitated. You will be less likely to be swindled—by anyone—if your money is in a trust. A designated trustee has to approve large withdrawals, which effectively creates a checks-and-balances system.

Early Bird Secret

Make Haste with Your Trust

If you decide that a living trust is right for you, don't procrastinate setting it up. There are good reasons not to wait. The most important may be the Medicare "look back." If you make a claim that you are unable to afford services and want Medicare to cover them, Medicare may insist upon looking back into your financial records to make sure that you have not transferred your assets recently. If you have moved money around in the last five years, you may not get the benefits you'd hoped for from Medicare.

Safe and Sound
The Necessity of a Safety Deposit Box

If you are worried about the security of your valuables, you might be in the market for a safety deposit box. This can be a strong box or safe that you keep somewhere in your home or it can be a box that you rent at your bank. The bank's box is less likely to be subject to burglary, fire, or water damage. But it is less easy to access, though only slightly. Some insurance companies will lower their premiums for items stored at the bank.

ITEMS THAT SHOULD BE STORED IN A SAFE DEPOSIT BOX:

Original documents including insurance policies; birth, marriage, divorce, and death certificates; deeds, titles, mortgages, leases; contracts; stocks; bonds; certificates of deposit; valuable, durable objects like jewelry, medals, rare stamps, coins, and other collectibles; photos of your home and its contents for insurance purposes; and anything else that is irreplaceable to you.

ITEMS THAT SHOULD <u>NOT</u> BE STORED IN A SAFE DEPOSIT BOX:

Anything that you might need at the last minute: Original documents including powers of attorney, living wills, medical directives, passports, funeral and burial wishes, and your will. You can put a copy of your will in a safe deposit box but keep the original elsewhere, because some states require a court order to open the safe-deposit box of a deceased person, and that can take time. The originals are better off at your home and with your lawyer.

It reduces taxes paid by your estate. You'll still pay estate taxes with a living trust but couples may be able to effectively raise their unified credit tax exemption with a trust.

You'll avoid probate. You'll save money, hassle, time, and publicity by avoiding probate.

You'll avoid a will contest. Wills are relatively easy to challenge. Trusts, however, are not. If you are concerned about this matter, a living trust may be ideal for you.

It may provide a Medicare cushion. Many seniors complain that the government seems to want them to be dirt poor before it will step up to the plate and pay for things that should be covered by Medicare. Families, naturally, worry about letting Mom drain her coffers to pay for medical treatments. A trust might offer a way around this dilemma. If Mom transfers nearly all her assets to a trust, then she may become eligible for Medicare treatments she otherwise wouldn't have been.

Making Major Changes

> The Dreamer's Guide to Life-Altering Lifestyle Makeovers

10

Starting a Second Career

It's true what they say: 60 is the new 40. So, for many seniors these days, retirement is simply the wrong word. Rebirth is more like it! Now is the time when you have the luxury to reinvent yourself. Try new things, travel to new places. Return to those activities you used to love that were almost forgotten in the swirl of raising children and pursuing your career. For many of us, it means considering significant changes in the way we live and support ourselves. And these changes can be exhilarating. This is your second act, and you are the star. And if you do want to slow down a little, now is a wonderful time when you can smell the roses and enjoy the grandkids. Whatever the next years have in store for you, you'll find our expert tips and suggestions in the coming pages to be worth their weight in gold!

Search your soul. Some people already know that they want to open that bait shop or become a nature photographer. Others aren't quite sure. The first step to deciding on a second act is figuring out exactly what you like and don't like. Assess your skills and your passions. Figure out what will translate to other jobs. One of the best aids in soul- and career-searching is the classic book *What Color Is Your Parachute?* by Richard Nelson Bolles, which will walk you through the process of figuring out what you really love and are suited for. There are also many Web sites that offer quizzes to help you in your search, including www.monster.com, which has one in its advice section, as does www.careerpath.com.

Stay put. The easiest way to have a second career might be to do so at the company where you already are, assuming you're still working. Is there a way for you to reduce your hours? Is there a different department you can work in that would excite you more? Could you work from home all the time or part of the time? Could you become a freelancer and sell your services to the company? There is a huge safety net associated with staying where you are known and appreciated. Consider simply tweaking your current job. There's lots of good advice and helpful tips for this at http://seniorliving.about.com.

Network. It's true what they say: it's all who you know. Think of the number of times you have made a sale or gotten a job or performed another transaction in your life thanks to a connection. Your second act job search will work the same way. Start talking to friends, clients, and acquaintances about what you are thinking of doing. See if anyone has any ideas for you or knows of any positions available or knows of anyone else you should be talking to.

Do your homework. If you *are* thinking of making a big change, do your homework first. Pick the brains of people who know more than you do. Read the trade papers of the field you are considering entering. Take a part-time job in the business if you can to make sure it really will suit you and that you'll acquire some of the skills needed before you make the leap. Consider companies that are friendly toward the over-50 crowd. You can find a list of these on the career section of the AARP Web site (www.aarp.org).

Review your finances. Make sure that any move you make will be advantageous to you. Can you take a pay cut? Or will a pay raise bump you into a higher tax bracket? Are you able to take out a loan to start your own business? How will this job change affect your Social Security benefits? Can you afford any training you may need to pursue your dream? Do you need to (and are you willing to) make a radical change like selling your home to finance your dream?

Early Bird Secret

Begin Your Job Search on the Web

There are loads of Web sites that can help you in your job search. Here is a handful of some of the best:

http://www.retirementjobs.com

http://www.civicventures.org/nextchapter/overview.cfm

http://www.retiredbrains.com

http://www.seniorjobbank.org

http://www.thingamajob.com

http://www.aarp.org/money/careers/employerresourcecenter/bestemployers

http://www.doleta.gov/seniors

http://careeronestop.org

Upgrade your skills. If you are looking to start over in a new field, do you need to go back to school to earn a degree? Apply for certification? Learn a new computer program? If so, now is the time to think about it. Ideally, you can take classes for your new career before you've quit your old one. Your current employer might even have a tuition reimbursement program you can use to pay for it. (If so, make sure that you don't have to stay for some length of time after taking classes.)

Qualities That Make You a Great Hire

The over-50 set deserves its props—we've earned them! Make sure that you stick up for yourself and your peers as you hunt for a job in your new field. There can occasionally be subtle (and not-so-subtle) resistance to hiring an older person, especially someone who is making a big change. If you encounter any, you might want to confront it head on. Seniors are well known to trump younger workers in many ways including:

Experience. You've been around the block and are not ruffled by workplace dramas, business cycles, and regime changes. You've already been there, done that. You are unflappable in the face of stormy weather. And your savvy means the company won't worry that you'll waste time on petty matters.

Work ethic. You have spent a lifetime getting up in the morning and getting things done. You are not a kid who came of age during the Internet bubble and expected things to be handed to you. You are dependable, perseverant, and focused. You are always appropriately dressed and behaved, and you project a good image, both internally and to clients.

Did You Know?

Size Does Matter! If you are sensing any age resistance to your plans to change careers, consider companies at both ends of the size spectrum. You may find that small companies are more creative, open-minded, and flexible. On the flip side, many large firms are good about maintaining programs and jobs that are geared toward seniors. The Wal-Mart greeter position is an example of this.

Customer service. You are mature and can relate to customers who are upset. After all, you've been impatient with shoddy service yourself. Your verbal skills are top-notch, meaning that you can communicate well and show empathy—just what customers need.

Loyalty. Younger employees have grown up believing that they have to jump from one job to another to get higher pay. Seniors are much less likely to agree. Retention saves companies a lot of money on training.

Time. Your kids are older now and maybe even out of the house. You are no longer juggling the demands of a young family with your job. You can devote more time and attention to your job than a younger person at a different stage of his or her life.

Motivation. Studies show that older workers are more highly motivated to succeed than younger ones. They have been shown to have a positive effect on product quality, cost control, and customer satisfaction. Take that, Junior!

Great Gigs for Seniors

What's next for you in the job market? If you are thinking about making a change, think seriously about these fields, which are magnets for seniors.

Consulting. You've got a lifetime's worth of knowledge in your field. It would be a shame to waste it. Why not hang out your shingle as a consultant? The job is flexible—you work whatever hours suit you, you take on only projects you like, and you set the pay rate. And you have all the contacts you need to get started—the clients and colleagues you already know.

Temp. You want to work part-time? Have flexible hours? Temping is all about flexibility. You are basically acting as a substitute worker. Many temp jobs pay well, from $10 to $20 an hour. And you can be a temp anywhere in the country and even the world. The largest temp service is Manpower, Inc. (www.manpower.com).

Government work. The U.S. government is very serious about non-discrimination. So if you are, say, a CPA and are looking for a new position, check the IRS for openings. If you are a teacher, look for a position at the board of education.

Eldercare. This subset of health care is growing steadily as longevity increases. You may be asked to offer companionship, personal care, and basic services like cooking and shopping to the elderly. Care may be in-home or in a facility.

Education. Teachers are badly needed, and if you have a bachelor's degree, it takes about a year to become certified to teach. Start with the U.S. Department of Education to learn more: http://www.ed.gov/admins/tchr-qual/recruit/altroutes/index.html. This concerns public schools. Certification requirements may be different—and easier—for some private schools.

Hospitality. If you are a people person, then hospitality careers might be right for you. If your first career was in a finance field or if you have an outgoing personality, then working in a casino might be the perfect fit. More seniors are finding work they love at these resorts. Those who find the fit ideal praise the sense of constant action and meeting new people.

Launching a New Business

Seniors today are younger at heart and in better health than ever before. So what's a vigorous, young 65-year-old to do in retirement? For many, the answer is to start your own business. The benefits of starting a business in retirement are many.

It will keep you active. Running a business keeps you on your toes. You've got to stay on top of news and trends, keep up your contacts, and generally be engaged in the world. You'll never worry about sitting around twiddling your thumbs. There is always work to be done if you have your own business.

You'll learn new skills. You will very likely have to learn new things as you launch your enterprise. You'll certainly learn something about accounting (whether you want to or not!), and you'll have to educate yourself on how businesses are run and the tools and technology of your new field—not to mention sales, merchandising, and customer service. All this helps to keep your brain in tip-top shape.

You'll earn extra income. You may have started your business for fun, and you may be running it for fun, but, hey, a little income is still welcome, right? And who's to say your little venture won't take off? Besides the financial rewards, when people pay you for your goods or services, it means that they like what you are offering. That's a great feeling.

Did You Know?

It's Never Too Late! Colonel Sanders was 65 years old when he set about franchising his little fried chicken restaurant. He ended up with a lot more than play money.

You'll reap tax benefits. There are wonderful tax benefits to running your own firm. If you set yourself up as a nature photographer, then your trip to the national park becomes a business trip. You should keep all your receipts and track your mileage because these are deductions if you itemize. If you and your wife are in business together and you have a monthly partners meeting in a nice restaurant, save that receipt! It's a write-off.

You'll be able to save even *more* for retirement. If your business takes off, you may be able to feather your nest a bit more. It might be worth your while to set up a retirement account like a Keogh or a simplified employee pension (SEP) plan. For instance, the law allows you to contribute 20 percent of net earnings to a SEP account each year.

Your Interview Skills

Refresh your interviewing skills before you look for a new job. Here are some of the best questions you might be asked in an interview:

Tell me about yourself.

Why are you interested in this industry? This company?

Tell me about your education.

How does what you've been doing apply to this job?

What do you like most about your current job/field? Why do you want to leave it?

What is your greatest strength?

What is your greatest weakness?

How do you work with others?

What experiences have you had in managing others?

How do you see yourself fitting in here?

Where do you see yourself in three years?

Do you have any questions for me?

When it comes time for you to ask questions, be prepared with the following:

What is the history of this position? Is it new? Are you replacing someone?

Which aspects of this job would you like to see performed better?

What do you see as the key challenges of the job?

Where can I go from this job, assuming that I succeed in it?

How would you describe your ideal candidate?

What are the company's short- and long-term objectives?

In what ways does the company excel? What are its limitations?

When and how will I be evaluated?

Who will I report to? Will anyone report to me?

What is the environment of the company or department?

When will you make the hiring decision? When may I call to follow up?

Enterprising Ideas for Entrepreneurs

Let's say that you know you want to run your own show. What kind of business should you start? There are a number of things to keep in mind when deciding to hang out your own shingle.

Stay in your current field. This is the path of least resistance and can mean an easy segue into entrepreneurship. You use all your current contacts, all the skills you've built up, all the same equipment. What could be easier? You can simply go freelance and take jobs as they come up, or you can become a consultant, which is a more formal way of being a freelancer. Many seniors find that their old firms are eager to hire them for outsourced work; most firms love to work with known quantities and former employees are just that. Staying in a familiar field will give you a baseline level of comfort.

Turn a hobby into a business. Have you been an avid calligrapher throughout the years and just haven't had time to devote to your passion? Now's the time! Seniors around the country are taking their crafting, sporting, and other leisure activities to the next level by milking them for cash. And they are delighted when it works! You would be quilting anyway, so it makes sense to get a little something extra for your efforts. You'll experience the thrill of knowing that other people are enjoying your talent and hard work.

Buy a business. You might consider stepping up to the plate and buying a business from someone who is retiring. The advantage is that the company usually has a built-in customer base, and you'll be inheriting all the tools, equipment, and leases you need to start right up. Think of this as being a hermit crab—you can move right into a fully furnished new shell. Unlike other options, this one requires some capital to get started. Have your lawyer carefully review the books and other documents before you sign on.

Do what you love. Your first career may have been filled with obligations. Let your next one be filled with pleasure. Choose a field that has always interested you, and you will be more likely to succeed. If work is fun, you are going to be eager to go to your place of business and willing to put in the hours it takes to give your new enterprise its best shot.

Reduce your risk. Having your own business means taking on some risk. Most entrepreneurs can tell you stories of the failed businesses they started before their successful ones took off. If you are in your 20s, you can afford to make mistakes because you have time to recover from them. If you are in your 60s, it's better to get things right on the first go. It's important, then, to make sure that you are conservative with your finances and that you are insured for anything that might expose you to undue risk.

Review your finances. Do whatever you can to keep the costs in check. Where are you going to get your start-up money if you need any? Experts advise you not to raid your retirement accounts. You would be better off borrowing money from a line of credit or home equity loan. Build your cash reserves well in advance of starting your business if you can. If you know that in five years you'll want to retire and try your hand at something new, now's the time to start socking away capital. Experts advise you to save double the amount you think you'll need to get started. Better safe than sorry.

Open a business checking and savings account. Make sure that your business has its own accounts for banking and credit. This way you'll be able to keep track of how it's doing and keep its finances separate from your personal ones.

Seniors Make Great Entrepreneurs!

Many retirees fall into entrepreneurship. They happen to see a need that is not being met and decide to address it themselves. And oftentimes the businesses set up relate to the senior community. Just as new moms start baby gear companies and new dog owners start fashion leash companies, many seniors discover opportunities that make sense for their peers.

Realize time is on your side. While retirees don't have the benefit of recovering from losses as easily as younger people do, they have the luxury of concentrating on their work as little or as much as they'd like. This lifestyle change works especially well for seasonal businesses. The retiree who opens a clam shack can pour his whole summer into the work, knowing he'll have the rest of the year to recover from all that hard work. A younger worker would be worried about how to make a living during the other months.

Consider your lifestyle. Are you brimming with energy or are you more low-key? Do you want a job that is going to let you really sink your teeth in, or are you looking for a distraction for a few hours a day? Do you want to take lots of vacations while you keep your business running? These lifestyle factors should be taken into account when you decide what kind of business to run. If you decide to open a bakery, you'd better be a really early riser (like 4 a.m.!) who is game for lots of physical labor. If you are going to do some bookkeeping, you can be on your porch in your bathrobe with your feet up. Make sure you know what your health and lifestyle is best suited for before you jump in.

Moving Down in House

After the kids move out, you may find that you have more house than you need. Many retirees decide to downsize their homes as they approach retirement for a number of good reasons.

Homes take work to maintain. Do you notice that by the time you are done dusting the last room in the house that the first one looks like it needs attention again? Do you find that the more space you have, the more clutter seems to accumulate, even if it's just you and your spouse living there? Does the expanse of lawn that used to represent games of catch and barbecues now just represent a lawn-mowing headache? A smaller home can mean a lot less headache and backache when it comes to maintenance.

Homes take money to maintain. The gutters need replacing. The burst pipe in the spare bathroom means a check to the plumber and the contractor. The high property taxes that were once well worth the money for the good school district no longer make sense because the kids are grown. A smaller home in a different neighborhood would require less money to maintain and the taxes would be lower. And what about heat? With the cost of oil going through the roof, wouldn't it be nice to have a cozy little ranch house instead of your drafty big Victorian?

Early Bird Secret

Make Your House Pay You!

Isn't it time your house paid you back? If you have paid off your mortgage or have a lot of equity in it, consider getting a reverse mortgage, and the bank will pay you to live in the house. You don't need to worry that you'll be thrown out at some point if you arrange for a mortgage that enables you to stay for as long as you are alive. The caveat: your heirs will not inherit the house. And it means that you will lose your equity in the house so that if you need to go to a care facility in 20 years, you can't sell the house to pay for it.

Your house is incompatible with your health. Those three flights of stairs used to be nothing to you. But if you have certain health issues—knee troubles, hip problems, or you get winded easily—do they really make sense?

It's good to make new memories. Out with the old; in with the new! Sometimes it's a good thing to have a fresh start, a clean slate. You are embarking on an exciting new phase of your life so think about if it might make sense to clear out the clutter and start again in a new space. Do you really need those life jackets you've kept in the basement since you sold your boat 20 years ago? We didn't think so.

You want to cash out. Property values go up and down, but if you've been in your home a long time, you have almost certainly seen yours go up. Maybe it's time to hang out the For Sale sign and listen to the sound of the cash register ring.

Selling Your Home—and Finding a New One

When the time comes for you to actually put the pedal to the metal and plan your move, take time to do it as painlessly as possible. Here are a few keys to a smooth move:

Consult a real estate agent. A real estate agent will give you a realistic sense of what you can expect to get from the house in the current market. The market has undergone some serious fluctuations in recent years, and an agent will be able to give you tips on things you can do to get the best possible price for your most important asset.

Declutter. Now is the time to unburden yourself of the many things you don't need. It also may be the time to make some money on a garage sale (see box on page 270), donate old things to charity (get a receipt in case you decide to take a tax deduction), divvy up mementos among the kids and friends, and keep only what you believe to be useful and beautiful. Decluttering is worth doing, even if you decide not to sell. It will clear your mind as well as your cellar.

Run the numbers. Determine how much you'll get for the house and how much it will cost to buy and maintain a new place. Consider the taxes, the maintenance, moving costs, and other things that might affect you.

Ka-Ching!

No More Pink Foam Hair Rollers

(And 46 Other Items You Own and Never Use That Add Up to a Great Yard Sale)

If you're considering downsizing, why not have a garage or yard sale to declutter and make some money in the process? Our experts gathered up 46 items that most frequently sit unused or are duplicated by newer models you have purchased.

1 Exercise equipment and sporting goods

2 Blenders

3 Bread machines

4 Microwave oven

5 Sewing machine

6 Small televisions

7 Stemware and flatware
Mismatched pieces get the toss

8 Kids books, toys, and clothes

9 Stereo components

10 Typewriters

11 DVDs and CDs

12 Books

13 Old magazines

14 Curling irons

15 Hotel soaps
Unused, unopened soaps and shampoos (you know you have a shoebox full!)

16 Occasional tables

17 Mismatched chairs

18 Old computer components—keyboards, monitors

19 Miscellaneous appliances and electronics—toasters, radios, toaster ovens, hair dryers

20 Costume jewelry (When exactly was the last time you wore the rhinestone ball earrings and matching three-inch flower pin?)

21 Odd pieces of dinnerware and serving platters

22 **Records**
If you haven't listened in one year, they're good to go

23 Fabric

24 Notions

25 Dress patterns

26 Art—real and otherwise

27 Lawn mower

28 Garden hoses

29 Tools, especially duplicates of items like hammers, saws, and screwdrivers

30 Muffin tins and other bakeware

31 **Mini blinds**
Broken, tangled, unnecessary

32 Old purses

33 Canvas tote bags

34 Draperies

35 Shot glasses, barware, coffee mugs

36 Luggage

37 Dining room table

38 Buffet and china cabinet

39 **Ceramic figurines**
How many Hummels do you need?

40 Rugs

41 Bottles: little bottles, Jim Beam, Avon, Kara Brooks, old medicine, Mrs. Butterworth, miniatures, fruit jars, baby food, and insulators

42 Camping gear

43 Needlework and other handmade items

44 Yarn, knitting needles, crochet hooks, and sweater and afghan pattern pamphlets

45 Comic books

46 Dolls and their clothing

Like, in your new place, do you still need a car? Think forward to the resale value of your new property as well. Will it be as easy to sell as you hope, if you need to move to a facility sometime in the future?

Make repairs. As your real estate agent will tell you, you should spiff up your home before you sell it because you'll get more money and sell it quicker this way.

Don't look for a gorgeous old property. Think new. Newer homes are easier to care for and usually easier to sell than older ones when the time comes.

Keep maintenance in mind. Your new home should be easy to care for. If you are moving to an apartment, you'll eliminate yard work and other property hassles. If you are moving to a house, make sure that the lawn is not expansive and the house is of a size that is manageable for you to handle and has fixtures that are up to date.

Think of your lifestyle. Look for a home that suits your lifestyle and that you can age into. If you love to walk, make sure the sidewalks in your neighborhood are well maintained and that the streets seem safe. If you just had a hip replaced, maybe stairs are not a good idea. If you have knee problems, make sure you can take a shower without having to climb over a high tub edge and that handles can be installed easily if you need them.

Remember taxes. If you moved to your current home in part because of the good schools, you may be paying more taxes than you need to be. Take a close look at the tax burden of homes while you shop. School districts make a big difference but so do streets. There may be a highly desirable street in your town where taxes are astronomical, whereas on a little cul-de-sac right off of that street the houses are just as nice, but taxes are much lower.

Relocating to a Retirement Community

Do these two words get you excited? They should. Once upon a time, your immediate response might have been "Ho hum" or "Not me" or even "Yikes!" By the time you are finished with this section, you will be more inclined to think *Love Boat*. Retirement communities these days are some of the most happening, social, and quickly growing spots in America.

Active/independent communities. These are residential spots with no medical or graduated support for seniors. It's an especially good option for couples with a wide age difference, where one is retired and the other still working. Many active communities may not be that different from the neighborhood you just left—you have your own home or apartment, you are surrounded by nice people, and you remain quite independent. There may be a clubhouse to belong to or perhaps a golf course. Your member fees mean that you may not need to deal with headaches like lawn mowing or snow removal, and the community may be gated or have a guard posted at the entrance. On the other hand, there may be some restrictions. These communities are for seniors so the policy toward children might limit the grandkids' visits.

Understanding the Facility's Fees

There are some variations, but most communities require an entrance fee, which must be paid in cash. (It is not something you can finance and is comparable to the cost of a house—from $40,000 all the way up to the millions for luxury properties.) Then residents pay a monthly maintenance fee, which may range from $800 to $5,000 (the high end, again, is the luxury option). The fee includes certain things like some meals and activities. When residents need more help with daily life, staffers attend to them in their own apartments. When their care needs to be stepped up, they move to the assisted-living wing of the residence. When they leave the community, either by choice or death, a portion of their entrance fee is returned to them or to their estate.

Continuing care retirement communities (CCRC). These communities offer the best of both worlds: independence *and* care when you need it. They create an even stronger sense of community than their active/independent counterparts because they usually have more common areas, more activities, and are generally more social. They are like cruise ships or college campuses—you can feel like you are in your own little universe within the grounds. And this can be a great thing. As you age and your care needs change, you won't need to uproot yourself. You will be able to get the care you need either in the same apartment or room or a new one within the same facility. This makes for an easy transition from independence to assisted care during a time of your life that might otherwise be difficult. Entrance levels vary at a CCRC. You usually have the choice to join with an extensive, modified, or fee-for-service contract. The extensive is the most

Retirement Community
Checklist

Before you visit retirement communities to which you're considering moving, make sure to have this list of questions in hand.

Financial

What's the entry fee? Is it refundable?

What is the daily or monthly rate?

Are there charges for additional services you may want or need?

Are utilities, phone, cable, and Internet services included?

Will there be many extras you'll pay for separately?

What type of notice period is required should you need or want to move?

How often are rates for accommodation and/or services increased?

What is the average annual rate of increase over the last few years?

What kinds of opportunities are available for a resident to receive further care as a condition or problem requires?

Is the facility connected with a nursing home or other kind of facility?

What are all the types of housing available (private versus shared, apartment, suite)?

Is the housing furnished? If so, what is included?

Is there a kitchen in your unit?

Are there restrictions on the types and amounts of personal belongings you may bring?

What happens if you are unable to pay for services?

What are the payment, billing, and credit policies?

What to Look for on Your Tour

Lifestyle

What are the admission requirements?

How close is the nearest hospital?

Is the community affiliated with any religious or cultural group?

How close are the churches, parks, and shopping centers?

How accessible is public transportation? Does the community offer it?

Do the residents stay year round? (You don't want to move to Vermont only to discover that the place clears out in the winter, leaving you nearly alone.)

How big is the facility? (Larger facilities may offer more activities, get-togethers, and transportation. Smaller communities may be more intimate and low-key.)

Are pets allowed?

What are your dining options? What kinds of meals are offered?

Can residents bring their own cars?

What are the facility's visiting hours? What types of accommodations are available for visitors? Are there any restrictions on having guests?

Do many residents take part in activities and outings?

How often are each resident's needs reassessed?

Things to Observe on Your Own

How clean is the facility? Does it look good? Does it smell?

How do the residents look? Friendly? Happy?

How do the staff look? Is the staff friendly? Are they courteous?

expensive, as it will cover unlimited long-term nursing care at an agreed-upon price, but if you live a long time, it might be the most economical in the long run. Modified care contracts cover a specific amount of long-term nursing care. Fee-for-service does not include long-term nursing care. It's inexpensive now, but it may not be in the future.

Assisted living. CCRCs include assisted-living accommodations and services, but facilities specifically for assisted living are strictly for people who absolutely do need assistance. Assisted living centers, just like the assisted living programs in CCRCs, offer residents some care with necessities like eating, bathing, dressing, doing chores, and taking medication. Other than these kinds of tasks, residents support themselves. Some medical care will be offered, but it won't be as intensive as what you'd find at a nursing home or hospital. One key difference between CCRCs and assisted living facilities is that in a CCRC you can plan ahead for the level of care you'll get and fix a price. When you enter an assisted living center, you pay for the services you need upon arrival. Deciding which one is right for you depends on your budget, risk tolerance, lifestyle, and health. If you think you'll be just fine on your own for a long time, it might pay to wait until you need an assisted living center. If you like the idea of establishing community ties in advance of your elder years and want to be sure that you'll get coverage however soon you'll need it, then a CCRC sounds like a better match.

Choosing the Right Locale

It may be time-consuming to visit every place you are considering, yet choosing a community is one of the biggest and most expensive decisions you might ever make.

Talk to the residents. It's a good idea to talk to a variety of people at the community. How long have they lived there? Are they happy? Would they change anything if they could? Were they surprised by anything about the place or the lifestyle? Do they have any advice for you?

Sleep over. Ask if you can spend the night. Nothing will give you a better sense of the place than an overnight visit. Make sure you take advantage of everything you can. Join or watch an activity. Try several dining options if possible. Soak up the atmosphere and see as much of the place as you can.

Make a return visit. Visit more than once. See the community in the morning and in the evening. And if you can see it in two different seasons, so much the better.

Make your tour comprehensive. Don't just see the rooms and common areas. Ask to see the treatment rooms, the kitchen, stairwells—as much as you can. Definitely visit the assisted-living accommodations in case you end up needing them.

Get the paperwork. This includes menus, activities lists, calendars, and other paperwork that will give you a sense of the lifestyle, as well as contracts and admission paperwork.

Hire a consultant. There are firms that will help you make this important decision. You will pay a fee for their services, of course, but considering the investment you'll be making, it may be well worth it.

Setting Up Residence in Another State

Moving is one of the most exciting adventures you can have at any age. And many seniors, when they start to think about downsizing, decide to not only move to a new home, but to a new state. And we're not just talking about snowbirds moving from the Northeast to Florida. Seniors these days are moving to some surprising places (Asheville, North Carolina, and Madison, Wisconsin, come to mind)—and loving it. Before you consider a move, make sure you figure out what you are looking for and determine which locations will best meet your changing needs. Here are some guidelines.

Job market. If you are planning to work in retirement, you need to keep an eye on the job market in your field. Is the economy where you are considering moving vibrant or sluggish? Is there a need for your skills in that market? Is there something else you'd like to do that will be supported by the local economy better?

Cost of living. What will it cost to live in a new state? Hawaii sounds great, but what do homes cost? The national median price of a home is about $215,000. How do the homes in your dream city compare? What does food cost? How are the taxes? And what is the price of a plane ticket to Georgia, where the grandkids are living? Make sure you do your homework and consider lifestyle factors. For instance, if you think you want to live on a farm someplace, figure out how long it will take you get to the grocery store. If you are moving from a city, you might be surprised by the amount of gas and automotive wear-and-tear from simple shopping tasks.

Taxes. Do you want to move to a state that has low taxes? Try Alaska, Florida, Nevada, South Dakota, Texas, Washington, and Wyoming. These states have no personal income tax. Consider New Hampshire and Tennessee, too; these tax only income from investments, not wages. If you love to shop, realize that five states don't have sales tax: Alaska, Montana, Delaware, New Hampshire, and Oregon. If you like the South and you don't like to pay property tax, then consider Alabama and Arkansas, which have some of the lowest property taxes in the country.

Early Bird Secret

Move within Shouting Distance

If the idea of making a big move is unappealing, then what about a small one? For example, if your primary residence is in New York City, you could be paying state and city taxes equal to 11 percent of your income, and that's not including federal taxes. Moving just 70 miles northeast to Pennsylvania could cut that state tax bill to less than 5 percent. You'd be just a pleasant day trip away from your old neighborhood and would save a bundle in the process.

Family. Most seniors say that they don't want to live more than three hours away from family. How close you want to stay to your family might be a big factor for you. Do you like flying to visit family and have the means for it? Do you prefer to drive? Will the family be more likely to want to visit you in one location versus another? Can you afford an extra guest room for visiting family and friends in one location over another?

Safety. How safe is the place you want to move to? Is there crime? What kind is it? Crime against people? Property? The housing bust has left many once-affluent neighborhoods abandoned. You may be able to get a good deal on a house, but is it really a good deal if you are worried about getting mugged when you walk to the mailbox?

Your lifestyle. Do you long to live someplace warm? Do you never want to use a windshield ice scraper again or shovel a walkway? The most popular sunshine states for seniors have consistently been Florida, California, Arizona, North Carolina, and Texas. You might be longing for rugged outdoorsy pursuits instead. Many people are drawn to states like Colorado, Washington, Idaho, Utah, Wyoming, West Virginia, and Tennessee. They cite the skiing, hiking, clean air, and absence of crowds as major attractions. Are you a city mouse or a country mouse? It used to be that retirees fled to the country. Now they are as likely to choose a city to settle down in. Cities are filled with places to go and people to see, and most have excellent public transit systems, which can make all the difference between a social butterfly and a hermit crab.

Entertainment and culture. Are there museums? Theaters? Golf courses? Public parks? How's the shopping? Is there a university nearby? Make sure you have a sense of what you'll do in your free time and that your hobbies dovetail nicely with what your home has to offer.

Medical care. As you age, you will likely need increased medical care. Can your new town offer what you might need? Make sure it will, especially if you already have health conditions that require care.

Is Moving Out of State a Good Idea for You?

The excitement of moving is undeniable. Before you move far away from where you are now, ask yourself these questions to make sure it really is the right choice for you.

Are you happy where you are now? If you are perfectly happy where you are now, what is the point of moving? If it's to save money, then perhaps there are other steps you can take that will ensure you can stay in your familiar stomping grounds. Make sure that you are not thinking of moving just because "everyone is doing it" or it seems like that's what you're supposed to do when you retire. Now is the time to do exactly what *you* want.

Are you active in and attached to your community?

If you are one of the regulars at your coffee shop, if you founded the local model airplane association, if you play senior softball twice a week, then maybe you are a joiner and would find similar events and ties wherever you move. Or maybe you have lived in your town for so long that you know everyone and feel really comfortable there. Some social butterflies thrive anywhere they go; others need the familiarity of their own garden. Which are you?

Have your friends moved away? Sometimes there seems to be a mass exodus from the neighborhood as friends retire and move away after their kids grow up. If this has happened to you, maybe you would be happier elsewhere. Sometimes neighbors retire together. If it doesn't matter where you live as long as you are among friends, then it might make sense to move with everyone else to the same area in Florida. If you find that you are making new friends in your old town, then it might be worth staying and just visiting your old friends a few times a year.

Is there someplace you've always wanted to live? If you have been deferring your dream of a bungalow in Los Angeles or a Cape Cod on, well, Cape Cod, then maybe now is the perfect time to indulge yourself. Search your heart and see if there is a tug pulling toward something you have always leaned toward. Then make sure you do the research before you take the leap.

Extraordinary
Savings

A *to* **Z**

In today's challenging economic climate, there are thousands of ways that seniors can save money besides simply getting a discount from merchants or big corporations. Use our A to Z guide to find innovative Early Bird ideas that will help put money back *in* your pocket. You'll discover ways to save every day, every week, every month, and every year. What type of baking dish should you use for maximum energy savings? How can you save big on a bag of potatoes at the grocery store? What does your television have to do with cooling costs? Can you make your newspaper subscription pay you back? Try any combination of these endlessly savvy tips, and you'll be amazed by the amount of money you've easily and painlessly put back in the bank.

Air conditioner

Don't work alone. Team up your air conditioner with a ceiling fan to spread cool air throughout the room. Using both at the same time lets you raise the air conditioner temperature by five degrees, which in turn lowers your cooling costs.

Stick with the program. Install a programmable thermostat for your air conditioner and cut down on your utility bill. Set it for several degrees warmer at night or when no one is home; you can save up to 10 percent on your cooling costs for every degree above 78 you raise the thermostat.

Don't light up your thermostat. Keep heat-generating appliances like lamps, computers, and televisions away from your air-conditioning thermostat. Their heat will trick the air conditioner into running longer.

Keep it clear. Make sure your air-conditioning vents are not blocked by furniture or other obstructions. (You don't want to pay to cool the back of your couch!)

Seal the leaks. Save on cooling costs by keeping the cool air you've paid for in your house. Seal or caulk dryer vents, pipes entering the house, and electrical outlets as well as drafty windows and doors. You'll keep warm air inside in the winter, too.

Shoot for the sky. Aim the vents of your room air conditioner at the ceiling, and let the cool air float down to you. You'll get more bang for your cooling buck (by cooling the room from top to bottom, rather than in just one spot), plus you'll have better air circulation as the cold air drifts down.

Airfare

Fly on Tuesdays, Wednesdays, and Saturdays. You'll generally find cheaper fares on these days. And be flexible about departure times and alternative airports, too—you'll save even more if you can accommodate the airlines' quirky schedules.

Take a companion. Look for special offers that allow you to bring a companion for half price. If it's a friend (and not your spouse, say), offer to split the savings you can get by booking two tickets together.

Wait until the last minute. This isn't normally sage advice for travelers, but it can work well for those with flexible schedules looking to save money on airfare (as well as hotels and cruises). Check out Travelzoo. com, SmarterTravel.com, 11thHourVacations. com, and LastMinuteTravel.com for good deals for procrastinators.

Night owls save on flights.

Book the best airfare just after midnight, East Coast time, when airlines cut prices on flights that are less than full. Calling your airline late at night can save you from $50 to $400.

Air freshener

Use a towel, not a spray can. Don't spend money on chemical scents that make you sneeze! You can eliminate odors in your house by soaking a hand towel in white vinegar, wringing it out completely, and swinging it over your head like a lasso a few times. You'll save the cost of air freshener and get a little exercise, too.

Alternative medicine

Make alternate arrangements. Surprisingly enough, alternative medicine—including acupuncture and massage therapy—may be less expensive than traditional treatments for some chronic health problems (depending on your insurance plan). Check your insurance policy for details.

Antacid

Don't be sour. Forget about spending money on antacid at the pharmacy next time you have heartburn, acid indigestion, sour stomach, or an upset stomach. Simply mix 1/2 teaspoon of baking soda into 1/2 cup of water (4 fluid ounces) until the baking soda dissolves completely. Then drink up for more settled times.

Appliances

The price will floor you. Ask your appliance retailer if you can buy the floor model of the appliance you want for a reduced price.

Don't be a fan. Shop for major purchases like appliances during sporting events like the Super Bowl or the World Series. Stores will be empty, and the salespeople will be ready and willing to negotiate so they can rack up some sales. You may easily knock at least 2 percent off the original purchase price of whatever you want to buy.

Art

Book it. Frame pictures from art books or magazines (that you own, of course) to spruce up your walls. Look for nice inexpensive frames to highlight your masterpieces.

Be faithful—to your bank.

Take money out of only your bank's ATM machine. You can be charged up to $3 by your bank for taking money out of another bank's machine, and then be charged again by the other bank. Don't pay another bank for access to *your* money.

ATM machine

Take only what you need. On average, consumers withdraw $60 per week from an ATM machine. And most consumers have no idea where that money goes. Figure out how much cash you really need each week, and take *only* that amount out of the ATM. You won't overspend because you won't have extra money in your wallet.

Bath

Just say no. Test the amount of water you use in a shower and compare it to the amount you use in a bath. Next time you shower, plug the bathtub and see how much water fills the tub. If there's less water than in your normal bath, you'll save money by taking a shower. Remember: an average bath uses 30 to 50 gallons of water, while a four-minute shower with a low-flow shower head uses only 10 gallons. Take short showers and save.

Battery

Baking soda for your car battery. Your car battery needs to be clean to keep working. You can remove corrosion and keep the battery clean with a mixture of 1 tablespoon baking soda and 1 cup of water. Use the solution to wash the outside of the battery (being careful not to let it get into the battery). Rinse it off with clean water and wipe to dry.

Belt

Cut it down to size. Don't toss a belt that no longer fits or doesn't work with your clothes. Size it to fit your pet as a collar.

Birdbath

Give the birds a bath (without taking one). Ignore fancy and expensive birdbaths at your garden or birding store. Just fashion an equally useful birdbath from an old pan on top of a flowerpot. Fill it with water and watch the birds flock to it.

Blinds

Be neutral. Buy blinds in a neutral color. You'll still be able to use them later if you change the color scheme of the room you're decorating now.

Books

Round up reading material. There's no need to buy books when you want to read something new. Organize an ongoing book swap with your church or a social or community group. Everyone brings in their latest and greatest reads and swaps them for others. Keep the books on an accessible shelf; you may need several shelves if your collection is a success!

Buy the latest bestselling books for half off.

Split the cost of one book with a friend (preferably at a discount), and give it to her to read when you've finished it. Then buy another one with the same friend, and let her read it first. It's like having your own private book club!

Boots and Shoes

Protect your sole. Make your boots and all your shoes last 10 times longer by going from the shoe store to the shoe repair and having sole protectors or heel and toe taps put on your new footwear. The protectors cost less than $20 and potentially save you hundreds since it's usually the soles that wear out first.

Let your footwear breathe. Don't store any shoes or boots in the attic or the basement during the off-season. The shifts in temperature will prematurely age them.

Place them in a closet that allows air to circulate and they'll last longer, saving you money and (yet another) a trip to the store.

Bottles as boot trees. Prolong the life of your boots by storing them with unusual boot trees. Put a clean, empty 1-liter soda bottle in each boot to help it retain its shape. You won't have to pay for boot trees or new boots.

Buttons

Old buttons, new look. Keep nice, fancy, or unusual buttons when you recycle or toss worn-out clothing. You can use them to change the look of a garment that's starting to bore you or to enliven a plain shirt that needs a little pizzazz.

Calendar

Save $15 by getting a calendar for free. Where? Try banks, insurance agencies, card stores, and your mail—you may find calendars from charities you support as well as from businesses you've used.

Candles

Keep your candles cold. Store your candles in the freezer for a longer burn life.

Car

Don't waste by waiting. If you plan to wait for someone in your idling car for more than one minute, turn the car off to save gas. You'll use less fuel starting up the car than leaving it on for even this short a time.

Warm your heart, not your car.

Today's cars do not need to be warmed up for more than 30 seconds. You car will warm up as you drive. If you warm it up in the driveway, you're just wasting gas.

Be an oily bird. Always ask your local lube center if it offers a senior discount or a multicar deal on oil changes. If it doesn't, keep asking until you find one that does.

Car wash

Fill up and wash up. Some gas stations offer free or cut-rate car washes when you stop to get gas.

Carpet

Go to pieces. Next time you need to replace your carpet, think about using carpet tiles for busy areas such as hallways and entryways. If a piece of the carpet gets stained or worn, you can simply replace the tile, rather than the whole carpet.

Pay more to pay less. Invest in a good-quality pad for under your carpet. It will protect the carpet from wear and tear, and let you buy a less expensive carpet.

Carpet cleaner

Salt it away. Don't use an expensive carpet cleaner next time you experience a nasty red wine spill on your carpet. Save that $5 to $10 and simply pour a pile of good old table salt on the spill. Leave the salt on until it dries, and then vacuum it up. The stain is gone!

Sprinkle on seltzer.

As soon as food hits your rug, wipe up the excess and then sprinkle it liberally with seltzer or club soda. Scrub with a brush, sprinkling on more seltzer or soda as needed. Blot dry with a towel.

Share it and save. Rent a carpet-cleaning machine for you and a neighbor, and split the cost. You can save big on a one-day rental.

Cash

Stash the cash. Cutting impulse spending can save big bucks, so if this is your personal bugaboo, try keeping only $20 to $40 in your wallet. The less you have in cash, the less you're likely to spend on impulse purchases. That $4 latte at the coffee shop will look a lot less appealing if it leaves you with only $16 for the rest of the day!

Cash register

Watch it like a hawk. Cash registers, as well as humans, make errors, so watch the register carefully to make sure it rings up the right price for the right item. You might get overcharged if the register mistakes your cream cheese for brie or if it hasn't been programmed with the current sale prices. Many grocery stores will give the item for free or at a sharp discount if the register (whether operated by a cashier or you on a self-checkout line) charges you the wrong amount.

Cat

It's the cat's meow. Save on vet bills by adding 1/8 to 1/4 teaspoon of olive oil to your cat's food. It will help prevent hairballs and keep your cat's digestive system purring along.

Cell phone

Talk *isn't* cheap. The average cell phone user faces a $60 bill each month, including taxes and miscellaneous fees. If you talk less than 200 minutes a month, you may be better off using a pay-as-you-go plan (as long as it charges 25 cents a minute or less). You can easily save $45 a month with a prepaid plan.

Extend your battery life. Try to run your battery out before recharging, at least every other time, for the longest battery life. Avoid buying a new cell phone battery and give your electric bill a break in the process by shutting your cell phone off before you go to sleep. Just remember to turn it back on in the morning!

Get the senior plan.

Verizon and AT&T both advertise a relatively inexpensive national senior cell-phone plan, but if you're buying your phone and setting up service with a regional carrier, be sure to ask about senior offers. If they say no, remind them that two of the majors have senior plans—one may be forthcoming for you.

Checks

Check it off your list. Is your bank charging a lot for printing your checks? If so, check out independent printers: most of them charge about half what your bank does for the same service. Try Checks Unlimited (800-210-0468 or www.checksunlimited.com) or Checks in the Mail (800-733-4443 or www.checksinthemail.com) or do an Internet search for "personal check printers," which will turn you up an additional range of printers such as www.checkswithstyle.com or www.checkworks.com. If you've ever wanted checks with John Deere tractors on them, an independent printer is the way to go!

Chicken

Buy it whole. Never buy chicken parts when you can buy the whole thing and make more meals from it, for pennies on the pound. Forget about fancy butchering: using strong kitchen shears, cut the chicken up the breast bone, up the back bone, and then cut those halves in half again. Cut off wings and legs, and you now have the kind of pieces that you'd pay hefty bucks for. Never again!

Coffee

Treat yourself—to a gift card. Buying a premium coffee regularly is the bugaboo of personal finance advisers, who see it as the ultimate waste of money, but it *is* okay to get one now and then. (Let's face it, they can be pretty tasty!) If you're inclined to overdo, buy a gift card for yourself for a budgeted amount each month, and enjoy every frothy, flavored cupful until the card runs out.

Cut the cost of home-brewed gourmet coffee. Even coffee made at home can be expensive, if you have expensive coffee tastes in fancy beans and roast. But you can mix the pleasure with savings if you combine one part of your favorite gourmet coffee with one part of a much less expensive store brand, and enjoy your high-end coffee tastes at a fraction of the cost.

Turn off the pot.

Nothing's better than a leisurely morning and a bottomless cup of coffee, but warming the coffee pot all morning isn't good for your electric bill—or your coffee, which will take on a flat, bitter flavor as all the essential oils evaporate. Brew directly into a thermal pot or pour your fresh-brewed coffee into a thermos, then turn off the coffee maker, and treasure your savings.

Pretend it's a day at the office. Even if you're drinking your coffee at home, think about buying it at an office supply superstore, such as Staples or Office Depot. You may find substantial savings on hot chocolate, tea, coffee, creamer, and sugar at the same place you get a good deal on your pencils and printer ink.

Coins

Hoard loose change. Dump your loose change into a jar at the end of every day, and once every six months or so (or while you can still lift the jar!), bring your change to a local bank that has a coin-counting machine. It's important to take them to a bank, which likely won't charge you a fee for the counting, rather than to one of the commercial coin-counting machines you see in grocery stores, which will deduct 10 percent of your hard-earned change. Ka-ching!

Computer

Think small to save big. Buy a laptop computer: it uses less energy than an Energy Star-rated desktop computer and monitor. A typical laptop draws from 15 to 25 watts when being used, while a conventional PC and monitor draw 150 watts. You'll be pleased with the evidence on your utility bill.

Go to sleep. Your computer continues to use energy even when you're not using it. In fact, you can cut its power demand by up to 90 percent if you make it automatically "sleep" after 20 or 30 minutes of non-use. (See your manual for programming instructions—it's usually a simple adjustment.) And when you finish a session of Internet surfing or e-mailing, turn it off altogether.

Confetti

Celebrate the savings. There's nothing more festive than a handful of confetti at a party, but don't spend money buying little bits of paper. Save leftover wrapping paper—even small pieces will work—and let your grandchildren use a hole punch or little scissors to create lots of circles or squares of colorful confetti. Use your homegrown confetti to celebrate family birthdays, News Year's Eve, or any happy occasion. (You can even vacuum it up into a clean hand vac to use again!)

Consignment shop

Pick your target carefully. One obvious way to cut back on clothing costs is to check out consignments shops. But don't choose just *any* consignment shop: find one close to a wealthy neighborhood, where you may be surprised at finding stacks of hardly or never-worn clothes, many from top designers and some items with the tags still on. You'll get amazing bargains on extraordinary clothes you won't find elsewhere.

Contact lenses

See your way through the mail. Save up to 50 percent on contact lenses and more on the necessary accessories (fluid and cleaning apparatus) by ordering through the mail.

You can order the exact type of lenses you currently wear—not a lesser brand—at a substantial discount by phone at 1-800-Contacts or online at www.1800contacts.com

Container gardening

Skimp on the soil. Save money on potting soil by using only as much as your plant needs—not what the deep container dictates. Put broken-up polystyrene chunks or packing "peanuts" at the bottom of the pot (making sure to keep the drainage hole clear), then add enough potting soil for your plant. You'll benefit from a lighter pot as well as a heavier wallet, and you'll find your pot drains better when it's not heavily packed with soil down to the bottom.

Create your own container.

You don't need to be restricted by traditional containers when choosing pots for your container gardening. Think about apple boxes, tin or colorful plastic buckets, bushel baskets, funky Italian tomato cans, an old trunk—any container that can have drainage holes drilled in the bottom.

Cottage cheese

Turn it on its head. Store your container of cottage cheese upside down in the refrigerator. It will last twice as long as if stored right side up.

Credit card

Edit your credit. Lose the temptation to spend by locking away your credit cards. Don't cancel them (it can hurt your credit score); instead, put them in a drawer, keeping only one in your wallet.

Dentist

Find a tooth trainee. If there's a local dental school near you, you may be able to get free or almost-free dental checkups and work done by supervised students (assuming your teeth are in good condition). Call to ask about the school's policy and go in for a cleaning to assess the school and see if you're comfortable. Chances are you can get excellent care for a fraction of the usual price.

Have a plan. Consider getting a dental plan rather than dental insurance. You pay an annual fee, ranging from $100 to $150, and get a 20 to 60 percent discount from participating dentists. Visit www.discount-dental.net or www.dentalplans.com to get more information and sign up.

Dentures

Do it yourself. Don't spend money over and over on expensive denture cleaning products. You can clean dentures easily and inexpensively at home with a soft toothbrush and a teaspoon of baking soda. Scrub gently and rinse in clear water. Then place the dentures in a small, microwave-proof container just big enough to hold them (a coffee mug, for example) and cover them with water. Add a tablespoon of white vinegar and microwave on high for two minutes. Allow to cool in the solution overnight, then in the morning rinse and wear. You can only do this if your dentures have *no metal parts*, but the microwave will kill bacteria far more effectively than anything you can buy.

Deodorant

Smell the savings. Save a fast few bucks by dusting baking soda under your arms instead of using commercial deodorant.

Detangler

Tame your hair for the price of conditioning it. Make your conditioner work overtime as a detangler. Simply mix 1 part conditioner with 5 parts water and spray the mixture on your wet hair, then comb. You'll be impressed by the versatility of your conditioner!

Directory assistance

411 for free. If you don't mind listening to a few ads, dial 1-800-373-3411 for free directory assistance. You'll save up to $2.50 per call.

Google it. Don't listen to a single ad. Dial 1-800-GOOG-411 (1-800-466-4411), say the place and number you're looking for, and Google can either give you the number or connect you directly—for free!

Try toll-free. Stop spending any money on phone calls that should be free. If you're calling any sort of national corporation and you don't have a toll-free number, call 1-800-555-1212 for free 800 directory assistance.

Discount store

Give it a hug. Discount stores tempt you not only with their excellent bargains, but also with their "I don't know what I was thinking when I bought this" impulse buys. How can you avoid these temptations? Avoid the shopping cart. Buy only what you can carry in your arms. You'll end up buying only what you really need and want.

Dishes

Pile it on. When you're stacking your dishes, use flattened coffee filters or paper towels between them (you can use the same ones over and over). You'll help prevent scratches and chips, which will make your dishes last longer, and you won't have to pay for overpriced "plate protectors."

Dishwasher

Laziness can pay off. Let your dishwasher do all the work. Wait until the machine is full to run it. Then happily note that if you had washed the dishes by hand, you would have used about two-thirds more water.

Let the disposal help the dishwasher. Prevent clogs in your dishwasher—and a plumber's bill—by running cold water through your disposal for 30 seconds before you use your dishwasher. The water will flush out any garbage caught in the disposal, which otherwise could get drawn into the dishwasher's drain line and possibly block it.

Disposal

Vinegar ice is nice for your disposal. Now and then, feed your garbage disposal a few frozen cubes of white vinegar and then flush with cold water after grinding. You'll help keep the disposal free of clogs and slow drains—and expensive repairs. The vinegar will also keep odors at bay.

Doctor

No longer the doctor's "office." You don't have to go to the doctor's office to get good medical help these days. Try going to CVS, Target, and Wal-Mart, many of which have opened in-store clinics, often run by nurse-practitioners. You don't need an appointment, and you'll get a diagnosis for about $25 to $60 (plus a prescription if you need one)—far less than a typical doctor's office visit.

Dollar bill

Go the paper route. Stop spending coins; they make you think you're not spending much. Instead, use only paper currency to buy everything, and put the change from all your daily purchases into a change bucket. You'll be likely to spend less and can save at least $20 a month with this trick.

Dry cleaning

Don't get taken to the cleaners. In fact, you can make out well with dry cleaners if you know when to go. Take in your drapes and bed linens in January, July, or August, when business is slow. Your local cleaner may offer a discount of around 15 percent on large items (or you can always ask for your senior discount if one isn't advertised); since drapes and bed linens can cost several hundred dollars to clean, you'll come out smelling like a rose.

Dryer

Keep it light. Dry lightweight fabrics with lightweight fabrics; save heavier fabrics for another load. The lightweight fabrics will dry faster when they're alone, so they'll spend less time in the dryer. You'll save time, energy, and money.

Keep it clean. A dirty lint filter forces your dryer to use 30 percent more energy to dry clothes. Clean the lint filter after every load and save a bundle.

Let it all hang out.

Try to use your dryer as infrequently as possible. Instead, hang your clothes on a clothes rack or clothesline to dry. Grandmother's ways were best! You'll save money on electricity, and your clothes (particularly those that contain elastic) will last longer, too.

Not the time for the timer. Stop using the timer when you dry your clothes. You can cut down on energy use by about 15 percent by using the moisture sensor instead. Besides, drying already dry clothes—which happens when you use the timer—can stress your clothes and reduce their lifespan.

Dryer sheet

Cut your softener in half. Half a dryer sheet works just as well as a whole one, so cut the sheet in half, and soften two loads for the price of one.

Don't just soften: clean! Put your used dryer sheets to work: dust your TV and computer screens, clean Venetian blinds, polish your bathroom taps, and wipe dry tile surfaces. You can even put them in shoes, wastebaskets, and laundry hampers for a fresh smell. You'll save money on all kinds of cleaning supplies.

DVD

A quart of milk, a burger, and…a movie? Looking to rent a recently released film? Free-standing video and DVD rental stores are falling by the wayside of new media and new ways to get films to customers. Check out your local grocery store or fast-food restaurant, where you can rent a new release from a Redbox kiosk for $1. If you typically rent one DVD a week, you can save up to $20 per month at a kiosk. Check out redbox.com to find a location near you.

Get it online and in the mail. Netflix has revolutionized movie rentals by mailing DVDs (with no shipping fee) to customers, who mail them back in a prepaid envelope when they're done. For a flat fee of $8.99 a month, you can get one DVD at a time, as many as you want in a month (they send the next one out when the first one is returned, typically in one business day), as well as unlimited viewing of online movies directly

through your computer, dispensing with the DVD and the mail altogether. Go to www.netflix.com and check out the movie rental of the future!

Check it out. Most large libraries now have a DVD section that offers an excellent selection of up-to-date and classic movies that can be checked out on your regular library card (although you may not find the very latest releases). The rules vary depending on your branch, but generally you can check out as many DVDs as you want for one week, with steep-for-a-library fines, such as $1 per day, beginning on the eighth day. So get those DVDs returned on time and take out a fresh batch!

Education

Study with the experts. Book groups are always a good way to learn about many topics, and the book groups at Barnes & Noble Book Clubs offer you an opportunity to learn from authors and experts—for free! Here you'll find a history book club, a mystery book club, a book club devoted to literature by women, and more. See what interests you at www.barnesandnoble.com/bookclubs.

Electrician

Save on service calls. Unless you have an electrical emergency, don't call the electrician every time you need something fixed. Since you pay a set (and often high) price for each service call, you'll save by having several tasks done at once.

Electronics

Keep the vampires at bay. Electronics and appliances that sport clocks or work by a remote use electricity, even when you're not using them. Chargers do, too. In fact, 40 percent of the energy used to run home electronics is devoured when these energy vampires aren't turned off! So literally pull the plug and pull down your energy costs.

'Tis the season to scoop up returns...and savings. Shop the clearance section of electronics stores after the holidays. It's a good time to find open-box merchandise or other returned items that can't be sold for full price. You may just find a very merry bargain!

Do some due diligence. A little research can pay you back in spades when it comes to buying new electronics. Whether you're ready for a new TV or you want to buy the grandkids the cutting-edge toy of the moment, go to www.google.com and click on "Shopping" at the top of the page. Type in the name of the item you want in the resulting search box, and Google will instantly pull up a list of all the prices for that item that can be found on the Internet, making comparison shopping a breeze!

Entertainment

The more the merrier. Find friends, colleagues, neighbors, and relatives who like the kinds of entertainment you like, and attend concerts, sporting events, and exhibitions for less. Just buy your tickets in bulk, and you'll score a 10 percent (or higher) discount.

Look up savings at the library. You know you can borrow books, CDs, DVDs, magazines, and even more at your library for free, but the library is also the place to find free or discounted passes to local zoos, museums, aquariums, and gardens. Stop by to see how entertaining your library can be.

Save in different seasons. Check out free concerts sponsored by your local community during the summer. During the holidays, look for free concerts at churches and colleges.

Usher in the arts.

Save up to $300 on season tickets to the symphony, opera, ballet, or theater by working as an usher at your local performance hall. Simply call the hall and ask if you can usher, or search the Internet with the words "volunteer," "usher," and the name of your town.

Practice, practice, practice. Many orchestras and other performing arts groups open their rehearsals to the public, free of charge. Find out what's available in your community, and pocket the cost of the performance.

Try out the tunes. Why spend money on an album when you don't know which tracks you'll like? Instead, tune in to Pandora.com and listen to hours of music you know you'll enjoy for free. Simply enter the name of the singer or the song you like, and Pandora will provide you with similar songs. You'll hear music you want, and the price is right.

Sign up for the season. If you plan to attend many symphony concerts, you should probably buy season tickets at senior rates—you'll pay less per ticket and get better seating. But because season tickets can get expensive, consider splitting the cost (and the number of concerts) with a friend. The same idea applies to theater and sporting events.

Exercise

Go back to school. Enroll in an academic class at a nearby community college, then use your college ID to exercise at the college gym. Even if your class costs $60, you'll save hundreds on your annual gym membership.

Wear Silver Sneakers. Check out www.silversneakers.com to find the nearest health club that participates in the Silver Sneakers program, which is covered by most Medicare health plans. If your plan covers it,

all you have to do is enroll at the health club. Most participating gyms and clubs also offer a senior adviser to help you get started and keep you on track.

A school with a pool. Does your local high school or middle school have a nice pool or gym? Your school district may offer memberships to use one or the other at off-hours, and some may let neighbors use the gym for free. Even if the school district imposes a fee, it's probably less for residents than non-residents—and be sure to ask if there's a senior discount!

Ride those (membership) cycles. If there's no Silver Sneakers gym that's convenient, watch the ads to get the best rates. Some gyms discount memberships at certain times each year. Some offer anniversary sales, while others cut their enrollment fees at the end of certain months to meet monthly quotas. Still others offer free enrollment to tie in to special times during the year, like Breast Cancer Awareness Month.

Clean or garden your way to health. You may never have thought of vacuuming or raking as good exercise, but you should. Depending on your weight (and your physical ability—don't overdo it!) one hour of serious housework can burn 172 calories, while washing and vacuuming your car for 40 minutes can consume 177 calories. Spend 20 minutes raking and you've burned 78 calories. Best of all, garden for one hour and you can burn 320 calories. Now, that's a savings on health club fees!

Pay up front. If you're trying to get serious about exercise (and equally serious about savings), sign up for a series of group classes or a number of sessions with a personal trainer. With or without a senior discount, you should be able to get at least 10 percent off the cost of individual classes or sessions.

Try out your workout. Many gyms offer a free pass, good for a week or two, that lets you try out their facilities before you sign up for membership. The pass works well on two levels: you get to see if the exercise club offers what you want, and you learn quickly if you're the type of person who will actually use a gym once you buy a membership. If the gym doesn't live up to your standards or you think you won't frequent the gym, pass on the membership and keep your money.

Get in on the ground floor. Keep your eyes open for new health clubs. You may be able to sign up for a heavily discounted membership if you're one of the first members.

Eyeglasses

Nail polish for your eyes. Next time you tighten the screw on your glasses (to avoid even bigger trouble), add a spot of clear nail polish across the top of the screw. Your fix will last longer—and your glasses will, too.

Buy two, pay less. Ask for a discount from your eyeglass provider if you plan to buy two pairs of frames at a time. You may even get a higher percentage off than the senior discount already provides.

Think inside the (big) box.

Check out warehouse clubs when you're checking out glasses. You'll be amazed by the selection, quality, and—above all—price. You can easily find a complete pair of glasses (frames and lenses) for under $150, about half what it would cost elsewhere. Be sure to ask if a senior discount can shave even more off the price.

Fan

Use your fan to keep you warm. Ceiling fans are energy-efficient lifesavers in the summer, but did you know that they're equally helpful in the winter? Use the reverse setting on your fan to push the warm air at the ceiling level back down to you.

Let it rest. Your bathroom fan may be doing more harm than good in the winter, if you let it run too long. According to the Department of Energy, a bathroom fan can suck all the nicely warmed air out of your house in just one hour. So give your fan and your furnace and your wallet a break.

Farmers' market

Shop often—and late. Farmers' markets have the freshest produce and good deals— but you can get even better deals if you shop late in the day. Sellers don't want to bring unsold produce back home, so they often sell their inventory at reduced prices before the market closes. You may find sweet savings of up to 80 percent.

Flowers

Send flowers long-distance, but save by going local. Bypass excessive shipping and processing charges from national floral services and order flowers from a florist in the recipient's town. Find the names and phone numbers of local florists by visiting locateaflowershop.com or try 1-800-GOOG-411, the free phone information service, and say the name of the town and "florist."

Chill your flowers. If you're spending money on cut flowers, you want them to brighten your home for as long as possible. Trim the stems, change the water daily, and put them in the refrigerator when you're asleep or at work. They'll last longer.

Preserve the beauty. Some fresh-cut flowers come with a little packet of preservative to add to the water, but if yours didn't, make your own by putting 2 teaspoons of sugar and 1 teaspoon of bleach in a quart of lukewarm water. The flowers will last for many days longer.

Freezer

Keep it full. Stock your freezer with water-filled plastic jugs if it isn't full. The frozen jugs will make your freezer more efficient (and your energy money well spent). Plus, you'll always have fresh water in a power outage.

Frosting

Bag it, freeze it, squeeze it. Don't toss leftover frosting. Put it into a small, strong plastic bag and throw it in the freezer. Next time you need to decorate baked goods, defrost the bag, mix a little water with the frosting, cut a small opening in a corner of the bag, and use it like a professional cake decorator!

Frozen food

Flash-freeze some savings. Yes, frozen food can be more expensive than dishes you make yourself, but it's a bargain compared to takeout or restaurant meals. If you eat out once or twice a week, skipping the restaurant meals and eating a fancy frozen meal instead can easily save you $20.

Buy frozen blueberries in season.

When fresh blueberries are in season, that's the time to also consider buying the frozen variety. Grocers often mark down frozen blueberries—and frozen versions of other fruits and vegetables—when they're in peak season.

Funeral

Think it through. Write down exactly what you want done for your funeral, memorial service, or burial arrangement. You'll save your family or estate money—they won't purchase what you didn't want—as well as additional grief by planning ahead.

Go yellow to save green. Do you know what your options are when planning your funeral? Most people don't. Look in the Yellow Pages of your phone book under "Funeral Services" for a local funeral consumer association, which will give you information about the least expensive options—options that could save you several thousand dollars. If you can't find it in your phone book, search online for "Funeral Consumers Alliance."

Get the information now. Don't choose a funeral home until you've either called several to compare prices of similar services or visited some to get an itemized price list. According to the government, you are entitled to this information by law.

Go to a discount price club for a casket. Yes, it's true: you can buy your casket online through a warehouse club, the same place you buy your paper towels in bulk. And you'll save money on it, too. Not all warehouse stores offer this service, but check online and you may turn up some significant savings.

Furnace

Stay in tune and save 10 percent. Get your furnace tuned up every two years. You can save about 10 percent on your heating bills if you maintain it correctly.

Filter out inefficiency. Keep your furnace running at maximum efficiency by changing the filter every two months, not once a season. Filters are cheap and easy to change—slip the old one out, slip the new one in. You can usually get a better deal if you buy them in multipacks at your local big-box store.

Furniture

Design your price. When buying big items like furniture, a senior discount may be harder to find. So find your own discount: You may not be a professional designer, but you can still ask for the designer's discount—usually 10 to 15 percent off. If the answer is no, request free delivery or a free trial period for the piece you've selected.

Try two for one. If you're shopping for a couch but could use a chair too, ask the salesperson what kind of deal you can get if you buy both. You may be able to score a worthwhile price break.

Garden gloves

Clean, not green. Buy an inexpensive pair of gardening gloves to cut down on cleaning costs. Use them to wipe dust and dirt from window blinds and shutters. Unlike expensive cleaning wipes, you can toss them in the laundry and use them again and again.

Gas

Join the online traffic. Visit GasBuddy.com, a Web site that monitors gas prices. Simply type in your zip code or city and state, and GasBuddy.com will tell you where you will find the least expensive gas near you. If you're able to save 20 cents a gallon, you'll pocket up to $12 per month.

Avoid wealthy neighborhood gas stations.

Not only do gas stations in these places pass the higher costs of the land beneath them on to the customer, the local residents might be a little less price sensitive—so the gas stations are more likely to charge more for their gas.

Follow the crowd. Avoid lonely gas stations in general and lonely gas stations off the highway in particular. They'll charge you more than gas stations at busy intersections or in bustling areas, where several are fighting to fill up your car.

Think ahead and save. Try to anticipate traffic flow and avoid quickly accelerating or braking. Steady driving can increase your fuel economy by as much as 20 percent.

Take the pedal *off* the metal. Drive 55 mph rather than 65 mph, and you'll burn 15 percent less gas per mile. And with today's gas prices, that 10 mph can easily translate into a savings of $200 or more per year.

Cruise to savings. Use cruise control and let the steady rate help improve your mileage by 7 percent (unless you're driving through lots of hills).

Pump it up. Make sure your tires are properly inflated. Check your owner's manual or the door jamb of your car for the correct PSI (pounds per square inch). Even one tire under-inflated by 2 PSI will increase your fuel consumption by 1 percent.

Get extra credit for filling up. Sign up for a credit card that gives you cash back for spending your hard-earned money at the gas pump. There are still a few cards out there that give you up to 5 percent back on gas and car maintenance costs.

Take the junk out of the trunk. Try to carry as light a load as possible in your car. Take out the shovel, the bags of salt, and any other heavy objects in your trunk. You'll increase your fuel economy by decreasing your load.

Spend on maintenance, save on gas. Have your mechanic check for old spark plugs, dirty air filters, low fluid levels, and any other problems that may put a drag on your fuel economy. According to the Department of Energy, a well-maintained car can increase fuel efficiency by as much as 17 percent.

Be cool about your air-conditioning. Use your air-conditioning only when you really need it. You may use up to 20 percent more fuel when you turn it on.

Wait for Wednesday. Buy your gas on Wednesdays. Prices may have settled back down by a few cents after rising for the weekend.

Made in the shade. Park your car in the shade or garage to save on fuel. Gas can evaporate when the car is sitting in the sun, particularly if the gas tank cap isn't screwed on as tightly as it should be.

Rise and shine and fill the tank. Two important facts: one, gas becomes denser at the coolest time of day. Two, you're charged by volume of gas, not density. You'll get more for your money if you buy your gas in the morning, when gas is most dense.

Gas cap

Does your cap fit? Almost 150 gallons of gas are vaporized every year because nearly 20 percent of cars on the road have damaged, loose, or missing gas caps. Is your gas cap in perfect condition? Ask your mechanic to check.

Gifts

Become a fan to get a fan. A great inexpensive gift for a grandchild who's also a sports fan: a fan mail package from his or her favorite sports team. Some packages are free, some cost up to $15 (depending on the team), and most contain a crowd-pleasing assortment of items such as bumper stickers, magnets, team photos, and more. Check out the Web site of your favorite team for ordering info.

Keep it in the family. Here's a gift idea that will thrill all your relatives, as well as your wallet. Gather favorite recipes, copy them, and create a family cookbook for everyone in your family.

Give a gift certificate—from you. Give a friend or family member a gift of your time. Whether the recipient needs babysitting, cooking, snow shoveling, or gardening, use your talents and your time to give a welcome (and inexpensive) present.

Celebrate Christmas all year. Buy half-price gifts after Christmas, and give them at birthdays, anniversaries, and so on. You can also buy holiday gift sets at bargain prices, take them apart, and either give the gifts separately or repackage them for the appropriate occasion.

The perfect photo-op.

Give grandchildren inexpensively framed photos of their parents at the recipient's current age—the goofier, the better. You'll provide laughs and memories for everyone at a picture-perfect price.

The gift of practicality. If you're on a budget and don't know what to give as a gift, choose an inexpensive practical gift that anyone would appreciate. Stamps, stationery, pens, cookies, coffee, and other simple, useful, and expendable gifts are particularly welcomed by those who don't have a lot of space.

Don't go empty-handed (or with an empty wallet). Holiday parties are great fun, but they can get expensive if you take a gift to each one. Save on hostess gifts by buying thoughtful presents in bulk: cocktail napkins, bars of scented soap, pretty candles, and so on.

Greeting cards

Send sentiments for less. Forget about buying traditional greeting cards at the stationery store. Instead, buy packages of greeting cards (either all-occasion or blank) at your warehouse club, craft store, discount store, or mass-merchandiser. At $2.29 per individual card, you can save around $10 by buying a multi-card package. You'll also save on gas by not running out to get a card every time you need one.

Make sentiments for nothing. Collect bits of scrap paper, fabric, clipped-out pictures from magazines—the sky's the limit—and make your own greeting cards. The effort will not only be appreciated, it might be framed!

It's like printing money. If you have a color printer, design and print your own gift cards, either with a simple word-processing program, or with a special paper and software package that offers you hundreds of designs and styles to make each card your own, available at stationery stores.

Groceries

Save hundreds with a pen and paper. How? Make a list of what you need before you head out to the grocery store, and stick to it. That way you won't be tempted by bite-sized marinated mozzarella balls or other unnecessary items. If you spent $5 on two frivolous items per shopping trip (that you may not use anyway), you'd waste at least $20 per month. Wouldn't you rather have that in your wallet?

Bag it. Save money and the environment by bringing your own bags to the grocery store. More and more stores are giving you money back for every bag you reuse.

Weigh in on savings. Whenever you buy potatoes or onions or any other produce by the bag rather than by the pound, weigh several bags and buy the heaviest one. You may get a 10 1/2-pound bag for the price of the 10-pound bag.

When old is new again. Don't fall for food described as "featured" in the aisles of your grocery store. The manager may just be promoting a commonly found food at its regular price.

Don't fall for limits. Keep your money in your purse when you see signs like "Limit six per customer." Stores know that customers will buy more of an item if they think there's a shortage—and there generally isn't.

Shop around (the store). You'll find necessities like meat, milk, and produce in the perimeter of the store. Less important prepackaged and preprocessed—and more expensive—items are generally in the center aisles. Stick to the perimeter.

Bigger isn't always better.

Grocery stores know that shoppers think the biggest box (of cereal or cookies or anything else) is the best deal—and often make the bigger package *more* expensive per portion than the smaller one! Always compare unit prices when shopping. You may be surprised where you'll find savings.

Be a latecomer. Visit your grocery store late in the day, when you may get unadvertised items on sale. Ask the butcher and the produce manager if they are cutting prices because of the late hour; smile sweetly and tell them you're looking for a senior discount. You may just get a great deal!

Double up. Try to stretch out the time between grocery-shopping trips. Instead of going once a week, go once every two weeks. You'll be forced to make your current food last longer and use up the food sitting patiently in the pantry and freezer.

Hair color

Lengthen the color of your locks.
Stretch out appointments for hair colorings or touch-ups by using a shampoo designed for color-treated hair. The color-enhancing shampoo won't cost much more than your regular shampoo, and it can easily save you $100 per year on colorings.

Don't stray too far. Be sure to stay within two shades of your natural hair color when you visit the salon. Your roots will blend into the colored hair better when it grows out, allowing more time between colorings.

Haircut

Return to school. Head to the nearest beauty school or salon training facility to get a salon-style haircut (and color) at a barbershop price. A supervised stylist-in-training will cut your hair; you'll cut the cost of an ongoing expense. Visit www.beautyschoolsdirectory. com to find a school near you.

Alternate and save. Can't give up your pricey haircuts? Consider alternating appointments at your usual salon with visits to a less expensive one, where you can get maintenance cuts for a fraction of what you normally pay—and be sure to inquire about senior discounts for cuts.

Cut down on your cuts. If you can't give up your expensive stylist, try stretching out the time between trips to the salon. Instead of getting a cut every four weeks, aim for every five and save the cost of three visits per year.

Trim your costs. If all you need is an easy trim, head over to a barbershop instead of your usual salon. You shouldn't have trouble finding a cut for under $20.

Try something new. Or at least try a new salon. Many salons just starting out need new customers, and they often offer deals for haircuts. You can save up to 50 percent on a haircut in a brand-new salon.

Save up to $20 by saying no. Whether you're getting your hair cut or colored, skip the blow-dry. Salons often charge big-time for drying your hair, so tell them not to. Keep the $20 in your pocket.

Hanger

Hang on to your hangers. Don't toss out a good hanger just because it has rough edges. Dab a little clear nail polish on the rough spot, and it's ready to go back to work.

Double up for savings.

Is your coat falling off its flimsy hanger? Don't spend money on fancy hangers. Simply tape two or three wire hangers together and hang your coat back up.

Holiday cards

Cut back on paper and postage. Send postcards rather than traditional greeting cards during the holidays. If you normally send 50 cards, you'll save almost $10 on postage alone.

Christmas times two. Cut the decorative front part off the Christmas cards you received last year and use them as Christmas postcards this year.

Hospital

Pack a bag. Try to bring toothpaste, aspirin, tissues, and other necessities from home next time you head to the hospital. You will be amazed by how much the hospital will charge you for such ordinary items.

Check your bill. Hospitals have been known to charge patients for procedures they never received, rooms never used, and medicine never administered. Check your hospital bill carefully, and question anything that doesn't look right.

Wait for your surgery. Ask to be admitted to the hospital on the day of your surgery, not before—you'll pay dearly for that extra day. Early admission generally benefits the staff, not you or your hospital bill.

Don't take the same test twice. Make sure your doctor sends all test results to the hospital so you won't be subjected to the same procedures again. You'll save money—and a lot of aggravation.

Free health care. Hospitals frequently offer skin cancer screenings, cholesterol tests, wellness seminars, and other services as a way to connect with their local community. Call your nearby hospital to find out what kinds of services they offer for free.

Hotel

Make it like home. Hotels can be expensive, and eating out only adds to the cost of your vacation. The next time you book a hotel, ask for a room that includes a kitchen. This may mean spending more on a suite, but once you factor in the cost of three meals a day at restaurants, it will also mean big savings—probably more than $50 a day. Try an extended-stay hotel for a good deal on a suite.

Call the hotel directly. You may save money on a phone call by dialing a hotel's toll-free number, but you may save a lot more on your hotel room by calling the hotel directly. Staffers at the hotel generally have more flexibility in giving discounts on room rates than those at the central reservations number, and they may be able to give you a better price than the official senior discount that the main reservation line offers.

Choose a business hotel for a leisure stay. Many fancy chain hotels that cater to business travelers find themselves with empty rooms on the weekends. They often drop their rates to entice customers. Call one of them for a good weekend deal.

Look beyond the room for savings. Just because you got a great deal on a hotel room doesn't mean you got the *best* deal. You need to look for the hotel's additional money-saving features. Does your room have a small refrigerator? Does the rate include free breakfast? Does the hotel offer free parking? A free Wi-Fi connection? Factor in these freebies when you choose your hotel, and your good deal will look great.

Visit off-season for big savings.

Summertime visits to popular ski areas often result in local hotels and resorts offering substantially reduced rates. Hiking, swimming, fishing, and golfing are popular activities at these places, so they're just as much of a blast in the summer as in the winter.

House

Time it right. If you're thinking of downsizing, shop for a house in the dead of winter when other home buyers are staying home. (If you live in the Sunbelt, shop in the heat of the summer for the same reason.) Even in a buyer's market, the time of year can make a big difference. Your off-season timing may just knock a hefty percentage off the in-season price.

Housekeeping

It bears repeating. Never spend money again on expensive household cleaners. Save yourself money over and over by substituting a simple 1-to-1 solution of white vinegar and water in a spray bottle for commercial cleaning products. You'll never buy the other stuff again. You'll be green, and your home will be clean as a whistle.

Ice cream

Free ice cream. One day, once a year, most Ben & Jerry's stores worldwide give away free ice cream cones. All free, all day, no limit. Check out benandjerrys.com to find out the specific day and the location of a store near you. If it's your birthday (and you can prove it), Baskin-Robbins will give you a free 2.5-ounce scoop, no matter what your age.

Ice pack

Freeze your costs. Do you need an ice pack for muscle aches and pains? Don't bother spending your money on the drugstore kind. Instead, make a reusable ice pack by mixing one part rubbing alcohol and two parts water in a sealable plastic bag, and freeze. Because it doesn't freeze solid, it's particularly handy to have for sore knees or elbows. It may help the pain to know you're saving at least $5 every time you pull it out of the freezer!

Use food for sore spots. Try putting a bag of frozen peas on an aching shoulder, or freeze a small ketchup packet from a fast-food restaurant to tuck onto a small, hard-to-reach sore spot. You have them in your house already—why not use them to save on ice packs from the pharmacy?

Insurance (car)

Buy in bulk. Buy your car and home insurance from the same company. Not only can you save up to 15 percent on separate car and home insurance costs, your insurance company will be less likely to drop you if you

have an accident—it will want to keep the rest of your business.

Hit the delete button. Make sure you're not paying double for the same insurance. Read your policies carefully to determine if you're paying for life insurance (which you already have) as part of your car insurance. Dump any double coverage that you find.

Take a class.

A defensive driving class, that is. You can get a 10 percent discount or more on your car insurance, and you'll learn how to stay away from trouble on the road, which may save you even more money in the long run. Ask your insurance provider, your state DMV, or the AARP for information on these classes.

Make your occupation work for you, even if you're retired. Ask your insurance company if it offers discounts for particular occupations. Some offer dollars off for teachers, engineers, and so on. See if your job, even your former job, has a payoff for you!

Update to keep costs down. Keep your insurance agent up to speed on changes that might affect your rates. Have you given up your extra car? Are you putting far less mileage on your car than when you commuted to work? Only using it for "pleasure" driving, never for business? Even little changes can save you money, so be sure to make that call each year.

Ask for any and all discounts. Your

insurance company or agent may not volunteer information about the many discounts available, so ask about discounts specifically: for car security systems, low mileage, a good driving record, safety features on your car, an older car, and more.

Keep quiet. Don't file small claims. If you

do, your insurance company is more likely to raise your rates. Absorb the cost of scratches in the paint, dings in the body, or a cracked windscreen (if you don't have specific replacement coverage) to keep your rates from going up, up, up—or your policy being canceled altogether.

Invitations

Don't supersize. Choose regular-size

invitations when you're planning a party. Oversized invitations will require additional postage (and will probably cost more, too).

Go high-tech. Send e-mail invitations to

your next party. Emily Post may not agree, but you'll save on the cost of postage and the cost of the invitations—and possibly even on the gas used going to the post office!

Jeans

Flip over your jeans. To make jeans last

longer, turn them inside out when you wash them (in cold water on the gentle cycle). If some of the dye escapes from the fabric during the wash, it has a better chance of being reabsorbed into the legs.

Patch 'em up. Are your favorite jeans soft

and comfortable and beautifully worn—and in danger of ripping? If so, reinforce the insides of the knees, the corners of pockets, and any other places that look likely to split with iron-on patches. You'll help make your beloved jeans last even longer.

Wash and dry with care. Don't toss

your jeans into the wash if you've worn them only once. Wait until they're dirty enough to need cleaning. And don't just throw them in the dryer, either. Use a no-heat setting, or better yet, hang them to dry, out of direct sunlight. You'll save wear and tear on your jeans and on your energy bill, too.

Jewelry

Fix it and forget it. Reset loose stones

in your costume jewelry easily and inexpensively with nail polish. Simply use clear nail polish as the glue; it's a quick fix that no one will detect.

Jewelry box

Do double duty. Why spend money on a

fancy jewelry box when any number of other organizers will serve the same purpose just as well or even better? Try using an ice-cube tray, a silverware tray, or a craft box designed for beads if you want to separate your jewelry. Hang your necklaces and bracelets from push-pins on a bulletin board. Put post earrings on a mesh pen holder or an upended colander. Your choices are unlimited (and the price is right!).

J

Jigsaw puzzle

A custom-made puzzle for the price of cardboard. Make a jigsaw puzzle by gluing leftover wallpaper or magazine photos, or even a picture you took yourself, enlarged on the computer, onto cardboard. When it dries, cut it up into the kinds of pieces— small or large, simple or complex—that you want for your puzzle. You'll save $10 to $20 just by using what you have on hand, and your grandkids will be thrilled.

Key

Lock out the locksmith. Make an extra set of house and car keys and give them to a trusted neighbor or friend. Next time you lose your keys or lock them in the house or car, you'll save yourself the expense of a locksmith.

Kitty litter

Make it cheap and easy. There's no need to spend a fortune on kitty litter. Just mix a 75-cent box of baking soda with an inexpensive brand of cat litter for immediate savings and the same odor effectiveness of the more expensive brands.

Keep it in your car.

Strange as it sounds, you should keep kitty litter in your trunk during the winter months. It provides excellent traction if you get stuck and is a lot cheaper than a tow truck.

Knee pad

Dig up your garden, not your pants. Save wear and tear on your pants when you garden by wrapping a plastic bag around each knee. You'll want to spend your money on beautiful flowers, not on a new pair of pants.

A mouse for inside and out. Use old computer mouse pads when you need to kneel in the garden. They'll cushion your knees just as well as cushions you buy at your garden store.

Laundry

A little care goes a long way. Turn dark-colored clothing inside out in the wash to prolong the color. Put lingerie and other fine washables in mesh bags to prevent snagging.

Keep it cold. Do your wash (including the rinse cycle) in cold water. A typical family of four can save $120 per year by not using hot water in the washing machine.

Give it a soak. Stained white tablecloths and napkins aren't destined for the dumpster or pricey store-bought solutions. Instead, soak them in a solution of water and 2 table-spoons of baking soda and launder as usual.

Lawn

Step on it. Don't waste water (and money) on your lawn; an average lawn requires just one hour of watering per week. How can you tell if yours is dry? Step on the grass. If the blades don't jump back up, you need to water. If they spring back, hold off on the sprinklers.

Offer an early drink. Water your plants and your lawn early in the morning. If you water later, the sun will burn off the moisture you so carefully put down before it has a chance to soak in.

Lawn mower

Leave it long. If you cut your grass too short, you'll cut down on saving water (and money). Set your mower blades to the 3-inch setting. Taller grass holds water longer than shorter grass.

Keep it "reel." If you have a small lawn, buy an old-fashioned push lawn mower—also known as a reel mower—rather than a fuel-powered mower. You'll easily save at least $100 on the transaction, you won't have to pay for gas or tune-ups, and you'll get great exercise every time you—or your lucky grandson!—mow the lawn.

Lighting

A bright idea. Install motion detector lights or timers on outdoor lights that may inadvertently get left on during the day. The automatic shut-off will give you peace of mind and a few extra dollars.

Convert to CFLs. Use compact fluorescent light (CFL) bulbs. They last 8 to 10 times longer than incandescent bulbs, put out less heat than incandescents, and, most importantly, use minimal energy. Putting CFLs in just a quarter of your fixtures may cut your lighting bill in half. Put them in all your fixtures and watch the savings skyrocket!

Dim the lights.

Save energy and money by using dimmer switches on your lights. If you dim an incandescent bulb 10 percent, you can save about 5 percent on electricity use. If you dim it 50 percent, you can save 25 percent on electricity. In both cases you'll also extend the life of the bulb.

Three ways to save. If you haven't yet converted to CFLs, use three-way bulbs in your light fixtures. Use the lowest wattage whenever possible, and you'll save on electricity costs.

Stick to the task. Rather than light an entire room when you're working in one corner, use efficient task lighting. It's an easy way to pay for only what you use.

Lotion

Stand your lotion on its head. Turn your almost-empty moisturizer bottle upside down. The lotion will fall into the cap, and you'll squeeze several more uses out of the bottle (you can do the same with shampoo and conditioner and any other cosmetic that will stand upside-down).

Magazine

Get your fix with a friend. Are you hooked on magazines but discovering that you have an expensive habit? Ask a few like-minded friends to each subscribe to one magazine, then swap the magazines so everyone gets to read them all. Depending on the number of magazines (and friends) involved, you could save a bundle.

Makeup

Cap your costs. Don't bother buying concealer if you already use foundation. You can find the perfect cover-up in the cap, where the foundation has settled. It's the right consistency, and you can't find a better color match!

Use it in a different form. If your lipstick is broken, don't give up on it. Instead, push the remainder of the lipstick down into the tube, and then use a lip brush to apply it. You can also put the broken bullet into a small empty makeup container, melt it with a blow-dryer, let it dry, then use it in its new form.

Take it off, take it all off. Try some extra moisturizer in place of your expensive makeup remover. It's a perfect substitute: It removes makeup quickly and easily for a lot less, and you don't have to buy extra products.

Match

Don't eat the match. Why spend money on extra-long matches when you probably have a perfectly good substitute on hand? Use a piece of dried spaghetti next time you need to light a hard-to-reach wick or multiple candles.

Meat

Tough it out. You know that tougher meats are less expensive than tender meats. But did you know that many butchers will run these cheaper cuts through the tenderizer if you ask? Your tough cut will turn into a more tender bite at no cost.

A wise buy for a wise guy (or gal). Boneless meat may cost more per pound, but it usually gives you more for your money than a cut filled with fat and bone.

Slice it thin to keep your wallet fat.

Ask your deli man or woman to slice your meat and cheese thinner than usual. You'll most likely use less in each sandwich you make, which is good for your wallet *and* your waistline.

Microwave

Zap it once to save twice. According to the U.S. Department of Energy and the Environmental Protection Agency, using your microwave oven for small portions can reduce your cooking energy by up to 80 percent. Plus, your air-conditioning costs will be lower in the summer if you use your microwave, since it doesn't generate heat the way your stove or oven does.

Mop

Flip it. After you've used your disposable mop pad, turn it over and use the other side. Then throw it away, knowing you've gotten twice your money's worth.

Movies

The early bird gets the...movie.

Want to see a first-run movie for less than the cost of a child's ticket (often for less than your senior discount price)? Check out A.M. Cinema, run by AMC Theatres, which offers movies for $4, $5, or $6 (depending on the theater and market) before noon on certain Fridays, Saturdays, Sundays, and holidays.

Movie magic for members. Costco members can buy movie tickets at discounted rates for theater chains including AMC, Cinemark, and Regal Entertainment. You buy in bulk (five tickets at a time) and save about $2 per ticket.

Free movies. Choose from hundreds of classic comedies, dramas, horror movies, musicals, Westerns, and more and watch them for free on *Entertainment Magazine*'s Web site, www.emol.org. Some of your favorite classics that are now in the public domain are available here, such as *My Man Godfrey* and *His Girl Friday*, as well as wonderful TV shows from days gone by, such as *The Honeymooners*. It's all easy to download (the site has detailed instructions if you need help) and perfectly legal, and, best of all, completely free.

Mulch

Chips all around. Rather than buying expensive garden mulch, contact your local tree doctor or sawmill, and ask them to deliver wood chips directly to your backyard. Biodegradeable, safe, and natural looking, this terrific mulch also may be free or much less expensive than buying bags of mulch.

Museum

Free art. Most private museums, both large and small, offer free admission on certain days or at certain times. And independent art gallery openings are usually free and open to the public. Plus you may score a free glass of wine, a cube of cheese, and a chance to talk to the artist.

Nails

Fingernails, that is. Stretch out the time between nail appointments: if you normally get your nails done once a week, mark your calendar to get them done once every two weeks instead. At $10 an appointment, you'll save $260 per year, not including tips! Ask the manicurist *not* to put a sealing topcoat on your nails. The thicker the coating, the faster it will peel off.

Very cool nails! Cold nail polish lasts longer and can be applied more smoothly. So take it out of the closet or medicine cabinet (or wherever you store it) and put it in the refrigerator.

Get more from your manicure. Your manicure will last longer if you clean your nails with vinegar. Use a cotton ball to apply the vinegar before you paint your nails, then enjoy the extra time you have before your next manicure.

Napkin

Cut from the right cloth. Sometimes it's hard to remember that cloth napkins still exist. They may require a little care, but they'll add a touch of elegance to your table—and more importantly, save you money over paper napkins in the long run.

National parks

Spend $10 to save hundreds. If you enjoy national parks, you'll enjoy the savings you can get with the America the Beautiful Senior Pass. As long as you're a citizen or permanent resident of the United States and at least 62 years old, you can buy this pass for $10 and get free or reduced admission to any federal recreation site—for the rest of your life! Get the pass from a national park, wildlife refuge, or participating federal recreation site or office.

Newspaper

Let's make a deal. Call your local newspaper and ask if it offers a discount for paying for your subscription a year in advance.

Pick and choose for less. Do you read only a few sections of the mammoth Sunday newspaper? If so, ask friends who always get the Sunday paper to give you the sections you like when they're done with them. You'll avoid waste—and the cost of the Sunday paper.

Save $4 on Sunday. If you're a news fiend, save money by swapping different Sunday newspapers with a friend. You read one in the morning, he reads the other, then you swap around noon. Or if you read only one Sunday newspaper, save several dollars by taking turns buying it. Just be sure to set a time to turn over the newspaper to your friend (and vice versa).

Dispense with the subscription altogether. Nearly all the major national newspapers in the United States can now be read online for free. You may have to register, which is also free, but in exchange you'll get news that's frequently updated, as well as additional photos, interactive graphics (at some sites), and, in many papers, additional articles and details there weren't room for in the printed paper.

Notary

A notary for nothing. Where can you get important documents notarized for free? Try your bank, the library, your employer, or a local government office. Call to make sure this service is offered (and that it's free) before you head out the door.

Obedience school

Sit, stay, save! Whether you enroll your dog in obedience school or train him yourself, you'll find savings in his good behavior. Because he'll be less likely to run into the street or eat things he shouldn't, you may save the price of medicine or even a big vet bill.

Odd job

Go the nonprofessional route. You don't always need an expensive professional to help you with jobs around the house. Call the job placement office at your local college to get students to help you with moving furniture, painting, gardening, lawn care, and more.

Orange juice

Cycling for sales. Start paying attention to when your grocery store puts your favorite brand of orange juice on sale. Chances are, you'll discover a pattern, or sales cycle. Soon you'll know when to buy orange juice and when not to. Sales cycles apply to ice cream, pasta, and cereal, too. When it's on sale, buy two or three and store them.

Outdoor furniture

Towel it off. Make your vinyl outdoor furniture last longer by sitting on a towel if you're wearing sunscreen. The sunscreen can eat away at the furniture's protective coating, allowing dirt to lodge permanently in the destroyed coating—making it impossible to clean. So sit on a towel and save yourself the cost of new furniture.

Oven

Keep it closed. Try not to open the oven door to check on the progress of your dish—the oven temperature drops by about 25 degrees every time you do (and you'll have to pay to get the heat back up to the right level). Use a good old-fashioned timer instead.

Turn it off and save.

Don't wait until your dish is completely cooked. Turn off the oven a few minutes before the recipe says you should. The heat left in the oven is sufficient for finishing the meal.

Choose your dish wisely. Use glass or ceramic baking dishes in your oven. Because glass conducts heat differently than metal, you can lower the temperature about 25 degrees (from the temperature the recipe says), and your food will still cook at the same rate.

Double your money. Save on energy bills by cooking two dishes in the oven at once. You can cook two items for the same meal—a chicken for dinner and brownies for dessert—or two items for two different meals, such as a roast for dinner and cinnamon rolls for breakfast the next day.

Over-the-counter medicine

Look past the packaging. Just as you save by buying generic prescription drugs, you can save by buying store brands of over-the-counter medications. Other than the packaging and, most importantly, the price, store brands are often no different from name-brand medications. Read the fine print to find the name and percentage of active ingredients—if they are the same as the active ingredients on the big-name brand, it's the same stuff. Ask the pharmacist, if you have any doubts.

Price your pills. And your gel caps and your capsules. You may find that each form of your medicine carries a different price tag. Choose the right form—and the right price—for you.

Overdraft protection

Guard your checking account. Sign up for overdraft protection at your bank, just in case. It usually costs nothing and saves you the possible expense of returned check fees.

Owner's manual

Save instructions to save money. Keep all owner's manuals, receipts, and warranties. You may be able to easily fix your appliance, tool, or electronic device by consulting the manual, or you may be able to get it fixed for free if you check your warranty. If you've lost the manual, these days you can probably find it online—search for the brand name and the type of product.

Packing material

Ship and save. Don't waste your money on bubble wrap or other shipping materials. Just insert a straw into an almost-closed zip-top bag, and inflate the bag. Remove the straw, zip the bag tightly shut, and use as packing material.

Painting

Roll up the savings. Put a plastic grocery bag completely around your roller pan, roller inside, when you're in the midst of paint jobs around the house. If you tie the bag closed around the pan, the paint will stay fresh for up to several days. When you're done, simply wash the roller and throw away the bag (and the pan, if it's a disposable one). You'll save time on clean-up and money on multiple roller pans.

Pantry

Stay organized. You'll save two ways if you keep your pantry organized: you won't go to the grocery store as often because you'll know what you have (thereby avoiding impulse purchases), and you won't buy the same item that's already sitting on your pantry shelf.

Paper towels

Mop up the savings. Stop using paper towels every time you have a spill. Use your handy dandy sponge and discover savings every time you keep a paper towel on the roll.

Go heavy duty.

Buy heavier weight paper towels, and use them the way you would if they were cloth: rinse them in water, squeeze them out, and drape them over the edge of the sink to live another day.

Pets

Lower the cost of a special diet. Did your vet put your pet on an expensive diet? If so, ask a nearby discount pet store if it can order what your pet needs for less than what the vet charges you. There may also be a generic version—ask at the store for any advice they can offer you to help keep your pet well and your wallet full!

Don't overfeed or overspend. An easy way to save money on pet food is by feeding your pet what is recommended and not overfeeding. Follow the guidelines on the package of food and adjust according to what your pet needs. You should be able to feel your pet's ribs, but his backbone shouldn't stick out.

Trade pet-sitting services. Do you have a friend with a pet? Ask her to swap pet-sitting services with you. She comes to your house to feed and exercise your pet when you're away, and you do the same for her. You both save on boarding costs, and your pets will be happier, too.

Spay and neuter for health and savings. You'll save money not caring for litters and by keeping your pet healthy. Female pets will have lower rates of breast, ovarian, and uterine cancer, and male pets will have lower rates of testicular cancer.

Take a shot at savings. Fido may need to be vaccinated, but he doesn't need the most expensive shot-giver around. Take him to a veterinary college, or even a pet store or mobile vaccination clinic (sponsored by a pet store) for reduced-cost vaccinations.

Place mat

Place a towel, not a mat. Use brightly colored dishtowels for slightly-oversized place mats. They're less expensive than fabric place mats and easier to clean. If you buy the dishtowels in bulk, you can save even more.

Hit the fabric shop. Like to sew? Even if you don't, most fabric shops offer bits and remnants of great material in pieces too small to sell by the yard at ridiculously low costs. Pick up what appeals to you, and sew a straight hem around the edge. Presto! Instant place mats!

Plants

Look forward to an eternal spring. Plant bulbs and perennials, which bloom year after year, rather than annuals that you have to replace every spring.

Save on seeds. Collect seeds in the fall that you can plant in the spring. Put dry seeds from flowers like zinnias and cosmos in a paper bag, and store the bag until you're ready to plant the seeds the following year. You'll have beautiful flowers for free!

Go native. Use local plants and flowers in your garden. Why? They require less fertilizer and water because they've already adapted to your soil.

Spring into action. Keep your eyes peeled for discarded plants during spring clean-up time. Many people rip out their perfectly good plants to make way for a new garden design. Pick up these discards when you see them.

Ask for help. Your local landscapers not only know a tremendous amount about gardening, they know where they're tearing out plants that will go to waste—unless you ask for them. Say that you'll pick up the greenery and cart it away, and you may get some wonderful new plants for free.

Know what's growing before you buy. It's springtime and those nasty weeds in your yard are starting to sprout…only they may not just be useless weeds: they might be purslane, or, if you live in the Southeast, ramps (wild leeks), and they cost a fortune at the grocery store. Caveat: always make sure that what you're planning on cooking is in fact edible. If you're not sure, pull a few and take them to your local horticultural specialist.

Buy this summer for next spring.

Once the spring and early summer perennials have bloomed and faded at the garden store, look out for terrific bargains on plants that have shed all their blossoms. They can often be bought for as much as 75 percent off. You can plant them in late summer, let them get well established, and then you'll have a stunning array of new flowers come next spring.

Prescription medicine

Get a $4 prescription. Target, Wal-Mart, and the pharmacies of many other stores across the United States, such as Hannaford grocery stores, have begun offering a list of more than 400 generic prescription drugs for $4 for a 30-day supply. The price of a 90-day supply is in the neighborhood of $10, depending on the pharmacy. You can get a list of the drugs available at the stores' Web sites or a printed copy at the stores' pharmacies. Ask your doctor if the drug he is prescribing is on the list—or if there's a suitable substitute on the list.

Buy at a wholesaler (even if you're not buying in bulk). Save money by filling your prescriptions at a wholesale club, even if you're not a member. The pharmacy may tack on a small fee, but you have the right under federal law to fill prescriptions at any pharmacy, so tell the person asking for your ID at the front door that you're only visiting the pharmacy. (And don't get carried away—you won't be able to buy anything else without a club membership ID.)

Do the splits. Ask your doctor if your tablets or pills can be split to save you money. You'll probably pay the same amount for the 10-milligram dose and 20-milligram dose, so if you buy the 20-milligram pills and split them in half, you've split your costs in half as well. (Note that you can't do this with time-release or long-acting pills or with capsules.) For best results, buy a pill-cutter at the drugstore, to make sure each pill is evenly divided.

Switch and save. Some pharmacies will reward you with discounts when you transfer your prescription from another drugstore. You may see advertised incentives to switch—like a gift card from your new drugstore.

Be loyal. You can score substantial savings if you're a repeat customer at a particular pharmacy. One major retailer we know offers discounts throughout the store for loyal pharmacy customers, and Kmart is testing a program that offers store-brand pain relief and cold medications for $1 if you purchase or refill a prescription at a Kmart pharmacy.

Ask for samples. Drug company representatives often shower doctors with samples of their medications, and your doctor is probably happy to share these free samples with you. Just ask if your doctor has any samples available. You'll save on a trip to the pharmacy, as well as on the prescription.

Go generic. You'll save big by using the generic version of your prescription drug. If a generic doesn't exist, ask you doctor if there is a similar, older drug that works just as well and is available as a generic.

Think like your insurance company. Request a copy of your insurance plan's formulary, or preferred drug list. You'll find drugs—both generic and brand name—that cost less and require a lower co-pay than drugs not on the list. Share the formulary with your doctor, and ask him to prescribe the drugs you need from the list, if possible.

Printer

Preview your savings. Don't automatically print a page from the Internet—it includes ads and icons you probably don't want. Instead, click on "print preview" or "print version" to see exactly what you're printing, then delete what you don't need. You'll save money on paper and ink as well as wear and tear on your printer.

Think about saving ink. Make your ink cartridge last longer by setting your printer to the lowest quality setting possible.

Double up. To save paper when you use your printer, try printing on both sides. Or print on the blank side of already used paper. Better yet, don't print out at all: store e-mail messages and other potential printouts on your computer.

Produce

Weigh in on savings. Use the produce scale to weigh the packages of produce you plan to buy. That 5-pound bag of apples may not really weigh 5 pounds; it may weigh less (and if it does you shouldn't buy it) or it may weigh more (and if it does you should march it right over to the cash register). Always make sure you're getting (at least) what you're paying for.

Shake it, baby.

The produce, that is. Many grocery stores spray fruits and vegetables to keep them looking fresh. But the water makes them heavier, and if you're paying for produce by the pound, you may be paying extra for water. Always give a head of lettuce, for example, a vigorous shake before bagging it up, and add up your savings.

Grow your own. There's no better way to save money and eat well than to grow some of your own produce. Instead of spending $10 a week on salad greens and vegetables and shelling out gas money to get to the grocery store, plant a few seeds in a small plot or in pots on your deck. You'll be mightily rewarded with fresh produce from April through November, depending on where you live.

Professional organization

Join the crowd. In addition to AARP, many professional associations offer discounts on health care, car rentals, and more to their members. Look at the type and quality of discount from the organizations for which you qualify to take advantage of these savings.

Quality

Always buy well if you can. It's true what they say: if you have a choice between buying something crafted well versus buying something shoddily produced, always opt for the better quality, if you can. It will last longer, won't have to be replaced, and likely won't have to be repaired as often as its cheaper sibling, thus saving you money in the long run.

Quantity

Two for one isn't always profitable. Before you grab "two for the price of one" in the grocery store, make sure that the individual price hasn't been elevated, too. And if you need only one (of anything), buy only one.

R

Radiator

Reflect on savings. Save on your heating bill by installing a heat reflector behind your radiator. (Create a reflector from foil-covered cardboard or by wrapping foam board in foil.) Make sure the foil faces away from the wall, and that the reflector is either the same size as the radiator or slightly larger. It will help push the warm air (that you've paid for) back out into your room.

Receipt

The thrill is gone. Shop only at stores that let you return merchandise, and always ask about their return policy. Hold on to receipts and don't cut tags off new purchases for two weeks. By the time two weeks have passed, you'll know if you really want the item you may have bought on impulse. If you're not wild about it, return it and stash the cash.

Refrigerator

Vacuum up the savings. Be sure to vacuum the coils at the bottom or back of your refrigerator twice a year to keep the appliance working efficiently. You'll pay more if your refrigerator needs to work harder because of dust in the coils.

Extra fridge in the basement?

Unless it's Thanksgiving or Christmas and you're entertaining a crowd, don't keep it cold "just in case." Pull the plug if it's empty, and sharply whittle away at your electric bill.

Rental car

Time it right. When renting a car, try to fly in and out of the airport at the same time of day. That way you can avoid paying for an extra day of rental when you've used only a few hours.

Take the shuttle to the car. Renting a car at the airport—particularly in big cities—can be expensive. You can use the free airport shuttle to avoid this cost two ways: first, take the shuttle to your hotel and rent a car there. You can save about 10 percent on taxes and fees alone. Second, take the shuttle to your hotel, and rent a car the next day, thereby saving the cost of a full day's rental.

Check your policy. You may not need liability coverage when you rent a car. Most insurance policies and some credit card companies offer liability coverage, so be sure to check your insurance and credit card policies before forking over money for what you may already have. Check for collision coverage, too.

Resort

You pay to play. That resort on the beach looks so appealing, with unlimited golf, tennis, and swimming. But wait: you don't play golf—so don't choose a resort that features golf. The cost of golf will be built into the cost of your room. Choose a resort that offers the services and activities you'll use.

Go off-season. Get dramatically reduced rates and less crowded beaches and golf courses by visiting resorts in the off-season. Time your visit just before or after the high-rate season, and you can save big.

Restaurant

Order small plates midday. There's no need to order expensive dinner-sized platters for lunch; they'll slow you down for the rest of the day and make you groggy by late afternoon. Instead, order two small plates from the appetizer side of the menu, and share them with a dining partner.

Start your restaurant meal at home. Enjoy an appetizer in your house before you go to a restaurant for dinner. You'll save on the first course and—if you have a substantial enough appetizer—may save even more by ordering a smaller entrée.

Eat for a week. Many communities offer "restaurant weeks," when you can dine at fancy restaurants for a very deep discount. During these promotional events, restaurants entice you with amazingly priced prix fixe meals—the same food you'd pay substan-

tially more for the rest of the year. Search online or watch your local media for details.

Go gourmet at home. Find several foodie friends and start a gourmet club. "Eat out" at a different house each week, rather than eating at a restaurant. You'll save a ton, and get exciting new food experiences as well.

Think before you drink. Order water instead of a soft drink when you go to a restaurant. Assuming you eat out once a week, you can save up to $100 per year.

Skip the dessert (but not really).

Don't pay for an overpriced dessert the next time you join friends for lunch at a restaurant. Pass on it, then pass by a bakery on your way home and enjoy a fabulous indulgence for a lot less.

Happy hour for your wallet. Check out restaurants and bars that offer happy hours. Along with buying inexpensive drinks, you may be able to create your dinner out of free hors d'oeuvres.

A restaurant's gift to you. Does your favorite restaurant give customers a free meal on their birthdays? If so, you can save the cost of a dinner on your special day. If not, find a restaurant that does!

Rewards program

Reward yourself. Join rewards programs whenever and wherever you can, whether offered by your credit card or an individual merchant or service you utilize often, to earn points every time you shop or travel. Then redeem your points for free merchandise, more travel, or services. Just be sure to note if the rewards program requires a membership fee, and determine if that fee is worth the rewards you earn.

Ribbon

Not just for the kitchen any more. Pull plastic wrap tight and twist it to make an unusual and inexpensive ribbon for your gift. It looks particularly festive atop a brightly colored package.

Do it again. High quality fabric ribbons can be used year after year. Just gently iron them, and they'll look brand new.

All that glitters is...ribbon! Shop tag sales for cheap garments with sparkling or colorful fabric and cut them up with pinking shears for beautiful ribbons. You'll spend less on the tag sale item than you will on new ribbon.

Rug

Stay away from chemicals. Whether it's an inherited Persian rug from your great aunt or a fabulous flea market find, steer clear of expensive industrial cleaners. If you find a troublesome stain, hold the rug up away from the floor, and pour warm water mixed with

baking soda through the stain (be prepared to catch the liquid on the underside with a bowl). Rinse with clear water and blot dry with a clean, soft towel.

Salt

Use kosher salt and save. Inexpensive kosher salt is not only tastier than regular table salt, it's more frugal. Why? Each flake or crystal of kosher salt is far bigger than its table salt cousin, meaning that a single pinch will go a very long way, saving you dough in the long run. (One box lasted one of our interviewees over a year.)

Sandwich

One is better than two. Share a sandwich with a friend when you're out and about and grabbing a quick lunch. One big sandwich costs less than two small sandwiches, so split the sandwich as well as the cost, and save!

Bring it from home. C'mon...bet your fridge is filled with assorted leftovers (ours is!). Why spend $5 for a mediocre sandwich from a deli when an inexpensive loaf of bread can be a vehicle for something you truly love?

Shades

Raise and lower to heat and cool. Save money on heating and cooling costs by using your shades and drapes strategically. In the summer, keep your shades and drapes closed on the sunny side of the house during the day and open at night. In the winter, keep them open during the day and closed at night.

Shampoo

Stretch your shampoo. You already know you should stock up on your favorite shampoo when it's on sale. What you may not know: you can alternate using your more expensive brand with a generic brand, and your hair will still look great.

Pump up the savings. Don't use extra shampoo and conditioner simply because the bottle lets you have more than you need. Pour your shampoo and conditioner into large pump bottles—they'll dole out smaller amounts so your hair care products will last longer.

Concentrate and save!

Most shampoos made today are super-concentrated. When you're nearing the bottom of the bottle, fill it halfway with water, tighten the cap, and shake. Depending on the product, you may have a few days to a few more weeks of shampoos ahead of you.

Shipping

Add up the savings. Whether you're shopping by catalog or on the Internet, find a friend who wants merchandise from the same retailer and place a single order, then split the shipping fees. Better yet, find several friends and place a big order so you get free shipping.

Shoes

Join Project SOS: Save Our Shoes. Double or triple the life of your shoes by repairing them, resoling them, and reheeling them when necessary. Why buy a new pair of shoes when you can save your favorite old pair with new soles for $20 to $50? And don't forget that a shoe repair shop can fix luggage, belts, and purses, too.

Keep 'em clean. Watch WD-40 work double duty: it cleans shoe leather *and* lubricates it so your shoes last longer. Ditto purses, briefcases, wallets, belts, riding saddles, bicycle seats, leather car interiors, and leather furniture. You get the point!

Preventive shoe care. Place foam insoles into all your shoes to save their insides. Buy inexpensive store-brand insoles, and replace them when they become dirty or worn. You'll save money on new shoes, and you'll have more comfortable shoes as a perk.

Shower

Go with the (low) flow. Invest in a low-flow showerhead, and save on water and heating costs. By spending $10 to $20 on a new showerhead, you can save about 7,300 gallons of water and $30 to $100 each year on your water and heating bills.

Soap

Dispense some soap and some savings. Don't just refill your soap dispenser with soap. Add one part hand soap and three parts water for a soap that cleans without cleaning out your wallet.

Go the old-fashioned body wash route. Instead of using a separate bar soap for your body and one for your face, buy an old-fashioned liquid body wash, such as pure castile soap—a tried and true multi-purpose favorite that's not only frugal, it's delightfully pure!

Socks

Getting dressed has never been so easy. Buy same-color socks in bulk. If the dryer eats one, you have an automatic match in your dresser drawer—and you won't need to buy a new pair of socks. Besides, you'll pay less buying packs of socks rather than individual pairs.

Soft drinks

Make your own. No, we're not kidding. Instead of buying chemical-packed flavored orange, grapefruit, or cherry soda, combine a splash of fresh juice with inexpensive club soda. Cheaper and healthier, by far.

Spices

Spice up your life for less. Never buy name-brand dried spices in the grocery store: you're paying for the bottles they're packed in. You can often buy spices in bulk at natural foods stores or ethnic groceries or visit online spice suppliers such as www.kalustyans.com or www.penzeys.com. Buy spices you use infrequently in smaller quantities. Store away from light in glass or metal containers.

Dry your own herbs for savings and flavor.

Have a leftover bunch of parsley (or cilantro, rosemary, or basil) in your fridge? Don't throw it away: dry it. Put the leaves on a clean baking sheet and place in a very slow oven (200°F) for 30 minutes. Remove, crumble, and store in an airtight jar, out of direct sunlight.

Sponge

Microwave your sponge. Make sure your sponge contains no metal fibers, and, if it doesn't, put your wet sponge in the microwave for one to two minutes on full power. You'll kill the bacteria that would normally make you toss the sponge. You'll use each sponge longer.

Sporting goods

Make an exchange. Look for school and community organizations that offer sporting goods swaps. You can also find sports stores that sell perfectly good second-hand athletic equipment, such as skis, for great prices.

Stockings

Freeze your hose. Panty hose, that is. Fill a plastic bag with water, drop in your new stockings, zip up the top, and toss the bag in the freezer. Thaw the concoction at room temperature. You'll strengthen the fibers in the stockings, cut down on runs, and save the cost of additional pairs of hose. You can continue protecting your stockings by refreezing them once a month, without water, for one night.

Stocking stuffer

Make Santa work all year. Buy stocking stuffers that aren't overtly seasonal at half off after Christmas, and you can use them as small Valentine's gifts, in Easter baskets, or as party favors throughout the year.

Storage

Store it well and save. Doesn't matter if it's food, sweaters, or garden tools: it pays to keep what you own stored carefully to avoid spoilage, moth damage, or rust. Double- and triple-wrap cold food items before freezing to prevent freezer burn; store sweaters in sealed plastic containers to prevent visitations from winged creatures; wipe down your garden tools with rubbing alcohol, dry them, and hang them until next year.

Stove

Stay small. Use small pots on small burners to save money on gas or electric costs. In fact, if you use a 6-inch pan on an 8-inch burner, you'll waste more than 40 percent of the energy. If you need to use a bigger pot, be sure to use a bigger burner; the pot won't heat evenly if you use it on a smaller one.

Cook on top. Your stove uses less energy than your oven, so try cooking meals on the stove as much as possible. Better yet, use a toaster oven, microwave, slow-cooker, or pressure-cooker.

Sweater

Buy one when you need one. Sweaters generally show up in stores around July, along with other fall clothes. Why do you need a sweater in July? Wait until October or November when you need one, and you can get the sweater for up to 75 percent less. The same idea applies to bathing suits, which go on sale in March and get marked down in July.

No sweat. You know that baby powder can be an effective deodorant, but did you know that it can also protect white shirts from sweat stains? Simply sprinkle it on the underarm areas of the shirt, then briefly iron. The baby powder will stop dirt and oil from staining the shirt. (This works for the collar, too.)

Tasting party

Excite your taste buds and your wallet. Host an international tasting party to learn more about ethnic food and wine. Have guests bring dishes and drinks to sample. You'll expand your culinary horizons, have fun, and avoid the high costs of sampling food and drink at restaurants and bars.

Taxes

Go directly to the source. You probably know that you can get free tax help over the phone from the IRS (1-800-829-1040), but did you know you can get free tax help in person at IRS walk-in sites? You can visit www.irs.gov, click on "Contact IRS," then click on "Contact my Local IRS Office," and find an IRS Taxpayer Assistance Center near you.

Get free tax help, in person.

You can take advantage of tax help at Tax Counseling for the Elderly, with 9,000 sites around the country. Call AARP at 1-888-227-7669 or visit the AARP Web site at www.aarp.org/money/taxaide for more information. You can search by zip code to find your nearest site for help.

Telephone

Go high-tech for (very) high savings. If you have DSL or a cable modem, download and install Skype software for free and call other Skype users all over the world from your computer—for free! You can also call the landlines and cell phones of non-Skype users at bargain rates. Visit www.skype.com for details.

Make saving a feature. How often do you use speed dialing? Has call forwarding come in handy? You probably don't need—or use—the many telephone add-ons that show up on your phone bill. Reevaluate each feature, drop several, and easily save $10 per month. Special offers from the phone company change all the time, so speak to a customer-service representative to evaluate your options—and be sure to ask if there are any senior discounts on phone service!

Television

Simplify and save. Do you really need over 100 television channels? If you trade your current cable package for basic cable, you may save up to $500 a year.

A super deal for the Super Bowl. Wait until the weeks before the Super Bowl for the best deal on a big-screen TV.

Thermostat

Lower the temperature and lower your costs. The Alliance to Save Energy says that you can subtract about 5 percent from your heating bill for every degree you lower your thermostat during the winter.

Get with the program. You've heard that programmable thermostats can save you money—but how much? If you invest $70 in an Energy Star programmable thermostat, you'll save more than twice that in its first year alone.

Don't exaggerate. In the morning, turn the thermostat up to the temperature you desire—not a higher temperature in the hopes that your house will warm up more quickly. It won't, and your furnace will have to work harder to reach a temperature you don't even want (and that will cost you more).

Toilet

Test for leaks. Add a drop of food coloring to the toilet tank. Wait a few minutes, then check to see if the color has shown up in the toilet bowl. If it has, you have a leak—and it may be costing you up to 200 gallons of water a day. Save water and money by fixing the leak.

Take up space to save.

If you have an older toilet, put a plastic bottle filled with water on the floor of the tank. Because the tank will require less water to fill, you'll save money on your water bill every time you flush. (Don't do this if you have a high-efficiency toilet.)

Tools

Priced for Dad, bought for you. Buy the tools you need when they go on sale around Father's Day in June.

Tag it. One of the best places to buy tools is at a tag sale. Keep your eyes peeled for everything from well-priced (but used) table saws and sanders to hammers with a history. Feel free to haggle.

Toothbrush

No cavities—and a free toothbrush. Be sure to ask your dentist for a free toothbrush next time—and every time—you go in for a check-up. Most dentists are happy to give you one, and some will also hand out free toothpaste, mouthwash, and dental floss.

Traveler's check

Use it when you don't travel. In your wallet, replace your emergency cash—that you may have used for impulse purchases—with a traveler's check. You're less likely to spend it than cash, which means you'll keep it for when you really need it (and not for something you really don't need).

Trees

Naturally cool your house...and your costs. Plant trees on the south, east, and west sides of your house, and save up to 25 percent on cooling costs. And here's an easy and inexpensive way to get trees: if you join the Arbor Day Foundation for $10, you'll receive 10 free trees! Just call 1-888-448-7337 or visit www.arborday.org.

Underwear

Stock up during seasonal sales cycles. Just as retailers reliably put seasonal items on sale, they do the same with necessities like underwear. Since you're always going to need underwear, socks, and so on, stock up when you see a sale.

Upholstered furniture

Pull the shades. Protect your upholstered furniture—and your investment in that furniture—by keeping it out of the sun. The sun can weaken the fabric's fibers and colors, so arrange your furniture to limit its exposure to sunlight, or simply shut the shades.

Vacuum the floor...and the couch... and the chair. Keep your upholstered furniture clean to save money. Vacuum it weekly to get rid of dirt and dust, which can act like sandpaper, grating on the fabric whenever anyone uses the furniture.

Utilities

Get audited—and like it! Ask your utility company for a free energy audit. A representative will come to your house and explain what you need to do to make your home more energy efficient. You can save $100 per year by sealing leaks in windows and doors and insulating ducts—all of which your energy audit will highlight. Your water company may provide this service for free, too.

Ask for off-peak rates. Find out if your utility company offers cheaper rates for running appliances at certain hours—usually off-peak—and save.

Stick *very* close to home.

Want to share your family heritage and introduce the grandkids to Italy, for example, without spending a dime on airfare? Throw an authentic Tuscan picnic in the privacy of your own home, complete with authentic food, photos, and history. Visit Netflix.com or Blockbuster.com to sign up and order informational videos about your chosen location. You'll have a ball and spend virtually nothing.

Vacation

Make the switch. Trade your house with someone looking to vacation in your area, and you'll save on lodging, car rental (you can trade cars, too), and restaurant bills (you have an entire kitchen at your disposal!). Even if you pay up to $100 to list your house on a home-exchange Web site such as www.digsville.com, www.homeexchange.com, www.homelink-use.com, or www.intervacusa.com, you still come out far ahead. (And don't forget that you can view listings for free.)

Stick close to home. Vacation in your hometown or a nearby area. Have you seen all the museums near you? Hiked on all the trails in local parks? Visited nearby historical sites that you learned about in school? View your hometown with a tourist's eyes, and you can have a great vacation at a fraction of what you normally spend.

Ask for (free) help. Call or visit the Web site of the visitors' center or Chamber of Commerce in the area where you'll be vacationing. You can get maps, sightseeing brochures, and information about lodging, restaurants, and local attractions—even money-saving offers—for free. Call local information for the phone number or search online for the name of the area plus "visitors' center" or "Chamber of Commerce."

Guide yourself to a great vacation. Bypass sightseeing tours that take you and your wallet for a ride. Instead, look for self-guided walking and driving tours at the visitors' center at your destination. You may find a free or inexpensive guided tour as well.

Vaccination

Flu-free. Call your local health department to ask if it offers seniors free or inexpensive flu immunizations. Since the government recommends that seniors should have a flu shot, you can often find reduced-rate or free flu shots for seniors at community centers and pharmacies.

Vacuum cleaner

Bag it. Prolong the life of your vacuum cleaner by changing the bag when it feels about two-thirds full. Otherwise, the motor will have to work harder, since the air sucked into the vacuum passes through a bag filled with dirt.

Veterinarian

Two for one. Find out if your vet offers a discount for a multiple-pet visit. Bring your two cats in at once, but pay for less than two visits.

Vintage goods

Older is better. Call it what you want: vintage, antique, or simply used, you'll find amazing bargains on clothes, furniture, and other previously owned goods at thrift stores like the Salvation Army or on sites like eBay.com. Not only will you get a great price, you'll also help the environment by buying items that might get tossed—and you won't be buying something that needs to be manufactured and transported. It's an all-around win!

Volunteer work

Work off your taxes. More and more communities are creating programs that allow seniors to volunteer at the library, as a tutor, or in other positions around town to deduct around $500 from their property taxes. Check with your local government to find out if it offers such a program.

Wall hanging

Look great and insulate. Think about energy savings next time you look for art for your walls. Using quilts or decorative rugs as wall hangings will help insulate interior walls and keep energy costs down.

Washing machine

Keep yours cool. Wash your laundry with cold water and save more than $40 per year if you have an electric water heater or $50 or more per year if you have a gas water heater.

Wash more to save more. Don't wash your clothes more often, just wash more clothes at once. You can save more than 3,400 gallons of water each year if you simply make sure your washing machine is full before you start it. If you need to wash a partial load, be sure to reduce the level of water accordingly.

Water

Bye-bye, bottled water. Save your money and the environment by passing by bottles of water in the grocery store. Instead, buy a reusable water bottle. Assuming a store-bought bottle of water costs $1, you'll recoup your costs after only eight or nine uses of the reusable bottle.

Pitch this idea. Keep a pitcher or bottle of water in the refrigerator so you'll always have cold water on hand. No more running the tap to get water that's cold enough to drink—and no more money down the drain!

Turn off the tap. Turn off the water for two minutes while you brush your teeth or shave and save five gallons of water—and shave a few dollars off your water bill, too.

Water heater

Wrap it up. Save more than $30 per year on your water-heating bill by wrapping your pre-2004 water heater in an insulating jacket.

Keep it hot… Don't let the hot water leaving the water heater cool down before it gets to the tap. You've paid to heat the water! Insulate the hot water piping for additional savings.

...and cool it down. Lower the temperature of your water heater to 120 degrees. You'll still get a steamy hot shower, but for a fraction of what you've been paying.

Turn it off. You may be on vacation, but your water heater isn't. Before you go, turn off your electric water heater or turn down your gas water heater. Your heating bills will enjoy the vacation, too.

Weather stripping

Seal it for savings. Don't pay to heat or cool the air outside your house. Put weather stripping around doors and windows and save about $30 per year in heating and cooling costs.

Wedding cake

Think small. If you're helping pay for a daughter's—or granddaughter's—wedding, suggest buying a small, exquisite wedding cake to cut in front of guests at the wedding reception, but serving a large sheet cake to guests. The fancy and elaborate cake for the photos may be small, but the savings will be large.

Weeds

Shoot 'em dead. Make your driveway and sidewalks last longer by zapping weeds in cracks. Save money in the process by using vinegar in a spray bottle rather than expensive weed killers.

Windows

Sparkling clean and saving. Walk right by window cleaning fluid next time you visit the store. Instead, make it yourself: Mix 1/2 cup ammonia or white vinegar with 1 gallon of water. Then use crumpled newspaper with your homemade cleaner to wash and dry your windows.

Wine

Make your case. Save 10 percent on your wine purchases by buying wine by the case. Many stores will give you 15 percent off if you pay cash. And don't think you have to buy 12 bottles of the same wine. At nearly every wine store, you can mix different kinds and still receive the discount.

Make ice, not waste.

Don't throw away the little bit of wine left in the bottle after dinner is over. Instead, pour it into an ice cube tray and transfer the frozen cubes to a zipper-lock bag. You can use the cubes later in recipes that call for wine.

Wineglasses

Split entertaining costs. Do you have a neighbor or friend who likes to entertain but would like to save a few dollars doing so? Ask if she'll buy matching wineglasses with you. You both buy 12, and lend them to each other as the need arises.

Wrapping paper

Wrap up the season with savings. Score big savings on wrapping, gift cards, and ribbons (as well as decorations and holiday cards) the day after Christmas. You can also save big on Easter wrap, Valentine's Day wrap, and so on immediately after those holidays, too. You'll usually save at least 50 percent, possibly more, and you can use everything you buy the following year.

Be plain. Try to buy solid-colored holiday wrapping paper when it's on sale—you'll be able to use it year-round for birthdays, anniversaries, baby showers, and so on. For example, you'll probably be able to buy solid red wrapping paper after Christmas for 50 percent off that you can use for Valentine's Day.

The copy machine is your friend. Save on gift wrap and make a big impression at the same time. Photocopy pictures of the recipient, tape the copies together, and use the sheets of paper as wrapping paper. Your gift wrap may even outshine your gift!

Map out the savings. Wrap gifts in colorful maps. You can use outdated maps you've used for travel in the past, maps sold cheap at tag sales, or maps you can get for free from AAA if you're a member.

Brides for the bride-to-be. Wrap an engagement gift or a wedding gift in the social pages (that feature wedding announcements) from your local newspaper. Save money on wrapping paper and create a conversation piece at the same time!

Double-duty. Wrap a housewarming gift in a brightly colored dishtowel. You'll save money on wrapping paper by making part of your gift the gift wrap.

Let the butcher and florist help. Buy a big roll of white butcher paper and large bolt of colorful ribbon from a florist supply store or craft store and you'll have plenty of wrapping material for the holiday season (and beyond).

X-ray

Examine your X-rays. Do you really need a complete set of X-rays every time (or every other time) you visit the dentist? Ask your dentist if you can skip a set of X-rays and save the cost.

Yard

Be a yardbird and save! Don't pay a pricey "landscape engineer" to do what will spend your calories while it saves your dough. Get out there and pull some weeds, plant some veggies, and care for your flowers. Most landscapers charge upward of $50 an hour; multiplied by an average of two hours and eight seasonal visits, you've just saved yourself $800!

Zipper

Zip up the savings. Don't automatically throw away a garment if the zipper stops working. Try surrounding it with Velcro; you'll avoid the work of ripping out the zipper and the cost of replacing the item.

Zipper pull

Replace it with style. If the zipper on your jacket or your purse is missing the zipper pull, don't toss it. Simply replace the pull with a small key chain (or just the metal ring of the keychain), a metal ring sporting a charm, or easiest of all, a paperclip.

Zoo

Join the animals. Don't let the high price of zoos keep you away from the lions and tigers and bears. Find out if your zoo offers a day of free admission or pay-what-you-wish donation (like Wednesdays at the Bronx Zoo), corporate days (where employees of certain organizations get free admission on designated days), or memberships that offer admission year-round (plus other goodies) for the set price of membership.

Y

Z

Index

I

Ice cream, 685

Iced tea, 413

Ice packs, 685

Identity theft, avoiding, 399, 403–4

ID requirements, 394

IHOP, 432, 437

Immigrant resources, for genealogy research, 601

Impulse spending, 666, 671

Income. *See* Finances

Income Gap Calculation, 618–19

Income tax. *See* Taxes

Independent retirement communities, 652–53

Indianapolis Zoo, 516

Information services, 459, 670–71

Informed consumers, 394, 396

Instant Hand Softener, 481

Insurance
    car, 395, 460–61, 685–86
    health, 612–16, 628, 638
    homeowners, 395
    life, 632–33
    long-term care, 632–34
    rental car, 395, 698

InterContinental Hotels Group, 568

International House of Pancakes (IHOP), 432, 437

International travel, 574–80

Internet access, 397, 398

Internet resources. *See also specific Web sites or topics*
    airfare deals, 395, 562
    clothing overstocks, 490–91
    craft projects, 587
    gas prices, 464, 679

    genealogy research, 598
    gourmet food purveyors, 431
    home stay lodging, 571–74, 707
    hotel bookings, 565
    job searches, 641
    movie tickets, 538
    online education, 397, 526–27
    phone service, 458
    retirement planning tools, 612, 621
    spectator sports tickets, 518
    theater tickets, 541

Interviews
    family, 590
    job, 645

Investments, 617–20. *See also* Finances

Invitations, 686

Isabella Stewart Gardner Museum, 543

J

Jack in the Box, 434

Jeans, 686

Jewelry and jewelry boxes, 686

JiffyLube, 464

Jigsaw puzzles, 687

Job interviews, 645

Job market, 641–43, 658

Junk mail, 399

K

Kennedy Center, 551

Keys, 687

KFC, 434

Kitchen utensils, 415, 444, 445

Kitty litter, 687

O

P

S